KT-571-435

TRENTINO-ALTO ADIGE
Pages 160–169

THE VENETO AND FRIULI
Pages 132–159

VENICE
Pages 80–131

EMILIA-ROMAGNA
Pages 246–261

UMBRIA
Pages 338–353

LE MARCHE
Pages 354–363

ABRUZZO, MOLISE AND PUGLIA
Pages 484–497

BASILICATA AND CALABRIA
Pages 498–505

NAPLES AND CAMPANIA
Pages 466–483

SICILY
Pages 506–527

Ancona

Pescara

L'Aquila

MA

Campobasso

Foggia

Bari

Napoli

Salerno

Potenza

Taranto

Catanzaro

Messina

Reggio di Calabria

Palermo

Catania

Agrigento

EYEWITNESS *TRAVEL GUIDES*

ITALY

DK

DORLING KINDERSLEY

LONDON • NEW YORK • STUTTGART • MOSCOW

A DORLING KINDERSLEY BOOK

ART EDITORS Vanessa Courtier, Annette Jacobs
PROJECT EDITOR Fiona Wild
EDITORS Francesca Machiavelli, Sophie Martin,
Helen Townsend, Nicky Tyrrell
DESIGNERS Jo Doran, Anthea Forlee,
Paul Jackson, Marisa Renzullo
MAP CO-ORDINATORS Michael Ellis, David Pugh
RESEARCHER Veronica Wood

MANAGING EDITOR Georgina Matthews
SENIOR ART EDITOR Sally-Ann Hibbard
DEPUTY EDITORIAL DIRECTOR Douglas Amrine
DEPUTY ART DIRECTOR Gaye Allen
SENIOR MANAGING ART EDITOR Gillian Allan

PRODUCTION CONTROLLER David Proffit
PICTURE RESEARCHER Naomi Peck
DTP DESIGNERS Siri Lowe, Tamsin Pender

MAIN CONTRIBUTORS
Ros Belford, Susie Boulton, Christopher Catling,
Sam Cole, Paul Duncan, Olivia Ercoli, Andrew Gumbel,
Tim Jepson, Ferdie McDonald, Jane Shaw

MAPS
Lovell Johns Ltd,
Dorling Kindersley Cartography

PHOTOGRAPHER
John Heseltine

ILLUSTRATORS
Stephen Conlin, Donati Giudici Associati srl, Stephen Gyapay,
Roger Hutchins, Maltings Partnership, Paul Weston, John Woodcock

•

Film outputting bureau Graphical Innovations (London)
Reproduced by Colourscan (Singapore)
Printed and bound by Graphicom (Italy)

First published in Great Britain in 1996
by Dorling Kindersley Limited
9 Henrietta Street, London WC2E 8PS

Copyright 1996 © Dorling Kindersley Limited, London

A CIP CATALOGUE RECORD IS AVAILABLE FROM THE BRITISH LIBRARY.
ISBN 0-7513-0105-1

•

Every effort has been made to ensure that the information in this
book is as up-to-date as possible at the time of going to press.
However, details such as telephone numbers, opening hours,
prices, gallery hanging arrangements and travel information are
liable to change. The publishers cannot accept responsibility for
any consequences arising from the use of this book.

We would be delighted to receive any corrections and
suggestions for incorporation in the next edition. Please write to:
Deputy Editorial Director, Eyewitness Travel Guides,
Dorling Kindersley, 9 Henrietta Street,
London WC2E 8PS.

◁ **Fertile wine-growing region around Panzano in Chianti, Tuscany**

CONTENTS

HOW TO USE
THIS GUIDE *6*

David **by Bernini, Rome**

INTRODUCING
ITALY

PUTTING ITALY
ON THE MAP *10*

A PORTRAIT OF
ITALY *16*

THE HISTORY
OF ITALY *38*

ITALY THROUGH
THE YEAR *62*

NORTHEAST ITALY

INTRODUCING
NORTHEAST ITALY *70*

VENICE *80*

VENICE STREET
FINDER *120*

THE VENETO
AND FRIULI *132*

TRENTINO-
ALTO ADIGE *160*

NORTHWEST ITALY

INTRODUCING
NORTHWEST ITALY *170*

Gondolas weaving through the maze of canals in Venice

A traditional small shop in
Volterra, Tuscany

Basilica of San Francesco in Assisi, started in 1228

HOW TO USE THIS GUIDE

THIS GUIDE helps you get the most from your visit to Italy, providing expert recommendations as well as detailed practical information. *Introducing Italy* maps the whole country and sets it in its historical and cultural context. The 15 regional chapters, plus *Rome*, *Florence* and *Venice*, describe important sights with the help of maps and images. Each section is introduced with features on regional architecture and food specialities. *Travellers' Needs* gives details on hotels and restaurants and the *Survival Guide* contains practical information on everything from transport to personal safety.

ROME

The centre of Rome has been divided into five sightseeing areas. Each area has its own chapter, which opens with a list of the sights described. All the sights are numbered and plotted on an *Area Map*. The detailed information for each sight is presented in numerical order, making it easy to locate within the chapter.

All pages relating to Rome have red thumb tabs.

A locator map shows where you are in relation to other areas of the city centre.

1 Area Map
For easy reference, the sights are numbered and located on a map. The sights are also shown on the Street Finder *on pages 433–41.*

Sights at a Glance lists the chapter's sights by category: Churches, Museums and Galleries, Historic Buildings, Streets and Piazzas.

2 Street-by-Street Map
This gives a bird's-eye view of the heart of each sightseeing area.

A suggested route for a walk is shown in red.

Stars indicate the sights that no visitor should miss.

3 Detailed information
All the sights in Rome are described individually. Addresses and practical information are provided. The key to the symbols used in the information block is shown on the back flap.

1 Introduction
The landscape, history and character of each region is described here, showing how the area has developed over the centuries and what it offers to the visitor today.

Italy Area by Area
Apart from Rome, Florence and Venice, Italy has been divided into 15 areas, each of which has a separate chapter. The most interesting towns and places to visit have been numbered on a *Pictorial Map*.

Each area of Italy can be identified quickly by its colour coding, shown on the inside front cover.

2 Pictorial Map
This shows the main road network and gives an illustrated overview of the whole region. All entries are numbered and there are also useful tips on getting around the region by car and train.

3 Detailed information
All the important towns and other places to visit are described individually. They are listed in order, following the numbering given on the Pictorial Map. Within each entry, information is given on the most important sights. The name of the provincial capital is given for smaller towns at the top of each entry.

Story boxes explore specific subjects further.

For all the top sights, a Visitors' Checklist provides the practical information you need to plan your visit.

4 Italy's top sights
These are given two or more full pages. Historic buildings are dissected to reveal their interiors; museums and galleries have colour-coded floorplans to help you locate the most interesting exhibits.

INTRODUCING
ITALY

Putting Italy on the Map

ITALY SITS AT THE HEART of the Mediterranean, shielded from the rest of Europe by the vast sweep of the Alps. The Po, its longest river, arcs across the industrial north, while the Apennine mountains split the boot-shaped peninsula down its length. Italy, with a population of 57.5 million governed from Rome, covers 301,268 sq km (116,320 sq miles) and includes Sicily and Sardinia.

Aerial view of Venice, showing the Grand Canal

◁ **View over Florence of the richly-decorated 15th-century Duomo and Campanile**

Satellite photograph of southern Europe and the Mediterranean

AUSTRIA
Graz
Klagenfurt
Balaton
HUNGARY
Cortina d'Ampezzo
Drau
Dráva
Belluno
Udine
SLOVENIA
LJUBLJANA
CROATIA
Danube

Treviso
Trieste
VENICE
dova

Ravenna
Rimini
Pesaro
SAN MARINO
Ancona

Gubbio
Perugia
Todi
Orvieto
Ascoli Piceno
Pescara
Isole Tremiti
BOSNIA AND HERZEGOVINA
Dubrovnik

Viterbo
itavecchia
L'Aquila
Sulmona
ROME
Anzio
Foggia
Benevento
Naples
Pompei
Amalfi
Bari
Brindisi
Lecce
Taranto
Isola d'Ischia
Isola di Capri
Agri

Greece Turkey Egypt
Greece

A
d
r
i
a
t
i
c
S
e
a

I o n i a n
S e a

Cosenza
Catanzaro

Isole Eólie o Lípari

Trapani
Palermo
Reggio di Calabria
SICILY
Catania
Siracusa

Isola di Pantelleria

Malta

KEY

▬▬	Motorway
▬▬	Major road
- - -	Ferry service
▬ ▪ ▬	International boundary

0 kilometres   200

0 miles   100

Northern Italy

Airline connections link the rest of Europe with the cities of Milan, Turin, Bologna, Pisa, Verona and Venice. Major roads and railways also provide excellent links to cities all over Europe. Transport services in the north are very efficient, with motorways and railways running down both coasts, and across the area's main east to west axis at the foot of the Alps. Milan, Verona and Bologna are the key transport hubs, while Florence forms the focus of links to the south.

Florence by Road
Good fast roads link Florence to Pisa to the west, Rome and Siena to the south, and Bologna to the north.

FLORENCE AND ENVIRONS

KEY

⛴	Ferry port
✈	Airport
FS	Main railway station
▪ ▪	International boundary
▬ ▬	Regional boundary
	Motorway
	Main road
	Railway line

0 kilometers   4

0 miles   2

VENICE

Venice by Road

Venice is joined to the mainland by a causeway. This provides easy access to motorway links with Verona and Padua.

Marco Polo

Mestre

N146

Canale Osellino

N14

Veneta

N11

Laguna

Santa Lucia

San Marco

Turkey-Egypt-Greece-Ancona

0 kilometres   4

0 miles   2

AUSTRIA

Cortina d'Ampezzo

Tolmezzo

N52

Cividale del Friuli

Udine

Pordenone

Gorizia

A4

Aquileia

Grado

Treviso

Trieste

SLOVENIA

VENICE

Mestre

Greece
Turkey
Egypt

Po
Delta

Ravenna

Rimini

SAN MARINO

Pèsaro

San Leo

Fano

Urbino

Urbania

Ancona

Jesi

Conero
Peninsula

Loreto

Greece

Ionian Islands

Cyprus

Turkey

Sibillini

Cortona

Gubbio

Grotte di
Frasassi

Lago
Trasimeno

Perugia

Assisi

Spello

Ascoli Piceno

Montefalco

Norcia

Todi

Spoleto

Orvieto

Isole Tremiti

Pescara

L'Aquila

Lanciano

ROME

VATICAN CITY

Sulmona

Scanno

San Severo

Sermoneta

Lucera

Sperlonga

Foggia

Terracina

Formia

Troia

Gaeta

Benevento

Brindisi

Caserta

0 kilometres   100

0 miles   50

Taranto

NAPLES

Monte
Vesuvio

Reggio di
Calabria

KEY TO COLOUR-CODING

Northeast Italy

Venice

The Veneto and Friuli

Trentino-Alto Adige

Northwest Italy

Lombardy

Valle d'Aosta and Piedmont

Liguria

Central Italy

Emilia-Romagna

Florence

Tuscany

Umbria

Le Marche

Southern Italy

I NTERNATIONAL AIRLINE services operate
to Rome, Naples and Palermo in
southern Italy. Transport links within
the region are generally slower than
in the north, particularly inland and
on the islands of Sicily and Sardinia.
Coastal road and rail links are
good, however, especially those
linking Rome and Naples, the
region's main transport hubs.
Two trans-Apennine motor-
ways offer the quickest
cross-country routes.

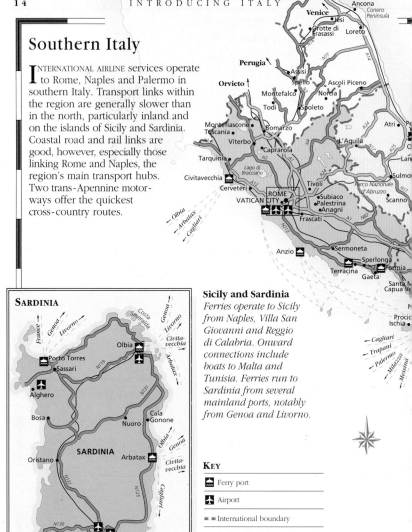

Sicily and Sardinia

*Ferries operate to Sicily
from Naples, Villa San
Giovanni and Reggio
di Calabria. Onward
connections include
boats to Malta and
Tunisia. Ferries run to
Sardinia from several
mainland ports, notably
from Genoa and Livorno.*

SARDINIA

Porto Torres · Sassari
Alghero
Bosa
Oristano
SARDINIA
Nuoro
Cala Gonone
Arbatax
Cagliari
Sant'Antioco
Olbia

KEY

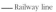 Ferry port

✈ Airport

▪ ▪ International boundary

▬ ▬ Regional boundary

▭ Motorway

▭ Main road

— Railway line

SICILIAN ISLANDS

Isole Eolie
Isole Egadi
Palermo
TUNIS
Pantelleria
SICILY
TUNISIA
Isole Pelagie
Malta

Palermo
Bagher
Monreale
Trapani
Erice
Isole Egadi
Marsala
Segesta
Selinunte
Agrigento

ROME AND ENVIRONS

0 kilometres 10

0 miles 5

Rome by Road

Motorway links approach Rome from Naples, Pescara and Florence. All feed into the city's ring road, the Grande Raccordo Anulare.

GRANDE RACCORDO ANULARE (GRA)

V. FLAMINIA

VIA CASSIA

VIA SALARIA

VIA NOMENTANA

A1

VATICAN CITY

FS

VIA AURELIA

VIA TIBURTINA

A24

VIA CASILINA

VIA APPIA NUOVA

A12

Leonardo da Vinci (Fiumicino)

Tevere (Tiber)

VIA CRISTOFORO COLOMBO

A2

Ciampino

Isole Tremiti

Vasto

Termoli

Rodi Garganico

Vieste

Gargano Peninsula

San Severo

Manfredonia

Lucera

Foggia

Troia

Trani

Bari

Albania

Greece

Egypt

A16

A14

N17

Benevento

Castel del Monte

Ruvo di Puglia

Melfi

Venosa

Alberobello

N379

Brindisi

Greece

Lagopesole

Caserta

Monte Vesuvio

Pompei

Salerno

Amalfi

Sorrento

Paestum

Cilento

A3

N407

Matera

Taranto

Metaponto

N7

Lecce

Greece

Galatina

Otranto

N18

Maratea

Rossano

N106

Cosenza

N407

A280

Sant'Eufemia Lamezia

Tropea

Stilo

Gerace

Isole Eolie

Naples

Messina

Villa San Giovanni

Milazzo

Tindari

Reggio di Calabria

Taormina

Naples

Malta

A20

A18

A19

Catania

Piazza Armerina

N117

Pantalica

Siracusa

Naples

Malta

Noto

0 kilometres 100

0 miles 50

KEY TO COLOUR-CODING

Rome and Lazio

Rome

Lazio

Southern Italy

Naples and Campania

Abruzzo, Molise and Puglia

Basilicata and Calabria

Sicily

Sardinia

A PORTRAIT OF ITALY

....

ITALY HAS DRAWN PEOPLE *in search of culture and romance for many centuries. Few countries can compete with its Classical origins, its art, architecture, musical and literary traditions, its scenery or food and wine. The ambiguity of its modern image is also fascinating: since World War II Italy has climbed into the top ten world economies, yet at its heart it retains many of the customs, traditions and regional allegiances of its agricultural heritage.*

Italy has no single cultural identity. From the northern snow-capped peaks of the Dolomites, to the long, rugged south-

Wedding Ferrari in typical Italian style

ern shores of Sicily, lies a plethora of distinctive regions and peoples. Politically, Italy is a young country: it did not exist as a unified nation state until 1861, and its 21 regions have maintained their cultural individuality. Visitors to Italy are often pleasantly surprised by the diversity of its dialects, cuisines, architecture and craftsmanship. There is also a larger regional division. People speak of two distinct Italies: the rich industrial north and the poorer agricultural south, known as *Il Mezzogiorno* or Land of the Midday Sun. The frontier separating the two is indeterminate, lying somewhere between Rome and Naples.

The north is directly responsible for Italy's place among the world's top industrial nations. It has been the powerhouse behind the Italian economic miracle, its success achieved by internationally renowned names such as Fiat, Pirelli, Ferragamo, Olivetti, Zanussi, Alessi and Armani. The south, in contrast, has high unemployment, earns less per capita

A secluded villa surrounded by cypress trees on a Tuscan hilltop

◁ Three sundials covering the façade of Palazzo del Governatore, on Piazza Garibaldi, Parma than the north, is in the grip of organized crime, and has some areas that rank among the most depressed in Europe.

The historic divide between north and south is a powerful factor in contemporary politics. The newly formed federalist party, the Northern League, has based its popular campaign on this split. The party gained enough votes in recent elections to be included in the national government. Those in favour of separation complain that the south is a drain on resources: Milan is seen as efficient and rich, while Naples is viewed as chaotic, dirty and corrupt.

History and geography have both contributed to the division. The north is closer in both location and spirit to Germany and France while the south has suffered a succession of invasions from foreign powers: Carthaginians and Greeks in ancient times, Saracens and Normans in the Middle Ages and until the middle of the last century, the Bourbons from Spain held sway.

TRADITION

Distinctive variations in Italy's regions have much to do with the mountainous landscape and inaccessible valleys.

Conversation at Palazzo Farnese

Tuscan and Ligurian hilltowns, for instance, have quite different silhouettes and farmhouses in Puglia are unlike those found in Emilia-Romagna.

For many travellers, the Italian journey comes to an end in Campania, in southern Italy. Further south the territory grows more foreign and the landscape, architecture, dialects, food, and even the appearance of the people, have closer affinities with the Eastern Mediterranean or North Africa than with Europe. In the far south, study of the local dialect has revealed traces of ancient Greek and old Albanian, preserved in tightly knit communities isolated by the rugged geography. Christianity and pagan ritual are closely linked; sometimes the Virgin is portrayed as a thinly disguised Demeter, the Earth goddess.

Throughout Italy, ancient techniques of husbandry endure and many livelihoods are closely connected to the land and the seasons. Main crops include wheat, olives and grapes; colourful Easter celebrations *(see p62)* pay tribute to the bounty of the soil. Although some of the north's postwar economic prosperity can be attributed to industry (especially car production in Turin), much of it has grown from the expansion of family-owned artisan businesses and the export of hand-made goods abroad. This is recognized as a distinct sector of the economy. The internationally successful retail clothes chain,

Café-goers relaxing in Marina di Pisa, Tuscany

Medieval skyscrapers emerging from the Tuscan landscape of San Gimignano

Benetton, is a recent example. The "Made in Italy" label, found on goods such as clothes, shoes and leather bags, guarantees a high standard.

Sophia Loren

CULTURE AND ARTS

The arts in Italy have had a long and glorious history and Italians are very proud of this. Given the fact that Italy has more than 100,000 monuments (archaeological sites, cathedrals, churches, houses and statues), all of which have major historical significance, it is not surprising that there is a shortage of funds to keep them in good repair. Many museums in Italy, particularly those in the south, are closed, or partially closed. You may find churches in Venice hidden behind permanent scaffolding or those in Naples shut due to recent earthquake damage. However, with tourism now accounting for 3 per cent of Italy's Gross Domestic Product, efforts are being made to put as many buildings and collections on show as possible.

The performing arts are also underfunded, yet there are some spectacular cultural festivals and other events. Opera is a forte, with almost every town of any size having its own opera house. Current stars include Luciano Pavarotti, and La Scala opera house in Milan shows world-class productions.

Cinema is another flourishing art form in Italy and has been so since its invention. The sets at Cinecittà, outside Rome, have been used by many famous directors such as Fellini,

Bernini's 17th-century Fontana del Tritone, Rome

Roadside stall near Positano, Campania

Pasolini, de Sica, Visconti and many others. Italian films have always been an important export, and continue to bring in money and acclaim from abroad. In Italy the arts belong to everyone: opera has traditionally been attended by people from all backgrounds, regardless of social status, as have cinemas and galleries.

SOCIAL CUSTOMS AND POLITICS

Italian society is still highly traditional, and Italians can be very formal. Between the generations degrees of familiarity exist: reserve *ciao* (hello or goodbye) for friends your age or younger, and greet older people with *piacere* (pleased to meet you), *buon giorno* (good day) or *buona sera* (good evening) and on parting, say *arrivederci* (goodbye). Strangers are met with a handshake, but family and friends receive a kiss.

Italian chic decrees that whatever clothes you wear should give the impression of wealth. If two people wear identical outfits, it is because Italians are conformists in fashion as in many other aspects of daily life.

Italian politics, in contrast, are not so well regulated. Governments in the

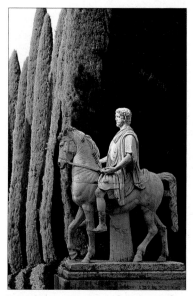

Italian chic, Armani style

postwar era have consistently been short-lived coalitions, and until recently, were dominated by the Christian Democrats. In 1993, however, Italy experienced a political crisis which blew its party system apart. Investigations in Milan into illegal party financing in 1992 revealed an organized network of bribery and corruption which exposed a huge number of politicians and businessmen. Among the disgraced was Giulio Andreotti, Christian Democrat leader and six times prime minister (until 1992), accused of colluding with the Mafia. Silvio Berlusconi, media tycoon and leader of the new Forza Italia party, became prime minister in 1994 but lasted only a short while as he, too, was accused of corrupt business practices.

MODERN LIFE

Food and football are the great constants; Italians live for both. Much time is spent on preparing food and eating. The Italian diet, particularly in the south, is among the healthiest in the world.

Statue of Emperor Domitian in the Vatican Gardens

The solution to heavy traffic in Rome's Piazza Barberini: motorbikes and scooters

Football is a national passion and inspires massive public interest and media attention, not least because it is a way of expressing regional loyalties.

As far as religion is concerned, the number of practising Catholics has been in decline for some years. Although Rome lies at the heart of world Catholicism, today many Italians are uninterested in religion and seem to rally to the altar only on saints' days or feast days.

The emphasis on conformity and a heartfelt commitment to the institution of the family remain key factors in Italian society despite the country's low, and falling, birth rate. Grandparents, children and grandchildren still live in family units, although this is becoming less common. All children are pampered but the most cherished ones are, more often than not, male. Women's Liberation fought a powerful campaign

Strolling through one of Bologna's many porticoes

in the 1960s and 1970s and did much to change attitudes to women in the workplace, particularly in the metropolitan areas of northern and central Italy. However, the idea that men should help with housework and the care of children is still a fairly foreign notion.

With the miracle of its postwar economic recovery, where industry and technology were united with design, Italy has become a modern-day success story. Although the economy has been dented by the worldwide recession of the early 1990s, together with the recent exposure of corruption in all walks of public life and unprecedented political upheaval, Italy appears unchanged to visitors from abroad. The ability of the country to hang on to its long-lasting regional identities and strong traditional values allows it to ride out any changes virtually unscathed.

Medieval and Early Renaissance Art

T HE STORY OF early Italian art, from the 13th century until the late 15th century, illuminates one of the richest periods in European art history. For the first time since Classical antiquity, painters and sculptors created a convincing pictorial space in which figures, modelled "in the round", were given life. Ethereal buildings were replaced by those firmly rooted in the real world, reproducing what artists actually saw. This revolution in art included the reintroduction of the fresco technique, giving artists huge surfaces for telling pictorial stories.

1235 Bonaventura Berlinghieri, *St Francis Altarpiece* (San Francesco, Pescia)

c.1305 Giotto di Bondone, *Meeting at the Golden Gate* (Cappella degli Scrovegni, Padua). Giotto broke away from the orna[te] Byzantine style to visualize naturalness and human emotions. His way of working would later be dubbed the Florentine style.

1285 Duccio di Buoninsegna, *Rucellai Madonna*, panel (Uffizi, Florence). Duccio dominated the Sienese painting style which combined bold linear movements with a new human intimacy.

1339 Lorenzetti, *Good Government Enthroned* (Palazzo Pubblico, Siena)

1220	1240	1260	1280	1300	1320
MIDDLE AGES				**FORERUNNERS TO RENAISSANCE**	
1220	1240	1260	1280	1300	1320

c.1259 Nicola Pisano, Pulpit (Baptistry, Pisa cathedral)

c.1328 Simone Martini, *Vision of St Martin* (Lower Church of San Francesco, Assisi)

c.1265 Coppo di Marcovaldo, *Madonna and Child* (San Martino ai Servi, Orvieto)

c.1297 Giovanni Pisano, Pulpit (Sant'Andrea, Pistoia)

c.1280 Cimabue, *Madonna Enthroned with Angels and Prophets*, also known as *Santa Trinità Madonna* (Uffizi, Florence)

c.1336 Andrea Pisano, *Baptism of St John the Baptist*, panel on the South Doors (Baptistry, Florence cathedral)

c.1291 Pietro Cavallini, *Last Judgment*, detail (Santa Cecilia, Trastevere, Rome)

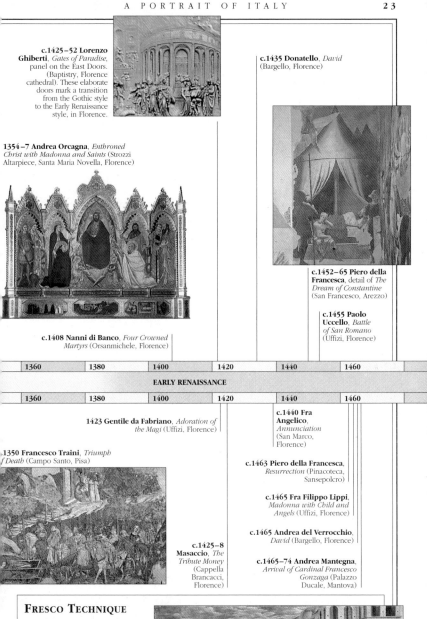

c.1425–52 Lorenzo Ghiberti, *Gates of Paradise*, panel on the East Doors. (Baptistry, Florence cathedral). These elaborate doors mark a transition from the Gothic style to the Early Renaissance style, in Florence.

c.1435 Donatello, *David* (Bargello, Florence)

1354–7 Andrea Orcagna, *Enthroned Christ with Madonna and Saints* (Strozzi Altarpiece, Santa Maria Novella, Florence)

c.1452–65 Piero della Francesca, detail of *The Dream of Constantine* (San Francesco, Arezzo)

c.1455 Paolo Uccello, *Battle of San Romano* (Uffizi, Florence)

c.1408 Nanni di Banco, *Four Crowned Martyrs* (Orsanmichele, Florence)

| 1360 | 1380 | 1400 | 1420 | 1440 | 1460 |

EARLY RENAISSANCE

| 1360 | 1380 | 1400 | 1420 | 1440 | 1460 |

1423 Gentile da Fabriano, *Adoration of the Magi* (Uffizi, Florence)

c.1440 Fra Angelico, *Annunciation* (San Marco, Florence)

1350 Francesco Traini, *Triumph f Death* (Campo Santo, Pisa)

c.1463 Piero della Francesca, *Resurrection* (Pinacoteca, Sansepolcro)

c.1465 Fra Filippo Lippi, *Madonna with Child and Angels* (Uffizi, Florence)

c.1465 Andrea del Verrocchio, *David* (Bargello, Florence)

c.1425–8 Masaccio, *The Tribute Money* (Cappella Brancacci, Florence)

c.1465–74 Andrea Mantegna, *Arrival of Cardinal Francesco Gonzaga* (Palazzo Ducale, Mantova)

FRESCO TECHNIQUE

Fresco, meaning "fresh", refers to the technique of painting onto a thin layer of damp, freshly laid plaster. Pigments are drawn into the plaster by surface tension and the colour becomes fixed as the plaster dries. The pigments react with the lime in the plaster to produce strong, rich colours, such as those in Masaccio's *The Tribute Money*.

The Tribute Money by Masaccio (Cappella Brancacci, Florence)

High Renaissance Art

THE HIGH RENAISSANCE in the late 15th century was marked by an increasing sense of realism in many religious works and the technical mastery of such renowned artists as Michelangelo, Leonardo da Vinci and Raphael. The different schools of Renaissance painting, while drawing on Classical models, produced varying styles: Florentine painting was noted for its cool clarity, while sensuous colour and warm light characterized many Venetian works. By the mid-16th century, however, these styles shifted to the fanciful, contorted imagery of Mannerism.

1481–2 Sistine Chapel wall frescoes painted by various artists.

c.1481–3 Pietro Perugino, *Christ Delivering the Keys of the Kingdom to St Peter*, wall fresco (Sistine Chapel, Rome)

c.1483–88 Andrea del Verrocchio, completed by Alessandro Leopardi, *Equestrian Monument of Bartolomeo Colleoni* (Campo dei Santi Giovanni e Paolo, Venice)

c.1485 Giovanni Bellini, *San Giobbe Altarpiece* (Accademia, Venice)

c.1503–1505 Leonardo da Vinci, *Mona Lisa* (Louvre, Paris)

c.1501 Andrea Mantegna, *Dead Christ* (Brera, Milan)

c.1495–8 Leonardo da Vinci, *Last Supper* (Santa Maria delle Grazie, Milan)

1505 Raphael, *Madonna of the Goldfinch* (Uffizi, Florence)

1519–26 Titian, *Madonna of the Pesaro Family* (Santa Maria Gloriosa dei Frari, Venice)

1508–12 Michelangelo, *Sistine Chapel ceiling* (The Vatican, Rome). Over 200 preliminary drawings were made for this incredible vision of God's power and humanity's spiritual awakening.

1480	1500	15

HIGH RENAISSANCE

1480	1500	15

1485 Leonardo da Vinci, *Virgin of the Rocks* (Louvre, Paris)

1499–1504 Luca Signorelli, *Damned Consigned to Hell* (Cappella Nuova, Orvieto cathedral)

1501–1504 Michelangelo, *David* (Galleria dell'Accademia, Florence)

1505 Giovanni Bellini, *Madonna and Child with Four Saints* (San Zaccaria altarpiece, Accademia, Venice)

c.1486 Leonardo da Vinci, *Uomo Vitruviano* (Accademia, Venice)

c.1508 Giorgione, *Tempesta* (Accademia, Venice)

1509 Raphael, *School of Athens* (Stanza della Segnatura, The Vatican, Rome). The scale, magnificence and harmony of this fresco represent the ideals of the High Renaissance. These ideals sought to express superhuman rather than human values.

1517 Sodo *Marriage of Alexander Roxana* (Vi. Farnesina, I

1516 Michela *Dying Slave* (Louvre, Paris)

1512–14 Raphael, *Ange Delivering St Peter from Prison*, detail from the *Liberation of St Peter from Prison* (Stanza d'Eliodoro The Vatican, Rome)

c.1480 Sandro Botticelli, *Birth of Venus* (Uffizi, Florence)

1528 Rosso Fiorentino, *Moses Defends the Daughters of Jethro* (Uffizi, Florence)

1530–32 Giulio Romano, *Ceiling and wall frescoes* (Sala dei Giganti, Palazzo del Tè, Mantova)

c.1532 Michelangelo, *"Blockhead" Captive* (Galleria dell' Accademia, Florence)

1534–5 Paris Bordone, *Fisherman Delivering the Ring* (Accademia, Venice)

c.1542 Titian, *David and Goliath* (Santa Maria della Salute, Venice)

c.1562–6 Jacopo Tintoretto, *Finding of the Body of St Mark* (Brera, Milan)

c.1550–54 Moretto, *Ecce Homo with Angel* (Pinacoteca Tosio Martinengo, Brescia)

1540	1560

MANNERISM

1540	1560

1538 Titian, *Venus of Urbino* (Uffizi, Florence)

1534–41 Michelangelo, *Last Judgment*, wall fresco (Sistine Chapel, Rome)

c.1535 Parmigianino, *Madonna and Angels* or *Madonna with the Long Neck* (Uffizi, Florence). Attenuated proportions and contrasting colours make this a fine example of the Mannerist style.

c.1546 Titian, *Portrait of Pope Paul III Farnese with his Nephews*, (Museo di Capodimonte, Naples)

1556 Veronese, *Triumph of Mordecai* (San Sebastiano, Venice)

c.1526–30 Correggio, *Assumption of the Virgin* (Dome of Parma cathedral). Neither a Mannerist nor High Renaissance painter, Correggio was a master of illusion, skilled at making ascending figures float convincingly, as seen in the fresco above.

c.1550 Agnolo Bronzino, *Portrait of Lucrezia Panciatichi* (Uffizi, Florence). Elongated features, such as Lucrezia's fingers, are typical of the exaggerated Mannerist style.

Italian Architecture

Corinthian capital

THE BUILDINGS OF ITALY span almost 3,000 years, drawing influences from a wide variety of sources. Etruscan and Roman buildings borrowed heavily from ancient Greece, while in later centuries Norman, Arabic and Byzantine styles coloured Italy's Romanesque and Gothic architecture. Classical ideals infused the country's Renaissance buildings, later giving way to the inspired innovations of the Baroque period.

Orvieto's Duomo *displays the ornate and intricate decoration, notably sculpture, common to many Romanesque and Gothic cathedrals. Building stretched from the 13th–16th centuries.*

The Basilica di San Marco

The Basilica di San Marco *(AD 832–1094) in Venice combines Classical, Romanesque and Gothic architecture, but its key inspiration was Byzantine (see pp106–9).*

200	400	600	800	1000
CLASSICAL		**BYZANTINE**		**ROMANESQU**
200	400	600	800	1000

Triumphal arches *such as Rome's Arch of Constantine (AD 313) were a uniquely Roman invention. Built to celebrate military victories, they were adorned with reliefs depicting episodes from successful campaigns (see p370).*

The round-arched Romanesque style emerged from the Dark Ages in structures such as the Duomo in Modena. The churches usually had simple interiors that derived from Roman basilicas.

The building of domes over square or rectangular spaces was a major development of the Byzantine era.

ETRUSCAN ARCHITECTURE

Virtually the only architectural memorials to the Etruscans are their necropolises (c.6th century BC), found primarily in Tuscany, Lazio and Umbria. Little else survives, probably because most day-to-day buildings were made from wood. The Etruscans' close cultural and trading ties with Greece, however, suggest their architecture would have borrowed heavily from Greek models. Rome, in turn, looked to Etruscan architecture for inspiration, and most early Roman public buildings were probably Etruscan in style.

Model of Etruscan temple with Classical Greek portico

The cathedral of Monreale *in Sicily, built in the 12th century, contains Norman elements blended with exotic Arabic and Byzantine decoration (see pp514–15).*

Bramante's *Tempietto at San Pietro in Montorio, Rome (begun in 1502) was a Renaissance tribute to the precise, Classical temples of ancient Rome* (see p370).

Baroque façades, *such as this one added to Syracuse's Duomo between 1728 and 1754, were often grafted onto older churches.*

Industrial innovations *in glass and metal were applied in new buildings, like Mengoni's imposing Galleria Vittorio Emanuele II (1865) in Milan* (see p188).

The Classical ideals of Rome and ancient Greece were reintroduced into Italian architecture during the Renaissance.

Papal patronage and the vigour of the Counter Reformation fuelled the Baroque, a period of architectural splendour, invention and exuberance.

The Mole Antonelliana (1863–97), in Turin, topped by a soaring granite spire, was for a time the tallest building in the world *(p216)*.

Torre Velasca's 26-floor tower in Milan (1950s) pioneered the use of reinforced concrete.

1400	1600	1800	2000
RENAISSANCE	BAROQUE	19th CENTURY	20th CENTURY
1400	1600	1800	2000

Siena's Duomo (1136–1382), an imposing Romanesque-Gothic cathedral, went through 200 years of architectural transformation *(see pp332–3)*.

Santa Maria Novella in Florence has a Renaissance façade (1456–70) by Alberti and a Gothic interior.

Gian Lorenzo Bernini (1598–1680), architect of St Peter's Square, was a dominant figure in Roman Baroque.

Andrea Palladio (1508–80) built Neo-Classical villas and palazzi. His style was imitated in Europe for over two centuries *(see p76)*.

Lantern

Inner shell

Outer skin of dome, supported by 24 ribs

Brunelleschi's dome *for the Duomo in Florence, completed in 1436, was a masterpiece of Renaissance design and ingenious engineering* (see p245).

The Gesù *in Rome was designed for the Jesuits by Vignola in 1568. With its powerful façade and lavish decoration it was the prototype for countless other Baroque churches* (see p371).

The Pirelli building *in Milan, built by Ponti and Nervi (late 1950s), is a great example of modern Italian architecture* (see p179).

Saints and Symbols in Italian Art

Saints and symbols are especially important in Italian art. They form part of an established visual language used by artists to narrate stories of the Bible and the Catholic church to church-goers. Paintings of the saints were the focus for prayer and each offered assistance in a particular aspect of daily life. Patron saints protected specific cities, or trades, and individuals who bore their name. Saints' days and religious festivals still play an important part in Italian life.

THE EVANGELISTS

The four evangelists, Matthew, Mark, Luke and John are each represented by a winged creature, standing for a divine mission.

Eagle (St John)

St Dominic is usually portrayed wearing the habit of his order. The lily is another of his attributes.

St Cosmas and St Damian are always shown together, dressed in physicians' clothing.

St Mark the Evangelist often holds his book of the Gospels.

St John carries a book of the Gospel bearing his name.

St Thomas Aquinas is usually shown with a star, barely visible in this painting on his Dominican habit.

St Lawrence carries a palm leaf as well as the gridiron on which he was roasted.

Virgin Enthroned with the Child and Saints (c.1450) was painted on dry plaster by the Dominican friar, Fra Angelico. It is on display at the Museo di San Marco, Florence (see p268).

The Virgin, usually shown in blue robes, is depicted as Mater Amabilis – the "Mother Worthy of Love".

St Peter Martyr, here with a palm leaf, is sometimes depicted with a head wound, carrying a sword.

SYMBOLS

In order to identify different saints or martyrs they were given "attributes" or symbols – particular objects to carry, or clothing to wear. These were items that played a particular role in their life story. Martyrs were known by their instruments of torture or death. Symbolism also appears in the sky, animals, flowers, colours and numbers.

The lamb symbolizes Christ, the Lamb of God, or in early Christian art, the sinner.

The skull is a "memento mori" to remind us of death and impermanence.

Winged man (St Matthew)

Winged lion (St Mark)

Winged ox (St Luke)

St Peter the Apostle, the "rock" on which the Christian church was founded, carries the keys to heaven.

St Catherine of Alexandria is shown here with a piece of the wheel on which she was martyred.

The Madonna, with the Christ Child, is an emblem of perfect motherly love.

Giovanni Bellini's painting of *Madonna and Child with Four Saints* (see p115)

St Jerome is always portrayed as an old man, often a hermit, whose life was devoted to scholarship.

Detail from **Madonna and Child with Four Saints**, *by Giovanni Bellini. The painting was produced for an altarpiece at San Zaccaria, Venice in 1505, where it is still on display.*

The angel, a messenger of God to man, is portrayed in this scene as a musician of Heaven.

St Lucy is depicted here holding her own eyes in a dish. She became the patron saint of the blind and symbolizes light.

***The lily**, flower of the Virgin, is the symbol of purity, resurrection, peace and chastity.*

***The cockle shell** most often represents pilgrimage. It is a particular attribute of St Roch.*

***The palm** represents, in Christian art, a martyr's triumph over death.*

Writers, Poets and Dramatists

ITALY HAS PRODUCED many writers (in Latin and Italian) who have won worldwide immortality. Each of them provides an illuminating insight into the country's turbulent past: the poets Virgil, Horace and Ovid give vivid accounts of the concerns and values of ancient Rome; medieval Florence and Tuscany are brought to life in the poetry of Dante and Petrarch and the salacious tales of Boccaccio. In less than a century these three great writers created a new literary language to rank with any in Europe. Italy's modern literature still commands international attention – Umberto Eco has to his credit one of the most widely read books of this century.

Primo Levi *(1919–87) gave an astonishing account of his survival of the Jewish Holocaust and World War II's aftermath in* The Truce *and* If This Is A Man.

Trentino Alto Adige

Valle d'Aosta and Piedmont

Lombardy

Liguria

Emilia-Romagna

Tuscany

Umberto Eco *(born 1932), a professor at the University of Bologna, wrote the novel* The Name Of The Rose, *which explored his passion for the Middle Ages. The book was made into a film in 1986.*

Giovanni Boccaccio *(1313–75) is notable for providing a fascinating social record of his era.* The Decameron, *his captivating collection of 100 short stories, is set in the plague-stricken Florence of 1348.*

Pinocchio, *written by Carlo Collodi in 1911, is one of the world's best known children's stories. "Collodi" was Carlo Lorenzini's pseudonym, taken after his mother's birthplace in Tuscany.*

Dante's *Divine* Comedy *(c.1321), is a journey through Hell, Purgatory and Paradise. It includes horrific accounts of the torments suffered by the damned.*

Venetian author Carlo Goldoni (1707–93) reacted against the satirical tradition of La Commedia dell'Arte, preferring to write more forgiving plays on contemporary Venice society.

CLASSICAL ROMAN WRITERS

Texts in Latin by Classical Roman philosophers, poets, dramatists and politicians are part of the bedrock of Western culture. Today the names Virgil *(The Aeneid)*, Ovid *(Metamorphoses)* and Pliny *(Historia Naturalis)* are literary legends. Fascinating histories such as Livy's *Early History of Rome*, Caesar's *Gallic Wars*, Tacitus's *Annals* and Suetonius's *The Twelve Caesars*, give us an invaluable window on the distant Roman past, as do the caustic *Satires* of Juvenal. Many Latin works owe their survival to the teams of medieval monks who diligently copied and illustrated them. In the Renaissance the stories of Ovid's *Metamorphoses* were plundered by many writers and the works of Cicero had a profound influence on prose style; Seneca was seen as a master of tragedy and Plautus's *Pot of Gold* served as a model for comedies.

Detail from medieval copy of Pliny's *Historia Naturalis*

Petrarch (1304–74), one of the earliest and greatest lyric poets, produced works which showed the first indications of Humanism.

St Francis of Assisi (1182–1226) was the first author to write in Italian instead of formal Latin. As well as letters and sermons, he wrote poems and songs, including the popular Canticle of the Sun.

Roman writer Alberto Moravia (1907–90) is usually labelled a "Neo-Realist". His novels and short stories focus on the corrupt values of contemporary society. Among his best known works are *Two Women* and *Agostino*.

Marche

ia

Lazio

Abruzzo, Molise and Puglia

Campania

Basilicata and Calabria

eneto Friuli

Sicily

The Sicilian Nobel Prize-winner, Luigi Pirandello (1867–1936), was preoccupied with the theme of multiple personality. Six Characters In Search Of An Author *is his most famous work.*

0 kilometres   200

0 miles   100

Music and Opera in Italy

BEFORE ITALY'S UNIFICATION, particularly during the 17th and 18th centuries, each major city had its own traditions of music-making. Rome, as the papal city, had musical traditions less hedonistic than elsewhere, and avoided opera. Florence had its day at the turn of the 16th century, with its celebrated *camerata* (groups set on reviving the traditions of Ancient Greek spectacle). Venice fostered church music on a grand scale, and Naples, during the 18th century, was renowned for comic opera. In the 19th century, Milan became the undisputed centre of Italian opera, centred on La Scala.

Stradivarius violin

THE MEDIEVAL AND RENAISSANCE PERIODS

THROUGH BOCCACCIO *(see p30)*, among others, it is known that singing, dancing and poetry often went hand in hand in medieval and Renaissance Italy. Italy concentrated on music as part of a spectacle rather than as a pure art form.

Important contributors to the music of these periods include Guido d'Arezzo (c.995–1050), a monk who perfected musical notation, and Francesco Landini (1325–97), one of the first known composers whose songs displayed a distinct concern for lyricism. The next 150 years were to be characterized by the *Ars Perfecta* style, culminating with composer Giovanni Palestrina (1525–94). His vocal style subjected dissonance to strict control, and it was employed for most church music. Madrigals (vocal settings of poems by Petrarch and other poets) were also popular.

La Pietà, Venice, where Vivaldi performed

The early 17th century saw Italian composers such as Carlo Gesualdo (c.1561–1613) and Claudio Monteverdi challenge these traditions by introducing more declamation and more of the unexpected.

THE BAROQUE ERA

CLAUDIO MONTEVERDI'S music straddled the transition from the Renaissance period to 17th-century Baroque. The word "baroque" means highly ornamented, even bizarre, and embellishment was rife. Monteverdi's madrigals began as standard pieces for four voices but ended up as mini-operas. This was due to the popularity of an individual instrumental style and the development of the *basso continuo* (a supporting organ, harpsichord or lute that unleashed the possibility for solos and duets). At this point, the beginnings of the string orchestra were in place.

A new fashion for declamation meant that various emotional states were being represented with sighs and sobs rather than just description. Monteverdi's *Vespers* followed others' in exploiting the stereophonic possibilities of San Marco in Venice by contrasting different forces

MAJOR ITALIAN COMPOSERS THROUGH THE AGES

Claudio Monteverdi *(1567–1643) was best known for his* Vespers *of 1610. Both his madrigals and operas are considered major landmarks in the development of music.*

Antonio Vivaldi *(1678–1741) wrote over 600 concertos, many of which are for the violin. The* Four Seasons, *a set of concertos, is among the best-selling classical music of all time.*

Gioachino Rossini *(1792–1868) was most famous for his comic operas, like* The Barber of Seville. *The romantic, expressive side of his more serious works was often overlooked.*

Luciano Pavarotti performing in the most modern surroundings

in different parts of the building. In the 1680s, Arcangelo Corelli (1653–1713) turned to classicism. Corelli was famous for the *Concerto Grosso,* a style that contrasted the solo string group with the full ensemble. He was followed by Antonio Vivaldi (1678–1741), who concentrated his efforts on developing the solo form of the *Concerto Grosso.* He used wind and plucked instruments as well as violins.

THE EMERGENCE OF OPERA

OPERA FIRST emerged during the wedding celebrations of Italy's 16th-century wealthy families. Monteverdi was the first composer to establish

Giuseppe Verdi (1813–1901), whose first works were for La Scala, was the most important opera composer of the 19th century. His most celebrated works include Rigoletto *and* Aida.

his work firmly in the opera repertoire. During the 17th century, Alessandro Scarlatti (1660–1725) formulated a model which consisted of an orchestral overture followed by a sequence of narrative, set as *recitative,* and interrupted by *da capo* (three-part) arias. Themes for the weightier *opera seria* were largely drawn from mythology, while the lighter *opera buffa* had stock scenes that sometimes owed a large debt to the traditions of Commedia dell'Arte. Famous for his comic operas, such as *The Barber of Seville,* was the composer Gioachino Rossini. Among other contributors, Vincenzo Bellini (1801–35) and Gaetano Donizetti (1797–1848) developed *bel canto* singing, a style stressing fine tone and ornamentation.

The two most prominent opera composers of the latter half of the 19th century were Giuseppe Verdi and Giacomo Puccini (1858–1924). Verdi often turned to the works of Shakespeare as well as to more recent subjects in order to form a basis for his work, while many composers, like Puccini, turned to the new trend of *verismo* (slices of contemporary realism) – *La Bohème* is one of the most refined examples of this style.

Puccini's *Tosca,* first staged in 1900

THE 20TH CENTURY

IN THE EARLY 20th century, Puccini's *La Fanciulla del West* (The Girl of the Golden West) brought cowboys into opera, *Turandot* looked towards the Orient and *Tosca* brought torture and murder. Some composers have attempted to emulate French and German music, and only a few Italian pieces, such as those by Ottorino Respighi (1879–1936), have been regularly performed. The most important name in Italian music today is Luciano Berio (born 1925), whose vocal and collage techniques have attracted numerous imitators. Berio also developed Music Theatre, a relatively new art form lying somewhere between drama and opera. Recently, however, Berio has continued the tradition of Grand Opera with his elaborate production of *Un Re in Ascolto.* But it is perhaps Luciano Pavarotti who must be credited with renewing an international interest in opera. His (often televised) performances with "Three Tenors" stars José Carreras and Placido Domingo have secured a massive world audience for opera.

The illuminated interior of Rome's Teatro dell'Opera

Italial Design

ITALY HAS HAD PHENOMENAL success evolving stylish, desirable forms for everyday objects. Its 20th-century achievements can be credited to a handful of forward-thinking industrial giants, such as Olivetti, willing to entrust important product decisions to a group of inspired designers, like Ettore Sottsass. The design genius was to rethink the function of consumer objects, apply new technology, and then make the result look seductive.

The streamlined *aesthetic of Italian design extends even to pasta; this Marille version was created by car designer Giorgio Giugiaro for Voiello in 1983.*

Sleek, sculptural *Alessi cutlery (1988), designed by Ettore Sottsass, combines maximum utility with elegance and aesthetic integrity.*

The Alessi kettle *(1985), designed by Michael Graves, achieved such popularity in its first year of production that over 100,000 were sold.*

One of the best *known coffeemakers is Bialetti's Moka Express. Although designed in 1930, it is still enormously popular today.*

Combining elegance *and function, the 1966 all-plastic Selene side chair was stackable and strong, and designed by Vico Magistretti for Artemide.*

The folding Cumano *table, designed by Achille Castiglione for Zanotta in 1979, is still revered as a "designer object".*

The Patty Difusa *chair, with unusual wooden arms that curve into legs, was designed by William Sawaya for Sawaya & Moroni in Milan.*

Pininfarina's streamlined *form for the Ferrari Testarossa (1986) pushes car design almost into the realms of sculpture.*

Light in weight, *and compact in shape, Olivetti's Valentine typewriter revolutionized the role of the desk typewriter. Designed by Ettore Sottsass in 1969, its portability allowed the user to work anywhere.*

Italian printer *Giambattista Bodoni (1740–1813) designed the sophisticated typeface that bears his name and is still popular 200 years after its creation.*

Milan's Giorgio Armani *is best known for his updating of classic items such as the jacket, creating a flattering, smart and comfortable, "deconstructed" look.*

The influential, *Rome-based, Valentino label has long excelled in sassy, well-tailored clothing, pitched at the very top end of the fashion market.*

Florence has a long *reputation as a producer of high quality crafts, particularly fashion accessories such as handbags, shoes, belts, jewellery and briefcases.*

Gucci's *image has had a major revamp. Their classic items, including shoes, are once again a revered totem for the fashion-conscious.*

The Artemide *company is renowned for combining metal and glass in many of their designs, especially lamps and lighting fixtures.*

Piaggio's innovative *Vespa scooter (1946), by Corradino d'Ascanio, provided cheap, fast and reliable transport at a time when few could afford the expense of a car. Hugely successful, the Vespa is still a common sight on Italy's streets.*

The Fiat 500 *(1957), like the Vespa, became a symbol of mobility and democratization, an expression of Italy's rapid postwar recovery.*

Scientists, Inventors and Explorers

I TALY HAS fostered a long tradition of important scientific thought and discovery, fuelled in the Renaissance by such men as Galileo, who searched for a new understanding of the universe. Meanwhile, explorers such as Columbus had set off to find new worlds, a move heralded in the 13th century by Marco Polo. The spirit of scientific enquiry continued up to the 20th century, with the invention of radio and pioneering work in the field of nuclear physics.

***Guglielmo Marconi** invented the first practical system for sending radio signals. In 1901, he succeeded in picking up a signal that had been sent to England from Newfoundland.*

Tren
Alto

Lombardy

The
and

Valle d'Aosta
and Piedmont

Liguria

Tuscan

__After deducing__ that an electric current made frogs' legs move, Alessandro Volta invented the electric battery, a "pile" of metal discs in contact with acid. He demonstrated it to Napoleon in 1801.

__Genoese-born__ Christopher Columbus sailed west from Spain in 1492. He reached the Indies in three months, navigating with such aids as an astrolabe.

__The explorer__ Amerigo Vespucci established that the New World was a separate land mass. A pamphlet wrongly described him as its discoverer, and so, in 1507, America acquired its name.

__Leonardo da Vinci__ was the ultimate Renaissance man, accomplished in both arts and sciences. He conceived his first design for a flying machine in c.1488, more than 400 years before the first aeroplane took off. This model is based on one of his technical drawings.

__The telescope__ enabled astronomers to produce accurate lunar maps. Domenico Cassini, astronomy professor at Bologna University, refined the instrument. In 1665 he traced the meridian line in the church of San Petronio.

| 0 kilometres | 200 |
| 0 miles | 100 |

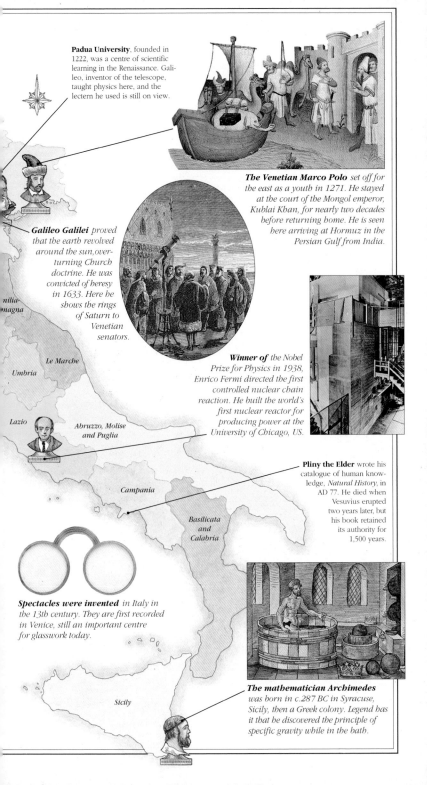

Padua University, founded in 1222, was a centre of scientific learning in the Renaissance. Galileo, inventor of the telescope, taught physics here, and the lectern he used is still on view.

The Venetian Marco Polo set off for the east as a youth in 1271. He stayed at the court of the Mongol emperor, Kublai Khan, for nearly two decades before returning home. He is seen here arriving at Hormuz in the Persian Gulf from India.

Galileo Galilei proved that the earth revolved around the sun, over-turning Church doctrine. He was convicted of heresy in 1633. Here he shows the rings of Saturn to Venetian senators.

nilia-magna

Le Marche

Umbria

Lazio

Abruzzo, Molise and Puglia

Winner of the Nobel Prize for Physics in 1938, Enrico Fermi directed the first controlled nuclear chain reaction. He built the world's first nuclear reactor for producing power at the University of Chicago, US.

Pliny the Elder wrote his catalogue of human know-ledge, *Natural History*, in AD 77. He died when Vesuvius erupted two years later, but his book retained its authority for 1,500 years.

Campania

Basilicata and Calabria

Spectacles were invented in Italy in the 13th century. They are first recorded in Venice, still an important centre for glasswork today.

Sicily

The mathematician Archimedes was born in c.287 BC in Syracuse, Sicily, then a Greek colony. Legend has it that he discovered the principle of specific gravity while in the bath.

TEMPLA DOMVM EXPOSITIS·VICOS·FORA·MOENIA·PONTES:
VIRGINEAM·TRIVII·QVOD·REPARARIS·AQVAM·
PRISCA·LICET·NAVTIS·STATVAS·DARE·COMMODA·PORTVS:
ET·VATICANVM·CINGERE·SIXTE·IVGVM:
PLVS·TAMEN·VRBS·DEBET:NAM·QVAE·SQVALORE·LATEBAT:
CERNITVR·IN·CELEBRI·BIBLIOTHECA·LOCO·

THE HISTORY OF ITALY

HE CONCEPT of Italy as a geographic entity goes back to the time of the Etruscans, but Italy's history is one of discord and division. Prior to the 19th century, the only time the peninsula was united was under the Romans, who by the 3rd century BC had subdued the other Italian tribes. Rome became the capital of a huge empire, introducing its language, laws and calendar to most of Europe before succumbing to Germanic invaders in the 5th century AD.

Julius Caesar

Another important legacy of the Roman empire was Christianity and the position of the pope as head of the Catholic church. The medieval papacy summoned the Franks to drive out the Lombards and, in AD 800, crowned the Frankish king Charlemagne Holy Roman Emperor. Unfortunately, what seemed to be the dawn of a new age turned out to be anything but. For five centuries popes and emperors fought to decide which of them should be in charge of their nebulous empire.

Meanwhile, a succession of foreign invaders – Normans, Angevins and Aragonese – took advantage of the situation to conquer Sicily and the south.

The north, in contrast, saw a growth of independent city states, the most powerful being Venice, fabulously wealthy through trade with the East. Other cities, such as Genoa, Florence, Milan and Siena, also had their days of glory. Northern Italy became the most prosperous and cultured region in western Europe and it was the artists and scholars of 15th-century Florence who inspired the Renaissance. Small, fragmented states, however, could not compete with great powers. In the 16th century Italy's petty kingdoms fell prey to a foreign invader, this time to Spain, and the north subsequently came under the control of Austria.

One small kingdom that remained independent was Piedmont, but during a war between Austria and France it fell to Napoleon in 1796. In the 19th century, however, it was Piedmont that became the focus for a movement towards a united Italy, a goal that was achieved in 1870, thanks largely to the heroic military exploits of Garibaldi. In the 1920s, the Fascists seized power and, in 1946, the monarchy was abandoned for today's republic.

16th-century map of Italy, of the kind used by Venetian and Genoese sailors

◁ **Fresco by Melozzo da Forlì of the court of Sixtus IV (1471–84), a powerful and worldly Renaissance pope**

The Age of the Etruscans

THE ETRUSCANS, who gave their name to Tuscany, were Italy's first major civilization. The frescoes, jewellery and pottery found in their tombs are evidence of a highly artistic, cultured people. Their origin is a mystery, as is their language, but from the 9th century BC they spread through central Italy, their chief rivals being the Greeks in the south. Etruria was never a unified state, just a loose confederation of cities. In the 6th century Etruscan kings ruled Rome, the city that would ultimately eclipse them.

ITALY IN 650 BC

▨	Etruscan kingdoms
☐	Greek colonies

The double flute was a speciality of the Etruscans. The instrument was played at festivals and funerals alike.

Terracotta Winged Horses
This beautiful relief of yoked horses (4th century BC) decorated the façade of the Ara della Regina temple at Tarquinia.

Bronze Sheep's Liver
The inscriptions served as a guide for telling the future from animals' entrails.

Terracotta Cremation Urn
The lid of the urn shows the deceased holding a writing tablet. The Etruscans intro-duced the alphabet to Italy.

TOMB OF THE LEOPARDS
Feasts and revelry are common themes in the frescoes that decorate Etruscan tombs. These musicians are from a tomb fresco (c.500 BC) at Tarquinia *(see p450)*.

TIMELINE

900 BC	800 BC	700 BC
9th century BC Pre-urban communities established along river valleys in Etruria	**c.700 BC** Growth of cities in Etruria; earliest Etruscan inscriptions	**616 BC** Etruscan become rulers of Rom
	753 BC Legendary date of foundation of Rome by Romulus	
c.900 BC First traces of Iron Age in Italy; Villanovan period		
c.800 BC Greeks settle in Sicily and south of Italy	**715–673 BC** Reign of the wise Numa Pompilius, second king of Rome	*Etruscan gold earrings*

A Boxing Match
Athletic competitions were held at funerals. This vase, which dates from about 500 BC, was made in Etruria, but imitates the Greek black-figure style of pottery.

The musicians and the dancer in the tomb painting are painted with a realism that indicates the influence of Greek art.

The lyre was made from a tortoise shell and played with a plectrum.

Apollo of Veii
This magnificent statue of Apollo (c.500 BC) shows the stylized facial features characteristic of Etruscan art.

Bronze Mirror
Wealthy Etruscans lived in great luxury. The women used polished bronze mirrors with engraved backs. This one shows Helen of Troy and the goddess Aphrodite.

WHERE TO SEE ETRUSCAN ITALY

Rock tombs *like these at Sovana (p336) are common in the volcanic tufa of central Italy.*

Tuscany, Lazio and Umbria are rich in Etruscan remains, especially tombs. There are huge necropolises in Lazio at Cerveteri and Tarquinia (p450). The latter also has an important museum. Other museums with major collections of Etruscan art and artefacts include the Villa Giulia (p430) and the Vatican's Museo Gregoriano (p412) in Rome, the Museo Archeologico in Florence (p274), the Museo Civico in Chiusi (p322) and the Museo Guarnacci in Volterra (p336).

Temple of Neptune
This fine temple at Paestum (5th century BC) is a legacy of Greek colonization of the south.

---

509 BC Last Etruscan king, Tarquinius Superbus, expelled from Rome; establishment of Roman Republic

450 BC Roman law codified in the Twelve Tables

Mixing bowl, imported from Greece

390 BC Gauls sack Rome; Capitol saved thanks to alarm sounded by cackling geese

0 BC   500 BC   400 BC

499 BC Battle of Lake Regillus; Romans defeat alliance of Latins and Etruscans

474 BC Etruscan fleet defeated by Greeks off Cumae; blow to Etruscan naval power

c.400 BC Gauls start to settle along valley of the Po

396 BC Veii, a major Etruscan city in present-day Lazio, falls to Rome

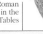

Relief of Capitoline geese, found in the Roman Forum

From Republic to Empire

From the scores of tribes inhabiting ancient Italy, one people, the Romans, emerged to conquer the peninsula and impose their language, customs and laws on the rest.

Roman mask and helmet (1st century BC)

Rome's success was due to superb skill in military and civil organization. The state was a republic ruled by two consuls, elected each year, but as the extent of Rome's conquests grew, power passed to generals such as Julius Caesar. The Republic became unworkable and Caesar's heirs became the first Roman emperors.

Cisalpine Gaul was annexed in 202–191 BC.

Etruria was in Roman hands by 265 BC.

Julius Caesar
The great general, conqueror of Gaul, returned to Italy in 49 BC to defeat his rival Pompey. His rise to absolute power signalled the end of the Republic.

Oscan Inscription
The languages of the peoples conquered by Rome lived on for centuries before being replaced by Latin. The Oscans lived in what is now Campania.

War Elephant
In 218 BC the great Carthaginian general Hannibal brought 37 elephants across the Alps – to spread alarm in the Roman ranks.

Roman Aqueduct
The Romans' talent for engineering found its most spectacular expression in huge aqueducts. These could be up to 80 km (50 miles) long, though for most of that distance the water ran underground.

High ground

Cleaning vent

Reservoir

Underground water channel

Arches carrying water across low ground

TIMELINE

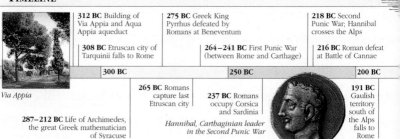

Via Appia

312 BC Building of Via Appia and Aqua Appia aqueduct	**275 BC** Greek King Pyrrhus defeated by Romans at Beneventum	**218 BC** Second Punic War; Hannibal crosses the Alps
308 BC Etruscan city of Tarquinii falls to Rome	**264–241 BC** First Punic War (between Rome and Carthage)	**216 BC** Roman defeat at Battle of Cannae

300 BC   **250 BC**   **200 BC**

265 BC Romans capture last Etruscan city

237 BC Romans occupy Corsica and Sardinia

Hannibal, Carthaginian leader in the Second Punic War

191 BC Gaulish territory south of the Alps falls to Rome

287–212 BC Life of Archimedes, the great Greek mathematician of Syracuse

Cicero Addresses the Senate
State business was debated in the Senate. The great orator Cicero (106–43 BC) argued for the Republic and against tyranny.

Roman Legionary
This bronze shows a legionary in standard kit of helmet, breastplate, leather kilt with iron plates, and greaves on his shins and sandals.

The Via Appia
was extended from Capua to Brindisi in 190 BC.

INIUM
ERIA

APUA — VIA APPIA
TARENTUM
Taranto
BRUNDISIUM
Brindisi

Sicily
became the first Roman province in 227 BC.

RHEGIUM
Reggio di Calabria

WHERE TO SEE ITALY FROM THE REPUBLICAN ERA

Republican structures are very rare, most having been rebuilt under the Empire. In Rome itself, two notable exceptions are the 2nd-century BC Temples of the Forum Boarium (p423). However, the legacy of the age to modern Italy is not hard to appreciate. Countless roads, such as the Via Appia Antica (p431), and towns were planned originally by Roman engineers. Two striking examples of towns with original Roman street plans are Lucca (pp310–11) and Como (p185).

***These huge basalt blocks** at Tharros in Sardinia (p535) were part of a Roman road.*

ROMAN ROADS

After conquering other tribes, the Romans imposed their authority by building roads along which legions could march rapidly to deal with any trouble. They also built towns. Many, such as Ariminum (Rimini), were "colonies", settlements for Roman citizens – often veteran legionaries.

Aerial View of Bologna
Roman street plans are still visible in city centres today. The route of the old Via Aemilia cuts straight through the centre of Bologna.

146 BC End of Third Punic War; Carthage destroyed

104 BC Slave revolt in Sicily

89 BC Social War: Rome's Italian allies granted citizenship

31 BC Octavian defeats Mark Antony at Battle of Actium

30 BC Suicide of Mark Antony and Cleopatra in Egypt

80 BC Building starts on the first Roman amphitheatre, at Pompei

| 150 BC | 100 BC | 50 BC |

168 BC End of Third Macedonian War; Romans now masters of Greece

73–71 BC Slave revolt led by Spartacus

44 BC Murder of Julius Caesar; end of Roman Republic

Milestone from the Via Aemilia

49 BC Caesar crosses the Rubicon and drives Pompey from Rome

45 BC Introduction of 12-month Julian calendar

The Golden Age of Rome

FROM THE AGE of Augustus to the reign of Trajan, Rome's power grew until her empire stretched from Britain to the Red Sea. Despite the extravagance of emperors such as Nero, taxes and booty from military campaigns continually refilled the Imperial coffers. Under the wiser rule of Trajan, Hadrian and Marcus Aurelius in the 2nd century AD, Roman citizens enjoyed wealth and comfort, with most of the work performed by slaves. Entertainment included visits to the baths, the theatre and the games. The town of Pompei, buried when Vesuvius erupted in AD 79, preserves many fascinating details of everyday life.

ROMAN EMPIRE IN AD 117

▢ *Maximum extent of the Empire*

Mosaic of Gladiators
Bloodthirsty gladiatorial combats were very popular. The gladiators were mostly slaves captured in war.

Frescoes of festoons and medallions

Trajan's Column
The carvings record Trajan's successful campaigns in Dacia (present-day Romania) in the first decade of the 2nd century AD.

The triclinium
(main dining room) had a beautiful frieze of cupids.

Roman Shops
Buildings in towns were lined with small shops open to the street, like this pharmacy. The front was closed with wooden panels and locked at night.

HOUSE OF THE VETTII

This reconstruction shows one of Pompei's finest houses *(see pp478–9)*. The Vettii were not aristocrats, but freedmen, former slaves, who had made a fortune through trade. The rooms were richly decorated with frescoes and sculptures.

TIMELINE

9 BC Dedication of Ara Pacis *(see p400)* in Rome to celebrate peace after wars in Gaul and Spain	**AD 17** Tiberius fixes boundary of Empire along the Rhine and Danube	*Bronze cooking pots from kitchen at Pompei*		**AD 79** Eruption of Vesuvius destroys Pompei and Herculane
50 BC	**AD 1**		**AD 50**	
27 BC Augustus takes title Princeps, in effect becoming the first Roman emperor	**AD 37–41** Reign of Caligula		**AD 67** Traditional date for martyrdom of St Peter and St Paul in Rome	**AD 80** Inaugura games in Colosseu
	AD 43 Roman conquest of Britain in reign of Claudius			
	AD 68 Deposition and suicide of Nero			

Augustus
The adopted son of Julius Caesar became the first emperor, reducing the Roman Senate to impotence and ruling by decree.

The atrium had a skylight in the roof with a pool that collected rainwater below.

Front entrance

WHERE TO SEE IMPERIAL ROME

The best places to discover how people lived are Pompei (pp478–9) and Herculaneum. Artefacts and works of art from the two sites are held at the Museo Archeologico in Naples (pp474–5), while local museums all over Italy contain statues and other remains. Famous sights in Rome include the Pantheon (p394) and the Colosseum (p383). Near Rome, Hadrian's Villa and Ostia (p451) are also fascinating places to visit, but the whole country preserves traces of Rome's glory – from the Arch of Augustus in Aosta (p207) to Villa Casale (p521) in Sicily.

The Forum (pp380–81), with its temples and law courts, was the centre of daily life in ancient Rome.

Reception room

Mosaic of a Banquet
The Romans ate reclining on low couches. A popular accompaniment for many dishes was garum, a salty sauce made of dried fish.

Peristyle or colonnade

The internal garden was a feature borrowed by the Romans from the Greeks.

Household Shrine
Religious rites were practised both in public and in private. This shrine from the House of the Vettii was dedicated to the lares, the household gods.

AD 117 Roman Empire reaches largest extent in reign of Trajan

AD 161–180 Reign of Marcus Aurelius

AD 193–211 Reign of Septimius Severus

AD 212 Roman citizenship extended to include people from all parts of the Empire

AD 100

AD 150

AD 200

1st century Amphitheatre Verona built

AD 125 Pantheon rebuilt by Hadrian

AD 134 Hadrian's Villa at Tivoli completed

Emperor Septimius Severus

AD 216 Baths of Caracalla completed in Rome

The Splitting of the Empire

Glass flask with Christian symbol (4th century AD)

A DECISIVE TURNING POINT in the history of the Roman Empire came with Emperor Constantine's conversion to Christianity in AD 312 and his decision to build a new capital at Constantinople (Byzantium). By the 5th century the Empire was split into two. Rome and the Western Empire could not stem the tide of Germanic invaders migrating southwards and Italy fell first to the Goths and later to the Lombards. The Eastern Empire retained nominal control over parts of Italy from its stronghold at Ravenna, which became the richest, most powerful city of the age, while the great palaces and arenas of Rome were reduced to ruins.

ITALY IN AD 600

- ▨ *Byzantine territories*
- ☐ *Lombard territories*

The Donation of Constantine
A medieval legend, encouraged by the papacy, tells how Constantine granted Pope Sylvester temporal power over Rome.

Belisarius was a general who won much of Italy back from the Goths.

Theodolinda of the Lombards
The 6th-century queen converted her people to orthodox Catholicism. Here, gold is melted for the church she built at Monza (see p178).

Justinian reigned from 527 to 565. He was a great lawgiver and one of the most powerful Byzantine emperors.

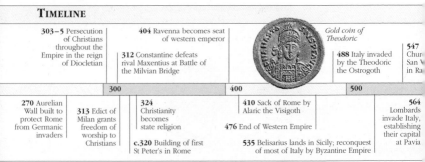

TIMELINE

303–5 Persecution of Christians throughout the Empire in the reign of Diocletian

312 Constantine defeats rival Maxentius at Battle of the Milvian Bridge

404 Ravenna becomes seat of western emperor

Gold coin of Theodoric

488 Italy invaded by the Theodoric the Ostrogoth

547 Chur San in Ra

300

400

500

270 Aurelian Wall built to protect Rome from Germanic invaders

313 Edict of Milan grants freedom of worship to Christians

324 Christianity becomes state religion

c.320 Building of first St Peter's in Rome

410 Sack of Rome by Alaric the Visigoth

476 End of Western Empire

535 Belisarius lands in Sicily; reconquest of most of Italy by Byzantine Empire

564 Lombards invade Italy, establishing their capital at Pavia

Charlemagne
The King of the Franks was invited by the pope to crush the Lombards. In return, he was crowned Holy Roman Emperor in AD 800.

Saracens Besieging Messina *(843)*
In the 9th century Sicily was conquered by Muslims from Africa. Saracen raiders even reached Rome, where Pope Leo IV built a new wall to defend the Vatican.

The emperor holds a large gold paten, the dish in which the bread is placed for Mass.

Maximian, Archbishop of Ravenna

Priests

THE COURT OF JUSTINIAN

Byzantine churches were decorated with glorious mosaics of coloured glass and gold leaf. This one from the apse of the church of San Vitale in Ravenna *(see p260)*, completed in 547, depicts members of the Imperial court.

WHERE TO SEE EARLY CHRISTIAN AND BYZANTINE ITALY

Though the fall of the Roman Empire led to war, famine and depopulation, the continuity of the Christian religion has preserved many monuments of the late Empire and Byzantine period. Rome has the catacombs *(p432)* and great basilicas, such as Santa Maria Maggiore *(p403)*. In Ravenna, the administrative capital of the Byzantine Empire, are the churches of San Vitale and Sant'Apollinare *(pp260–61)* with their magnificent mosaics. Sicily and the south also preserve many Byzantine churches, while the finest example of late Byzantine architecture is San Marco in Venice *(pp106–9)*.

Stilo *in Calabria has a beautiful Byzantine church, the Cattolica* (p504), *dating from the 10th century.*

Santa Costanza *in Rome* (p431) *was built in the 4th century as the mausoleum of Constantine's daughter. Late Roman mosaics decorate the vaults.*

---

95 Lombards [con]trol two [en]ds of Italy

752 Lombard King Aistulf takes Byzantine stronghold of Ravenna

774 Charlemagne conquers Italy and takes Lombard crown

800 Charlemagne crowned Holy Roman Emperor in St Peter's

878 Saracens capture city of Syracuse from Byzantine Empire and gain control of Sicily

| 600 | 700 | 800 | 900 |

Gregory the [G]reat (reigned 590–604)

99 Pope Gregory negotiates [pe]ace between the Lombards [an]d the Byzantine Empire

754 Pope appeals to Franks for help; King Pepin invades Italy and defeats Lombards

6th-century Lombard gold helmet in the Bargello museum, Florence (see p275)

The Rise of Venice

Enrico Dandolo, Doge of Venice (c.1120–1205)

MEDIEVAL ITALY saw waves of foreign invaders joining in the struggle for power between popes and emperors. In the confusion, many northern cities asserted their independence from feudal overlords. The most powerful was Venice, governed by its doge and Great Council, which grew rich through trade with the East and by shipping Crusaders to fight the Saracens in the Holy Land. Its maritime rivals on the west coast were Genoa and Pisa.

MEDITERRANEAN IN 1250

— *Genoese trade routes*

Venetian trade routes

Matilda of Tuscany
Matilda, Countess of Tuscany (1046 – 1115) supported the radical Pope Gregory VII against the Emperor Henry IV. When she died, she left her lands to the church.

Basilica San Marco

Doge's Palace

Canopy over the half-deck

Sails – for added speed

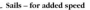

The oars, pulled by slaves, were the principal means of propulsion.

Venetian Galley
The galleys used by Venice, both as warships and for carrying cargo, were similar to ancient Greek vessels.

The columns of San Marco and San Teodoro had been erected in the 12th century.

MARCO POLO'S DEPARTURE FOR CHINA

Venice traded in Chinese silks and spices imported via the Middle East, but no Venetian had been to China before Marco Polo's father Nicolò. Marco Polo set off with his father in 1271, returning 25 years later with fantastic tales of his time at the court of Kublai Khan.

TIMELINE

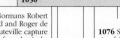

Medieval students

1000 Doge of Venice, Pietro Orseolo II, defeats Dalmatian pirates in Adriatic

11th century School of Law at Bologna develops into Europe's first university

1139 Naple[s] incorporated int[o] Kingdom of Sicily

1000	1050	1100

1030 Norman knight Rainulf granted county of Aversa by Duke of Naples

1061 Normans Robert Guiscard and Roger de Hauteville capture Messina from the Arabs

1063 San Marco in Venice rebuilt

1084 Normans sack Rome

1076 Salerno, last Lombard city, falls to Normans

1073–85 Pope Gregory VII reforms church and papacy

1115 Death of Countess Matilda

1130 [Roger] II crow[ned] king of Sicily

St Francis of Assisi
(1181–1226)
In The Dream of Pope Innocent III *by Giotto, painted around 1290–1295, St Francis holds up the tottering edifice of the Roman church. The Franciscans' rule of poverty brought about a religious revival in reaction to the wealth of the church.*

WHERE TO SEE EARLY MEDIEVAL ITALY

Of the many churches built in this period, especially fine examples are Venice's San Marco (p106), Sant'Antonio (p152) in Padua and the Duomo in Pisa (p314). The Leaning Tower (p316) also dates back to the 12th century. Medieval castles include Frederick II's Castel del Monte in Puglia (p493) and Castello dell'Imperatore in Prato.

***Castello dell' Imperatore**, Prato, was built about 1240.*

Monastery of Sant'Apollonia

Today's Riva degli Schiavoni

Nicolò Polo, his brother Maffeo and son Marco prepare to embark. They sailed first to Acre in the Levant.

Fourth Crusade
Discord between the leaders of the crusade and Pope Innocent III culminated in the sacking of Constantinople in 1204.

Frederick II
(1194–1250)
The emperor kept a court of poets and scholars in Sicily. He won Jerusalem from the Arabs by diplomacy, but was constantly at war with the pope and the cities of Lombardy.

1155 Frederick Barbarossa crowned Holy Roman Emperor

1198 Frederick II becomes king of Sicily

1204 Sacking of Constantinople

1209 Franciscan Order founded

1216 Dominican Order founded

1250 Death of Frederick II

1260 Urban IV invites Charles of Anjou to rule Naples and Sicily

1265 Birth of Dante

| 50 | 1200 | 1250 |

Frederick Barbarossa dressed as a Crusader

1220 Frederick II crowned Holy Roman Emperor

1237 Lombard League defeat Frederick at Battle of Cortenuova

1228 Gregory IX excommunicates Frederick II; struggle between Guelphs (the papal party) and Ghibellines (supporters of the emperor)

1271 Marco Polo sets off on journey to China

The Late Middle Ages

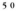

OLD FEUDS BETWEEN pope and emperor thrived throughout the 14th century, kept alive by two warring factions – the Guelphs, who backed the papacy, and the Ghibellines, who favoured Imperial power. The cities of Lombardy and Tuscany used the political confusion to grow in strength. It was against this turbulent backdrop that a great new age in painting was inspired by artists such as Duccio and Giotto. Also at this time the Florentine poets Dante and Petrarch laid the foundations of Italian literature.

Sienese bishop's staff

ITALY IN 1350

- ▨ *Papal States*
- ☐ *Holy Roman Empire*
- ▨ *Angevin Kingdom of Naples*

MEDIEVAL TOWN SQUARE

Throughout central Italy, the town square was an expression of civic pride and independence. Towns, such as Perugia *(see pp342–3)*, tried to overshadow their rivals in the splendour of their town halls. The centre of Perugia has changed little since the 14th century when the town's main rival was Siena.

The campanile or bell tower

A griffin, symbol of Perugia

Condottieri
Cities paid condottieri, *leaders of bands of mercenaries, to fight their wars. Siena hired Guidoriccio da Fogliano, seen here in a fresco by Simone Martini (1330).*

The main chamber of the town hall, the Sala dei Notari, is decorated with the coats of arms of Perugia's mayors.

Dante's Inferno
One of the harshest punishments in Dante's vision of hell is reserved for corrupt popes, such as Boniface VIII (reigned 1294–1303), who are placed upside down in fiery pits.

The Fontana Maggiore was begun in 1275 and includes panels by Nicola Pisano. Prominently placed, it is an emblem of the town's wealth.

TIMELINE

1282 Sicilian Vespers; uprising against French rule in Palermo; 2,000 French soldiers killed

1282 Peter of Aragon lands at Trapani, conquers Sicily and is crowned king in Palermo

1296 Work begins on the Duomo in Florence

1298 Marco Polo returns from China to Venice

The poet and scholar Petrarch

1304 Birth of Petrarch

1309–43 Reign of Robert the Wise of Naples

1309 Clement V moves papacy to Avignon

1310 Work begins on Palazzo Ducale in Venice

1313 Birth of Boccaccio

1321 Dante completes *La Divina Commedia*

1337 Death of Giotto

1275   **1300**   **1325**

The Black Death
Bubonic plague reached Italy in 1347, carried on Genoese ships from the Black Sea. It killed over a third of the population, reducing the remainder to a state of superstitious terror.

WHERE TO SEE LATE MEDIEVAL ITALY

Many central Italian cities and towns have public buildings from the 13th and 14th centuries; among the most impressive are Palazzo Vecchio *(p283)* in Florence and Siena's Palazzo Pubblico *(p330)*. Smaller towns that preserve much of their medieval character include Volterra *(p324)* and the walled Monteriggioni *(p324)* in Tuscany, Gubbio *(p342)* and Todi *(p349)* in Umbria and Viterbo *(pp448–9)* in Lazio. The Duomo in Orvieto *(pp348–9)* is a fine example of a late 13th-century Gothic cathedral.

Piazza dei Priori in Volterra (p324) is one of the most beautiful medieval squares in Italy.

The cathedral was started in 1350 and used to include an outside pulpit in the square.

Construction of Alessandria
Almost all towns were ringed with strong walls. This fresco (1407) by Spinello Aretino is a valuable record of medieval building techniques.

Return of Pope Gregory XI to Rome *(1377)*
For 70 years the popes had lived in Avignon, protected by the French kings, while nobles and republicans fought for control of Rome.

1343 Simon Boccanegra becomes first doge of Genoa; Giovanna I Queen of Naples

1347–9 Black Death

Medieval doctor

1378–1415 Period of Schism, with rival popes and antipopes in Rome and Avignon

1380 Genoese fleet surrenders to Venetians at Chioggia

1350	1375	1400

1354 Cola di Rienzo killed in Rome

1385 Gian Galeazzo Visconti becomes ruler of Milan

1406 Pisa annexed by Florence

1347 Cola di Rienzo tries to re-establish Roman Republic

1377 Gregory XI returns from Avignon to Rome

The Renaissance

Leonardo da Vinci (1452–1519)

FIFTEENTH-CENTURY ITALY saw a flowering of the arts and scholarship unmatched in Europe since the days of Greece and Rome. Architects turned from the Gothic to Classical models for inspiration, while painting, with its new understanding of perspective and anatomy, produced a generation of artists that included such giants as Leonardo da Vinci, Raphael and Michelangelo. The patronage for this cultural "rebirth" came from the wealthy families that ruled the city states of the north, led by the Medici of Florence. In spite of intense rivalry, they oversaw a period of uneasy stability out of which the Renaissance grew.

ITALY IN 1492

	Republic of Florence
	Papal States
	Aragonese possessions

Handing over the Keys of St Peter
Perugino's fresco in the Sistine Chapel (see p416) links the authority of the pope to the New Testament and, through the Classical buildings in the background, to ancient Rome.

Galeazzo Maria Sforza was the son of Milan's ruler.

Piero de' Medici, Lorenzo's father, was given the nickname "the Gouty".

Self-portrait of the artist

Execution of Savonarola *(1498)*
Having assumed the leadership of Florence in 1494, the fanatical monk was hanged, then burned for heresy in Piazza della Signoria.

TIMELINE

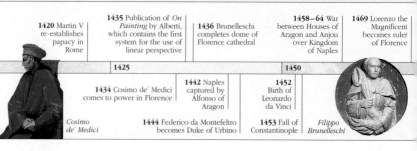

1420 Martin V re-establishes papacy in Rome

1435 Publication of *On Painting* by Alberti, which contains the first system for the use of linear perspective

1436 Brunelleschi completes dome of Florence cathedral

1458–64 War between Houses of Aragon and Anjou over Kingdom of Naples

1469 Lorenzo the Magnificent becomes ruler of Florence

1425

1450

1434 Cosimo de' Medici comes to power in Florence

1442 Naples captured by Alfonso of Aragon

1452 Birth of Leonardo da Vinci

Cosimo de' Medici

1444 Federico da Montefeltro becomes Duke of Urbino

1453 Fall of Constantinople

Filippo Brunelleschi

The Battle of Pavia (1525)
The French King Francis I was captured at this battle against the army of the Hapsburg Emperor Charles V, who won control of Italy.

THE PROCESSION OF THE MAGI

Benozzo Gozzoli's fresco (1459) in the Palazzo Medici-Riccardi, Florence, depicts members of the Medici family and other contemporary notables. It contains many references to a great church council held in Florence in 1439.

WHERE TO SEE RENAISSANCE ITALY

Many cities were flourishing centres of the arts in the 15th century. None can rival Florence *(pp262–303)* with its great palazzi and the Uffizi gallery *(pp278–81)*, but Venice *(pp80–131)*, Urbino *(pp360–61)* and Mantua *(p199)* all preserve great treasures. In Rome, do not miss the Vatican's Sistine Chapel and Raphael Rooms *(pp414–17)*.

The Spedale degli Innocenti *by Brunelleschi in Florence* (p269) *shows the Classical symmetry and restraint of Renaissance architecture.*

Humanism
Carpaccio's painting of St Augustine is thought to show Cardinal Bessarion (c.1395–1472), one of the scholars who revived interest in Classical philosophy, especially Plato.

Lorenzo de' Medici (the Magnificent) was depicted as one of the three kings travelling to Bethlehem.

Pope Julius II
During his reign (1503–13), the worldly Julius made the papacy a major power in European politics. Raphael's portrait shows him as a shrewd, old statesman.

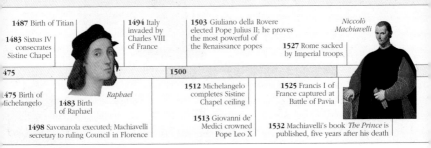

1483 Sixtus IV consecrates Sistine Chapel

1487 Birth of Titian

1494 Italy invaded by Charles VIII of France

1503 Giuliano della Rovere elected Pope Julius II; he proves the most powerful of the Renaissance popes

Niccolò Machiavelli

1527 Rome sacked by Imperial troops

475   1500

1475 Birth of Michelangelo

1483 Birth of Raphael

Raphael

1512 Michelangelo completes Sistine Chapel ceiling

1513 Giovanni de' Medici crowned Pope Leo X

1525 Francis I of France captured at Battle of Pavia

1498 Savonarola executed; Machiavelli secretary to ruling Council in Florence

1532 Machiavelli's book *The Prince* is published, five years after his death

The Counter Reformation

Gian Lorenzo Bernini

AFTER THE SACK OF ROME in 1527, Italy was at the mercy of Charles V, Holy Roman Emperor and King of Spain. Pope Clement VII, who had opposed Charles, crowned him emperor in Bologna. In response to the growing threat from Protestantism, a series of reforms, known as the Counter Reformation and backed by the Inquisition, imposed rigid orthodoxy. New religious orders, such as the Jesuits, were set up to take the battle for men's souls far overseas. The missionary spirit of the age inspired the dramatic forms of the Baroque.

ITALY IN 1550

☐ Spanish possessions
☐ States allied with Spain

Emperor Charles V and Pope Clement VII
The two former enemies settled their differences and the future destiny of Italy in the Treaty of Barcelona (1529).

The Virgin Mary intervenes on the side of the Christians.

BAROQUE STUCCO DECORATION

This stucco relief by Giacomo Serpotta (c.1690) in the Oratory of Santa Zita in Palermo is a magnificent example of Late Baroque exuberance. The subject is a favourite of the period, the Battle of Lepanto, a great naval triumph for the combined forces of Christendom against the Turks (1571).

The centre of the ingenious creation is, in effect, a framed painting in perspective.

Baroque Architecture
Guarino Guarini's decoration of the dome of the Chapel of the Holy Shroud in Turin (see p213) was completed in 1694.

The young boy rests his hand on a helmet, symbol of the victorious Christians.

TIMELINE

1530–37 Alessandro de' Medici ruler of Florence

1542 Inquisition established in Rome

Andrea Palladio

1545–63 Council of Trent sets out agenda of Counter Reformation

1580 Death of architect Palladio

1589 Palestrina publishes setting of the Latin Hymnal

1600 Philosopher Giordano Bruno burnt for heresy in Rome

1550

1575

1540 Founding of Jesuit Order

1541 Michelangelo completes *Last Judgment* in Sistine Chapel

1529 Charles V crowned Holy Roman Emperor in San Petronio, Bologna

1571 Victory over Turkish fleet at Battle of Lepanto

1564 Birth of Galileo

1560 San Carlo Borromeo appointed Bishop of Milan

Giovanni Pierluigi da Palestrina

Trial of Galileo
The great astronomer was often in trouble with the Inquisition. He was summoned to Rome in 1633 and forced to deny that the Earth and planets moved round the sun.

Lepanto was the last major sea battle in which Venetian galleys played an important role.

Cherubs, a favourite motif in Baroque decoration

St Ignatius Loyola
The Spanish saint was the founder of the Jesuits – sanctioned by the pope in Rome in 1540.

The turban, symbol of the defeated Turks

Revolt of Masaniello *(1647) High taxes made Spanish rule in Naples unpopular. A proposed tax on fruit sparked off this failed revolt.*

WHERE TO SEE BAROQUE ITALY

The Ecstasy of St Teresa *by Bernini (p402) has the dynamic theatricality characteristic of the best Baroque sculpture.*

The Baroque is strongly associated with Rome and in particular with its great public spaces such as Piazza Navona *(pp388–9)* and the many churches by Borromini and Bernini. Other cities and towns with striking Baroque architecture include Lecce *(pp496–7)* in Puglia, Palermo *(pp510–13)*, Noto *(p527)* and Syracuse *(pp526–7)* in Sicily, and Turin *(pp212–17)*.

1626 New St Peter's consecrated in Rome	**1669** Venice loses island of Crete to the Turks	**1694** Andrea Pozzo completes ceiling fresco for the church of Sant'Ignazio in Rome
1631 Duchy of Urbino absorbed by Papal States		**1678** Birth of Vivaldi
1625	**1650**	**1675**
1633 Galileo condemned by papal authorities	**1647** Revolt in Naples in response to tax on fruit	**1693** Eastern Sicily ruined by earthquake that kills 5 per cent of the island's population
1642 *L'Incoronazione di Poppea* by Monteverdi	**1669** Major eruption of Mount Etna	**1674** Revolt against Spanish rule in Messina

The Grand Tour

The Romantic poet Shelley, visitor to Italy

THE TREATY of Aix-la-Chapelle in 1748 marked the start of 50 years of peace. It was about this time that Italy, with its great art treasures and Classical ruins, including the newly excavated Pompei, became Europe's first great tourist destination. Young English "milords" visited Rome, Florence and Venice as part of a new type of pilgrimage, the Grand Tour; while artists and poets sought inspiration in Rome's glorious past. In 1800, Napoleon, who conquered and briefly united Italy, threatened to destroy the old order, but in 1815 the status quo was restored.

Charles III's Fleet at Naples *(1753)*
Ruler of Naples from 1734 to 1759, when he became King of Spain, Charles attempted genuine political reforms.

Goethe in the Roman Campagna
Goethe toured Italy in the 1780s. Great poets who followed his example included the Romantics Keats, Shelley and Byron.

Farnese Hercules
(see p475)

Venetian Carnival
The colourful folklore of Carnival attracted many tourists, but Venice's days of greatness were over. In 1797, the proud maritime republic was ceded to Austria by Napoleon.

The Dying Galatian
(see p376)

GALLERY OF VIEWS OF ANCIENT ROME BY PANNINI

Giovanni Pannini (1691–1765) painted views Roman ruins for foreigners. This painting i capriccio, an imaginary scene incorporating many well-known views and Classical statue

TIMELINE

1713 Treaty of Utrecht gives Naples and Sardinia to Austria and Sicily to Piedmont

1725 *The Four Seasons* by Vivaldi

Medici coat of arms

1735 Peace of Vienna confirms Charles III as King of the Two Sicilies (Naples and Sicily)

1755 Corsica sold Genoa to Fra

1748 First excavation at Pompei

1700

1720

1740

1707 Birth of playwright Carlo Goldoni

1720 Piedmont and Sardinia united under House of Savoy; Sicily passes to Austria

1737 End of Medici dynasty in Florence; Grand Duchy of Tuscany passes to Austrian House of Lorraine

Antonio Vivaldi, great Venetian composer

View of the Roman Forum by Piranesi
The popular series of etchings Vedute di
Roma *(Views of Rome) by Giovanni Battista
Piranesi (1720–78) inspired a new interest
in excavating the ruins of ancient Rome.*

The Colosseum was as popular
a subject in the 18th century
as it is on today's
picture postcards.

The Laocoön
(see p407)

View of the Pantheon
(see p394)

WHERE TO SEE
18TH-CENTURY ITALY

The 18th century produced two of Rome's
best-loved tourist attractions: the Spanish
Steps *(p399)* and the Trevi Fountain *(p400).*
It was also the age of the first purpose-built
museums, including the Vatican's Museo
Pio-Clementino *(p411).* The Neo-Classical
sculpture of Antonio Canova (1757–1822)
was immensely popular during this period.
His tomb is in Santa Maria Gloriosa dei Frari
in Venice *(pp94–5).* Of Neo-
Classical buildings, the most
imposing is a vast monument
to enlightened despotism:
the Palazzo Reale at
Caserta *(p480).*

***Pauline Borghese**, Napoleon's sister, was the
model for Antonio Canova's* Venus *(1805) in
the Villa Borghese collection in Rome (p429).*

Napoleon
*When Napoleon
conquered Italy
in 1800, he was seen
by many as a
liberator. The
enchantment
wore off as he
took priceless
works of art
back to Paris.*

Congress of Vienna *(1815)*
*The conference decided that Austria should
keep Lombardy and Venice, thereby sowing
the seeds of the Italian unification movement.*

	La Scala Opera House, Milan (see p187) **1778** La Scala opened in Milan	**1796–7** Napoleon's first campaign in northern Italy	**1800–1801** Napoleon conquers Italy **1808** Murat becomes King of Naples	**1809** Pope Pius VII exiled from Rome
760	**1780**		**1800**	
1773 Pope dissolves Jesuit Order	**1780** Joseph II succeeds to Austrian throne; minor reforms in Lombardy		**1806** Joseph Bonaparte becomes King of Naples	
1765–90 Reign of Leopold Grand Duke of Tuscany, who introduces enlightened reforms	**1797** Venice given to Austria by Treaty of Campo Formio; France controls rest of northern Italy		**1815** Congress of Vienna restores status quo in Italy, though Austria keeps Venice	

The Risorgimento

THE WORD "RISORGIMENTO" (resurgence) describes the five decades of struggle for liberation from foreign rule, culminating in the unification of Italy in 1870. In 1848, patriots rose up against the Austrians in Milan and Venice, the Bourbons in Sicily and the pope in Rome, where a republic was declared. Garibaldi valiantly defended the republic, but all the uprisings were too localized. By 1859, the movement was better organized with Vittorio Emanuele II at its head. Two years saw the conquest of all but Venice and Rome, both of which fell within a decade.

Vittorio Emanuele

ITALY IN 1861

☐ *Kingdom of Italy*

The guns were rusty, old converted flintlocks.

Giuseppe Mazzini
(1805–72)
An exile for much of his life, Mazzini fought alongside Garibaldi to unite Italy as a republic, rather than a kingdom.

The red shirt was the badge of the Garibaldini.

Italian Railways
The short railway line from Naples to Portici was opened in 1839. Politically fragmented, Italy was slow to create an effective rail network.

Revolt of Messina
When, in 1848, Messina revolted, Ferdinand II subjected the town to a savage bombardment, earning himself the nickname King Bomba.

TIMELINE

1831 Insurrection in Romagna and Le Marche against papal rule

1840 First major railway links established

1849 Accession of Vittorio Emanuele II as ruler of Piedmont

1820	1830	1840	1850

1820s Carbonari secret society active in Papal States

1831 Mazzini founds *Giovine Italia* (Young Italy) movement

Daniele Manin, hero of the Venetian uprising of 1848

1847 Economic crisis

1848 Revolutions throughout Italy

1849 Republic of Rome crushed by French troops

1852 Cavour becomes prime minister of Piedmont

Battle of Solferino *(1859)*
With the help of a French army led by Napoleon III, the Piedmontese won Milan and Lombardy from the Austrians.

Two old paddle steamers brought the Thousand from Quarto near Genoa.

WHERE TO SEE RISORGIMENTO ITALY

Almost every town in Italy honours the heroes of the Risorgimento with a Via Garibaldi, a Via Cavour, a Piazza Vittorio, a Via Mazzini and a Via XX Settembre (the date of the fall of Rome in 1870). Many cities also have Risorgimento museums. One of the best is in Turin *(p215)*.

The Victor Emmanuel Monument (p374) *is a prominent, but largely unloved, Roman landmark.*

Count Camillo di Cavour *(1810–61)*
Cavour's diplomacy as prime minister of Piedmont ensured that the House of Savoy became rulers of the new Italy. He also coined the word "Risorgimento".

The skiffs were lent by other ships moored in Marsala harbour.

Giuseppe Verdi *(1813–1901)*
Composers such as Verdi, Donizetti and Rossini made the 19th century the great era of Italian opera. Verdi's early operas inspired the Risorgimento.

GARIBALDI AND THE THOUSAND

Giuseppe Garibaldi (1807–82) was a leader of courage and genius. In 1860, he landed at Marsala with 1,000 volunteers. The garrison at Palermo surrendered, Sicily fell and he went on to conquer Naples, thus presenting Vittorio Emanuele with half a kingdom.

Twentieth-Century Italy

F ASCISM UNDER MUSSOLINI (1922–43) promised the Italians greatness, but delivered only humiliation. In spite of this, Italy has become one of Europe's leading economies with a standard of living undreamt of at the turn of the century. This has been achieved in the face of great obstacles. Since 1946, the Republic has passed through many crises: a series of unstable coalitions, the terrorist outrages in the 1970s and, most recently, corruption scandals involving numerous ministers and officials.

1936 Fiat produces first "Topolino" car

1922 Fascists march on Rome; Mussolini invited to form government

1918 Austrian advance halted at the river Piave, just north of Venice

1940 Italy enters World War II

1943 Allies land in Sicily; Italy signs armistice and new Badoglio government declares war on Germany

1915 Italy enters World War I

1900 Assassination of King Umberto I

1911–12 Italy conquers Libya

1900	1920	1940

1900	1920	1940

1908 Earthquake destroys many towns and villages in Calabria and eastern Sicily; Messina almost completely razed to the ground; over 200,000 die

1936 Italy conquers Abyssinia; pact with Germany, forming anti-Communist "Axis"

1920s Postwar years see continued emigration to the United States. Here, emigrants cheer as they reach New York aboard the *Giulio Cesare*

1943 Mussolini imprisoned, then freed by Germans

1946 Referendum in which Italy votes to become a republic; Christian Democrat party forms first of a long series of coalition governments

1917 Defeat at Caporetto on Italy's northeastern border; Italian troops, such as these Alpini, retreat to defensive positions

1909 In his *Futurist Manifesto*, Filippo Marinetti condemns all traditional art as too static. His idea of a new dynamic art is expressed in works such as Umberto Boccioni's bronze *Unique Forms of Continuity in Space*

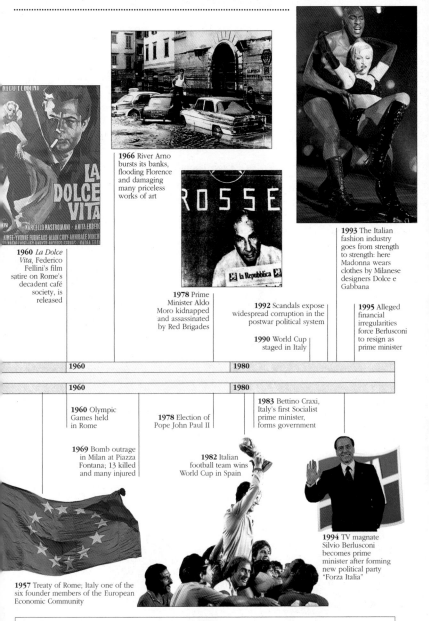

1960 *La Dolce Vita*, Federico Fellini's film satire on Rome's decadent café society, is released

1966 River Arno bursts its banks, flooding Florence and damaging many priceless works of art

1978 Prime Minister Aldo Moro kidnapped and assassinated by Red Brigades

1992 Scandals expose widespread corruption in the postwar political system

1990 World Cup staged in Italy

1993 The Italian fashion industry goes from strength to strength: here Madonna wears clothes by Milanese designers Dolce e Gabbana

1995 Alleged financial irregularities force Berlusconi to resign as prime minister

1960 **1980**

1960 **1980**

1960 Olympic Games held in Rome

1978 Election of Pope John Paul II

1983 Bettino Craxi, Italy's first Socialist prime minister, forms government

1969 Bomb outrage in Milan at Piazza Fontana; 13 killed and many injured

1982 Italian football team wins World Cup in Spain

1994 TV magnate Silvio Berlusconi becomes prime minister after forming new political party "Forza Italia"

1957 Treaty of Rome; Italy one of the six founder members of the European Economic Community

ITALIAN CINEMA SINCE WORLD WAR II

The social problems of Italy in the late 1940s inspired a wave of cinema that came to be known as Neo-Realism. Leading exponents included Roberto Rossellini, who made *Roma Città Aperta* (1945), Vittorio de Sica, the director of *Bicycle Thieves* (1948), and Luchino Visconti. Since that time, the major Italian directors have cultivated their own personal styles.

Vittorio de Sica (1902–74)

Visconti's later films, such as *Death in Venice* (1971), concentrate on formal beauty and decadence, while Federico Fellini's *La Dolce Vita* (1960) and *Roma* (1972) depict life as a grotesque carnival. Italy also produces many less serious, commercial films. Most are for local consumption, but Sergio Leone's westerns of the late 1960s achieved worldwide popularity.

ITALY THROUGH THE YEAR

Throughout Italy, the variety of local character and colour is astonishing. This is mainly due to the survival of regionalism, particularly in the southern parts of the country. Old traditions, customs and lifestyles are still greatly respected and there is a deep attachment to the land, which is reflected in a healthy interest in the food and produce, as well as a perseverance of seasonal religious and secular events. Annual festivals, whether in rural or urban areas, range from wine-tasting and gastronomic celebrations to elaborate commemorations of every patron saint imaginable.

SPRING

THE ITALIAN SPRING begins early, particularly in the south. City streets and main sights are rarely overcrowded (except at Easter in Rome). The weather, however, can be unpredictable and wet in the central and northern parts of the country. Spring specialities, such as asparagus, spinach and artichokes, begin to feature on restaurant menus. This is a season of great celebration; festivals and fairs abound, especially in Sicily, and the Easter papal address always draws massive crowds to St Peter's.

Tuscan asparagus

MARCH

Mostra Vini Spumanti, *(mid-Mar)*, Madonna di Campiglio, Trentino-Alto Adige. Fair celebrating sparkling wine.
Sa Sartiglia, Oristano, Sardinia. Three-day carnival ending on Shrove Tuesday.

Procession of the Grieving Madonna on the isle of Procida

Su e zo per i ponti *(second Sun)*, Venice. Marathon-style race through the city's streets, up and down the bridges.

APRIL

Procession of the Grieving Madonna *(Good Friday)*, Procida, Campania. A colourful religious procession throughout the island.
Holy Week *(Easter Week)*. Numerous Easter celebrations from Palm Sunday to Easter Sunday, throughout the country.
Papal Address *(Easter Sunday)*, Rome. The Pope makes his Easter address from the Vatican.
Dance of the Devils and Death *(Easter Sunday)*, Prizzi, Sicily. Dance recital symbolizing the attempts of evil to vanquish the forces of God.
Scoppio del Carro *(Easter Sunday)*, Florence. Firework display is lit by a mechanical dove in front of the Duomo.
Festa della Madonna che Scappa in Piazza *(Easter Sunday)*, Sulmona, Abruzzo. A meeting between the Virgin and the Risen Christ is enacted.
Festa degli Aquiloni *(first Sun after Easter)*, San Miniato, Tuscany. Kite lovers perform aerial acrobatics at this festival.
Festa di San Marco *(25 Apr)*, Venice. St Mark, the patron saint of Venice, is commemorated by a gondola race across St Mark's Basin.
Mostra Mercato Internazionale dell'Artigianato *(last week)*, Florence. An important European exhibition of arts and crafts.

Spring strawberries

Scoppio del Carro (Explosion of the Carriage) festival in Florence

Sagra Musicale Lucchese *(Apr–Jul)*, Lucca, Tuscany. Extensive festival of sacred music, held in the city's many Romanesque churches.

MAY

Festa di Sant'Efisio *(1 May)*, Cagliari, Sardinia. Paraders in traditional Sardinian costume.
Festa dei Ceri *(5 May)*, Gubbio, Perugia. Festival, including a race with four teams carrying large candles.
Festa di San Domenico Abate *(6 May)*, Cocullo, Abruzzo. Includes a procession with a statue of St Dominic covered with live snakes.
Festa della Mela *(late May)*, Ora (Auer), Trentino-Alto Adige. This annual "Festival of the Apple" takes place in a town known as the "gateway to the Dolomites".
Greek Drama in Theatre *(May–Jun)*, Syracuse, Sicily. Festival of Greek drama.
Maggio Musicale *(May–Jun)*, Florence. This is the city's biggest arts festival, including music, drama and dance.

Street carpeted with flowers for the Infiorata in Genzano

SUMMER

Summer brings the crowds to Italy, particularly the cities. Italians, however, flee and head for the coast, usually in August. The queues for tourist attractions can be long and hotels are often fully booked. Festivals vary; religious events are interspersed with those of the arts and local folklore.

JUNE

Festa della Fragola
(1 Jun), Borgo San Martino, Alessandria. Musical and folkloric performances in celebration of the strawberry.
Biennale *(Jun – Sep)*, Venice. The world's biggest exhibition of contemporary art, which takes place during odd-numbered years only.
Infiorata *(early Jun)*, Genzano, Castelli Romani. A procession through streets carpeted with flowers in this town just south of Rome.
Festa di San Giovanni
(mid-Jun – mid-Jul), Turin, Piedmont. Festival in honour of the city's patron saint, John, dating from the 14th century.
Calcio Storico Fiorentino
(24 Jun), Florence. Procession of people in 16th-century-style costumes; firework displays.

Festa di Sant'Andrea
(27 Jun), Amalfi, Campania. Fireworks and processions.
Festa dei Due Mondi
(late Jun – early Jul), Spoleto, Umbria. International festival of drama, music and dance.
Gioco del Ponte *(last Sun)*, Pisa. "The Bridge Parade" of marchers in antique armour.
Tevere Expo *(end Jun)*, on the Tiber, Rome. Arts and crafts, food and wine stalls, folk music and fireworks.

JULY

Corsa del Palio *(2 Jul)*, Siena. Tuscany's most famous event *(see p331)* presents a medieval flag-waving exhibition and horse race.
Festa della Madonna della Bruna *(first Sun)*, Matera, Basilicata. A lively procession of clergymen and knights in costume.
Festa dei Noiantri *(last two weeks of Jul)*, Rome. A colourful race of the city's horse-drawn carriages.
Festa della Santa Maria del Carmine *(16 Jul)*, Naples. A sumptuous festival featuring the illumination of the city's *campanile* (bell tower).
International Film Festival *(Jul – Aug)*, Taormina, Sicily.

Musician from Florence's Calcio

The Sienese Palio in action

Opera Festival *(Jul – Aug)*, Verona, Veneto. Renowned opera festival *(see p137)* overlapping with the **Shakespeare Festival**, providing music, drama, opera and dance.

AUGUST

Medieval Palio *(first week – end Aug)*, Feltre, Veneto. Parades and archery competitions, medieval-style.
Festa del Mare *(15 Aug)*, Diano Marina, Liguria. This "Festival of the Sea" boasts a spectacular firework display.
Corsa del Palio *(16 Aug)*, Siena, Tuscany. See July entry.
Festa dei Candelieri
(16 Aug), Sassari, Sardinia. "Festival of the Candle", dating from the 16th century.
Venice Film Festival
(late Aug – early Sep). International festival on the Lido.
Rossini Festival *(Aug – Sep)*, Pèsaro, Le Marche. A celebration of the composer's work, in his birthplace.
Settimane Musicali di Stresa *(late Aug – end Sep)*, Stresa, Lombardy. Four weeks of concerts and recitals.

Sun, sand and sea – essential ingredients of a Tuscan beach holiday

AUTUMN

Autumn is a slow, gentle season in Italy but that doesn't mean there are fewer festivals and fairs. In addition to the various religious events at this time of year, gastronomic festivals are especially popular, commemorating such delectables as chestnuts, local cheeses, sausages and mushrooms. Autumn is the season of the *vendemmia*, the grape harvest, which is often used as an excuse for village festivities at which the latest local wines flow freely.

The climate *(see pp68–9)* in late autumn is often cold and wet in the north. The south, however, can be quite warm right through October.

Advertisement for the September
Palio in Asti, Piedmont

SEPTEMBER

Sagra dell'Uva *(early Sep)*, Rome. Harvest festival with grapes at bargain prices and lots of folk entertainment.
Neapolitan Song Contest *(7 Sep)*, Piazza di Piedigrotta, Naples. Usually entered by couples; the singer often plays a mandolin, while their partner plays the castanets.
Festa di San Sebastiano e Santa Lucia *(1–3 Sep)*, Sassari, Sardinia. Includes a contest where competitors improvise short poems.
Procession of the Macchina di Santa Rosa *(3 Sep)*, Viterbo, Lazio. Commemoration of the saint's body being transported to the Church of Santa Rosa in 1258.

The widely cultivated olive tree

Giostra del Saracino *(first Sun)*, Arezzo, Umbria. Joust of the Saracen and knights, dating from the 13th century.
Regata Storica *(first Sun)*, Venice. A procession of historic boats followed by a colourful gondola race.
Human chess game *(second week)*, Marostica, near Vicenza. A popular costumed game held in the main square every even year.
Rassegna del Chianti Classico *(second week)*, Chianti, Tuscany. Celebration of the local wines.
The Miracle of San Gennaro *(19 Sep)*, Naples. Re-enactment of the liquefaction of the saint's blood, in a lively mass at the Duomo.
Palio *(third Sun)*, Asti, Piedmont. Includes a costumed medieval procession and bareback horse racing.

OCTOBER

Amici della Musica *(Oct–Apr)*, Florence, Tuscany. The "Friends of Music" concert season begins.
Fiera del Tartufo *(first Sun)*, Alba, Piedmont. A variety of events centred around the locally grown white truffle.
Festa di San Francesco *(4 Oct)*, Assisi, Umbria. Feast in honour of the saint.
Wine festivals *(first week)*, Castelli Romani, Lazio.
Sagra del Tordo *(last Sun)*, Montalcino, Tuscany. Celebration of the thrush; costumed archery contests.
Festa dell'Uva *(dates vary)*, Bolzano, Trentino-Alto Adige. Grape festival with live music and a costumed procession featuring allegoric charts.

A roast chestnut stall in autumn

NOVEMBER

Festa dei Popoli *(Nov–Dec)*, Florence, Tuscany. Film festival showing films in their original languages with Italian sub-titles.
Festa della Salute *(21 Nov)*, Venice. Cherished by Venetian locals, this feast gives thanks to the Virgin Mary in memory of a 1630 plague.

The human chess game in the town square of Marostica

WINTER

THERE ARE FAIRS, markets and religious events up and down the country at this time of year. Neapolitan Christmas cribs are famous and nearly every church has one. The Christmas holiday itself is low key; more is made of other religious events such as the liquefaction of San Gennaro's blood in Naples and the Carnevale in Venice.

Rome during one of its rare snowfalls

DECEMBER

Festa di Sant'Ambrogio
(early Dec), Milan. The official opening of La Scala Opera season *(see p187).*
Festa della Madonna di Loreto *(10 Dec)*, Loreto, Le Marche. Celebration of the Virgin's Holy House.
La Befana *(mid-Dec – mid-Jan)*, Rome. Well-known Christmas and children's fair held in Piazza Navona.
The Miracle of San Gennaro *(19 Dec)*, Naples. See September.
Christmas fair *(mid-Dec)*, Naples. Fair selling crib figures and decorations.
Fiaccole di Natale *(Christmas Eve)*, Abbadia di San Salvatore, Tuscany. Features carols and processions in memory of the first shepherds.
Midnight Mass *(24 Dec)*, at churches all over the country.
Christmas Day *(25 Dec)*, St Peter's Square, Rome. Public blessing by the pope.

La Befana at Piazza Navona, Rome

JANUARY

Capodanno *(1 Jan)*, all over the country. New Year's Day is celebrated with fireworks and volleys from hunters firing into the air to scare off ghosts and spirits of the old year and welcome in the new.
La Befana *(mid-Dec – mid-Jan)*, Rome. The Christmas and children's fair continues.
Pitti Immagine Uomo, Pitti Immagine Donna, Pitti Immagine Bimbo, Fortezza da Basso, Florence. Month of international fashion shows for women, men and children.
Festa di San Sebastiano *(20 Jan)*, Dolceacqua, Liguria. A laurel tree covered with colourful communion hosts is carried through town.

Carnevale, Viareggio

Festa d'o' Cippo di Sant'-Antonio *(17 Jan)*, Naples. A procession for St Anthony, protector of animals.
Carnevale *(22 Jan – 7 Feb)*, Viareggio, Tuscany. A carnival famous for lively floats, often inspired by topical themes.
Fair of St Orsa *(30 – 31 Jan)*, Aosta, Valle d'Aosta. A popular exhibition of traditional arts and crafts.

FEBRUARY

Carnevale *(first ten days of Lent, finishing Shrove Tuesday)*, Venice. The famous pre-Lent festival, meaning "farewell to meat". A variety of events is organized, but anyone can buy a mask and participate while watching an array of gorgeous costumes on show.
Sagra delle Mandorle in Fiore *(first or second week)*, Agrigento, Sicily. Annual almond blossom celebration.
Bacanal del Gnoco *(11 Feb)*, Verona. Traditional masked procession with both international and local allegorical floats. Masked balls are held in the town's squares.
Carnevale *(dates vary)*, Mamoiada, Sardinia. Processions include *mamuthones* wearing sinister black masks.

Carnevale revellers in Venice

The Sporting Year

FOOTBALL IS BY FAR the most important sport in Italy, uniting the country when the national team (*Azzurri*) play. Other sports throughout the year also attract a large following, so fans are never at a loss for varied activities. For most big sporting events, tickets can be obtained for cash at club outlets such as the venue itself. Agencies provide hard-to-get tickets at often higher prices. Beware of the inevitable touts at popular events as their expensive tickets may not be valid.

World Cup mania

Calcio Fiorentino, one of Italy's few indigenous sports, is said to be the medieval precursor of modern football.

Coppa Italia football final

Memorial d'Aloia rowing competition, Umbria

Italian Tennis Open, Rome

Giro d'Italia is one of the world's most prestigious cycling races. Gianni Bugno, left, won in 1992 and 1993.

The professional Water polo season takes place from March through to July. The Canottieri Napoli team play consistently well through the championship.

January	February	March	April	May	June

Indoor Athletics Championships

International Showjumping, Rome

Swimming is a popular competitive water sport and the Indoor Championships are held in February. Olympic medallist Luca Sacchi is one of Italy's top swimmers.

The Italian leg of the Circuito Mondiale in Mugello. Luca Cadalora was champion in 1991.

Although the San Marino Grand Prix is not technically an Italian motor race, it is held each May at Imola, near the home of Ferrari (see p252).

Italian Outdoor Swimming Championships are held each year in July. Top swimmer Giorgio Lamberti and his team mates, pictured above, celebrate a relay team victory.

Italy has some of the best ski resorts in Europe and hosts the middle stages of the World Ski Cup each winter. Above is Alberto Tomba, winner of the 94–95 Cup.

The Italian Grand Prix, held annually at Monza, is Italy's round of the international Formula One World Championship. Jean Alesi, near right, is one of the country's top drivers.

Trofeo dei Templi rowing competition, Sicily

The San Remo Car Rally, held each year in October, was made famous by driver Micky Biason and the Lancia Delta Integrale.

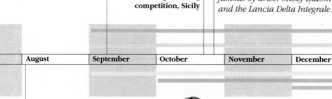

	August	September	October	November	December

Roberto Baggio, below right, in action at the 1994 World Cup

na Palio e p331), d on 2 y and 16 gust

The Italian football season runs from September through to June. It culminates with the Coppa Italia final, which is equivalent to the British FA Cup. Italy's football obsession, however, reaches fever pitch when the World Cup takes place every four years.

KEY TO SPORTING SEASONS

▨	Football
▨	Water polo
▨	Rugby
▨	Basketball
▨	Volleyball
▨	Skiing

The Outdoor Athletics Championship has become very popular in recent years, especially the steeplechase, where Francesco Panetta made his name.

The Climate of Italy

THE ITALIAN PENINSULA has a varied climate falling into three distinct geographical regions. Cold Alpine winters and warm, wet summers characterize the northern regions. In the extensive Po Valley, arid summers contrast with freezing, damp winters. The rest of Italy has a pleasant climate with long, hot summers and mild winters. Cooler weather along the backbone of the Apennines can bring snow during the winter months.

TRENTINO-ALTO ADIGE

°C			
16	28	17	
4	17	5	5
			-5
6 hrs	8 hrs	4 hrs	2 hrs
67 mm	100 mm	83 mm	20 mm
month Apr	Jul	Oct	Jan

Average monthly maximum temperature

Average monthly minimum temperature

Average daily hours of sunshine

Average monthly rainfall

LOMBARDY

°C			
18	28	17	
8	18	10	6
			-1
5 hrs	9 hrs	5 hrs	3 hrs
74 mm	78 mm	89 mm	64 mm
month Apr	Jul	Oct	Jan

VALLE D'AOSTA AND PIEDMONT

°C			
17	26	17	
6	15	7	7
			-2.5
5 hrs	9 hrs	4 hrs	3 hrs
95 mm	87 mm	85 mm	45 mm
month Apr	Jul	Oct	Jan

LIGURIA

°C			
18	28	21	
11.5	20	14	12
			6.5
7 hrs	9 hrs	8 hrs	4 hrs
66 mm	30 mm	74 mm	69 mm
month Apr	Jul	Oct	Jan

TUSCANY

°C			
17	29	20	
8	16	15	10
			2
8 hrs	11 hrs	6 hrs	5 hrs
72 mm	30 mm	90 mm	65 mm
month Apr	Jul	Oct	Jan

SARDINIA

°C			
19	29	22	
10	20	14	14
			7
8 hrs	11 hrs	6 hrs	4 hrs
31 mm	7 mm	48 mm	50 mm
month Apr	Jul	Oct	Jan

EMILIA-ROMAGNA

°C			
17	30	16	
8.5	19	10	4
			-1
6 hrs	11 hrs	5 hrs	3 hrs
58 mm	39 mm	81 mm	46 mm
month Apr	Jul	Oct	Jan

Aosta · Milano · Brescia · Verona · Trento · Torino · Parma · Modena · Genova · Livorno · Olbia · Sassari · Cagliari

THE VENETO AND FRIULI

°C

17	28 / 18	18	
7	7	9	7
			0

7 hrs	9 hrs	4 hrs	2 hrs

112 mm	108 mm	134 mm	90 mm

| month | Apr | Jul | Oct | Jan |

LE MARCHE

°C

16	27 / 20	19	
9	9	13	8.5
			3

6 hrs	10 hrs	5 hrs	3 hrs

56 mm	55 mm	77 mm	67 mm

| month | Apr | Jul | Oct | Jan |

UMBRIA

°C

19	29 / 16	19	
6	6	9	8
			1

5 hrs	10 hrs	6 hrs	3 hrs

79 mm	44 mm	92 mm	75 mm

| month | Apr | Jul | Oct | Jan |

ABRUZZO, MOLISE AND PUGLIA

°C

18	28 / 20	21	
10	10	14	13
			6

6 hrs	10 hrs	6 hrs	4 hrs

47 mm	27 mm	68 mm	61 mm

| month | Apr | Jul | Oct | Jan |

ROME AND LAZIO

°C

18	29 / 19	22	
9	9	13	12
			4.5

6 hrs	10 hrs	7 hrs	5 hrs

51 mm	21 mm	95 mm	87 mm

| month | Apr | Jul | Oct | Jan |

NAPLES AND CAMPANIA

°C

19	30 / 21	22	
12	12	18	13
			7

7 hrs	11 hrs	6 hrs	4 hrs

58 mm	12 mm	68 mm	85 mm

| month | Apr | Jul | Oct | Jan |

SICILY

°C

19	29 / 20	24	
12	12	16	15
			9

8 hrs	11 hrs	7 hrs	4 hrs

29 mm	7 mm	59 mm	59 mm

| month | Apr | Jul | Oct | Jan |

BASILICATA AND CALABRIA

°C

18	29.5 / 18.5	21.5	
9.5	9.5	14	13
			6.5

6 hrs	10 hrs	5 hrs	4 hrs

70 mm	13 mm	86 mm	90 mm

| month | Apr | Jul | Oct | Jan |

Trieste

Ancona

L'Aquila · Pescara

MA

Campobasso

Foggia

Bari ·

Napoli · Potenza · Taranto

Catanzaro

Messina · Reggio di Calabria

Palermo

Catania

· Agrigento

NORTHEAST ITALY

Northeast Italy at a Glance

THE SHEER VARIETY TO BE FOUND in northeast Italy makes it a fascinating area to explore. The majestic Dolomites dominate the north, straddling Trentino-Alto Adige and the Veneto, and are dotted with medieval castles and modern skiing resorts. On the plain, the cities of Verona, Vicenza and Padua are all noted for outstanding architecture and museums, while the rural hinterland boasts beautiful villas. The incomparable and spectacular city of Venice, with its magnificent monuments, rises from the lagoon. Further east, in Friuli, there are important Roman remains. This map pinpoints some of the highlights.

Castel Tirolo,
Merano

TRENTINO-ALTO ADIGE
(See pp160–69)

Palazzo Pretorio,
Trento

The Veneto

Alto Adige *is a dramatic region of snow-covered mountain valleys scattered with forbidding castles and onion-domed churches in the Tyrolean style (see pp164–5).*

The Dolomites *(see pp78–9) form the spectacular backdrop to many towns in northeast Italy, among them Trento, the region's capital (see pp168–9).*

Ponte Scaligero,
Verona

La Rotonda,
Vicenza

```
0 kilometres        40
0 miles        20
```

Verona *is one of the loveliest cities in the Veneto, boasting the Castelvecchio and a Roman arena now used for performances of opera (see pp136–41).*

Vicenza, *a model Renaissance city, is dominated by the buildings of Palladio, such as the Palazzo della Ragione and La Rotonda (see pp144–7).*

◁ **Dusk over the atmospheric city of Verona**

Udine *in Friuli is an interesting city which centres on the elegant Piazza della Libertà. The piazza contains imposing statues, such as this colossal Hercules, and the Porticato di San Giovanni (see pp156–7).*

Friuli-Venezia Giulia

Porticato di San Giovanni, Udine

Aquileia, *once a splendid Roman city, is filled with ancient remains, such as this Mausoleum. Its Basilica houses early Christian mosaics (see p158).*

THE VENETO AND FRIULI
(See pp132–59)

Basilica mosaic

VENICE
(See inset)

Padua *boasts several major sights, among them the Basilica di Sant'Antonio and the Cappella degli Scrovegni with its frescoes by Giotto (see pp148–53).*

Basilica di Sant'Antonio, Padua

Basilica di San Marco *in Venice is one of Europe's finest Byzantine buildings, with a magnificent gilded interior (see pp106–9).*

VENICE
(See pp80–131)

The Palazzo Ducale is a masterpiece of Venetian Gothic architecture
(see pp110–13).

Basilica di San Marco

Palazzo Ducale

0 kilometres   1

0 miles   0.5

Regional Food: Northeast Italy

Gelati

MANY TRADITIONAL SPECIALITIES of the Veneto are dominated, not surprisingly, by fresh fish and seafood from Lake Garda and the Venetian lagoon. This is complemented by seasonal produce – peas, courgettes, asparagus from Bassano del Grappa, radicchio from Treviso – and meat and cheese from the mainland. Pasta is eaten throughout the northeast, but more typical is polenta, made from maize flour, and also the many types of risotto. The influences from neighbouring countries and trading partners may be tasted in the sweet and sour, spicy or pickled dishes found throughout the region, from the mountains in the north to the beaches of the south.

Radicchio alla Griglia *is a dish of slightly bitter red endive leaves from Treviso which are grilled lightly over a hot fire.*

Crab

Mussels   Bream

Squid

Prawns

Scallops

Red mullet

Antipasto di Frutti di Mare *is a mixed seafood platter, dressed with a little olive oil and lemon juice. It is a particular favourite in Venice, where the seafood comes fresh from the lagoon.*

Fiori di Zucchini, *a seasonal delight, are courgette flowers stuffed with delicate fish mousse then fried in a light batter.*

Brodo di Pesce, *or fish soup, is typically Venetian and served all along the coast. It usually contains a mixture of fish, and is sometimes flavoured with saffron from Friuli.*

Risotto alle Seppie *contains cuttlefish ink, which colours the rice a dramatic black in this traditional risotto.*

Risi e Bisi, *a soft and liquid risotto – almost a thick soup – is made of rice with fresh peas and small pieces of bacon.*

Carpaccio, *wafer-thin slices of raw beef sprinkled with oil, is here served with rocket leaves and slivers of Parmesan cheese.*

Zuppa di Cozze *is a classic way of cooking mussels, with a delicious sauce of white wine, garlic and parsley.*

Spaghetti alle Vongole *often appears on coastal menus: it is spaghetti with fresh clams in a piquant, chilli-pepper sauce.*

Polenta, *like pasta, is a filling staple of the Italian diet. Made from maize, it is often grilled and served with a tasty sauce.*

Sarde in Saor *is a traditional Venetian dish of grilled fresh sardines accompanied by a sweet and sour sauce.*

Anguille in Umido *are eels, gently stewed in an aromatic tomato sauce flavoured with white wine and garlic.*

Fegato alla Veneziana *is a traditional Venetian speciality of tender calf's liver, lightly cooked on a bed of onions.*

Tiramisù, *Italy's most famous dessert, is a wonderfully rich blend of coffee-soaked sponge cake and mascarpone cheese.*

THE WINES OF THE NORTHEAST

The Veneto produces large quantities of everyday wines – red, white and rosé *(chiaretto)*. When choosing an unknown white, you might select a Bianco di Custoza rather than an anonymous Soave. But don't rule out Soave; there are some fine examples, notably by Pieropan and Anselmi. The best whites from the northeast come from Friuli, where winemakers Puiatti, Schiopetto, Jermann and Gravner excel in their craft. Trentino-Alto Adige too, produces some crisp whites. Much light and fruity red wine is produced near Bardolino and Valpolicella, with some outstanding bottles coming from Allegrini and Masi. Recioto della Valpolicella is a rich, sweet dessert wine, while Recioto Amarone is less sweet, but stronger still.

Recioto Amarone *is a rich and full-bodied red wine, full of fruit and very high in alcohol.*

Bianco di Custoza *is a dry white "super Soave" from the eastern shores of Lake Garda. Good white wine producers in the Veneto region include Pieropan, Anselmi, Maculan, Tedeschi, Allegrini and Cavalchina.*

Prosecco *is the Veneto's own sparkling wine, and a delightful aperitivo. It may be secco (dry) or amabile (medium-sweet).*

Bianco di Custoza

Collio Pinot Bianco

Pieropan *produces some of Soave's finest quality wine. The single-vineyard wines from this renowned estate are excellent.*

Collio Pinot Bianco *is a superb, fragrant white wine made in the Collio hills next to the Slovenian border. Puiatti is a top producer.*

Understanding Architecture in Venice and the Veneto

TRADE CONTACT WITH THE EAST led medieval Venice to develop its own exotic style – known as Venetian Gothic – blending Byzantine domes and Islamic minarets with European Gothic pointed arches and quatrefoils. In the 16th century, Palladio introduced his interpretations of Classical architecture through a series of churches, public buildings and rural villas in Venice and the Veneto. The 17th century brought the Baroque style, though its exuberance was tempered by Palladio-influenced restraint.

Andrea Palladio (1508–80)

THE ARCHITECTURE OF VENICE: BYZANTINE TO BAROQUE

Onion-shaped cupolas capping the main domes

Upper loggia with copies of the Four Horses of St Mark

Statues added in the 15th century

Byzantine-style façade mosaics

Central portal modelled on the Roman triumphal arch

The Basilica di San Marco, *western Europe's finest Byzantine church (completed 11th century), was given lavish treatment to make it a dazzling shrine for the relics of St Mark, the Evangelist, and a fitting symbol of Venetian aspirations (see pp106–9).*

THE GENIUS OF PALLADIO

Doric columns supporting the ground floor, Ionic above

Shaded loggias for escaping the heat

Palazzo Chiericati is a huge mansion of 1550, its simple style borrowed from the ancient Roma It was once surrounded by water reflect the statues of Classical deiti along its roof (see p146).

Arcades linking the wings to the central block

Symmetrical façade

Villa Barbaro at Maser was one of the villas designed by Palladio from the 1550s when it became fashionable for rich Venetians to acquire rural estates. This villa is typical, combining a working farm, housed in the side wings, with the elegant buildings of a country house (see p143).

WHERE TO SEE THE ARCHITECTURE

A vaporetto trip along the Grand Canal in Venice *(see pp84–7)* is a splendid way of getting an overview of Venetian architecture. Ca' d'Oro, Ca' Rezzonico and Ca' Pesaro may also be visited as they contain museums and a visit to the Basilica di San Marco

Typical Venetian Gothic window

and the Palazzo Ducale is a must. There are numerous examples of Palladio's architecture in the Veneto, but the star is the Villa Barbaro *(see p143)*. Several of his villas line the Brenta Canal (see p154), and the town of Vicenza *(see pp144–7)* is full of his buildings, including La Rotonda, his famous villa.

Arcading influenced by the Palazzo Ducale

Florid tracery inlaid with azure

Finials once covered in gold leaf

Keystones carved as helmeted heads

Deep recesses creating play of light and shade

Swags of fruit, ribbons and flowers

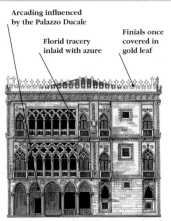

Ca d'Oro, the 15th-century "House of Gold", reveals Moorish influence in its roof finials and sinuous pointed arches (see p90).

The 17th-century Ca' Pesaro typifies the Venetian Baroque style – Classical columns and rich, but subtle ornamentation (see p85).

Giant composite columns

Istrian marble, chosen to catch the changing light of the lagoon

Statues and memorials to patrons of the church

San Giorgio Maggiore, built in 1559–80, is marvellously sited at the entrance to the Venetian inner harbour. It broke from the prevailing Gothic style, introducing the clean simplicity and harmonious proportions of Classical architecture to Venice, and more resembles an ancient Roman temple than a Christian church (see p116).

Pediment with coat of arms

Sundials at each end

The Dolomites

THE DOLOMITES ARE THE MOST DISTINCTIVE and beautiful mountains in Italy. They were formed of mineralized coral which was laid down beneath the sea during the Triassic era, and uplifted when the European and African continental plates dramatically collided 60 million years ago. Unlike the glacier-eroded saddles and ridges of the main body of the Alps, the pale rocks here have been carved by the corrosive effects of ice, sun and rain, sculpting the cliffs, spires and "organ pipes" that we see today. The eastern and western Dolomites, separated by the town of Bolzano, have slightly different characteristics; the eastern section is the more awe-inspiring, especially the Catinaccio (or Rosengarten) range which is particularly beautiful, turning rose pink in the dawn sunlight.

Onion dome, a common local feature

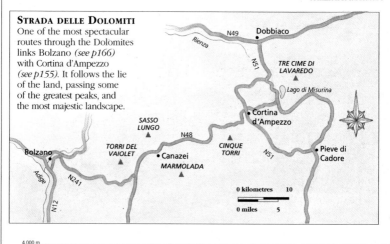

STRADA DELLE DOLOMITI

One of the most spectacular routes through the Dolomites links Bolzano *(see p166)* with Cortina d'Ampezzo *(see p155)*. It follows the lie of the land, passing some of the greatest peaks, and the most majestic landscape.

N49   Dobbiaco

Rienza

N51

TRE CIME DI LAVAREDO

Lago di Misurina

Cortina d'Ampezzo

SASSO LUNGO

N48

Bolzano

TORRI DEL VAIOLET

CINQUE TORRI

N51

Pieve di Cadore

Canazei

MARMOLADA

Adige   N241

N12

0 kilometres 10

0 miles 5

DISTINCTIVE PEAKS OF THE DOLOMITES

The peaks of the eastern Dolomites include several with distinctive shapes and some of the highest mountains in the range. Many are easily identifiable and have been individually named.

4,000 m (13,123 ft)

3,000 m (9,842 ft)

2,000 m (6,562 ft)

1,000 m (3,281 ft)

Approximate heights

Marmolada 3,343 m (10,968 ft)

Sasso Lungo 3,179 m (10,430 ft)

Cinque Torri 2,366 m (7,762 ft)

*The **Cinque Torri** or Five Towers rise from a single base between Canazei and Cortina d'Ampezzo.*

***Sasso Lungo**, part of the Gruppo di Sella, is a tall peak easily recognized by its distinctive scar.*

***Marmolada** is the highest peak in the Dolomite chain. A chair-lift ascends from the south side of the lake.*

Lago di Misurina is a large and beautiful lake lying beside the resort of Misurina. The crystal clear waters reflect the surrounding mountains, mirroring various peaks such as the distinctive Tre Cime (Three Peaks) di Lavaredo, in shimmering colours.

Outdoor activities in this area of dramatic landscapes include skiing in winter, and walking and rambling along the footpaths, and to picnic sites, in summer. Chair-lifts from the main resorts provide easy access up into the mountains themselves, transporting you into some breathtaking scenery.

NATURE IN THE DOLOMITES

Forests and meadows support a breathtaking richness of wildlife in the region. Alpine plants, which flower between June and September, have evolved their miniature form to survive the harsh winds.

The Flora

Gentian seeds are used to make a bitter local liqueur.

The red mountain lily thrives on sunbaked slopes.

The pretty burser's saxifrage grows in clusters on rocks.

Horned rampion has distinctive pink flower heads.

The Fauna

The ptarmigan changes its plumage from mottled brown in summer to snow white in winter for effective camouflage. It feeds on mountain berries and young plant shoots.

The chamois, a shy mountain antelope prized for its soft skin, is protected in the national parks, where hunting is forbidden.

Roe deer are very common as their natural predators – wolves and lynx – have now died out. Their keen appetite for tree saplings causes problems for foresters.

Torri del Vaiolet
2,243 m
(7,375 ft)

Tre Cime di Lavaredo
2,999 m
(9,839 ft)

The Torri del Vaiolet is part of the beautiful Catinaccio range, known for its colour.

Tre Cime di Lavaredo or Drei Zinnen dominate the valleys north of the Lago di Misurina.

VENICE

L YING IN THE *extreme northeast of Italy, Venice, gateway to the Orient, became an independent Byzantine province in the 10th century. Exclusive trading links with the East and victory in the Crusade of 1204 brought wealth and power, which were only gradually eroded by European and Turkish rivals. Today, Venice's ties are with the local Veneto region which stretches from the flat river plains to the Dolomites.*

Venice is one of the few cities in the world that can be truly described as unique. It survives against all the odds, built on a series of low mud banks amid the tidal waters of the Adriatic, and regularly subject to floods. During the Middle Ages, under the leadership of successive doges, Venice expanded its power and influence throughout the Mediterranean to Constantinople (modern Istanbul). The immense wealth of the city was celebrated in art and architecture throughout the city.

The riches of St Mark's alone bear witness to Venice's position as a world power from the 12th to 14th centuries. After slowly losing ground to the new states of Europe, however, it fell to Napoleon in 1797. Finally, Venice joined the Kingdom of Italy in 1866, so bringing unity to the country for the first time in its history. Today, Venice has found a new role. Her palazzi have become museums, shops, hotels and apartments and her convents have been turned into centres for art restoration. Yet little of the essential fabric of Venice has altered in 200 years. The city's sounds are still those of footsteps and the cries of boatmen. The only engines are those of barges delivering supplies or waterbuses ferrying passengers between stops. The same well-worn streets are still trodden. More than 12 million visitors a year succumb to the magic of this improbable place whose "streets are full of water" and where the glories of the past are evident at every turn.

A busy street on the island of Burano, with its distinctive, brightly painted houses

◁ Gondola prows, with their characteristic *ferri*, and Santa Maria della Salute in the background

Exploring Venice

Venice is divided into six ancient administrative districts or *sestieri*: Cannaregio, Castello, San Marco, Dorsoduro, San Polo and Santa Croce. Visitors usually start at Piazza San Marco, heading for the magnificent Basilica and the Palazzo Ducale, probably the busiest part of the city. You can walk to most places in Venice itself, and take a ride on a waterbus to any of the islands.

SIGHTS AT A GLANCE

0 metres   500

0 yards   500

KEY

	Street-by-Street: San Polo *pp92 – 3*
	Street-by-Street: Dorsoduro *pp98 – 9*
	Street-by-Street: Piazza San Marco *pp104 – 5*
✈	International airport
FS	Railway station
⛴	Ferry boarding point
⛴	*Vaporetto* boarding point
	Traghetto crossing *(see p636)*
	Gondola mooring
i	Tourist information

Santa Maria della Salute, at the mouth of the Grand Canal

SEE ALSO

- *Street Finder* pp120–29
- *Where to Stay* pp542–4
- *Where to Eat* pp578–9

LOCATOR MAP

THE LAGOON

GETTING AROUND

The only road into Venice is the N11 from Mestre which carries you over the causeway to Piazzale Roma where car parks and bus stops are situated. Rail travellers will arrive at Santa Lucia station on the Grand Canal. In the city, public transport is by *vaporetto*, or waterbus – the best for sightseeing being the No.1 which travels the length of the Grand Canal *(see pp130–31)*.

The Grand Canal: Santa Lucia to the Rialto

THE BEST WAY to view the Grand Canal as it winds through the heart of the city is from a *vaporetto*, or waterbus. Several lines travel the length of the canal *(see p623)*. The palaces lining the waterway were built over a span of five centuries and present a panoramic survey of the city's history, almost all bearing the name of some once-great Venetian family.

San Marcuola
The church was rebuilt in the 18th century, but the planned new façade overlooking the canal was never completed.

San Geremia houses the relics of St Lucy, once kept in the church of Santa Lucia where the railway station now stands.

Palazzo Labia
Between 1745–50, Giambattista Tiepolo decorated the ballroom with scenes from the life of Cleopatra.

Canale di Cannaregio

Palazzo Corner-Contarini

San Marcuo

FS **Ferrovia**

Ponte degli Scalzi

Fondaco dei Turchi
A warehouse for Turkish traders in the 17th–19th centuries, this is now the Natural History Museum.

San Simeone Piccolo
This 18th-century domed church is based on the Pantheon in Rome.

THE GONDOLAS OF VENICE

The gondola has been a part of Venice since the 11th century. With its slim hull and flat underside, the craft is perfectly adapted to negotiating narrow, shallow canals. There is a slight leftward curve to the prow, which counteracts the force of the oar, preventing the gondola from going round in circles.

In 1562 it was decreed that all gondolas should be black to stop people making an ostentatious show of their wealth. For special occasions they are decorated with flowers. Today, gondola rides are expensive and usually taken by tourists *(see p623)*. However, *traghetti* (gondola ferries) are a cheap, convenient way of crossing the Grand Canal.

Gondolas tied up by steps

Ca' d'Oro
*The delicate Gothic tracery of the
façade makes this a striking
landmark. Its art collection
(see p90) includes Bernini's
model for a fountain (c.1648).*

LOCATOR MAP

☐ *See Venice Street Finder
maps 1, 2, 3*

Palazzo Vendramin Calergi
*This is one of the finest
early Renaissance palaces
in Venice. The German
composer Richard Wagner
(left) died here in 1883.*

The Pescheria has
been the site of a busy
fish market for six
centuries.

Palazzo Sagredo
*Graceful Veneto-Byzantine and
Gothic arches are both featured
on the waterfront façade.*

**Palazzo Michiel dalle
Colonne** takes its name from
its distinctive colonnade.

San Stae

The Rialto Bridge
(see p93) spans
the canal in the
commercial heart
of the city.

San Stae
*The façade
of this Baroque
church is richly
adorned with
statues. It is a popu-
lar concert venue.*

Ca' d'Oro

Ca' Pesaro
*The huge, stately Baroque
palace today houses a
gallery of modern art and
the Oriental Museum.*

Rialto

The Grand Canal: the Rialto to San Marco

Aᴼᵀᴱᴿ ᴾᴬˢˢᴵᴺᴳ the Rialto, the canal doubles back on itself along a stretch known as La Volta (the bend). It then widens out and the views become more spectacular approaching San Marco. Façades may have faded and foundations frayed with the tides, yet the canal remains, in the words of the French ambassador in 1495, "the most beautiful street in the world".

Palazzo Mocenigo
Lord Byron stayed in this huge 18th-century palace in 1818.

Sant' Angelo

San Tomà

Palazzo Garzoni
is a renovated Gothic palace, now part of the university.

Ca' Rezzonico
Now a museum of 18th-century Venice (see p99), the palace was the last home of the poet Robert Browning, seen here with his son Pen.

San Samuele

Ca' Rezzonico

Palazzo Grassi
The elegant palazzo dates from the 1730s. Bought by Fiat in 1984, it is now used for art exhibitions.

Ponte dell'Accademia

Accademia

Palazzo Capello Malipiero
The palace was rebuilt in 1622. Beside it stands the 12th-century campanile of San Samuele.

Accademia
The world's greatest collection of Venetian paintings is housed here in the former Scuola della Carità (see pp102–3), which has a Baroque façade by Giorgio Massari.

Palazzo Barbaro
Novelist Henry James wrote The Aspern Papers *here in 1888.*

The Riva del Vin is the quay where wine *(vin)* used to be unloaded. It is one of the few spots where you can sit and relax on the banks of the Grand Canal.

Palazzo Barzizza, rebuilt in the 17th century, preserves its early 13th-century façade.

Peggy Guggenheim Collection
A one-storey palazzo houses Guggenheim's great modern art collection (see p100).

Santa Maria della Salute
The vast weight of this Baroque church is supported by over one million timber piles (see p101).

Palazzo Gritti-Pisani
The former home of the Gritti family is now the luxury Gritti Palace Hotel (see p544).

Harry's Bar, founded in 1931 by Giuseppe Cipriani, is famous for its cocktails.

Palazzo Dario
Beautiful coloured marbles give the 1487 palace a highly individual façade. Legend has it the building is cursed.

The Dogana di Mare (customs house), built in the 17th century, is crowned by two bronze Atlases supporting a golden globe topped by a weathervane.

Travelling slowly along the Grand Canal by gondola ▷

Madonna dell'Orto, with 15th-century façade statues of St Christopher and the Apostles

Madonna dell'Orto ❶

Campo Madonna dell'Orto. **Map** 2 F2. 🇮🇹 041-71 99 33. 🚤 Madonna dell'Orto. ⏰ 9:30am–noon, 4:30–7pm daily (Oct–Mar: 5pm).

THIS LOVELY Gothic church, founded in the mid-14th century, was dedicated to St Christopher, patron saint of travellers, to protect the boatmen who ferried passengers to the islands in the northern lagoon. A 15th-century statue of the saint, recently restored by the Venice in Peril fund, still stands above the main portal. The dedication was changed and the church reconstructed in the early 15th century, following the strange discovery, in a nearby vegetable garden *(orto)*, of a statue of the Virgin Mary said to have miraculous powers.

The interior, faced almost entirely in brick, is large, light and uncluttered. Immediately on the right stands a magnificent painting by Cima da Conegliano, *St John the Baptist and Other Saints* (c.1493). The vacant space in the chapel opposite belongs to Giovanni Bellini's *Madonna with Child* (c.1478), which was stolen for the third time in 1993.

The church's greatest remaining treasures are the works of art by Tintoretto, who was a parishioner of the church. His tomb, which is marked with a plaque, lies with that of his children, in the chapel to the right of the chancel. The most dramatic of his works are the towering masterpieces that decorate the chancel (1562–4).

On the right wall is the *Last Judgment*, whose turbulent content caused John Ruskin's wife, Effie, to flee the church in horror. In *The Adoration of the Golden Calf* on the left wall, the figure carrying the calf, fourth from the left, is believed to be a portrait of the artist. Inside the chapel of San Mauro, off the end of the right nave, stands a statue of the Madonna by Giovanni de' Santi. It was restored by the Venice in Peril fund, and inspired the rededication of the church.

Ca' d'Oro ❷

Calle Ca' d'Oro. **Map** 3 A4. 🇮🇹 041-523 87 90. 🚤 Ca' d'Oro. ⏰ 9:30am–1:30pm daily. 🎫

IN 1420 Marino Contarini, a wealthy patrician, commissioned the construction of what he hoped would be the city's most magnificent palace *(see p77)*. The building's intricate carving was entrusted to a team of Venetian and Lombard craftsmen, while the façade was beautifully adorned with the most elaborate and expensive decorative finishes of the day, including gold leaf, vermilion and ultramarine.

Tullio Lombardo's *Double Portrait*

Over the years the palace was extensively remodelled, and by the 18th century was in a state of semi-dereliction. In 1846 it was bought by the Russian Prince Troubetzkoy for the famous ballerina Maria Taglioni. Under her direction the palace suffered barbaric restoration, losing, among other things, its staircase and much of its original stonework. It was finally rescued by Baron Giorgio Franchetti, a wealthy patron of the arts, who bequeathed both the building and his private art collection to the state in 1915.

Pride of place on the first of the gallery's two floors goes to Andrea Mantegna's *St Sebastian* (1506), the artist's last work, which occupies a special alcove of its own. Elsewhere, the floor's main exhibits are ranged around the *portego* (gallery). This is largely dominated by the vivid 15th-century *Double Portrait* (c.1493) by the sculptor Tullio Lombardo; Sansovino's lunette of the *Madonna and Child* (c.1530); and several bronze reliefs by the Paduan Andrea Briosco, "Il Riccio" (1470–1532). Rooms leading off the *portego* to the right contain numerous bronzes and medallions, with some examples by Pisanello and Gentile Bellini. Paintings here also include the famous *Madonna of the Beautiful Eyes*, attributed to Giovanni Bellini, a *Madonna and Child*, attributed to Alvise Vivarini (both late 15th century), and Carpaccio's *Annunciation* and *Death of the Virgin* (both c.1504). A room to the left of the *portego* contains non-Venetian paintings, notably a *Flagellation* by Luca Signorelli (c.1480). A lovely staircase leads to the second floor, which opens with a room hung with tapestries. It has bronzes by Alessandro Vittoria and paintings by

The magnificent Gothic façade of the Ca' d'Oro, or House of Gold

Titian and Van Dyck. The *portego* displays frescoes (c.1532) by Pordenone from the cloister of Santo Stefano, while an anteroom contains damaged frescoes by Titian and Giorgione taken from the Fondaco dei Tedeschi.

Giovanni Bellini's 1513 altarpiece in San Giovanni Crisostomo

San Giovanni Crisostomo ❸

Campo San Giovanni Crisostomo. **Map** 3 B5. 041-522 71 55. Rialto. 11am–12:30pm, 3–5pm daily.

THIS PRETTY little terracotta-coloured church lies in a bustling quarter close to the Rialto. Built between 1479 and 1504, it is a lovely Renaissance design, the last work of Mauro Coducci.

The interior, which is built on a Greek-cross plan, is dark and intimate. The light meter illuminates Giovanni Bellini's *St Jerome with Saints Christopher and Augustine* (1513) above the first altar on the right. This was most probably Bellini's last painting, executed when he was in his eighties.

Over the high altar hangs Sebastiano del Piombo's *St John Chrysostom and Six Saints* (1509–11).

Santa Maria dei Miracoli ❹

Campo dei Miracoli. **Map** 3 B5. 041-528 39 03. Rialto. 10am–noon, 3–6pm Mon–Sat.

AN EXQUISITE masterpiece of early Renaissance architecture, the Miracoli is the favourite church of many Venetians and the one where they like to get married. Tucked away in a maze of alleys and waterways in eastern Cannaregio, it is small and somewhat elusive.

Often likened to a jewel box, Santa Maria dei Miracoli is decorated in various shades of marble, with some fine bas reliefs and sculpture. It was built in 1481–9 by the architect Pietro Lombardo and his sons to enshrine *The Virgin and Child* (1408), a painting believed to have miraculous powers. The picture, by Nicolò di Pietro, can still be seen above the altar.

The interior of the church is embellished by pink, white and grey marble, at its best when lit up by rays of pale

Decorative column from inside Santa Maria dei Miracoli

sunshine. It is crowned by a barrel-vaulted ceiling (1528) which has 50 portraits of saints and prophets. The balustrade, between the nave and the chancel, is decorated by Tullio Lombardo's carved figures of St Francis, Archangel Gabriel, the Virgin and St Clare.

The screen around the high altar and the medallions of the Evangelists in the cupola spandrels are also Lombardo's work. Above the main door, the choir gallery was used by the nuns from the neighbouring convent, who entered the church through an overhead gallery. The Miracoli has recently undergone a major restoration programme, which was funded by the American Save Venice organization.

SANTA MARIA DEI MIRACOLI
This beautifully proportioned façade is composed of decorated panels and multicoloured polished marble.

Carving of saint

The semi-circular crowning lunette emphasizes the church's jewel-box appearance.

A false loggia is formed of Ionic arches, inset with windows. The marble used was reportedly left over from the building of San Marco.

Virgin and Child by **Giorgio Lascaris**

The marble panels are fixed to the bricks by metal hooks. This method prevents the build-up of damp and salt water behind the panels, and dates from the Renaissance.

Street-by-Street: San Polo

THE RIALTO BRIDGE and markets make this area a magnet for visitors. Traditionally the city's commercial quarter, it was here that bankers, brokers and merchants conducted their affairs. Streets are no longer lined with stalls selling spices and fine fabrics, but the food markets and pasta shops are unmissable. Away from the bridge, streets quickly become less crowded, leading to tiny piazzas and quiet churches.

The Rialto Markets have existed for centuries, and are renowned for their produce. The Pescheria sells fresh fish and seafood.

The 17th-century church of San Cassiano houses a carved altar (1696) and a *Crucifixion* by Tintoretto (1568).

Sant'Aponal has a façade decorated with worn Gothic reliefs. The church was founded in the 11th century, but is now deconsecrated.

The Frari

San Silvestro

San Giovanni Elemosinario is an inconspicuous church that was rebuilt in the early 16th century, although its campanile dates from the end of the 14th century. Inside it are interesting frescoes by Pordenone.

KEY

– – – Suggested route

| 0 metres | 75 |
| 0 yards | 75 |

STAR SIGHT

★ Rialto

LOCATOR MAP
*See Venice Street Finder
maps 2, 3, 6, 7*

The lively Erberia, selling fresh fruit and vegetables

San Giacomo di Rialto's
clock face (1410), which
has sadly been a poor
time-keeper over the
years, adorns one
of Venice's oldest
churches.

**Market
entrance**

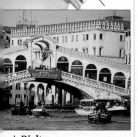

★ **Rialto**
*One of Venice's most
famous sights, the bridge
offers fine views of the
Grand Canal, and marks
the heart of the city* ❺

Rialto ❺

Ponte di Rialto. **Map** 7 A1. 🚤 *Rialto.*

THE RIALTO takes its name
from *rivo alto* (high bank)
and was one of the first areas
of Venice to be inhabited. A
banking and then market
district, it remains one of the
city's busiest and most
bustling areas. Locals and
visitors alike jostle among the
colourful stalls of the Erberia
(fruit and vegetable market)
and Pescheria (fish market).

Stone bridges were built in
Venice as early as the 12th
century, but it was not until
1588, after the collapse, decay
or sabotage of earlier wooden
structures, that a solid stone
bridge was designed for the
Rialto. Completed in 1591, the
new bridge remained the only
means of crossing the Grand
Canal until 1854, when the
Accademia bridge was built.

Few visitors leave Venice
without crossing the famous
bridge. It is a wonderful place
to watch and photograph the
constant activity of boats on
the Grand Canal below.

San Giacomo dell'Orio ❻

Campo San Giacomo dell'Orio.
Map 2 E5. ☎ *041-524 06 72.*
🚤 *Riva di Biasio or San Stae.*
🕐 *8am–noon, 5–7pm Mon–Sat.*

THIS CHURCH is a focal point
of a quiet quarter of Santa
Croce. The name "dell'Orio"
(locally dall'Orio) may derive
from a laurel tree *(alloro)*
that once stood near the
church. San Giacomo was
founded in the 9th century,
rebuilt in 1225 and thereafter

repeatedly modified, resulting
in a mixture of architectural
styles. The campanile, basilica
ground plan and Byzantine
columns survive from the 13th
century. The ship's keel roof
and the columns are from the
Gothic period, and the apses
are Renaissance.

In order to gain access to
the Veronese ceiling and altar
paintings in the new sacristy,
apply to the custodian.

San Polo ❼

Campo San Polo. **Map** 6 F1.
☎ *041-523 76 31.* 🚤 *San Silvestro.*
🕐 *8am–noon, 3:30–6:30pm
Mon–Sat, 8am–noon Sun.*

FOUNDED IN THE 9th century,
rebuilt in the 15th and
revamped in the early 19th
in Neo-Classical style, the
church of San Polo is worth
visiting for the lovely Gothic
portal and the Romanesque
lions at the foot of the 14th-
century campanile – one
holds a serpent between its
paws, the other a human head.

Inside, follow the signs for
the *Via Crucis del Tiepolo* –
14 pictures of the Stations
of the Cross (1749) by the
painter Giandomenico Tiepolo:
many include vivid portraits
of Venetian life. The church
also has paintings by
Veronese, Palma il Giovane
(the Younger) and a dramatic
Last Supper by Tintoretto.

**A Romanesque lion at the base of San
Polo's 14th-century campanile**

Santa Maria Gloriosa dei Frari 🔞

MORE COMMONLY KNOWN as the Frari (a corruption of Frati, meaning brothers), this vast Gothic church dwarfs the eastern area of San Polo. The first church on the site was built by Franciscan friars in 1250–1338, but was replaced by a larger building completed in the mid-15th century. The airy interior is striking for its sheer size and for the quality of its works of art, including masterpieces by Titian and Giovanni Bellini, a statue by Donatello and several grandiose tombs.

Foscari Monument
Doge Foscari died in 1457, after a long and eventful 34-year reign.

The campanile
is 83 m (262 ft) high, the tallest in the city after that of San Marco.

★ Assumption of the Virgin
Titian's glowing and spectacular work (1518) draws the eye through the monk's choir, to the altar, and heavenwards.

Rood Screen
(1475)
Pietro Lombardo and Bartolomeo Bon carved the rood screen and its decorative marble figures.

Entrance

The ***Madonna di Ca' Pesaro*** (1526) shows Titian's mastery of light and colour.

★ Monks' Choir
This consists of three-tiered stalls (1468), carved with bas reliefs of saints and Venetian city scenes.

FLOORPLAN

The Frari's imposing cruciform interior, which is 90 m (295 ft) long, holds 12 sights that should not be missed.

VISITORS' CHECKLIST

Campo dei Frari. **Map** 6 D1.
041-522 26 37. San Tomà.
9–11:45am, 2:30–5:30pm
Mon–Sat, 3–5:30pm Sun &
public hols. except for those
attending mass & on public hols.
frequent.

KEY TO FLOORPLAN

1 Tomb of Canova
2 Monument to Titian
3 *Madonna di Ca' Pesaro* by Titian
4 Choir stalls
5 Corner Chapel
6 Tomb of Monteverdi
7 Tomb of Doge Nicolò Tron
8 High altar with *Assumption of the Virgin* (1518) by Titian
9 Tomb of Doge Francesco Foscari
10 *John the Baptist* (c.1450) by Donatello
11 B Vivarini's altar painting (1474), Bernardo Chapel
12 *Madonna and Child with Saints* (1488) by Bellini

★ Madonna and Child
The sacristy's altarpiece (1488) by Bellini, with its sublime use of colour, is one of Venice's most beautiful Renaissance paintings.

The former monastery, which houses the State Archives, has two cloisters, one in the style of Sansovino, another designed by Palladio.

Tomb of Canova
Canova designed, but never constructed, a Neo-Classical marble pyramid like this as a monument for Titian. After Canova's death in 1822, the sculptor's pupils used a similar design for their master's tomb.

STAR SIGHTS

★ Assumption of the Virgin by Titian

★ Madonna and Child by Bellini

★ Monks' Choir

Scuola Grande di San Rocco ●

Restored main entrance to the Scuola di San Rocco

FOUNDED IN HONOUR of San Rocco (St Roch), a saint who dedicated his life to helping the sick, the Scuola started out as a charitable confraternity. Construction began in 1515 under Bartolomeo Bon and was continued by Scarpagnino until his death in 1549. The work was financed by donations from Venetians keen to invoke San Rocco's protection and the Scuola quickly became one of the wealthiest in Venice. In 1564 its members decided to commission Tintoretto to decorate its walls and ceilings. His earliest paintings, the first of over 50 works he eventually left in the Scuola, fill the small Sala dell'Albergo off the Upper Hall. His later paintings occupy the Ground Floor Hall, immediately within the entrance.

Tintoretto's magnificent *Crucifixion*, painted in 1565 for the Sala dell'Albergo in the Scuola di San Rocco

GROUND FLOOR HALL

THE GROUND FLOOR cycle was executed in 1583–7, when Tintoretto was in his sixties, and consists of eight paintings illustrating the life of Mary. The series starts with an *Annunciation* and ends with an *Assumption*, which has been poorly restored.

The tranquil scenes of *The Flight into Egypt*, *St Mary Magdalene* and *St Mary of Egypt* are remarkable for their serenity. This is portrayed most

Detail from *The Flight into Egypt* (1582–7) by Tintoretto

lucidly by the Virgin's isolated spiritual contemplation in the *St Mary of Egypt*. In all three paintings, the landscapes are rendered with rapid strokes, and are an important part of the composition.

UPPER HALL AND SALA DELL'ALBERGO

SCARPAGNINO'S great staircase (1544–6), with its upper flight decorated with two vast paintings commemorating the plague of 1630, leads to the Upper Hall. Here, biblical subjects decorate the ceiling and walls, painted by Tintoretto from 1575–81.

The ceiling paintings portray scenes from the Old Testament. The three large and dynamic square paintings in the centre show episodes from the Book of Exodus: *Moses Strikes Water from the Rock*, *The Miracle of the Bronze Serpent* and *The Fall of Manna in the Desert*. These all allude to the charitable

aims of the Scuola in alleviating thirst, sickness and hunger respectively. All three paintings are crowded compositions displaying much violent movement.

The vast wall paintings in the hall feature episodes from the New Testament, linking with the ceiling paintings. Two of the most striking paintings are *The Temptation of Christ*, which shows a handsome young Satan offering Christ two loaves of bread, and *The Adoration of the Shepherds*. Like *The Temptation of Christ*, *The Adoration* is composed in two halves, with a female figure, shepherds and ox below, and the Holy Family and onlookers above.

The beautiful carvings below the paintings were added in the 17th century by sculptor Francesco Pianta. The figures are allegorical and include (near the altar) a caricature of Tintoretto with his palette and brushes, representing Painting. Near the entrance to the Sala dell'

Detail from _The Temptation of Christ_ (1578–81) by Tintoretto

VISITORS' CHECKLIST

Campo San Rocco. **Map** 6 D1.
(_041-523 48 64._ ** San Tomà.**
** _Apr–Oct: 9am–5pm daily;_
Nov–Mar: 10am–1pm Mon–Fri,
10am–4pm Sat & Sun (last adm:
30 mins before closing).
** _1 Jan, Easter, 25 Dec._ **

Albergo, there is a self-portrait (1573) by Tintoretto. The Sala dell'Albergo itself is a small room containing the most breathtaking of his master-pieces – the _Crucifixion_ (1565). Henry James remarked of this painting: "no single picture contains more of human life; there is everything in it, including the most exquisite beauty." Tintoretto began the cycle of paintings in this room in 1564, when he won the commission with the ceiling painting _San Rocco in Glory_. On the wall opposite the _Crucifixion_ are paintings of episodes from the Passion: _Christ before Pilate, The Crowning with Thorns_ and _The Ascent to Calvary._

The easel painting _Christ Carrying the Cross_ was once attributed to Giorgione, but is now believed to be by Titian.

San Rocco ⑩

Campo San Rocco. **Map** 6 D1.
** _San Tomà._ ** _7:30am–12:30pm daily, 3–5pm Sun._

SHARING THE LITTLE square with the celebrated Scuola Grande di San Rocco is the church of the same name. Designed by Bartolomeo Bon in 1489 and largely rebuilt in 1725, the exterior has suffered from a mixture of architectural styles. The façade, similar in concept to the Scuola, was added in 1765–71.

Inside, the chancel is decor-ated with a series of paintings by Tintoretto depicting scenes from the life of San Rocco.

San Pantalon ⑪

Campo San Pantalon. **Map** 6 D2.
** _San Tomà._ ** _8–11am, 4–6:30pm Mon–Sat._

Fumiani's epic ceiling painting (1680–1740) in San Pantalon

THE OVERWHELMING feature of this late 17th-century church is its vast painted ceiling, dark, awe-inspiring and remarkable for its illusionistic effect of height. The ceiling comprises a total of 40 scenes, and admirers claim that this is the world's largest work of art on canvas.

The scenes show the martyrdom and apotheosis of the physician St Pantalon. The artist, Gian Antonio Fumiani, took 24 years (1680–1704) to achieve the masterpiece, before allegedly falling to his death from the scaffolding.

KEY TO PAINTINGS

☐ **GROUND FLOOR HALL 1** The Annunciation; **2** The Adoration of the Three Kings; **3** The Flight into Egypt; **4** The Massacre of the Innocents; **5** St Mary Magdalene; **6** St Mary of Egypt; **7** The Presentation in the Temple; **8** The Assumption.

☐ **UPPER HALL WALLS 9** San Rocco; **10** St Sebastian; **11** The Adoration of the Shepherds; **12** The Baptism of Christ; **13** The Resurrection; **14** The Agony in the Garden; **15** The Last Supper; **16** The Vision of San Rocco; **17** The Miracle of the Loaves and Fishes; **18** The Resurrection of Lazarus; **19** The Ascension; **20** Christ Heals the Paralytic; **21** The Temptation of Christ.

☐ **UPPER HALL CEILING 22** Moses Saved from the Waters; **23** The Pillar of Fire; **24** Samuel and Saul; **25** Jacob's Ladder; **26** Elijah on a Chariot of Fire; **27** Elijah Fed by the Angels; **28** Daniel Saved by the Angels; **29** The Passover; **30** The Fall of Manna; **31** The Sacrifice of Isaac; **32** The Miracle of the Bronze Serpent; **33** Jonah Emerges from the Whale; **34** Moses Strikes Water from the Rock; **35** Adam and Eve; **36** Three Children in the Furnace; **37** God Appears to Moses; **38** Sampson Brings out Water from the Jawbone of an Ass; **39** The Vision of the Prophet Ezekiel; **40** The Vision of Jeremiah; **41** Elisha Distributes Bread; **42** Abraham and Melchizedeck.

Ground Floor Hall

Upper Hall

Street-by-Street: Dorsoduro

THE SESTIERE OF DORSODURO was built up on a stratum of solid subsoil – the name means "hard backbone". It has as its focal point the lively Campo Santa Margherita, the largest open space in this part of Venice. The square bustles with activity, particularly in the morning when the market stalls are open, and in the evening when it is the haunt of students from nearby Ca' Foscari, now part of Venice university. The surrounding streets contain some architectural stunners, notably Ca' Rezzonico and the Scuola Grande dei Carmini, which has decorations by Tiepolo. Of the area's waterways, the delightful Rio San Barnaba is best appreciated from the Ponte dei Pugni, near the barge selling fruit and vegetables – itself a time-honoured Venetian sight. Alongside the Rio Terrà Canal there are some lively cafés and a fascinating shop selling masks for Carnevale.

Santa Margherita

Campo Santa Margherita is an ideal place for relaxing in a café.

Palazzo Zenobio, built at the end of the 17th century, has been an Armenian college since 1850. With permission, visitors can see the fine 18th-century ballroom.

Scuola Grande dei Carmini contains nine ceiling panels (1739–44) in the hall on the upper floor, painted by Tiepolo for the Carmelite confraternity.

Santa Maria dei Carmini has a Gothic side porch carved with Byzantine reliefs.

Rio San Barnaba, flanked by Fondamenta Gherardini, is one of the prettiest canals in the *sestiere*.

KEY

– – – Suggested route

0 metres   50
0 yards   50

LOCATOR MAP
*See Venice Street Finder
maps 5, 6*

Tiepolo's *New World* fresco, part
of a series in Ca' Rezzonico

★ **Ca' Rezzonico**
*The ballroom covers the width
of the palazzo once owned
by Browning* ⓬

Palazzo Giustinian
was home to
Wagner in 1858.

Ca' Foscari
was completed in
1437 for Doge
Francesco Foscari.

RIO DI CA' FOSCARI
C D ASEO
C SAONERI
GAZEN
C FOSCARI
CANAL GRANDE
C DELLA VIDA
CALLE BERNARDO
C D BOTTEGHE
CAMPO
SAN
BARNABA
CALLE DEL TRAGHETTO

Ponte dei Pugni was
a traditional scene of
fist fights between rival
factions. They were
finally banned in 1705
for being too violent.

San Barnaba is a thriving
community, with its own
floating barge stall crammed
with fresh fruit and vegetables.
It is a focal point for tourists
and locals alike.

Ca' Rezzonico ⓬

Fondamenta Rezzonico 3136.
Map 6 E3. 🚃 *041-522 45 43.*
🚤 *Ca' Rezzonico.* ⭕ *Apr–Sep:
10am–5pm; Oct–Mar: 10am–4pm
Sat–Thu.* ⬤ *1 Jan, 1 May,
25 Dec.* 📷

THIS PALAZZO HOUSES the
museum of 18th-century
Venice, its rooms furnished
with frescoes, paintings and
period pieces taken from other
palaces or museums. Building
began with Longhena (architect
of La Salute, *see p101*) in 1667,
but the funds of the Bon
family, who commissioned it,
ran dry before the second
floor was started. In 1712 the
unfinished palace was bought
by the Rezzonico family of
Genoa. A large portion of
their fortune was spent on the
completion of the palace.

The Rezzonico family sold it
on, in 1888, to the famous
poet Robert Browning and his
son, Pen. The outstanding
attraction in the palace today
is Giorgio Massari's ballroom,
which occupies the entire
breadth of the building. It
is adorned with gilded
chandeliers, carved
furniture by Andrea
Brustolon and a ceiling
with *trompe l'oeil* frescoes.
Other rooms have frescoes
by Giambattista Tiepolo,
including his lively
Nuptial Allegory (1758),
and one by his son,
Giandomenico, originally
in his villa at Zianigo.

There are paintings by
Longhi, Guardi, and – rare in
Venice – Canaletto. On the top
floor is a reconstructed 18th-
century apothecary's shop
and a puppet theatre.

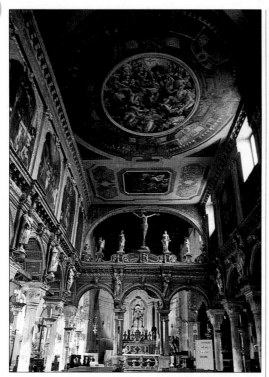

Nave of San Nicolò dei Mendicoli, one of the oldest churches in Venice

San Nicolò dei Mendicoli **⓭**

Campo San Nicolò. **Map** 5 A3.
📞 041-528 59 52. 🚊 San Basilio.
🕐 10am–noon, 4–6pm Mon–Sat;
for morning services only on Sun.

CONTRASTING WITH the remote and rundown area around it, this church still remains one of the most charming in Venice. Founded in the 7th century, it has been rebuilt extensively over the years. The little porch on the north flank is 15th century and once sheltered the beggars, or *mendicanti*, who gave the church its name.

Thanks to the Venice in Peril fund, in the 1970s the church underwent one of the most comprehensive restoration programmes since the floods of 1966. Flooding had become such a problem that the priest often ferried himself around the church in a coracle (a small wicker boat). The floor, which was 30 cm (1 ft) below

the level of the canals, was rebuilt and raised slightly to prevent further flood damage. The roofs and lower walls were reconstructed, and paintings and statues restored.

The interior is delightfully embellished, particularly the nave with its 16th-century gilded wooden statues. These include the figure of San Nicolò himself. On the upper walls is a series of paintings of the life of Christ (c.1553) by Alvise dal Friso and other pupils of Veronese.

Outside, a small column supports a stone lion, in a humbler echo of the Column of San Marco in the Piazzetta.

San Sebastiano **⓮**

Campo San Sebastiano. **Map** 5 C3.
📞 041-28 24 87. 🚊 San Basilio.
🕐 2:30–5:30pm daily.

THIS CHURCH HAS one of the most homogeneous interiors in the whole of Venice. The splendour was created by Veronese who, from 1555 to 1560 and again in the 1570s, was commissioned to decorate the sacristy ceiling, the nave ceiling, the frieze, the east end of the choir, the high altar, the doors of the organ panels and the chancel.

The paintings, which are typical of the artist, are rich and radiant, with sumptuous costumes and colours. Those on the sacristy ceiling depict the *Coronation of the Virgin* and the *Four Evangelists*.

Of the other paintings, the finest are the three which tell the story of Esther, Queen of Xerxes I of Persia, famous for securing the deliverance of the Jewish people.

Appropriately, the artist is buried in the church. His tomb is situated in front of the beautifully paved chapel to the left of the chancel.

Accademia **⓯**

See pp102–3.

Peggy Guggenheim Collection **⓰**

Palazzo Venier dei Leoni. **Map** 6 F4.
📞 041-520 62 88. 🚊 Accademia.
🕐 11am–6pm Wed–Mon.
⬤ 25 Dec. 📷

INTENDED AS A four-storey palace, the 18th-century Palazzo Venier dei Leoni in fact never rose beyond the ground floor – hence its nickname, *Il*

The truncated palazzo housing the Peggy Guggenheim Collection

Palazzo Nonfinito (The Unfinished Palace). In 1949 the building was bought as a home by the American millionairess Peggy Guggenheim (1898–1979), a collector, dealer and patron of the arts.

A perspicacious and high-spirited woman, she initially befriended, and then furthered the careers of, many innovative abstract and Surrealist artists. One was Max Ernst, who became her second husband. The collection consists of 200 fine paintings and sculptures, each representing the 20th century's most influential modern art movements. The dining room has notable Cubist works of art, including *The Poet* by Pablo Picasso, and an entire room is devoted to Jackson Pollock, who was "discovered" by Guggenheim. Other artists represented are Braque, Chagall, de Chirico, Dalí, Duchamp, Léger, Kandinsky, Klee, Mondrian, Miró, Malevich, Rothko, Bacon and Magritte, whose Surreal *Empire of Light* (1953–4) shows a night scene of a darkened house in a wooded setting with a bright day sky above. The sculpture collection, which includes Constantin Brancusi's elegant *Bird in Space* (c.1923), is laid out in the house and garden.

Constantin Brancusi
Bird in Space

Perhaps the most provocative piece is Marino Marini's *Angelo della Città* (Angel of the Citadel, 1948), located on the terrace overlooking the Grand Canal. This shows a prominently displayed man sitting on a horse, erect in all respects. Embarrassed onlookers avert their gaze to enjoy views of the Grand Canal.

The Guggenheim is one of the most visited sights of Venice, and the best place in the city to see modern art. Light-filled rooms and the large modern canvases provide a striking contrast to the Renaissance paintings which usually form the highlights in most Venetian churches and museums. A bonus for English speakers is the team of assistants, who are often visiting arts graduates from Britain.

The garden has been paved and features an array of sculptures. Peggy Guggenheim's ashes are also preserved here, near the place where her pet dogs were buried. A shop and restaurant are housed in buildings off the garden. Call for information on temporary exhibits.

The Baroque church of Santa Maria della Salute, at the mouth of the Grand Canal

Santa Maria della Salute ⑰

Campo della Salute. **Map** 7 A4.
📞 *041-522 55 58.* 🚊 *Salute.*
🕐 *8:30am–noon, 3–5pm daily.*
📷 *to sacristy.*

THE GREAT BAROQUE church of Santa Maria della Salute, standing at the entrance of the Grand Canal, is one of the most imposing architectural landmarks of Venice. Henry James likened it to "some great lady on the threshold of her salon".

Interior of the Salute with the octagonal space at its core

The church was built in thanksgiving for the city's deliverance from the plague epidemic of 1630, hence the name *Salute*, which means health and salvation.

Each November, in celebration, worshippers light candles and approach across a bridge of boats spanning the mouth of the Grand Canal for the occasion.

Baldassare Longhena started the church in 1630 at the age of 32, and worked on it for the rest of his life. It was not completed until 1687, five years after his death.

The interior is comparatively sober. It consists of a large octagonal space below the cupola and six chapels radiating from the ambulatory. The large domed chancel and grandiose high altar dominate the view from the main door.

The altar's sculptural group by Giusto Le Corte represents the Virgin and Child giving protection to Venice from the plague. The best of the paintings are in the sacristy to the left of the altar: Titian's early altarpiece of *St Mark Enthroned with Saints Cosmas, Damian, Roch and Sebastian* (1511–12) and his dramatic ceiling paintings of *Cain and Abel, The Sacrifice of Abraham and Isaac* and *David and Goliath* (1540–9). *The Wedding at Cana* (1551) on the wall opposite the entrance is a major work by Jacopo Tintoretto.

Accademia ⑮

SPANNING FIVE CENTURIES, the matchless
collection of paintings in the Accademia
provides a complete spectrum of the Venetian
school, from the medieval Byzantine period
through the Renaissance to the Baroque and
later. The basis of the collection was the
Accademia di Belle Arti founded in 1750 by
the painter Giovanni Battista Piazzetta. In
1807 Napoleon moved the collection to these
premises, and enriched it with works of art
removed from churches and monasteries.

The Tempest
*In this enigmatic landscape (c.1507),
Giorgione was probably creating a
fantasy rather than portraying
any specific subject.*

KEY TO FLOORPLAN

- ☐ Byzantine and International Gothic
- ☐ Renaissance
- ☐ Baroque, Genre and Landscape
- ☐ Ceremonial Painting
- ☐ Temporary exhibitions
- ☐ Non-exhibition space

The courtyard (1561)
designed by Palladio

The former church
of Santa Maria
della Carità

**Feast in the House
of Levi (1573) by
Paolo Veronese**

**Audio-visual
display room**

Entrance

**Madonna and Child between
St John the Baptist and a Saint**
*In this beautiful painting (c.1504),
Giovanni Bellini places the figures in
spacious landscape, so marking a new
phase in his development.*

Coronation of the Virgin
*Paolo Veneziano's polyptych (1325)
has a central image of the Virgin
surrounded by a panoply of religious
scenes. This detail shows episodes
from the Life of St Francis.*

Healing of the Madman (c.1496) by Vittore Carpaccio

VISITORS' CHECKLIST

Campo della Carità. **Map** 6 E3.
041-522 22 47.
Accademia. 9am–2pm
Mon–Sat, 9am–1pm Sun &
public hols (last adm: 30 mins
before closing). 1 Jan, 1 May,
25 Dec.

BYZANTINE AND INTERNATIONAL GOTHIC

R<small>OOM 1 SHOWS</small> the influence of Byzantine art on the early Venetian painters. In Paolo Veneziano's glowing *Coronation of the Virgin* (1325), the linear rhythms are unmistakably Gothic, but the gold background and central panel are distinctly Byzantine.

In contrast, *The Coronation of the Virgin* (1448) by Michele Giambono reveals a delicate naturalism, typical of the International Gothic style.

RENAISSANCE

T<small>HE RENAISSANCE</small> came late to Venice, but by the second quarter of the 15th century it had transformed the city into a thriving art centre rivalling Florence and Rome. Central to Venetian art in the 15th century was the *Sacra Conversazione*, in which the Madonna is portrayed with various saints in a harmonious composition. Giovanni Bellini's altarpiece for San Giobbe (c.1487) in room 2 is one of the finest examples of this subject.

In contrast, the High Renaissance exuberance of Paolo Veronese is exemplified in the monumental *Feast in the House of Levi* (1573). The painting occupies a whole wall in room 10. Tintoretto's huge masterpiece *The Miracle of St Mark Freeing a Slave* (1548) is also on display here.

BAROQUE, GENRE AND LANDSCAPE

V<small>ENICE LACKED</small> native Baroque painters, but a few non-Venetians kept the Venetian school alive in the 17th century. The most notable was the Genoese Bernardo Strozzi (1581–1644). The artist was a great admirer of the work of Veronese, as can be seen in his *Feast at the House of Simon* (1629) in

room 11. Also represented in this room is Giambattista Tiepolo, the greatest Venetian painter of the 18th century.

The long corridor (12) and the rooms that lead from it are largely devoted to light-hearted landscape and genre paintings from the 18th century. Among them are pastoral scenes by Francesco Zuccarelli, works by Marco Ricci, scenes of Venetian society by Pietro Longhi and a view of Venice by Canaletto (1763). This is a fine example of his sense of perspective.

CEREMONIAL PAINTING

R<small>OOMS 20 and 21</small> return to the Renaissance, featuring two great cycles of paintings from the late 16th century. The detail in these large-scale anecdotal canvases provides a fascinating glimpse of the life, customs and appearance of Venice at the time.

Room 20 houses *The Stories of the Cross* by Venice's leading artists. In room 21, minutely detailed *Scenes from the Legend of St Ursula* (1490s) by Carpaccio mix reality and imagination by linking episodes from the life of the saint to the settings and costumes of 15th-century Venice.

Feast in the House of Levi (1573) by Paolo Veronese

Street-by-Street: Piazza San Marco

THROUGHOUT ITS LONG history Piazza San Marco has witnessed pageants, processions, political activities and countless Carnival festivities. Visitors flock here in their thousands for two of the city's most important historic sights – the Basilica and the Palazzo Ducale. These magnificent buildings complement lesser sights, such as the Campanile, Museo Correr and Torre dell'Orologio, not to mention the gardens of the Giardinetti Reali, open-air orchestras, elegant cafés – notably Quadri and Florian's – and numerous smart shops.

Lion of St Mark

Torre dell'Orologio
The clock tower, with hidden clockwork figures, dates from the Renaissance **20**

Gondolas are moored in the Bacino Orseolo, named after Doge Pietro Orseolo who established a hospice for pilgrims here in 977.

The Piazza was described by Napoleon as the "most elegant drawing room in Europe".

MERCERIE

PROCURATIE VECCHIE

PIAZZA SAN MARCO

PROCURATIE NUOVE

Museo Correr
Giovanni Bellini's Pietà *(1455–60) is one of many masterpieces hanging in the galleries of the Correr* **22**

Harry's Bar has attracted American visitors since Giuseppe Cipriani and his friend Harry set it up in 1931. Shown here is Ernest Hemingway, one of the bar's many famous patrons.

San Marco Vallaresso

★ Basilica di San Marco
This 13th-century façade mosaic shows the body of St Mark being carried into the basilica ⑱

LOCATOR MAP
See Venice Street Finder map 7

The Campanile
The present Campanile replaced one that collapsed in 1902 ㉑

The Bridge of Sighs (1600) was built as a passageway between the Palazzo Ducale and the prison. It reputedly took its name from the sighs of prisoners being led to trial.

CALLE LARGA SAN MARCO

RIO DEL

Ponte della Paglia

PALAZZO

PIAZZETTA

MOLO SAN MARCO

★ Palazzo Ducale
Once home to Venice's rulers, and to the offices of State, the Doges' Palace is a triumph of Gothic architecture ⑲

San Marco Giardinetti

The vaulting of the stairway in the magnificent Libreria Sansoviniana (1588) is decorated with frescoes and gilded stucco. The national library of St Mark is housed here.

| 0 metres | 75 |
| 0 yards | 75 |

The Zecca, designed by Sansovino and started in 1537, was the city mint until 1870, and gave its name to the *zecchino* or Venetian ducat.

STAR SIGHTS

★ Basilica di San Marco

★ Palazzo Ducale

Basilica di San Marco ⑱

VENICE'S FAMOUS BASILICA blends the architectural and decorative styles of East and West to create one of the greatest buildings in Europe. The exterior owes its almost Oriental splendour to countless treasures from the Republic's overseas empire. Among these are copies of the famous bronze horses, brought from Constantinople in 1204, and a wealth of columns, bas reliefs and coloured marbles studded across the main façade. Mosaics from different epochs adorn the five door-ways, while the main portal is framed by some of Italy's loveliest Romanesque carving (1240–65).

The Pentecost Dome, showing the Descent of the Holy Ghost as a dove, was probably the first dome to be decorated with mosaics.

St Mark and Angels
The statues crowning the central arch are additions from the early 15th century.

The elegant arches echo those of the lower floor, forming a repeat pattern.

★ Horses of St Mark
The four horses are replicas of the gilded bronze originals, now protected inside the Basilica's museum.

STAR FEATURES

★ Façade Mosaics

★ Horses of St Mark

Romanesque carvings adorn the arches of the main portal.

Entrance

★ Façade Mosaics
A 17th-century mosaic shows the body of St Mark being taken from Alexandria, reputedly smuggled past Muslim guards under slices of pork.

Baldacchino

The fine alabaster columns of the altar canopy, or baldacchino, are adorned with scenes from the New Testament.

The Ascension Dome
features a magnificent 13th-century mosaic of Christ surrounded by angels, the 12 Apostles and the Virgin Mary.

St Mark's body, believed lost in the fire of AD 976, supposedly reappeared in this spot in 1094, when the new church was consecrated.

The Mosaic Pavement
shows beautiful pictures of birds and beasts, some of which are allegorical.

St Mark's Treasury

The Tetrarchs

This charming sculptured group in porphyry (4th-century Egyptian) is thought to represent Diocletian, Maximian, Valerian and Constantine. Collectively they were the Tetrarchs, appointed by Diocletian to help rule the Roman Empire.

THE BUILDING OF ST MARK'S

Built on a Greek cross plan and crowned with five huge domes, this is the third church to stand on the site. The first, which enshrined the body of St Mark in the 9th century, was destroyed by fire. The second was pulled down in favour of a church reflecting Venice's growing power. The present design was inspired by the Church of the Apostles in Constantinople and was completed and decorated over the centuries. From 1075, all ships returning from abroad had, by law, to bring back a precious gift to adorn "the House of St Mark". The mosaics inside are mostly 12th–13th century and cover 4,240 sq m (45,622 sq ft). Some were later replaced by such artists as Titian and Tintoretto. Until 1807 St Mark's was the doge's private chapel, used for ceremonies of State, after which it succeeded San Pietro di Castello as the cathedral of Venice.

13th-century carving of a grape harvester on the main portal

Exploring the Basilica

S T MARK'S MAGNIFICENT INTERIOR is clad with dazzling
mosaics, which begin in the *narthex*, or atrium of
the Basilica, and culminate in the glittering panels of
the Pentecost and Ascension domes. The Genesis
Cupola in the atrium has a stunning Creation of the
World described in concentric circles. The *pavimento*
or floor is also patterned with mosaics in marble and
glass. Steps from the atrium lead to the Museo Marciano,
home to the Basilica's famous horses. Other treasures
include the jewel-encrusted Pala d'Oro, behind the high
altar, the Nicopeia icon and the
precious hoards of silver, gold
and glassware in the Treasury.

Madonna di Nicopeia
*This Byzantine icon,
looted in 1204, is one of
Venice's most revered images.*

**The Porta dei
Fiori** or Gate
of Flowers is
decorated with
13th-century
reliefs.

**Cappella
dei Mascoli**

**North
side aisle**

★ **Pentecost Dome**
*Showing the Apostles
touched by tongues of
flame, the Pentecost Dome
was lavishly decorated
in the 12th century.*

Atrium

**Steps to
Museo Marciano**

**Cappella
Zen**

Baptistry

★ **Treasury**
*A repository
for precious
artefacts from
both Italy and
Constantinople,
the treasury
houses objects
such as this
11th-century
silver-gilt coffer.*

★ **Ascension Dome**
*A mosaic of Christ in Glory decorates the
enormous central dome. This masterpiece
was created by 13th-century Venetian
craftsmen, who were strongly influenced
by the art and architecture of Byzantium.*

★ **Pala d'Oro**
The altar-piece, created in the 10th century by medieval goldsmiths, is made up of 250 panels such as this one.

The sacristy door (often locked) has fine bronze panels by Sansovino which include portraits of himself with Titian and Aretino.

The Altar of the Sacrament is decorated with mosaics of the parables and miracles of Christ dating from the late 12th or early 13th century.

The columns of the inner façade are thought to be fragments of the first basilica.

South side aisle

STAR FEATURES

★ **Pala d'Oro**

★ **Treasury**

★ **Ascension and Pentecost Domes**

MOSAICS

CLOTHING THE DOMES, walls and floor of the Basilica are over 4,000 sq m (43,000 sq ft) of gleaming golden mosaics. The earliest, dating from the 12th century, were the work of mosaicists from the East. Their delicate techniques were soon adopted by Venetian craftsmen, who gradually took over the Basilica's decoration, combining Byzantine inspiration with Western influences. During the 16th century, many sketches by Tintoretto, Titian, Veronese, and other leading artists were reproduced in mosaic.

Among the most dazzling mosaics – many of which have been heavily restored – are those in the 13th-century central Ascension Dome and the 12th-century Pentecost Dome over the nave.

PALA D'ORO

BEYOND THE CAPPELLA di San Clemente lies the entrance to the most valuable treasure of San Marco: the Pala d'Oro. This jewel-spangled altarpiece, situated behind the high altar, consists of 250 enamel paintings on gold foil, enclosed within a gilded silver Gothic frame. Originally commissioned in Byzantium in AD 976, the altarpiece was further embellished over the

centuries. Napoleon stole some of the precious stones in 1797, but the screen still gleams with pearls, rubies, sapphires and amethysts.

MUSEO MARCIANO

STEPS FROM the atrium, signposted Loggia dei Cavalli, take you up to the church museum, where the gallery offers a splendid view into the basilica. The gilded bronze horses, housed in a room at the far end of the museum, were stolen from the top of the Hippodrome (ancient racecourse) in Constantinople (modern Istanbul) in 1204 but their origin, either Roman or Hellenistic, remains a mystery. Also on show are mosaics, medieval manuscripts and antique tapestries.

BAPTISTRY AND CHAPELS

THE BAPTISTRY was added by Doge Andrea Dandolo (1343–54), who is buried here, along with Sansovino, who designed the font. The adjoining Cappella Zen became a funeral chapel for Cardinal Zen in 1504 in return for a bequest to the State.

In the left transept the Cappella dei Mascoli is decorated with scenes from the life of the Virgin Mary, while the third chapel in the same transept houses the icon of the Madonna of Nicopeia. Looted in 1204, she was once carried into battle at the head of the Byzantine army.

Noah and the Flood, atrium mosaics from the 13th century

Palazzo Ducale ⑲

Mars by Sansovino

THE PALAZZO DUCALE (Doges' Palace) was the official residence of each Venetian ruler (doge) and was founded in the 9th century. The present palace owes its external appearance to the building work of the 14th and early 15th centuries. To create their airy Gothic masterpiece, the Venetians broke with tradition by perching the bulk of the palace (built in pink Veronese marble) on top of an apparent fretwork of loggias and arcades (built from white Istrian stone).

★ **Giants' Staircase**
This 15th-century staircase is crowned by Sansovino's statues of Mars and Neptune, symbols of Venice's power.

Sala del Senato

Sala del Collegio

Anticollegio

The Arco Foscari
has copies of Antonio Rizzo's 15th-century Adam and Eve.

Main entrance

★ **Porta della Carta**
This 15th-century Gothic gate is the principal entrance to the palace. From it, a vaulted passageway leads to the Arco Foscari and the internal courtyard.

Courtyard

★ **Sala del Maggior Consiglio**
This vast hall was used as a meeting place for members of Venice's Great Council. Tintoretto's huge Paradise *(1590) fills the end wall.*

Sala dello Scudo
The walls of this room, once part of the doge's private apartments, are covered with maps of the world. In the centre of the room are two giant 18th-century globes.

VISITORS' CHECKLIST

Piazzetta. **Map** 7 C2.
041-522 49 51. San Marco. Mar–Sep: 9am–7pm daily; Oct–Feb: 9am–4pm daily (last adm: 1 hr before closing).
1 Jan, 1 May, 25 Dec.

Sala delle Quattro Porte

Sala del Consiglio dei Dieci

Sala della Bussola

Torture Chamber
Interrogations took place in the Torture Chamber. Suspects were hung by their wrists from a cord in the centre of the room.

The Bridge of Sighs

Drunkenness of Noah
This early 15th-century sculpture, symbolic of the frailty of man, is set on the corner of the palace.

The Ponte della Paglia, built of Istrian stone, has a pretty balustrade of columns and sculpted pine cones.

The Loggia
Each arch of the ground level portico supports two arches of the loggia, which commands fine views of the lagoon.

STAR FEATURES

★ **Giants' Staircase**

★ **Porta della Carta**

★ **Sala del Maggior Consiglio**

Exploring the Palazzo Ducale

A TOUR OF THE PALAZZO DUCALE takes you through a succession of richly decorated chambers and halls, arranged over three floors, culminating with the Bridge of Sighs and the prisons. Unless you are visiting the state apartments (only accessible during exhibitions), the fixed itinerary works down from the top floor.

Jacopo and Domenico Tintoretto's *Paradise*, one of the world's largest paintings, in the Sala del Maggior Consiglio

SCALA D'ORO AND COURTYARD

A PASSAGE from the Porta della Carta opens into the palace courtyard. Ahead lies Antonio Rizzo's 15th-century Giants' Staircase, at the top of which the new doge would be crowned with the *zogia* or dogal cap. The ticket office and palace entrance are to the left. The Scala d'Oro (golden staircase), which leads to the palace's upper floors and the start of the set itinerary, takes its name from the elaborate gilt stucco vault created by Alessandro Vittoria (1554–8).

SALA DELLE QUATTRO PORTE TO THE SALA DEL SENATO

T HE FIRST ROOM, the Sala delle Quattro Porte, boasts a ceiling designed by Palladio and frescoed by Tintoretto. The end walls of the next room, the Anticollegio, are decorated with mythological scenes by Tintoretto, while Veronese's masterly *Rape of Europa* (1580), opposite the window, is one of the palace's most dramatic works. The adjoining Sala del Collegio

was the hall where the doge and his counsellors met to receive ambassadors and discuss matters of State. Embellishing the magnificent ceiling are 11 paintings (c.1577) by Veronese. In the next room, the Sala del Senato, the doge and some 200 senators discussed foreign affairs. The ceiling and wall paintings are by Tintoretto and his pupils.

A bocca di leone for denunciations

SALA DEL CONSIGLIO DEI DIECI TO THE ARMERIA

T HE ITINERARY returns through the Sala delle Quattro Porte to the Sala del Consiglio dei Dieci. This was the meeting room of the powerful Council of Ten, founded in 1310 to protect State security. Two fine works by Veronese adorn the ceiling: *Age and Youth*

Dialectic (c.1577) by Veronese in the Palazzo Ducale's Sala del Collegio

and *Juno Offering the Ducal Crown to Venice* (both 1553–4). In the Sala della Bussola, offenders awaited their fate in front of the Council of Ten. The room's *bocca di leone* (lion's mouth), was used to post secret denunciations. The wooden door here leads to the State Inquisitors' Room and thence to the torture chamber and prisons. The Armoury – one of the finest such collections anywhere in Europe – occupies the following rooms.

SALA DEL MAGGIOR CONSIGLIO

T HE SCALA DEI CENSORI takes you to the second floor and past the Sala del Guariento and Antonio Rizzo's statues of Adam and Eve (1480s) to the magnificent Sala del Maggior Consiglio. A vast chamber, it was used as a meeting place for the Great Council and for grand State banquets. By the mid-16th century the Great Council had around 2,000 members. Any Venetian of high birth over 25 was entitled to a seat unless he married a commoner. Tintoretto's huge *Paradise* (1587–90) occupies the eastern wall. Measuring 7.45 by 24.65 m (25 by 81 ft), it is one of the largest paintings in the world. The itinerary then continues in more sombre vein, crossing the Bridge of Sighs to enter the dank world of the prisons.

Torre dell'Orologio ⑳

Piazza San Marco. **Map** 7 B2. 🚊 *San Marco.* 🔴 *for restoration.*

THIS RICHLY decorated clock tower on the north side of the piazza was built in the late 15th century. Mauro Coducci is thought to have worked on the design. With its display of the phases of the moon and the signs of the zodiac, the gilt and blue enamel clock face was designed with

The clock face of the Torre dell'Orologio

seafarers in mind. According to a gruesome local legend, once the clock was completed, the two inventors of the complex mechanism had their eyes gouged out to prevent them from ever creating a replica.

On the upper level, the winged lion of St Mark stands against a star-spangled blue backdrop. At the very top the two huge bronze figures, known as the *Mori*, or Moors, because of their dark patina, strike the bell on the hour.

Campanile ㉑

Piazza San Marco. **Map** 7 B2. ☎ *041-522 40 64.* 🚊 *San Marco.* 🔴 *9:30am–7pm daily.* 🔴 *3 weeks Jan.* ♿

FROM THE TOP of St Mark's campanile, high above the piazza, visitors can enjoy sublime views of the city, the lagoon and, visibility permitting, the peaks of the Alps. It was from this viewpoint that Galileo demonstrated his telescope to Doge Leonardo Donà in 1609. To do so he would have climbed the internal ramp. Access these days is via a lift.

The first tower, completed in 1173, was built as a lighthouse to assist navigators in the lagoon. It took on a less benevolent role in the Middle Ages, when offenders were imprisoned – and in some cases left to die – in a cage

hung near its summit. With the exception of several 16th-century renovations, the tower survived unharmed until 14 July 1902 when, with little warning, its foundations gave way and it suddenly collapsed. The only casualties were the Loggetta at the foot of the tower and the custodian's cat. Donations for reconstruction came flooding in and the following year the foundation stone was laid for a campanile *"dov' era e com'era"* ("where it was and as it was"). The new tower was finally opened on 25 April (the Feast of St Mark) 1912.

Museo Correr ㉒

Procuratie Nuove. Entrance in Ala Napoleonica. **Map** 7 B2.
☎ *041-522 56 25.* 🚊 *San Marco.* 🔴 *10am–5pm Wed–Mon.* 🔴 *1 Jan, 1 May, 25 Dec.* ♿

TEODORO CORRER bequeathed his extensive collection of works of art to Venice in 1830, thus forming the core of the city's fine civic museum.

Its first rooms form a suitably Neo-Classical backdrop for early statues by Antonio Canova (1757–1822). The rest of the floor covers the history of the Venetian Republic, with maps, coins, armour and a host of doge-related exhibits.

Young Man in a Red Hat *(c.1490) by Carpaccio in the Museo Correr*

The second floor contains the picture gallery, whose collection is second only to that of the Accademia.

The paintings are hung chronologically, enabling you to trace the evolution of Venetian painting, and to see the influence that Ferrarese, Paduan and Flemish artists had on the Venetian school.

The gallery's most famous works are by Carpaccio: *Portrait of a Young Man in a Red Hat* (c.1490), and *Two Venetian Ladies* (c.1507). The latter is traditionally, but probably incorrectly, known as *The Courtesans* because of the ladies' low-cut dresses. The Museo del Risorgimento on the same floor looks at the history of Venice until unification with Italy in 1866.

The ceiling of Santo Stefano, built in the form of a ship's keel

Santo Stefano ㉓

Campo Santo Stefano. **Map** 6 F2. ☎ *041-522 50 61.* 🚊 *Accademia or Sant'Angelo.* 🔴 *8am–noon, 4–7pm Mon–Sat; 7:30am–12:30pm, 6–8pm Sun.*

DECONSECRATED six times on account of the blood spilled within its walls, Santo Stefano – one of Venice's loveliest churches – is now remarkably serene. Built in the 14th century, and altered in the 15th, the church has a carved portal by Bartolomeo Bon and a campanile with a typical Venetian tilt. The interior has a splendid ship's keel ceiling, carved tie-beams, and a sacristy crammed with valuable paintings.

Santi Giovanni e Paolo ㉔

K NOWN MORE COLLOQUIALLY as
San Zanipolo, Santi Giovanni
e Paolo vies with the Frari *(see
pp94–5)* as the city's greatest
Gothic church. Built by the
Dominicans in the 14th century,
it is striking for its vast scale and
architectural austerity. Known as
the Pantheon of Venice, it houses
monuments to no fewer than 25
doges. Among these are several
fine works of art, executed by the
Lombardi family and other
leading sculptors.

The bronze statue is
a monument to Doge
Sebastiano Venier,
who was Com-
mander of
the Fleet at
Lepanto.

The Nave
*The cross-vaulted
interior is tied by
wooden beams
and supported by
stone columns.*

**★ Tomb of Nicolò
Marcello**
*This magnificent
Renaissance
monument to Doge
Nicolò Marcello
(died 1474) was
sculpted by Pietro
Lombardo.*

The doorway, which
is decorated with
Byzantine reliefs and
carvings by Bartolomeo
Bon, is one of Venice's
earliest Renaissance
architectural works.

Entrance

★ Tomb of Pietro Mocenigo
*Pietro Lombardo's superb
tomb (1481) commemorates
the doge's military pursuits
when he was Grand Captain
of the Venetian forces.*

★ Polyptych by Bellini
*This painting (c.1465) shows
St Vincent Ferrer, a Spanish
cleric, flanked by St
Sebastian and St Christopher.*

The Baroque high altar, begun in 1619, is attributed to Baldassare Longhena.

16th-century altar statues by Vittoria

16th-century frescoes attributed to Palma il Giovane

★ **Tomb of Andrea Vendramin**
Lombardo's masterpiece (1476–8) takes the form of a Roman triumphal arch.

STAR FEATURES

★ **Doges' Tombs**

★ **Polyptych by Bellini**

Statue of Colleoni ㉕

Campo Santi Giovanni e Paolo.
Map 3 C5. 🚉 *Ospedale Civile.*

Bartolomeo colleoni, the famous condottiere or commander of mercenaries, left his fortune to the Republic on condition that his statue was placed in front of San Marco. A prominent statue in the piazza would have broken with precedent, so the Senate cunningly had Colleoni raised before the Scuola di San Marco instead of the basilica. A touchstone of early Renaissance sculpture, the equestrian statue of the proud warrior (1481–8) is by the Florentine Andrea Verrocchio, but was cast in bronze after his death by Alessandro Leopardi. The statue has a strong sense of power and movement which arguably ranks it alongside the works of Donatello.

Santa Maria Formosa ㉖

Campo Santa Maria Formosa.
Map 7 C1. 🚉 *Rialto.*

Designed by Mauro Coducci in 1492, this church is unusual in having two main façades – one overlooking the campo, the other the canal. The bell tower or campanile, added in 1688, is noted for the grotesque face at its base. Two paintings stand out in the interior: a triptych (1473) by Bartolomeo Vivarini and Palma il Vecchio's *St Barbara* (c.1510). St Barbara was the patron saint of artillerymen, hence the pair of cannons at the base of the painting.

San Zaccaria ㉗

Campo San Zaccaria. **Map** 8 D2.
📞 *041-522 12 57.* 🚉 *San Zaccaria.*
🕐 *10am–noon, 4–6pm daily.* 💰 *to chapels only.*

Set in a quiet square just a stone's throw from the Riva degli Schiavoni, the church of San Zaccaria is a successful blend of flamboyant Gothic

Palma il Vecchio's *St Barbara* (c.1510) in Santa Maria Formosa

and Classical Renaissance styles. Founded in the 9th century, its façade was later rebuilt by Antonio Gambello in Gothic style. When Gambello died in 1481, Mauro Coducci completed the upper section, adding many of its Renaissance panels.

The interior's artistic highlight is Giovanni Bellini's serene and sumptuously coloured *Madonna and Child with Saints* (1505) in the north aisle. A door off the right nave leads to the Chapel of St Athanasius which in turn leads to the Chapel of San Tarasio. The chapel contains vault frescoes (1442) by the Florentine Andrea del Castagno, and polyptychs (1443–4) by Antonio Vivarini and Giovanni d'Alemagna.

A Renaissance panel by Coducci on the façade of San Zaccaria

Scuola di San Giorgio degli Schiavoni 28

Calle Furlani. **Map** 8 E1.
041-522 88 28. San Zaccaria.
9:30am–12:30pm Tue–Sun;
also 3–6:30pm Tue–Sat. 1 Jan,
1 May, 25 Dec.

WITHIN THIS small gem are some of the finest paintings of Vittore Carpaccio. They were commissioned at the height of his career by the Schiavoni, or Dalmatian Slav community in Venice.

The Scuola was established in 1451 and rebuilt in 1551. It has changed very little since. The exquisite frieze, executed between 1502 and 1508, shows scenes from the lives of patron saints: St George, St Tryphone and St Jerome. Each episode of the narrative cycle is remarkable for its vivid colouring, minutely observed detail and historic record of Venetian life. Outstanding among them are *St George Slaying the Dragon, St Jerome Leading the Tamed Lion to the Monastery* and *The Vision of St Jerome*.

San Giovanni in Bragora 29

Campo Bandiera e Moro. **Map** 8 E2.
041-520 59 06. Arsenale.
8–11am, 3–5pm daily.

THE EXISTING church is essentially Gothic (1475–9) and the intimate interior contains major works of art that demonstrate the transition from Gothic to early Renais-

Old sail factory
Arsenale Vecchio, 12th–13th century
Corderia
Arsenale Nove, 14th century

18th-century engraving of the Arsenale

sance. Bartolomeo Vivarini's altarpiece *Madonna and Child with Saints* (1478) is unmistakably Gothic. Contrasting with this is Cima da Conegliano's large-scale *Baptism of Christ* (1492–5), which adorns the main altar.

Arsenale 30

Map 8 F1. Arsenale or Tana.
Museo Storico Navale Campo San Biagio. **Map** 8 F3. 041-520 02 76.
9am–1pm Mon–Sat. 1 Jan, 1 May, 25 Dec & religious hols.

THE ARSENALE was founded in the 12th century and by the 16th had become the greatest naval shipyard in the world, capable of constructing a whole galley in 24 hours, using an assembly-line system. Surrounded by crenellated walls, it was like a city within a city. Today the site is largely disused. Its impressive 15th-century gateway, twin towers

and guardian lions can be viewed from the campo or bridge outside. The gateway was built by Antonio Gambello and is often cited as Venice's first Renaissance construction. For a better view of the docks and warehouses inside the walls, *vaporetto* number 23 or 52 will take you through the heart of the Arsenale Vecchio.

Around the corner, in Campo San Biagio, the **Museo Storico Navale** charts Venetian naval history from the heyday of the Arsenale to the present.

San Giorgio Maggiore 31

Map 8 D4. 041-528 99 00.
San Giorgio. 9am–noon, 2:30–5pm. **Fondazione Cini** for exhibitions only.

APPEARING LIKE a stage set across the water from the Piazzetta is the little island of San Giorgio Maggiore. The

St George Slaying the Dragon (1502–8) by Carpaccio, in the Scuola di San Giorgio degli Schiavoni

church and monastery, constructed between 1559–80, are among Andrea Palladio's greatest architectural achievements. The church's temple front and the spacious, serene interior with its perfect proportions and cool beauty are typically Palladian (see pp76–7). These qualities are echoed by the church of Il Redentore on the nearby island of Giudecca, built by Palladio in 1577–92.

The colonnaded exterior of Murano's Basilica dei Santi Maria e Donato

On the chancel walls of San Giorgio Maggiore, you will see two fine paintings by Tintoretto: *The Last Supper* and *Gathering of the Manna* (both 1594). In the Chapel of the Dead is his last work, *The Deposition* (1592–4), finished by his son Domenico.

The top of the campanile affords a superb panorama of the city and lagoon. Looking down, you can see the monastery cloisters, now part of the **Fondazione Cini**, a cultural centre that hosts international exhibitions.

Palladio's San Giorgio Maggiore

Murano ③②

🚢 *52 from San Zaccaria; 12, 13, 23 from Fondamente Nuove.*

LIKE THE CITY of Venice, Murano comprises a cluster of small islands, connected by bridges. It has been the centre of the glassmaking industry since 1291, when the furnaces and craftsmen were moved here from the city because of the risk of fire and the disagreeable effects of smoke. Some of the houses on the water date from this period.

🏛 Museo Vetrario
Palazzo Giustinian, Fondamenta Giustinian. 🖪 *041-73 95 86.* ◯ *10am–5pm (Oct–Mar: 4pm) Thu–Tue.*

In the 15th and 16th centuries Murano was the principal glass-producing centre in Europe and today, most tourists visit for glass alone. The Museo Vetrario in the Palazzo Giustinian houses a fine collection of antique pieces. The prize exhibit is the dark blue Barovier wedding cup (1470–80), with enamel work by Angelo Barovier.

🏛 Basilica dei Santi Maria e Donato
Fondamenta Giustinian. 🖪 *041-73 90 56.* ◯ *9am–noon, 4–6:30pm daily.*

The architectural highlight of the island is the Basilica dei Santi Maria e Donato, with its lovely colonnaded apse. Despite some heavy-handed restoration undertaken in the 19th century, this 12th-century church still retains much of its original beauty. Visitors should note the Gothic ship's keel roof, the apse with its mosaic Madonna and the beautiful medieval mosaic floor, which dates from 1140.

Burano ③③

🚢 *12 from Fondamente Nuove; 14 from San Zaccaria.*

BURANO IS THE MOST colourful of the lagoon islands and can be distinguished from a distance by the tilting tower of its church. In contrast with the haunting Torcello, the island is densely populated, its waterways fringed with brightly painted houses, such as the Casa Bepi.

The main thoroughfare is Via Baldassare Galuppi, named after the Burano-born composer. It features traditional lace and linen stalls and open-air trattorias serving fresh fish.

🏛 Scuola dei Merletti
Piazza Baldassare Galuppi. 🖪 *041-73 00 34.* ◯ *Tue–Sun.* ● *1 Jan, 24 & 25 Dec.*

Venetian glass goblet

The people of Burano are fishermen and lacemakers by tradition. You can indeed still see fishermen scraping their boats or mending nets, but today lacemakers are rare. In the 16th century, however, the local lace was the most sought after in Europe – it was so delicate it became known as *punto in aria* ("points in the air"). After a slump in the 18th century, the industry revived and a lace-making school, or Scuola dei Merletti, was set up in 1872. Although authentic Burano lace is hard to find nowadays, you can watch it being made by Burano women at the school. There is also a museum attached which displays fine examples of antique lace.

The multicoloured Casa Bepi on the island of Burano

Torcello ❸

ESTABLISHED BETWEEN the 5th and 6th centuries, the island of Torcello boasts the oldest building in the lagoon – the cathedral of Santa Maria dell'Assunta. Founded in AD 639, it contains some splendid ancient mosaics. The adjoining church of Santa Fosca, of pure Byzantine design, is another mark of Torcello's former glory – before being eclipsed by Venice it had a population of 20,000.

★ Apse Mosaic
The 13th-century Madonna, set against a gold background, is one of the most beautiful mosaics in Venice.

★ Doomsday Mosaics
The highly decorative 12th-century mosaic of the Last Judgment *covers the west wall.*

Pulpit
The present basilica dates from 1008, but includes earlier features. The pulpit contains 7th-century fragments.

The Roman sarcophagus
below the altar is said to contain the relics of St Heliodorus.

★ Iconostasis
The exquisite Byzantine marble panels of the rood screen are carved with peacocks, lions and flowers.

Nave Columns
Two rows of slender marble columns, 18 in all, separate the three naves. Their finely carved capitals date from the 11th century.

Torcello's Last Canals
Silted canals and malaria hastened Torcello's decline. One of the remaining waterways runs from the vaporetto stop to the basilica.

VISITORS' CHECKLIST

No. 14 from San Zaccaria.
Santa Maria dell'Assunta
041-73 00 84. 10am–12:30pm, 2–6:30pm daily.
Campanile to the public.
Santa Fosca 041-73 00 84.
10am–12:30pm, 2–6:30pm daily. for mosaics. **Museo dell'Estuario** 041-73 07 61.
10am–12:30pm, 2–5:30pm (Oct–Apr: 4pm) Tue–Sun.
public hols.

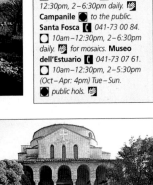

The altar was rebuilt in 1939 and stands below a 15th-century wood relief of *Santa Fosca Sleeping.*

The central dome and cross sections are supported by columns of Greek marble with Corinthian capitals.

Santa Fosca
Built in the 11th and 12th centuries on a Greek-cross plan, the church has a serene Byzantine interior with a central pentagonal apse.

The Portico of Santa Fosca, with its elegant stilted arches, is built on three sides of the church, and probably dates from the 12th century.

Vaporetto **boarding point**

The Museo dell'Estuario houses many old church treasures.

STAR FEATURES

★ Apse Mosaic

★ Doomsday Mosaics

★ Iconostasis

Attila's Throne
It was said that the 5th-century king of the Huns used this marble seat as his throne.

VENICE STREET FINDER

ALL THE MAP REFERENCES given for sights, hotels and restaurants in Venice refer to this section of the book. The key map below shows which areas of the city are covered by the Street Finder. The first figure of the map reference indicates which map to turn to, and the letter and number which follow are for the grid reference. Standard Italian spelling has been used on all the maps in this book,

but when exploring Venice you will find that the names on many street signs are written in Venetian dialect. Mostly this means only a slight variation in spelling (as in the word Sotoportico/Sotoportego below), but some names look totally different. For example, the church of Santi Giovanni e Paolo *(see map 3)*, is frequently signposted as "San Zanipolo". A further map showing the vaporetto routes follows the street maps.

RECOGNIZING STREET NAMES

The signs for street *(calle)*, canal *(rio)* and square *(campo)* will soon become familiar, but the Venetians have a colourful vocabulary for the maze of alleys which makes up the city. When exploring, the following may help.

FONDAMENTA S.SEVERO	**RIO TERRA GESUATI**
Fondamenta is a street that runs alongside a canal, often named after the canal it follows.	**Rio Terrà** is a filled-in canal. Similar to a *rio terrà* is a *piscina*, which often forms a square.

SOTOPORTEGO E PONTE S.CRISTOFORO

Sotoportico or Sotoportego means a covered passageway.

SALIZADA PIO X	**RIVA DEI PARTIGIANI**
Salizzada is a main street (formerly a paved street).	**Riva** is a wide *fondamenta*, often facing the lagoon.

RUGAGIUFFA	**CORTE DEI DO POZZI**
Ruga is a street lined with shops.	**Corte** means a courtyard.

RIO MENUO O DE LA VERONA

Many streets and canals in Venice often have more than one name: *o* means "or".

1

5

Canal

Grand

```
0 metres        500
0 yards         500
```

MURANO
(Inset on maps 3–4)

4

8

KEY TO STREET FINDER

- Major sight
- Place of interest
- Railway station
- Ferry boarding point
- *Vaporetto* boarding point
- *Traghetto* crossing
- Gondola mooring
- Bus terminus
- Tourist information
- Hospital with casualty unit
- **P** Parking
- Police station
- Church
- Synagogue
- Post office
- Railway line

SCALE OF MAP PAGES

| 0 metres | 200 |
| 0 yards | 200 |

SCALE OF MURANO INSET

| 0 metres | 500 |
| 0 yards | 500 |

Canale de

Canale Colambola

PONTE DELLA LIBERTA

FONDAMENTA DI SACCA SAN GIROLAMO
SACCA DI
SAN GIROLAMO
CALLE LARGA DEI PENITENTI

CALLE FERAU
CALLE DEL FORNER
FONDAMENTA CASE NUOVE
FONDAMEN
Rio d
FONDA

CPLO DELLE
COOPERATIVE

CALLE TINTORIA
FONDAMENTA
RIO

Ponte dei
Tre Archi

Canale di Cannaregio

FONDAMENTA CO. S. N.
CALLE DELLE BECCARIE
CRO D
BECCARE
CD. SCARLATTO
CALLE D. TINTOR
CD. MAGAZEN
CD. GLORI
CALLE DELLA CERERIA
CALLE CANNE
CALLE BISCOTELLA

Ponte dei
Tre Archi

Rio di San Giobbe
GIOBBE
FMTA SAVO
San
Giobbe
CAMPO
SAN GIOBBE
CALLE MADONNA
FONDAMENTA
R.TD. CREA
CALLE BUSELLO
CALLE CENDON
CALLE SAL

Rio della Crea

CALLE PRIULI DETTA DEI CAVALLETTI
CALLE CARMELITANI

CALLE PE
CALLE DELLA

Scalzi

FMTA D. SCAL
Pon
degli S

Stazione Ferrovie
dello Stato
Santa Lucia

SIMEON
CALLE TRAGH
DI SANTA LUCIA
CALLE BERGAMASCH

i

Ferrovia

FONDAMENTA SAN

FONDAMENTA SANTA LUCIA

Can. d. Santa Chiara
FONDAMENTA DI SANTA CHIARA
C.VOLTO DI SANTA
CHIARA

Piazzale
Roma

FONDAMENTA CROCE
FONDAMENTA
MONASIERO
GIARDINO
EX PAPADOPOLI
CORTE CASE NUO
CAMPO

1   A   B   C

1

2

3

4

5

A   5   B   C

1

RIG RAVANO
C. TOSCANA
CALLE DOGANA DI TERRA
CALLE DI PARADISO
CALLE DELLO STORIONE
CALLE MADONNA
Ponte di Rialto
Fóndaco dei Tedeschi
C. PINDEMONTE
C.D. FORNO
C. DI PIOMBO
C. DI BORGOLOCO
CALLE TREVISANA
CALLE PINELLI

R T SAN SILVESTRO
RIVA DEL VIN
Rialto
SAL.NO X
CAMPO SAN BARTOLOMEO
C.D. ZOCCO
C. CINIMMATI
C. MARTINENGO
C. DEL DOSE
CAMPO SANTA MARIA FORMOSA
CALLE LUNGA S. MARIA FORMOSA

C BISSA
C PONTE S ANTONIO
CAMPO SAN LIO
C DE VELE
C.D. NAVE
San Bartolomeo
CALLE D. STAGNERI
SALIZZADA SAN LIO

San Silvestro
RIVA DEL CARBON
CALLE LARGA MAZZINI
R.D. FERRO
Santa Maria della Fava
RIO C.MPO D. FAVA
S Maria della Fava
MERCERIA S SALVATORE
CALLE
C.D. FAVA
C. MONDO NUOVO
S Maria Formosa

Palazzi Dandolo Sarsetti
RIO DELL'OVO
CORTE TEATRO
C. TEATRO
CALLE BEMBO
RAMO
San Salvatore
CALLE SANT'ANTONIO
C.D. MEZZO
Rio di Santa Maria Formosa

Fondazione Querini Stampalia

San Salvatore
CORTE TEATRO
CALLE SAN LUCA
C.D. SCALE
MERCERIA SAN ZULIAN
C.D. ACQUE
Rio di San Lorenzo
CASSELLERIA
CALLE D. BANDE
RUGA GIUFFA

Palazzo Loredan
RIO DI
CALLE GRIMANI
CALLE CAVALLI
SAL.GALLIPOLI
CAMPO SAN LUCA
C. MAGAZEN
DE MORTI
DELLE BALLOTTE
C. DELLA
RIO DEL MEGIO
Rio di San Zulian
C. D. MEGIO
San Zulián
Museo Guidi

SAN MARCO
CALLE SAN PATERNIAN
CAMPO MANIN
SAL S PATERNIAN
C DELLE COLONNE
C.D. PRETI
RIO TERRA DELLE COLONNE
MERCERIA
C. SPADARIA
C.D. SPECCHIERI
CALLE LARGA SAN MARCO
CALLE DELLA CHIESA
CALLE DEL FIGHER

CALLE CORTESIA
C.D. CORTESIA
R.T.D. ASSASSINI
CALLE SAN LUCA
C. DELLE LOCANDE
C. FUSERI
RIO DI SAN LUCA
C. GALLO
CALLE FIUBERA
C.D. LOCOLO
CALLE CANONICA
Museo Diocesano
SAL SAN PROVOLO

Palazzo Contarini del Bóvolo
Fuseri
CHIESA SAN FANTIN
C.D. FABBRI
Procuratie
PIAZZETTA DEI LEONCINI
RIO DEL PALAZZO
CALLE DEGLI ALBANESI
CALLE DELLE RASSE
Rio del Vin
Hotel Danieli

2

Palazzo Verona
C.PELLA VERONA
R. d'
CALLE DEL FRUTTAROL
CALLE DEL BARCAROLI
CALLE VENIER
C. DI PISCINA
Rio di Bacino Orseolo
Rio
delle
Torre dell'Orologio
PROCURATIE VECCHIE
Basilica San Marco
Palazzo Ducale
Ponte dei Sospiri
Fo del

La Fenice
San Fantin
CPO C.D. LA CHIESA
SAN FANTIN
Rio dei Barcaroli
CALLE DI PISCINA
CALLE BOGNOLO
C. VENEZIANA
C.D. SALVADEGO
C.BEL
FREZZERIA
PIAZZA SAN MARCO
Campanile
Museo Correr
Procuratie Nuove
Museo Archeologico
Ponte della Paglia
San Z

3

CALLE D. FENICE
CALLE DELLE VESTE
PISCINA SAN MOISE
CALLE DEL CARRO
SAL SAN MOISE
CALLE LARGA XXII MARZO
RM PRIMO CT CONTARINA
Zecca
Libreria Sansovintiana
Colonne di San Marco e San Teodoro

Santa Maria del Giglio
CAMPO DEL TRAGHETTO
CALLE DELLE OSTREGHE
CALLE DELL'ALBERO
CALLE DEL PESTRIN
San Moisè
C. BAROZZI
CALLE DEL TRAGHETTO
Ridotto
Harry's Bar
FONDAMENTA DELLE FARINE
San Marco
Bacino di San Marco

4

Salute
CAMPO DELLA SALUTE
FMTA DOGANA ALLA SALUTE

CALLE ABAZIA
CALLE DELLA LANZA
C RIO MORTI
C DI MEZZO
CALLE DEL MEZZO
Santa Maria della Salute
Dogana di Mare

C R TERRA
RT D. CATECUMENI
RIO TERRA A' SALONI
RAMO SQUERO
CALLE QUERINI
FONDAMENTA ZATTERE AI SALONI

6

5

Zitelle
FONDAMENTA DELLE ZITELLE
Le Zitelle
FONDAMENTA SAN GIOVANNI
CAMPO NANI E BARBAR

GIUDECCA

Venice Vaporetto Routes

ROUTES AROUND THE LAGOON

Laguna Veneta

Torcello ⑭
Mazzorbo ⑫
Burano ⑫ ⑭
See main map
⑬
⑬ ⑬
Treporti ⑬ ⑭
Sant' Erasmo ⑬
Vignole ⑬
Punta Sabbioni ⑭ ⑭ ⑰
San Nicolò ⑭ ⑰
Santa Maria Elisabetta ① ⑥ ⑭ ㊶ ㊷
Casino ㊷

MARE ADRIATICO

The Vaporetto Routes

The ACTV network runs regular services around the city and out to most of the islands. Some services are circular; others extend their routes during the high season. More details of the different types of vaporetti *and how to use them are given on pages 636–7.*

Canale delle Sacche

Sant'Alvise ㊷
Ponte dei Tre Archi ㊷
Ponte delle G...
San Ma...
Ferrovia ① ③ ④ ㊷ ㊶ FS
Riva di Biasio ①
Tronchetto B ③ ④ ㊶
Automezzi Venezia-Lido ⑰
Piazzale Roma ① ④ ㊷ ㊶ ㊶
San Tomà ① ㊶
San Sa...
Ca' Rezzonico ① ㊶
Accademia ① ㊶
Santa Marta ㊷ ㊶ ㊶
San Basilio ㊶
Zattere ⑯ ㊷ ㊶

Bacino della Stazione Marittima

Canale di Fusina
Fusina P
Sacca Fisola ㊷ ㊶
Sant'Eufemia ㊷ ㊶
Palan... ㊶

Canale della Giudecca

GIUDECCA

0 metres   500
0 yards   500

MURANO

Venier 🔲 52 52̈

Museo 🔲 52 52̈

Navagero 🔲 23 52 52̈

Serenella 52 52̈ 🔲

Faro 🔲 12 13 23 52 52̈

Colonna 🔲 23 52 52̈

Canale degli Angeli

Canale dei Marani

Burano
Sant'Erasmo

52, 52̈

23, 52, 52̈

12, 13, 23

12, 13, 23, 52, 52̈

12, 13, 23, 52, 52̈

52, 52̈

Cimitero 🔲 23 52 52̈

SAN
MICHELE

12, 13, 23, 52, 52̈

52

Canale delle Fondamente Nuove

23, 52, 52̈

nna
rto

12 13 23 52 52̈ 🔲
Fondamente
Nuove

Ca' d'Oro 🔲 ①

Ospedale 23 52 52̈ 🔲

Celestia 23 52 52̈ 🔲

an
tro

① ③ 82 🔲
Rialto

Grande

San Zaccaria 🔲
⑭ ⑳ 23 52 52̈ 82

Arsenale 🔲 ①

Tana 23 52 52̈ 🔲

1, 3, 4, 6, 17, 20, 23, 52, 52̈

23

a Maria
giglio

San Marco
① ③ ④ 82 🔲

1, 3, 4

82

3, 4, 10, 17, 52, 52̈

① 🔲
Salute

Canale

82

52, 52̈

70

🔲 82
San Giorgio

20

di

① 82 🔲
Giardini/Biennale

1, 6, 14, 17, 23, 52

82

3, 4, 17, 52, 52̈

82

52, 52̈

SAN
GIORGIO
MAGGIORE

San

52 52̈ 82 🔲
Zitelle

Marco

Sant'Elena
① ⑭ 23 52

entore

La Grazia
San Clemente

San Servolo
San Lazzaro

See inset map

KEY

🔲 12	*Vaporetto* route
🔲 82	Seasonal addition to route
🔲	Ferry boarding point
🔲	*Vaporetto* boarding point
FS	Railway station
P	Parking

ROUTES

① Piazzale Roma – Lido

③ Circular – clockwise (seasonal)

④ Circular – anticlockwise (seasonal)

⑥ San Zaccaria – Lido

⑩ Venice – San Clemente

⑫ Venice – Burano

⑬ Venice – Treporti

⑭ Venice – Torcello

⑭ Venice – Punta Sabbioni

⑯ Venice – Fusina (seasonal ferry)

⑰ Venice – Lido (car ferry)

⑳ Venice – San Lazzaro

23 Circular (seasonal)

52 Zitelle – Murano – Lido

52̈ Murano – Piazzale Roma

82 Circular (seasonal to Lido)

THE VENETO AND FRIULI

THE VENETO IS A REGION OF TREMENDOUS CONTRASTS, *encompassing the breathtaking natural beauty of the Dolomites, Lake Garda (Italy's largest lake) and the rolling Euganean Hills, and the man-made delights of magnificent ancient cities such as Verona, Vicenza and Padua. Neighbouring Friuli-Venezia Giulia lines the border with Slovenia to the east, taking in the Carnic Hills in the north, the Roman town of Aquileia and the bustling Adriatic port of Trieste.*

The Romans built frontier posts on this fertile land of silt deposits, and these survive today as the cities of Vicenza, Padua, Verona and Treviso. Strategically placed at the hub of the empire's road network, the cities prospered under Roman rule, but suffered in the wave of Germanic invasions of the 5th century AD.

The region's fortunes revived under the benign rule of the Venetian empire. The medieval cities of the Veneto lay on important trade routes such as the Serenissima, the road connecting the flourishing port·cities of Venice and Genoa, and the Brenner Pass, used by commercial travellers crossing the Alps from northern Europe. Wealth from agriculture, commerce and the spoils of war paid for the beautification of these cities through the building of Renaissance palaces and public buildings, many designed by the Veneto's great architect, Andrea Palladio. His palazzi and villas are telling symbols of the leisured existence once enjoyed by the area's aristocrats.

Today the Veneto is a thriving wine exporter, textile producer and agricultural centre, and Friuli is a focus for new technology, while remaining largely agricultural. Both regions are popular tourist destinations, despite lying a little in the shadow of Venice, and boast an abundant and enchanting variety of attractions.

A leisurely *passeggiata* in one of Verona's ancient streets

◁ **The Renaissance bridge by Palladio at Bassano del Grappa in the Veneto**

Exploring the Veneto and Friuli

THE FLAT LANDSCAPE of the Veneto plain is dramatically off-set by the spectacular Dolomite mountains which form the northwestern border to the Veneto. Friuli, Italy's most northeasterly region, lies tucked up against Austria to the north and Slovenia to the east. Both the Veneto and Friuli are bordered to the south by the Adriatic, with its beaches and ports, which provide a contrast with the area's gently rolling countryside, the vast stretch of Lake Garda and the many attractive resorts and ancient towns.

View of Verona from the Teatro Romano

Innsbruck

CORTINA D'AMPEZZO ⑬
PIEVE CADO

DOLOMITI

Cordevole

PARCO NAZIONALE DEL DOLOMITI BELLUNESI

BELLU ⑫

Trento   FELTRE

VITTORI VENET

Piave

RIVA DEL GARDA

ASIAGO

ASOLO ④

CONEGLI

Bolzano Trento

BASSANO DEL GRAPPA ③

RECOARO TERME

MAROSTICA

TREVISO ⑩

THIENE

A31

Brenta

N53

N47

CASTELFRANCO VENETO ⑤

LAKE GARDA ②

GARDA

VICENZA ⑥

A4

VENICE

PESCHIERA DEL GARDA

VERONA ①

Brescia

SOAVE

LONIGO

PADUA ⑦

BRENTA CANAL ⑨

Laguna Vene

VILLAFRANCA DI VERONA

Adige

ABANO TERME

EUGANEAN HILLS ⑧

Bacchiglione

Mantova

MONSELICE

CHIOGG

N10

N454

Adige

A13

ROVIGO

Po di Vene

N516

N309

Po

N482

N16

Po

Ravenna

Ferrara Bologna

KEY

▭	Motorway
▭	Major road
▭	Minor road
▭	Scenic route
≈	River
☀	Viewpoint

0 kilometres   25

0 miles   20

SEE ALSO

- **Where to Stay** pp544–7

- **Where to Eat** pp580–82

GETTING AROUND

An extensive rail network and good bus services make this region easy to explore by public transport, though only buses operate around Lake Garda. Motorways and main roads provide good links between the main cities. The Venice Simplon-Orient-Express train, which operates from London to Venice, offers a novel approach to the area.

The bridge at Cividale del Friuli

A mountain chalet in Cortina d'Ampezzo

SIGHTS AT A GLANCE

Verona ❶

V ERONA IS A VIBRANT trading centre, the second biggest city in the Veneto region (after Venice) and one of the most prosperous in northern Italy. Its ancient centre boasts many magnificent Roman ruins, second only to those of Rome itself, and fine palazzi built of *rosso di Verona*, the local pink-tinged limestone, by the city's medieval rulers. Verona has two main focal points: the massive 1st-century AD Arena, which is still the setting for major events, and Piazza Erbe with its colourful market.

Scaligeri statue in Castelvecchio

One of the main attractions, however, is the church of San Zeno Maggiore *(see pp140–41)*, which boasts unusual medieval bronze door panels: they are carved with extraordinary scenes, some biblical, others on the life of San Zeno.

View of Verona from the Museo Archeologico

Verona's Rulers

In 1263 the Scaligeri began their 127-year rule of Verona. They used ruthless tactics in their rise to power, but once established, the Scaligeri family brought peace to a city racked by civil strife and inter-family rivalry. They proved to be relatively just and cultured rulers – the poet Dante was welcomed to their court in 1301, and dedicated the final part of his epic *Divine Comedy* to the ruling Cangrande I. Today their legacy remains in their ornate tombs and in Castelvecchio.

In 1387 Verona fell to the Visconti of Milan, and a succession of outsiders – Venice, France and Austria – then ruled the city until the Veneto was united with Italy in 1866.

Verona's enormous Roman Arena seen from Piazza Brà

KEY

FS	Railway station
🚌	Bus terminus
P	Parking
ℹ	Tourist information
✝	Church

Ponte Scaligero, part of the old defence system of Castelvecchio

VISITORS' CHECKLIST

255,000. ✈ Villafranca 14 km (9 miles) SW. 🚉 Porta Nuova, Piazza XXV Aprile. 🚌 Piazza Cittadella. 🅸 Piazza Erbe 38 (045-59 28 28). 🕒 daily. 🎫 Combined or single ticket valid for churches. 🎭 Apr: VinItaly wine fair; Jun–Aug: Estate Teatrale Veronese; Jul–Aug: Opera Festival.

♣ Castelvecchio

Corso Castelvecchio 2. **(** 045-59 44 34. 🕒 Tue–Sun. 🎫 ♿

This impressive castle, built by Cangrande II between 1355 and 1375, now houses one of the finest art galleries in the Veneto outside Venice. It is arranged to give striking views of the castle itself as well as the exhibits displayed within.

The first section contains a wealth of late Roman

and early Christian material – silver plate, 5th-century brooches, glass painted with a portrait of Christ the Shepherd in gold, and the carved marble sarcophagus of Saints Sergius and Bacchus (1179).

The section on medieval and early Renaissance art vividly demonstrates the influence of northern art on local painters: the emphasis is on brutal realism as opposed to serene idealism. The late Renaissance works include a fine collection of 15th-century Madonnas.

Jewellery, suits of armour, swords and shield bosses, Veronese's *Deposition* (1565) and a portrait painting attributed to either Titian or to Lorenzo Lotto are on display in further sections.

Outside, a walkway offers views of the river Adige and the medieval **Ponte Scaligero** crossing it, and of the 14th-century equestrian statue of Cangrande I which once graced his tomb *(see p138).*

♫ Arena

Piazza Brà. **(** 045-59 65 17. 🕒 Tue–Sun. ● public hols. 🎫 📷 ♿

Verona's Roman amphitheatre, completed in AD 30, is the third largest in the world, after Rome's Colosseum and the amphitheatre at Santa Maria

Capua Vetere, near Naples. The interior, still virtually intact, could hold almost the entire population of Roman Verona, and visitors came from across the Veneto to watch gladiatorial combats and mock battles. Since then, the Arena has seen executions, fairs, bullfights, and theatre and opera productions.

♫ San Fermo Maggiore

Via San Fermo. **(** 045-800 72 87. 🕒 daily. 🎫

San Fermo Maggiore is not one but two churches: this is most clearly seen from the outside, where the apse has pointed Gothic elements rising above a sturdy Romanesque base. The lower church, begun in 1065 by Benedictine monks on the site of an earlier sanctuary, has frescoes on the simple arcades.

The more impressive upper church dates from 1313 and is covered with a splendid ship's keel roof. The interior also boasts much medieval fresco work including a 14th-century section by Stefano da Zevio depicting Musician Angels. Nearby is the Brenzoni mausoleum (c.1440) by Giovanni di Bartolo, and above it a 1426 fresco of the *Annunciation* by Pisanello (1377–1455).

The 11th-century apse of the lower church of San Fermo Maggiore

Exploring Verona

S INCE THE DAYS OF THE ROMAN EMPIRE, Piazza Erbe – built on the site of the ancient Roman forum – has been the centre of Verona. Many of the city's fine palazzi, churches and monuments are nearly as ancient, many dating from the medieval period.

The fountain, erected in the 14th century at the centre of Piazza Erbe

🏛 Piazza Erbe

Piazza Erbe is named after the city's old herb market. Today's stalls, shaded by umbrellas, sell everything from herb-flavoured roast suckling pig in bread rolls to succulent fresh-picked fruit or delicious wild mushrooms.

At the northern end of Piazza Erbe stands the Baroque **Palazzo Maffei** (1668), surmounted by statues. In front of it rises a column supporting the **Venetian lion**, which marks Verona's absorption, in 1405, into the Venetian empire. On the west side is the **Casa dei Mercanti**, a largely 17th-century building which dates originally from 1301. Opposite, coloured wall frescoes are still visible above the cafés.

The **fountain** in the middle of the piazza is often overshadowed by the market stalls, though the statue at its centre dates from Roman times. It serves as a reminder that this piazza has been used as a market place for 2,000 years.

🏛 Piazza dei Signori

Torre dei Lamberti 📞 045-803 27 26. ☐ Tue–Sun. ◯ public hols. 📷 ♿

In the centre of the square stands an elegant 19th-century **statue of Dante**, whose gaze seems fixed on the forbidding **Palazzo del Capitano**, once the home of Verona's military

commanders. Beside it is the equally intimidating **Palazzo della Ragione**, the palace of Reason, or law court; both were built in the 14th century. The courtyard of the law court has a handsome external stone staircase, added in 1446–50. Fine views of the Alps can be had by climbing the 84-m (275-ft) **Torre dei Lamberti**, which rises from the western side of the courtyard.

Behind the statue of Dante is the **Loggia del Consiglio** (1493), the council chamber topped by statues of Roman worthies born in Verona: they include Pliny the Elder, the natural historian, and Vitruvius, the architectural theorist.

The square is linked to Piazza Erbe by the Arco della Costa, or the Arch of the Rib, named after the whale rib long ago hung beneath it.

The frescoed Renaissance façade of the Loggia del Consiglio on Piazza dei Signori

🔒 Tombs of the Scaligeri

Via Arche Scaligeri.

Beside the entrance to the tiny Romanesque church of **Santa Maria Antica**, once the parish church of the powerful Scaligeri family, lie a profusion of bizarre tombs of the one-time rulers of Verona.

Over the entrance to the church is the impressive tomb of Cangrande I (died 1329), surmounted by an equestrian statue of the ruler, a copy of the original which is now in Castelvecchio (see p137).

The other Scaligeri tombs are next to the church, behind a wrought-iron fence which incorporates the ladder emblem of the family's original name (della Scala, meaning "of the steps"). Towering above the fence are the tombs of Mastino II (died 1351) and Cansignorio (died 1375), splendidly decorated with a profusion of tiny Gothic spires. Other members of the Scaligeri family lie within a series of plainer tombs which stand nearer the church wall.

14th-century Scaligeri tomb

🔒 Sant'Anastasia

Piazza Sant'Anastasia. 📞 045-800 43 25. ☐ daily. 📷 ♿

The huge and lofty church of Sant'Anastasia was begun in 1290. Faded 15th-century frescoes and carved scenes from the life of St Peter Martyr adorn its Gothic portal.

Inside, there are two notable holy water stoups, supported on figures of beggars, known locally as i gobbi (the hunchbacks). These figures were carved a century apart: the earlier one (on the left) dates from 1495.

The sacristy, off the north aisle, is home to the fine but unfortunately damaged fresco of St George and the Princess (1433–8) by Pisanello.

ROMEO AND JULIET

The tragic story of Romeo and Juliet, two young lovers from rival families (the Capulets and the Montagues in Shakespeare's play), was written by Luigi da Porto of Vicenza in the 1520s and has inspired countless poems, films, ballets and dramas.

At the **Casa di Giulietta** (Juliet's house), No. 27 Via Cappello, Romeo is said to have climbed to Juliet's balcony: in reality this is a restored 13th-century inn. Crowds throng to see the simple façade, and stand on the small marble balcony. The run-down house dubbed the **Casa di Romeo** stands a few streets away in Via Arche Scaligeri, east of Piazza dei Signori.

The so-called **Tomba di Giulietta** is displayed in a crypt below the cloister of San Francesco al Corso on Via del Pontiere. The stone sarcophagus lies in an extremely atmospheric setting.

The so-called Casa di Giulietta

⛪ Duomo
Piazza Duomo. 📞 045-59 56 77.
🕐 daily. 📷 ♿

Verona's cathedral was begun in 1139 and is fronted by a magnificent Romanesque portal carved by Nicolò, one of the two master masons responsible for the façade of San Zeno (see pp140–41). Here he sculpted the sword-bearing figures of Oliver and Roland, two of Charlemagne's knights, whose exploits were much celebrated in medieval poetry. Alongside them stand evangelists and saints with wide eyes and flowing beards. To the south there is a second Romanesque portal carved with Jonah and the Whale and with comically grotesque caryatids.

The highlight of the interior is Titian's lovely *Assumption* (1535–40), and outside there is a Romanesque cloister in which the excavated ruins of earlier churches are visible. The 8th-century baptistry, or San Giovanni in Fonte (St John of the Spring), was built from Roman masonry; the marble font was carved in 1200.

🎭 Teatro Romano
Rigaste Redentore 2. 📞 045-800 03 60. 🕐 Tue–Sun. 📷

This theatre was built in the 1st century BC; little now survives of the original stage area, but the semicircular seating area remains largely intact. It offers entrancing views over the city: in the foreground is the only one of three Roman bridges to have survived, though it was rebuilt after World War II.

🏛 Museo Archeologico
Rigaste Redentore 2. 📞 045-800 03 60. 🕐 Tue–Sun. 📷

A lift carries visitors from the Teatro Romano up the cliffs to the monastery above, now an archaeological museum.

The exhibits around the tiny cloister and in the old monks' cells include mosaics, pottery, glass and tombstones. There is also a fine bronze bust of the ambitious first Roman emperor, Augustus (63 BC–AD 14), who succeeded in overcoming his opponents, including Mark Antony and Cleopatra, to become the sole ruler of the Roman world in 31 BC.

Statuary and formal hedges in the Renaissance Giardino Giusti

🌿 Giardino Giusti
Via Giardino Giusti 2. 📞 045-803 40 29. 🕐 daily. 📷 ♿

This is one of Italy's finest Renaissance gardens. It was laid out in 1580 and, as with other gardens of the period, there is a deliberate juxtaposition of nature and artifice: the formal lower garden of clipped box hedges, gravel walks and potted plants contrasts with wilder, natural woods above.

John Evelyn, an English author and diarist who visited Verona in 1661, thought this the finest garden in Europe.

⛪ San Giorgio in Braida
Lungadige San Giorgio. 📞 045-834 02 32. 🕐 daily.

This lovely domed Renaissance church was begun in about 1530 by Michele Sanmicheli. The altar includes the famous *Martyrdom of St George* (1566) by Veronese, and above the west door is the *Baptism of Christ*, usually attributed to Tintoretto (1518–94).

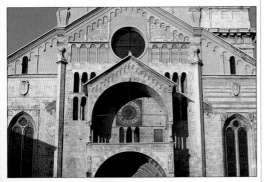

The imposing façade of Verona's Duomo, Santa Maria Matricolare

Verona: San Zeno Maggiore

Detail from San Zeno's façade

SAN ZENO, built in 1123–35 to house the shrine of Verona's patron saint, is the most ornate Romanesque church in northern Italy. The façade is adorned with an impressive rose window, marble reliefs, and a graceful porch canopy. The highlight, however, is the fascinating 11th- and 12th-century bronze door panels. A squat tower just north of San Zeno is said to cover the tomb of King Pepin of Italy (777–810).

Nave Ceiling
The nave has a magnificent example of a ship's keel ceiling, so called because it resembles the inside of an upturned boat. This ceiling was constructed in 1386 when the apse was rebuilt.

The bell tower, started in 1045, reached its present height of 72 m (236 ft) in 1178.

Altarpiece by Mantegna
The Madonna's halo in Andrea Mantegna's altarpiece of the Virgin and Child with saints (1457–59) echoes the shape of the church's rose window.

Former washroom

★ Cloister (1123)
The arches are rounded Romanesque on one side, pointed Gothic on another.

Crypt
The vaulted crypt contains the tomb of San Zeno, appointed first bishop of Verona in AD 362, who died in AD 380.

Nave and Main Altar
The plan of the church is modelled on an ancient Roman basilica, the Hall of Justice. The main altar is situated in the raised sanctuary where the judge's throne would have stood.

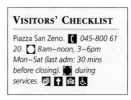
Striped brickwork is typical of Romanesque buildings in Verona. Courses of local pink brick are alternated with ivory-coloured tufa.

The rose window, dating from the early 12th century, symbolizes the Wheel of Fortune: figures on the rim show the rise and fall of human luck.

BRONZE DOOR PANELS

The 48 bronze panels of the west doors are primitive but forceful in their depiction of biblical stories and scenes from the life of San Zeno. Those on the left date from 1030 and survive from an earlier church on the site; those on the right were made after the earthquake in 1137. The panels are the work of three separate craftsmen, and are linked with masks. Huge staring eyes and Ottoman-style hats, armour and architecture feature prominently. Among the scenes, some of which are unclear, are Adam and Eve, Salome dancing for the head of John the Baptist, and a startling Descent into Limbo.

Descent into limbo   Christ in Glory   Human head

The Romanesque porch is one of the finest examples of the style in northern Italy. Since 1138 it has shielded biblical bas reliefs, above the west doors, from the elements.

Marble side panels, which were carved in 1140, depict events from the Life of Christ (to the left of the doors) and scenes from the Book of Genesis (to the right).

★ West Doors
Each of the wooden doors has 24 bronze plates nailed on to make the doors look like solid metal. A multi-coloured bas relief above them depicts San Zeno, flanked by the people of Verona, vanquishing the devil.

STAR FEATURES

★ **West Doors**

★ **Cloister**

Lake Garda ❷

VISITORS' CHECKLIST

Brescia, Verona & Trento. **i** *Via Roma 8, Gardone Riviera (0365-29 04 11).* **FS** *Peschiera del Garda & Desenzano del Garda.* **⛴** *to all towns.* **Villa il Vittoriale**, *Via Vittoriale 12, Gardone.* **C** *0365-201 30.* ☐ *Tue–Sun.* 🎫 **Rocca Scaligera**, *Sirmione.* **C** *030-91 64 68.* ☐ *Tue–Sun.* 🎫 ✒

GARDA, THE LARGEST AND EASTERNMOST of the Italian lakes, borders three regions: Trentino to the north, Lombardy to the west, and the Veneto to the south and east. The low-lying countryside around the southern stretches becomes increasingly dramatic further north, until impressive rocky cliffs, sometimes swathed in pines, hug the shoreline of the northern tip. Numerous sporting facilities, the many sights to explore, and the splendid scenery of snow-capped mountains help make the lake a favourite summer playground.

Eastern tip of Sirmione Peninsula
Beyond the town is a path which follows the rim of the peninsula, passing boiling sulphur springs.

Riva's waterfront is dominated by an old fortress of the Scaligeri. Windsurfers favour this resort because of the consistent offshore winds.

Gardone is noted for its exotically-planted park and for the Villa il Vittoriale, the Art Deco home of the poet Gabriele d'Annunzio, which is filled with curiosities.

The Republic of Salò was established here by Mussolini in 1943. The cathedral in this elegant and attractive town of pastel-painted houses contains an altarpiece by Veneziano.

The hydrofoils,
catamarans and steamers which ply the lake offer glimpses of villas and gardens which cannot be seen from the coastal road.

Riva del Garda · Torbole

Limone sul Garda

Campione del Garda · Malcesine

Assenza

Brenzone

Gargnano · Castelletto

Bogliaco

Maderno

Gardone Riviera

Salò · Torri del Benaco

Portese

Garda

Manerba · Bardolino
Moniga

Lazise

Padenghe sul Garda · Sirmione

Desenzano

Peschiera

The streets of Malcesine cluster below an imposing medieval castle. A cable car climbs to the summit of Monte Baldo (1,745 m/5,725 ft), offering far-reaching views.

0 kilometres 2

0 miles 1

The lake is named after this long-established town.

Bardolino gave its name to the well-known red wine.

Peschiera's attractive enclosed harbour and fortress were built by the Austrians in the 1860s, during the Italian Wars of Independence.

KEY

- • • • Steamer route
- • • • Car ferry
- ⛵ Sailing club or centre
- **i** Tourist information
- ✹ Viewpoint

Sirmione
A fascinating medieval castle, the Rocca Scaligera, dominates the town of Sirmione. At the tip of the peninsula lie Roman ruins.

The 16th-century wooden bridge by Palladio at Bassano del Grappa

Bassano del Grappa ❸

Vicenza. 🕌 *39,000.* 🚆 🚌
🛈 *Largo Corona d'Italia 35 (0424-52 43 51).* 🛒 *Thu & Sat.*

T HIS PEACEFUL TOWN lies at
the foot of Monte Grappa.
The river Brenta, which flows
through the town, is straddled
by the graceful Ponte degli
Alpini, which was designed in
1569 by Palladio. It is built of
timber to allow it to flex when
hit by the spring meltwaters.
Bassano is well known for its
majolica products (decorated
and glazed earthenware), some
of which are on display in the
Palazzo Sturm. The town is
also synonymous with Italy's
preferred after-dinner drink,
the clear spirit known as
grappa. It is produced from
the lees *(graspa)* left over from
wine production; information
about the process is given in
the **Museo degli Alpini**.

🏛 **Palazzo Sturm**
Via Ferracina. 📞 *0424-52 22 35.*
🕐 *Fri–Sun.* 🔲
🏛 **Museo degli Alpini**
Via Anagarano 2. 📞 *0424-52 31 21.*
🕐 *Tue–Sun.*

Asolo ❹

Treviso. 🕌 *2,000.* 🚌 🛈 *Via Santa Caterina 258 (0423-52 41 92).* 🛒 *Sat.*

A SOLO IS beautifully sited
among the cypress-clad
foothills of the Dolomites. This
tiny walled town was once
ruled by Queen Caterina
Cornaro (1454–1510), the

Venetian wife of the King of
Cyprus, who poisoned her
husband so that Venice would
gain Cyprus. Cardinal Pietro
Bembo, a poet, coined the
verb *asolare* to describe the
bittersweet life of enforced
idleness she endured in exile
here. Among others who have
fallen in love with the narrow
streets and grand houses was
poet Robert Browning, who
named a volume of poems
Asolanda (1889) after Asolo.

ENVIRONS: At Masèr, 10 km
(6 miles) east of the town,
stands the magnificent **Villa
Barbaro** *(see pp76–7)*. It was
designed by Palladio in about
1555, in conjunction with the
artist Veronese, and perfectly
blends symmetry and light,
airy rooms with sumptuous
trompe l'oeil frescoes. Statuary
and a small pool add interest
to the gardens outside.

🏯 **Villa Barbaro**
Masèr. 📞 *0423-92 30 04.*
🕐 *Tue, Sat, Sun & public hols.* 🔲

Castelfranco Veneto ❺

Treviso. 🕌 *30,000.* 🚌
🛈 *Via Francesco M Preti 39 (0423-49 50 00).* 🛒 *Thu am & Fri am.*

F ORTIFIED IN 1199 by rulers of
Treviso as a defence against
the neighbouring Paduans, the
historic core of this town lies
within well-preserved walls. In
the **Casa di Giorgione**, said to
be the birthplace of the painter
Giorgione (1478–1511), about
whom little is known, there is
a museum devoted to his life.
Giorgione innovatively used
landscape to create mood,
adding figures to intensify the
atmosphere – for instance in
his mysterious, most famous
work, *The Tempest (see p102)*.
Another of his few directly
attributable works hangs here
in the **Duomo**: the *Madonna
and Child with Saints Liberal
and Francis* (1504).

ENVIRONS: About 8 km (5
miles) northeast of the town,
at the village of Fanzolo, lies
the **Villa Emo** (c.1555). It
was designed by Palladio,
and is a typical example of
his work: a cube flanked by
two symmetrical wings (used
to store the estate's grain).
Inside there are lavish
frescoes by Zelotti.

🏯 **Casa di Giorgione**
Piazzetta del Duomo. 📞 *0423-49 12 40.* 🕐 *Tue–Sun.*
🔵 *public hols.* 🔲 🔲
🏯 **Villa Emo**
Fanzolo di Vedelago. 📞 *0423-47 64 14.* 🕐 *Mar–Oct: Tue, Sat & Sun.* 🔲

Fresco (c.1561) by Veronese adorning the Villa Barbaro near Asolo

Street-by-Street: Vicenza ⑤

Face at No. 21 Contrà Porti

VICENZA IS KNOWN as the city of Andrea Palladio (1508–80), who started out as a mere stonemason and became the most influential architect of his time. Walking around the city it is intriguing to study the evolution of his distinctive style. In the centre is the monumental basilica he adapted to serve as the town hall, nearby is the Teatro Olimpico, and all around are the palaces he built for Vicenza's wealthy citizens.

Loggia del Capitaniato
This covered arcade was designed by Palladio in 1571.

Contrà Porti
is bordered by some of the most elegant palazzi in Vicenza.

Palazzo Valmarana Braga
Palladio's impressive building of 1566 is decorated with giant pilasters and sculpted scenes. It was not completed until 1680, 100 years after the architect's death.

San Lorenzo

Piazza Stazione

CORSO ANDREA PALLADIO

CONTRA CAVOUR

VIA BATTISTI

CONTRA P LAMPERTICO

CONTRA GARIBALDI

C MUSCHERIA

CONT PESC V

CONTRA SAN ANTONIO

PIAZZA DEL DUOMO

Duomo
Vicenza's cathedral was rebuilt after bomb damage during World War II left only the façade and choir entirely intact.

Andrea Palladio
This memorial to Vicenza's most famous son is usually surrounded by market stalls.

0 kilometres 2

0 miles 1

KEY

– – – Suggested route

STAR SIGHT

★ **Piazza dei Signori**

A large hall is all that remains of the 15th-century Palazzo della Ragione.

Santa Corona

Teatro Olimpico Museo Civico

Torre di Piazza, built in the 12th century, is an impressive 82 m (269 ft) high.

The lion of St Mark gazing down on Piazza dei Signori

★ **Piazza dei Signori**

Palladio's elegant buildings flank the Piazza dei Signori, including the majestic two-tier colonnades of the 16th-century "Basilica", built around the old Palazzo della Ragione.

The Quartiere delle Barche contains numerous attractive palaces built in the 14th-century Venetian Gothic style.

Ponte San Michele
This elegant stone bridge, built in 1620, provides lovely views of the surrounding town.

La Rotonda Monte Berico Villa Valmarana ai Nani

Piazza delle Erbe, the city's market square, is overlooked by a 13th-century prison tower.

Casa Pigafetta
This striking 15th-century house was the birthplace of Antonio Pigafetta, who in 1519 set sail round the world with Magellan.

🏛 Piazza dei Signori

Basilica 0444-32 36 81. Tue–Sun & religious hols.

This square at the heart of Vicenza is dominated by the Palazzo della Ragione, often referred to as the **Basilica**. Its green, copper-clad roof is shaped like an upturned boat with a balustrade bristling with the statues of Greek and Roman gods. The colonnades were designed by Palladio in 1549 as a facing to support the city's 15th-century town hall, which had begun to subside. This was Palladio's first public commission, and a great success. Beside it stands the 12th-century Torre di Piazza.

The **Loggia del Capitaniato**, to the northwest, was built by Palladio in 1571: the Loggia's upper rooms contain the city's council chamber.

🏛 Contrà Porti

Contrà (an abbreviation of *contrada*, or district) is the Vicenza dialect word for street. On one side of the Contrà is a series of pretty Gothic buildings with painted windows and ornate balconies, reminiscent of Venice and a reminder that Vicenza was once part of the Venetian empire.

Several elegant Palladian palazzi stand on this street. Palazzo Porto Barbarano (No. 11), Palazzo Thiene (No. 12) and Palazzo Iseppo da Porto (No. 21) illustrate the sheer variety of Palladio's style – all share Classical elements but each is unique. An intriguing detail is that Palazzo Thiene appears to be of stone, though it is in fact built of cheap, light-weight brick, cleverly rendered to look like masonry.

Exploring Vicenza

VICENZA, THE GREAT PALLADIAN CITY and one of the wealthiest cities in the Veneto, is celebrated the world over for its splendid and varied architecture; it also offers the visitor elegant shops and cafés to visit.

Carpione's ceiling fresco in the large entrance hall of the Museo Civico

🏛 Museo Civico

Piazza Matteotti. **(** 0444-32 13 48.
🔲 Tue – Sun. 🈺 &

The excellent Museo Civico is housed in **Palazzo Chiericati** (*see p76*) by Palladio, built in 1550. Inside is a fresco by Giulio Carpione of a naked charioteer, representing the Sun, who appears to fly over the entrance hall. The upstairs rooms hold many excellent pictures. Among the Gothic altarpieces from churches in Vicenza is Hans Memling's *Crucifixion* (1468–70), the central panel from a triptych whose side panels are now located in New York.

Other rooms contain works by the local artist Bartolomeo Montagna (c.1450–1523).

✠ Santa Corona

Contrà Santa Corona. **(** 0444-32 36 44. 🔲 daily.

This great Gothic church was built in 1261 to house a thorn donated by Louis IX of France and said to be from Christ's Crown of Thorns. The Cappella Porto houses the tomb of Luigi da Porto (died 1529), author of the novel *Giulietta e Romeo*, on which Shakespeare based his famous play. Notable paintings include Giovanni Bellini's *Baptism of Christ* (c.1500) and the *Adoration of the Magi* (1573) by Paolo Veronese.

🎭 TEATRO OLIMPICO

Piazza Matteotti. **(** 0444-32 37 81.
🔲 daily. 🈺 &

Europe's oldest surviving indoor theatre is a fine and remarkable structure, largely made of wood and plaster, and painted to look like marble. Palladio began work on the design in 1579, but he died the following year. His pupil, Vincenzo Scamozzi, took over the project, completing the theatre in time for its opening performance of Sophocles' tragic drama, *Oedipus Rex*, on 3 March 1585.

Odeon Frescoes
The gods of Mount Olympus, after which the theatre is named, decorate the Odeon, a room used for music recitals.

The Anteodeon contains frescoes depicting the theatre's opening performance, and oil lamps from the original stage set.

Main ticket office

Stage Set
Scamozzi's scenery represents the Greek city of Thebes. The streets are cleverly painted in perspective and rise at a steep angle to give the illusion of great length.

The Auditorium
was designed by Palladio to resemble the outdoor theatres of ancient Greece and Rome, such as the Arena at Verona (*see p137*), with a semi-circle of "stone" benches and a ceiling painted to portray the sky.

⛪ San Lorenzo

Piazza San Lorenzo. ⬜ *daily.*

The portal of this church is a
magnificent example of Gothic
stone carving, richly decorated
with the figures of the Virgin
and Child, and St Francis and
St Clare. Inside there are fine
tombs, and damaged frescoes.
The lovely cloister, north of
the church, is an attractive,
flower-filled haven of calm.

⛪ Monte Berico

Basilica di Monte Berico. ⬜ *daily.*
Refectory ⬜ *with permission only.*

Monte Berico is the green,
cypress-clad hill to the south
of Vicenza to which wealthy
residents once escaped, in the
heat of summer, to enjoy the
cooler air and pastoral charms
of their country estates. Today,
shady *portici*, or colonnades,
adorned with shrines, line the
wide avenue linking central
Vicenza to the basilica on top
of the hill. The domed basilica

La Rotonda (1550–52), most famous of all Palladio's works

itself, built in the 15th century
and enlarged in the 18th, is
dedicated to the Virgin who
appeared here during the
1426–8 plague to announce
that Vicenza would be spared.

The ornate interior contains
a moving *Pietà* fresco (1500)
by Bartolomeo Montagna, a
fossil collection in the cloister,
and Veronese's fine painting,
*The Supper of St Gregory the
Great* (1572), in the refectory.

epics of Homer and Virgil. In
the separate Foresteria (guest
house), the 18th-century
frescoes depicting peasant life
and the seasons, painted by
Tiepolo's son, Giandomenico,
are equally decorative but
imbued with an earthy realism.

The villa can be reached by
an enjoyable, ten-minute walk
from the basilica on Monte
Berico. Head downhill along
Via Massimo d'Azeglio to the
high-walled convent on the
right where the road ends,
then take Via San Bastiano.

🏛 La Rotonda

Via Rotonda 29. 📞 *0444-32 17 93.*
Villa ⬜ *15 Mar–15 Oct: Wed.*
Garden ⬜ *Tue & Thu.*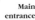

This perfectly symmetrical
villa, also known as the
Villa Capra Valmarana, is
the epitome of Palladio's
architecture *(see pp76–7)*,
and also the most famous
of his villas. The design,
consisting of a dome
rising above a cube,
is both simple and
visually satisfying. It
received immediate
acclaim for the way it blends
so perfectly with its surroundings, creating a gentle echo of
the hilly landscape. A pleasant
contrast exists between the
terracotta roof tiles, the white
walls and the green lawns.

The villa, built in 1550–52,
has inspired many copies in
cities as far away as London,
St Petersburg and Delhi. Fans
of *Don Giovanni* will enjoy
spotting locations used in
Joseph Losey's 1979 film.

To reach La Rotonda, follow
the path that passes beside the
Villa Valmarana ai Nani.

The façade statues of stately
toga-clad figures are portraits
of sponsors who paid for the
theatre's construction.

The courtyard giving
access to the Teatro is
decorated with ancient
sculptures. These were
donated by members of
the Olympic Academy,
the learned body that
built the theatre.

**Main
entrance**

**The Baroque hilltop church,
the Basilica di Monte Berico**

🏛 Villa Valmarana ai Nani

Via San Bastiano. 📞 *0444-54 39 76.*
⬜ *mid-Mar–Nov: Tue–Sun pm.* 📷

The wall alongside the Villa
Valmarana (which was built
in 1688 by Antonio Muttoni)
is topped by figures of dwarfs
which give the building its
name *ai Nani* (of the Dwarfs).

Inside, the walls are covered
with gravity-defying frescoes
by Tiepolo, in which the fleshy
and pneumatic gods of Mount
Olympus float about on clouds
watching scenes from the

Street-by-Street: Padua ❼

PADUA (PADOVA) is an old university town with an illustrious academic history. Rich in art and architecture, it has two particularly outstanding sights. The magnificent Cappella degli Scrovegni *(see pp150–51)*, north of the city centre, is famous for Giotto's lyrical frescoes. Close to the railway station, it forms part of the complex incorporating the Eremitani church and museums. The Basilica di Sant'Antonio, which forms the focal point in the southern part of the city, is one of the most popular pilgrimage destinations in Italy.

Palazzo del Capitanio
Built between 1599 and 1605 for the head of the city's militia, the tower incorporates an astronomical clock made in 1344.

Piazza dei Signori is bordered by attractive arcades which house small speciality shops, cafés and old-fashioned wine bars.

Corte Capitaniato, a 14th-century arts faculty (open for concerts), contains frescoes which include a rare portrait of the poet Petrarch.

Ufficio di Turismo

Loggia della Gran Guardia
This fine Renaissance building dating from 1523 once housed the Council of Nobles. It is now used as a conference centre.

★ Duomo and Baptistry
The 12th-century baptistry of the Duomo contains one of the most complete medieval fresco cycles to survive in Italy, painted by Giusto de' Menabuoi in 1378.

The Palazzo del Monte di Pietà has 16th-century arcades and statues enclosing a medieval building.

KEY

– – – Suggested route

0 kilometres   2

0 miles   1

STAR SIGHT

★ Duomo and Baptistry

VISITORS' CHECKLIST

🚶 250,000. 🚆 Piazzale della
Stazione. 🚌 Piazza Boscetti.
ℹ️ Riviera dei Mugnai 8 (049-
875 06 55). 🗓️ daily. 🎭 Oct–
Apr: concert season.

Caffè Pedrocchi
*Built like a Classical temple,
the Caffè Pedrocchi has
been a famous meeting
place for students and
intellectuals since it
opened in 1831.*

A bronze statue
of a woman
(1973) by Emilio
Greco stands at
the centre of
this largely
pedestrianized
square.

Stazione
Chiesa degli Eremitani
Cappella degli Scrovegni
Museo Civico

PIAZZA CAVOUR

VIA GORIZIA

ZZA DELLA FRUTTA

VIA OBERDAN

PTTA GARZERIA

VIA VIII FEBBRAIO

V SAN CANZIANO

IAZZA DELLE ERBE

Basilica di Sant'Antonio
Orto Botanico

Padua University
*Founded in 1222, this
is Italy's second oldest
university. Elena Piscopia
was the first woman
graduate, in 1678.*

lazzo
lla Ragione,
e medieval court of justice,
ntains magnificent frescoes.

**Piazza
delle Erbe**
*There are some
excellent views to be
had over the market
place from the 15th-
century loggia, which
runs alongside the
13th-century Palazzo
della Ragione.*

🏛️ Duomo and Baptistry

Piazza Duomo. **Baptistry** 049-
66 28 14. 🗓️ daily (Nov – Mar:
Tue – Sun). 🎫

The Duomo was built in 1552
to plans partly by Michelangelo, on the site of an earlier,
14th-century cathedral. Beside
it stands a domed baptistry
(c.1200). The interior is entirely decorated with vibrant
frescoes painted by Giusto
de' Menabuoi, dating from
around 1378. The frescoes
depict episodes from the
Bible, including scenes of
the Creation, the Miracles, the
Passion, the Crucifixion and
the Resurrection of Christ.

🏛️ Palazzo della Ragione

Piazza delle Erbe. 049-820 50 06.
🗓️ daily. 🎫 ♿
The "Palace of Reason", which
is also known as the Salone,
was built in 1218 to serve as
Padua's law court and council
chamber. The vast main hall
was originally decorated with
frescoes by Giotto, but fire
destroyed his work in 1420.
The Salone is breathtaking in
its sheer size. It is the largest
undivided medieval hall in
Europe, 80 m (260 ft) long,
27 m (90 ft) wide and 27 m
(90 ft) high. Frescoes painted
in 1420–25 by Nicola Miretto
cover its walls: the fascinating
panels – 333 of them – depict
the months of the year, with
appropriate gods, signs of
the zodiac and seasonal
activities. A 1466 copy of
the huge Gattamelata
statue *(see p152)* by
Donatello stands at
one end of the hall,
emphasizing the
impressive vastness
of the Salone.

🏛️ Caffè Pedrocchi

Via VIII Febbraio 2.
049-875 20 20.
🗓️ daily.
Caffè Pedrocchi
opened in 1831, and became
famous throughout Italy as
the café that never closed its
doors. Today people come as
much to talk, play cards or
watch the world go by as to
eat or drink. The upstairs
rooms, decorated with florid
Moorish, Egyptian, medieval,
Greek and other styles, are
used for concerts and lectures.

Padua: Cappella degli Scrovegni

ENRICO SCROVEGNI built this chapel in 1303, hoping thereby to spare his dead father, a usurer, from the eternal damnation in hell described by the poet Dante in his *Inferno*. The interior of the chapel is entirely covered with beautiful frescoes of scenes from the life of Christ, painted by Giotto between 1303 and 1305. As works of great narrative force, they exerted a powerful influence on the development of European art.

The Nativity
The naturalism of the Virgin's pose marks a departure from Byzantine stylization, as does the use of natural blue for the sky, in place of celestial gold.

Expulsion of the Merchants
Christ's physical rage, the cowering merchant and the child hiding his face show an animation that is characteristic of Giotto's style.

The Coretti
Giotto painted the two panels known as the Coretti as an exercise in perspective, creating the illusion of an arch with a room beyond.

View towards altar

West entrance   North side   Altar   South side   West entrance

GALLERY GUIDE
The scenes, which are depicted in sequence, are fully explained on a small board, printed in several languages with a basic numbered key, which the custodian will offer you on entry to the chapel. Owing to the size of the chapel, the number of visitors at any one time is restricted, and as a consequence, long queues can build up at peak times. The duration of visits is also timed when it gets busy. To avoid such restrictions, it is best to arrive early or late in the day.

KEY
- Episodes of Joachim and Anna
- Episodes from the Life of Mary
- Episodes from the Life and Death of Christ
- The Virtues and Vices
- The Last Judgment

The Last Judgment

This scene fills the entire west wall of the chapel. Its formal composition is closer to Byzantine tradition than some of the other frescoes, with parts probably painted by assistants. A model of the chapel is shown (centre left, at the bottom) being offered to the Virgin by Scrovegni.

Mary is Presented at the Temple
Giotto sets many scenes against an architectural background, using the laws of perspective to give a sense of three dimensions.

Injustice
The Vices and Virtues are painted in monochrome. Here Injustice is symbolized by scenes of war, murder and robbery.

View towards entrance

Lament over the Dead Christ
Giotto's figures express their grief in different ways: some huddle together, another gestures wildly.

GIOTTO

The great Florentine artist Giotto (1266–1337) is regarded as the father of Western art. His work, with its sense of pictorial space, naturalism and narrative drama, marks a decisive break with the Byzantine tradition of the preceding 1,000 years. He is the first Italian master whose name has passed into posterity, and although he was regarded in his lifetime as a great artist, few of the works attributed to him are fully documented. Some may have been painted by others, but his authorship of the frescoes in the Scrovegni Chapel need not be doubted.

Exploring Padua

PADUA IS A CITY OF MANY ATTRACTIONS, with a rich history: this is reflected in the major museum complex which occupies a group of 14th-century monastic buildings attached to the church of the Eremitani, a reclusive Augustinian order. The admission ticket includes entry to the Cappella degli Scrovegni *(see pp150–51)*, which stands on the same site. Padua is, in addition, the setting for one of Italy's most important churches – the splendid Basilica di Sant'Antonio – and for one of the earliest universities to be founded in Italy.

15th-century *Angels in Armour* by Guariento, Museo Civico Eremitani

🏛 Chiesa degli Eremitani and Museo Civico Eremitani

Piazza Eremitani. 049-65 48 51. daily. 1 Jan, 24–6 Dec.

The Eremitani church was built from 1276 to 1306, and contains magnificent roof and wall tombs. Among them is that of Marco Benavides (1489–1582), a professor of law at the city university, whose Renaissance tomb was the work of Ammannati (1511–92), an architect from Florence. Celebrated frescoes (1454–7) by Mantegna, portraying scenes from the lives of St James and St Christopher, were destroyed during a bombing raid in 1944. Two scenes from this magnificent series survive in the Cappella Ovetari, south of the sanctuary: *The Martyrdom of St James* and *The Martyrdom of St Christopher*.

A 1st-century AD tomb in the archaeological collection

The Museo Civico Eremitani comprises a coin collection, an archaeological section and a wonderful art gallery.

Among the treasures in the Bottacin section there are some very rare Roman medallions and an almost complete set of Venetian coinage.

The rich archaeological collection contains interesting Roman tombs, fine mosaics and impressive life-size statues. Renaissance bronzes include the comical *Drinking Satyr* by Il Riccio (1470–1532).

The beautiful 14th-century Crucifix from the Cappella degli Scrovegni is displayed in the Quadreria Emo Capodilista, as well as works by Giotto, and 15th-to 18th-century paintings from the Venetian and Flemish schools.

⛪ Basilica di Sant'Antonio

Piazza del Santo.

This exotic church, with its minaret-like spires and Byzantine domes, is also known as Il Santo. It was built from 1232 to house the remains of St Anthony of Padua, a preacher who modelled himself on St Francis of Assisi. Although he was a simple man who rejected worldly wealth, the citizens of Padua built one of the most lavish churches in Christendom to serve as his shrine.

The influence of Byzantine architecture is clearly visible in the basilica's outline: a cone-shaped central dome rises above seven encircling domes; the façade combines Gothic and Romanesque elements.

Inside, the high altar features Donatello's magnificent reliefs (1444–5) on the miracles of St Anthony, and his statues of the Crucifixion, the Virgin and Paduan saints. The tomb of St Anthony, hung with offerings, lies in the north transept; large marble reliefs depicting the saint's life, carved in 1505–77 by various artists, adorn the walls around it. A lively fresco scene of the Crucifixion by Altichiero da Zevio (1380s) adorns the south transept.

🏇 Statue of Gattamelata

Beside the entrance to the basilica stands one of the great works of the Renaissance: a statue of the mercenary soldier Gattamelata. This gritty portrait was created in 1443–52, in honour of a man who during his life did great service to the Venetian Republic. The artist Donatello won fame for the monument, the first equestrian statue made on such a large scale since Roman times.

The Basilica di Sant'Antonio, and Donatello's statue of Gattamelata

✠ Scuola del Santo and Oratorio di San Giorgio

Piazza del Santo. 📞 049-66 39 44.
🕐 daily. 🎫 ♿

Five excellent frescoes, including the earliest documented paintings by Titian, are to be found in these two linked buildings. The Scuola del Santo contains two scenes from the life of St Anthony, which were painted by Titian in 1511. The works in the San Giorgio oratory, delightful saints' lives and scenes from the life of Christ, were executed by Altichiero da Zevio and Jacopo Avenzo, who painted them in 1378–84.

❧ Orto Botanico

Via Orto Botanico 15. 📞 049-65 66 14. 🕐 Apr–Oct am. 🎫 ♿

Padua's botanical garden, the oldest in Europe, was founded in 1545 and still retains much of its original appearance. The gardens and hothouses here were used to cultivate the first lilac trees (1568), sunflowers (1568) and potatoes (1590) to be grown in Italy.

✠ Palazzo del Bo

Via Marzolo 8. 📞 049-828 31 11.
🕐 daily: am. 🎫

The historic main university building, named after a tavern called *Il Bo* (the ox), originally housed the medical faculty, renowned throughout Europe. Among its famous teachers and students was Gabriele Fallopio (1523–62), after whom the Fallopian tubes are named.

From the 16th-century courtyard, guided tours continue to the pulpit Galileo used when he taught physics here from 1592 until 1610; the wooden anatomy theatre, built in 1594 and now the oldest surviving medical lecture theatre in the world, is also visited.

The 16th-century anatomy theatre in the old medical faculty of the university's Palazzo del Bo, Padua

The Euganean Hills, formed by ancient volcanic activity

Euganean Hills ❽

FS 🚌 to Terme Euganee, Montegrotto Terme. 🛈 Viale Stazione 60, Montegrotto Terme (049-79 33 84).

THE CONICAL Euganean Hills, remnants of long-extinct volcanoes, rise abruptly out of the surrounding plain. Hot water springs bubble up out of the ground at Abano Terme and Montegrotto Terme where scores of establishments offer thermal treatments, ranging from mud baths to immersion in the hot sulphurated waters. Spa cures originated in Roman times; remains of the original baths and theatre are still visible at Montegrotto Terme.

⛪ Abbazia di Praglia

Via Abbazia di Praglia, Bresseo di Teolo. 📞 049-990 00 10.
🕐 Tue–Sun.

The Benedictine monastery at Praglia, 6 km (4 miles) west of Abano Terme, is a peaceful haven in the tree-clad hills where the monks grow herbs and restore manuscripts. They also lead guided tours of the dignified Renaissance church (1490–1548), which is noted for its beautiful cloister. There are also richly carved stalls in both the choir and the refectory, and paintings and frescoes by Zelotti, a 16th-century painter from Verona, in the dome of the church and the refectory.

⬛ Casa di Petrarca

Via Valleselle 4, Arquà Petrarca.
📞 0429-71 82 94. 🕐 Tue–Sun. 🎫

The picturesque town of Arquà Petrarca, on the southern edge of the Euganean Hills, is named in honour of Francesco Petrarca, the medieval poet known in English as Petrarch (1303–74). Petrarch spent the last few years of his life here, living in a house frescoed with scenes from his lyrical poems, overlooking a landscape of olive groves and vineyards. He lies buried in a simple sarcophagus in front of the church.

The Casa di Petrarca (part 14th century) in Arquà Petrarca

✠ Villa Barbarigo

Valsanzibio. 📞 0444-913 00 42.
🕐 Mar–Nov. 🎫

To the north of Arquà is the 18th-century Villa Barbarigo at Valsanzibio, which boasts one of the finest Baroque gardens in the Veneto. These were planned by Antonio Barbarigo in 1669, and are a grandiose mix of statuary, fountains, a maze, formal parterres, lakes and avenues of cypress trees.

The 16th-century Villa Foscari at Malcontenta, beside the Brenta Canal

Brenta Canal 9

Padua and Venezia. **FS** *Venezia Mestre, Dolo, Mira.* to Mira, Dolo and Strà. **I** *Via Don Minzoni, Mira (041-42 49 73).* **Canal trips on *Il Burchiello:*** Via Trieste 42, Padua. **(** 049-66 09 44.

OVER THE CENTURIES, in order to prevent the Venetian lagoon silting up, the rivers flowing into it were diverted. The river Brenta was canalized in two sections: the older branch, between Padua and Fusina (just west of Venice), dates back to the 16th century and flows for a total of 36 km (22 miles). Its potential as a transport route was quickly realized, and fine villas were built along its length.

Today many of these elegant buildings can still be admired – the N11 road runs alongside most of the canal's length – and three of them open their doors to the public. The 18th-century **Villa Pisani** at Strà has an extravagant frescoed ceiling by Tiepolo. The **Villa Widmann-Foscari** at Mira (itself a pretty village) was built in 1719 but altered in the 19th century, and contains an interior decorated in French Rococo style. In the village of Malcontenta is the well-known **Villa Foscari**, or Villa Malcontenta, one of Palladio's loveliest villas *(see pp76–7)*.

It was built in 1560 and the interior was decorated with magnificent frescoes by Zelotti.

These villas may also be visited as part of an indulgent 8.5-hour guided tour from Padua, travelling to Venice (or, on alternate days, from Venice to Padua) along the river in a leisurely fashion on board the *Burchiello* motor launch – the cost for the one-way journey, however, is fairly prohibitive.

Villa Pisani
Via Pisani, Strà. **(** 049-50 20 74. daily.
Villa Widmann-Foscari
Via Nazionale 420, Mira Porte.
(0330-26 15 10. Tue–Sun.
Villa Foscari
Via dei Turisti, Malcontenta.
(041-547 00 12. Tue & Sat am. Dec–Mar.

Treviso 10

82,000. **FS** **I** *Via Toniolo 41 (0422-54 76 32).* Tue & Sat am.

DESPITE COMPARISONS with Venice, the lovely fortified city of Treviso has its own very distinctive character.

A good place to start a tour of the streets, some lined with attractive balconied houses beside willow-fringed canals, is **Calmaggiore**. The street links the Duomo with the Palazzo dei Trecento, the rebuilt 13th-century town hall.

The **Duomo** was founded in the 12th century but rebuilt several times. Inside, Titian's *Annunciation* (1570) vies for attention with the striking *Adoration of the Magi* fresco (1520) by Titian's arch rival, Il Pordenone. More paintings by Titian and other artists of the Renaissance may be seen in the **Museo Civico**.

The bustling fish market, which dates back to medieval times, is held on an island in the middle of Treviso's river Sile; this arrangement allows the remains of the day's trading to be flushed away instantly.

The bulky Dominican church of **San Nicolò**, nestling by the 16th-century city wall, contains interesting tombs and frescoes, including, on a wall of the chapter house, the first-ever depiction of spectacles in art. A magnificent tomb (1500) by Antonio Rizzo is framed by a fresco of pageboys (c.1500) by Lorenzo Lotto.

Museo Civico
Borgo Cavour 24. **(** 0422-513 37. Tue–Sun.

The houses of the medieval town of Treviso overlook ancient canals

The façade and entrance to the Renaissance Palazzo dei Rettori in Belluno

Conegliano ⓫

Treviso. 🏠 35,000. 🚌 ℹ️ *Via Colombo 45 (0438-212 30).* 🚢 *Fri.*

CONEGLIANO lies among Prosecco-producing vineyards, and winemakers from all over Italy learn their craft at Conegliano's renowned wine school. Via XX Settembre, the winding and arcaded main street, is lined with fine 15th- to 18th-century palazzi, many in the Venetian Gothic style or decorated with fading frescoes. The **Duomo** contains the town's one great work of art, an altarpiece painted by local artist Cima da Conegliano (1460–1518) depicting the *Virgin and Child with Saints* (1493).

A mythical statue on Conegliano's theatre

Reproductions of Cima's most famous works are on show in the **Casa di Cima**, the artist's birthplace. The detailed landscapes in the background of his paintings were based on the hills around the town; the same views can still be seen from the gardens surrounding the Castelvecchio (old castle).

🏠 Casa di Cima
Via Cima. 📞 *0438-226 60.* ☐ *Sat & Sun.* 📷

Belluno ⓬

🏠 36,000. 🚇 🚌 ℹ️ *Via Rodolfo Pesaro 21 (0437-94 00 83).* 🚢 *Sat.*

PICTURESQUE BELLUNO, capital of Belluno province, serves as a bridge between the two different parts of the Veneto, with the flat plains to the south and the Dolomite peaks to the

north. Both are encapsulated in the views to be seen from the 12th-century **Porta Ruga** at the southern end of Via Mezzaterra, the main street of the old town. More spectacular still are the views from the bell tower of the 16th-century **Duomo** (subsequently rebuilt). The nearby baptistry houses a font cover with the figure of John the Baptist carved by Andrea Brustolon (1662–1732). Brustolon's works also grace the churches of San Pietro (on Via San Pietro) and Santo Stefano (Piazza Santo Stefano). North of Piazza del Duomo stands the city's most elegant building, the **Palazzo dei Rettori** (1491) – once home to the town's Venetian rulers – and the 12th-century **Torre Civica**, all that now survives of a medieval castle.

The **Museo Civico** contains paintings by Bartolomeo Montagna (1450–1523) and Sebastiano Ricci (1659–1734), and a notable archaeological section. North of the museum is Belluno's finest square, **Piazza del Mercato**, with its arcaded Renaissance palaces and its fountain of 1410.

South of the town are the ski resorts of the Alpe del Nevegal; in the summer a chair lift operates from Faverghera up the flank of the mountain to a height of 1,600 m (5,250 ft) offering extensive views.

🏛 Museo Civico
Via Duomo 16. 📞 *0437-94 48 36.* ☐ *Tue–Sat.* ● *Sat pm Oct– mid-Apr, public hols.*

Cortina d'Ampezzo ⓭

Belluno. 🏠 7,000. 🚌 ℹ️ *Piazzetta San Francesco 8 (0436-32 31).* 🚢 *Tue & Fri.*

ITALY'S TOP SKI RESORT, much favoured by the smart set from Turin and Milan, is well supplied with restaurants and bars. Cortina is set amid the extremely dramatic scenery of the Dolomites *(see pp78–9)*, which explains part of the resort's attraction: all around, crags and spires thrust their distinctive weather-beaten shapes above the trees.

Cortina benefits from better than average sports facilities, thanks to hosting the 1956 Winter Olympics. In addition to downhill and cross-country skiing, there is also a ski jump and a bobsleigh run for those who favour something more adventurous than usual, as well as an Olympic ice stadium, several swimming pools, tennis courts and riding facilities.

During the summer months, Cortina becomes an excellent base for walkers. Information on trails and guided walks is available from the tourist office or, during the summer, from the Club Alpino Italiano next door *(see p625)*.

Corso Italia in Cortina d'Ampezzo, Italy's most important ski resort

Traditional copper pans on display in the Museo Carnico in Tolmezzo

Tolmezzo ⑭

Udine. 🏠 10,000. 🚌 **ℹ** Via Umberto I 15, Arta Terme (0433-92 92 90). 🅿 Mon.

Tolmezzo is the capital of the Carnia region, named after the Celtic tribe that inhabited the area around the 4th century BC. The town is surrounded by the high peaks of the Carnic Alps, including the pyramidal Monte Amariana (1,906 m – 6,253 ft) to the east. The best place to begin a tour of the region is the **Museo delle Arti Popolari**, which has displays of local costumes, crafts, textiles and agriculture.

Southwest of the town, a scenic road climbs 14 km (8.5 miles) to the ski resort of **Sella Chianzutan**, a good base for walking in the summer. More resorts line the road, west of Tolmezzo, to **Ampezzo**, at which point a minor road heads north through the gorge of the River Lumiei. Following this road to the Ponte di Buso bridge and the **Lago di Sàuris** is an excellent introduction to the majestic Carnic Alps.

Above this point the road is often impassable in winter, but in summer there are flower-filled meadows all along the road up to Sella di Razzo, and then back along the **Pesarina Valley**, via Comeglians and Ravascletto. Returning south, **Zuglio** was once the Roman town of Forum Iulii Carnicum, guarding the road over the pass. Today it is worth a detour for the remains of its Roman basilica, baths and forum.

🏛 Museo delle Arti Popolari
Piazza Garibaldi 2.
📞 0433-432 33. 🕐 Tue–Sun.
🔴 1 Jan, 1 May, 25 Dec. 🔖

Pordenone ⑮

Udine. 🏠 49,000. 🚊 🚌 **ℹ** Corso Vittorio Emanuele II 30 (0434-52 12 18). 🅿 Wed & Sat.

Old Pordenone consists of one long street, the **Corso Vittorio Emanuele**, lined with pretty arcaded houses of pink brick, some with the faded traces of decorative frescoes on their façades. The 13th-century **Palazzo Comunale** forms a striking conclusion to the street with its eccentrically shaped roofline of curves and minaret-like side towers, and its 16th-century clocktower. Opposite is the **Museo Civico**, housed in the 17th-century Palazzo Ricchieri, where works by the local artist Il Pordenone (1484–1539) are on display.

Around the corner stands the **Duomo**, which contains the lovely altar painting of the *Madonna della Misericordia* (1515) by Il Pordenone. The bell tower beside the Duomo is a fine example of Romanesque decorative brickwork.

🏛 Museo Civico
Corso Vittorio Emanuele 51. **📞** 0434-39 23 11. 🕐 Tue–Sun. 🔴 public hols. 🔖 ♿

Udine ⑯

🏠 99,000. 🚊 🚌 **ℹ** Piazza I Maggio 7 (0432-50 47 43). 🅿 Sat.

Udine is a city of varied and surprising architecture. In the centre lies **Piazza della Libertà**, where the Palazzo del Comune (1448–56), built of pink stone in Venetian Gothic style, stands beside the Art Deco Caffè Contarena (1915). Opposite, the Renaissance symmetry of the Porticato di San Giovanni is interrupted by the Torre dell'Orologio (Clock Tower, 1527) crowned by two bronze Moors who strike the hours. Note also the fountain of 1542, the two 18th-century statues, and the column supporting the Lion of St Mark.

Rising behind the square is a 26-m (85-ft) hill which offers sweeping views over the city. Beyond the **Arco Bollani**, a gateway designed by Palladio in 1556, steps lead up to the 16th-century castle, now the **Musei Civici e Galleria di Storia e Arte Antica**, which houses the city's fine art and archaeology collections.

South of Piazza Matteotti, where the market is held, at the end of Via Savorgnana, stands the **Oratorio della Purità**, and the **Duomo** with its octagonal bell tower. Both contain important paintings and frescoes by Giambattista Tiepolo (1696–1770). More of Tiepolo's work can be seen in the **Palazzo Arcivescovile**, which the artist decorated with frescoes.

Lago di Sauris, an artificial lake lying in the Carnic Alps above Tolmezzo

The arcaded Porticato di San Giovanni on Piazza della Libertà, Udine

ENVIRONS: Outside Codroipo, 24 km (15 miles) west, rises the imposing **Villa Manin**. A road passes through the villa's grounds, so its massive size can be seen even when the house – once the retreat of Ludovico Manin, the last doge of Venice (1725–1802) – and its magnificent gardens are closed to the public.

🏛 **Musei Civici e Galleria di Storia e Arte Antica**
Castello di Udine. 📞 0432-50 28 72.
🕐 Tue–Sat (Sun am). ● 1 Jan, 1 May, 25 Dec. 📷 ⓑ

🏛 **Palazzo Arcivescovile**
Piazza Patriarcato. 📞 0432-250 03.
🕐 Wed–Sun. 📷 ⓑ

🏛 **Villa Manin**
Passariano. 📞 0432-90 66 57.
Gardens 🕐 Wed–Fri pm, Sat & Sun. ● 25 & 26 Dec. 📷 ⓑ

Cividale del Friuli ⑰

Udine. 🚶 11,000. 🚆 🚌
🔼 Corso Paolino Aquileia 10 (0432-73 13 98). 🚐 Sat.

A GATE IN THE medieval walls of Cividale leads down the main street and straight to the dramatic ravine of the River Natisone, which splits the town in two and is spanned by the arch of the medieval **Ponte del Diavolo** (Devil's Bridge).

Above the river's north bank stands the **Tempietto Longobardo** (Lombardic Chapel), a very rare example of an 8th-century church decorated with reliefs of saints, modelled in stucco. The town's history is traced in the excellent **Museo**

Archeologico Nazionale, which contains the excavated remains of buildings from a Roman town, and a collection of Lombardic items including jewellery, ivory and weapons.

Next door is the **Duomo**, rebuilt in 1453 after a fire, with its beautiful silver altarpiece (13th century). The **Museo Cristiano**, off the south aisle, contains sculptures from the original church: of particular interest is the altar donated by Ratchis, the Lombardic Duke of Friuli and later King of Italy (737–44), which is finely carved with scenes from the Life of Christ, including a charming Nativity. There is in addition the unusual baptismal font of Patriarch Callisto (737–56): this octagonal structure, with a roof supported by pillars, is decorated with symbols of the Evangelists.

🔒 **Tempietto Longobardo**
Piazzetta San Biagio. 📷

Interior view of the Tempietto Longobardo in Cividale del Friuli

🏛 **Museo Archeologico Nazionale**
Palazzo dei Provveditori Veti, Piazza del Duomo 13. 📞 0432-73 11 19.
🕐 daily am. ● 1 Jan, Easter, 1 May, 25 Dec. 📷

🏛 **Museo Cristiano**
Piazza del Duomo. 🕐 daily. ⓑ

Gorizia ⑱

🚶 40,000. 🚆 🚌 🔼 Via Diaz 16 (0481-53 38 70). 🚐 Thu.

G ORIZIA WAS AT the centre of fierce fighting during both world wars and was split in two by the 1947 Treaty of Paris, leaving part in Italy, part in Yugoslavia (now Slovenia).

The town's arcaded streets and pastel-painted houses, many with balconies full of flowers, have been carefully restored following substantial damage during World War II. A visit to the modern Museo Provinciale della Grande Guerra (Museum of the Great War), housed in the basement of the **Museo Provinciale**, provides a fascinating introduction to the realities of war. The museum uses videos, photographs, and life-size mock-ups of trenches, gun emplacements and latrines to show the waste, squalor and heroism of war.

Rooms on the upper floor of the museum house temporary exhibitions and items from the town's art collection, which includes works by local artists.

On a mound nearby rises the castle, encircled by 16th-century fortifications. From here there are extensive views stretching over the town to the mountains beyond.

The Lion of Venice above the entrance to Gorizia's castle

ENVIRONS: To the southwest of Gorizia, scenic country roads pass through the foothills of the **Carso**, a limestone plateau stretching down to Trieste. The plateau is dotted with fields enclosed by drystone walls, and gouged with tunnels, caves and underground rivers.

🏛 **Museo Provinciale**
Borgo Castello 3. 📞 04831-53 39 26.
🕐 Tue–Sun. 📷 ⓑ

The attractive harbourside at Grado, along the coast south of Aquileia

Aquileia ⑲

Udine. 🏰 3,500. 🚌 ℹ️ *Piazza Capitolo 4 (0431-91 94 91).* 🚃 *Tue.*

AQUILEIA, now little more than a village but encircled by the ruins of palatial villas, baths, temples and market buildings, provides a poignant reminder of the lost splendour of the Roman Empire.

It was here that Emperor Augustus received Herod the Great, King of Judea, in 10 BC, and it was here too, in AD 381, that the early Christian church held a major council attended by the learned saints Ambrose and Jerome to settle doctrinal issues. In the 5th century, however, the town was abandoned following several sackings. Fortunately, substantial parts of the early Christian basilica have survived, which contain the town's particular treasure: ornate floor mosaics.

⛪ Basilica

Piazza del Capitolo. **0431-845 58.** ⭕ *daily.* ⚫ *1 Jan, 1 May, 25 Dec.*
The basilica was founded in about AD 313 and much of the original structure still survives, including the magnificent floor mosaics of the nave and of the **Cripta degli Scavi** below. The designs are a delightful mixture of geometric patterns, biblical stories and scenes from everyday life in 4th-century Aquileia. There is a lively portrayal of the tale of Jonah, particularly where he is swallowed by an extraordinary sea monster: the fishing boats are meanwhile surrounded by a rich array of creatures of the deep, including wide-eyed dolphins and squid.

🏛 Museo Archeologico Nazionale

Via Roma 1. **0431-910 16.** ⭕ *daily.* ⚫ *1 Jan, 1 May, 25 Dec.* 🏷
The mosaics in the basilica continue a tradition of crafts-

manship that flourished in the city from the 2nd century AD. Additional examples of mosaics and stone carvings from the Classical era (1st to 3rd centuries) are on display in this museum, together with glass, amber, and a collection of flies, beautifully worked in gold, that once formed the adornment of a Roman matron's veil.

🏛 Museo Paleocristiano

Località Monastero. **0431-911 31.** ⭕ *daily am.* ⚫ *1 Jan, 1 May, 25 Dec.*
This museum, which stands not far from Aquileia's ancient harbour beside the once-navigable River Natissa, focuses on the development of art during the early Christian era (4th to 6th centuries).

ENVIRONS: The resort of **Grado**, like Venice, sits on a group of low islands in the middle of the Adriatic lagoon, attached to the mainland by a long, narrow causeway. The town grew into a port for Aquileia in the 2nd century and was used as a haven by Aquileia's citizens during the troubled period of the barbarian invasions. Today, Grado is one of the most popular seaside resorts on the Adriatic, with good seafood restaurants, a long sandy beach and a yachting harbour.

At the centre of the old town stands the **Duomo**: the interior contains 6th-century frescoes in the apse, which are similar in style to those covering the vaults of San Marco in Venice *(see pp106–9).* Nearby, in the little church of **Santa Maria delle Grazie**, there are yet more 6th-century mosaics.

SYMBOLISM IN EARLY CHRISTIAN ART

Christians were persecuted until their religion was granted official status by Constantine the Great in AD 313. Prior to this they had developed a language of secret symbols to express their beliefs, many of which can be seen in the mosaics and marble tomb chests of Aquileia. Many of these and other symbols later found their way into popular bestiaries and folk art.

Part of the 4th-century floor mosaic in the basilica at Aquileia

The Winged figure of Victory holding a laurel wreath was a Classical symbol of triumph, and holiness. Later, it came to represent Christ's resurrection, and more generally, victory over death.

Trieste ㉒

👥 *235,000.* ✈ 🚆 🚌 ℹ️ *Via San Niccolò (040-36 98 81).* 🎪 *Tue–Sun.*

TRIESTE IS AN atmospheric city, tucked up next to Slovenia, with a long, bustling harbour lined with handsome buildings and lapped by the waves of the Adriatic Sea.

🏛️ Acquario Marino

Via Campo Marzio 5. 📞 *040-30 62 01.* ◻ *Tue–Sun (Oct–Apr: am only).* ⬤ *public hols.* 📷 ♿

The city's aquarium, along the harbour near the fish market, is one of the most popular attractions in Trieste. It contains examples of the fascinating marine life in the Adriatic.

♜ Castello di San Giusto

Piazza Cattedrale 3. 📞 *040-31 36 36.* ◻ *Tue–Sun.* ⬤ *1 Jan, 25 Dec.* 📷

Up above the harbour stands a hilltop castle – built by the city's Venetian governors from 1368 – set on a terrace from which there are sweeping views over the Gulf of Trieste.

The Castello del Miramare on the bay of Trieste

The interior of the castle now houses a museum containing 19th-century drawings and prints of Trieste, and a collection of weapons and armour.

🔒 Basilica Paleocristiana

Via Madonna del Mare 11. 📞 *040-436 31.* ◻ *Wed am.*

Beside the castle lie the substantial ruins of the Roman basilica or law court built around AD 100. Note the stone magistrates' bench and throne.

🔒 Duomo

Piazza Cattedrale. ◻ *daily.* ♿

In the church of **San Giusto**, the city's Duomo, the magistrates' bench and throne of the Roman basilica were reinterpreted to become the seat of the bishop and clergy. Here there are two thrones and benches, because the building was formed in the 14th century by linking two 5th-century churches that had been built beside each other. The two apses are decorated with very fine 13th-century mosaics in the Venetian style.

🏛️ Museo di Storia dell'Arte

Palazzo Economo, Piazza della Libertà 7. 📞 *040-436 31.* ◻ *Mon–Sat.* ⬤ *public hols.* 📷

The important archaeological collection held here provides fascinating evidence of Trieste's extensive trade links with the ancient Greek world.

13th-century mosaics in the apse of San Giusto, Trieste's Duomo

ENVIRONS: From **Villa Opicina**, just north of Trieste, sweeping views may be had over the city, its bay and south down the coast of Slovenia. A little beyond, at Borgo Grotta Gigante, lies the **Grotta del Gigante**, a huge cavern filled with stunning "organ pipe" formations and tall columns of stalagmites.

At Grignano, 8 km (5 miles) northwest of the city, stands the **Castello del Miramare**, a white castle set in lush green gardens beside the sparkling blue Adriatic. It was built by the Hapsburg Archduke Maximilian in 1856–60 as his summer retreat, a few years before he was assassinated in Mexico. It is still furnished in contemporary style.

🏞️ Grotta del Gigante

Via Machiavelli 17, Borgo Grotta Gigante. 📞 *040-32 73 12.* ◻ *Tue–Sun.* 📷

♜ Castello del Miramare

Miramare, Grignano. 📞 *040-22 41 43.* ◻ *daily.* ♿

***The Tortoise** hiding in his shell represented darkness and ignorance, while the cockerel, who crows at dawn, signified light and enlightenment.*

***ICHTHUS, or fish**, was an acronym for* Iesous CHristos THeou Uios Soter *– Jesus Christ, Son of God, Saviour, in Ancient Greek.*

***Colourful birds**, such as peacocks, symbolized immortality and the glorious transformation of the soul when it arrives in Heaven.*

TRENTINO-ALTO ADIGE

HE ITALIAN-SPEAKING *Trentino – named after Trento, the regional capital – and the German-speaking Alto Adige or Südtirol (South Tyrol, the region bordering the upper reaches of the River Adige) differ dramatically in culture. However, they do share one feature in common: the majestic Dolomites that form the back-drop to every town and village, covered in snow for six months of every year and carpeted with exquisite Alpine plants for the other six.*

The region's mountains have been cut by glaciers into a series of deep, broad valleys. Many of these face south, so it remains unusually warm and sunny, even in winter. Travellers have passed up and down these valleys for generations – as confirmed by the extraordinary discovery, in 1991, of a 5,000-year-old man's body found emerging from the surface of a melting glacier in Alto Adige. The frozen corpse wore leather boots, stuffed with hay for warmth, and was armed with a copper ice pick.

The paths that Neolithic man once trod became major road networks under the Romans, when many of the region's cities were founded. By the Middle Ages, Alto Adige had established its very own distinctive culture under the Counts of Tyrol, whose land (later appropriated by the Hapsburgs) straddled both sides of today's Italian/Austrian border. The Tyrolean nobility built the castles that still line the valleys and the mountain passes, in order to protect travellers from brigands.

Another ancient legacy is the tradition of hospitality to be found in the numerous guesthouses along the valleys. Many of these are built in the distinctive Tyrolean style, with beautiful timber balconies for making the most of the winter sun, and overhanging roof eaves to keep snow at a distance. Cosy in winter, with log fires and warming food, and offering marvellous views, they make the ideal base for enjoying the region's mountain footpaths and ski slopes.

Skiers enjoying the slopes around Monte Spinale, near Madonna di Campiglio, in Trentino

◁ **A typical view of the Dolomites between Bressanone and Ortisei, in Alto Adige**

Exploring Trentino-Alto Adige

Trentino-alto adige is a region where unspoiled nature is complemented by a wealth of sporting opportunities. The tributary valleys feeding into the Adige valley contain lakes, rivers and streams, and also woodland, vineyards and Alpine pasture full of butterflies, birds and flowers. South of the region rise the distinctive limestone peaks of the Dolomites, while further north the area becomes more mountainous still, enclosed finally by the splendid heights of the Alps.

Via Ponte Aquila in Bressanone

Sights at a Glance

Key

▬▬ Motorway

▬▬ Major road

▬▬ Minor road

▬▬ Scenic route

〜 River

☆ Viewpoint

0 kilometres 25

0 miles 10

Cortina d'Ampezzo
Belluno

Castel Tirolo above the town of Merano

View of the Dolomites from Madonna di Campiglio

GETTING AROUND

The region's main artery is the
Brenner Pass road: it runs from
Austria in the north, following
the River Adige from Bolzano to
Trento, and southwards on to
Verona. Both the motorway and
the main road beside it are
among the busiest in Europe,
and the valley roads can also be
congested during the ski season.
Winter driving can be hazard-
ous, requiring special tyres and
snow chains. Trains and coaches
also serve the main towns, but
car transport is more effective.

SEE ALSO

• *Where to Stay* pp547–9

• *Where to Eat* pp582–4

Abbazia di Monte Maria, founded in the 12th century, near Malles Venosta

Malles Venosta ❶

MALS IM VINSCHGAU

Bolzano. 🏘 4,600. FS 🚌
ℹ Piazza Peter Glückh 3 (0473-83 11 90). 🛒 Wed.

MALLES VENOSTA sits in high border country, close to Switzerland and Austria, and was a customs control point during the Middle Ages. As a legacy, the town has several Gothic churches, whose spires and towers give the town an appealing skyline, mirroring the jagged peaks that rise all around. The oldest is the tiny church of **San Benedetto**, a 9th-century Carolingian building on Via San Benedetto, with frescoes portraying its patrons.

ENVIRONS: The medieval **Castel Coira** (Churburg) rises at Sluderno (Schluderns), 4 km (2.5 miles) southeast of Malles. It was built to guard the road to Val Venosta, which runs by the River Adige, and it now contains an excellent collection of weapons and armour.

Clinging to the mountainside 5 km (3 miles) north of Malles, just above the town of Burgusio (Burgeis), is the Benedictine **Abbazia di Monte Maria** (Marienberg), founded in the 12th century but enlarged in the 18th and 19th. The church's crypt shelters an outstanding series of 12th-century frescoes.

♠ **Castel Coira**
Churburg, Sluderno. 📞 0473-61 52 41. 🕐 mid-Mar–Nov: Tue–Sun. 🎫

🏠 **Abbazia di Monte Maria**
Road to Malles. 📞 0473-83 13 06.
🕐 Mon–Fri (Apri–Sept: Sat am also).
● public hols. **Donation**.

Merano ❷

MERAN

Bolzano. 🏘 40,000. FS 🚌
ℹ Corso della Libertà 35 (0473-23 52 23). 🛒 Tue & Fri.

MERANO IS AN attractive spa town to which Austrians, Germans and Italians come to drink the waters, take therapeutic baths and stroll through the riverside gardens – before taking coffee and pastries in one of the Belle Epoque cafés. On Corso Libertà, a street of smart shops and hotels, stands the **Kurhaus** or Spa Hall built in 1914, now a concert venue. The 15th-century **Castello Principesco** was home to the Hapsburg Archduke Sigismund

The Art Nouveau façade of the Kurhaus in Merano

and is still furnished in period style. Inviting gardens line the River Passirio, which winds its way through the town. The Passeggiata Lungo Passirio d'Inverno (Winter Walk) lines the north bank to the Roman bridge, Ponte Romano; the Passeggiata d'Estate (Summer Walk) on the south bank leads to the medieval Ponte Passirio.

ENVIRONS: The romantic 12th-century **Castel Tirolo**, home of the Counts of Tyrol who gave their name to the Tyrol region, lies 4 km (2.5 miles) to the north. It now houses a museum of Tyrolean history.

♠ **Castello Principesco**
Via Galilei. 📞 0473-23 78 34.
🕐 Apr–Oct: Mon–Fri & Sat am. ●
public hols. 🎫

♠ **Castel Tirolo**
Via Castello 24, Tirolo. 📞 0473-22 02 21. 🕐 mid-May–Oct: daily. 🎫

Vipiteno ❸

STERZING

Bolzano. 🏘 5,500. FS 🚌
ℹ Piazza Città 3 (0472-76 53 25).
🛒 5th & 20th of every month.

VIPITENO, SURROUNDED by mineral-rich valleys, is very Tyrolean in feel. On Via Città Nuova, lined with fine mansions, rise the Gothic **Palazzo Comunale**, containing Renaissance sculpture and paintings, and the Torre dei Dodici, the symbol of the town. Wood carvings in the

Wrought-iron si Vipiteno

Museo Multscher are by Hans Multscher; the Bavarian sculptor came to Vipiteno in 1456-8 to carve the altar for the parish **church**, which lies just south of the town.

To the west, the charming **Val di Racines** includes waterfalls and a natural rock bridge.

🏛 **Palazzo Comunale**
Via Città Nuova. 📞 0472-76 51 08.
🕐 Mon–Fri. ● public hols. 🎫 ♿
🏛 **Museo Multscher**
Via della Commenda. 🕐 May–Oct: Mon–Sat. ● public hols. ♿
Donation.

The medieval castle dominating the town of Brunico

Brunico ❹
BRUNECK

Bolzano. 🏘 *12,000.* FS 🚌 ℹ *Via Europa (0474-55 57 22).* 🚂 *Tue.*

THE ATTRACTIVE TOWN of Brunico, overlooked by the imposing form of its medieval **castle** (altered in the 15th and 16th centuries) retains 14th-century fortifications and a network of narrow streets that can only be explored on foot. The church of **St Ursula**, northwest of St Ursula's Gate, contains a series of outstanding mid 15th-century altar reliefs of the Nativity. In the **Museo Etnografico di Teodone**, the town's folklore museum, there are displays on traditional agricultural life and on local costumes; it also provides an opportunity to visit a 16th-century farmhouse and barn.

St Ursula's Gate sundial, Brunico

🏛 **Museo Etnografico di Teodone**
Via Duca Teodone 24. 📞 *0474-55 20 87.* ◯ *mid-Apr–Oct: Tue–Sat.* ● *public hols.* 🚫 🚻 *ground floor.*

Bressanone ❺
BRIXEN

Bolzano. 🏘 *17,000.* FS 🚌 ℹ *Viale Stazione 9 (0472-83 64 01).* 🚂 *Mon.*

THE NARROW MEDIEVAL alleys of Bressanone cluster around the cathedral and the palace of the prince-bishops who ruled the town for much of its history. The **Duomo**, on Piazza del Duomo, was rebuilt in the 18th century but retains its 12th-century cloister, decorated with superb 15th-century frescoes. The lavish interiors of Palazzo Vescovile, the bishops' Renaissance palace, house the **Museo Diocesano**. It contains precious items from the Middle Ages, as well as the **Museo dei Presepi**, with its collection of wooden crib figures that are carved locally.

ENVIRONS: At Velturno (Feldthurns), just 8 km (5 miles) southwest, stands the Renaissance **Castello di Velturno**, the summer retreat of the rulers of Bressanone noted for its frescoed rooms. A little over 3 km (2 miles) north of Bressanone lies the **Abbazia di Novacella**, a picturesque group of fortified monastic buildings with an outstanding series of cloister frescoes. Further north up the valley, at **Rio di Pusteria** (Mühlbach), the remains of a 16th-century fortified barrier can be seen to the east of the town. The barrier funnelled ancient travellers through the customs post that divided Tyrol from the Görz district.

High above Rio di Pusteria, to the southeast, looms the massive outline of the **Castello di Rodengo** (Rodeneck). The castle contains wonderful 13th-century frescoes showing battle scenes, the Last Judgment and courtly episodes from the *Iwein* romance by Hartmann von Aue, the medieval poet.

🏛 **Museo Diocesano**
Palazzo Vescovile, Piazza Hofburg. 📞 *0472-83 05 05.* ◯ *mid-Mar–Oct: Mon–Sat.* 🚫

🏛 **Museo dei Presepi**
Palazzo Vescovile, Piazza Hofburg. 📞 *0472-83 05 05.* ◯ *mid-Dec–mid-Feb & mid-Mar–Oct: daily.* ● *24, 25 Dec.* 🚫

♟ **Castello di Velturno**
Velturno. 📞 *0472-85 55 25.* ◯ *Mar–Nov: Tue–Sun.* 🚫 🚻 *ground floor.*

🏰 **Abbazia di Novacella**
Varna. 📞 *0472-83 61 89.* ◯ *Mon–Sat.* ● *public hols.* 🚫

♟ **Castello di Rodengo**
Rodengo. 📞 *0472-45 40 56.* ◯ *May–mid-Oct: Tue–Sun.* 🚫

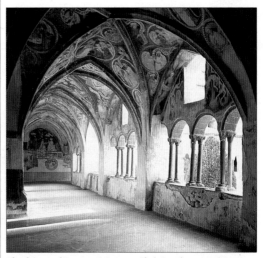

The cloisters of Bressanone Duomo with their 15th-century frescoes

The Baroque interior of the church of St Ulrich in Ortisei

Bolzano **6**
BOZEN

🏠 98,000. 🚉 🚌 ℹ️ *Piazza Walther 8 (0471-97 06 60).* 🚐 *Sat.*

B OLZANO, THE CAPITAL of the Alto Adige, is the gateway between the Italian-speaking Trentino region and the German-speaking Alto Adige or Südtirol, and has a marked Tyrolean atmosphere. The old centre, **Piazza Walther** at its core, is dominated by the Gothic **Duomo** (15th century), with its multicoloured roof of mosaic-patterned tiles, and its spire pierced by elaborate tracery. The importance of wine to the local economy – hills clothed in vineyards surround the town – is reflected in the "wine door" inside the Duomo, which is carved with many figures busily at work among vine tendrils.

The Duomo spire, Bolzano

In the middle of Piazza Walther stands a statue of Walther von der Vogelweide, the 13th-century troubadour – born, according to legend, in the Bolzano area. North of the square, the streets are lined with ornate houses adorned with intricate gables, balconies and oriel windows; traces of frescoes decorate their pastel-painted façades. The outdoor market starts at Piazza Grano, forming inviting arrays of local produce which continue along the arcaded Via dei Portici.

This street continues to the **Museo Civico**, where South Tyrolean history is introduced through domestic interiors, wood carvings and costumes. The **Chiesa dei Domenicani** (Dominican church), on Piazza Domenicani, has 14th-century *Triumph of Death* frescoes and a frescoed cloister.

🏛 Museo Civico
Via Cassa di Risparmio 14. 📞 *0471-97 46 25.* 🕐 *Tue – Sat.* ⬤ *public hols.* ♿ 📷

Ortisei **7**
SANKT ULRICH

Bolzano. 🏠 4,200. 🚌 ℹ️ *Via Rezia 1 (0471-79 63 28).* 🚐 *Fri.*

O RTISEI IS THE prosperous main resort for the pretty Val Gardena and Alpe di Siusi region, and a major centre for woodcarving; good examples

of local craftsmanship may be seen in shops throughout the town, in the **Museo della Val Gardena** (which also focuses on local archaeology), and in the church of **St Ulrich**.

To the south is the beautiful and popular **Alpe di Siusi** (Seiser Alm) region, noted for its Alpine meadows, balconied farmsteads and onion-domed churches. The best way to explore the area is by cableway from Ortisei: visitors can climb the 2,518-m (8,260-ft) high Monte Seceda, where a sign-posted 30-minute walk leads to the Odle group of Dolomites.

🏛 Museo della Val Gardena
Via Rezia 83. 📞 *0471-79 75 54.* 🕐 *Jul – Aug: daily; Feb – Apr, Jun, Sep & Oct: Tue – Fri pm.* ⬤ *1 Jan, Easter, 1 May, 25 Apr.* 📷

Canazei **8**

Trento. 🏠 1,700. 🚌 ℹ️ *Via Roma 34 (0462-611 13).* 🚐 *Sat.*

L OCATED AT THE BASE of some of the highest and most awe-inspiring groups of peaks, Canazei is a good base for exploring the Dolomites. In summer, chair-lifts climb to viewpoints where the beauty of the encircling mountains can be appreciated to the full. One of the most popular viewpoints is Belvedere I, reached by cableway from Via Pareda in Canazei itself: the cliffs of the Sella group are visible to the north, with Sasso Lungo

Skiers enjoying views of the Dolomites above Canazei

to the west and Marmolada, the highest of the Dolomitic peaks at 3,343 m (10,965 ft), rising to the south.

ENVIRONS: At **Vigo di Fassa**, 13 km (8 miles) southwest, the **Museo Ladino** focuses on the Ladin-speaking people of the Fassa valley. Though Ladin – a German-influenced Italian dialect – is no longer widely spoken, the ancient traditions (costumes, music) still thrive.

🏛 Museo Ladino
Frazione San Giovanni, Vigo di Fassa.
📞 0462-642 67. **●** for restoration.

Cavalese ❾

Trento. **🚶** 3,600. **🚌** **ℹ** Via Fratelli Bronzetti 60 (0462-24 11 11).
📅 last Tue of month.

The frescoed façade of the Palazzo della Magnifica Comunità

CAVALESE IS THE chief town in the Val di Fiemme, a pretty region of flower-filled pastures, wooded valleys and Tyrolean architecture. At the centre of the town stands the **Palazzo della Magnifica Comunità**. Originally built in the 13th century, this was the seat of the medieval governing council which ruled the area as a semi-autonomous region. Today the panelled interiors contain medieval paintings by local artists, and an archaeology collection. Most visitors come for the excellent summer and winter resort facilities, and to climb, by cable car, to the 2,229 m (7,311 ft) top of **Alpe Cermis**, the mountain that rises to the south of the town.

ENVIRONS: The church in **Tesero**, the next village east, bears a 15th-century fresco by an unknown painter depicting Sabbath-breakers. The church

Vines growing on the terraced slopes of the Cembra valley

itself, dating back to 1450, has a flurry of Gothic vaulting, and a modern representation of the Crucifixion painted against a background of the village.

At **Predazzo**, about 13 km (8 miles) east, the good **Museo Geologico e Mineralogico** explains the local geology.

🏛 Palazzo della Magnifica Comunità
Piazza Battisti 2. **📞** 0462-34 03 65.
◯ Easter, Jul–Aug & 23 Dec–6 Jan: daily pm. **●** 15 Aug, 25 Dec.
🏛 Museo Geologico e Mineralogico
Piazza Santi Filippo e Giacomo 2.
📞 0462-50 23 92. **◯** 20 Dec–6 Jan & mid-Jun–mid-Sep: Mon–Sat; Mar–mid-Jun & mid-Sep–Oct: Mon–Fri pm. **●** public hols.

San Martino di Castrozza ❿

Trento. **🚶** 600. **🚌** **ℹ** Via Passo Rolle 165 (0439-76 88 67).

THE RESORT OF San Martino occupies one of the most scenic and accessible valleys in the southern Dolomites, making it very popular with walkers and skiers. Chairlifts rise to the peak of **Alpe Tognola** (2,163 m, 7,095 ft), southwest of the town, and up the **Cima della Rosetta** (2,609 m, 8,557 ft) to the east. Both offer magnificent views of the Pale Group of Dolomitic peaks, a stirring sight as the massive rock peaks, split by glaciers, rise

Piramidi di Segonzano, near Cembra

above a sea of green meadows and woodland. San Martino is almost entirely surrounded by forest, which once supplied the Venetian Republic with timber for ships. The forest is now protected, and as a result this is one place where it is possible to see Alpine flowers, mushrooms, birds and other wildlife with relative ease.

Cembra ⓫

Trento. **🚶** 1,500. **🚌** **ℹ** Viale IV Novembre 3 (0461-68 31 10).
📅 Wed.

THE WINE-PRODUCING town of Cembra nestles on the terraced slopes of a scenic valley of flower-filled villages. Some 6 km (4 miles) east of Cembra stand the **Piramidi di Segonzano**, a rare series of erosion pillars, some over 30 m (100 ft) high, each topped by a rock. The footpath to the pillars is well signposted, with informative noticeboards along the way explaining the formation of the bizarre columns, which are similar in appearance to giant termites' nests. Their setting amid bird-filled woodland makes the steep climb up to the site well worthwhile. A further reward is the fine view, from the top of the hill, along the Cembra valley and westwards as far as the Brenta group of Dolomites.

📷 Piramidi di Segonzano
Strada Statale 612 to Cavalese.
📞 0461-68 31 10. **◯** daily. **♿**

The impressive falls of the Cascate di Nardis, Madonna di Campiglio

Madonna di Campiglio ⑫

Trento. 🚶 1,100. 🚌 ℹ️ *Via Pradalago 4 (0465-420 00).* 🗓️ *Jun–Sep: Tue & Thu.*

MADONNA DI CAMPIGLIO is the chief resort in the Val Meledrio. Nestling between the Brenta and Adamello groups of Dolomitic peaks, it makes the perfect base for walking or skiing amid the magnificent mountain terrain. Cableways radiate out from the town in every direction, giving easy access to the peaks.

ENVIRONS: The church at **Pinzolo**, 14 km (9 miles) south, has a well-preserved fresco depicting a *Dance of Death* (1539). The inevitable march of the figures, both rich and poor, is underlined by a text written in local dialect.

North of Pinzolo, the road west from Carisolo leads to the verdant and popular, yet unspoilt, **Val Genova**. About 4 km (2 miles) along the valley is the spectacular **Cascate di Nardis**, a waterfall that plunges down 90 m (300 ft). The two masses of rock at the bottom are said to be the forms of petrified demons.

Trento ⑬

🚶 105,000. 🚆 🚌 ℹ️ *Via Alfieri 4 (0461-98 38 80).* 🗓️ *Thu.*

TRENTO, THE CAPITAL of the region to which it gave its name, is also the most attractive town in Trentino: it has a fine Romanesque cathedral and a richly decorated castle, and streets lined with handsome Renaissance mansions. Trento is noted as the venue for the **Council of Trent** (1545–63), set up by the Catholic Church to consider reforms that might encourage breakaway groups, in particular the German Protestants, to return to the fold. The reforms, which ushered in the period of the Counter Reformation, were only partly successful.

The **Duomo**, site of some of the Council meetings, was built in robust Romanesque style from the 13th century. It was three centuries before it was completed, in 1515, but the builders maintained architectural harmony by ignoring Gothic and Renaissance styles entirely. The result is a church of unusual integrity, noble and assured. The Duomo stands on **Piazza Duomo**, the city's main square, which was first laid out by the Romans as their central market place or forum. Trento's Roman name, Tridentum, is commemorated in the figure of Neptune who stands holding his trident at the top of the 18th-century fountain, which stands in the middle of the main square.

🏛 Museo Diocesano Tridentino

Piazza Duomo 18. (0461-23 44 19. ◑ *Mon–Sat.* ● *public hols.* 🚫 &

This museum is housed in the **Palazzo Pretorio**, an imposing medieval building that stands on the eastern side of Piazza Duomo. Its contents include early ivory reliquaries, Flemish tapestries and paintings depicting the Council of Trent.

♠ Castello del Buonconsiglio

Via Bernardo Clesio. (0461-23 37 70. ◑ *Tue–Sun (Oct–Mar: Tue–Sat).* ● *1 Jan, 15 Aug, 25 Dec.* 🚫 &

This large castle, built in the 13th century and later enlarged

Inner courtyard of the Magno Palazzo

with additional buildings, is part of the defences of the town. Trento was an important frontier on the main road linking Italy to northern Europe, and thick walls still encircle the town.

The southern section of the castle consists of the magnificent **Magno Palazzo** (1530), built for the ruling prince-bishops of Trento, who were given extensive powers by the Holy Roman Emperor in order to foster loyalty and discourage defection to the pope. The lavish decoration (which includes frescoes of virile satyrs and nymphs by Gerolamo Romanino, 1531–2) speaks of massive wealth and a luxurious lifestyle. The fine rooms, now the setting for the **Museo Provinciale**, contain paintings, ceramics and 15th-century wood carvings, and prehistoric, Etruscan and Roman items. The **Torre dell'Aquila** (Eagle Tower) nearby contains frescoes painted around

Palazzo Pretorio and the Duomo in Trento's main square

The commanding form of the Campana dei Caduti in Rovereto

1400. They depict the Months of the Year in charming detail: the month of January, for instance, has some delightful snowballing scenes.

ENVIRONS: Immediately to the west of Trento a scenic round-trip along a winding road leads up the north flank of **Monte Bondone** and back, via **Vezzano,** down the western slopes. The views along the route are magnificent, in particular from Vaneze and Vason. East of Trento, Pergine marks the start of the **Val Sugana**, a broad valley with attractive and popular lakes. In the hills north of Lake Levico lies the spa town of **Levico Terme**, distinguished by elegant Neo-Classical buildings set amid beautifully wooded parkland.

Rovereto ⓮

Trento. 🏔 *33,000.* 🚌 🚍 🚹 *Via Dante 63 (0464-43 03 63).* 🚙 *Tue.*

ROVERETO WAS at the centre of fierce fighting during World War I, after which the Venetian castle (built in 1416) that dominates the town was transformed into the **Museo Storico della Guerra**, a war museum covering all periods of history. The displays include several highlights, among them sections devoted to war-time humour, spying and propaganda. Contemporary photographs tell the story of this century's two world wars in harrowing detail. Near the entrance to the museum, stairs lead out onto the castle roof for a view of the town's war

memorial – the **Campana dei Caduti** (Bell of the Fallen). One of the largest bells in Italy, it was cast from melted-down cannons at the end of World War II and then mounted in an imposing temple-like building above the town; it is rung daily at sunset. From the memorial there are extensive views over the valley. Below the war museum stands the **Museo Civico**, housing collections on archaeology, art, natural history and folklore.

ENVIRONS: A little over 8 km (5 miles) north of Rovereto is the prominent landmark of **Castel Beseno**, rising on a hill to the east. This enormous castle, by far the largest in the region, was built and rebuilt from the 12th century to the 18th to guard the junction of the three valleys. The ruins are undergoing restoration: 16th-century frescoes may be seen.

To the south of Rovereto, the main road passes through a valley littered with massive house-sized boulders created by landslips; these are known as the **Ruina Dantesca**, because they are mentioned in Dante's *Inferno* (XII, 4–9).

🏛 **Museo Storico della Guerra**
Via Castelbarco 7. 📞 *0464-43 81 00.* 🕐 *Apr–Jul & Sep–Nov: Tue–Sun.* 🖼

🏛 **Museo Civico**
Borgo Santa Caterina. 📞 *0464-43 90 55.* 🕐 *Tue–Sat.* 🖼

🏰 **Castel Beseno**
Besenello. 📞 *0464-23 37 70.* 🕐 *Apr–Oct: Tue–Sun.* 🖼 🖼

Castello di Avio ⓯

Via Castello, Sabbionara d'Avio. 📞 *0464-68 44 53.* 🚍 🚌 *to Vo, then 2 km (1 mile) walk.* 🕐 *Feb–Sep: 10am–1pm, 2–6pm Tue–Sun; Oct–Nov: 10am–1pm, 2–5pm Tue–Sun.* 🖼

Castello di Avio in its lush setting

CASTLES LINE THE Adige valley all the way to the Brenner Pass, but few are as accessible as the Castello di Avio, southwest of Ala. It was founded in the 11th century but considerably extended in the 13th, and now clings to the flank of the valley, offering far-reaching views. The castle is being restored but remains open so that visitors can watch the work in progress. Among the numerous frescoes with secular themes is a rare series in the Casa delle Guardie (the Sentry House) depicting 13th-century battle scenes.

The extensive walls enclosing Castel Beseno above Rovereto

NORTHWEST ITALY

Northwest Italy at a Glance

THE NORTHWEST OF ITALY is made up of three very different geological characteristics: the jagged Alps, the flat plain, and the undulating shoreline of the Mediterranean. Within this varied landscape, some of it still wild and unspoilt, lie extremely rich and diverse vestiges of the area's substantial cultural heritage. The major sights, in the regions of Valle d'Aosta and Piedmont, Liguria and Lombardy, are shown on this map.

Valle d'Aosta

Parco Nazionale del Gran Paradiso

Basilica di Sant'Andrea, Vercelli

Mole Antonelliana, Turin

VALLE D'AOSTA AND PIEDMONT
(See pp202–21)

Piedmont

LIGURIA
(See pp222–3)

The Parco Nazionale del Gran Paradiso *is a beautiful wilderness, and the habitat of rare Alpine fauna and flora (see pp208–9).*

The capital of Piedmont *is Turin, an elegant and bustling city of splendid Baroque architecture. Its skyline is dramatically dominated by the Mole Antonelliana (see p216).*

San Remo *is a typical Riviera resort, with palm trees and a casino. The onion-domed outline of the Russian church adds an exotic flavour to the town (see p226).*

The casino, San Remo

The Basilica di Sant'Andrea *in Vercelli is an important Romanesque building, one of the earliest to use Gothic elements (see p220).*

◁ **Typical shuttered Ligurian façades in Santa Margherita Ligure**

LOMBARDY
(See pp180–201)

a, Lake
iore

Duomo, Milan

Certosa di
Pavia

Isola Bella *is an enchanting island on romantic Lake Maggiore. Nearby lies beautiful Lake Como (see pp184–5).*

Milan's Duomo, *with its distinctive bristling spires, is one of the many architectural gems in this stylish city (see pp187).*

Portofino

Portofino *is one of Italy's most exclusive resorts. Nestling in a creek, its pretty pastel-coloured houses surround a yacht-filled harbour (see p233).*

The Certosa di Pavia, *a charming Carthusian monastery, includes a richly decorated Gothic church with a magnificent Renaissance façade, and a series of attractive cloisters (see pp196–7).*

0 kilometres   50

0 miles   25

Regional Food: Northwest Italy

RICHNESS AND HEARTINESS characterize the food of northwest Italy, an area dominated by the presence of the Alps. Here, unlike in the rest of Italy, butter is used in cooking as much as oil. The area is the home of rice growing in Italy, and risotto naturally features prominently on local menus, complementing the ubiquitous pasta dishes. Cheeses are also a speciality, as are truffles – which grow in the clay soil of Piedmont –

Grissini

and nuts of all types. Garlic, saffron, basil and wine are other favourite ingredients in the aromatic sauces. Grissini, the crisp breadsticks found on every restaurant table, originate in Turin.

Onion and Herb Focaccia is made from dough enriched with olive oil; it may also be baked plain, or with olives or tomato.

Bresaola, wafer-thin slices of cured raw beef, is served as an antipasto with olive oil and a squeeze of lemon.

Farinata is a flat bread made of oil and chickpea flour. It is relatively thin, similar to a pancake and eaten as a snack.

Green peppers

Orange peppers

Red peppers

Bagna Cauda

Spring onions

Celery

Yellow peppers

Bagna Cauda is an anchovy-based dip flavoured with garlic, olive oil, butter and sometimes truffles. It is served hot, usually over a warming stove, and eaten with sliced raw vegetables which are dipped into it. It is a speciality of Piedmont.

Risotto alla Milanese is a rich and delicious Milanese dish of rice, white wine, onion, saffron and grated Parmesan cheese.

Trenette al Pesto, a Genoese speciality, consists of noodles with a sauce of basil, garlic, pine nuts, Parmesan and oil.

Pansôti with Walnut Sauce is Ligurian, spinach-and-egg filled pasta, with a sauce of nuts, garlic, herbs, ricotta cheese and olive oil.

Manzo al Barolo *is a Piedmont dish of lean beef marinated in red wine and garlic, then stewed gently for extra tenderness.*

***Cacciucco**, found on Ligurian menus, is a rich stew of mixed fish and seafood cooked with wine, garlic and herbs.*

Costolette alla Milanese *are veal cutlets dipped in egg and breadcrumbs, fried in butter and served with lemon.*

Ossobuco *is shin of veal with marrow bone in a tomato and wine sauce, with a hint of garlic, anchovy and lemon.*

Fagiano Tartufato *– stuffed pheasant – is filled with white truffles and pork fat; it is then wrapped in bacon and roasted.*

Spezzatino di Pollo *is a chicken quarter cooked with tomato sauce containing wine and, sometimes, truffles.*

CHEESE

The lush Alpine meadows in the northwest help to produce some of the finest cheeses in Italy. They include the blue-veined yet mild Gorgonzola; the delicate Mascarpone, a cream cheese much used in desserts; and Taleggio, a soft, creamy cheese to be eaten young, all from Lombardy. Fontina, a semi-hard cheese made in the Valle d'Aosta, has a nutty, slightly sweet taste.

Fontina   Taleggio

Gorgonzola

Spinaci alla Piemontese, *a side order, is a blend of spinach, anchovies, butter and garlic, with croutons.*

Amaretti *are light and delicious macaroon-type biscuits, usually taken with coffee, made from almonds and egg whites. They are often wrapped in pretty coloured paper.*

Torta di Nocciole, *a Piedmontese nut tart, includes hazelnuts, eggs and butter among its ingredients.*

Zabaglione *is a frothy concoction of egg, sugar and Marsala wine, accompanied by sponge fingers. It is served hot or cold.*

Panettone *from Milan is a light yeast cake which contains candied fruit. It is traditionally eaten at Easter and Christmas.*

The Wines of Northwest Italy

Medieval illustration of a grape crusher

Grapes are grown throughout the northwest – from the cliffs of Liguria to the steep mountainsides of Valle d'Aosta. The best wines, however, come from Piedmont, in particular the Langhe hills southwest of Turin, source of two of Italy's finest reds: the rich, powerful, long-lived Barolo and Barbaresco. Both of these are now showing the benefits of modern techniques and a renewed interest in high-quality wine making. Lighter, everyday red wines that go well with the local cuisine include Dolcetto and the popular Barbera. Another Piedmont speciality is sparkling *spumante*, Italians' instinctive choice whenever there is something around to celebrate.

Castiglione Falletto in the heart of Piedn

Barbera d'Alba *comes from the adaptable Barbera grape, which can grow on almost any slope. Its ubiquitous nature means that the wines it yields can be light and full of fruit, as well as dense, strong and full-flavoured. Good producers include Aldo Conterno, Voerzio, Pio Cesare, Altare, Gaja, Vajra and Vietti.*

Dolcetto *is grown in seven different areas. Dolcetto d'Alba has a delicious perfume and deep purple colour. Best drunk within two years, it ranges in flavour from fresh and fruity to the rich, concentrated plumminess of some of the top wines, such as those produced by Giuseppe Mascarello.*

Barolo, *prized the world over for its complex array of flavours and firm tannins, is made from the Nebbiolo grape and may take up to 20 years to mature. Vigna Colonnello is a top Barolo from Aldo Conterno, made only in the best years like 1993, 1990 and 1989.*

PIEDMONT

MONFERRATO

LANG

- Turin
- Chieri
- Canale
- Bart
- Al
- Bra
- Saluzzo
- Barolo
- Cast
- Falle
- Dogliani
- Cuneo
- Mondovi

KEY

☐ Barolo

☐ Barbaresco

☐ Other vineyard areas

0 kilometres   25

0 miles   15

The white truffle of Alba is an autumn speciality from the Langhe hills. Highly prized for its earthy scent, it is excellent with Barolo.

Moscato d'Asti is an excellent aperitivo or light dessert wine made from the aromatic, fruity Moscato grape. It is light in alcohol with a gently sweet finish and may have a slight sparkle. Ideal for refreshing the palate after a hearty Piedmontese meal, Araldica's versatile Moscato is delicious when served well chilled.

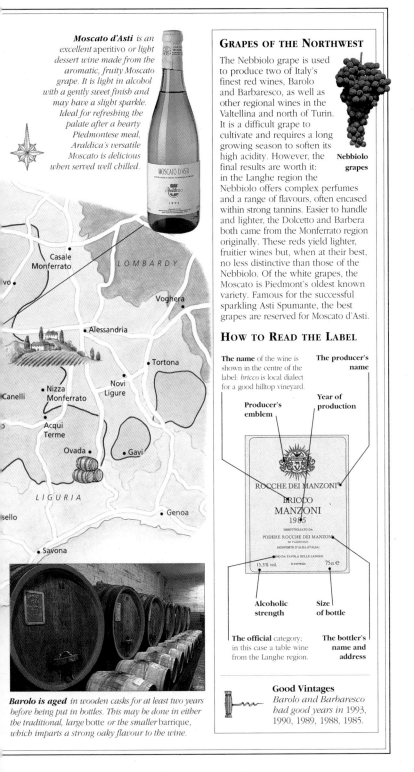

GRAPES OF THE NORTHWEST

The Nebbiolo grape is used to produce two of Italy's finest red wines, Barolo and Barbaresco, as well as other regional wines in the Valtellina and north of Turin. It is a difficult grape to cultivate and requires a long growing season to soften its high acidity. However, the final results are worth it: **Nebbiolo grapes** in the Langhe region the Nebbiolo offers complex perfumes and a range of flavours, often encased within strong tannins. Easier to handle and lighter, the Dolcetto and Barbera both came from the Monferrato region originally. These reds yield lighter, fruitier wines but, when at their best, no less distinctive than those of the Nebbiolo. Of the white grapes, the Moscato is Piedmont's oldest known variety. Famous for the successful sparkling Asti Spumante, the best grapes are reserved for Moscato d'Asti.

HOW TO READ THE LABEL

The name of the wine is shown in the centre of the label: *bricco* is local dialect for a good hilltop vineyard.

The producer's name

Producer's emblem

Year of production

ROCCHE DEI MANZONI
BRICCO
MANZONI
1985

IMBOTTIGLIATO DA
PODERE ROCCHE DEI MANZONI
IN VALENTINO
MONFORTE D'ALBA (ITALIA)
VINO DA TAVOLA DELLE LANGHE

13,5% vol.   R 84798CN   75 cl ℮

Alcoholic strength

Size of bottle

The official category; in this case a table wine from the Langhe region.

The bottler's name and address

Good Vintages
Barolo and Barbaresco had good years in 1993, 1990, 1989, 1988, 1985.

Barolo is aged in wooden casks for at least two years before being put in bottles. This may be done in either the traditional, large botte or the smaller barrique, which imparts a strong oaky flavour to the wine.

Understanding Architecture in Northwest Italy

ALTHOUGH THE BUILDINGS of the northwest tend to be solid and imposing – a result partly of the more severe climate – there is no distinctive architectural stamp as there is around Venice, Florence or even in Rome. Instead, a variety of buildings in different styles, many borrowed or reinterpreted from elsewhere, are dotted across the area: enchanting medieval castles, outstanding Romanesque and Gothic buildings, unusual Baroque structures. The northwest is also rich in modern architecture – in terms of both design and materials – influenced by the region's industrial developments and its strong flair for innovative design, which also often draws its inspiration from earlier architectural styles.

Castello Sforzesco, 1451–66 *(see p186)*

CHARACTERISTICS OF NORTHWEST ITALIAN ARCHITECTURE

Double row of defensive walls

Wooden balcony

Few windows

Massive square tower

Pointed turret

Battlements

Castello di Fénis, one of the finest castles in the Valle d'Aosta, is a 14th-century fortress with asymmetrical towers, turrets and crenellated walls. Frescoes adorn the interior (see p207).

Alternating bands of marble

Rose window

Lions support columns and porch above

Elaborate carving

Rose window

Octagonal drum influenced by the Duomo in Florence

Highly ornate façade

Patterned marble design

Cappella Colleoni, Bergamo (1476), mixes Renaissance elements with rich decoration in the Gothic manner (see p193).

Monza's Duomo (1390s) typifies the Lombard style of Romanesque architecture with its marble stripes and ornate carving (see p193).

Massive scale

Ornate window surrounds

Rotunda

Balcony

Curved brickwork

Palazzo Carignano is perhaps the finest product of Turin's idiosyncratic Baroque school. Guarini's masterpiece (1679) boasts an extraordinary undulating brick façade and a fine rotunda (see p215).

WHERE TO SEE THE ARCHITECTURE

The road to Aosta is flanked by numerous medieval castles *(see p206)* while inspirational Romanesque and Gothic churches are found in Lombardy – at Monza *(p193)*, Pavia *(p195)*, Milan *(pp186–193)*, and Como *(pp184–5)*. The 15th-century Certosa di Pavia *(pp196–7)* is a must, as well as the charming city of Mantova *(p199)*. Turin *(pp212–16)* is famous for its unique Baroque school, and Bergamo for its exuberance. Architecture from the last two centuries is best represented in Milan and Turin, and in Genoa some exciting new redevelopment projects are taking place.

Renzo Piano's mast structure (1992) in Genoa's redeveloped port

19TH–20TH CENTURY ARCHITECTURE

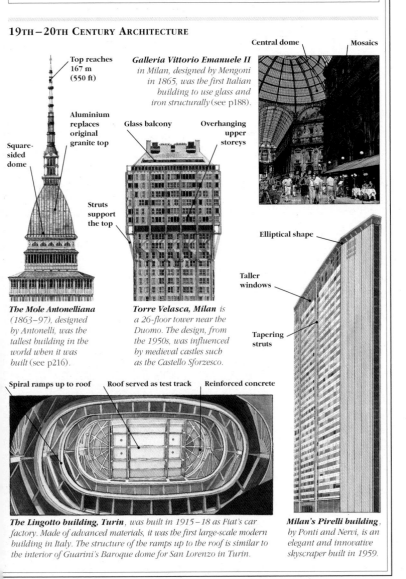

Top reaches 167 m (550 ft)

Aluminium replaces original granite top

Square-sided dome

Struts support the top

The Mole Antonelliana (1863–97), designed by Antonelli, was the tallest building in the world when it was built (see p216).

Galleria Vittorio Emanuele II in Milan, designed by Mengoni in 1865, was the first Italian building to use glass and iron structurally (see p188).

Glass balcony

Overhanging upper storeys

Torre Velasca, Milan is a 26-floor tower near the Duomo. The design, from the 1950s, was influenced by medieval castles such as the Castello Sforzesco.

Central dome

Mosaics

Elliptical shape

Taller windows

Tapering struts

Spiral ramps up to roof Roof served as test track Reinforced concrete

The Lingotto building, Turin, was built in 1915–18 as Fiat's car factory. Made of advanced materials, it was the first large-scale modern building in Italy. The structure of the ramps up to the roof is similar to the interior of Guarini's Baroque dome for San Lorenzo in Turin.

Milan's Pirelli building, by Ponti and Nervi, is an elegant and innovative skyscraper built in 1959.

LOMBARDY

THE REGION OF LOMBARDY *stretches from the Alps, on the border with Switzerland, down through the romantic lakes of Como and Maggiore to the broad, flat plain of the River Po. It is an area of lakeside villas with azalea-filled gardens, of wealthy towns with imposing palazzi and highly decorated churches, and of efficient, modern industry and large-scale agriculture, the financial heart of Italy. At its centre stands Milan, the style-conscious capital of Lombardy.*

The region was named after the Lombards or Longobards, a barbarian tribe that invaded Italy in the 6th century AD. During the Middle Ages, Lombardy was part of the Holy Roman Empire, but not always loyal to its German emperors. The canny Lombards, who had developed a profitable talent for banking and commerce, resented any outside interference with their cosy prosperity.

The 12th century saw the rise of the Lega Lombarda, or Lombard League, a band of forceful separatists founded to counter the brutal imperialism of Frederick Barbarossa (their modern incarnation is the Lega Nord political party). Power was then seized by the region's great families, most notably the Visconti and the Sforza of Milan.

These dynasties also became great patrons of the arts, commissioning exquisite palaces, churches and artworks, many of which can still be seen. Bergamo, Mantova and Cremona – not to mention Milan itself – contain a remarkably rich array of art treasures. Here are such pinnacles of European civilization as the charterhouse at Pavia, Leonardo da Vinci's *Last Supper* and the magnificent paintings of the Pinacoteca di Brera in Milan.

Lombardy – famous as the birthplace of Virgil, Monteverdi, Stradivarius and Donizetti – today offers visitors the contrasting pleasures of lyrical lakeside landscapes (resorts on lakes Como and Maggiore have attracted poets, aristocrats and gamblers for centuries) and beautiful, bustling cities.

Strolling through Milan's enormous Galleria Vittorio Emanuele II

◁ **The peaceful shores of the beautiful Lake Como, southwest of Bellagio**

Exploring Lombardy

THE ENORMOUS PLAIN of the River Po runs through much of Lombardy, providing a landscape that is flat and perfectly suited to the consequent expansion of industry in the region. This is, however, also a region of great contrasts. To the north, in a still unspoilt setting in the foothills of the mountains, lie the dreamy lakes Como and Maggiore, as well as the dramatic valleys and peaks of the Parco Nazionale dello Stelvio around Bormio and Sondrio. Further south, busy industrialized areas give way to huge tracts of agriculture dotted with towns of great beauty such as Cremona, Mantova and Pavia, which offer a rich and splendid array of cerebral pleasures.

SIGHTS AT A GLANCE

Bergamo **5**
Brescia **9**
Certosa di Pavia
  pp196–7 **12**
Cremona **13**
Lago d'Iseo **8**
Lake Como **1**
Lake Maggiore **2**
Lodi **10**
Mantova **15**
Milan (Milano)
  pp186–93 **3**
Monza **4**
Parco Nazionale dello
  Stelvio **6**
Pavia **11**
Sabbioneta **14**
Val Camonica **7**

SEE ALSO

- **Where to Stay** pp549–51

- **Where to Eat** pp584–6

Passo di Gavia in the Parco Nazionale dello
Stelvio on the eastern fringes of Lombardy

0 kilometres   25

0 miles   20

A view of Isola Bella on Lake Maggiore

The colourful façade of the Cappella Colleoni in Bergamo

KEY

▬▬	Motorway
▬▬	Major road
▬▬	Minor road
▬▬	Scenic route
≈	River
☆	Viewpoint

GETTING AROUND

Milan has two international airports, which are obvious gateways into northern Italy, and the vast and flat Lombard plain has its advantages when it comes to transport: roads and railway lines criss-cross it and make trips between the larger towns very easy. The lakes, however, are better visited by car, as only two main towns are served by trains, though there are bus and boat services around the shores. The Parco Nazionale dello Stelvio and the mountains are more remote still, but offer good tourist facilities.

Lake Como ❶

SET IN AN IDYLLIC LANDSCAPE of mountains and rugged hillsides, and shrouded in an almost eerie calm, Lake Como has for centuries attracted visitors who come here for relaxation, inspiration, walks in the hills or to go boating. The long and narrow lake, crafted into a wishbone shape by glacial erosion, offers fine views up to the Alps and down to the prosperous towns of Como and Lecco.

The northern stretches are wilder and less populated than the southern part, offering visitors great tranquillity.

View of the lake near Como

Menaggio is one of a string of popular resorts lining the west bank.

Varenna, a ferry port, is overlooked by a ruined 11th-century castle. At Fiumelatte, just south, there is a foaming stream, the "river of milk".

Villa Carlotta nestles among lush gardens with lovely views.

Cernobbio was a favourite resort of the exiled Queen Caroline of England in the early 19th century.

Domaso
Gravedona
Cólico

Dervio

Menaggio
Varenna
Griante
Fiumelatte
Tremezzo
Bellagio
Mezzegra

Onno

Cernobbio
Como

Lecco

N36 · N340d · N340 · N583

Bellagio
This delightful resort on the cusp of the lake's two arms has elegant lakeside promenades and cafés.

The southeastern arm of the lake is also called the Lago di Lecco.

Lecco, home to the 19th-century novelist, Manzoni.

The scenic route just south of Bellagio climbs a hill to offer far-reaching lake views.

| 0 kilometres | 15 |
| 0 miles | 10 |

Como
The town, which gave its name to the lake, boasts a fine Duomo in mixed Gothic and Renaissance styles, with carvings on its façade.

KEY

•••	Car ferry route
•••	Ferry route
🔱	Sailing and boating centre
🛈	Tourist information
▰	Motorway
▬	Major road
▭	Minor road
☀	Viewpoint

Tadoline's copy (1834) of Canova's
Cupid and Psyche in Villa Carlotta

Exploring Lake Como

In the heart of **Como** lies the
elegant Piazza Cavour. Nearby
rises the beautiful 14th-century
Duomo, with its 15th- and
16th-century reliefs and paintings, and fine tombs. The
18th-century dome is by
Turin's famous Baroque
architect, Juvarra. Next to the
Duomo stand the 13th-century
Broletto (town hall), charmingly striped in white, pink
and grey, and the tall Torre del
Comune. **Villa Carlotta** is an
elegant 18th-century summer-
house, known for its gardens.
In springtime, rhododendrons,
camellias and azaleas burst
into colour in this pretty
setting. Inside, the villa houses
a collection of sculptures.

Lecco, a small industrial
town lying to the south of the
lake's eastern arm, was the
birthplace of Liberal Catholic
writer Alessandro Manzoni
(1785–1873). The author's
childhood home, the **Casa
Natale di Manzoni** is devoted
to memorabilia of his life and
works. In Piazza Manzoni, a
monument depicts scenes
from his most famous novel, *I
Promessi Sposi (The Betrothed)*
– set partly in 17th-century
Lecco as well as Milan.

🏛 **Villa Carlotta**
Tremezzo, Como. [C] *0344-404 05.*
[clock] *daily.* ● *Nov–mid-Mar.* [icons]
🏛 **Casa Natale di Manzoni**
Largo Caleotto, Lecco. [C] *0341-48
14 47.* [clock] *Tue–Sun.* ● *1 Jan, Easter,
1 May, 15 Aug, 25 Dec.* [icons]

Lake Maggiore ➋

Verbania. [FS] [bus] [boat] *Stresa, Verbania,
Baveno & the islands.* [i] *Via Principe
Tommaso 70/72, Stresa (0323-304 16).*

LAKE MAGGIORE is a long
expanse of water that
nestles right up against the
mountains and stretches away
into Alpine Switzerland; it is
warmer in atmosphere and
more unashamedly romantic
than Lake Como. The gently
sloping shores are dotted with
verbena vegetation – from
which the ancient lake
derived its Roman
name, Verbanus – as
well as camellias and
azaleas. In the centre
lie the delightful
Borromean islands,
mini-paradises named
after the chief patron
of the lake, Cardinal
Carlo Borromeo.

A huge copper
statue of the cardinal
stands in **Arona**, the
town where he was
born in 1538. It is
possible to climb up
and look out over the
lake through his eye
sockets and ear holes.
Arona also boasts a
ruined castle and a
chapel, Santa Maria,
that was dedicated to
the famous Borromeo family.

Further up the western coast
of the lake is **Stresa**, the chief
resort and main jumping-off
point for visits to the islands;
the town is full of villas and
verdant gardens, where many
visitors take a stroll. Behind
Stresa, a cable car ride away,
rises Monte Mottarone, a
snow-capped peak offering

The statue of Carlo
Borromeo in Arona

spectacular panoramic views
of the surrounding mountains,
including Monte Rosa.

The **Borromean islands**,
lying at the centre of the lake
near Stresa, are small jewels
of natural beauty augmented
by artificial grottoes, architectural follies and landscaped
parks. The **Isola Bella** is
home to the 17th-century
Palazzo Borromeo and its
splendid garden of landscaped
terraces, fountains, peacocks,
statues and grottoes. Isola
Madre is largely given over to
a botanical garden.
San Giovanni is the
most exclusive and
smallest of the isles,
with a villa which
once belonged to
the conductor
Arturo Toscanini
(1867–1957).

The lake becomes
quieter towards the
Swiss border, but
continues to be
lined with attractive
villas. The **Villa
Taranto**, on the
outskirts of Ver-
bania, houses an
exotic botanical
collection.

About 3 km (2
miles) west of
Cannobio, a market
town near Switzer-
land, is the dramatic gorge
and tumbling waterfall of the
Orrido di Sant'Anna, which
can be reached by boat.

🏛 **Palazzo Borromeo**
Isola Bella. [boat] *from Stresa.* [C] *0323-
305 56.* [clock] *Apr–Sep: daily.* [icon]
🏛 **Villa Taranto**
Via Vittorio Veneto, Verbania. [C] *0323-
55 66 67.* [clock] *Apr–Oct: daily.* [icons]

Isola Bella's 17th-century Palazzo Borromeo and garden on Lake Maggiore

Milan ❸

CENTRE OF FASHION, business and – in recent years – political scandal, Milan has a bustling, businesslike feel about it. It is smart rather than attractive, a city of wealth as opposed to imagination, the heartland of the Italian economy. To the Goths who took it over from the Romans it was "Mailand", the land of May, a place of warmth and inspiration. It has long been an important trading centre at the junction of transalpine routes, and a prize for powerful dynasties. Today, it is the place to see Italy at its most stylish.

Detail from the Duomo

♣ Castello Sforzesco
Piazza Castello. **☎** 02-62 08 39 46. ◯ Tue–Sun. 🔒 public hols. 🖼 ♿
The first castle on this site was built by the Visconti family, but demolished when their reign ended in the mid-15th century. Milan's new ruler, Francesco Sforza, built in its place this Renaissance palace, which combines a forbidding exterior with a delightful interior. The castle is based on a series of courtyards, the most beautiful of which, the Cortile della Rocchetta, is a graceful arcaded square designed by Bramante and Filarete. The palace now contains, together with sections on Applied Arts, Archaeology and Coins, the **Civiche Raccolte d'Arte Antica**. This fine collection of furniture, antiquities and paintings includes Michelangelo's unfinished sculpture, known as the

Michelangelo's *Rondanini Pietà* (c.1564) in the Castello Sforzesco

Rondanini Pietà. The canvases in the picture collection, dating from the Renaissance to the 18th century, are particularly impressive. The Cappella Ducale contains Gothic frescoes by an unknown artist.

🏛 Museo Poldi-Pezzoli
Via Alessandro Manzoni 12. **☎** 02-79 48 89. ◯ Tue–Sat. 🖼
Giacomo Poldi-Pezzoli was a wealthy nobleman who, on his death in 1879, bequeathed his magnificent art collection to the state. Its most famous painting is the 15th-century Renaissance *Portrait of a Young Woman* by Antonio Pollaiuolo, though there are also works by Piero della Francesca, Botticelli and Mantegna, among others. The applied arts section is richly endowed with fascinating items ranging from rugs and lace to glass, enamels and porcelain, as well as sculpture, jewellery and sundials, displayed in fine settings.

***Portrait of a Young Woman* by Pollaiuolo, Museo Poldi-Pezzoli**

SIGHTS AT A GLANCE

```
0 metres        500
0 yards         500
```

KEY

M	Underground station
🚌	Bus terminus
P	Parking
ℹ	Tourist information
✚	Church

🎭 Teatro alla Scala

Piazza della Scala. 📞 02-86 18 31 44. 🎭 **Museo Teatrale** 📞 02-805 34 18. 🕐 Mon–Sat. 📷

The Neo-Classical opera house, known popularly as La Scala, opened in 1778 and is one of the most prestigious opera houses in the world. With the largest stage in Europe, it hosts sumptuous and magnificent productions, featuring the greatest singers.

The façade of the world-famous Teatro alla Scala

VISITORS' CHECKLIST

🚶 1,465,000. ✈ Malpensa 55 km (34 miles) NW; Linate 8 km (5 miles) E. 🚉 Stazione Centrale, Piazza Duca d'Aosta. 🚌 Piazza Castello. 🛈 Via Marconi 1 (02-80 96 62); Stazione Centrale (02- 669 05 32). 🛒 daily, major market on Sat. 🎉 7 Dec: Sant'Ambrogio.

🏛 Duomo

Piazza del Duomo. 📞 02-86 46 34 56. 📷 for roof. ♿

Situated at the very heart of Milan is its giant cathedral, one of the largest Gothic churches in the world at 157 m (514 ft) long and, at its widest point, 92 m (301 ft) across. It was begun in the 14th century under Prince Gian Galeazzo Visconti but not completed until more than 500 years later.

The building's most startling feature is the extraordinary roof, with its 135 spires and innumerable statues and gargoyles; and from which, on a clear day, there are far-reaching views to the Alps.

Below, the façade incorporates a dazzling assortment of styles from Gothic through to Renaissance and Neo-Classical. The bronze doors are faced with bas reliefs recounting episodes from the life of the Virgin, the life of Sant' Ambrogio, and scenes retelling the history of Milan. Note, around the apse, the delicate Gothic tracery of the windows.

Inside, the aisles are divided by giant pillars and lit from all sides by remarkable stained glass. Look out for the Visconti family symbol – a serpent swallowing a man – in the fine tracery of the apse windows. Among the many tombs and statues is a depiction of San Bartolomeo Flayed, carrying his skin.

The treasury, lying beneath the main altar, contains much medieval gold and silver-work. In addition, excavations have revealed remains of the original 4th-century baptistry.

Tickets to performances are usually sold out months in advance, but you can visit the adjoining **Museo Teatrale** to admire sets and costumes of past productions, portraits of conductors and theatrical items dating back to Roman times. There is also a good view of the auditorium, with its *trompe l'oeil* effects, gilded box galleries and its enormous chandelier.

The Gothic Duomo, crowned with spires

Exploring Milan

IN ADDITION TO THE GREAT MONUMENTS in Milan, such as the cathedral and the castle, there is a host of varied and interesting museums, churches and civic buildings which provide an enthralling mix of old and new. This chic and busy metropolis offers plenty of opportunities for cultural activities, gastronomic adventures, designer-fashion shopping or just strolling about, Milan-style.

The glass ceiling and dome covering the Galleria Vittorio Emanuele II

⚜ Galleria Vittorio Emanuele II

Main entrances on Piazza del Duomo and Piazza della Scala.

This ornate shopping arcade, known as *Il Salotto di Milano* (Milan's drawing room), was designed by the architect Giuseppe Mengoni in 1865. The galleria had a tragic start, however, as Mengoni fell to his death from the roof not long before its inauguration in 1877 (a year before the arcade was actually finished). The city's glitterati are nevertheless attracted to its stylish shops, cafés and restaurants, which include Il Salotto, said to serve the finest coffee in all Milan, and the elegant Savini, which is one of the city's most prestigious restaurants.

The galleria itself has a floor plan in the shape of a Latin cross, with an octagonal centre adorned with mosaics representing four continents (Europe, America, Africa and Asia), together with others representing Art, Agriculture, Science and Industry. Its finest feature is its metal and glass roof, crowned with a magnificent central dome. The roof was the first structure in Italy to use metal and glass in a structural way, rather than just decoratively. The floors are decorated with mosaics of the signs of the zodiac; locals may be seen stepping on the genitals of Taurus the Bull, in order to bring good luck.

🏛 Museo del Duomo

Palazzo Reale, Piazza del Duomo 14.
📞 02-86 03 58. ☐ *Tue – Sun.*
⬤ *25 Dec.* ▨

The museum lies south of the Duomo in the Palazzo Reale (Royal Palace), for centuries home to the Visconti and other families that ruled Milan. It charts the complicated history of the Duomo from its origins in the 14th century (and the pre-existing church on its site) until the 1886 competition held to redesign its façade.

Among the exhibits there are interesting 16th- and 17th-century wooden models of the cathedral, and many of the original medieval sculptures – including figures thought to be Gian Galeazzo Visconti and Galeazzo Maria Sforza. There are in addition stained glass windows, paintings, tapestries and a pair of very elaborately carved choir stalls. Another section has displays focusing on some of the 20th-century amendments to the cathedral.

🏛 Civico Museo d'Arte Contemporanea

Palazzo Reale, Piazza del Duomo 12.
📞 02-62 08 39 43. ☐ *Tue – Sun.*
⬤ *Easter.* ♿

The Museum of Contemporary Art (or CIMAC), housed on the second floor of the Palazzo Reale, is a refreshingly up-to-date gallery. It opened in 1984 and is still in the process of expanding, but the emphasis is heavily on Italian works: from the 19th century to pieces by members of the Futurist movement (Umberto Boccioni in particular), from abstract art to the more diverse productions of the present day. Look out for works by Carlo Carrà (1881–1966), Filippo De Pisis (1896–1956), Giorgio Morandi (1890–1964) and Tancredi, as well as those by more familiar artists such as Modigliani (1884–1920) and De Chirico (1888–1978).

Still Life (1920) by Giorgio Morandi in the Museo d'Arte Contemporanea

Among the non-Italian artists are Post-Impressionists (Van Gogh, Cézanne, Gauguin), Picasso – a bequest of 30 etchings – and Matisse, Klee, Mondrian and Kandinsky.

🏛 Pinacoteca Ambrosiana

2 Piazza Pio XI. 📞 02-86 45 14 36. 🔴 for restoration until April 1996.

The Ambrosiana is home to the magnificent library of Cardinal Federico Borromeo, whose 30,000 manuscripts survive to this day. Come to admire the 5th-century illustrated *Iliad*, early editions of Dante's *Divine Comedy* (1353) and Leonardo's *Atlantic Codex* (15th century).

The building also houses an interesting art gallery, originally bequeathed by Borromeo on his death in 1618. The collection of paintings and sculpture attests to the cardinal's broad-ranging if slightly quirky taste, and now ranges from 14th-century pieces to works of the early 19th century. Among the canvases are the *Portrait of a Musician* attributed to Leonardo da Vinci (1452–1519) and the exquisite *Portrait of a Young Woman*, attributed to his pupil, Ambrogio da Predis. Other masterpieces include the *Madonna of the Canopy* by Botticelli (15th century), a cartoon version of Raphael's Vatican fresco, *The School of*

Fruit Basket (c. 1596) by Caravaggio in the Pinacoteca Ambrosiana

Athens (16th century), and Caravaggio's *Fruit Basket* (the first painting in Italy to have a still life as its subject). There is also a strong collection of Venetian art, with paintings by Tiepolo, Titian, Giorgione and Bassano, and panel paintings by the late 15th-century Lombard painter, Bergognone.

🏛 San Satiro

Via Torino. 📞 02-86 68 83. 🔴 daily.

This unassuming church, its full title Santa Maria presso San Satiro, is one of the most beautiful Renaissance buildings in Milan. It stands on the site of a 9th-century sanctuary,

little of which remains apart from the Cappella della Pietà (off the left aisle), beside an 11th-century bell tower.

The interior appears to be in the shape of a Greek cross. This, however, is an illusion created by various *trompe-l'oeil* effects in stucco, as space restrictions led Bramante (who became entrusted with its construction in the late 15th century) to choose a T-shaped plan. Above the altar is a 13th-century fresco. An octagonal baptistry containing terracottas lies off the right aisle. The church's façade was finished only in the 19th century.

DESIGNER FASHION IN MILAN

Italians are famous for the attention they pay to their self-image, and here in Milan, Italian chic can be seen in the cluster of top-name shops which occupy the Quadrilatero, the parallelogram of streets delineated by Via Monte Napoleone, Via Sant'Andrea, Via della Spiga and Borgospesso.

Unlike the Paris fashion scene, which concentrates on flamboyant, often outrageous new designs for women, Milan is more understated in its stylishness: well-cut suits, elegant accessories, chic but wearable shoes. In a sense, the Quadrilatero merely reflects an up-market version of the fashions seen in the streets of any town in Italy: the values of style and comfort are the same; only the astronomical prices serve as a reminder that this is the shopping terrain of the glamorous and very well-heeled.

Dress by Valentino

Via Monte Napoleone, focus of Milan's smartest shops

Milan: Pinacoteca di Brera

MILAN'S FINEST art collection is held in an imposing 17th-century building, the Palazzo di Brera. This is where, in the 18th century, the Accademia di Belle Arti was founded; the picture collection developed alongside the academy. Inside the Brera hang some of the finest examples of Italian Renaissance and Baroque painting, including major works by Piero della Francesca, Mantegna, Bellini, Raphael, Tintoretto, Veronese and Caravaggio. The collection also includes 20th-century works by some of Italy's most famous modern artists.

Mother and Son *(c.1917)*
The metaphysical paintings of Carlo Carrà show a dream world full of strange and obscure symbols.

Portrait of Moisè Kisling
Modigliani's angular portrait of 1915 reflects his interest in African sculpture.

Twin staircases lead up to the first-floor entrance of the Pinacoteca.

★ The Kiss *(1859)*
Francesco Hayez's painting is one of the most reproduced works of Italian 19th-century art. Patriotic and sentimental, it became a symbol of the optimism surrounding the unification of Italy.

The bronze statue (1809) by Canova depicts Napoleon as a demi-god with Victory in his hand.

KEY TO FLOORPLAN

- ☐ 15th- to 16th-century Italian painting
- ☐ 16th- to 17th-century Dutch and Flemish painting
- ☐ 17th-century Italian painting
- ☐ 18th- to 19th-century Italian painting
- ☐ 20th-century Italian painting and sculpture
- ☐ Non-exhibition space

Works by Rembrandt, Rubens and Van Dyck are among the non-Italian artists on show.

VISITORS' CHECKLIST

Via Brera 28. 02-72 26 31.
Lanza, Monte Napoleone &
Duomo. 60, 61. 9am–
5:30pm Tue–Sat, 9am–1pm Sun
& public hols (last adm: 30 mins
before closing). 1 Jan, 1
May, 25 Dec.

★ **Dead Christ by Mantegna**
*The subtle lighting and dramatic
perspective of this lamentation by
Mantegna (1431–1506) make it
one of his greatest masterpieces.*

GALLERY GUIDE

*The collection is displayed in 38 rooms,
and was first built up by paintings from
churches, later from acquisitions. Not
all of it is permanently on view – this is
due to restoration work and research.*

Twinned columns
support the arcades
in the courtyard.

The stone façade
presents a regular
and slightly austere
appearance.

**Madonna della
Candeletta** *(c.1490)
This painting by Carlo
Crivelli was the central
part of a polyptych. It is
richly detailed with
much distinctive
ornamentation.*

**Main entrance
from Via Brera**

★ **Marriage
of the Virgin
by Raphael**
*This graceful
altarpiece was
painted in
1504. The cir-
cular temple is
signed with
the artist's
name.*

STAR PAINTINGS

★ **Dead Christ
by Mantegna**

★ **Marriage of the
Virgin by Raphael**

Milar: Southwest of the Centre

S OME OF MILAN'S FINEST TREASURES are to be found in its religious buildings: the ancient monasteries and churches make up some very fine architectural ensembles in themselves, as well as incorporating important ruins and relics dating back to Roman times. It is also in Milan that one of the most famous images in the world is to be found: Leonardo's evocative masterpiece, the *Last Supper*.

San Lorenzo Maggiore viewed from the northeast

The entrance to Sant'Ambrogio, flanked by unequal bell towers

🔒 Sant'Ambrogio

Piazza Sant'Ambrogio 15. 02-86 45 08 95. daily.
Sant'Ambrogio, or St Ambrose, is the patron saint of Milan, a man who was so eloquent that bees were said to fly into his mouth, attracted by his honey tongue. As bishop of Milan in the 4th century, he worked hard to avoid a schism in the church. This is the basilica that he began building in AD 379, though most of it today is 10th-century Romanesque. A medieval gateway leads to the bronze doors of the entrance, flanked by two bell towers. Inside, note the fine rib vaulting and the beautiful pulpit, and the striking 9th-century altar decorated with gold, silver

and precious gems, crowned by a canopy. In a chapel off the south aisle, fine mosaics line a stunning cupola. Down in the crypt lies the tomb of Sant'Ambrogio himself.

Up above the portico, a small museum contains architectural fragments, tapestries and paintings relating to the church.

🔒 San Lorenzo Maggiore

Corso di Porta Ticinese. 02-837 54 76. daily.
This church contains the most important collection of Roman and early Christian remains in Milan. The octagonal basilica was built in the 4th century, above what was probably a Roman amphitheatre, and subsequently rebuilt in the 12th and 16th centuries.

In front of the church stands a row of 16 Roman columns and, in commemoration of his Edict, a statue of the Emperor Constantine. Fine 4th-century mosaics adorn the Cappella di Sant'Aquilino, a Romanesque chapel, which also contains two early Christian sarcophagi. Other Roman architectural elements, which were incorporated into the building of this church, may be seen in a chamber below the chapel.

🔒 Santa Maria delle Grazie

Piazza Santa Maria delle Grazie 2. 02-498 75 88. **Cenacolo** Tue – Sun am. public hols.
This beautiful 15th-century Renaissance convent, its lovely apse and calm small cloister designed by Bramante, contains one of the key images of western civilization: the *Cenacolo (Last Supper)* by Leonardo da Vinci. The image captures the moment at which Christ tells His disciples that one of them will betray Him. Note, however, that the Christ figure is unfinished: Leonardo did not consider himself to be worthy enough to complete it.

The artist also spurned the standard fresco technique of painting on wet plaster, applying tempera to the dry wall instead. The result is full of subtlety but has deteriorated badly: it is almost impossible to stop the paint flaking off, and restoration has proved difficult. The painting is now protected by a complex filtering system.

Leonardo da Vinci's *Last Supper* (1495–7) adorning the refectory wall of Santa Maria delle Grazie

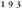

THE EDICT OF MILAN

Milan was founded by the Romans in AD 222, and quickly grew to be an important city at the junction of different trading routes. As the Roman Empire grew and then split into two, emperors began to neglect Rome for the better-placed Mediolanum (literally, city in the middle of the plain). It was here that Emperor Constantine declared his edict of AD 313, in which Christianity was officially recognized, thus effectively making it the religion of the empire. The emperor is said to have been converted following a vision, but by the 4th century adopting Christianity was the only way to unite the now disparate empire.

Emperor Constantine

Monza ❹

Milano. 🏛 125,000. 🚈 🚌
🛈 Palazzo Comunale, Piazza Carducci (039-32 32 22). 🛆 Thu & Sat.

THESE DAYS MONZA is merely a satellite of Milan, famous for its international Formula One **Autodromo**, which lies inside a vast and beautiful park on the edge of Monza. The park also includes an elegant Rococo hunting lodge called the Villa Reale, and a large golf course. At one time, however, Monza was one of the most important towns in Lombardy: Theodolinda, the 6th-century Lombard queen, built its first cathedral and bequeathed her treasure to the town.

At the heart of the town centre is the present **Duomo**, with its notable green and white 14th-century façade and beautiful 15th-century frescoes portraying Theodolinda's life. Behind the high altar is the small Iron Crown, believed to have belonged to Emperor

Constantine: it is prized for the iron strip, said to have been one of the nails from the cross of Christ. More local treasures may be found in the Duomo's **Museo Serpero**, including a silver hen standing over seven tiny chicks – which symbolize Lombardy and the seven provinces it ruled – and a relic said to be John the Baptist's tooth.

🚗 **Autodromo**
Parco di Monza. 📞 039-248 21.
⬜ daily. ⬤ 25 Dec. 🅿 ♿
⛪ **Duomo**
Piazza Duomo. 📞 039-32 34 04. **Museo Serpero** ⬜ Tue–Sun. 🅿

Bergamo ❺

🏛 150,000. 🚈 🚌 🛈 Via Papa Giovanni XXIII 106 (035-24 22 26). 🛆 Mon & Sat.

BERGAMO IS A DELIGHTFUL hilltop town that owes much of its artistic inspiration and architectural splendour to the influence of Venice, which ruled it from the 15th to the late 18th century. The town is divided into two distinct parts: Bergamo Alta crowning the hill, with its cluster of attractive medieval and Renaissance buildings; and the more modern and airy Bergamo Bassa lying below.

The jewel of the upper town is **Piazza Vecchia**, containing one of the most appealing architectural ensembles in the region. Its buildings include the 12th-century Torre del Comune with its fine clock and curfew bell that rings every night at 10pm, the late 16th-century Biblioteca Civica and the attractive 12th-century Palazzo della Ragione, or law courts, adorned with a statue of the lion of Venice.

The arcades of the Palazzo della Ragione lead to Piazza del Duomo, the square of the Neo-Classical Duomo, which is dominated by the façade of the **Cappella Colleoni**

Leonello d'Este (c.1440) by Pisanello in the Accademia Carrara, Bergamo

Detail from the Cappella Colleoni

(see p178). The chapel was built in 1476 to house the tomb of Bergamo's famous political leader, Bartolomeo Colleoni. The chapel is flanked by two 14th-century buildings: an octagonal baptistry and the porch leading to the Romanesque basilica of Santa Maria Maggiore. The basilica's austere exterior contrasts with its Baroque interior, which contains the tomb of Gaetano Donizetti (1797–1848), the operatic composer who was born in Bergamo.

The **Galleria dell'Accademia Carrara** is the highlight of Bergamo Bassa, a major picture gallery with a fine collection of works by Venetian masters and local artists, as well as masterpieces from the rest of Italy: 15th-century works by Pisanello, Crivelli, Mantegna, Giovanni Bellini and Botticelli; 16th-century paintings by Titian, Raphael and Perugino; 18th-century canvases by Tiepolo, Guardi and Canaletto. Major artists represented from the rest of Europe include Holbein, Dürer, Brueghel and Velázquez.

🏛 **Galleria dell'Accademia Carrara**
Piazza dell'Accademia. 📞 035-39 94 26. ⬜ Wed–Mon. ⬤ public hols. 🅿

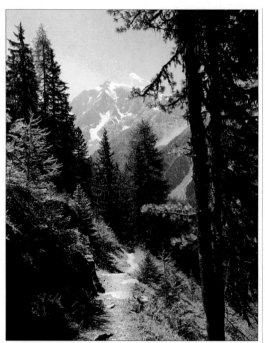

A leafy pathway through the Parco Nazionale dello Stelvio

Parco Nazionale dello Stelvio ⑥

Trento, Bolzano, Sondrio & Brescia.
🚌 *from Bormio to Santa Caterina &
Madonna dei Monti.* 🛈 *Via Monte
Braulio 56, Bormio (0342-90 51 51).*

THE STELVIO, Italy's largest
national park, is the gateway from Lombardy to the
strangely beautiful, glacier-
strewn Dolomite mountains.
The glaciers are dotted with
more than 50 lakes, and dominated by craggy peaks such as
Gran Zebrù, Cevedale and
Ortles – the tallest mountain
here at 3,905 m (12,811 ft).
The dramatic, winding roads of
the Stelvio are the dread of
cyclists in the annual Giro
d'Italia, Italy's answer to the
Tour de France. For walkers,
the area provides virtually
unlimited hiking at all levels,
and access to remote areas still
populated by ibexes, marmots,
chamois and eagles. The only
real population centre is at
Bormio, which boasts every
winter and summer sports
facility you could hope for, and
is a good base from which to

explore the area. The town's
interesting **Orto Botanico** provides an introduction to some
of the species of mountain
plants found in the region.

🌢 Orto Botanico
Via Monte Braulio, Bormio. ☐ *Oct–
Jun: Mon–Sat, Jul–Sep: daily.* 🈸

Val Camonica ⑦

Brescia. 🚆 🚌 *Capo di Ponte.*
🛈 *Via Briscioli, Capo di Ponte
(0364-420 80).*

THIS ATTRACTIVE BROAD valley
formed by a glacier is the
setting for an extraordinary

series of prehistoric carvings
on rock. These form an astonishing outdoor mural from the
Lago d'Iseo to Capo di Ponte
and beyond, and the entire
valley has been declared a
cultural protection zone by
UNESCO. More than 180,000
engravings from the Neolithic
era until early Roman times
have been discovered, some as
recently as the 1970s; the best
are in the **Parco Nazionale
delle Incisioni Rupestri**
around Capo di Ponte. Don't
miss the Naquane rock which
is carved with nearly 1,000
figures from the last Ice Age.
The **Museo Archeologico di
Val Camonica** at Cividate
Camuno focuses on, among
other things, the Roman settlement in the valley.

🏛 Museo Archeologico di Val Camonica
Via Nazionale, Cividate Camuno.
📞 *0364-34 43 01.* ☐ *Tue–
Sun am.* ♿

Lago d'Iseo ⑧

Bergamo & Brescia. 🚆 🚌 ⛴ *Iseo.*
🛈 *Lungolago Marconi 2, Iseo
(030-98 02 09).*

THIS GLACIATED LAKE lying in
wine-producing country is
not only surrounded by tall
mountains and waterfalls, but
also boasts a mini-mountain
of its own, in the form of the
island of Monte Isola. Along
the shores of the lake are a
clutch of fishing villages such
as Sale Marasino and Iseo itself. From Marone, on the east
bank of the lake, a road leads
to the village of **Cislano**,
about 5 km (3 miles) away.
Here, extraordinary spire-like
rock formations rise from the

Prehistoric engraving of a mounted hunter and stag in the Val Camonica

The partly Renaissance Ponte Coperto, straddling the River Ticino at Pavia

ground, each spire topped by a boulder. These distinctive erosion pillars, one of the strangest and most beautiful natural wonders in Lombardy, are known locally as the 'Fairies of the Forest'.

Brescia ❾

🏛 200,000. FS ⛴ 🛈 Corso Zanardelli 34 (030-434 18). 🛒 Sat.

LOMBARDY'S SECOND city after Milan boasts a rich artistic heritage, ranging from Roman temples to the triumphalist Mussolini-era architecture of its main square, Piazza Vittoriale. The major sights include the Roman ruins around Piazza del Foro, consisting of the **Tempio Capitolino** – a three-part Capitoline temple, now incorporating a museum – and a theatre; the **Pinacoteca Civica Tosio Martinengo**, containing works by Raphael, Lorenzo Lotto and local artists; and the **Duomo** on Piazza Paolo, with its 11th-century core and white 17th-century exterior. One of the relics in the Duomo is the banner from the *Carroccio*, or sacred ox cart, which served as a symbol for the medieval Lega Lombarda. **Piazza della Loggia**, where the market is held, is named after the attractive Renaissance loggia, built partly by Palladio. The 18th-century church of San Nazaro e San Celso on Corso Matteotti contains a lovely altarpiece by Titian.

⋂ Tempio Capitolino
Via Musei 57a. ☎ 030-460 31.
🕒 Tue–Sun. ⬤ 1 Jan, 1 May, 1 Nov, 25 Dec. ♿

🏛 Pinacoteca Civica Tosio Martinengo
Via Martinengo da Barco.
☎ 030-377 49 99. 🕒 Tue–Sun. ⬤ 1 Jan, 1 May, 1 Nov, 25 Dec. ♿

Lodi ❿

Milano. 🏛 43,000. FS ⛴
🛈 Piazza Broletto 4 (0731-42 13 13).
🛒 Wed, Thu, Sat & Sun.

THIS IS A CHARMING medieval town of pastel-coloured houses with wrought-iron gateways, pretty courtyards and gardens. Just off Piazza Vittoria, the arcaded square on which the 12th-century Duomo stands, is the fine Renaissance church of the **Incoronata**. The magnificent octagonal interior is entirely decorated with wall paintings and gilding, and crowned with a dome. One of the chapels has 15th-century works by Bergognone.

Pavia ⓫

🏛 81,000. FS ⛴ 🛈 Via Fabio Filzi 2 (0382-272 38). 🛒 Wed & Sat.

DURING PAVIA'S golden age, the city was the Lombards' capital, and later witnessed coronations of Charlemagne and Frederick Barbarossa. Even after it lost its status to Milan in 1359, Pavia

The Roman Tempio Capitolino in Brescia

remained an important city, and great churches, tall towers and other monuments still stand as a testimony to this.

Aside from the magnificent Charterhouse *(see pp196–7)* just north of Pavia, there is the sandstone **Basilica di San Michele** off Corso Garibaldi. The building was founded in the 7th century but largely rebuilt in the 12th after being struck by lightning. Its façade is decorated with friezes of fantastic animals, and inside there are intricate carvings on the columns; a chapel to the right of the main altar contains a 7th-century silver crucifix.

In the centre of the town, around Piazza della Vittoria, stand several ancient monuments. These include the medieval **Broletto** (town hall) with its 16th-century façade and the **Duomo**, begun in 1488 and worked on in turn by Amadeo, Leonardo da Vinci and Bramante. The dome was added in the 1880s. The 11th-century Torre Civica, which stood next to it, collapsed suddenly in 1989. Crossing the river is the **Ponte Coperto**, a Renaissance covered bridge with a consecrated church halfway along it. The bridge was rebuilt after World War II.

Pavia is also the site of one of Europe's oldest (1361) and most respected universities, now residing around a series of Neo-Classical courtyards off Strada Nuova. This road continues northwards to the 14th-century castle, now home to Pavia's **Museo Civico**.

Northwest of Piazza Castello is the 12th-century church, **San Pietro in Ciel d'Oro**. It no longer boasts the fine gilded ceiling from which it derives its name, but does still contain a magnificent shrine to St Augustine, whose bones were allegedly brought to Pavia from Carthage in the 8th century. The body of Boëthius (c.480–524), an important philosopher, is buried down in the crypt.

🏛 Museo Civico
Castello Visconteo, Piazza Castello. ☎ 0382-338 53.
🕒 Tue–Fri am & Sat. ⬤ public hols. ♿ ♿

Certosa di Pavia ⓬

THE CHARTERHOUSE 8 km (5 miles) north of Pavia is the pinnacle of Renaissance architecture in Lombardy, a gloriously decorated Carthusian monastery built over 200 years. It was conceived as a monument to Gian Galeazzo Visconti, the Milanese ruler who founded the complex in 1397 and who, until his early death, had ambitions to become king of all Italy. This splendid shrine was created by the great 15th-century craftsman Giovanni Antonio Amadeo, among others, who used innovative techniques of relief work and multi-coloured decoration.

The choir stalls (15th century) are deeply carved and inlaid with intricate marquet

The tomb of Galeazzo Vis (1351–14 in the tran

Pietradura Altar
Several of the 17th-century altars in the chapels have lavish designs worked in semi-precious stones ("pietradura").

The grilles date from c.1660.

The side chapels are richly decorated with marble, *trompe l'oeil* frescoes and ornate altars and altarpieces.

The interior of the church is largely Gothic.

★ Frescoes by Bergognone (c.1494)
This striking portrait of Christ is one of several frescoes by Bergognone in the transept and chapels, together with an altar painting of Sant'Ambrogio.

Tomb of Ludovico il Moro and Beatrice d'Este
This realistic marble portrait of Ludovico and his child bride was begun by Cristoforo Solari in 1497, some 11 years before Ludovico's death.

Great Cloister
This huge cloister is reached through the Small Cloister. It is framed on three sides by the two-storey monks' cells, each backed by a small garden. A hatch beside the door permits food to be delivered without any communication.

Monk's cell

VISITORS' CHECKLIST

Viale del Monumento, Pavia.
0382-92 56 13. from
Pavia. Certosa. Both followed
by 1 km (half a mile) walk.
9–11:30am, 2:30–5:30 pm
(Oct–Mar: 6pm) Tue–Sun & Mon
public hols (last adm: 30 mins
before closing). **Donation** to
guide.

The New Sacristy is painted with colourful ceiling frescoes.

This delightful, arcaded Small Cloister, with fine terracotta ornamentation, contains a small garden, planted in formal designs.

★ Renaissance Façade
The 15th-century lower part of the façade is profusely decorated with statues and carvings of Roman emperors, saints (here St Peter), apostles and prophets. The upper part dates from 1500.

Main entrance to the Certosa

★ Altarpiece by Perugino
The six-panel altarpiece was painted in 1499 but now only one panel – that depicting God the Father – is original; it is flanked by two paintings by Bergognone.

STAR FEATURES

★ Renaissance Façade

★ Altarpiece by Perugino

★ Frescoes by Bergognone

The Duomo on Piazza del Comune, Cremona

Cremona ⑬

🏛 76,000. 🚉 🚌 ℹ️ *Piazza del Comune 5 (0372-232 33).* 🛒 *Wed & Sat.*

CREMONA, A MAJOR agricultural market, is famous above all for music, thanks to native sons such as the composer Claudio Monteverdi (1567–1643) and the violin-maker Stradivarius. The town itself is dominated by the beautiful Piazza del Comune, bordered by outstanding buildings.

The main attraction is the exuberant part-Romanesque **Duomo**, and its bell tower – said to be the tallest medieval tower in Italy – known as the **Torrazzo**; the two are linked by a Renaissance loggia. The wonderful façade is dominated by the large 13th-century rose window and by a number of intricate touches, including a small portico with statues of the Virgin and saints. Inside, the Duomo is sumptuously decorated with magnificent early 16th-century frescoes and Flemish tapestries, as well as paintings in the side chapels. The top of the Torrazzo offers sweeping views. Outside the Duomo, note the pulpit where itinerant preachers, including San Bernardino of Siena, used to speak to onlookers.

Next to the Duomo stands an octagonal 12th-century baptistry, while on the other side

of the piazza rise the arcades of the late 13th-century **Loggia dei Militi** where the town's military commanders once met, now a war memorial.

The **Palazzo del Comune** is the other major building on the square. It was rebuilt in the 13th century (the windows are more recent) and now contains four rare violins: one each by Guarnieri del Gesù, Andrea and Niccolò Amati, and Stradivarius. The **Museo Stradivariano** displays drawings, models and violins that were made by the master craftsman. The **Museo Civico**, housed in a 16th-century palazzo, contains paintings, wood carvings, the cathedral's treasure, ceramics and a section on archaeology. On the eastern outskirts of the town, on the road to Casalmaggiore, lies the Renaissance church of **San Sigismondo**. It was here that Francesco Sforza married Bianca Visconti in 1441, and the church was subsequently rebuilt (from 1463) in honour of the event. The interior is richly decorated with

16th-century paintings, altarpieces and frescoes by artists of the Cremona school (Campi family, Gatti and Boccaccino).

🏛 **Torrazzo**
Piazza del Comune. ⏱ *Easter–1 Nov. daily.* 📷
🏛 **Palazzo del Comune**
Piazza del Comune. 📞 *030-221 38.* ⏱ *Tue–Sun.* ● *public hols.* 📷 ♿
🏛 **Museo Stradivariano**
Via Palestro 17. 📞 *030-46 18 86.* ⏱ *Tue–Sun.* ● *public hols.* 📷
🏛 **Museo Civico**
Via Ugolani Dati 4. 📞 *030-46 18 85.* ⏱ *Tue–Sun.* ● *public hols.* 📷

Sabbioneta ⑭

Mantova. 🏛 4,600. 🚉 🚌 ℹ️ *Via Vespasiano Gonzaga 31 (0375-520 39).* 🛒 *Sep–Jun: 1st Sun of month.* ✉️ *apply to the tourist information centre.* 📷

SABBIONETA is the result of a delightful experiment in the theory of Renaissance architecture. It was built by Vespasiano Gonzaga (1531–91) as an ideal city, and its hexagonal walls contain a perfect grid of streets and buildings designed on a human scale. The finest buildings include the splendid Teatro Olimpico designed by Scamozzi, the Palazzo Ducale and the frescoed Palazzo del Giardino, which may be visited as part of a tour of the town.

ANTONIO STRADIVARI AND HIS VIOLINS

Cremona is where the violin was developed. The instrument-maker Andrea Amati made the first ones in the 1530s, and they soon became popular with the royal courts throughout Europe because of their superior tone to the medieval fiddle.

It was Antonio Stradivari, known as Stradivarius (1644–1737) – the pupil of Andrea Amati's grandson

19th-century engraving of Antonio Stradivari

Niccolò – who raised the level of craftsmanship to genius. He used to go walking in the forests of the Dolomites in search of the perfect wood for his instruments. Stradivarius produced more than 1,100 violins in his workshop, of which more than 400 exist to this day and remain unrivalled by modern techniques or equipment. The main stopping-off points on a Stradivarius tour of Cremona are the Museo Stradivariano, the violin room in the Palazzo del Comune, and the great man's tombstone on Piazza Roma.

The ceiling of the Camera degli Sposi, by Mantegna, in the Palazzo Ducale

Mantova ⑮

🏛 55,000. 🚉 🚌 🛈 *Piazza Andrea Mantegna 6 (0376-32 82 53).* 🚍 *Thu.*

MANTOVA IS A STRIKING if stern-looking place of fine squares and aristocratic architecture, bordered on three sides by lakes formed by the swollen banks of the River Mincio. The climate can be humid as a result, but Mantova (Mantua) more than makes up for it with a keen sense of cultural history: it was the birthplace of the poet Virgil and playground for three centuries of the Gonzaga dukes. It was also the birthplace of the artist Mantegna, the refuge where Shakespeare sent Romeo into exile from Verona, and the setting for Verdi's opera *Rigoletto*. These links are all celebrated in street names, signposts and monuments around the town. The theatrical connections are enhanced by the 18th-century **Teatro Scientifico Bibiena**, on Via Accademia, which Mozart's father thought was the finest he had ever seen.

Mantova is focused on three attractive main squares: Piazza dell'Erbe, Piazza del Broletto, named after the 13th-century building adorned with a statue of the poet Virgil, and the cobbled Piazza Sordello. On one side of Piazza Sordello is the **Duomo**, with an 18th-century façade and fine interior stuccoes by Giulio Romano (c.1492–1546); on another side, the forbidding façade of the Palazzo Bonacolsi, with its tall prison tower. Piazza dell'Erbe

is dominated by the **Basilica di Sant'Andrea** (15th century), designed largely by Alberti, the early Renaissance architect and theorist, and now flanked by an arcade of shops. The square is also notable for the appealing 11th-century Rotonda di San Lorenzo, and the part-13th-century Palazzo della Ragione with its 15th-century clock tower.

Detail from the 15th-century clock tower on Piazza dell'Erbe

🏛 Palazzo Ducale

Piazza Sordello. 📞 *0376-32 02 83.* ⏰ *Mon–Sat & Sun am for guided tours only.* 🔴 *1 Jan, 1 May, 25 Dec.* 🎟

The highlight of Mantova is the Palazzo Ducale, the vast home of the Gonzaga family which covers the entire northeastern corner of the town and incorporates Castello San Giorgio – a 14th-century fortress – and a basilica, as well as the palace proper. Amid the splendours are many impressive works of

art: they include an unfinished series of 15th-century frescoes by Pisanello, retelling episodes from the Arthurian legends; a large portrait by Rubens (17th century) of the ducal family in the Salone degli Arcieri; and – most absorbing of all – the frescoes by Mantegna in the **Camera degli Sposi** (1465–74). These portray Lodovico Gonzaga and members of his family and court in all their magnificence *(pp200–201)*. The entire room is decorated with images of people, animals and fantastic landscapes, and completed by a light-hearted *trompe l'oeil* ceiling of figures, *putti* and a blue sky.

🏛 Palazzo del Tè

Viale Tè. 📞 *0376-32 32 66.* ⏰ *Tue–Sun.* 🔴 *1 Jan, 1 May, 25 Dec.* 🎟 🛗

At the other end of the town stands another extraordinary palace, the early 16th-century Palazzo del Tè, built by Giulio Romano for the Gonzaga family as a base from which they could go horse riding in the surrounding countryside. Here the artworks conspire with the architecture to produce striking effects: in the **Sala dei Giganti**, for instance, the frescoed Titans appear to be tearing down the very pillars of the room itself. Also remarkable is the Camera di Psiche, decorated with scenes from the *Golden Ass* by Apuleius, and said to celebrate Federico II's love for his mistress. Other rooms are lavishly painted with horses and signs of the Zodiac.

The 13th-century façade of Palazzo Ducale overlooking Piazza Sordello

15th-century fresco, by Mantegna, from the Camera degli Sposi in the Palazzo Ducale ▷

VALLE D'AOSTA AND PIEDMONT

PIEDMONT AND THE NEIGHBOURING VALLE D'AOSTA *are – apart from Turin and its cultural splendours – essentially countryside. To the north lie the Alps, with ski resorts such as Courmayeur, and the wild stretches of the Parco Nazionale del Gran Paradiso. To the south lie the vineyard-clad hills around Barolo, and seemingly endless fields of grain and rice, used in the local dish, risotto.*

The northwest is also rich in culture. From the 11th century to the 18th, both the verdant Valle d'Aosta and Piedmont were part of the French-speaking principality of Savoy and enjoyed the influences of both sides of the Alpine divide. Even today, French and dialectal variants are still spoken in the remote valleys of Piedmont and in much of the Valle d'Aosta. It was only under Duke Emanuele Filiberto in the 16th century that the region was brought definitively into the Italian sphere of influence; and later it was to play the key role in the Risorgimento *(see pp58–9)*, the ambitious movement that united the whole country under a king from Piedmont. The vestiges of this history are to be found in the medieval castles of the Valle d'Aosta and the extraordinary clusters of chapels known as *sacri monti* dotted around the foothills of the Alps. The town of Vercelli also spawned a school of painting, which is in evidence in the small parish churches and excellent fine art collections in the region. The most impressive architecture in the northwest, however, is undoubtedly to be found in Turin, a much underrated and surprisingly elegant Baroque city which boasts, among other things, one of the best Egyptian museums in the world. Piedmont is also known for its industry – Fiat in Turin, Olivetti in Ivrea, the wool trade in Biella – but it has not forgotten its agricultural roots, and food and drink play an important role in the life of the region: the hills of southern Piedmont produce many of the great Italian red wines.

Taking vermouth in one of Turin's cafés

◁ **The 13th-century Châtelard castle in the Valle d'Aosta**

Exploring Valle d'Aosta and Piedmont

THE VAST FLAT PLAIN of the Po, covered with the watery expanse of rice fields around Vercelli and Novara, eventually gives way, in the west, to the majestic heights of the Alps. Turin, the largest city in the area and the capital of Piedmont, stands at the edge of the plain, nestling almost in the shadow of the mountains. Further northwest, attractive Alpine valleys headed by dramatic peaks provide the setting for the traditional villages, ancient towns and castles around Aosta. The Parco Nazionale del Gran Paradiso is an unspoilt tract of breathtaking scenery.

Rice fields around Vercelli

SIGHTS AT A GLANCE

Turin, the capital of Piedmont, in the valley of the Po

GETTING AROUND

There is no motorway access from France into northwest Italy, though the tunnel under the Simplon or Sempione Pass provides a direct rail route from Switzerland. From the rest of Italy, however, there are excellent motorway connections across the plain to Turin and up to Aosta. The region is well served with rail links, and there are buses between the main towns and to some of the outlying resorts. Getting around the mountains is more difficult, making the car the most efficient method of transport.

St Pierre castle in the Valle d'Aosta

SEE ALSO

- *Where to Stay* pp551–4

- *Where to Eat* pp586–8

| 0 kilometres | 25 |
| 0 miles | 20 |

KEY

	Motorway
	Major road
	Minor road
	Scenic route
	River
	Viewpoint

Monte Bianco ❶

Aosta. **FS** *Pré-St-Didier.*
🚌 *Courmayeur.* **ℹ** *Piazzale Monte Bianco 13, Courmayeur (0165-84 20 60).*

M ONTE BIANCO – Mont Blanc
as it is also known – the tallest mountain in the Alps at 4,810 m (15,780 ft), dominates the western Aosta valley and its attractive all-year resort, **Courmayeur**. The cable car ride up to the Aiguille du Midi from Entrèves, 5 km (3 miles) further north, offers one of the most spectacular views in the Alps. From Pré-St-Didier, below Courmayeur, the **Little St Bernard Pass** with its small glaciers, forests and ravines can be explored.

Colle del Gran San Bernardo ❷

Aosta. **FS 🚌** *Aosta.* **ℹ** *Strada Statale Gran San Bernardo 13, Etroubles (0165-785 59).*

T HE GREAT ST BERNARD pass is
synonymous with the hardy mountain rescue dogs that have been trained locally by

Catholic monks since the 11th century. The **Monks' Hospice**, founded around 1050 by St Bernard of Aosta, lies just over the Swiss border (bring your passport), on the shores of a lovely lake; the dogs are still being trained there. The pretty Great St Bernard valley itself includes the town of Etroubles, set in a forest of conifers, the hamlet of St-Oyen with its pretty parish church, and the resort of St-Rhémy-en-Bosses.

A St Bernard dog

🏠 Monks' Hospice
Colle San Bernardo, Switzerland.
📞 *00 41 26-87 12 36.*
🕐 *Jun–Sep: daily.*

Monte Cervino ❸

Aosta. **FS 🚌** *Breuil Cervinia.*
ℹ *Via Carrel 29, Breuil Cervinia (0166-94 91 36).*

T HE DISTINCTIVE triangular
peak of Monte Cervino (the Matterhorn) rises to 4,478 m (14,691 ft) and is easily recognizable. Below the mountain lies a scattering of attractive villages like Antey-St-André, Valtournenche (which gave its

name to the valley) and the resort of **Breuil-Cervinia**. From Breuil a cable car rises up to the Cime Bianche, offering dramatic views over the surrounding mountains. This entire area is a paradise for both skiers and walkers.

Monte Rosa ❹

Aosta. **FS** *Verrès.* **🚌** *St-Jacques.*
ℹ *Route Varasc, Champoluc (0125-30 71 13).*

M ONTE ROSA overlooks the
beautiful Gressoney and Ayas valleys. The rolling lower Ayas valley is dominated by the ruins of the Romanesque **Castello di Graines**, perched on a large rock. Higher up, the resort of Champoluc has a cable car connection with the striking **Testa Grigia** (3,315 m, 10,873 ft). The Gressoney valley is home to the Walser people, who speak an obscure German dialect. At the bottom of the valley, near Pont-St-Martin with its Roman bridge, lies **Issime**: the 16th-century church here has a fresco of the Last Judgment on its façade.

🏠 Castello di Graines
Graines, Strada Statale 506.
🕐 *daily.* **♿**

MEDIEVAL CASTLES AND FORTS IN THE VALLE D'AOSTA

The mountains alone provided insufficient protection to the fragmented kingdoms that covered the Valle d'Aosta in the Middle Ages. The medieval lords, who ruled ruthlessly over their small domains, built castles to enforce their often fragile power. Of the many built, 70 castles survive in some form to this day. You will pass a number of them if you drive into Italy by the Mont Blanc tunnel; they stretch from Aosta to Pont-St-Martin.

Originally Aosta castles were designed to be defensive and threatening, such as the looming tower of **Montmayer**, perched high on a huge rock by the Valgrisenche valley. Nearby, the equally forbidding dark tower of **Ussel** throws a melancholy, brooding watchfulness over the valley.

Fénis and **Verrès** represent an important shift in the function of the feudal castle. Both Fénis, a splendid 14th-century showpiece *(see p178)*, and Verrès were not just important military outposts but also examples of palatial opulence and good living. **Issogne** too furthered this luxurious trend with its elaborate frescoes, loggias and fountains.

Decoration was also important to Vittorio Emanuele II, owner of **Sarre**, who turned the halls of his fortress into a plush hunting lodge. The owners of **Châtelard**, set in some of the highest vineyards in Europe, placed fine wine production alongside military aims.

The strategically sited 14th-century castle at Verrès

The 12th-century cloister, with 40 carved columns of darkened marble, in Sant'Orso

Aosta ❺

🏛 37,000. ⏚ ▭ ℹ Piazza Chanoux 8 (0165-23 66 27). 🔔 Tue.

LYING ON A PLAIN surrounded by dramatic mountains, the town of Aosta provides a remarkable mixture of ancient culture and spectacular, rich scenery. The Romans captured it from Salassian Gauls in around 25 BC, and Aosta is still dotted with fine Roman architecture built in honour of Emperor Augustus – indeed the town was once called *Augusta Praetoria*, and its name only evolved into Aosta over the centuries. The medieval town was later fortified by the Challant family and then by the Dukes of Aosta, who added towers to the old Roman walls.

Modern Aosta is a bustling place with rambling suburbs, a crossroads for local industries and tourists on their way to the mountains. The centre, how-ever, still consists of a delightful grid of large squares and sur-prising architectural treasures, which justify Aosta's nickname of "Rome of the Alps".

⋔ Roman Ruins
Roman Theatre, Via Baillage. ☐ daily. ● 25 Dec. **Amphitheatre**, Convento di San Giuseppe, Via dell'Anfiteatro. 📞 0165-36 21 49. ☐ by appt only. 📷 ♿ **Roman Forum**, Piazza Giovanni XXIII. ☐ daily. ● 25 Dec.
During Roman times, entry to Aosta was over the **bridge** to the east of the town (beyond the modern bridge) and through the **Arch of Augustus**. This triumphal arch is today marred only by a roof added in the 18th century. Ahead stands the **Porta Pretoria**, its

double row of stone arches flanked by a medieval tower; the gateway originally stood about 2.5 m (8 ft) higher than at present. Equally well preserved is the town's **Roman Theatre**, with a section of its 20-m (65-ft) high façade. The elliptical **Amphitheatre**, a little to the north, is reached through the convent of San Giuseppe. In the old town, next to the cathedral, lies the **Roman Forum**, or market place, with its huge cryptoporticus: the function of this impressive underground gallery, with its massive arches, remains the object of speculation.

Detail of a medieval mosaic on the floor of Aosta's Duomo

⋔ Duomo
Piazza Giovanni XXIII. ☐ daily. **Museo del Tesoro** ☐ Apr–Sep: daily; Oct–Mar: Sun & public hols pm. 📷 ♿
This relatively modest shrine to St John the Baptist was first built in the 12th century, but has been altered many times since. The interior is Gothic, with finely carved 15th-century

choir stalls, and floor mosaics depicting sacred and pagan scenes. Next door, the **Museo del Tesoro** contains a rich collection of statuettes and reliquaries, and a number of impressive medieval tombs.

⋔ Sant'Orso
Via Sant'Orso. 📞 0165-26 20 26. ☐ daily. ♿
East of the town walls is the architectural highlight of Aosta: a medieval complex of church buildings. Sant'Orso itself has a simple and unusual Gothic façade characterized by a thin, very tall portal. The interior has 11th-century frescoes, a crypt of the same date holding the tomb of St Orso, patron saint of Aosta, and a beautiful **cloister** with columns and capitals carved into highly detailed figures and animals.

ENVIRONS: The castle at **Fénis** *(see p206)*, 12 km (8 miles) east, is one of the few castles in the Aosta valley with a well-preserved interior, including beautiful frescoes and wooden galleries. **Issogne**, 38 km (23 miles) southeast, is the setting for another highly decorated castle, remodelled around 1490. It is filled with frescoes and decorative motifs, including a wrought-iron fountain in the shape of a pomegranate tree.

♜ Castello di Fénis
Fénis. 📞 0165-76 42 63. ☐ daily. ● 1 Jan, 25 Dec. 📷
♜ Castello di Issogne
Issogne. 📞 0125-92 93 73. ☐ daily. ● 1 Jan, 25 Dec. 📷

Some of the impressive ruins standing in the Roman Forum in Aosta

Parco Nazionale del Gran Paradiso ❻

A BREATHTAKING WILDERNESS of dramatic mountains and lush meadows, the Gran Paradiso is Italy's foremost national park, created in 1922 from part of a former royal hunting reserve of the House of Savoy. It is mainly a summer resort for walkers due to its unspoiled scenery, rare wildlife and unusual Alpine flowers, though there is also cross-country skiing during the winter months. The king of the park is the ibex, a relative of the deer family all but extinct in the rest of Europe. The park is also prized by naturalists for its chamois, ptarmigan, golden eagles, rare butterflies and marmots.

Castello di Aymavilles
The 18th-century core of this castle is framed by medieval corner towers.

Goletta Waterfall
is an impressive cascade near the Lago di Goletta.

Male Ibex
The ibex lives largely above the tree line. Groups are often seen around Col Lauson at dawn and dusk, and also around Pont in June.

Val di Rhêmes-Notre-Dame
This peaceful and broad valley offers magnificent scenery with waterfalls and fast-flowing streams running from the glacier at its head.

ARVIER
VILLENEUVE
AVI
Pondel
Rhêmes-St-George
VAL DI RHÊMES
VAL SAVARENCHE
Valsavarenche
Rhêmes-Notre-Dame
Eaux-Rousses
LA
Pont
GRAN PARADISO
4,061 m
(13,320 ft)
Ceresole Reale

Cascata di Balma
This tall, dramatic waterfall, situated a little to the east of the rustic village of Lillaz, is best observed after the spring snow melt.

Cogne is the main resort and a good base from which to explore the park. Maps of the park's routes and footpaths are available here.

Lillaz is sedate and off the beaten track; while Valnontey and Cogne are two of the busiest resorts.

VISITORS' CHECKLIST

Piemonte and Valle d'Aosta.
🛈 Segreteria Turistica, Via Umberto I 1, Noasca (0124-90 10 70). Other information offices at Ceresole Reale & Cogne. ☐ Jul, Aug & public hols. FS Aosta & Pont Canavese. 🚌 from Aosta or Pont Canavese to the different valleys. ☑ **Paradisia Alpine Garden**, Valnontey, Cogne. 📞 0165-740 40. ☐ mid-Jun–mid-Sep: daily. 🖪 ♿ 📷

★ Paradisia Alpine Garden
The botanic garden contains a collection of Alpine plants, including the delicate "twinflower".

STAR SIGHTS

★ **Paradisia Alpine Garden**

★ **Valnontey**

0 kilometres   5

0 miles   5

★ Valnontey
This lovely valley, after which the resort is named, provides dramatic views of glaciers and easy access to various footpaths.

KEY

🛈 Tourist information

═ Main road

❀ Viewpoint

The small resort of Ceresole Reale under winter snow

Lake Ceresole Reale ❼

Torino. 🚌 to Ceresole Reale.
ℹ Apr – Oct: Corso Vercelli 1, Ivrea (0124-95 31 86); Nov – Mar: Comune di Ceresole (0124-95 31 21).

ON THE SOUTHERN, Piedmont side of the extensive Parco Nazionale del Gran Paradiso (see pp208–9) lies the small resort of Ceresole Reale, on the shores of a spectacular mountain lake. The route from Cuorgne goes through the rolling countryside of the Canavese and follows the N460 along a narrow gorge with a cascading stream. At **Noasca**, a spectacular waterfall may be seen high above the houses.

Ceresole Reale lies in a basin surrounded by meadows and forests of larch, and framed by mountains – the Gran Paradiso range to the north, Levanna to the southwest – which are reflected in the clear waters of the lake. The lake itself is actually a dammed reservoir, providing energy to supply Turin with electricity. This nevertheless unspoiled corner is a good base for walking, climbing and hiking, and also offers facilities for skiing during the winter.

Via Lattea ❽

Torino. FS Oulx. 🚌 to Sauze d'Oulx.
ℹ Piazzale Agnelli 4, Sestriere (0122-75 51 70).

THE CLOSEST RING of mountain resorts to Turin, and as a consequence popular for weekend excursions, is known colloquially as the Via Lattea or "milky way". Villages like **Bardonecchia** and **Sauze d'Oulx** preserve traditional old stone and wood buildings that have been a feature of the region for centuries. The small church in Bardonecchia has, in addition, a fine 15th-century carved choir. In contrast, the super-modern complex at **Sestriere** has been purpose-built to accommodate skiers in winter and hikers in summer.

From Bardonecchia a chairlift operates some of the way up **Punta Colomion**, which rises immediately to the south of the resort. The summit, at 2,054 m (6,738 ft), offers fine views, and numerous hiking and walking possibilities.

Susa ❾

Torino. 🏛 7,000. FS 🚌 ℹ Corso Inghilterra 39 (0122-62 24 70). 🛒 Tue.

THIS ATTRACTIVE mountain town flourished in Roman times: the **Arch of Augustus**, built in 8 BC and still standing, commemorates the alliance between the local Gaulish

The impressive part-Roman gateway, Porta Savoia, in Susa

chieftain and the Emperor Augustus. Other relics from the Roman period include two arches of an aqueduct, sections of an amphitheatre and traces of the old town walls. **Porta Savoia**, an imposing Roman gateway dating from the 4th century, was remodelled in the Middle Ages.

Most of the historic centre of the town is medieval, including the castle of Countess Adelaide and the **Duomo**, both originally 11th century. The Duomo, much altered since then, houses a polyptych (c.1500) attributed to Bergognone, and a precious 14th-century Flemish triptych portraying the Virgin and Saints. South of the town lies the Gothic church of **San Francesco**, surrounded by an area of early medieval houses.

A street in the traditional village of Bardonecchia, on the Via Lattea

Carved capitals on the Porta dello Zodiaco at the Sacra di San Michele

Sacra di San Michele ⑩

Strada Sacra San Michele. ▮ 011-93 91 30. ▮ Jul–Aug from Avigliana & Turin. ▮ 9–12am, 3–6pm Tue–Sun.

THIS SOMEWHAT forbidding abbey complex is perched dramatically on a ridge halfway up Monte Pirchiriano, at a height of 610 m (2,000 ft). The monastic community here was founded around the year 1000, possibly on the site of a previous sanctuary, though the exterior looks every bit as much a fortress as the spiritual refuge that it was for 600 years.

During its prime, the abbey attracted pilgrims on their way to Rome, and as a result it grew enormously wealthy and powerful, controlling over 100 other abbeys in Italy, France and Spain. It was also subsequently attacked and looted several times, despite being fortified, before falling into decline and eventually being suppressed in 1662.

The sanctuary is reached by climbing 154 steep steps hewn out of the rock, which offer wonderful views over the surrounding countryside and up to the Alps. At the very top of this stairway, known as the Scalone dei Morti (Stairway of the Dead), is the Romanesque Porta dello Zodiaco, a doorway profusely carved with creatures and symbols relating to the signs of the Zodiac. Beyond the doorway a few more steps lead into the church itself, which dates from the 12th– 13th centuries and incorporates traces of an earlier building. The interior houses 15th- and 16th-century paintings and frescoes, and a 16th-century triptych by the Piedmontese artist Defendente Ferrari. The crypt holds the tombs of the early dukes and princes of the House of Savoy-Carignano.

Avigliana ⑪

Torino. ▩ 9,500. ▤ ▭ ▮ Piazza del Popolo 6 (011-93 86 50). ▮ Thu.

ON A FINE DAY, this small town perched beside two glacier-fed lakes and encircled by tall mountains looks breath-takingly beautiful. Avigliana is overlooked by a castle, first erected in the mid-10th century but now in ruins, which was once the home of the Counts of Savoy. Until the early 15th century the town was one of their favourite bases.

The medieval houses here are largely unspoiled, particularly in the two main squares, Piazza Santa Maria and Piazza Conte Rosso. Other buildings of note are the Casa della Porta Ferrata on Via Omonima, and the 15th-century Casa dei Savoia on Via XX Settembre.

The church of San Giovanni (13th–14th century) contains early 16th-century paintings by Defendente Ferrari.

Pinerolo ⑫

Torino. ▩ 36,000. ▤ ▭ ▮ Viale Giolitti 7–9 (0121-79 55 89). ▮ Wed & Sat.

PINEROLO LIES in an attractive setting beside hills at the confluence of the Lemina and Chisone valleys. The town was the capital of the Acaia family, a branch of the House of Savoy, and in the 14th and 15th centuries it was known for the cultural atmosphere that prevailed here under the family's patronage. However, the town enjoyed none of the stability of Turin: it was occupied by the French five times between the 15th and 18th centuries. During the 17th century the French demolished many of the town's ancient buildings in order to make Pinerolo a defensive stronghold; among the political prisoners allegedly held here was the notorious "Man in the Iron Mask". Today the town is a busy centre of commerce.

A number of monumental buildings do remain, however. The **Duomo**, at the centre of the town, was remodelled in Gothic style in the 15th–16th centuries and has a fine portal and an impressive bell tower. Via Principi d'Acaia climbs up to the 14th-century palace of the Princes of Acaia, and to the 15th-century church of **San Maurizio**, where the Acaia princes are buried; beside it rises a 14th-century bell tower.

The medieval arcades surrounding Piazza Conte Rosso in Avigliana

Turin ⑬

MENTION TURIN (Torino) and most people will think of industry and comfortable north Italian prosperity. It is certainly an economic powerhouse but it is also a town of enormous grace and charm, with superb Baroque architecture and excellent museums, set against the dramatic scenery of the foothills of the Alps. Turin is also, of course, the home of the famous Turin Shroud, the Fiat car company, and the Juventus football team.

Exploring Turin

Though settled by the Romans (**Porta Palatina** is an impressive 1st-century AD relic), and the seat of a university since the Middle Ages, Turin came into its own only after 1574, when Emanuele Filiberto of Savoy moved his capital here. Three centuries of steady prosperity ensued. Turin then became the power base for Italy's unification movement and, from 1861 to 1865, the capital of the newly united country. Subsequently its main

The Fiat car factory logo

power was economic. The car company **Fiat** (Fabbrica Italiana Automobili Torino), was established here in 1899 and grew to be one of the biggest firms in Europe. After World War II, Turin attracted thousands of poor Italians from the south who came to work in its factories. Though there have been social conflicts and labour disputes as a result, managers and workers do unite over football: the Juventus team is owned by the much-revered Fiat boss, Gianni Agnelli.

Statue of Emperor Augustus in front of the Roman Porta Palatina

🏛 Duomo

Piazza San Giovanni. ◯ daily. ⬛
The cathedral, built in 1498 and dedicated to St John the Baptist, is the only example of Renaissance architecture in Turin. The sober square bell

TURIN TOWN CENTRE

Armeria Reale ⑤
Duomo ②
Mole Antonelliana ⑨
Museo Egizio and
  Galleria Sabauda ⑦
Palazzo Carignano ⑧
Palazzo Madama ⑥
Palazzo Reale ④
Porta Palatina ①
San Lorenzo ③

0 metres   500
0 yards   500

KEY

P Parking

ℹ Tourist information

✝ Church

FS Railway station

The 15th-century Duomo, with the Cappella della Sacra Sindone beyond

tower, which predates the rest of the church by 30 years, stands in refreshing contrast to Turin's sumptuous Baroque buildings; its top was designed by Filippo Juvarra in 1720. Inside, the Duomo is heavy with statuary and paintings. Through a black marble arch on the right side of the church is the **Cappella della Sacra Sindone** (Chapel of the Holy Shroud), which is actually incorporated into the Palazzo Reale *(see p216)*. The chapel is a remarkable feat, designed by Guarino Guarini (1624–83) with an extraordinary mesh-like cupola; the exterior view is equally eccentric. On top of the altar is the urn containing the famous Shroud itself.

🏛 Palazzo Madama

Piazza Castello. 📞 011-54 38 23.
⬤ for restoration until 1998.

Turin's main square once contained a medieval castle which incorporated elements of the original Roman city walls. The castle was later enlarged and remodelled, and a new façade by Juvarra was added, at the request of a royal widow, in the 18th century. The Palazzo Madama – as it was subsequently renamed – now sits in the centre of the square with a stately, balustraded façade.

The interior, with its grand staircase and first floor, both designed by Juvarra,

is home to the **Museo Civico d'Arte Antica**. This extensive collection contains treasures which range in date from the Graeco-Roman era to the 19th century. The display includes the famous and mysterious *Portrait of an Unknown Man* by Antonello da Messina (15th century) among the paintings and sculptures, and reproductions of the Duc de Berry's beautiful *Book of Hours* from c.1420. Other sections contain displays of jewellery, majolica and glass, complementing the textiles and furniture.

The façade of the Palazzo Madama, designed by Filippo Juvarra in 1718–21

THE TURIN SHROUD

Detail of the mysterious 12th-century Turin Shroud

The most famous – and most dubious – holy relic of them all is kept in Turin's Duomo. The shroud, said to be the winding-sheet in which the body of Christ was wrapped after His crucifixion, owes its fame to the fact that the shroud bears the imprint of a crucified man with a wound in his side, and bruises from what might have been a crown of thorns.

The shroud is one of the most famous medieval relics. Its early history is unclear, but the House of Savoy was in possession of it around 1430, and had it displayed in Guarini's chapel from 1694. The "original" shroud – which sits in a silver casket inside an iron box within a marble coffer inside the urn on the chapel altar – is not on view, though a replica is, together with a welter of scientific explanations as to the shroud's possible origins. In 1988, however, the myth of the shroud was exploded: a carbon-dating test showed that it dates back no further than the 12th century. The shroud nevertheless remains an object of religious veneration.

Exploring Turin

THE CITY OF TURIN IS BLESSED with numerous interesting museums, which are housed in splendid palazzi and civic buildings. The centre itself is relatively small, with broad, straight streets, often bordered with cafés and shops, which are pleasant places to stroll along. The city is also famous for its innovative cuisine and boasts some of the country's finest restaurants.

Granite statue of Ramses II (13th century BC) in the Museo Egizio

🏛 Museo Egizio

Via Accademia delle Scienze 6.
📞 011-561 77 76. ⏱ Tue–Sun.
⬤ 1 Jan, 1 May, 25 Dec. 📷

Turin owes its magnificent Egyptian Museum – one of the most important in the world – largely to the Piedmont-born Bernardo Drovetti, who was stationed in Egypt as French Consul General at the time of the Napoleonic Wars. It was the booty he brought back that formed the basis of this very fine collection of Egyptian arte-facts. On the ground floor, the items on display include monumental sculptures and reconstructed temples; upstairs, there are collections of papyrus and everyday objects. Among the most impressive sculptures are a black granite Ramses II (13th century BC, or 19th dynasty), the slightly earlier Amenophis II, and the basalt figure of Gemenef-Har-Bak, a vizier from the 26th dynasty. The Sala della Nubia contains a breathtaking reconstruction of the 15th-century BC **Rock Temple of Ellessya**.

Extraordinary wall and tomb paintings are displayed on the upper floor, together with items of daily use such as the tools used for measuring, weaving, fishing and hunting. The 14th-century BC Tomb of Kha and Merit, complete with the food, tools and ornaments buried with them for the afterlife, is particularly fascinating. The papyrus collection is beautiful and of enormous interest to scholars: these documents have been vital to modern understanding of Egyptian language, customs and history – one document, the *Papiro dei Re* (Royal Papyrus), crucially lists all the pharaohs up to the 17th dynasty, with their dates.

G Ferrari's *St Peter and a Donor* (16th century), Galleria Sabauda

🏛 Galleria Sabauda

Via Accademia delle Scienze 6.
📞 011-54 74 40. ⏱ Tue–Sun am.
📷 ♿

The Palazzo dell'Accademia delle Scienze, the building by Guarini in which the Egyptian Museum is housed, is also home to the House of Savoy's main painting collection. The top two floors are the setting for a stunning array of works by Italian, French, Flemish and Dutch masters.

The collection was originally begun in the second half of the 15th century, and has been expanded over the centuries since. It is grouped in regional schools and contains a section on Piedmontese painting, which is not often represented in other galleries: this includes four canvases by Gaudenzio Ferrari (c.1480–1546) and two early 16th-century paintings by Defendente Ferrari. Among works of particular interest from other Italian schools are Antonio and Piero Pollaiuolo's 15th-century *Tobias and the*

Detail from an 18th-dynasty papyrus Book of the Dead, Museo Egizio

Archangel Raphael, and a late 15th-century study of the *Birth of Venus* by one of Botticelli's students. Mantegna, Bellini, Bronzino, and Veronese are among other Italian artists represented.

The section on Dutch and Flemish art includes Jan Van Eyck's *St Francis* (15th century) and Rembrandt's *Old Man Sleeping* (17th century), as well as portraits by Van Dyck, which include a study of Charles I's children, and his *Principe Tommaso di Savoia-Carignano* (1634). Among the French works on display are 17th-century landscape paintings by Claude Lorrain and Poussin.

🏛 Palazzo Carignano

Via Accademia delle Scienze 5. 📞 011-562 11 47. ⬜ daily. ⬤ 1 Jan, 25 Dec. 📷 ♿

The façade of Palazzo Carignano by Guarini

This Baroque palazzo is not only Guarini's masterpiece, it is arguably the finest building in Turin, with its magnificent undulating brick façade and ornate rotunda. It was originally constructed in 1679 for the Carignano family – an offshoot of the main House of Savoy – but came into its own in the 19th century. The first king of Italy, Vittorio Emanuele II, was born here in 1829; and after Italy was unified in 1861 by a series of referendums, the former royal residence was used as the country's first national parliament building.

The palazzo is now home to the **Museo Nazionale del Risorgimento**, which through paintings and a collection of artefacts (housed in the rooms where history was made), tells the story of unification. It introduces Mazzini, Cavour and Garibaldi – key figures in the Risorgimento (*see pp58–9*).

Spacious arcades on Turin's lively Via Roma

🚋 Via Roma

Via Roma is Turin's main street, running through the heart of the historic centre. It leads from Piazza Castello at its northern end down through Piazza San Carlo to the distinctive arched façade of Stazione Porta Nuova, which forms a focal point at the southern end. The station was built in 1868 and looks out over the green and pleasant gardens of the 19th-century Piazza Carlo Felice. The square is framed by shops and cafés and provides an excellent vista up Via Roma from a calm vantage point. Via Roma itself is a magnificent concourse lined with stylish fashion shops and shaded arcades, interrupted only by cobbled squares, crisscrossed by tramlines. A grid pattern of side streets branch off either side of Via Roma, revealing additional shopping arcades.

🚋 Piazza San Carlo

This square halfway along Via Roma comprises an ensemble of Baroque architecture so sophisticated as to earn it the

nickname of "Turin's drawing room". At the southern end rise the twin churches of Santa Cristina and San Carlo; both were built in the 1630s though **Santa Cristina** has a Baroque façade, crowned with statues, which was designed by Juvarra in the early 18th century.

At the centre of the square stands a 19th-century statue of Emanuele Filiberto resheathing his sword. The work, by Carlo Marocchetti, has become an emblem of the city. At the corners of the square, frescoes depict the Holy Shroud. The **Galleria San Federico**, in the square's northwestern corner, is a stylish shopping arcade.

Piazza San Carlo is known for its society cafés. In one such establishment, in 1786, Antonio Benedetto Carpano invented the drink known as vermouth, which is still very popular in Turin today.

🌳 Parco del Valentino

Corso Massimo D'Azeglio. ⬜ daily. 📷
Borgo Medioevale 📞 011-669 93 72. ⬜ daily. 📷 ♿
Orto Botanico ⬜ daily. 📷 ♿
This park beside the river contains the **Borgo Medioevale**, a complex of buildings resembling a medieval village and castle, which was built for an exhibition in the late 1880s. The buildings show different types of design and construction, based on traditional houses and castles which can be found scattered throughout Piedmont and in the Valle d'Aosta.

The **Orto Botanico**, beside the medieval complex, is an impressive botanical garden in a pleasant setting.

Looking south across the elegant Piazza San Carlo, "Turin's drawing room"

Turin: Symbols of the City

Turin's architecture mirrors the city's transition from monarchic power to industrial power. Witness the ostentation of the Baroque apartments of the Savoy royal family; and contrast them with the futuristic Mole Antonelliana, a tall structure, which heralded the dawn of the modern industrial age. Much of Turin's history in the 20th century has been dominated by the motor car: Fiat made Turin its home and, despite some industrial unrest, the city's workers replied by rewarding it with success. For the curious, Turin's motor museum is worth a visit, as it maps out the history of Italian car design.

The 19th-century tower, Mole Antonelliana, dominating Turin

🏛 Mole Antonelliana

Via Montebello 20. ☎ 011-817 04 96.
🕐 Tue–Sun. ⬤ public hols. 📷

This eccentric building is the Turin equivalent of the Eiffel Tower in Paris: an unmissably tall landmark that serves no clear purpose except perhaps to act as a signature for the city as a whole. It looks a bit like a glorified lightning conductor: indeed an electric storm struck down the top 47 m (155 ft) in 1954, which was subsequently rebuilt. The 167-m (550-ft) Mole, by Alessandro Antonelli (1798–1888), was originally planned to be a synagogue, but the city finished it in 1897 and used it to house the city's museum. The Mole ("massive structure") – for a time the tallest building in the world – became a symbol of Italian unity. Today it is an exhibition hall with a viewing platform halfway up, reached by lift, which affords excellent views over the city and to the Alps.

Inside the dome of San Lorenzo

🏛 Palazzo Reale

Piazzetta Reale. ☎ 011-436 14 55.
🕐 Tue–Sun. ⬤ 1 Jan, 1 May, 25 Dec. 📷 ♿

The Palazzo Reale was the seat of the Savoy royal family from 1646 until the unification of Italy. Behind the austere façade, designed by Amedeo di Castellamonte, lie richly decorated state apartments; the ceilings were painted by Morello, Miel and Seyter in the 17th century. The many splendid furnishings, tapestries and ornaments date from the 17th to the 19th centuries; they include the elaborate Chinese Cabinet by Juvarra, the Alcove Room, the lavishly decorated Throne Room, and the innovative Scala delle Forbici, or Scissor Stairs, created by Juvarra in 1720. Behind the palace are extensive gardens, which extend northwards.

To the left of the main entrance to the palace is **San Lorenzo**, the former royal chapel. This fine Baroque building (1667–80) is by architect Guarino Guarini, its ornate interior boasting another of his extraordinary, geometric domes.

A lavishly decorated gallery in the 17th-century Palazzo Reale, a royal home until unification

🏛 Armeria Reale

Piazza Castello 191. ☎ 011-54 38 89.
🕐 Tue–Sun am (also Tue & Thu pm).
⬤ 1 Jan, 1 May, 25 Dec. 📷

One wing of the Palazzo Reale, on the northern side of the main square, provides the splendid setting for one of the most extensive and breathtaking collections of arms and armoury in the world.

The armoury originally belonged to the House of Savoy, and was opened to the public in 1837. The fine rooms, such as the splendid Galleria Beaumont, designed by Juvarra in 1733, hold treasures ranging in date from Roman and Etruscan times to the 19th century. The collection has some particularly magnificent medieval and Renaissance items from some of the greatest armourers and gunsmiths in the world, including a pistol of Charles V. One section is devoted largely to Oriental arms and armour.

The adjoining but separate Royal Library contains a collection of drawings and manuscripts, including a self-portrait by Leonardo da Vinci.

Environs: About 3 km (2 miles) out of the city centre lies a colossal hall built in the 1960s for the famous **Museo dell'Automobile**. Founded by two motoring pioneers in 1932, it now houses over 150 veteran, vintage and classic cars. The collection includes glorious Bugattis, Maseratis, Lancias, Fiats and also a number of fine foreign cars. The first petrol-driven car made in Italy (1896) is kept here, as well as the first Fiat (1899) and the 1929 Isotta Fraschini *coupé de ville* that was used to transport Gloria Swanson in the Hollywood film *Sunset Boulevard*. Note also that a large number of the sports cars from the 1950s have the steering wheel on the right – ie British – side: this brief trend was in deference to the great British car makers such as Aston Martin.

There is also a library and a documentation centre which are both open to the public.

Designs from 1949 for the Ferrari 166 MM

🏛 **Museo dell'Automobile**

Corso Unità d'Italia 40. (011-67 76 56. ⬤ *Tue–Sun.* ⬤ *1 Jan, 25 Dec.* ♿

Stupinigi ⑭

Piazza Principe Amedeo 7, Stupinigi. (011-358 12 20. 🚌 *63 to Piazza Caio Mario & then 41.* ⬤ *Tue–Sun.* ⬤ *public hols.* ♿

An interior view of the 18th-century Palazzina di Caccia di Stupinigi

I N 1729–30 THE ARCHITECT Filippo Juvarra (1676–1736) designed the magnificent hunting lodge of Stupinigi – also known as the Palazzina di Caccia di Stupinigi, or the Villa Reale di Stupinigi – at a beautiful location 9 km (5 miles) southwest of Turin.

It was created for Vittorio Amedeo II and is one of the very finest hunting lodges, built on an impressive scale, reminiscent of the palace of Versailles in France.

The dynamic and complex plan incorporates semicircles and an octagon, with the main block consisting of a dome rising above a circular building from which wings jut out, not unlike the arms of a windmill.

The mass of the central section is lightened by balustrading topped with urns and figures, while the dome is crowned with an 18th-century bronze figure of a stag.

The huge interior includes rooms sumptuously decorated with *trompe l'oeil* paintings and frescoes on a hunting theme – the 18th-century *Triumph of Diana*, for instance, in the main *salone*. About 40 of those rooms house the interesting **Museo d'Arte e di Ammobiliamento**, a museum specializing in 17th- and 18th-century furniture and furnishings. Many of the ornate items on display in these rooms were originally kept in other former royal residences.

Outside there are extensive grounds, which feature an elegant combination of spectacular broad avenues, parkland and colourful formal parterres.

Basilica di Superga ⑮

Strada Basilica di Superga 73, Comune di Torino. (011-898 00 83. Ⓕ Ⓢ *Sassi.* 🚌 *79 from Sassi.* ⬤ *8:30am–noon, 3–5pm daily.* **Tombs** ⬤ *Fri, public hols.* **Donation.**

O N A HILL to the east of Turin, reachable by car or by railway, stands the superb Baroque basilica of Superga, built by Juvarra in 1717–31. The commission came from Duke Vittorio Amedeo II, in fulfilment of a vow made to the Virgin Mary in 1706 while the French were besieging the duke and his army in Turin.

The beautiful yellow and white façade is dominated by a large portico designed like a Classical temple, with a high dome immediately beyond. It is flanked by twin bell towers on either side. The interior is magnificent, decorated in light blue and yellow, and contains numerous fine paintings and carvings of interest.

Underneath the basilica lies the great mausoleum which houses the tombs of the kings of Sardinia and of various princes and dukes of Savoy. Turin's 1949 aircrash victims, including the city's football team, are also remembered on a plaque behind the basilica.

One of the other benefits of visiting the basilica is the breathtaking views it affords over both Turin and the surrounding countryside.

The imposing façade of the 18th-century Baroque Basilica di Superga designed by Filippo Juvarra

The 17th-century Basilica dell'Assunta dominating Sacro Monte, Varallo

Santuario d'Oropa 🄰

Via Santuario d'Oropa 480, Comune di Biella. 🄲 015-245 59 20.
🄵🄢 Biella. 🚌 from Biella. ⭘ daily. ♿

PERCHED ABOVE the wool town of Biella stands the tranquil church and hospice complex of Oropa, a series of three squares surrounded by pale buildings with stone-shingled roofs, cut into the forested hillside.

The sanctuary, which dates largely from the 17th and 18th centuries, was originally founded in the 4th century by Sant' Eusebio, Bishop of Vercelli. It was intended as a hospice for the poor, and to honour the "Black Madonna" which he had brought back from the Holy Land. The Madonna, said to be the work of St Luke himself, is the object of some of the biggest and most important pilgrimages in the region.

The statue of the Madonna is kept in the restored **Chiesa Vecchia** (Old Church), whose façade was designed by Filippo Juvarra (1676–1736). Beyond it, at the top of the complex, rises the imposing mass of the Neo-Classical **Chiesa Nuova** (New Church), which was begun in 1885 but completed only in 1960.

Behind this church, a footpath leads to the cable car up to Monte Mucrone, from where there is good walking countryside and a small, attractive mountain lake. On a hill southwest of the complex stand 19 chapels, a dozen of which date from between 1620 and 1720. They contain frescoed scenes which depict the life of the Virgin.

Domodossola 🄷

Verbania. 🏛 20,000. 🄵🄢 🚌
🄸 Corso Ferraris 49 (0324-48 13 08).
🄴 Sat.

DOMODOSSOLA is an attractive mountain town of Roman origin. At its centre lies the **Piazza del Mercato**, or market square, framed by attractive arcades and houses dating from the 15th and 16th centuries.

The Ossola valley, where the town lies, sits in an Alpine landscape of pasture and forest sliced by rivers and streams, dotted with dams. Pretty villages north of Domodossola include the resort of **Bagni di Crodo**, with its cold-water mineral spas, and **Baceno**, where the 14th–16th century church – the most important in the region – contains fine frescoes and wood carvings.

Further north still, the Antigorio and Formazza valleys are planted with fig trees and vineyards. Just before La Frua, spectacular waterfalls drop about 145 m (475 ft) when the waters are not being harnessed for power. The idyllic, wooded Valle Vigezzo, east of Domodossola, also offers some breathtaking scenery.

Varallo 🄸

Vercelli. 🏛 7,900. 🄵🄢 🚌
🄸 Corso Roma 38 (0163-5512 80).
🄴 Tue.

THE SMALL TOWN and tourist resort of Varallo lies half-way up the attractive Sesia valley, and boasts a remarkable church, **Santa Maria delle Grazie**. The late 15th-century church is notable for its beautiful frescoed wall depicting the Life of Christ and *trompe l'oeil* architectural elements; the paintings are the work of Gaudenzio Ferrari (1484–1546).

A long stairway behind the church (and also a cableway) climbs up to the even more extraordinary **Sacro Monte**, a religious community built at an altitude of about 610 m (2,000 ft). This "Sacred Mount" was founded as a sanctuary of the New Jerusalem in 1486 and sponsored by the Archbishop of Milan, San Carlo Borromeo.

The Basilica dell'Assunta, with a 19th-century façade, is set in a tranquil courtyard with palm trees and a fountain; the interior is a riot of ornate Baroque architecture. Dotted around it are over 40 chapels representing the sacred sites of Jerusalem, with statues and painted figures positioned in front of frescoed backdrops painted by Gaudenzio Ferrari, Tanzio da Varallo and others.

Christ Condemned (16th century) in a chapel at Varallo's Sacro Monte

The interior of the church of San Giulio in the middle of Lake Orta

Lake Orta ⓳

Novara. FS 🚍 ⛴ Orta.
ℹ️ Via Olina 9, Orta San Giulio (0322-91 19 37).

L AKE ORTA IS ONE of Italy's least visited lakes – unjustly, as it is delightfully set among the foothills of the Alps.

The lake's main resort is **Orta San Giulio**, a small town with a historic centre containing handsome palazzi, and houses decorated with wrought-iron balconies. In the lakeside **Piazza Principale** stands the Palazzo della Comunità, a frescoed building of 1582 resting on arcades. At the top of a mound stands the 15th-century church of **Santa Maria Assunta** (rebuilt in the 17th century), with a Romanesque doorway and an interior that is richly decorated with 17th-century frescoes and paintings.

Above Orta San Giulio is the sanctuary of **Sacro Monte**, built from 1591 to 1770 and dedicated to St Francis of Assisi. A winding path, offering lovely views of the lake,

climbs to the church. The path is lined by 21 chapels, most of them Baroque, in which frescoes and life-size figure groups by various artists depict scenes from the life of St Francis.

In the middle of the lake rises the picturesque **Isola San Giulio**. The island was said to have been liberated from snakes and monsters by the 4th-century Christian preacher Julius, from whom the island's name derives. A basilica stands on the island to this day; it is notable for its 12th-century black marble pulpit decorated with wild animals and birds, and for the 15th-century frescoes – including one attributed to Gaudenzio Ferrari, of the *Virgin and Child Enthroned*.

Novara ⓴

🏃 105,000. FS 🚍 ℹ️ Via Dominioni 4 (0321-39 84 94). 🏪 Mon, Thu & Sat.

Fresco detail of a horseman (17th century) by Morazzone in San Gaudenzio, Novara

N OVARA HAS DISTANT origins as the Roman city of Nubliaria – meaning "surrounded in mist". Nowadays its delightful arcaded streets and

squares, and historic buildings, exude a quiet affluence. Many of the most important buildings stand around Piazza della Repubblica. They include the beautiful Renaissance courtyard of the **Broletto** (town hall), which attracts many art students, who come to sketch its graceful 15th-century red-brick arcades and covered stairway. The buildings now house a small **Museo Civico**, comprising an archaeological section, a picture gallery and a modern art gallery.

Across the piazza rises the **Duomo**, rebuilt by the architect Alessandro Antonelli in around 1865 in Neo-Classical style, with a huge central doorway. The interior contains dramatic Renaissance paintings of the Vercelli school and Flemish tapestries, as well as the remains of an earlier sanctuary on this site: these include the frescoed 12th-century chapel of San Siro and the 15th-century cloisters. The octagonal **Baptistry** next door dates in part from the 5th century and is painted with medieval frescoed scenes of the terrible Apocalypse.

A few streets away stands the church of **San Gaudenzio**. It is strikingly crowned by an elongated four-tiered dome and spire, designed by Antonelli, and reminiscent of his Mole Antonelliana in Turin (see p216). At the top of the spire, which is 121 m (400 ft) high, is a statue of San Gaudenzio himself. Inside, the late 16th-century church contains a fine collection of Renaissance and Baroque paintings by artists from Piedmont: these include a notable 17th-century battle scene by Tanzio da Varallo, a 16th-century altarpiece by Gaudenzio Ferrari, and a fresco painting by Pier Francesco Morazzone (c.1572–1626).

🏛 **Museo Civico**
Via Fratelli Rosselli 20. 📞 0321-62 70 37. 🕐 Tue–Sun. 🔴 public hols. 🉐
⛪ **Baptistry**
Piazza della Repubblica. 📞 0321-39 30 31. 🕐 ask at the Curia Arcivescovile.

View across Lake Orta to the Isola San Giulio

Vercelli ㉑

🏃 50,000. FS ▦ 🛈 Viale Garibaldi 90 (0161-25 78 88). ♿ Tue & Fri.

VERCELLI IS THE RICE capital of Europe, set in a vast plain of paddy fields that give rise to millions of plates of risotto each year. The paddies provide a sight of shimmering sheets of water stretching far into the distance. Vercelli itself also developed its own school of painting in the 16th century, and has one major architectural treasure, the 13th-century **Basilica di Sant'Andrea**.

The Basilica, standing just across from the railway station, is famous as the first example of Italian architecture to be influenced by the Gothic style of northern France – note the beautiful vaulted nave and the flying buttresses, typical Gothic elements. Overall, however, the Basilica remains a stunning achievement in Romanesque architecture, built from 1219 to 1227 as part of an abbey for the papal legate Cardinal Guala Bicchieri. The façade, curiously, changes colour halfway up, the blue-grey of the lower part turning to red and white in the twin towers; these are linked by a double arcade. A carving attributed to Antelami (12th century) adorns the central lunette.

The three-aisled interior is gently illuminated through rose windows. The muted decoration is largely focused on the vaulting, which is supported by tall, slender shafts. Off the north side is the simple 13th-century cloister, beautifully framed by arcades rising from clustered columns.

Vercelli's other important historic buildings are not far away, including the imposing 16th-century **Duomo**, the **Ospedale Maggiore** (13th century), and the church of **San Cristoforo**, with frescoes and a particularly fine Madonna (both c.1529) painted by Gaudenzio Ferrari. The **Museo Civico Borgogna** is the best place to admire the masterpieces of the Vercelli school. The main shopping street, Corso Libertà, has a handful of attractive 15th-century houses and courtyards.

🏛 Museo Civico Borgogna

Via Antonio Borgogna 8. 📞 0161-25 27 76. 🕐 Tue–Fri pm, Sat & Sun am. ⬤ 1 Jan, 15 Aug, 1 Nov, 25 Dec. **Donation.**

The 13th-century cloisters of the Basilica di Sant'Andrea in Vercelli

Asti ㉒

🏃 74,000. FS ▦ 🛈 Piazza Alfieri 34 (0141-53 03 57). ♿ Wed & Sat.

MOST OFTEN ASSOCIATED only with sweet *spumante* (sparkling) wine, Asti is in fact at the centre of Italy's most prestigious wine region *(see*

Detail of the carving on the 15th-century porch at the entrance to the Duomo in Asti

pp176–7) and also a tranquil and noble city of medieval towers, elegant churches and warm red roofs.

Just north of the main railway station lies the Piazza del Campo del Palio, the largest square in Asti and the site of its annual horse race. The race, held towards the end of September to coincide with the local wine fair, rivals the Palio in Siena *(see p331)* for outrageous horsemanship and medieval pageantry.

Beyond this square lies another, the triangular-shaped **Piazza Alfieri**. A statue here commemorates the local poet and dramatist Vittorio Alfieri (1749–1803), in whose honour both this square and the main street were renamed.

Corso Alfieri runs the entire length of the old city centre. At its eastern end stands the 15th-century church of **San Pietro in Consavia**, with terracotta decoration and 17th-century frescoes, and an attractive cloister. Beside it is the circular Romanesque **baptistry** which dates back to the 10th–12th centuries; it was once the church of the knights of the Order of St John of Jerusalem, who established their headquarters here.

West of Piazza Alfieri is the **Collegiata di San Secondo**, (13th–15th century) named after Asti's patron saint, which houses a Renaissance polyptych by Gandolfino d'Asti and 15th-century frescoes. The area around the western section of Corso Alfieri contains a few of the medieval towers for which the town was once famous; they include the Torre dei Comentini, the very elegant Torre Troyana and, at the far

The watery expanses of the rice fields around Vercelli

...end, the Torre Romana. This was built on the ruins of a tower in which San Secondo, a Roman soldier, was held. The nearby 14th-century Gothic **Duomo** has a 15th-century porch and, inside, 18th-century frescoes, stoups made from ancient capitals, and two 12th-to 13th-century carvings on the west corner of the transept.

Cuneo ㉓

🏘 *56,000.* FS ⛴ 🛈 *Corso Nizza 17 (0171-69 32 58).* 🛒 *Tue.*

Cuneo derives its name from *cuneato*, meaning wedge-shaped, which describes the sliver of land that the town occupies at the confluence of two rivers, the Gesso and the Stura di Demonte. In early November the town hosts the regional cheese fair, with unusual local cheese varieties.

The market town centres on an enormous main square, **Piazza Galimberti**, with its old arcades, where the traders come to hawk their wares every Tuesday. Much of the town was rebuilt in the 18th and 19th centuries, providing Cuneo with wide, tree-lined boulevards, though the impressive viaduct which takes the railway line into town dates from the 1930s. The deconsecrated 13th-century church of **San Francesco** has a fine 15th-century portal. The 18th-century church of **Santa Croce** has an unusual concave façade by Francesco Gallo.

Cuneo is a good base for exploring the pretty local valleys, such as the Valle Stura where rare flowers grow.

Bossea ㉔

Località Bossea, Comune Frabosa Soprana. 📞 *0174-34 92 40.* FS *Mondovì.* 🚌 *from Mondovì.* ⭕ *daily for guided tours only.* 📷

Some 25 km (16 miles) south of Mondovì, near the end of a scenic route which follows the valley of the Torrente Corsaglia up into the Maritime Alps, are the caves of Bossea, some of the finest in all Italy. The series of caves contain remarkable and beautiful stalactite columns and shapes that have formed over many thousands of years. Guided tours lead through different chambers – some of them surprisingly vast – following the underground rivers and lakes. The skeleton of a prehistoric bear, *Ursus spelaeus*, which was discovered in the caves, may also be seen on display.

Bring a sweater – the temperature rarely rises above 9° C (50° F).

The Castello di Casotto in the hills above the resort of Garessio

Garessio ㉕

Cuneo. 🏘 *4,000.* FS 🚌 🛈 *Via al Santuario 2 (0174-811 22).* 🛒 *Fri.*

One of the prettier resorts of the Maritime Alps, Garessio is no more than a sprinkling of houses spread out over the hills, surrounded by woods of chestnut trees. It is also a popular spa.

According to local legend, the waters here have miraculous powers: in about AD 980 an octogenarian nobleman called Aleramo found instant relief from his painful kidney and circulatory problems by drinking the mineral-rich water. Since then, the waters have been drunk for their remedial properties – linked in particular with the relief of diuretic and digestive problems – and for their refreshing taste.

Environs: About 16 km (10 miles) west of Garessio stands the **Castello di Casotto**, the dramatically-sited summer palace used by the House of Savoy. The royal family used to come here to enjoy the local mineral water, the attractive scenery and the exceptionally pure air of the hills.

The town of **Ormea**, 12 km (7 miles) southwest, is interesting for its ruined 11th-century castle, its church with late 14th-century Gothic frescoes, and its attractive houses.

⛫ Castello di Casotto
Garessio. 📞 *0174-35 11 31.* ⭕ *daily.* 📷

Market day in the enormous Piazza Galimberti at the centre of Cuneo

LIGURIA

L IGURIA IS A LONG, THIN COASTAL STRIP *nestling at the foot of vine-covered mountains. Here pastel-coloured houses bask in the Mediterranean sun, while their gardens, flourishing in the mild climate, are a riot of colourful plants. In contrast with resorts like Portofino and even San Remo, the bustling city of Genoa, for centuries a trading port of immense power, is the only major population centre.*

Genoa has a long history as a seafaring power, achieving greatness first as a trading post with ancient Greece and Phoenicia, and later, as the capital of a small commercial empire that at one stage eclipsed even Venice. The great sea admiral Andrea Doria came from Genoa, as did the 15th-century explorer of the Americas, Christopher Columbus.

Genoa's rise began in the 12th century, when it succeeded in beating back the Saracen pirates that plagued the Ligurian coast. From then on, the maritime republic prospered, profiting from the Crusades to set up trading posts in the Middle East and marshalling its naval might to humble its rivals. The golden age lasted until the 16th century and the glorious reign of Andrea Doria, who enriched the city further by financing the wars of Genoa's European allies through the good offices of the city's bank. Factionalism among the ruling aristocracy, however, and foreign conquest, first by the French in 1668 and then the Austrians in 1734, led to the region's decline. It was only in the early 19th century, with unification fervour spreading thanks to native son Giuseppe Mazzini and the revolutionary Garibaldi, that Liguria ever recaptured a glimpse of its former prominence.

Today, sheltered by the steep slopes that rise up from the sea, houses of faded elegance lie all along the coast, particularly in San Remo, where aristocrats came to spend the winter in gracious mansions at the end of the 19th century.

Green shutters and rich ochre walls characterize the houses of Portofino

◁ Rugged cliffs tumble into the sea along Liguria's Riviera Levante

Exploring Liguria

L IGURIA DIVIDES NEATLY into two parts. The western coastline, known as the Riviera Ponente, is a thin strip of coastal plain stretching across to the French border, while the eastern coastline, or Riviera Levante, is more rugged and picturesque, descending directly into the sea. Between the two lengths of coast lies the region's capital and biggest port, Genoa (Genova). The faded elegance of the tranquil coastal villages contrasts with this cramped and busy port which snakes along the coast, hemmed in between the sea and the mountains rising steeply behind it.

Stag motif of the city of Cervo, above the cathedral doors

Genoese street market selling fruit and vegetables

SIGHTS AT A GLANCE

KEY

════ Motorway

──── Major road

──── Minor road

──── Scenic route

≈ River

⚡ Viewpoint

0 kilometres 25

0 miles 10

Nice
Monaco →

The smart resort of San Remo on the Riviera Ponente, west of Genoa

SEE ALSO

- **Where to Stay** pp554–5

- **Where to Eat** pp589

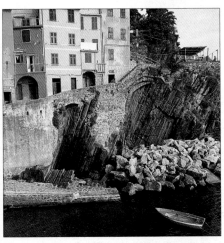

Houses wedged into the cliffs in Riomaggiore, Cinque Terre

GETTING AROUND

If you keep to the coast, transport in Liguria is straightforward. The A10 motorway, becoming the A12 at Genoa, and a mainline railway hug the shore from the French border to Tuscany. The main stations along the route are at Ventimiglia, San Remo, Imperia, Savona, Genoa and La Spezia. There are good road and rail links between Genoa and Milan and Turin. Access to inland Liguria is harder because of the mountains. Bus services link many of the coastal towns with the prettiest hill villages. If you have a car you can explore some of the countryside by following the smaller routes, such as the N28 from Imperia towards Garessio in Piedmont, the N334 from Albisola or the N456 from Voltri towards Milan.

The spectacular gardens of the
Villa Hanbury near Ventimiglia

Balzi Rossi **1**

Imperia. **FS** *Ventimiglia & Mentone.*
*from Ventimiglia to Ponte San
Luigi & then a ten-minute walk.*

AN UNASSUMING promontory
is the setting for some of
the most important caves in
northern Italy. Guided tours
lead through the traces of the
cave-dwelling civilization of
pre-Iron Age Liguria. The caves
contain excavated burial sites
where the dead were adorned
with sea-shells. The **Museo
Nazionale dei Balzi Rossi**
contains tools, weapons and
stone-etched female figures
dating from 100,000 years
ago. There is also a reproduc-
tion of an etching of a horse
found in one of the caves.

🏛 Museo Nazionale dei
Balzi Rossi

Via Balzi Rossi 9, Frazione di Balzi
Rossi. **[** *0184-381 13.* ◯ *daily.*
● *1 Jan, 1 May, 25 Dec.* 🈶 🕭

Villa Hanbury **2**

Corso Monte Carlo 43, Località La
Mortola. **[** *0184-22 95 07.*
FS *Ventimiglia.* *from Ventimiglia.*
◯ *daily (Oct–Mar: Thu–Tue).* 🈶 🕭

IN 1867 THE ENGLISH botanist
Sir Thomas Hanbury and
his brother bought this villa on
the Mortola promontory. They
took full advantage of the
exceptionally mild and sunny
Ligurian climate to establish a
garden of exotic plants along
the sloping pathways of the
enchanting seaside villa.
   The collection, which
Hanbury had himself gathered
on trips to Africa and Asia, has
since grown to number more
than 3,000 varieties of tropical
flora including rubber trees,
palms and wild cacti.
   The garden is now run by
the state and is one of the
most impressive botanical
gardens in Italy. Even in winter
visitors will find a wealth of
colour and vegetation here.

Dolceacqua **3**

Imperia. 🏠 *1,900.* **FS** **i** *Via
Patrioti Martiri 58 (0184-20 66 66).*
● *Thu.*

THIS PRETTY wine-producing
village, 8 km (5 miles)
north of Ventimiglia, is built
on either side of the churning
River Nervia, its two halves
joined by an arching 33-m
(108-ft) medieval stone bridge.
The highlight is the ruined
castle (12th–15th century)
inhabited for a while in the
16th century by the powerful
Doria family from Genoa. The

two square towers at the front
dominate the village. The
terraced vineyards in the surrounding hills produce
bunches of grapes for general
consumption as well as for a
robust red wine known as
Rossese or vino di Dolceacqua.

San Remo **4**

Imperia. 🏠 *60,000.* **FS**
i *Largo Nuvoloni 1 (0184-57 15 71).*
📧 *Tue & Sat.*

The Casinò Municipale in San
Remo, completed in 1906

SAN REMO IS a pleasant resort
of faded elegance where
late 19th-century aristocrats
first discovered the pleasures
of the Italian Riviera. The
composer Tchaikovsky, Alfred
Nobel (the father of modern
explosives) and the nonsense
poet Edward Lear all stayed in
the stuccoed mansions of the
palm-lined seafront avenue, the
Corso dell'Imperatrice. The
focus of the town, then as
now, is the Casino. A little
further down the Corso stands
the ornate onion-domed
Russian Orthodox church.
   An enchanting flower market
is held on Corso Garibaldi
early in the mornings, while
rising up on the hill called La
Pigna are the winding streets
and pastel-coloured shutters
of the old town. A funicular
railway climbs up to Monte
Bignone, which has excellent
views over the Riviera.

Bussana Vecchia **5**

Imperia. Off San Remo–Arma di
Taggià road.

BUSSANA VECCHIA is a marvellously atmospheric ghost
town. In February 1887 an
earthquake shook the village,
reducing its Baroque church

The village of Dolceacqua with its medieval bridge and ruined castle and surrounding houses to ruins. (One survivor, Giovanni Torre del Merlo, went on to invent the ice-cream cone).

The town was rebuilt as Bussana Nuova about 2 km (1 mile) closer to the sea. Since then the old village has been taken over by artists, who have restored some interiors, providing a venue for summer concerts and exhibitions.

Cervo ❻

Imperia. 🏛 *1,400*. FS 🚌
ℹ *Piazza Castello 1 (0183-40 81 97).*
🚢 *Thu.*

CERVO IS THE PRETTIEST of the many seafront villages just east of Imperia, with a narrow complex of streets and houses rising dramatically up from the shingle beach. At the top of the village stands the concave Baroque façade of **San Giovanni Battista**. In front of the church, in July and August, they hold charming chamber orchestra performances. The church is also known as the "*corallina*", after the coral fishing which once brought prosperity for the local people. Now Cervo is an unassuming but characteristic Ligurian holiday resort, with unspoilt hotels near the beach.

The 5th-century Baptistry at Albenga

San Giovanni Battista at Cervo

Spectacular rock formations in the grottoes of Toirano

Albenga ❼

Savona. 🏛 *21,000*. FS 🚌
ℹ *Via Bernardo Ricci (0182-55 47 52).* 🚢 *Wed.*

UNTIL THE Middle Ages, the Roman port of Albium Ingaunum played an important maritime role.

The sea, however, gradually moved further out, leaving the town, now called Albenga, stranded on the Centa River. Most striking now is its Romanesque brick architecture, in particular the three 13th-century towers clustered around the cathedral of **San Michele**. The cathedral's interior was restored to its medieval form in the late 1960s. To the south is an intriguing 5th-century **Baptistry** with a ten-sided exterior and octagonal interior. Inside, the original 5th-century blue and white mosaics of doves represent the 12 apostles. To the north of the cathedral is the small Piazza dei Leoni, named after its three stone lions.

In a 14th-century palace on Piazza San Michele is the **Museo Navale Romano** founded in 1950 following the salvage of a Roman ship that had sunk offshore around 100–90 BC. The museum contains ancient amphorae as well as exhibits salvaged from more recent shipwrecks.

⛪ Baptistry
Piazza San Michele. ☎ *0182-512 15.*
☐ *Tue–Sun.* ⬤ *1 Jan, Easter, 25 Dec.* 🏷

🏛 Museo Navale Romano
Piazza San Michele 12. ☎ *0182-512 15.* ☐ *Tue–Sun.* ⬤ *1 Jan, Easter, 25 Dec.* 🏷

Grotte di Toirano ❽

Piazzale delle Grotte, Toirano.
☎ *0182-980 62.* 🚌 *from Albenga to Borghetto Santo Spirito.* FS *to Borghetto Santo Spirito or Loano then bus.* ☐ *9am–noon, 2–5pm daily.*
⬤ *mid-Nov–mid-Dec & 25 Dec.* 🏷

BENEATH the delightful medieval hilltown of Toirano lies a series of extraordinary caves containing relics of Paleolithic life dating from 80,000 BC.

Guided tours through the **Grotta della Basura** (Witch's Cave) reveal remarkable prehistoric human and animal footprints, and a collection of ancient bear bones and teeth in the "bear cemetery".

The **Grotta di Santa Lucia**, which can also be visited by guided tour, reveals the full beauty of the luminous yellow and grey stalactites and stalagmites that have formed there.

The **Museo Preistorico della Val Varatella** at the entrance to the Grotta della Basura has a small display of finds from the caves, as well as a model of a prehistoric bear.

🏛 Museo Preistorico della Val Varatella
Piazzale delle Grotte. ☎ *0182-980 62.*
☐ *daily.* ⬤ *15 Nov–15 Dec & 25 Dec.* 🏷

Street-by-Street: Genoa ❾

THERE IS SOMETHING refreshingly rough-edged about Genoa (Genova in Italian), Italy's most important commercial port. In contrast to the genteel resorts along the neighbouring coast, the narrow streets of the old town are the haunts of sailors and streetwalkers.

With its natural harbour and the mountains to protect it, Genoa rose to prominence as a sea-based power. During the 16th century the Doria family cemented Genoa's importance, and also proved astute patrons of the arts.

Palazzo Bianco

Piazza San Matteo
The houses and church of San Matteo were built by the Doria family in 1278. Palazzo Quartara has a bas relief of St George above the doorway.

The port and Palazzo Reale

San Lorenzo
The black and white striped Gothic façade of the Duomo dates from the early 13th century.

Palazzo Ducale
Once the seat of the doges of Genoa, this elegant building with its two fine 16th-century courtyards and arcades now contains a major arts and cultural centre.

San Donato has a splendid 12th-century octagonal bell tower.

Sant'Agostino
The 13th-century church and convent were bombed during World War II, but the bell tower remains. The cloisters now house sculpture like this fragment from the tomb of Margaret of Brabant by Pisano (1311).

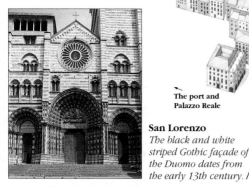

KEY

– – – – Suggested route

| 0 metres | 100 |
| 0 yards | 100 |

VICO TRE RE MAGI

Il Gesù
This Baroque church, built between 1589 and 1606, is also known as the church of Santi Ambrogio e Andrea.

VISITORS' CHECKLIST

765,000. Cristoforo Colombo 6 km (4 miles) W. Stazione Principe, Piazza Acquaverde. Stazione Marittima, Ponte dei Mille. Via Roma 11 (010-54 15 41); Stazione Principe (010-246 26 33). Mon, Wed & Thu. 25 Jun: Sagra di San Pietro; Jul: Genova Si Apre (concerts, shows & exhibitions); Oct: Fiera Nautica.

Piazza De Ferrari is the site of the Neo-Classical Banco di Roma and the Accademia, as well as the restored Teatro Carlo Felice.

The bronze fountain in Piazza De Ferrari was constructed in 1936.

Porta Soprana
The eastern gateway to the city has curved outer walls and stands close to the site of Christopher Columbus's house.

Sant'Andrea
The 12th-century cloisters standing in a small garden are all that remain of the convent that once stood here.

19th-century lion guarding the steps leading to the Duomo

San Lorenzo (Duomo)
Piazza San Lorenzo. 010-29 68 17. daily. **Museo del Tesoro** 010-29 66 95. Mon, Wed, Fri, Sun. public hols.

The Duomo, with its black and white striped exterior, blends virtually every architectural style Genoa has ever known, from the 12th-century Romanesque side portal of San Giovanni to the Baroque touches of some of its side chapels. The three portals at the west end are in French Gothic style. The most sumptuous of the chapels is dedicated to St John the Baptist, patron saint of Genoa; it includes a 13th-century sarcophagus that once contained the saint's relics. Steps lead down from the sacristy to the **Museo del Tesoro di San Lorenzo** which houses such treasures as the Roman green glass dish said to have been used at the Last Supper, and a blue chalcedony plate on which the head of John the Baptist was allegedly served up to Salome.

The Port
The port is the heart of Genoa and the origin of its wealth and power as a seafaring city state in the 11th and 12th centuries. It is a workaday place, given over to container shipping, and ringed by busy roads and 1960s wharves and office buildings.

Among the vestiges of its medieval glory is the **Lanterna** lighthouse (restored in the 1540s) near the Stazione Marittima. In the old days fires would be lit at the top of the Lanterna to guide ships into port. Today, regeneration of the port is in part due to the modern conference centre designed by Renzo Piano *(see p179)*. The best way to see the port is from the sea; boats, giving guided tours, depart from Ponte dei Mille.

Exploring Genoa

VISITORS ARE WELL REWARDED when they explore Genoa – a city proud of its history and legends. The palaces of the Via Balbi and Via Garibaldi, and the paintings and sculptures dotted around the city in churches and museums, are among the finest in northwestern Italy. The environs, too, provide scenic and relaxing locations for excursions along the coast or in the steep hills behind.

The courtyard of the University on Via Balbi

♙ Sant'Agostino
Piazza Sarzano 35. **010-20 16 61.**
◯ Tue–Sat pm. ● public hols.
Museo di Architettura e Scultura Ligure ◯ Tue–Sat & Sun am.
● public hols. ▨ ⚐
The Gothic church of Sant'Agostino was begun in 1260, but bombed to pieces in World War II. It is now deconsecrated and all that remains of the original building is the fine Gothic bell tower, decorated with coloured tiles. The monastery, of which the church of Sant'Agostino was

once a part, was also bombed. What remained were two ruined cloisters – one of which forms the only triangular building in Genoa. The cloisters have recently been reconstructed and converted into the **Museo di Architettura e Scultura Ligure**. It contains the city's collection of architectural pieces and fragments of sculpture, as well as frescoes – all salvaged from Genoa's other destroyed churches. The finest piece is a magnificent fragment from the tomb of Margaret of Brabant. Margaret, who died in 1311, was the wife of Emperor Henry VII who invaded Italy in 1310. Carved by Giovanni Pisano around 1313, the sculptures from her tomb were restored and repositioned in 1987. The figures, whose garments are arranged in simple folds, seem to be helping Margaret to lay down to rest.

⊞ Palazzo Reale
Via Balbi 10. **010-247 06 40.**
◯ daily. ● 1 Jan, 1 May, 25 Dec.
▨ ⚐
This austere-looking residence, used by the Kings of Savoy from the 17th century onwards, has a highly ornate Rococo interior – notably its ballroom and its Hall of Mirrors. Among the paintings are works by Parodi and Carlone and a *Crucifixion* by Van Dyck. The lovely garden, which slopes down towards the old port, includes an intriguing cobblestone mosaic around the central fountain, depicting houses and animals.
  Opposite the palace is the old **University** (1650) designed by the architect Bartolomeo Bianco, as was much of Via Balbi. The large building brilliantly overcomes Genoa's hilly topography, and is constructed on four levels.

⊞ Palazzo Bianco
Via Garibaldi 11. **010-29 18 03.**
◯ Tue–Sun am. ▨ **Palazzo Rosso** ◯ as for Palazzo Bianco. ▨
The Palazzo Bianco is situated on Genoa's most beautiful street, the **Via Garibaldi**, where there are numerous fine 16th-century mansions and palazzi. The Palazzo Bianco contains the city's prime collection of paintings, including the works of many Genoese artists such as Luca Cambiaso, Bernardo Strozzi, Domenico Piola and Giovanni Benedetto Castiglione. Better-known artists featured here

A portrait of Columbus, Villa Doria in Pegli

CHRISTOPHER COLUMBUS IN GENOA

The name of Christopher Columbus, the explorer of the New World, is in evidence all over Genoa. His statue greets you as soon as you emerge in Piazza Acquaverde from Porta Principe railway station; various public buildings bear his name; even the airport is called Aeroporto Cristoforo Colombo. In the 17th-century Palazzo Belimbau, built on top of the old city walls, is a series of frescoes by the Genoese artist Tavarone celebrating the explorer's life and you can see three of his letters in the Sala del Sindaco in Palazzo Tursi (the city hall) on Via Garibaldi. It is not certain whether Columbus (c.1451–1506) was born in Genoa, in Savona 15 km (9 miles) to the west or outside Italy altogether. However, city registers mention his father, a weaver, and different family homes within the city. The small ivy-clad house next to the Porta Soprana may have been Columbus's childhood home, where he first discovered his passion for the sea.

The house where Columbus may have lived

The romantic gardens at Villa Durazzo-Pallavicini in Pegli

include Filippino Lippi (a lovely *Madonna with Saints*), Veronese, Van Dyck and Rubens. Across the street in the **Palazzo Rosso** are more paintings, including work by Dürer and Caravaggio, as well as ceramics, furniture and coins. Upstairs in the *piano nobile* the rooms are adorned with 17th-century frescoes by Genoese artists such as de Ferrari and Piola.

⚏ Staglieno Cemetery
Piazzale Resasco, Staglieno. ☎ 010-87 01 84. ☐ daily. ☐ public hols. ☐

Fine tomb architecture from the huge Staglieno Cemetery

This grandiose cemetery, just over the hills northeast of Genoa along the Bisagno River, is so big (160 ha, 395 acres) that it has its own internal bus system. Founded in 1844, its tombs and monuments make up an eerie city of miniature cathedrals, Egyptian temples and Art Nouveau palaces. Its most famous resident is Giuseppe Mazzini, the Genoese revolutionary who died not far from Pisa in 1872.

ENVIRONS: Until World War II, **Pegli**, 6 km (4 miles) west of the city centre, was a popular weekend retreat for rich Genoese wanting to get away from it all. Now it forms part of the metropolis, but nevertheless maintains an air of tranquillity thanks to its parks and two villas, the 19th-century **Villa Durazzo-Pallavicini** and the 16th-century **Villa Doria**. The latter now houses a naval history museum celebrating Genoa's glorious past: you can see globes, compasses, astrolabes, maps, model ships and a portrait of Columbus ascribed to Ghirlandaio, probably dating from 1525. The Villa Durazzo-Pallavicini houses an archaeological museum which relates the pre-Roman history of the Ligurian coast. The villa's garden is landscaped with romantic grottoes, pavilions and fountains.

Nervi, 8 km (5 miles) to the east of the city, is another former resort town, famous for its sea-front promenade, the **Passeggiata Anita Garibaldi** (named after Garibaldi's Brazilian wife). The walk crosses the Nervi torrent and follows a route that has been cut into the rock face, giving panoramic views

of the coast. The lush **Parco Municipale** is another feature of Nervi. It once formed the grounds of two aristocratic villas – the Villa Serra and the Villa Gropallo. The gardens contain some rare species of exotic and Mediterranean trees.

The Villa Serra on Via Capolungo now houses the **Galleria d'Arte Moderna** featuring modern Italian painting. The **Villa Luxoro** on Via Aurelia is notable for its collection of clocks, fabrics, furniture and lace. The area is also famous as Garibaldi's departure point when he set off for Sicily with his *Mille* (the famous "Thousand" men) to bring about the unification of Italy. A large monument at Quarto dei Mille, about 3 km (2 miles) back towards the city, marks the place where the volunteers met in May 1860 to follow the intrepid revolutionary *(see pp58–9)*.

⛪ Villa Doria
Piazza Bonavino 7, Pegli. ☎ 010-696 98 85. ☐ Tue–Sat & 1st & 3rd Sun of month. ☐ public hols. ☐ ☐

⛪ Villa Durazzo-Pallavicini
Via Pallavicini 11, Pegli. ☎ 010-698 10 48. ☐ Tue–Sat & 2nd & 4th Sun of month. ☐ public hols. ☐ ☐

⛪ Galleria d'Arte Moderna
Villa Serra, Via Capolungo 3, Nervi. ☎ 010-28 26 41. ☐ Tue–Sat. ☐ public hols. ☐

⛪ Villa Luxoro
Via Mafalda di Savoia 3, Nervi. ☎ 010-32 26 73. ☐ Tue–Sat. ☐ public hols. ☐

Pini (c.1920) by Rubaldo Merello in the Galleria d'Arte Moderna at Nervi

Pastel-coloured houses near the pebbly beach at Camogli

Camogli ⓾

Genova. 🏠 6,500. 🚊 🚌 ⛴
ℹ️ *Via XX Settembre 33 (0185-77 10 66).* 🛒 *Wed.*

BUILT ON A pine-wooded slope, Camogli is an attractive fishing village where sea-shells adorn the pastel-painted walls of the houses, and the smell of frying fish wafts out from the small restaurants into the streets. Near the pebble beach and fishing port is the medieval Castello della Dragonara, a castle now containing the **Acquario Tirrenico** which displays 22 tanks of sea creatures.

Camogli celebrates its famous festival of the Blessing of the Fish on the second Sunday of May when sardines are fried in a huge pan 4 m (13 ft) in diameter. The fish is distributed free to all-comers.

fff Acquario Tirrenico
Castello della Dragonara. 📞 0185-77 33 75. 🕐 *Sat, Sun & public hols.* 📷

Portofino Peninsula ⓫

Genova. 🚌 ⛴ *Portofino.* ℹ️ *Via Roma 35 (0185-26 90 24).*

PORTOFINO IS THE most exclusive harbour and resort town in Italy, crammed with the yachts of the wealthy. You can reach Portofino by road (cars are not allowed into the village), or boat, from the resort of Santa Margherita Ligure. Above the town are the church of **San Giorgio**, containing relics said to be of the dragon-slayer, and a castle.

On the other side of the peninsula, which you have to reach on foot (a two-hour walk) or by boat, is the **Abbazia di San Fruttuoso**, named after a 3rd-century saint whose followers were shipwrecked here and, according to local folklore, protected by three lions. The white abbey buildings, set among pines and olive trees, date mostly from the 11th century, although the imposing Torre dei Doria was added 500 years later. You can take a boat to

The 16th-century castle jutting into Rapallo harbour

try to locate the **Cristo degli Abissi**, a bronze statue of Christ that sits on the sea bed near San Fruttuoso, acting as a protector of sailors. Further west along the coast is Punta Chiappa, a rocky promontory famous for the changing colours of the sea.

fff Abbazia di San Fruttuoso
San Fruttuoso. 📞 *0135-77 27 03.* 🕐 *Tue–Sun (Dec–Feb: public hols & the day before only).* ● *Nov.* 📷

Rapallo ⓬

Genova. 🏃 30,000. 🚊 🚌 ⛴
ℹ️ *Via Diaz 9 (0185-545 73).* 🛒 *Thu.*

HISTORIANS KNOW Rapallo as the place where two treaties – one between Italy and Yugoslavia, the other between Germany and Russia – were signed after World War II. Film buffs might recognize it as a location for *The Barefoot Contessa*, filmed here in 1954. Its villas still have a patrician feel to them, as do the riding stables, golf course and tennis courts. The palm-lined esplanade ends in a small 16th-century **castle**, in which art exhibitions are now occasionally held. Above the village is the 16th-century **Santuario di Montallegro**, which houses a Byzantine icon said to possess miraculous powers.

fff Santuario di Montallegro
Montallegro. 📞 *0185-23 90 00.* 🕐 *daily.*

Large yachts moored in Portofino's famous harbour

The dramatic coastline near Corniglia in the Cinque Terre

Cinque Terre ⓲

La Spezia. 𝐅𝐒 to all towns. 🚤 Monterosso, Vernazza. 🛈 Via Figina, Monterosso (0187-81 75 06).

THE CINQUE TERRE is a protected stretch of rocky coastline on the Riviera di Levante which extends from Monterosso al Mare to Riomaggiore at its southeastern tip. The name refers to five dramatically situated villages which apparently cling to the very edge of vertiginous cliffs: Monterosso al Mare, Vernazza, Corniglia, Manarola and Riomaggiore. The villages were once only accessible by sea and today there is still no road that links them all. An ancient footpath known as the Sentiero Azzurro follows the coast, joining the villages and offering superb views of the distinctive green terraced vineyards that produce the local dry white Cinque Terre wines.

The villages remain spectacularly self-contained, hemmed in by steep cliffs, though they are now suffering from some depopulation. **Monterosso al Mare**, on the northwestern edge of the Cinque Terre, is the largest of the five villages and overlooks a wide bay with its own sandy beach. **Vernazza**, further down the coast, has streets linked by steep steps or *arpaie*. **Corniglia**, perched at the pinnacle of rocky terraces, seems untouched by the passage of time, as does **Manarola** which is linked by the famous Via dell'Amore, or Lovers' Lane, to **Riomaggiore**, a 15-minute walk away. Riomaggiore, like Monterosso, is one of the more accessible villages by road, allowing it to cater better for visitors.

Portovenere ⓴

La Spezia. 𝐀 4,600. 🚌 🚤 🛈 Piazza Bastreri (0187-79 06 91). 🚤 Mon.

NAMED AFTER VENUS herself, Portovenere is one of the most romantic villages on the Ligurian coast with its cluster of narrow streets lined with pastel-coloured houses. In the upper part of the village is the 12th-century church of San Lorenzo. A sculpture over the doorway here depicts the martyr-

Above the doorway of San Lorenzo in Portovenere

dom of the saint who was roasted alive on a grill. On the stone promontory that curls out into the sea stands the small, black and white 13th-century church of **San Pietro**. From here, or from the 16th-century castle on top of the cliffs on the northwestern side of the village, there are glorious views of the Cinque Terre and the small island of Palmaria which lies about 400 m (1,300 ft) offshore.

Lerici ⓯

La Spezia. 𝐀 13,000. 🚌 🚤 🛈 Via Gerini 40 (0187-96 73 46). 🚤 Sat.

THIS STRETCH OF COAST, along the Gulf of La Spezia, was once popular with such English-language literati as Yeats and DH Lawrence. The village of San Terenzo, across the bay from Lerici, was where the poet Shelley spent the last four years of his life. It was from his home, the Casa Magni, that he set out in 1822 on a fatal voyage to meet Leigh Hunt in Livorno. Tragically, he was shipwrecked near Viareggio and drowned.

Lerici, once a small fishing village and now a popular resort, sits on the edge of a beautiful bay, and has a pleasant beach overlooked by pastel-coloured houses. It has a forbidding medieval **castle** which was built by the Pisans and later passed to the Genoese. Apparently carved out of the cliff, it dominates the holiday villas below.

⚓ **Castello di Lerici**
Piazza San Giorgio. 📞 010-96 51 08. 🔓 daily. 📷 ♿

The harbour of Vernazza in the Cinque Terre

A stunning view of Manarola on the Sentiero Azzurro, Cinque Terre ▷

CENTRAL ITALY

Central Italy at a Glance

T HE CENTRAL REGIONS of Italy are popular
with visitors because they offer a range
of beautiful landscapes and towns rich in
culture and history, including outstanding
churches, towers and palaces. Emilia-
Romagna is home to the impressive Po
Delta that provides a haven for wildlife.
Tuscany is dominated by Florence,
one of Italy's most celebrated centres.
Umbria and Le Marche offer gentle
pastoral countryside and
picturesque hilltowns. The
major sights of this rewarding
area are shown here.

*__The Leaning Tower__ of Pisa
and the Duomo (see pp314–16),
splendid examples of 12th- and
13th-century architecture, are
decorated with Arabic-inspired,
complex geometric patterns.*

**Leaning Tower
of Pisa**

TUSC *(See pp3*

FLORENCE
(See pp262–303)

Duomo, Campanile and Baptistry

Uffizi

Palazzo Pitti

*__The Duomo__ and the
Baptistry, set in the
heart of Florence,
dominate the city
(see pp272–4). The
dome dwarfs many
surrounding buildings.*

*__The Uffizi__ contains
a superb collection of
Florentine art from
Gothic to High Renais-
sance and beyond
(see pp278–81).*

The Palazzo Pitti,
begun in 1457 for the
banker Luca Pitti,
became the main resi-
dence of the Medici. It
now houses their treas-
ures (see pp294–5).

0 kilometres   1

0 miles   0.5

0 kilometres

0 miles   25

◁ **Autumn colour in Tuscany, in the hills of the Val d'Orcia, south of Siena**

The church of San Vitale in Ravenna is a gem of Byzantine art and architecture (see p260). It contains brilliantly preserved mosaics from the 6th century.

EMILIA-ROMAGNA
(See pp246–61)

San Vitale, Ravenna

The Palazzo Ducale in Urbino was built by Duke Federico, the town's 15th-century ruler, to plans by Laurana (see pp360–61). This Renaissance palace now houses the Galleria Nazionale delle Marche.

SAN MARINO

Palazzo Ducale, Urbino

LE MARCHE
(See pp354–63)

UMBRIA
(See pp338–53)

NCE
et)

Duomo, Siena

Basilica of San Francesco, Assisi

Giotto's fresco cycle from the Basilica of San Francesco in Assisi was executed in the 13th century (see pp344–7). The church is visited by thousands of pilgrims each year.

Siena, a medieval town steeped in tradition, centres around the Campo, the large piazza shaped like a scallop shell (see pp328–33). The lively horse race, the Corsa del Palio, is held here in July and August.

Regional Food: Central Italy

THE FOOD OF TUSCANY, UMBRIA and Le Marche is simple but often hearty. Packed with flavour, it is based on peasant cooking that relies heavily on olive oil, tomatoes, beans, hams and salamis. Meanwhile, the traditional dishes in Emilia-Romagna tend to be more elaborate, using ingredients such as cream, interesting meats – including game, Parma ham and mortadella – and excellent quality cheeses such as Parmesan. Fresh fish and seafood is available along the coasts, but is often more expensive than meat.

Artichoke

Balsamic vinegar *from Modena in Emilia-Romagna is renowned throughout the world. Aged for up to seven years in oak barrels, the dark, smooth vinegar is used to flavour soups, stews and salad dressings.*

Wild boar salami

Mortadella

Cooked ham (*prosciutto cotto*)

Parma ham

Cured meats and hams *form an important part of the cuisine of central Italy. The most famous is Parma ham from Emilia-Romagna, where the pigs are fattened on the whey left over from making Parmesan cheese.*

Panzanella, *a refreshing summer salad, is made of juicy tomatoes, onion, garlic and oil-soaked bread, garnished with fresh basil.*

Tortelloni, *a larger version of tortellini, may be stuffed with meat or cheese and served with a rich sauce.*

Liver paste

Tomato paste

Olive paste

Anchovy paste

Crostini *are delicious snacks made from rounds of toast topped with anchovy, olive, liver or tomato paste. Bruschetta is grilled bread rubbed with garlic and drizzled with olive oil.*

Spaghetti al Ragù *is a traditional dish from Bologna. The pasta is topped with a generous portion of beef and tomato sauce.*

Cannelloni *is another form of stuffed pasta. Large pasta tubes may be filled with meat or cheese and spinach, and then coated with tomato or cheese sauce before being baked.*

Baccalà *is a simple, flavourful dish of dried salt cod prepared with garlic and garnished with parsley. In Tuscany, tomatoes are often added.*

Bistecca alla Fiorentina, *grilled over an open fire, is a large, tender steak that can be seasoned with oil and herbs and garnished with fresh lemon.*

Scottiglia di Cinghiale *is prepared with wild boar chops. This dish is particularly popular in the Maremma area of southern Tuscany.*

Torta di Limone *is one of the richer desserts that come from Emilia-Romagna. It is prepared with lemons and fresh cream.*

Torta di Riso *is a traditional Tuscan dessert consisting of rice cake served with a simple fruit sauce and seasonal fruit.*

Pecorino

Parmesan

Cheeses *are used in many recipes, but may also be served with fruit as a main course or at the end of a meal.*

Panforte

Panforte *is a dense, dark cake spiced with cinnamon and cloves. Ricciarelli are made from ground almonds, orange peel and honey.*

Cantucci *are sweet Tuscan biscuits often served together with* vin santo, *a traditional dessert wine.*

Ricciarelli

MUSHROOMS AND TRUFFLES

Wild mushrooms are considered a great delicacy in central Italy, and a range of fresh and dried mushrooms are frequently used in cooking. Fresh mushrooms are available in the autumn when restaurants are often packed with locals tasting seasonal mushroom dishes. Prized black truffles *(tartufi neri)* with a rich flavour and firm texture are expensive and used sparingly, as are funghi porcini. Porcini may be served grilled as a main course, used on pizza, in stuffed pasta or served as a vegetable dish, sautéed gently with garlic.

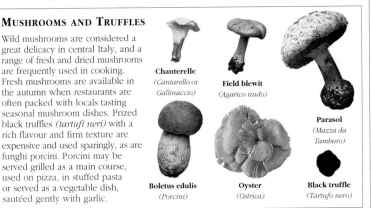

Chanterelle
(Cantarello or Gallinaccio)

Field blewit
(Agarico nudo)

Parasol
(Mazza da Tamburo)

Boletus edulis
(Porcini)

Oyster
(Ostrica)

Black truffle
(Tartufo nero)

The Wines of Central Italy

**Roman mosaic
of a bird
eating grapes**

VINEYARDS ARE SEEN EVERYWHERE in Central Italy, from the rolling cypress-fringed hills of Tuscany to the flatter, Lambrusco-producing plains of Emilia-Romagna. The finest red wines are made in the hills of southeastern Tuscany: Chianti Classico, Brunello di Montalcino and Vino Nobile di Montepulciano. Today's innovative mix of modern and traditional techniques is steadily improving the quality of much of the region's wine.

*Chianti Classico
is the heart of the
Chianti zone. Chianti
may be light and fruity
or dense and long-
lived – price is the
usual guide. Rocca
delle Macie is very
reasonably priced.*

*Vernaccia di San
Gimignano is a Tuscan
white wine with a long,
distinguished history.
Traditionally a golden,
often oxidized wine, it is
now also produced in a
fresher style, for early
drinking. Teruzzi e
Puthod make
consistently
good Vernaccia.*

**Vino Nobile di
Montepulciano** *is made
from the same grapes as
Chianti. It can be of superior
quality, hence its claim to
be a "noble wine". The
vineyards are set around
the delightful hilltop
village of Montepulciano.*

Parma

Modena

Bologna

EMILIA-ROMAGNA

Pistoia

Lucca

Florence

Pisa

Greve

San Gimignano

Siena

TUSCANY

Montepu...

Montalcino

Brunello di Montalcino
*is made from Sangiovese,
Brunello being its local
name. Its firm tannins
may need up to ten
years to soften before
the rich, spicy flavours
are revealed. Rosso di
Montalcino, on the
other hand, can be
enjoyed much younger.*

0 kilometres   50

0 miles   25

VINO DA TAVOLA

During the 1970s innovative wine makers set out to create new, individual wines even though under the existing rules they would be labelled as simple table wine. A trend which started with Antinori's Tignanello (a Sangiovese-Cabernet Sauvignon blend), this approach has reinvigor-ated Tuscan wine, to produce some exciting variations.

SASSICAIA
1985
TENUTA SAN GUIDO

**Sassicaia, a red
wine made from
the Cabernet
Sauvignon grape**

Chianti estate at Badia a Passignano in Tuscany

KEY

- ☐ Chianti
- ☐ Chianti Classico
- ☐ Vernaccia di San Gimignano
- ☐ Brunello di Montalcino
- ☐ Vino Nobile di Montepulciano
- ☐ Orvieto Classico
- ☐ Orvieto
- ☐ Verdicchio dei Castelli di Jesi
- ☐ Lambrusco

Rimini

Pèsaro

Urbino

LE MARCHE

Jesi

Ancona

Gubbio

UMBRIA

erugia

Assisi

GRAPES OF CENTRAL ITALY

The versatile Sangiovese grape dominates wine making in Central Italy. It is the main grape in Chianti, in Vino Nobile di Montepulciano, in Brunello di Montalcino, and in many of the new-style *Vino da Tavola* wines. Of the established whites, Trebbiano and Malvasia head the list. Imported varieties such as white Chardonnay and red Cabernet Sauvignon are playing an increasing role, often being used to complement and enhance native varieties.

Sangiovese grapes

HOW TO READ THE LABEL

Producer's name

The DOCG name is a reliable guide to the origin of the wine.

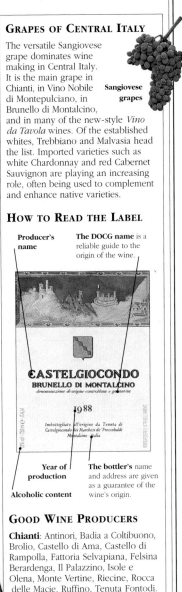

CASTELGIOCONDO
BRUNELLO DI MONTALCINO
denominazione di origine controllata e garantita

1988

Imbottigliato all'origine da Tenuta di Castelgiocondo dei Marchesi de' Frescobaldi Montalcino - Italia

Year of production

The bottler's name and address are given as a guarantee of the wine's origin.

Alcoholic content

GOOD WINE PRODUCERS

Chianti: Antinori, Badia a Coltibuono, Brolio, Castello di Ama, Castello di Rampolla, Fattoria Selvapiana, Felsina Berardenga, Il Palazzino, Isole e Olena, Monte Vertine, Riecine, Rocca delle Macie, Ruffino, Tenuta Fontodi.
Brunello di Montalcino: Argiano, Altesino, Caparzo, Castelgiocondo, Costanti, Il Poggione, Villa Banfi.
Vino Nobile di Montepulciano: Avignonesi, Le Casalte, Poliziano. In **Umbria**: Adanti, Lungarotti.

Verdicchio is a dry white wine from Le Marche with a crisp, slightly salty taste. In recent years the introduction of the single vineyard Verdicchio, such as Umani Ronchi's CaSal di Serra, has won much acclaim.

Orvieto Classico is a popular Umbrian white wine. This fresh, dry (Secco) version from the Antinori estate is a good example of a modern-style Orvieto. The wine also comes in a sweeter form, known as Abboccato.

Good Chianti Vintages
1993, 1990, 1988, 1985, 1983, 1975, 1971, 1970, 1967, 1964, 1961.

Understanding Architecture in Central Italy

CENTRAL ITALY has countless fine Renaissance buildings, many of them concentrated in and around Florence. Their clear lines, elegant simplicity and harmonious proportions came out of a re-evaluation of the past. Turning their backs on the Gothic style, the architects of the Renaissance returned to Classical Rome for inspiration. Most of the large buildings had been started by the late 15th century, paid for by the Catholic Church or by powerful noble families, such as the Medici of Florence.

The Palazzo Ducale in Urbino (begun 1465)

RELIGIOUS BUILDINGS

Arched bays trisect the façade.

Pope Pius II's coat of arms

One of 12 roundels by Luca della Robbia

Small circular windows

Square plan topped by small dome

Symmetrical floorplan is based on a Greek cross.

Harmonious proportions

Pienza's Duomo *was built by Bernardo Rossellino in 1459 for Pope Pius II as part of his vision of the ideal Renaissance city* (see p323).

The Pazzi Chapel *of Santa Croce in Florence (1433) is one of Brunelleschi's most famous works, decorated with terracotta roundels by Luca della Robbia* (see pp276–7).

Santa Maria della Consolazione *in Todi, begun in 1508, owes much to the ideas of the architect Bramante* (see p349).

TOWN AND COUNTRY HOUSES

The cornice was designed to cast a shadow over the face of the palace around midday.

Wedge-shaped masonry

Strong horizontal line

Square windows are found only on the ground floor.

The Palazzo Strozzi *in Florence (1489–1536) is typical of many Tuscan city palaces* (see p318). *The three storeys are given equal importance, and the massive rusticated stonework conveys the impression of strength and power* (see p285).

WHERE TO SEE THE ARCHITECTURE

The simple canons of the Renaissance were interpreted differently away from the hotbed of artistic thought and cultural endeavour of Florence, which has the greatest number of churches and palaces. Alberti's Tempio Malatestiano at Rimini *(see p258)* evokes the sobriety of ancient Roman architecture yet seeks to

Vista in the Boboli Gardens, Florence

reinterpret it in his own unique fashion. Urbino's Palazzo Ducale *(pp360–61)* perfects the grace and polish of the era and is a truly noble period residence. On a smaller scale are the planned Renaissance centres of elegant towns such as Ferrara *(p253)*, Pienza *(p323)* and Urbania *(p359)*. All three centres are examples of enlightened patronage, and pay homage to the art of antiquity.

The weight of the lantern prevents the dome from springing apart.

Timber ribs provide the main support.

Outer shell

Inner shell

The top edge of the frieze divides the façade in two.

Classical triangular pediment

Volute connects the lower and upper parts.

The Duomo in Florence is crowned by the revolutionary dome (1436) by Brunelleschi, which had to be built without scaffolding due to its size. The timber structure is covered by an inner and outer shell (see pp270–71).

The façade of Santa Maria Novella in Florence (1458–70) was designed by Leon Battista Alberti. He incorporated some of the existing Gothic features into an overall design typical of the Renaissance (see pp288–9).

The villa at Poggio a Caiano (1480) was re-designed in the Renaissance by Giuliano da Sangallo (see pp318). The graceful, curved staircase was added around 1802.

Clock, a later addition

Classical frieze

Classical colonnade derived from a Classical temple

Classical portico

EMILIA-ROMAGNA

EMILIA-ROMAGNA is the heartland of central Italy, a broad corridor through the hills and plains of the Po Valley that marks the watershed between the cold north of the Alps and the hot Mediterranean south. With its rich agricultural land, historical cities and thriving industry, it is one of the most prosperous areas in Italy.

Most of the major towns in Emilia-Romagna lie near the Via Aemilia, a Roman road built in 187 BC that linked Rimini on the Adriatic coast with the garrison town of Piacenza. Prior to the Romans, the Etruscans had ruled from their capital, Felsina, located on the site of present-day Bologna. After the fall of Rome, the region's focus moved to Ravenna, which became a principal part of the Byzantine Empire administered from Constantinople.

During the Middle Ages pilgrims heading for Rome continued to use the Via Aemilia. Political power, however, passed to influential noble families – the Malatesta in Rimini, the Bentivoglio in Bologna, the d'Este in Ferrara and Modena, and the Farnese in Parma and Piacenza. Great courts grew up around the families, attracting poets such as Dante and Ariosto, as well as painters, sculptors and architects. Many of their works still grace the medieval centres of these towns.

Modern Emilia-Romagna, cobbled together from separate Papal States in 1860, was given its present borders in 1947. Emilia, covering the western half of the region, is traditionally associated with a more northern outlook and a tendency towards the left in politics. Romagna, with its capital at Ravenna, has always turned to the south for artistic, cultural and political inspiration.

The entire region has a reputation as a great gastronomic centre. Agriculture has long thrived on the Po's alluvial fringes, earning the Pianura Padana (Po Plain) epithets such as the "bread basket" and "fruit bowl" of Italy. Pigs still outnumber humans in many areas, and some of the country's most famous staples – Parma ham and Parmesan cheese – originate here.

The medieval Palazzo del Comune in Ferrara

◁ The Fontana del Nettuno (Neptune's Fountain) in Bologna

Exploring Emilia-Romagna

EMILIA-ROMAGNA is a chequerboard of fields and plains between the Po river to the north and the forest-covered Apennine mountain slopes to the south. The best place to begin a tour of the region is centrally situated Bologna. Modena, its long-time rival, boasts one of the country's loveliest Romanesque cathedrals. Parma has a more provincial feel and Ferrara, too, has an easy-going air. Castell'Arquato offers a taste of the smaller villages that dot the hills south of the Po.

Piazza Cavalli, Piacenza's central square

SEE ALSO

• **Where to Stay** pp555–7

• **Where to Eat** pp590–91

Reed-lined shores along the Po Delta

SIGHTS AT A GLANCE

GETTING AROUND

Excellent road and rail links, aided by predominantly flat terrain, make this region quick and easy to get around. Bologna is connected by the A1 to Florence and by the A13 to Ferrara and Venice. The busy A1 links Bologna with Milan via Piacenza, Fidenza and Parma. The A15 connects Parma with La Spezia, and the A21 joins Piacenza and Cremona. Fast, frequent train services run along almost parallel routes.

The beach at Cesenatico, north of Rimini on the Adriatic coast

KEY

Motorway

Major road

Minor road

Scenic route

River

Viewpoint

0 kilometres 25

0 miles 20

The 13th-century Palazzo Pretorio in Castell'Arquato

Piacenza ●

🏠 105,000. 🚆 🚌 🛈 *Piazzetta dei Mercanti 7 (0523-32 93 24).* 🗓 *Wed & Sat.*

PIACENZA TRACES its history back to Roman times. Located near the Po, it served as a fortified camp protecting the Emilian plain from invasion by both Hannibal and the Gauls. The centre is still based on the Roman plan.

Little visited by tourists, Piacenza has a pleasantly understated old centre that is full of fine medieval and Renaissance buildings. Pride of place goes to two bronze equestrian **statues** in the central Piazza Cavalli, the work of the 17th-century sculptor Francesco Mochi, a pupil of Giambologna. Lauded as masterpieces of Baroque sculpture, the statues represent Alessandro Farnese, a soldier of fortune, and his son, Ranuccio: both were rulers of 16th-century Piacenza.

Behind the statues is the red-brick **Palazzo del Comune**, also known as "Il Gotico", an evocatively battlemented Lombard-Gothic palace begun at the end of the 13th century.

The **Duomo**, at the end of Via XX Settembre, has a rather leaden Lombard-Romanesque exterior (begun in 1122), and a 14th-century campanile. The interior features Guercino's painted cupola and medieval frescoes that adorn the apse and transepts. There are also frescoed saints near the main door, painted to resemble members of the congregation.

The **Museo Civico** offers an eclectic mixture of sculpture and paintings – the star among these is the *Madonna and Child with John the Baptist* by Botticelli (1444–1510). There is also an armoury and archaeology section. The highlight here is the so-called *Fegato di Piacenza*, an Etruscan bronze representation of the sheep livers once used by priests for divination, inscribed with deities' names.

🏛 Museo Civico
Palazzo Farnese, Piazza Cittadella. 📞 *0523-32 82 70.* 🕐 *Tue–Sun.* ⬛ *public hols.* ♿

Detail from façade of Duomo in Fidenza

Castell'Arquato ●

Piacenza. 🏠 4,500. 🚌 🛈 *Viale Remondini 1 (0523-80 30 91).* 🗓 *Mon.*

TUCKED INTO THE FOLDED hills between Fidenza and Piacenza, Castell'Arquato is among the prettiest of the villages scattered around the countryside south of the Po. Day visitors come at the week-ends to escape Emilia's larger cities, thronging the restaurants and bars around the beautiful **Piazza Matteotti**. The best medieval building on the piazza is the 13th-century **Palazzo Pretorio**, a venerable Romanesque basilica. The impressive **Rocca Viscontea** (14th century), a former Visconti fortress, is situated on Piazza del Municipio. The village's hilltop site offers good views, particularly over the verdant Arda valley to the east.

Fidenza ●

Parma. 🏠 23,000. 🚆 🚌 🛈 *Piazza Duomo 2 (0524-840 47).* 🗓 *Wed & Sat.*

LIKE MANY TOWNS hugging the line of the Po, Fidenza owed its early prominence to the Via Aemilia (the old Roman road). The town assumed greater importance as a medieval way station for pilgrims en route to Rome. Today Fidenza is visited for its superb **Duomo** on Piazza Duomo (13th century), a composite piece of architecture that embraces Lombard, Gothic and transitional Romanesque elements. The most immediately eye-catching feature is the opulent façade, probably created by the craftsmen who worked with Benedetto Antelami on Parma's Duomo. Inside, the walls are dotted with fragments of medieval frescoes, while the crypt contains the relics of San Donnino, the Duomo's patron.

Interior of Parma Baptistry

Parma ❹

🏛 175,000. 🚇 🚌 ℹ *Piazza Duomo 5 (0521-23 47 35).*
🛒 *Wed & Sat; Thu (flea).*

FEW ITALIAN TOWNS are as urbane or prosperous as Parma, not only a byword for fine food and good living but also a treasure trove of excellent paintings, superlative sculpture and fine medieval buildings. It boasts one of Italy's top opera houses and a panoply of elegant shops and first-rate bars and restaurants.

The Lombard-Romanesque **Duomo** on Piazza Duomo, among the greatest in northern Italy, is renowned for the painting of the *Assumption* (1534) that fills its main cupola, by Emilian artist, Antonio da Correggio. The nave is adorned with the work of pupils of Correggio. The south transept features a carved frieze (1178) by Benedetto Antelami, who was responsible for much of the exquisite **Baptistry** (1196) just south of the cathedral. The reliefs inside and outside the latter – particularly those describing the months of the year – are among the most important of their age in Italy.

East of the Duomo is the church of **San Giovanni Evangelista** (rebuilt 1498– 1510) whose dome features a fresco (c.1520) of the *Vision of St John at Patmos* by Correggio. Frescoes by Parmigianino, a pupil of Correggio, can be seen here and in the 16th-century church of **Madonna della Steccata** on Via Dante.

🏛 Palazzo Pilotta

Piazzale della Pilotta 15. **Galleria**
📞 0521-23 33 09. 🕐 Mon–Sun am.
🔴 1 Jan, 1 May, 25 Dec.
📷 ♿ **Museo** 📞 0521-23 37 18. 🕐 Tue –Sat.
🔴 as above. 📷

This vast palace was built for the Farnese family during the 16th century, and was rebuilt after bomb damage from World War II. The palace comprises several parts, including the **Teatro Farnese** (1628), a copy of Palladio's ravishing theatre in Vicenza, built entirely of wood.

Both Parmigianino and Correggio are represented in the palace's **Galleria Nazionale**. The gallery also contains works by Fra Angelico, Bronzino and El Greco, and two gargantuan paintings by Ludovico Carracci: the *Apostles at the Sepulchre* and the *Funeral of the Virgin* (both late 16th century).

The **Museo Archeologico Nazionale**, on the lower floor, has exhibits from Velleia, an Etruscan necropolis, and from prehistoric sites in the hills around Parma.

🏛 Camera di San Paolo

Via Melloni. 📞 0521-23 33 09.
🕐 daily. 🔴 1 Jan, 1 May, 25 Dec.
📷 ♿
Originally the refectory of the Benedictine convent of San Paolo, this room was frescoed by Correggio in 1518 with mythological scenes.

Campanile and Baptistry in Parma

THE MAKING OF PARMESAN CHEESE AND PARMA HAM

No cheese is as famous or as vital to Italy's cuisine as Parmesan *(Parmigiano)*. There are two types: the superior Parmigiano-Reggiano and the lower-quality Grana. The cheese is made using techniques that have barely altered in centuries. Partially skimmed milk is added to whey, to promote fermentation, and rennet is used to curdle the milk. The cheese is then salted and shaped. Parmesan is not only used in cooking but is delicious eaten on its own, or with pears – an Italian speciality.

Shop selling Parmesan cheese and Parma ham

Parma ham owes its excellence to techniques perfected over many years and to the special conditions in which it is cured. It is made from pigs fattened on whey left over from the making of Parmesan cheese. The meat has a character that requires little more than salt and pepper to produce the famous *prosciutto crudo*. The breezy hills of Langhirino, south of Parma, are ideal for curing the hams, which are aged for up to ten months. Each ham is branded with the five-pointed crown of the old Duchy of Parma.

Flora by Carlo Cignani (1628–1719) in the Galleria Estense in Modena

Modena ❺

🏛 *175,000.* 🚉 🚌 🛈 *Piazza Grande (059-20 66 60).* 🚗 *Mon.*

To MOST ITALIANS Modena means fast cars, for both Ferrari and Maserati have factories in its industrial outskirts. Monuments to an earlier age, however, make this one of Emilia's most enticing historic destinations. A thriving colony since Roman times, the city rose to medieval prominence on the back of its broad agricultural hinterland and the arrival in 1598 of the d'Este nobles from Ferrara. This family continued to rule the city until the 18th century.

🔒 Duomo

Corso Duomo. 📞 *059-21 60 78.* ⏱ *daily.*
Modena's superlative **Duomo** rises alongside the old Roman Via Aemilia (now Via Emilia). One of the region's greatest Romanesque buildings, it was founded by Countess Matilda of Tuscany, ruler of Modena in the 11th century. It was designed by Lanfranco and dedicated to San Geminiano, the city's patron saint, whose stone coffin lies under the

choir. The exterior's most noticeable feature is the **Torre Ghirlandina**, a perilously leaning tower begun at the same time as the Duomo and completed two centuries later. It was once home to Modena's famous *Secchia*, a wooden bucket whose theft from Bologna in 1325 supposedly provoked war between the two cities. It also inspired the mock epic poem *La Secchia Rapita* (The Stolen Bucket) by the 17th-century poet Tassoni, and became the symbol of an ongoing rivalry between the cities.

The large reliefs on the Duomo's impressive main (west) façade are the work of the mysterious 12th-century sculptor, Wiligelmus.

The highlight of the rather severe interior is a large carved *tribuna* (rood screen) decorated with 12th-century scenes from the Passion.

🏛 Palazzo dei Musei

Largo di Porta Sant'Agostino.
Galleria Estense 📞 *059-22 21 45.* ⏱ *Tue – Fri & Sun.* ● *1 Jan, 31 Jan, Easter, 25 Apr, 25 Dec.* ♿
Biblioteca Estense 📞 *059-22 22 48.* ⏱ *Mon–Sat.* ● *public hols.*
Northwest of the Duomo, and reached through an attractive warren of old streets, stands the Palazzo dei Musei. Formerly an arsenal and workhouse, it is now home to the cream of the city's museums and galleries. Its finest section is the **Galleria Estense**, given over to the d'Este's private art collection, which was transferred here when the city of Ferrara, the family's former dominion, became part of the Papal States. Most of the paintings are by

Emilian and Ferrarese artists (notably Reni and the Carracci) but there are also works here by Bernini, Velázquez, Tintoretto and Veronese.

Among the permanent displays in the **Biblioteca Estense**, the d'Este Library, are a 1481 edition of Dante's *Divine Comedy*, and dozens of fascinating maps and diplomatic letters, many dating back centuries. A map dated 1501 was among the first to show the 1492 voyage by Columbus to the New World. The jewel of the collection is the magnificent illuminated Borso d'Este Bible, with gloriously decorated pages containing over 1,200 miniatures by 15th-century artists of the Ferrara school, most notably Taddeo Crivelli and Franco Russi.

The Torre Ghirlandina in Modena

ENVIRONS: The **Ferrari** factory, 20 km (12 miles) to the south, was founded by Enzo Ferrari in 1945. The FIAT-owned manufacturer now produces around 2,500 cars annually. The **Galleria Ferrari** has a small exhibition featuring memorabilia, a reconstruction of the founder's study, classic engines and many vintage cars.

🏛 Galleria Ferrari

Via Dino Ferrari 43, Maranello.
📞 *0536-94 32 04.* ⏱ *Tue – Sun.* ● *1 Jan, 25 Dec.* 📷 ♿

Ferrari 250 SWB, produced between 1959 and 1962

Ferrara ❻

140,000. FS ☎ ℹ *Corso Giovecca 21 (0532-20 93 70).* 📅 *Mon & Fri.*

THE D'ESTE DYNASTY has left an indelible mark on Ferrara, one of the region's greatest walled towns. The noble family took control of the town under Nicolò II in the late 13th century, holding power until 1598, when the family was forced by the papacy to move to Modena.

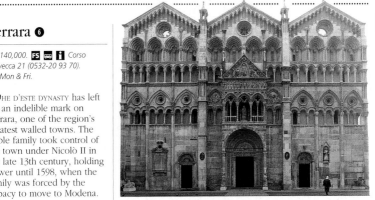

Façade of the Duomo in Ferrara

♠ Castello Estense

Largo Castello. ☎ *0532-29 92 79.* ○ *Tue–Sun.* 🎫
The family's dynastic seat, with its moats, towers and battlements (begun 1385), looms over the town centre. Ferrante and Giulio d'Este were

The impressive medieval Castello Estense in Ferrara

incarcerated in its draughty dungeons for plotting to overthrow Alfonso I d'Este. Parisina d'Este, wife of the ruthless Nicolò III, was executed here for having an affair with Ugo, her illegitimate stepson.

⊞ Palazzo del Comune

Piazza Comunale.
Bronze statues of Nicolò III and Borso d'Este, one of Nicolò's reputed 27 children, adorn this medieval palace (begun 1243). Both are copies of the 15th-century originals by Leon Battista Alberti.

🏛 Museo della Cattedrale

Cattedrale di Ferrara. ☎ *0532-20 74 49.* ○ *daily.* ● *public hols.* **Donation.**
Ferrara's 12th-century **Duomo** is a Romanesque-Gothic hybrid designed by Wiligelmus. Fine reliefs on the façade depict

vivid scenes from the Last Judgment. The excellent **museum** contains a fine set of marble reliefs of the *Labours of the Months* (late 12th century), two painted organ shutters (1469) of *St George* and the *Annunciation* by Cosmè Tura, and the *Madonna of the Pomegranate* (1408) by Jacopo della Quercia.

⊞ Palazzo Schifanoia

Via Scandiana 23. ☎ *0532-641 78.* ○ *daily.* ● *25, 26 Dec.* 🎫
This d'Este summer retreat, begun in 1385, is famous for its Salone dei Mesi (Room of the Months), whose walls display murals by Tura and other Ferrarese painters with scenes of the different months. They were commissioned by Borso d'Este, who appears in many of the panels.

🏛 Museo Archeologico Nazionale

Palazzo di Ludovico il Moro, Via XX Settembre 124. ☎ *0532-662 99.* ● *for restoration until 1997.*
The most interesting exhibits here are artefacts that were excavated from Spina, a Greco-Etruscan trading post near Comacchio on the Po Delta.

🏛 Palazzo dei Diamanti

Palazzo dei Diamanti, Corso Ercole I d'Este 21. ☎ *0532-20 58 44.* ○ *Tue–Sun am.* ● *1 Jan, 1 May, 25 Dec.* 🎫
Named after the diamond motifs on its façade, the Palace of Diamonds houses a modern art gallery, a museum devoted to the Risorgimento, and the Pinacoteca Nazionale, which contains works from leading Renaissance exponents of the Ferrara and Bologna schools.

THE D'ESTE FAMILY DYNASTY

During their medieval heyday, the d'Este family presided over one of Europe's leading courts, combining the roles of blood-crazed despots with enlightened Renaissance patrons. Nicolò III, for example, had his wife and her lover brutally murdered. Alfonso I (1503–34) married Lucrezia Borgia, descendant of one of Italy's most notorious families, while Ercole I (1407–1505) attempted to poison a nephew who tried to usurp him (and eventually had him executed). At the same time the d'Este court attracted writers like Petrarch, Tasso and Ariosto, and painters such as Mantegna, Titian and Bellini. Ercole I also rebuilt Ferrara, creating one of Europe's finest Renaissance cities.

Portrait of Alfonso I d'Este by Titian (c.1485–1576)

Street-by-Street: Bologna ❼

Detail of façade from San Petronio

T HE HISTORIC city centre of Bologna is a handsome ensemble of brick buildings and charming porticoed streets. Medieval palaces are clustered around the two central squares, Piazza Maggiore and Piazza del Nettuno, flanked to the south by the churches of San Petronio and San Domenico. Here, too, is the venerable Archiginnasio, part of the university of Bologna and one of the oldest in Europe. Further afield, the skyline is etched by the Asinelli and Garisenda towers, and by the campanile of Santo Stefano.

Fontana di Nettuno
The famous Neptune fountain (1566) was designed by Tommaso Laureti and decorated with magnificent bronze figures by Giambologna.

The Palazzo del Podestà (13th century) was remodelled in 1484.

Tourist information

Railway station
↑ Ferrara

Modena ←

VIA UGO BASSI

VIA DELL'INDIPENDENZA

VIA RIZZOLI

VIA OREFICI

VIA IV NOVEMBRE

PIAZZA MAGGIORE

★ **San Petronio**
The Martyrdom of St Sebastian (15th century) in the Cappella di San Sebastiano is by Lorenzo Costa of the Ferrarese School.

Archiginnasio

VIA D'AZEGLIO

VIA DELL'ARCHIGINNASIO

VIA FARIN

Piazza Cavour
The flagged medieval streets and shady porticoed buildings found in this pleasant piazza are typical of Bologna's elegant city centre.

PIAZZA CAVOUR

VIA

VIA GARIBALDI

San Domenico
(1251) is dedicated to St Dominic, who is buried here in a magnificent tomb.

STAR SIGHT

★ **San Petronio**

San Giacomo Maggiore
The Triumph of Death *fresco by Costa (1483–6) adorns the Cappella Bentivoglio.*

Pinacoteca Nazionale

Museo di Anatomia Umana Normale

VIA ZAMBONI
VIA BENEDETTO XIV
Ravenna
VIA SAN VITALE
STRADA MAGGIORE
ZA DI RTA GNANA
VIA SANTO STEFANO
Firenze

Torri degli Asinelli e Garisenda
The colossal towers are two of the few remaining towers begun by Bologna's important families in the 12th century.

Abbazia di Santo Stefano
The Fontana di Pilato, or Pilate's fountain, in the courtyard features a basin with Lombard inscriptions from the 8th century.

KEY

– – – Suggested route

0 kilometres 150
0 miles 150

🔒 San Giacomo Maggiore
Piazza Rossini. 📞 051-22 59 70.
🕐 daily.

This Romanesque-Gothic church, begun in 1267 but altered substantially since, is visited mainly for the Cappella Bentivoglio, a superb family chapel founded by Annibale Bentivoglio in 1445 and consecrated in 1486. Pride of place naturally goes to a portrait with subtle characterization of the patrons by Lorenzo Costa (1460–1535), who was also responsible for the frescoes of the *Apocalypse*, the *Madonna Enthroned* and the *Triumph of Death*. The chapel's altarpiece, depicting the *Virgin and Saints with Two Angel Musicians* (1488), is the work of Francesco Francia. The Bentivoglio family is further glorified in the tomb of Anton Galeazzo Bentivoglio (1435) opposite the chapel. It was among the last works of the noted Sienese sculptor, Jacopo della Quercia. The Oratory of Santa Cecilia features frescoes on the lives of Santa Cecilia and San Valeriano by Costa and Francesco Francia (1504–6).

The Bentivoglio tomb (1435) by Jacopo della Quercia

Exploring Bologna

Monuments to Bologna's rich cultural heritage are scattered across the city, from the leaning towers and the church of San Petronio in the old centre to the Pinacoteca Nazionale in the university district.

⛫ Torri degli Asinelli e Garisenda

Piazza di Porta Ravegnana. ⭘ *daily.* 🖼

The famous Torri Pendenti, or leaning towers – Torre degli Asinelli and Torre Garisenda – are among the few survivors of the original 200 that once formed the skyline of Bologna. Both were begun in the 12th century, though there were probably earlier towers on the site – Dante mentioned a pair of towers here in his *Inferno*. Torre Garisenda was shortened as a safety measure within only a few years of its construction, and still leans some 3 m (10 ft)

from the vertical. At 97 m (318 ft) tall, Torre Asinelli is the fourth highest tower in Italy after those in Cremona, Siena and Venice. Its 500-step ascent offers fine views over Bologna's pantiled rooftops to the hills beyond.

🔒 Abbazia di Santo Stefano

Via Santo Stefano. 【 *051-22 32 56.* ⭘ *daily.*

Santo Stefano is a curious collection of four medieval churches (originally seven) jumbled together under one roof. The 11th-century church of the Crocifisso provides little

Exterior of the Abbazia di Santo Stefano

🔒 SAN PETRONIO

Piazza Maggiore. 【 *051-22 21 12.* ⭘ *daily.* ♿

Dedicated to the city's 5th-century bishop, this church ranks among the greatest of Italy's brick-built medieval buildings. Founded in 1390, it was originally intended to be larger than St Peter's in Rome, but its size was scaled down when the church authorities diverted funds to the nearby Palazzo Archiginnasio. The resulting financial shortfall left the church decidedly lopsided, with a row of columns on its eastern flank that were intended to support an additional internal aisle. The project's financial profligacy, nonetheless, was said to have been instrumental in turning Martin Luther against Catholicism.

The altarpiece of the *Martyrdom of St Sebastian* is from the late Ferrarese School.

The pink and white interior adds to the overall light and airy effect.

The canopied main portal features beautiful biblical reliefs (1425–38) by Jacopo della Quercia.

Gothic Interior
The interior is airy, with graceful pillars supporting the roof. Twenty-two chapels, shielded by screens, open off the nave. In 1547 the Council of Trent (see p168) was temporarily moved here due to the plague.

Entrance

Unfinished upper façade

The meridian line, along the 60th meridian between the north and south poles, was traced in 1655 by the astronomer Gian Domenico Cassini.

The stained glass windows (1464–6) in this chapel are by Jacob of Ulm.

more than a corridor to polygonal San Sepolcro, the most appealing of the quartet. Also dating from the 11th century, its centrepiece is the tomb of St Petronius, a marvellously overstated affair modelled on the Holy Sepulchre of Jerusalem. The courtyard contains the so-called Fontana di Pilato, an 8th-century basin.

Santi Vitale e Agricola dates originally from the 5th century, making it the oldest church in the city. It was rebuilt in the 8th and 11th centuries. Inside are the sarcophagi of Saints Vitalis and Agricola, martyred in the 4th century. Santa Trinità features a small museum of minor paintings and religious artefacts, including wooden statues of the *Adoration of the Magi* painted by Simone dei Crocifissi (c.1370).

Bell tower

Choir Stalls
The exquisite inlaid choir stalls of the Chapel of the Holy Sacrament were made by Raffaello da Brescia in 1521.

🏛 Pinacoteca Nazionale

Via delle Belle Arti 56.
📞 *051-24 32 49.*
🕐 *Tue – Sun am.*
● *1 Jan, Easter, 1 May, 15 Aug, 25 Dec.* 📷

Bologna's principal art gallery, and one of northern Italy's most important collections, stands on the edge of the city's university district, a bustling area of bars, bookshops and cheap restaurants. The gallery is mainly dedicated to work by Bolognese painters, notably Vitale da Bologna, Guido Reni, Guercino and the Carracci family. Members of the Ferrarese School are also represented, in particular Francesco del Cossa and Ercole de' Roberti. The two highlights are Perugino's *Madonna in Glory* (c.1491) and Raphael's famous *Ecstasy of St Cecilia*, painted around 1515, both artists having worked in Bologna.

The *Ecstasy of St Cecilia* (c.1515) by Raphael in Bologna's Pinacoteca Nazionale

🏛 Museo di Anatomia Umana Normale

Via Irnerio 48. 📞 *051-24 44 67.*
🕐 *Mon – Fri.* ● *25 Dec, 1 Jan, Easter, 1 May.* ♿

Although well off the standard tourist itineraries, the Museum of Human Anatomy is one of the more memorable of Bologna's smaller museums. Originally established as an anatomy theatre in 1742, the building became a museum in 1907, and now consists of an occasionally gruesome collection of visceral waxworks. There are numerous models of organs, limbs and flayed bodies. Sculpted rather than made from casts, these objects have an artistic as well as scientific appeal. The models were used as medical teaching aids until the 19th century.

⛪ San Domenico

Piazza di San Domenico.
📞 *051-640 04 11.* 🕐 *daily.*
Bologna's San Domenico can lay claim to being the most important of Italy's many Dominican churches. Begun in 1221, after St Dominic's death, it was built to house the body of the saint, who died here and lies buried in a tomb known as the Arca di San Domenico. A magnificent composite work, the tomb's statues were executed by Nicola Pisano; the reliefs of scenes from the *Life of St Dominic* were the work of Nicola Pisano and his assistants; the canopy (1473) is attributed to Nicola di Bari; while the figures of the angels and Saints Proculus and Petronius are early works by Michelangelo. The reliquary (1383) behind the sarcophagus contains St Dominic's head.

Arca di San Domenico in the Basilica di San Domenico

Fresco of Malatesta and St Sigismund (1451) by Piero della Francesca in the Tempio Malatestiano, Rimini

Faenza ❽

Ravenna. 🏛 *54,000.* 🚉 🚌
ℹ️ *Piazza del Popolo 1 (0546-252 31).* 🏪 *Tue, Thu & Sat.*

FAENZA IS SYNONYMOUS with the **faïence** ceramic-ware to which it gave its name. Renowned across Europe for over 500 years, the pottery, with its distinctive blue and ochre colouring, is still made in countless small factories around the town.

The highlight of Faenza is the **Museo Internazionale delle Ceramiche**, one of the largest ceramic collections in Italy. Its exhibits feature not only examples of local ware, but also pottery from other countries and other periods, including Roman ceramics and medieval majolica. There is also a section devoted to the modern ceramic art of Picasso, Matisse and Chagall.

🏛 **Museo Internazionale delle Ceramiche**
Viale Baccarini 19. 📞 *0546-212 40.*
🕐 *Tue–Sun.* ⬛ *1 Jan, Easter, 25 Apr, 1 May, 15 Aug, 25 Dec.* 📷

Rimini ❾

🏛 *130,000.* 🚉 🚌 ℹ️ *Piazza Fellini 3 (0541-245 11).* 🏪 *Wed & Sat.*

RIMINI WAS ONCE a quaint seaside resort, whose innocent charms were celebrated in the early films of Federico Fellini, the director born and raised here. Today it is the largest beach resort in Europe. The seafront, which continues unbroken for almost 15 km (9 miles), is lined with clubs, restaurants and bars. The crowded beaches are clean and well groomed, though entrance fees are charged at the private beaches.

Rimini's old quarter, by contrast, is pleasantly quiet. Its charming cobbled streets gather around **Piazza Cavour**, dominated by the 14th-century **Palazzo del Podestà**. The town's finest building is the **Tempio Malatestiano**, built as a Franciscan church but converted in 1450 by Leon Battista Alberti, the great Florentine architect, into one of Italy's great Renaissance monuments. The work was commissioned by Sigismondo Malatesta (1417–68), a descendant of Rimini's ruling medieval family, and reputedly one of the most debauched and evil men of his time. Ostensibly designed as a chapel, the Tempio eventually became little more than a monument to Malatesta. Inside there are sculptures by Agostino di Duccio and a fresco (1451) by Piero della Francesca of Malatesta kneeling before St Sigismund (1451).

The entwined initials of Malatesta and his fourth wife, Isotta degli Atti, provide a recurring decorative motif, and there are reliefs depicting scenes of bacchanalian excess and oddities such as strangely posed elephants (a Malatesta family emblem). All this led Pope Pius II to condemn the building as "a temple of devil-worshippers", and to burn Malatesta's effigy for what the papal charge against him described as acts of "murder, violation, adultery, incest, sacrilege and perjury".

ENVIRONS: Further along the coast, away from Rimini, the resorts become relatively quieter. **Cesenatico**, 18 km (11 miles) north, offers all the usual facilities yet the beaches are less crowded.

🏛 **Tempio Malatestiano**
Via IV Novembre. 🕐 *daily.* ♿

Ravenna ❿

🏛 *135,000.* 🚉 🚌 ℹ️ *Via Salara 8–12 (0544-354 04).* 🏪 *Wed & Sat.*

MOST PEOPLE VISIT Ravenna for its superb mosaics from the Byzantine period (*see pp260–61*), but the town itself is a surprisingly pleasant medley of old streets, fine shops and peaceful piazzas.

Façade of the Renaissance Tempio Malatestiano in Rimini

Piazza del Popolo, Ravenna's central square

The **Museo Nazionale** features a wide range of icons, paintings and archaeological displays. The best place to relax and take a break from sightseeing is Piazza del Popolo, a lovely ensemble of medieval buildings.

Museo Nazionale
Via Fiandrini. 0544-344 24.
Tue–Sun.

Po Delta ⓫

Ferrara. FS Ferrara. to Goro or Gorino. from Porto Garibaldi, Goro & Gorino. Via Buonafede 12, Comacchio (0533-31 01 47).

THE PO IS ITALY'S longest river. Its vast basin covers some 15 per cent of the country and supports around a third of the nation's population. Although ravaged in many places by industrial pollution, at its finest it offers beautifully subtle landscapes – rows of poplar trees across misty fields and long views over soft brown soils. There are also vistas over the shifting sands of its vast delta, an estuary of marshes, dunes and islands.

The Po Delta is known to Italian naturalists as the "Italian Camargue". There are plans to turn the entire region – some 30,000 ha (74,000 acres) – into a national park that would stretch from the edge of the Venetian lagoon to the coastal pine woods that lie around Ravenna.

Wetland areas such as the **Valli di Comacchio** north of Ravenna are already nature reserves, a winter home to thousands of breeding and migrating birds. Ornithologists gather here to see gulls, coots, bean geese and black terns, and far rarer species such as the white egret, hen harrier and pygmy cormorant. **Comacchio**, the nearest settlement, is one of several fishing villages dotted around the area. Its most famous catch is eels, often caught using methods like water gates that date back as far as Roman times.

Other nature reserves include the **Bosco della Mesola**, a tract of ancient woodland planted by the Etruscans and cared for over the centuries by generations of monks. You can walk or cycle through its shady canopy, with excellent opportunities for spotting large herds of deer that wander throughout the woodland.

For a good look at the entire region, follow the N309 – part of the old Via Romea pilgrimage trail to Rome – that runs north to south through some 100 km (62 miles) of the proposed park. Numerous smaller lanes branch off into the wilderness. There are also boat trips to some of the delta's more remote corners: key departure points include the villages of Ca' Tiepolo, Ca' Vernier and Taglio di Po.

Hen harrier, found in the Po Delta

The peaceful landscape along the banks of the river in the Po Delta

A Tour of Ravenna

Rome's power declined, Ravenna was made the capital of the Western Empire (AD 402), a prominence it retained during the Ostrogoth and Byzantine rule in the 5th and 6th centuries. Ravenna is renowned for its early Christian mosaics – the town had converted to Christianity in the 2nd century AD and was made a bishopric in the 4th century AD. The mosaics span the years of Roman and Byzantine rule, offering comparisons between Classically inspired designs and later Byzantine motifs.

R AVENNA ROSE to power in the 1st century BC under the Emperor Augustus, who built a port and naval base at nearby Classis. As

Mosaic detail from San Vitale

The Good Shepherd ②
This mosaic adorns the tiny Mausoleo di Galla Placidia. Begun in 430, this exquisite building probably never received the remains of Placidia, wife of a barbarian emperor.

San Vitale ①
San Vitale's apse mosaics (526–547) show Christ, San Vitale (being handed a martyr's crown), two angels and Bishop Ecclesius, who began the church (see pp46–7).

Baptism of Jesus ③
The 5th-century Battistero Neoniano (Neonian Baptistry) is named after the bishop who may have commissioned its decoration, including this beautiful mosaic. It was built near the remains of a Roman bathhouse and is Ravenna's oldest monument.

Battistero degli Ariani ⑤
The cupola of this late 5th-century baptistry has a mosaic showing the Apostles ringed around a centrepiece depicting the Baptism of Christ.

VISITORS' CHECKLIST

San Vitale & Mausoleo di Galla Placidia, Via Fiandrini. 0544-342 66. Apr–Sep: 9am–7pm daily; Oct–Mar: 9am–4:30pm (last adm: 15 mins before closing). 1 Jan, 25 Dec.
Battistero Neoniano, Via Battistero. 0544-21 85 59. as above. 1 Jan, 25 Dec.
Tomba di Dante, Via Dante. Apr–Sep: 9am–7pm daily; Oct–Mar: 9am–noon, 2–5pm daily (last adm: 15 mins before closing). 1 Jan, 25 Dec.
Battistero degli Ariani, Via degli Ariani. 0544-344 24. Apr–Sep: 8:30am–7pm daily; Oct–Mar: 8:30am–4:30pm (last adm: 15 mins before closing). 1 Jan, 1 May.
Sant'Apollinare Nuovo, Via di Roma. 0544-390 81. Apr–Sep: 9am–7pm daily; Oct–Mar: 9am–4:30pm (last adm: 15 mins before closing). 1 Jan, 25 Dec.
Combined ticket also available.

Sant'Apollinare Nuovo ⑥
This glorious 6th-century church, named after Ravenna's first bishop, is dominated by two rows of mosaics. Both show processions of martyrs and virgins bearing gifts for Christ and the Virgin.

Tomba di Dante ④
Dante's wanderings around Italy after his exile from Florence eventually brought him to Ravenna, where he died in 1321. A lamp in his sepulchre (1780) is fed by oil given by the city of Florence.

KEY

– – – Suggested route

P Parking

Tourist information

0 metres 200
0 yards 200

FLORENCE

FLORENCE IS A VAST AND BEAUTIFUL *monument to the Renaissance, the artistic and cultural reawakening of the 15th century. Writers such as Dante, Petrarch and Machiavelli contributed to its proud literary heritage, though it was the paintings and sculptures of artists such as Botticelli, Michelangelo and Donatello that turned the city into one of the world's greatest artistic capitals.*

While the Etruscans had long settled the hills around Fiesole, Florence first sprang to life as a Roman colony in 59 BC. Captured by the Lombards in the 6th century, the city later emerged from the Dark Ages as an independent city state. By the 13th century a burgeoning trade in wool and textiles, backed by a powerful banking sector, had turned the city into one of Italy's leading powers. Political control was wielded first by the guilds, and later by the Florentine Republic. In time, power passed to leading noble families, of which the most influential were the Medici, a hugely wealthy banking dynasty. Florence, and later Tuscany, remained under the family's almost unbroken sway for three centuries. During this time the city was at the cultural and intellectual heart of Europe, its cosmopolitan atmosphere and wealthy patrons providing the impetus for a period of unparalleled artistic growth. Artists, sculptors and architects flocked to the city, filling its streets, churches and palaces with some of the world's greatest Renaissance works. By 1737 the Medici had died out, leaving the city under Austrian (and briefly Napoleonic) control until Italian Unification in 1860. Between 1865 and 1871 Florence was the capital of the new Kingdom of Italy. In recent history its streets and artistic heritage were ravaged by the Arno floods of November 1966.

Florentines strolling in front of Ponte Vecchio (1345), the old bridge lined with shops spanning the Arno

◁ **The dome of Florence's Duomo, completed in 1436, designed by Brunelleschi**

Exploring Florence

H ISTORIC FLORENCE is a surprisingly compact area, and the majority
of the sights described on the following pages can easily be
reached on foot. Most visitors head for the Duomo, the city's
geographical and historical focus, ideally placed to explore
the Campanile, Baptistry and Museo dell'Opera del Duomo.
To the south is Piazza della Signoria, long the city's political
heart, flanked by the Palazzo Vecchio, Florence's town
hall, and the Uffizi, one of Italy's leading art galleries.
To the east lies the church of Santa Croce, home
to frescoes by Giotto and the tombs of some of
Florence's greatest men. To the west stands
Santa Maria Novella, the city's other great
church, also adorned with fresco-filled
chapels. Across the Ponte Vecchio, and
the Arno – the river that bisects the city –
is the district of Oltrarno, dominated
by Santo Spirito and the vast Pitti
Palace, containing galleries
with works by great Renaissance artists including
Raphael and Titian.

**Bell tower,
Palazzo
Vecchio**

GETTING AROUND

Florence has an excellent bus service,
including electric buses, making
public transport both convenient
and fast. The compact city centre,
which is closed to traffic, is easily
negotiated on foot.

KEY

▨	Street-by-Street: Around San Marco *pp266–7*
▨	Street-by-Street: Around the Duomo *pp270–71*
▨	Street-by-Street: Around Piazza della Repubblica *pp284–5*
▨	Street-by-Street: Around Oltrarno *pp292–3*
FS	Railway station
P	Parking
ℹ	Tourist information
—	City walls

Ponte Vecchio with Ponte Santa Trìnita in the foreground

LOCATOR MAP

SIGHTS AT A GLANCE

Churches

*Cappella Brancacci
pp290–91* **25**
Cappelle Medicee **19**
Convento di San Marco **2**
*Duomo and Baptistry
pp272–4* **7**
Ognissanti **24**
Orsanmichele **8**
Santissima Annunziata **3**
Santa Croce **10**
Santa Felicita **28**
San Lorenzo **18**
Santa Maria Novella **21**
San Miniato al Monte **30**
Santo Spirito **26**

Buildings, Monuments and Squares

Mercato Centrale **20**
Palazzo Antinori **22**
Palazzo Davanzati **16**
Palazzo Rucellai **23**
Palazzo Strozzi **17**
Palazzo Vecchio **15**
Piazza della Signoria **14**
Piazzale Michelangelo **29**
Ponte Vecchio **12**
Spedale degli Innocenti **5**

Museums and Galleries

Bargello **9**
Galleria dell'Accademia **1**
Museo Archeologico **4**
Museo dell'Opera del
Duomo **6**
Museo di Storia della
Scienza **11**
Palazzo Pitti pp294–5 **27**
Uffizi pp278–81 **13**

SEE ALSO

| 0 metres | 500 |
| 0 yards | 500 |

Street-by-Street: Around San Marco

THE BUILDINGS in this part of Florence once stood on the fringes of the city, serving as stables and barracks. The Medici menagerie of lions, elephants and giraffes was housed here. Today it is a student quarter and the streets are often busy with young people attending the university or the Accademia di Belle Arti, the world's oldest art school, founded in 1563.

Santissima Annunziata
This fine Renaissance church has an opulent Baroque interior ❸

Palazzo Pandolfini was designed by Raphael in 1516.

★ Convento di San Marco
The Annunciation (c.1445) is an example of Fra Angelico's exquisite fresco decoration ❷

Sant'Apollonia features a fresco of the *Cenacolo* (Last Supper) by Andrea del Castagno (1450).

VIA DELLA DOGANA

VIA DELLA PIRA

VIA CAVOUR

VIA DEGLI ARAZZIERI

VIA SAN GALLO

PIAZZA DI SAN MARCO

VIA GIORGIO LA PIRA

VIA CESARE BATTISTI

VIA RICASOLI

Luigi Cherubini
(1760–1842), the Florentine composer, trained at the Conservatorio.

PIAZZA DELLA SANTISSIMA ANNUNZIATA

KEY

– – – Suggested route

0 metres   50

0 yards   50

Galleria dell'Accademia
This detail is from a 14th-century altarpiece, the Madonna and Saints, *by an unnamed master* ❶

Giambologna's statue of Duke Ferdinando I was cast by Tacca in 1608.

LOCATOR MAP
See Florence Street Finder map 2

Part of the 15th-century *Cassone Adimari* by Lo Scheggia in the Accademia

Spedale degli Innocenti
Opened in 1444, the city orphanage by Brunelleschi was decorated with cameos by Andrea della Robbia **5**

The Giardino dei Semplici was opened in 1543.

Museo Archeologico
Many of the Etruscan objects in the museum were originally in the Medici collections **4**

VIA GINO CAPPONI

STAR SIGHTS

★ **Convento di San Marco**

★ **Galleria dell'Accademia**

Galleria dell'Accademia ❶

Via Ricasoli 60. **Map** 2 D4. 055-238 86 12. 9am–7pm Tue–Sat, 9am–2pm Sun. 1 Jan, 1 May, 25 Dec.

THE ACADEMY OF FINE ARTS, founded in 1563, was the first school established in Europe specifically to teach the techniques of drawing, painting and sculpture. The art collection displayed here was formed in 1784 with the aim of providing material for students to study and copy.

The most famous work on display is Michelangelo's *David* (1504), a colossal nude of the biblical hero who killed the giant Goliath. The sculpture was commissioned by the city to be placed in Piazza della Signoria, but it was moved to the Accademia for safe-keeping in 1873. One copy now stands in its original position (*see pp282–3*) and a second is located on Piazzale Michelangelo. The *David* statue established Michelangelo, at the age of 29, as the foremost sculptor of his time.

Michelangelo's other masterpieces include the *Quattro Prigioni* (the Four Prisoners), sculpted between 1521 and 1523 and intended to adorn the tomb of Pope Julius II. The statues were presented to the Medici family in 1564 by the artist's nephew, Leonardo. The muscular figures struggling to free themselves from the stone are among the most dramatic of Michelangelo's works. The statues were subsequently moved to the Grotta Grande in the Boboli Gardens, where casts of the originals can now be seen.

The Accademia also contains an important collection of paintings by 15th- and 16th-century Florentine artists, among them Filippino Lippi, Fra Bartolomeo, Bronzino and Ridolfo del Ghirlandaio. The major works include the *Madonna del Mare* (Madonna of the Sea), attributed to Botticelli (1445–1510), and *Venus and Cupid* by Jacopo Pontormo (1494–1556), based on a preparatory drawing by Michelangelo. Also here is an elaborately painted wooden chest, the *Cassone Adimari* (1440–45) by Lo Scheggia, the step-brother of Masaccio. Originally part of a wealthy bride's trousseau, the wooden chest is decorated with details of Florentine life, clothing and architecture. A scene of the bridal party appears on the chest in front of the Baptistry.

The Salone della Toscana (Tuscany Room) features more modest paintings and sculptures by 19th-century members of the Accademia and plaster models by the sculptor, Lorenzo Bartolini.

Michelangelo's *David*

The light and airy former library, designed by Michelozzo

Convento di San Marco ❷

Piazza di San Marco. **Map** 2 D4.
📞 055-238 86 08. ⏰ 7am–12:30pm, 4–8pm. 🚻 📷 **Museo di San Marco**
📞 055-238 85. ⏰ 9am–2pm Tue–Sun. ⬛ 1 Jan, 1 May, 25 Dec. ♿ 📷

THE CONVENT OF SAN MARCO was founded in the 13th century and enlarged in 1437 when Dominican monks from nearby Fiesole moved there at the invitation of Cosimo il Vecchio. He paid a considerable sum to have the convent rebuilt by his favourite architect, Michelozzo, whose simple cloisters and cells provide the setting for a remarkable series of devotional frescoes (c.1438–45) by Florentine painter and Dominican friar, Fra Angelico. The convent and art collections have been arranged to form the interesting **Museo di San Marco**.

Beyond the ticket office lies the magnificent **Chiostro di Sant'Antonino** by Michelozzo, a cloister named after the convent's first prior, Antonino Pierozzi (1389–1459), who later became the Archbishop of Florence. Most of the faded frescoes here describe scenes from the saint's life by Bernardino Poccetti. The panels in the corner are by Fra Angelico. A door in the cloister's right side leads to the **Ospizio dei Pellegrini** (Pilgrims' Hospice), a room where pilgrims and visitors were offered hospitality. Today it houses the museum's free-standing paintings, including two famous

A detail from Fra Angelico's poignant _Deposition_ (c. 1440)

masterpieces: Fra Angelico's _Deposition_ (c.1435–40), an altarpiece painted for the church of Santa Trinita, and the _Madonna dei Linaiuoli_, commissioned by the Linaiuoli (flaxworkers' guild) in 1433.

In the courtyard, right of the convent's former bell, is the vaulted **Sala Capitolare** (Chapter House), decorated with a noted but over-restored _Crucifixion and Saints_ (1440) painted by Fra Angelico.

Covering one wall of the small **Refettorio** (refectory) is a fresco of the _Last Supper_ (c.1480) by Domenico Ghirlandaio. Stairs from the courtyard lead to the first floor, where you suddenly see Fra Angelico's _Annunciation_ (c.1445), thought by many to be among the city's most beautiful Renaissance paintings. Beyond, ranged around three sides of the cloister, are the **Dormitory Cells**. These 44 tiny monastic cells are frescoed with scenes from _The Life of Christ_ by Fra Angelico and assistants (1439–45). The cells numbered 1 to 11 are generally attributed to Fra Angelico personally, as is the lovely fresco of the Madonna and Saints on the right of the corridor _(see p28)_.

Cells 12–14 were once occupied by Savonarola, the zealous Dominican monk who became Prior of San Marco in 1491. Among other deeds, Savonarola incited Florentines to rebel against the Medici and was responsible for the burning of many works of art. Denounced as a heretic, he was burned at the stake in Piazza della Signoria in 1498.

Along the third corridor lies an airy colonnaded hall, formerly a public **library** designed by Michelozzo in 1441 for Cosimo il Vecchio. Beyond it lie two cells (38 and 39) which were used by Cosimo when he went on retreat here. Each is decorated with two frescoes (the other cells have only one), and they are both larger than any of the neighbouring rooms.

Fra Angelico's allegorical fresco, the _Mocking of Christ_ (c. 1442), showing Jesus blindfolded and being struck by a Roman guard

The Birth of the Virgin (1514) by del Sarto in Santissima Annunziata

Santissima Annunziata ❸

Piazza della Santissima Annunziata.
Map 2 E4. 📞 *055-239 80 34.*
🕐 *7am–noon, 4–7pm Mon–Sat,*
4–5:30pm Sun. ♿

FOUNDED BY the Servite order in 1250, the church of the Holy Annunciation was later rebuilt by Michelozzo between 1444 and 1481. Its atrium contains a celebrated if slightly faded series of frescoes by the Mannerist artists Rosso Fiorentino, Andrea del Sarto and Jacopo Pontormo. Perhaps the finest of its panels are *The Journey of the Magi* (1511) and *The Birth of the Virgin* (1514) by Andrea del Sarto.

The heavily decorated, dark interior has a frescoed ceiling completed by Pietro Giambelli in 1669. Here is one of the city's most revered shrines, a painting of the Virgin Mary begun by a monk in 1252 but miraculously completed by an angel, according to devout Florentines. Newly-wed couples traditionally visit the shrine (on the left as you enter the church) to present a bouquet of flowers to the Virgin and to pray for a long, fruitful marriage.

A door from the north transept leads to the **Chiostrino dei Morti** (Cloister of the Dead), so called because it was originally used as a burial ground. Today it is best known for del Sarto's fresco, *The Madonna del Sacco* (1525).

The church is situated on the northern flank of **Piazza della Santissima Annunziata**, one of the finest Renaissance squares in Florence. Designed by Brunelleschi, the delicate nine-bay arcade fronts the Spedale degli Innocenti to its right, while at the centre of the square stands a bronze equestrian statue of Duke Ferdinando I. Started by Giambologna, it was finished in 1608 by his assistant Pietro Tacca (who designed the highly-stylized bronze fountains in the square).

Museo Archeologico ❹

Via della Colonna 38. **Map** 2 E4.
📞 *055-235 75.* 🕐 *9am–2pm Tue–Sat, 9am–1pm Sun.* ⬤ *some public hols.*

THE ARCHAEOLOGICAL MUSEUM in Florence is in a palazzo built by Giulio Parigi for the Princess Maria Maddalena de' Medici in 1620. It now exhibits an outstanding collection of Etruscan, Greek, Roman and Egyptian artefacts, although parts of the collection are being restored following the flood in 1966. The first floor contains a splendid series of Etruscan bronzes as well as the famous *Chimera* (4th century BC), a mythical lion with a goat's head imposed on its body and a serpent for a tail. Equally impressive is the 1st-century *Arringatore* bronze

Etruscan warrior, Museo Archeologico

found near Lake Trasimeno in Umbria. It is inscribed with the name of Aulus Metellus. A large section on the second floor is dedicated to Greek vases, notably the famed François Vase, found in an Etruscan tomb near Chiusi.

Spedale degli Innocenti ❺

Piazza della Santissima Annunziata 12.
Map 2 E4. 📞 *055-247 93 17.*
🕐 *8:30am–2pm Mon, Tue, Thu–Sat,*
8am–1pm Sun. ⬤ *public hols.*

Part of Brunelleschi's arcaded loggia, Spedale degli Innocenti

NAMED AFTER Herod's biblical Massacre of the Innocents, the "Hospital" opened in 1444 as Europe's first orphanage. Part of the building is still used for this purpose. Brunelleschi's arcaded loggia is decorated with glazed terracotta roundels, added by Andrea della Robbia around 1498, showing babies wrapped in swaddling bands. At the left end of the portico you can see the *rota*, a rotating stone cylinder on which anonymous mothers could place their unwanted children and ring the bell for them to be admitted to the orphanage.

Within the building lie two elegant cloisters: the **Chiostro degli Uomini** (Men's Cloister), built between 1422 and 1445 and decorated with *sgraffito* roosters and cherubs, and the smaller Women's Cloister (1438). A small upstairs gallery contains a handful of fine works, including terracottas by della Robbia and pictures by Botticelli, Piero di Cosimo and Domenico Ghirlandaio.

Street-by-Street: Around the Duomo

WHILE MUCH OF FLORENCE was rebuilt during the Renaissance, the eastern part of the city retains a distinctly medieval feel. With its maze of tiny alleys, it is an area that would still be familiar to Dante (1265–1321), whose birthplace probably lay somewhere among its hidden lanes. The poet would recognize the Badia Fiorentina where he first glimpsed

Stained glass window from the Duomo

Beatrice, as well as the gaunt outlines of the Bargello opposite. He would also be familiar with the Baptistry, one of the city's oldest buildings, though he would not know the Campanile nor the Duomo, whose foundations were laid in the poet's old age.

★ Duomo and Baptistry
The exteriors of the Duomo and Baptistry are richly decorated with marbles and reliefs, such as this detail from the Duomo's façade **7**

The Loggia del Bigallo (1358) is where abandoned children were once left. They were then sent to foster homes if they remained unclaimed.

PIAZZA DI SAN GIOVANNI

PIAZZA DEL DUOMO

VIA DELL' OCHE

VIA S. ELISABETTA

VIA

VIA DE' MEDICI

VIA ROMA

VIA D. SPEZIALI

VIA DE' CALZAIUOLI

VIA DE'

V.D. TAVOLINI

V.D. CIMATORI

V. DE' LAMBERTI

CALIMALA

VIA PORTA ROSSA

Orsanmichele
The church's niche carvings depict patron saints of trade guilds, such as this copy of Donatello's St George **8**

KEY

– – – Suggested route

0 metres   100

0 yards   100

Via dei Calzaiuoli, lined with smart shops, is the city's liveliest street.

Piazza della Signoria

Museo dell'Opera del Duomo
Works from the Duomo, Campanile and Baptistry are displayed in this museum

Pegna sells a range of fine wines, oil and honey.

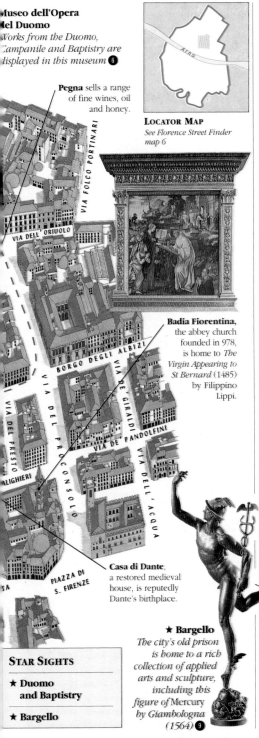

LOCATOR MAP
See Florence Street Finder map 6

Badia Fiorentina, the abbey church founded in 978, is home to *The Virgin Appearing to St Bernard* (1485) by Filippino Lippi.

Casa di Dante, a restored medieval house, is reputedly Dante's birthplace.

★ **Bargello**
The city's old prison is home to a rich collection of applied arts and sculpture, including this figure of Mercury by Giambologna (1564) ❾

STAR SIGHTS

★ **Duomo and Baptistry**

★ **Bargello**

Carving from Luca della Robbia's choir loft in the Museo dell'Opera

Museo dell'Opera del Duomo ❻

Piazza del Duomo 9. **Map** 2 D5 (6 E2).
📞 055-239 87 96. ◯ Apr–Oct: 9am–7:30pm Mon–Sat; Nov–Mar: 9am–6pm Mon–Sat (last adm: 40 mins before closing). ◯ 25 Dec, 1 Jan, Easter. 🎟 📷

THE CATHEDRAL Works Museum, second only to the Bargello in its collection of sculpture, houses items removed over the years from the exteriors of the Duomo, Campanile and Baptistry.

Its first two rooms are devoted to Brunelleschi and to the Duomo's construction, displaying tools used by 15th-century masons and a model created during the building of the cathedral dome.

The main ground floor room has a facsimile of Arnolfo di Cambio's original façade for the cathedral, together with statues such as Donatello's *St John* (1408–15) and Arnolfo di Cambio's striking *Madonna of the Glass Eyes* (1296), both originally created for its niches.

Michelangelo's *Pietà* (before 1555) has pride of place on the staircase, a fitting prelude to the magnificent white marble choir lofts by Donatello and Luca della Robbia on the upper floor. The former dwarfs Donatello's remarkable *La Maddalena* statue (1455), a counterpoint to his figure of the prophet Abakuk (1423–5), in the same room. Close by stand four of Ghiberti's cleaned and restored Baptistry door panels *(see p274),* surrounded by a beautiful medley of paintings and silverware.

Duomo and Baptistry ❼

Sir John Hawkwood by Paolo Uccello, in the Duomo

Rising above the heart of the city, the richly-decorated Duomo – Santa Maria del Fiore – and its orange-tiled dome have become Florence's most famous symbols. Typical of the Florentine determination to lead in all things, the cathedral is Europe's fourth largest church, and to this day it still remains the city's tallest building. The Baptistry, with its celebrated bronze doors, may date back to the 4th century, making it one of Florence's oldest buildings. The Campanile, designed by Giotto in 1334, was completed in 1359, 22 years after his death.

Campanile
At 85 m (276 ft), the Campanile is 6 m (20 ft) shorter than the dome. It is clad in white, green, and pink Tuscan marble.

Gothic windows

The Neo-Gothic marble façade echoes the style of Giotto's Campanile, but was only added in 1871–87.

★ **Baptistry**
Colourful 13th-century mosaics illustrating the Last Judgment *decorate the ceiling above the octagonal font, where many famous Florentines, including Dante, were baptized. The doors are by Andrea Pisano (south) and Lorenzo Ghiberti (north, east).*

North Doors

East Doors
(See p274)

Main entrance

South Doors

Campanile Reliefs
Reliefs by Andrea Pisano on the Campanile's first storey depict the Creation of Man, and the Arts and the Industries. Illustrated here are scenes representing hunting, weaving and law-giving.

The top of the dome offers spectacular views over the city.

★ Dome by Brunelleschi
Brunelleschi's dome, finished in 1463, was the largest of its time to be built without scaffolding. The outer shell is supported by a thicker inner shell that acts as a platform for it.

The *Last Judgment* frescoes (1572–4) by Vasari were completed by Zuccari.

VISITORS' CHECKLIST

Piazza del Duomo. **Map** 2 D5 (6 E2). (055-29 45 14. ■ 1, 11, 17, 23a. ◯ 10am–5:30pm daily. ✝ ◯ & **Crypt & Dome** ◯ 9am–6pm Mon–Fri, 8:30am–5pm Sat, 1–5pm Sun. ◯ *religious hols.* ◯ **Campanile** (055-230 28 85. ◯ Apr–Oct: 9am–7:30pm daily; Nov–Mar: 9am–5pm daily (last adm: 40 mins before closing). ◯ 1 Jan, Easter Sun, 25 Dec. ◯ **Baptistry** ◯ 1:30–6pm Mon–Sat, 9am–1:30pm Sun & religious hols. ✝ ◯

Bricks were set between marble ribs in a self-supporting herringbone pattern – a technique Brunelleschi copied from the Pantheon in Rome.

Chapels at the East End
The three apses, crowned by smaller copies of the dome, have five chapels each. The 15th-century stained glass is by Ghiberti.

The marble sanctuary around the High Altar was created by Baccio Bandinelli in 1555.

Entrance to the 463 steps leading up to the dome

Marble Pavement
The colourful, intricately inlaid pavement (16th century) was designed in part by Baccio d'Agnolo and Francesco da Sangallo.

Dante Explaining the Divine Comedy (1465)
This painting by Michelino shows the poet outside Florence against a backdrop of Purgatory, Hell and Paradise.

STAR FEATURES

★ Dome by Brunelleschi

★ Baptistry

The East Doors of the Baptistry

LORENZO GHIBERTI'S FAMOUS bronze Baptistry doors were commissioned in 1401 to mark the city's deliverance from the plague. Ghiberti was chosen to make a set of new doors after a competition that involved seven leading artists, including Donatello, Jacopo

Ghiberti's winning panel

della Quercia and Brunelleschi. The trial panels by Ghiberti and Brunelleschi are so different from Florentine Gothic art of the time, notably in the use of perspective and individuality of figures, that they are often regarded as the first works of the Renaissance.

"GATE OF PARADISE"

Having spent 21 years working on the North Doors, Ghiberti was commissioned to make the East Doors (1424 –1452). Michelangelo enthusiastically dubbed them, the "Gate of Paradise". The original ten relief panels showing scriptural subjects are now exhibited in the Museo dell'Opera del Duomo (*see p271*); those on the Baptistry are copies.

Abraham and the Sacrifice of Isaac
The jagged modelled rocks symbolizing Abraham's pain are carefully arranged to emphasize the sacrificial act.

Joseph Sold into Slavery
Ghiberti, a master of perspective, formed the architectural elements in shallower relief behind the figures to create the illusion of depth in the scene.

KEY TO THE EAST DOORS

1	2
3	4
5	6
7	8
9	10

1 Adam and Eve are Expelled from Eden
2 Cain Murders his Brother, Abel
3 The Drunkenness of Noah and his Sacrifice
4 Abraham and the Sacrifice of Isaac
5 Esau and Jacob
6 Joseph Sold into Slavery
7 Moses Receives the Ten Commandments
8 The Fall of Jericho
9 The Battle with the Philistines
10 Solomon and the Queen of Sheba

Detail of carvings by Donatello on the wall of Orsanmichele

Orsanmichele ⑧

Via dei Calzaiuoli. **Map** 3 C1 (6 D3).
◯ 9am–noon, 4–6pm daily. ♿

BUILT IN 1337 as a grain market, Orsanmichele was later converted into a church which took its name from *Orto di San Michele*, a monastic garden long since vanished. The arcades of the market became windows, which have since been bricked in, but the original Gothic tracery can still be seen. The decoration of the church was entrusted to Florence's major *Arti* (guilds). Over 60 years they commissioned sculptures of their patron saints to adorn the 14 exterior niches, though today many of the original figures have been replaced by copies. Among the sculptors at work here were Lorenzo Ghiberti, Donatello and Verrocchio.

The beautifully tranquil interior contains an opulent 14th-century altar by Andrea Orcagna, a *Virgin and Child* by Bernardo Daddi (1348) and a statue of the *Madonna and Child with St Anne* by Francesco da Sangallo (1522).

Bargello ⑨

Via del Proconsolo 4. **Map** 4 D1
(6 E3). 📞 055-238 86 06. 🚌 19.
◯ 9am–2pm Tue–Sun. ⬤ 1 Jan,
25 Apr, 1 May, 25 Dec (some rooms may be closed during winter). 💶 📷
♿ ground floor only.

FLORENCE'S second-ranking museum after the Uffizi, the Bargello contains a wonderful medley of applied arts and Italy's finest collection of Renaissance sculpture. Begun in 1255, the fortress-like building was initially the town hall (making it the oldest seat of government in the city), but later became a prison and home to the chief of police (the *Bargello*). It also became known for its executions, which took place in the main courtyard until 1786, when the death sentence was abolished by Grand Duke Pietro Leopoldo. Following extensive renovation, the building opened as one of Italy's first national museums in 1865.

The key exhibits range over three floors, beginning with the Michelangelo Room, superbly redesigned after extensive damage during the 1966 flood. Three contrasting works by Michelangelo lie dotted around the room, the most famous a tipsy-looking *Bacchus* (1497), the sculptor's first large free-standing work. Close by is a powerful bust of *Brutus* (1539–40), the only known portrait bust by Michelangelo, and a beautifully delicate circular relief depicting the *Madonna and Child* (1503–5).

Brunelleschi's *Sacrifice of Isaac* (1402) in the Bargello

Countless works by other sculptors occupy the same room. Among them is an exquisite *Mercury* (1564) by the Mannerist genius, Giambologna, as well as several virtuoso bronzes by the sculptor and goldsmith, Benvenuto Cellini (1500–71).

Across the courtyard, full of fragments and the coats of arms of the Bargello's various incumbents, two more rooms contain exterior sculptures removed from sites around the city. The courtyard's external staircase leads to the first floor, which opens with a wonderfully eccentric bronze menagerie by Giambologna. To the right is the Salone del Consiglio Generale, a cavernous former courtroom that contains the cream of the museum's Early Renaissance sculpture. Foremost among its highlights is Donatello's heroic *St George* (1416) – the epitome of "youth, courage and valour of arms" in the words of Vasari. Commissioned by the Armourers' Guild, the statue was brought here from Orsanmichele in 1892. At the centre of the room, in direct contrast, is Donatello's androgynous *David* (c.1430), famous as the first free-standing nude by a Western artist since antiquity. Among the room's more easily missed works, tucked away on the right wall, are two reliefs depicting *The Sacrifice of Isaac* (1402). Created by Brunelleschi and Lorenzo Ghiberti respectively, both were entries in the competition to design the Baptistry doors.

Beyond the Salone, the Bargello's emphasis shifts to the applied arts, with room after room devoted to rugs, ceramics, silverware and a host of other beautiful *objets d'art*. The most celebrated of these rooms is the Salone del Camino on the second floor, which features the finest collection of small bronzes in Italy. Some are reproductions of antique models, others are small copies of Renaissance statues. Giambologna, Cellini and Antonio del Pollaiuolo are among those represented.

Donatello's *David* (c.1430) in the Bargello

Bacchus (1497) by Michelangelo

Santa Croce ⓾

THE GOTHIC CHURCH of Santa Croce contains the
tombs and monuments of many famous
Florentines, among them Michelangelo, Galileo
and Machiavelli, as well as radiant early 14th-
century frescoes by Giotto and his gifted pupil
Taddeo Gaddi. In the cloister alongside the church
stands the Cappella de' Pazzi (Pazzi Chapel), a
Renaissance masterpiece
designed by Filippo
Brunelleschi.

**Tomb of Leonardo
Bruni** *(1447)
Rossellino's effigy of
this great humanist was
unusual in its sensitive
realism and lack of
monumental pomp.*

**Tomb of
Michelangelo** *(1570)
Vasari's tomb figures
represent Painting,
Sculpture and
Architecture.*

Annunciation **by
Donatello (15th century)**

**Tomb of
Machiavelli**

**The Neo-
Gothic
façade**
by Niccolò
Matas was
added in
1863.

**Tomb of
Galileo**

**Entrance
to church**

Exit

**Entrance to
Cloister and
Cappella
de' Pazzi**

**Entrance
to Museo**

Cimabue's Crucifixion
*Badly damaged in the flood
of 1966, this 13th-century
masterpiece is among the
highlights of the museum
(museo), as is Taddeo
Gaddi's magnificent* Last
Supper *(c.1355–60).*

★ Cappella de' Pazzi
*Brunelleschi's domed
chapel with Classical
proportions was begun
in 1443. The roundels
(c.1442–52) are by
Luca della Robbia.*

**The Neo-Gothic
campanile** was
added in 1842.

The Cappella Baroncelli,
frescoed by Taddeo Gaddi
between 1332 and 1338,
contains the first true night
scene in Western art.

Sacristy

★ Cappella Bardi Frescoes
*Giotto frescoed the Bardi
and Peruzzi chapels to the
right of the high altar
between 1315 and 1330.
This touching scene from
the left hand wall of the
chapel shows* The Death
of St Francis *(1317).*

STAR FEATURES

★ **Cappella Bardi
Frescoes**

★ **Cappella de' Pazzi**

Museo di Storia della Scienza ⓫

Piazza de' Giudici 1. **Map** 4 D1 (6 E4).
055-29 34 93. 9:30am–1pm
Mon–Sat, 2–5pm Mon, Wed, Fri.
1 Jan, 25 Apr, 1 May, 24 Jun.

THIS LIVELY and superbly
presented museum devotes
numerous rooms on two floors
to different scientific themes,
illustrating each with countless
fine displays and a panoply
of old and beautifully made
scientific instruments. It is
also something of a shrine to
the Pisa-born scientist, Galileo
Galilei (1564–1642),
and features two of
his telescopes, as
well as large-
scale reconstruc-
tions of his
experiments
into motion,
weight, velocity
and acceleration.
These are some-
times demonstrated
by the attendants. Other
exhibits come from
the Accademia del
Cimento (Academy
for Experimentation),
which was founded in 1657
by Grand Duke Ferdinand II
in memory of Galileo.

The first few rooms are
devoted to astronomical,
mathematical and navigational
instruments, with galleries
concentrating on Galileo,
telescopes and optical games.
Some of the loveliest exhibits
are in room 7, which is
crammed with early maps,
globes and astrolabes, and
among the antique micro-
scopes, thermometers and
barometers in the rooms
beyond. The second floor is
slightly less arresting, but

**Astrolabe,
Museo di Storia
della Scienza**

there are some fine old clocks,
mathematical instruments,
calculators, a horrifying
collection of 19th-century
surgical instruments, weights
and measures, and some
graphic anatomical models.

Ponte Vecchio ⓬

Map 4 D1 (6 E4).

PONTE VECCHIO, the oldest
surviving bridge in the city,
was built in 1345, the last in a
succession of bridges and fords
on the site that dated back to
Roman times. Designed by
Giotto's pupil Taddeo
Gaddi, its pictur-
esque shops were
originally the
domain of
blacksmiths,
butchers and tan-
ners (who used
the river as a con-
venient place for
disposing of waste).
They were reviled for
their noise and stench
and were eventually
evicted in 1593 by
Duke Ferdinando I –
replaced by jewellers and
goldsmiths who were able to
pay higher rents. The
elevated Corridoio Vasariano
runs along the eastern side of
the bridge, above the shops.
Giorgio Vasari designed the
corridor in 1565 to allow the
Medici family to move about
their residences without
having to mix with the public.
This was the city's only bridge
to escape destruction during
World War II and visitors
today come as much to admire
the views as to browse among
the antique shops and
specialized jewellery shops.

Ponte Vecchio viewed from the Ponte Santa Trìnita

Uffizi ⓮

THE UFFIZI, Italy's greatest art gallery, was built in 1560–80 to house offices *(uffici)* for Duke Cosimo I. The architect Vasari used iron as reinforcement, which enabled his successor, Buontalenti, to create an almost continuous wall of glass on the upper storey. This was used as a gallery for Francesco I to display the Medici art treasures. The collection was divided up in the 19th century: ancient objects went to the archaeological museum and sculpture to the Bargello, leaving the Uffizi with a matchless collection of paintings.

Main staircase

Entrance hall

Entrance

Bacchus *(c.1589)*
Caravaggio's early work depicts the god of wine as a pallid, debauched youth. The mood of dissipation is echoed in the decaying fruit, one of Western art's earliest still-life paintings.

Corridor ceilings are frescoed with 1580s "grotesques" copied from Roman grottoes.

Annunciation *(1333)*
The Sienese painter Simone Martini was strongly influenced by French Gothic art, and this is one of his masterpieces. The two saints are by Martini's pupil and brother-in-law, Lippo Memmi.

Buontalenti staircase

GALLERY GUIDE
The Uffizi art collection is on the top floor of the building. Greek and Roman sculptures are displayed in the broad corridors (East, Arno, West) running round the inner side of the building. The paintings are hung in rooms off the corridors in chronological order to reveal the development of Florentine art from Byzantine to High Renaissance and beyond. Gothic art is in rooms 2–6; Early Renaissance in 7–14; High Renaissance and Mannerism in 15–29; and later paintings in 30–45.

Ognissanti Madonna *(c.1310)*
Giotto's grasp of spatial depth and substance in this altarpiece was a milestone in the mastery of perspective.

KEY TO FLOORPLAN
- ☐ East Corridor
- ☐ West Corridor
- ☐ Arno Corridor
- ☐ Gallery rooms 1–45
- ☐ Non-exhibition space

The Duke and Duchess of Urbino *(c.1465–70)*
*Piero della Francesca's portraits of Federico da Montefeltro
and his wife Battista Sforza were painted after Battista died
aged 26. Her portrait was probably based on her death mask.*

The Tribune,
decorated in
red and gold,
contains the
works most
valued by
the Medici.

The Birth of Venus *(c.1485)*
*Botticelli shows the goddess of love flanked by
Zephyrus, god of the west wind, who blows
the risen Venus to shore on a half-shell. The
myth may symbolize the birth of beauty
through the divine fertilization of matter.*

The Holy Family *(1456)*
*Michelangelo's paint-
ing, the first to break
with the convention
of showing Christ
on the Virgin's lap,
inspired Mannerist
artists through its
expressive handling
of colour and posture.*

**Vasari's Classical Arno
façade** (begun 1560)

The Vasari Corridor
is a passageway
across the Arno to
the Pitti Palace.

**The Venus of
Urbino** *(1538)*
*Titian's sensuous nude,
inspired by Giorgione's
Sleeping Venus, may in
fact be a portrait of a
courtesan deemed
sufficiently beautiful
to be a goddess.*

Exploring the Uffizi

THE UFFIZI offers not only the chance to see the world's greatest collection of Italian Renaissance paintings, but also the opportunity to enjoy masterpieces from as far afield as Holland, Spain and Germany. Accumulated over the centuries by the Medici, the collection was first housed in the Uffizi in 1581, and eventually bequeathed to the Florentine people by Anna Maria Lodovica, the last of the Medici.

GOTHIC ART

PAST THE STATUES and antiquities of room 1, the Uffizi proper opens in style with three altarpieces of the *Maestà*, or Madonna Enthroned, by Giotto, Duccio and Cimabue, some of Italy's greatest 13th-century painters. Each work marks a stage in the development of Italian painting away from the stilted conventions of Byzantium to the livelier traditions of Gothic and Renaissance art. The shift is best expressed in Giotto's version of the subject (known as the *Ognissanti Madonna*), where new feeling for depth and naturalistic detail is shown in the range of emotion displayed by the saints and angels, and by the carefully evoked three-dimensionality of the Virgin's throne.

Giotto's naturalistic influence can also be seen among the paintings of room 4, which is devoted to the 14th-century Florentine School, an interesting counterpoint to the Sienese paintings of Duccio and his followers in room 3. Among the many fine paintings here are works by Ambrogio and Pietro Lorenzetti, and Simone Martini's *Annunciation*.

Room 6 is devoted to International Gothic, a highly decorative style that represented the height of Gothic expression. It is exemplified by Gentile da Fabriano's exquisite, glittering *Adoration of the Magi* painted in 1423.

EARLY RENAISSANCE

A NEW UNDERSTANDING of geometry and perspective during the 15th century increasingly allowed artists to explore the complexities of space and depth. None became more obsessed with these new compositional possibilities than Paolo

Madonna and Child with Angels **(1455–66) by Fra Filippo Lippi**

Uccello (1397–1475), whose picture of *The Battle of San Romano* (1456) in room 7 is one of the gallery's most fevered creations.

Room 7 also contains two panels from 1460 by Piero della Francesca, another artist preoccupied with the art of perspective. The panels, which are among the earliest Renaissance portraits, depict the Duke and Duchess of Urbino on one side and representations of their virtues on the other.

While such works can seem coldly experimental, Fra Filippo Lippi's *Madonna and Child with Angels* (1455–66), in Room 8, is a masterpiece of warmth and humanity.

Sandro Botticelli's allegorical painting, *Primavera* (1480)

Like many Renaissance artists, Lippi uses a religious subject to celebrate earthly delights such as landscape and feminine beauty. A similar approach is apparent in the works of Botticelli, whose famous paintings in rooms 10–14 are for many the highlight of the gallery. In *The Birth of Venus*, for example, Venus takes the place of the Virgin, expressing a fascination with Classical mythology common to many Renaissance artists. The same is true of the *Primavera* (1480), which breaks with Christian religious painting by illustrating a pagan rite of spring.

Detail from *The Annunciation* **(1472–5) by Leonardo da Vinci**

HIGH RENAISSANCE AND MANNERISM

ROOM 15 FEATURES works attributed to the young Leonardo da Vinci, notably a sublime *Annunciation* (1472–5), which reveals hints of his still emerging style, and the *Adoration of the Magi* (1481), which remained unfinished when he left Florence for Milan to paint *The Last Supper* (1495–8).

Room 18, better known as the Tribune, was designed in 1584 by Buontalenti in order to accommodate the best-loved pieces of the Medici collection. Its most famous work is the so-called Medici Venus (1st century BC), a Roman copy of a Greek statue deemed to be the most erotic in the ancient world. The copy proved equally salacious and was removed from Rome's Villa Medici by Cosimo III to keep it from corrupting the city's art students. Other highlights in

room 18 include Agnolo Bronzino's portraits of *Cosimo I* and *Eleonora di Toledo*, both painted around 1545, and Pontormo's *Charity* (1530) and the portrait of *Cosimo il Vecchio* (1517).

Rooms 19 to 23 depart from the gallery's Florentine bias, demonstrating how rapidly Renaissance ideas and techniques spread beyond Tuscany. Painters from the German and Flemish schools are well-represented, together with painters from Umbria like Perugino, but perhaps the most captivating works are the paintings by Venetian and northern Italian artists such as Mantegna, Carpaccio, Correggio and Bellini.

Room 25, which returns to the Tuscan mainstream, is dominated by Michelangelo's *Holy Family* or Doni Tondo (1456), notable for its vibrant colours and the Virgin's unusually twisted pose. The gallery's only work by Michelangelo, it was to prove immensely influential with the next generation of painters, especially Bronzino (1503–72), Pontormo (1494–1556) and Parmigianino (1503–40). The last of these was responsible for the *Madonna of the Long Neck* (c.1534) in room 29. With its contorted anatomy, unnatural colours and strange composition, this painting is a masterpiece of the style that came to be called Mannerism. Earlier, but no less remarkable masterpieces in rooms 26 and 28 include Raphael's sublime

Madonna of the Goldfinch (1506) by Raphael

Madonna of the Long Neck (c.1534) by Parmigianino

Madonna of the Goldfinch (1506) and Titian's notorious *Venus of Urbino* (1538), censured by Mark Twain as the "foulest, the vilest, the obscenest picture the world possesses". Others hold it to be one of the most beautiful nudes ever painted.

LATER PAINTINGS

VISITORS, already sated by a surfeit of outstanding paintings, are often tempted to skim through the Uffizi's final rooms. The paintings in rooms 30 to 35 – which are mainly from the Veneto and Emilia-Romagna – are mostly unexceptional, but the gallery's last rooms (41–45) contain paintings that compare favourably with those that have gone before. Room 43 has three works by Caravaggio: *Medusa* (1596–8), painted for a Roman cardinal; *Bacchus* (c.1589), one of the artist's earliest works; and the *Sacrifice of Isaac* (c.1590), whose violent subject is belied by the painting's gentle background landscape. Room 44, dedicated to Rembrandt and northern European painting, features Rembrandt's *Portrait of an Old Man* (1665) and two self-portraits of the artist as a young and old man (painted in 1634 and 1664, respectively). Canaletto, Goya, Tiepolo and other 18th-century artists bring the gallery to its conclusion.

Piazza della Signoria ⑭

Savonarola (1452–98)

Piazza della signoria and Palazzo Vecchio have been at the heart of Florence's political and social life for centuries. The great bell once used to summon citizens to *parlamento* (public meetings) here, and the square has long been a popular promenade for both visitors and Florentines. The piazza's statues (some are copies) commemorate the city's major historical events, though its most famous episode is celebrated by a simple pavement plaque near the loggia: the execution of the religious leader Girolamo Savonarola who was burnt at the stake.

David
This copy of the famous Michelangelo statue symbolizes triumph over tyranny. The original (see p267) stood in the piazza until 1873.

Heraldic Frieze
The crossed keys on this shield represent Medici papal rule.

Salone dei Cinquecento *(1495)*
This vast chamber contains a statue of Victory by Michelangelo and frescoes by Vasari describing Florentine triumphs over Pisa and Siena.

Sala dei Gigli

Fontana di Nettuno, Ammannati's fountain (1575) of the Roman sea god surrounded by water nymphs, commemorates Tuscan naval victories.

Entrance to Palazzo Vecchio

The Marzocco is a copy of the heraldic lion of Florence carved by Donatello in 1420. The original is in the Bargello.

★ Palazzo Vecchio (completed 1332)
This Republican frieze over the palace entrance is inscribed with the words, "Christ is King", implying that no mortal ruler has absolute power.

★ The Rape of the Sabine Women by Giambologna
(1583) The writhing figures in Giambologna's famous statue were carved from a single block of flawed marble.

The Uffizi

The Loggia dei Lanzi
(1382), designed by Orcagna, is named after the Lancers, the bodyguards of Cosimo I who were billeted here.

Roman statues, possibly of emperors, line the Loggia.

★ Perseus by Cellini
This bronze statue (1554) of Perseus beheading Medusa was intended to warn Cosimo I's enemies of their probable fate.

STAR FEATURES
★ Palazzo Vecchio
★ Perseus by Cellini
★ The Rape of the Sabine Women by Giambologna

Palazzo Vecchio ⑮

Piazza della Signoria. **Map** 4 D1 (6 D3). 055-276 83 25. 19, 23, 31, 32. 9am–7pm Mon–Wed, Fri & Sat, 8am–1pm Sun (last adm: 1 hr before closing). 1 Jan, Easter, 1 May, 15 Aug, 25 Dec.

THE "OLD PALACE" still fulfils its original role as Florence's town hall. It was completed in 1322 when a huge bell, used to call citizens to meetings or warn of fire, flood or enemy attack, was hauled to the top of the imposing bell tower. While retaining much of its medieval appearance, the interior was remodelled for Duke Cosimo I when he moved into the palace in 1540. Leonardo and Michelangelo were asked to redecorate the interior, but it was Vasari who finally undertook the work, incorporating bombastic frescoes (1563–5) of Florentine achievements. Michelangelo's statue of *Victory* (1525) graces the Salone dei Cinquecento, which also boasts a tiny Studiolo (study) decorated from 1569 to 1573 by 30 of Florence's leading Mannerist painters. Other highlights include the Cappella di Eleonora, painted by Bronzino (1540–45); the loggia, with its views over the city; and the Sala dei Gigli (Room of Lilies) containing Donatello's *Judith and Holofernes* (c.1455) and frescoes of Roman heroes (1485) by Ghirlandaio.

A copy of Verrocchio's Putto fountain in Vasari's courtyard

Street-by-Street: Around Piazza della Repubblica

UNDERLYING THE STREET PLAN of modern Florence is the far older pattern of the ancient Roman city. Nowhere is this more evident than in the grid of narrow streets around Piazza della Repubblica, site of the old Roman forum. This pivotal square housed the city's main food market until the 1860s, when redevelopment tidied up the area, and added the triumphal arch that now stands in today's café-filled square.

Santa Trìnita has frescoes by Ghirlandaio on the Life of St Francis (1486), depicting events that took place in this area. Here, a child is revived after falling from the Palazzo Spini-Ferroni.

Palazzo Spini-Ferroni

Ponte Santa Trìnita was built in wood in 1290 and then rebuilt by Ammannati in 1567 to celebrate the defeat of Siena.

Palazzo Strozzi
This monumental palazzo dominates the square ⑰

Santi Apostoli
was reputedly founded by Charlemagne.

Palazzo Davanzati
Frescoes with exotic birds decorate the Sala dei Pappagalli, which was once the dining room of this 14th-century palazzo ⑯

KEY

– – – Suggested route

0 metres   200
0 yards   200

LOCATOR MAP
*See Florence Street Finder
maps 5, 6*

Piazza della Repubblica, which dates from the 19th century, is lined by some of Florence's oldest and best known cafés.

Mercato Nuovo, the "New Market" (1547), now deals mainly in souvenirs.

Palazzo di Parte Guelfa was the headquarters of the Guelphs, the dominant political party of medieval Florence.

Ponte Vecchio
(See p277)

Detail of a frieze illustrating a medieval romance in Palazzo Davanzati

Palazzo Davanzati ⑯

Via Porta Rossa 13. **Map** 3 C1 (5 C3).
📞 *055-238 86 10.* 🕐 *9am–2pm
Tue–Sun.* ⬤ *some public hols.* 📷

THIS WONDERFUL MUSEUM, also known as the Museo dell'Antica Casa Fiorentina, uses original fittings and furniture to recreate the ambience of a typical 14th-century town house. The peaceful inner courtyard, linked by stairs to the upper floors, contains a well and a pulley system, something of a luxury in medieval Florence, when most households drew their water from public fountains. All the rooms have something of interest, but the most beautiful are the Sala dei Pappagalli, named after its frescoed parrot (*pappagallo*) motifs; the gloriously decorated Sala Pavoni, or Camera Nuziale (Wedding Room); and the upper floor kitchen, a rustic room with fine views.

Palazzo Strozzi ⑰

Piazza degli Strozzi. **Map** 3 C1 (5 C3).
**Piccolo Museo di Palazzo
Strozzi** ⬤ *for restoration.*

SHEER SIZE accounts for the impact of the Palazzo Strozzi, and although it is only three storeys high, each floor exceeds the height of a normal palazzo. It was commissioned by the wealthy banker Filippo Strozzi, who had 15 buildings demolished to make way for the palazzo. He hoped it would rival the Medici palaces elsewhere in the city. Strozzi died in 1491, just two years after the first stone was laid.

Work on the building continued until 1536, with three major architects contributing to its design – Giuliano da Sangallo, Benedetto da Maiano and Simone del Pollaiuolo (also known as Cronaca). The exterior, built of huge rusticated masonry blocks, remains unspoiled. Look out for the original Renaissance torch-holders, lamps and the rings for tethering horses that still adorn the corners and façades. A small museum off the courtyard records the building's history, but the palace is now primarily used as an exhibition venue (a large antique fair is held here biennially in late September).

Exterior of Palazzo Strozzi, with masonry block rustication

San Lorenzo ⑱

San Lorenzo was the parish church of the Medici family, and in 1419 Brunelleschi was commissioned to rebuild it in the Classical style of the Renaissance. Almost a century later Michelangelo submitted some plans for the façade, and began work on the Medici tombs in the Sagrestia Nuova. He also designed a library, the Biblioteca Mediceo-Laurenziana, to house the family's collection of manuscripts. The lavish family mausoleum, the Cappella dei Principi, was started in 1604.

Cappella dei Principi
The Medici mausoleum, behind the high altar, was begun in 1604 by Matteo Nigetti, and forms part of the Cappelle Medicee.

The huge dome by Buontalenti echoes that of the Duomo *(see pp272–3).*

The Old Sacristy was designed by Brunelleschi and decorated by Donatello.

Campanile

Biblioteca Staircase
Michelangelo's Mannerist staircase, one of the artist's most innovative designs, was built by Ammannati in 1559.

Michelangelo designed the desks and ceiling of the Biblioteca, where exhibitions of Medici manuscripts are often held.

The cloister garden is planted with box hedges, pomegranate and orange trees.

The Martyrdom of St Lawrence
Bronzino's vast Mannerist fresco of 1659 is a bravura, choreographed study of the human form, rather than a reverential response to the agony of the saint.

Entrance to church

A simple stone slab marks
the unostentatious grave of
Cosimo il Vecchio
(1389–1464), founder
of the Medici dynasty.

The Cappelle Medicee
complex comprises the
Cappella dei Principi and its
crypt, the Sagrestia Nuova
(see p287).

Pulpits by Donatello
*The bronze pulpits in the
nave were Donatello's last
works. Completed by his
pupils in 1460, the reliefs
capture the flinching pain of
Christ's Passion and the
glory of the Resurrection.*

**St Joseph and Christ
in the Workshop**, a
striking work showing
the young Christ with
his father, is by Pietro
Annigoni (1910–88),
one of the few modern
artists whose work is
seen in Florence.

Michelangelo submitted
several designs for the
façade of San Lorenzo, but
it remains unfinished.

**The Tomb of the Duke of Nemours
(1520–34) by Michelangelo in the
Cappelle Medicee's New Sacristy**

Cappelle Medicee ⑲

Piazza di Madonna degli Aldobrandini.
Map 1 C5 (6 D1). 📞 055-238 85.
🚌 many routes. ◯ 9am–2pm
Tue–Sat, 9am–1pm Sun & public hols.
◯ 1 Jan, 1 May, 25 Dec. 🎟 📷 ⛪

THE MEDICI CHAPELS divide
into three distinct areas.
Beyond the entrance hall lies
a low-vaulted crypt, a suitably
subdued space for the brass-
railed tombs of numerous
lesser Medici. From here
steps lead to the octagonal
Cappella dei Principi
(Chapel of Princes), a vast
family mausoleum begun
by Cosimo I in 1604. Little
in Florence is so opulently
decorated: the ceiling is
garishly frescoed and the walls
are smothered in huge swathes
of semi-precious *pietre dure*
(inlaid stone). Spaced around
the walls are the tombs of six
Medici Grand Dukes. From

here a corridor leads to
Michelangelo's **New Sacristy**,
designed as a counterpoint
to Brunelleschi's Old Sacristy
in San Lorenzo. Three groups
of statues, all carved by
Michelangelo between 1520
and 1534, stand around the
walls: that on the near left
hand wall is *The Tomb of the
Duke of Urbino* (grandson
of Lorenzo the Magnificent),
showing the Duke deep in
thought. Opposite is *The
Tomb of the Duke of Nemours*
(Lorenzo's third son). Close to
the unfinished *Madonna and
Child* (1521) is a simple tomb
containing Lorenzo the
Magnificent and his murdered
brother, Giuliano (died 1478).

Mercato Centrale ⑳

Piazza del Mercato Centrale. **Map** 1 C4
(5 C1). ◯ 7am–2pm daily (also:
Sep–Jun: 4–8pm Sat).

AT THE HEART of the San
Lorenzo street market is
the bustling Mercato Centrale,
Florence's busiest food
market. It is housed in a vast
two-storey building of cast-
iron and glass, built in 1874
by Giuseppe Mengoni.
  The ground floor stalls sell
meat, poultry, fish, salamis,
hams, cheeses and excellent
olive oils. There are also
Tuscan takeaway foods such as
porchetta (roast suckling pig),
lampredotto (pig's intestines)
and *trippa* (tripe). Fresh fruit,
vegetables and flowers are sold
on the top floor: look out for
wild mushrooms and truffles
in the autumn, and baby
artichokes in early spring.

Yellow courgette flowers and other vegetables in the Mercato Centrale

Santa Maria Novella ㉑

THE CHURCH of Santa Maria Novella was built by the Dominicans between 1279 and 1357. The lower Romanesque part of its façade was incorporated into one based on Classical proportions by the pioneering Renaissance architect Leon Battista Alberti in 1456–70. The Gothic interior contains superb frescoes, including Masaccio's powerful *Trinity*. The famous Green Cloister, frescoed with perspective scenes by Paolo Uccello, and the dramatically decorated Spanish Chapel now form a museum.

The arcade arches are emphasized by grey and white banding.

Monastic buildings

The Nave
The piers of the nave are spaced closer together at the altar end. This trick of perspective creates the illusion of an exceptionally long church.

Cappellone degli Spagnuoli, the chapel used by the Spanish courtiers of Eleonora of Toledo, has frescoes of salvation and damnation.

Chiostro Verde takes its name from the green base used in Uccello's frescoes, which were sadly damaged by the 1966 floods.

Trinity by Masaccio
This pioneering fresco (c.1428) is renowned as a masterpiece of perspective and portraiture. The kneeling figures flanking the arch are the painting's sponsors, judge Lorenzo Lenzi and his wife.

Entrance

Entrance to museum

Cappella Strozzi
The 14th-century frescoes by Nardo di Cione and his brother Andrea Orcagna were inspired by Dante's epic poem, The Divine Comedy.

Ghirlandaio's *Madonna della Misericordia* (1472) in Ognissanti

The Strozzi Tomb is by Benedetto da Maiano (1493).

Cappella di Filippo Strozzi features Filippino Lippi's frescoes of St John raising Drusiana from the dead and St Philip slaying a dragon.

Cappella Tornabuoni
Ghirlandaio's famous fresco cycle, The Life of John the Baptist *(1485), peoples the biblical episodes with Florentine aristocrats in contemporary dress.*

Palazzo Antinori ㉒

Via de' Tornabuoni. **Map** 1 C5 (5 C2). ● *to the public.* **Cantinetta Antinori** ⏰ *12:30–2:30pm, 7–10:30pm Mon–Fri.*

PALAZZO ANTINORI was built in 1461–6 and is one of the finest small Renaissance palazzi in Florence. It was acquired by the Antinori in 1506 and has remained with the family ever since. The dynasty owns many estates all over Tuscany and Umbria, producing a range of wines, oils and liqueurs that can be sampled – along with fine Tuscan dishes – in the wine bar off the main courtyard, called the Cantinetta Antinori.

Palazzo Rucellai ㉓

Via della Vigna Nuova 16r. **Map** 1 C5 (5 B2). ☎ *055-21 33 70.* ● *10am–7:30pm Thu–Tue, 10–11:30pm Fri & Sat.* ⏰ *some public hols.* 🖼 ♿

BUILT IN 1446–57, this is one of the most ornate Renaissance palaces in the city. It was commissioned by Giovanni Rucellai, whose enormous wealth derived from the import of a rare and costly red dye made from lichen found only on the island of Majorca. The dye was called *oricello*, from which the name Rucellai is derived.

Giovanni commissioned several buildings from the architect Leon Battista Alberti, who designed this palace as a virtual textbook illustration of the major Classical orders.

The palazzo now houses the Museo Alinari. The Alinari brothers began taking pictures of Florence in the 1840s, not long after the invention of photography. They supplied high-quality prints, postcards and art books to foreigners on the Grand Tour who flocked to Florence during the 19th century. The museum mounts changing exhibitions from its vast archives, offering a fascinating insight into Florence's history of the last 150 years.

Ognissanti ㉔

Borgo Ognissanti 42. **Map** 1 B5 (5 A2). ☎ *055-239 87 00.* ⏰ *7:30am–noon, 4–6:30pm daily.* ♿

OGNISSANTI, or All Saints, was the parish church of the Vespucci, one of whose members, the 15th-century navigator Amerigo, gave his name to the New World. The young Amerigo is depicted in Ghirlandaio's fresco of the *Madonna della Misericordia* (1472) in the second chapel on the right between the Virgin and the man in the red cloak. Amerigo realized that the land discovered by Columbus was a new continent, not the eastern shore of the Indies. He made two voyages, and the letters he sent back enabled cartographers to draw the first maps of the new land.

Ognissanti is also the burial place of Botticelli. His fresco of *St Augustine* (1480) is on the south wall. Alongside the church is a cloister and refectory with Ghirlandaio's fresco of *The Last Supper* (1480).

Cappella Brancacci ㉕

THE CHURCH of Santa Maria del Carmine is famous for the Brancacci Chapel, which contains frescoes on *The Life of St Peter* commissioned by the Florentine merchant Felice Brancacci around 1424. Although the paintings were begun by Masolino in 1425, many of the scenes are by his pupil, Masaccio (who died before completing the cycle) and by Filippino Lippi, who completed the work in 1480. Masaccio's revolutionary use of perspective, his narrative drama and the tragic realism of his figures placed him in the vanguard of Renaissance painting. Many great artists, including Leonardo and Michelangelo, later visited the chapel to study his pioneering work.

In every scene, St Peter is distinguished from the crowds as the figure in the orange cloak.

St Peter Healing the Sick
Masaccio's realistic portrayal of cripples and beggars was revolutionary in his time.

The grouping of stylized figures in Masaccio's frescoes reflects his interest in the sculpture of Donatello.

Masaccio's simple style allows us to focus on the figures central to the frescoes without distracting detail.

Expulsion of Adam and Eve
Masaccio's ability to express emotion is well illustrated by his harrowing portrait of Adam and Eve being driven out of the Garden of Eden, their faces wracked by misery, shame and the burden of self-knowledge.

KEY TO THE FRESCOES: ARTISTS AND SUBJECTS

☐ Masolino

☐ Masaccio

☐ Lippi

1	2	3	7	8	9
4	5	6	10	11	12

1 Expulsion of Adam and Eve
2 The Tribute Money
3 St Peter Preaching
4 St Peter Visited by St Paul
5 Raising the Emperor's Son;
St Peter Enthroned
6 St Peter Healing the Sick

7 St Peter Baptizing the Converts
8 St Peter Healing the Cripple;
Raising Tabitha
9 Temptation of Adam and Eve
10 St Peter and St John Giving Alms
11 Crucifixion; Before the Proconsul
12 The Release of St Peter

VISITORS' CHECKLIST

Piazza del Carmine. **Map** 3 A1
(5 A4). ☎ 055-238 21 95. ☐ 15.
◯ 10am–5pm Mon, Wed–Sat,
1–5pm Sun (last adm: 30 mins
before closing). ● 25 Dec. ▨

**Masolino's *Temptation
of Adam and Eve*** is
gentle and decorous, in
contrast with the
emotional force of
Masaccio's painting on
the opposite wall.

Woman in a Turban
*The freshness of Masaccio's
original colours is seen in
this rediscovered roundel,
hidden behind the altar
for 500 years.*

St Peter is depicted
against a background
of Florentine buildings.

Two Figures
*Masolino's work tends to be more
formal, less naturalistic and less
animated than that of Masaccio.*

Before the Proconsul
*Filippino Lippi was called in to complete the cycle of
frescoes in 1480. He added this emotional scene
showing the Proconsul sentencing St Peter to death.*

Street-by-Street: Oltrarno

Medici coat of arms

FOR THE MOST PART, the Oltrarno is a homely area of small houses, quiet squares and shops selling antiques, bric-a-brac and foodstuffs. The Via Maggio, a busy thoroughfare, breaks this pattern, but step into the side streets and you escape the bustle to discover a corner of old world Florence. The restaurants serve authentic, reasonably priced food, and the area is full of studios and workshops restoring antique furniture. Among the things to see are Santo Spirito and Palazzo Pitti, one of the city's largest palaces, whose medley of museums contains an art collection second only to that of the Uffizi.

Santo Spirito
Brunelleschi's simple church was completed after the architect's death ㉖

Cenacolo di Santo Spirito, the old refectory of a monastery that once stood here, contains a dramatic fresco attributed to Orcagna (c.1360).

Palazzo Guadagni (1500) was the first in the city to be built with a roof-top loggia, setting a trend among the aristocracy.

Palazzo di Bianca Cappello (1579) is covered in ornate *sgraffito* work and was the home of the mistress of Grand Duke Francesco I.

Masks and murals are handmade at this shop, Frieze of Papier Mâché.

LOCATOR MAP
*See Florence Street Finder
maps 3, 5*

The 16th-century fountain
and gargoyle in Piazza de' Frescobaldi were
designed by Buontalenti, as was the façade
(1593–4) of the nearby church of Santa Trìnita.

Ponte Vecchio
(see p277)

BORGO SAN JACOPO

V. D. RAMAGLIANTI

CANELLA

O SPRONE

VIA DE' GUICCIARDINI

**Palazzo
Guicciardini**
was the
birthplace of
historian
Francesco
Guicciardini.

★ **Palazzo Pitti**
*Several museums are contained in this massive
palazzo, including an outstanding collection
of paintings. This painting of Palazzo Pitti
was made by Giusto Utens in 1599* ㉗

KEY

– – – Suggested route

0 metres   100

0 yards   100

STAR SIGHTS

★ **Palazzo Pitti**

Santo Spirito ㉖

Piazza di Santo Spirito. **Map** 3 B2
(5 B4). 055-21 00 30. 8:30am–
noon, 4–6pm Thu–Tue.

THE AUGUSTINIAN foundation
of this church dates from
1250. The present building,
dominating the northern end
of the pretty Piazza di Santo
Spirito, was designed by the
architect Brunelleschi in 1435,
but not completed until the
late 15th century, well after
his death. The unfinished
modest façade was added
in the 18th century.

Inside, the harmony of the
proportions has been somewhat spoiled by the elaborate
Baroque baldacchino and the
High Altar, which was finished
in 1607 by Giovanni Caccini.
The church has 38 side
altars, decorated with 15th-
and 16th-century Renaissance
paintings and sculpture,
among them works by
Cosimo Rosselli, Domenico
Ghirlandaio and Filippino
Lippi. The latter painted a
magnificent *Madonna and
Child* (1466) for the Nerli
Chapel in the south transept.

In the north aisle, a door
beneath the organ leads to
a vestibule with an ornate
coffered ceiling. It was
designed by Simone del
Pollaiuolo, more commonly
known as Cronaca, in 1491.
The sacristy adjoining the
vestibule, in which 12 huge
columns are crammed into a
tiny space, was designed by
Giuliano da Sangallo in 1489.

**Interior of Santo Spirito with
colonnaded aisle**

Palazzo Pitti ㉗

THE PALAZZO PITTI was originally built for the banker
Luca Pitti. The huge scale of the building, begun in
1457 and attributed to Brunelleschi, illustrated Pitti's
determination to outrival the Medici family through its
display of wealth and power. Ironically, the Medici
later purchased the palazzo when building costs
bankrupted Pitti's heirs. In 1550 it became the main
residence of the Medici, and subsequently all the rulers
of the city lived here. Today the richly decorated rooms
exhibit countless treasures from the Medici collections.

Judith (1620–30) by Artemisia
Gentileschi

The Three Ages of Man (c.1510),
attributed to Giorgione

GALLERIA PALATINA

THE PALATINE GALLERY, which
forms the heart of the Pitti
museum complex, contains
countless masterpieces by
artists such as Botticelli, Titian,
Perugino, Andrea del Sarto,
Tintoretto, Veronese, Giorgione
and Gentileschi. The works
of art, accumulated by the
Medici Grand Dukes, are still
hung much as the Medici
wished, regardless of subject
or chronology. The gallery
consists of 11 main salons, the
first five of which are painted
with allegorical ceiling frescoes
glorifying the Medici. Begun
by Pietro da Cortona in 1641,
they were completed in 1665
by his pupil, Ciro Ferri. Room 1

(Sala di Venere) contains
Antonio Canova's statue of
the *Venus Italica* (1810),
commissioned by Napoleon
to replace the *Venus de'
Medici* (which was to be
taken to Paris). Room 2
(Sala di Apollo) features
Titian's *Portrait of a
Gentleman* (1540), perhaps
the finest of several
paintings by the
artist in the
gallery. Still finer
pictures adorn
rooms 4 and 5,
including some
canvases by
Perugino, Andrea
del Sarto and a host
of paintings by
Raphael. The most
beautiful of the last
group are Raphael's

High Renaissance *Madonna
della Seggiola* or Madonna
of the Chair (c.1514–15), and
the *Donna Velata* or Veiled
Woman (c.1516), whose
model was reputedly
the artist's mistress.
Other excellent
paintings in the
remaining gallery
rooms include
Fra Filippo
Lippi's lovely
*Madonna and
Child*, painted in the
mid-15th century, and
The Sleeping Cupid
(1608) by Caravaggio.

*Madonna of the
Chair* (c.1515) by
Raphael

Galleria Palatina

**The Museo degli
Argenti**, or the
silverware museum,
also displays
precious *objets
d'art.*

**The
Boboli
Gardens**

**Entrance to museums
and galleries**

Brunelleschi designed the
palace façade, which was
eventually extended to three
times its original length.

**Appartamenti
Monumentali**

**The Galleria
d'Arte Moderna**
is a 30-room
gallery featuring
paintings from the
years 1784 to 1924

The Palmieri Rotonda **by Giovanni Fattori (1825–1908)**

APPARTAMENTI MONUMENTALI

THE STATE APARTMENTS on the first floor of the south wing of the palazzo were built in the 17th century. They are decorated with frescoes by various Florentine artists, a series of portraits of the Medici by the Flemish painter Justus Sustermans, who worked at the court between 1619 and 1681, and a group of 18th-century Gobelins tapestries. In the late 18th and early 19th centuries, the apartments were completely revamped in Neo-Classical style by the Dukes of Lorraine when they succeeded the Medici dynasty as the rulers of Florence.

The apartments are lavishly appointed with ornate gold and white stuccowork ceilings and rich decoration, notably on the walls of the Parrot Room, which are covered with an opulent crimson fabric detailed with a bird design. The apartments have been extensively restored in accordance with the original plans and designs.

The Throne Room of the Appartamenti Monumentali

Galleria del Costume

A copy of Giambologna's *Oceanus Fountain* (1576)

OTHER COLLECTIONS

OPENED IN 1983, the Galleria del Costume reflects the changing taste in the courtly fashion of the late 18th century up to the 1920s. It also hosts many special exhibitions. The same admission ticket gives access to the Museo degli Argenti (Silverware Museum), housed in rooms formerly used by the Medici as summer apartments. The family's lavish and occasionally dubious taste is reflected in the vast array of precious objects on display. These embrace beautiful examples of Roman glassware, ivory, carpets, crystal, amber, and fine works by Florentine and German goldsmiths. Pride of place goes to 16 *pietre dure* vases (decorated with hard or semi-precious inlaid stone), once owned by Lorenzo the Magnificent.

The highlights of the Galleria d'Arte Moderna (Modern Art Gallery) are the paintings of the *Macchiaioli* (spot-makers), a group of Tuscan artists with a style similar to the French Impressionists.

Piazza della Signoria depicted in precious stones

THE BOBOLI GARDENS

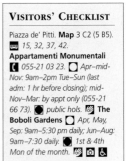

The Boboli Gardens, a lovely place to escape the rigours of sightseeing, were laid out for the Medici after they bought the Palazzo Pitti in 1549. An excellent example of stylized Renaissance gardening, they were opened to the public in 1766. The more formal parts of the garden, nearest the palazzo, consist of box hedges clipped into symmetrical geometric patterns. These lead to wilder groves of ilex and cypress trees, planted to create a contrast between artifice and nature. Countless statues adorn the gardens, particularly along the Viottolone, an avenue of cypress trees planted in 1637. High above the gardens stands the Forte di Belvedere, designed by Buontalenti in 1590 for the Medici Grand Dukes.

**The Virgin from *The Annunciation*
(1528) by Pontormo**

Santa Felicita 28

Piazza di Santa Felìcita. **Map** 3 C2
(5 C5). ☎ *055-21 30 18.* ⏰ *8am–
noon, 3:30–6:30pm daily.* 📷

THERE HAS BEEN a church on
this site since the 4th century. The present structure,
begun in the 11th century,
was remodelled in 1736–9
by Ferdinando Ruggieri, who
retained Vasari's earlier porch
(added in 1564) as well as
many of the church's original
Gothic features.

The Capponi family chapel
to the right of the entrance
contains two works by
Jacopo da Pontormo: *The
Annunciation* and *The
Deposition.* Painted between
1525 and 1528, the frescoes'
strange composition and
remarkable colouring make
them two of Mannerism's
greatest masterpieces.

Piazzale
Michelangelo 29

Piazzale Michelangelo. **Map** 4 E3.
🚌 *12, 13.*

OF ALL THE GREAT Florentine
viewpoints – such as
the Duomo and Campanile –
none offer such a magnificent
panorama of the city as
Piazzale Michelangelo. Laid
out in the 1860s by Giuseppe
Poggi, and dotted with copies
of Michelangelo's statues, its
lofty balconies attract endless
tour buses, countless visitors
and the inevitable massed
ranks of souvenir sellers.
Nonetheless, this bustling
square remains an evocative
spot, particularly at dusk,
when the sun sets over the
Arno and distant Tuscan hills.

San Miniato
al Monte 30

Via del Monte alle Croci. **Map** 4 E3.
☎ *055-234 27 31.* 🚌 *12, 13.*
⏰ *8am–noon, 2–7pm daily (Oct–
Mar: 2:30–6pm).* ● *public hols.* ♿

SAN MINIATO is one of the
most beautiful Romanesque
churches in Italy. Begun in
1018, it was built over the
shrine of San Miniato (St
Minias), a rich Armenian
merchant beheaded for his
beliefs by Emperor Decius in
the 3rd century. The façade,
begun around 1090, has the
geometric marble patterning
typical of Pisan-Romanesque
architecture. The statue on
the gable shows an eagle
carrying a bale of cloth, the
symbol of the powerful Arte
di Calimala (guild of wool
importers), who financed the
church in the Middle Ages.

**The façade of the church of San
Miniato al Monte**

The 13th-century mosaic
shows Christ, the Virgin
and St Minias. The same
protagonists appear in the
apse mosaic inside the
church, which sits above a
crypt supported by columns
salvaged from ancient Roman
buildings. The floor of the
nave is covered with seven
mosaic panels of animals and
signs of the Zodiac (1207).

Other highlights in the
church include Michelozzo's
free-standing Cappella del
Crocifisso (1448) and the
Renaissance Cappella del
Cardinale del Portogallo (1480)
with terracotta roundels (1461)
on the ceiling by Luca della
Robbia. There is a fresco cycle
of *Scenes from the Life of St
Benedict* (1387) by Spinello
Aretino in the sacristy.

Ponte Vecchio and the Arno from the heights of Piazzale Michelangelo

FLORENCE STREET FINDER

Map references given for sights in the Florence section refer to the maps on the following pages. Where two references are provided, the one in brackets relates to the large-scale maps, 5 and 6. References are also given for Florence hotels *(see pp557–9)* and restaurants *(see pp591–3)*, and for useful addresses in the *Travellers' Needs* and *Survival Guide* sections at the back of the book. The map below shows the area of Florence covered by the *Street Finder*. The symbols used for sights and other features on the *Florence Street Finder* maps are listed below. Streets in Florence have double sets of numbers: red numbers are for businesses, and black or blue for domestic residences.

SCALE OF MAPS 1–2 & 3–4

| 0 metres | 250 |
| 0 yards | 250 |

1:12,000

SCALE OF MAPS 5–6

| 0 metres | 150 |
| 0 yards | 150 |

1:7000

| 0 kilometres | 1 |
| 0 miles | 0.5 |

KEY TO STREET FINDER

	Major sight	ⓘ	Tourist information	⊠	Post office
	Place of interest	✚	Hospital with casualty unit	═	Railway line
FS	Railway station	🚓	Police station		One-way street
🚌	Bus terminus	✝	Church	━	City walls
P	Parking	✡	Synagogue		

SEE PAGES
5, 6 FOR
ENLARGEMENT
OF THIS AREA

SEE PAGES
5, 6 FOR
ENLARGEMENT
OF THIS AREA

1

2

3

4

5

PIAZZA DI VERZAIA

BORGO SAN FREDIANO

VIALE LUDOVICO ARIOSTO

VIA DELL'ORTO

VIA DEL LEONE

VIA DEL CAMALDOLI

PIAZZA DE' NERLI

PIAZZA DEL CARMINE

PIAZZA PIATTELLINA

PIAZZA TORQUATO TASSO

Cappella Brancacci (Santa Maria del Carmine)

VIA SAN GIOVANNI

VIA DEI CARDATORI

VIA DEL TESTOTONE

VIA DI CAMALDOLI

VIA DEL DRAGO D'ORO

S. ONOFRIO

VIA LORENZO BARTOLINI

VIA DEL PIAGGIONE

PIAZZA DEL TIRATOIO

VIA DEL CESTELLO

San Frediano in Cestello

PIAZZA DI CESTELLO

LUNGARNO SODERINI

Pescaia di S. Rosa

Pte alla Carraia

Fiume Arno

PIAZZA CARLO GOLDONI

V.D. VIGNA NUOVA

V.D. PURGATORIO

VIA DEL PARIONE

Palazzo Corsini

LUNGARNO CORSINI

VIA DE' TORNABUONI

Palazzo Strozzi

PIAZZA STROZZI

V.D. ANSELMI

PIAZZA REPUBB

Orsan

PIAZZA DE' DAVANZATI

V.P.TA ROSSA

Merca Nuov

PIAZZA NAZARIO SAURO

BORGO DELLA STELLA

VIA DI SANTO SPIRITO

Santa Trinita

P. DI S. TRINITA

Palazzo Bartolini-Salimbeni

Palazzo Spini-Ferroni

Ponte S. Trinita

LUNGARNO GUICCIARDINI

LUNGARNO D. ACCIAIOLI

Santi Apostoli

Ponte Vecchio

BORGO SAN JACOPO

VIA SANTA MONICA

VIA SANT'AGOSTINO

VIA MAFFIA

Santo Spirito

Cenacolo di Santo Spirito

VIA DE' COVERELLI

VIA DELLO SPRONE

VIA DE' VELLUTI

PIAZZA DI S. FELICITÀ

PIAZZA DI FRESCOBALDI

VIA DI SANTA MARIA

VIA S. AGOSTINO

VIA SANT'AGOSTINO

VIA CHIESA

VIA DELLE CALDAIE

PIAZZA DI SANTO SPIRITO

VIA MAZZETTA

VIA DELLE CALDAIE

VIA DE' PRESTO DI SAN MARTINO

VIA DE' SERRAGLI

VIA DEL CAMPUCCIO

VIA SANTA MARIA

VIA ROMANA

GIARDINO TORRIGIANI

VIA S. FRANCESCO POVERINO

VIA VILLANI

VIA MINIMA

VIA GIANO DELLA BELLA

VIA DEL CASONE

VIALE FRANCESCO PETRARCA

VIA DEL CAMPUCCIO

SDRUCCIOLO DE' PITTI

VIA MAGGIO

VIA DELLO SPRONE

VIA TEGOLAIO

V.D. GUICCIARDINI

Palazzo Pitti

PIAZZA DE' PITTI

PIAZZA DI SAN FELICE

Santa Felicita

Museo La Specola

GIARDINO DI BOBOLI

Forte di Belvedere

VIA DEL BOBOLINO

VIA DEL MONTE

V. SERUMIDO

VIA DEL ROSSO

VIA D'IPPOLITO PINDEMONTE

VIA VINCENZO MONTI

VIA UGO FOSCOLO

VIA PIETRO METASTASIO

VIA GIOVANNI PRATI

PIAZZA DELLA CALZA

PIAZZALE DELLA PORTA ROMANA

VIA DEL MASCHERINO

VIA D. MADONNA D. PACE

VIA DEL BALUARDO

VIA DELLE CAMPORA

VIA SENESE

VIA CANTAGALLI

VIALE NICCOLÒ MACHIAVELLI

VIA FARINATA DEGLI UBERTI

VIALE DEL POGGIO IMPERIALE

VIA DANTE DA CASTIGLIONE

VIA MICHELE DI LANDO

VIALE NICCOLÒ MACHIAVELLI

VIA DI SAN LEON

VIA S. PAOLO

VIA SCAGNI

VIA DI SANT'ILARIO A COLOMBAIA

VIA BENEDETTO DA FOIANO

PIAZZALE GALILEO

VIA SENESE

VIA LORENZO BELLINI

VIA LORENZO MAGALOTTI

VIA BENEDETTO CASTELLI

VIA DEL GELSOMINO

VIA LEONARDO XIMENES

V.LE EVANGELISTA TORRICELLI

VIA DI SAN LEONARDO

VIA V. VIVIANI

VIA GUGLIELMO RIGHINI

VIA GIOVANNI ALFONSO BORELLI

VIA

TUSCANY

RENOWNED *for its art, history and evocative landscape, Tuscany is a region where the past and present merge in pleasant harmony. Hilltowns gaze across the countryside from on high, many encircled by Etruscan walls and slender cypress trees. Handsome palaces testify to the region's wealth while medieval town halls indicate a long-standing tradition of democracy and self-government.*

In the countryside, among the vineyards and olive groves, there are hamlets and farmhouses, as well as fortified villas and castles that symbolize the violence and intercommunal strife that tore Tuscany apart during the Middle Ages. Several imposing castles and villas were built for the Medici family, the great patrons of the Renaissance who supported eminent scientists, such as Galileo.

Northern Tuscany, and the heavily populated plain between Florence and Lucca, is dominated by industry, with intensively cultivated land between the cities and the wild mountainous areas. The area centred around Livorno and Pisa is now the region's economic hub. Pisa, at the height of its powers, dominated the western Mediterranean from the 11th to the 13th centuries.

Its navy opened up extensive trading routes with North Africa, and brought to Italy the benefits of Arabic scientific and artistic achievement. During the 16th century the Arno estuary began to silt up, ending Pisan power.

At the heart of central Tuscany lies Siena, which was involved in a long feud with Florence. Its finest hour came with its victory in the Battle of Montaperti in 1260, but it was devastated by the Black Death in the 14th century and finally suffered a crushing defeat by Florence in the siege of 1554–5.

Northeastern Tuscany, with its mountain peaks and woodland, provided refuge for hermits and saints, while the east was home to Piero della Francesca, the early Renaissance painter whose timeless and serene works are imbued with an almost religious perfection.

A timeless view and way of life in Casole d'Elsa, near San Gimignano in central Tuscany

◁ The complex architecture of Pisa's Duomo (begun in 1063) and the Leaning Tower (begun in 1173)

Exploring Tuscany

Tuscan cities such as Florence, Siena and Pisa, together with smaller towns like Lucca, Cortona and Arezzo, contain some of Italy's most famous artistic treasures. Medieval villages such as San Gimignano, with its famous towers, or Pienza, a tiny Renaissance jewel, sit at the heart of the glorious pastoral countryside for which the region is equally renowned. Elsewhere landscapes range from the spectacular mountains of the Alpi Apuane to the gentle hills of Chianti.

SIGHTS AT A GLANCE

View of Cortona in eastern Tuscany

0 kilometres   25

0 miles   20

Cypress trees, a classic feature of the Tuscan landscape

Verona
Venezia
Bologna

PRATO
10

ARTIMINO
11   Arno   **13** FIESOLE

FLORENCE

VALLOMBROSA

RADDA IN
CHIANTI

SANSEPOLCRO
15

4
MIGNANO   **14**   AREZZO

23   MONTERCHI

MONTERIGGIONI   **22** SIENA
21
CRETE SENESI   CORTONA
                                 16

                                 Perugia

26
SAN GALGANO

PIENZA
20   **19**   **18** MONTEPULCIANO
MONTALCINO   CHIUSI
                       17

MASSA
MARITTIMA

MONTE
AMIATA

MAREMMA
31

SOVANA
29
30
PITIGLIANO

MONE
         MARSILIANA

MONTE
ARGENTARIO   ORBETELLO
32
         Roma

GETTING AROUND

Motorways or fast dual
carriageways link Florence,
the hub of Tuscany's road and
rail network, to Siena, Pisa,
Lucca and the south. The Via
Aurelia and A12 motorway serve
the Tuscan coast. Rural roads,
however, can be slow and
winding. Rail links are good,
and connect most major towns.

Key

▬▬▬	Motorway
▬▬▬	Major road
▭▭▭	Minor road
▬▬▬	Scenic route
≈	River
✲	Viewpoint

Carrara ❶

Massa Carrara. 🏠 70,000. FS 🚌
🛈 Piazza Gino Menconi 6b (0585-
63 22 18). 🛒 Mon.

INTERNATIONALLY renowned for
its marble quarries, Carrara's
almost flawless white stone
has been prized for centuries
by famous sculptors from
Michelangelo to Henry Moore
(the stone for Michelangelo's
David came from Carrara). The
region's 300 or more quarries
date back to Roman times,
making this one of the oldest
industrial sites in continuous
use in the world. Many of the
town's marble-sawing mills
and workshops welcome
visitors, offering them the
chance to see the ways in
which marble and quartz are
worked. These techniques –
along with marble artefacts old
and new – can be seen at the
Museo Civico del Marmo.

Local marble is put to good
use in the town's **Duomo** in
Piazza del Duomo, particularly
in the fine Pisan-Romanesque
façade with its delicate rose
window. The cathedral square
also contains Michelangelo's
house, used by the sculptor

A quarry in the marble-bearing hills around Carrara

during his visits to select blocks
of marble. The town has some
lovely corners to explore, in
particular the elegant Piazza
Alberica. Most visitors head
for the stone quarries that are
open to the public at nearby
Colonnata and at **Fantiscritti**
(take one of the regular town
buses or follow the signs to
the "Cave di Marmo"). The
latter features a small museum
with displays of various marble
quarrying techniques.

🏛 **Museo Civico del Marmo**
Viale XX Settembre. 📞 0585-84 57
46. ⏷ Mon–Sat (Oct–Mar am only).

Garfagnana ❷

Lucca. FS 🚌 Castelnuovo di
Garfagnana. 🛈 Castelnuovo di
Garfagnana (0583-64 43 54).

A LOVELY VERDANT, silent
valley wedged between
the Orecchiella mountains
and the Alpi Apuane, the
Garfagnana region can be
explored from **Seravezza**,
Barga or **Castelnuovo di
Garfagnana**. While the town
of Barga makes the prettiest
base, thanks to its tawny
stone cathedral and charming
streets, Castelnuovo is more
convenient for drives and
walks in the surrounding
mountains. **San Pellegrino in
Alpe** in the Orecchiella has a
fascinating folklore museum,
the **Museo Etnografico**. It is
easily seen in conjunction with
the **Orto Botanico Pania di
Corfino** at the headquarters
of the **Parco dell'Orecchiella**
at Pania di Corfino, with its
collection of local Alpine trees.

To the west, the Apuan Alps
are protected by the Parco
Naturale delle Alpi Apuane, an
area whose spectacular jagged
peaks and wooded valleys are
criss-crossed by hiking trails
and scenic mountain roads.

🏛 **Museo Etnografico**
Via del Voltone 15, San Pellegrino in
Alpe. 📞 0583-64 90 72. ⏷ Jun–
Sep: daily. 🖼
🌿 **Parco dell'Orecchiella**
Centro Visitatori, Orecchiella.
📞 0583-61 90 98. ⏷ Jul–mid-Sep:
daily; mid-Sep–Jun: by appt only. ♿
🌿 **Orto Botanico Pania
di Corfino**
Parco dell'Orecchiella. 📞 0583-61
90 98. ⏷ mid-Jun–mid-Sep: daily.

The Parco Naturale delle Alpi Apuane on the edge of the Garfagnana

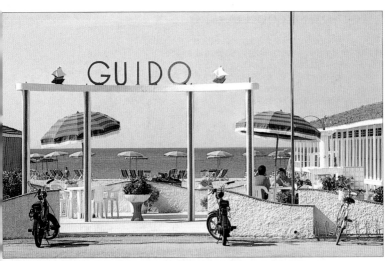

One of many seaside cafés lining the waterfront in the popular beach resort of Viareggio

Bagni di Lucca ❸

Lucca. 🚶 7,400. 🚌 ℹ️ *Via Umberto I 139 (0583-879 46).* 🅰️ *Wed & Sat.*

Aᴌᴌ ᴏᴠᴇʀ ᴛᴜsᴄᴀɴʏ there are hot springs of volcanic origin, like Bagni di Lucca. The Romans first exploited the springs and built bath complexes where army veterans, who settled in towns including Florence and Siena, could relax. More spas came into prominence in the Middle Ages and the Renaissance, and have continued to be recommended for relieving a variety of ailments, such as arthritis.

Tuscan spas really came into their own in the early 19th century when Bagni di Lucca reached its heyday as one of Europe's most fashionable spas, frequented by emperors, kings and aristocrats. Visitors came not only for thermal cures, but also for the **Casino** (1837), one of Europe's first licensed gambling houses. These days the town is rather sleepy, and its main sights are the 19th-century monuments, including the Neo-Gothic **English Church** (1839) on Via Crawford and the **Cimitero Anglicano** (Protestant Cemetery) on Via Letizia.

Eɴᴠɪʀᴏɴs: Southeast of Bagni di Lucca lies another popular spa town, **Montecatini Terme**. Developed in the 18th century, this town is one of the most interesting with a wide range of spa architecture, from Neo-Classical to Art Nouveau spa establishments.

Viareggio ❹

Lucca. 🚶 55,000. 🚆 🚌 ℹ️ *Viale Carducci 10 (0584-96 22 33).* 🅰️ *Thu.*

Kɴᴏᴡɴ ғᴏʀ ɪᴛs ᴄᴀʀɴɪᴠᴀᴌ, held in January and early February, this is also the most popular of the resorts on the Versilia coast. Its famous "Liberty" (Art Nouveau) style of architecture can be seen in the grand hotels, villas and cafés built in the 1920s after the resort's original boardwalk and timber chalets went up in flames in 1917. The finest example of the architecture is the **Gran Caffè Margherita** at the end of Passeggiata Margherita, designed by the prolific father of Italian Art Nouveau, Galileo Chini.

Torre del Lago Puccini ❺

Lucca. 🚶 11,000. 🚆 🚌 ℹ️ *Via Marconi 225 (0584-35 98 93).* 🅰️ *Fri & Sun.*

A ɢᴌᴏʀɪᴏᴜs ᴀᴠᴇɴᴜᴇ of lime trees, the Via dei Tigli, connects Viareggio with Torre del Lago Puccini, once the home of the opera composer Giacomo Puccini (1858–1924). He and his wife are buried in their former home, now the **Museo Villa Puccini**, a small museum that features the piano on which the maestro composed many of his best known works. Equal prominence is given to the villa's original fittings, including the gun room that housed Puccini's hunting rifle. **Lago Massaciuccoli**, an important nature reserve for rare and migrant birds, provides a pretty backdrop for open-air performances of Puccini's works.

🏛 **Museo Villa Puccini**
Piazzale Belvedere Puccini. 📞 *0584-34 14 45.* ⬜ *daily.* 🚫 ♿

Near Puccini's lakeside home at Torre del Lago Puccini

Street-by-Street: Lucca ❻

Lucca's regular grid of streets still follows the pattern of the former Roman colony founded in 180 BC. Great, solid ramparts, built in the 16th to 17th century, help to shut out traffic, making the city a pleasant place to explore on foot. San Michele in Foro – one of the town's many fine Pisan-Romanesque churches – stands on the site of the Roman forum (*foro*), the city's main square laid out in ancient times. It is still Lucca's main square today.

San Frediano / Palazzo Pfanner

Tourist information

Casa di Puccini
Giacomo Puccini (1858–1924), composer of some of the world's most popular operas, including La Bohème, *was born in this house.*

Piazza Napoleone
This sprawling square is named after Napoleon, whose sister, Elisa Baciocchi, ruled Lucca from 1805 to 1815.

Railway station

★ **San Michele in Foro**
The extraordinary Pisan-Romanesque façade (11th to 14th century) has three tiers of twisted or carved columns, each one different from the rest.

San Giovanni

The Museo dell'Opera del Duomo, a new museum, features treasures removed from San Martino.

Star Sights
★ **San Martino**
★ **San Michele in Foro**

Key

– – – Suggested route

0 metres   300
0 yards   300

In Via Fillungo,
Lucca's main
shopping street,
several shop fronts
are decorated
with Art Nouveau
details.

Torre dei Guinigi /

Villa Bottoni

Pinacoteca Nazionale

Giardino Botanico

n Martino

*a's beautiful 11th-century
mo is one of the outstand-
xamples of the exuberant
n-Romanesque style.*

Apostles from the mosaic on the façade of San Frediano in Lucca

🔒 San Frediano

Piazza San Frediano. 🔲 daily.
San Frediano's striking façade
features a colourful 13th-
century mosaic, *The Ascension*,
a fine prelude to the church's
wonderfully atmospheric interior. Pride of place goes to a
splendid Romanesque font on
the right, its sides carved with
scenes from the Life of Christ
and the story of Moses. Note
the scene of Moses and his
followers (dressed as medieval
knights) as they pass through
the divided Red Sea. In the
second chapel in the north
aisle, Aspertini's frescoes
(1508–9) tell the story of
Lucca's precious relic, the
Volto Santo – a carving said
to date from the time of the
Crucifixion. The fine altarpiece
(1422) in the fourth chapel of
San Frediano's north aisle is
by Jacopo della Quercia.

🔒 San Michele in Foro

Piazza San Michele. 🔲 daily.
Built on the site of the old
Roman forum *(foro)*, San
Michele's wonderfully rich
mixture of twisted marble
columns and Cosmati work
(inlaid marble) adorns one of
the most exuberant Pisan-
Romanesque façades in
Tuscany. Built between the
11th and 14th centuries, its
decoration is overwhelmingly
pagan. Only the huge winged
figure of St Michael on the
pediment marks this out as a
church. The interior has little

of interest except for the
beautiful painting of *Saints
Helena, Jerome, Sebastian
and Roch* by Filippino Lippi
(1457–1504).

🏛 Casa di Puccini

Via di Poggio. 🔲 0583-58 40 28.
🔲 Tue–Sun. 🖼
The fine 15th-century house
in which Giacomo Puccini
(1858–1924) was born is now
a shrine to the great opera
composer. It contains portraits
of Puccini, costume designs
for his operas and the piano
he used when composing his
last opera, *Turandot*.

🏛 Via Fillungo

Lucca's principal shopping
street winds its way through
the heart of the city towards
the Anfiteatro Romano. A good
place to stroll, its northern
end has several shops with
Art Nouveau ironwork, and
halfway down lies the de-
consecrated church of San
Cristoforo, built in the 13th
century, with a lovely interior.

**One of the many bars and shops
along Via Fillungo**

Exploring Lucca

L UCCA'S PEACEFUL NARROW LANES wind among the medieval buildings, opening suddenly to reveal churches, tiny piazzas, and many other reminders of the city's long history, including a Roman amphitheatre.

Medieval buildings mark the outline of Lucca's old Roman amphitheatre

⌂ Anfiteatro Romano
Piazza del Anfiteatro.
Roman *Luca* was founded in 180 BC, and stones from the ancient Roman amphitheatre have been ransacked over the centuries to build churches and palaces, leaving only a handful of original fragments studded into today's arena-shaped Piazza del Mercato. Slum housing clogged the piazza until 1830, when it was cleared on the orders of Marie Louise, the city's Bourbon ruler of that time. It was then that the amphitheatre's original shape was revealed, a graphic and evocative reminder of Lucca's rich Roman heritage. Low archways at the piazza's cardinal points mark the gate through which beasts and gladiators would once have entered the arena.

🏛 Museo dell'Opera del Duomo
Via Arcivescovado. 【 0583-49 05 30.
🕐 Tue – Sun. 🖼 ♿
The museum, housed in the former Archbishop's Palace (14th century), displays the treasures of the Duomo of San Martino. These include the 11th-century carved stone head

---

⛪ SAN MARTINO
Piazza San Martino. 【 0583-95 70 68. 🕐 daily.
Lucca's extraordinary cathedral, dedicated to St Martin, was built subsequent to the campanile, hence the façade's cramped and asymmetric appearance. The main portals contain outstanding 13th-century carvings by Nicola Pisano and Guidetto da Como. The Tempietto inside houses the Volto Santo, a revered 13th-century effigy believed by medieval pilgrims to have been carved at the time of the Crucifixion.

Façade
The cathedral façade is decorated with Romanesque sculptures and colonnading (1204).

The campanile was begun in 1060 as a defensive tower.

Ghirlandaio's painting of *The Madonna and Saints* (1449–94) is in the Sacristy.

Domed chapels encircling the apse

Romanesque blind arcades and carved capitals

Tomb of Ilaria del Carretto
This beautiful portrait in marble by Jacopo della Quercia (1405–6) is of the youthful bride of Paolo Guinigi.

Matteo Civitali's marble Tempietto (1184)

Circular clerestory windows, in the nave and above the aisle roof, illuminate the church's unusually tall nave.

Nicola Pisano (1200–78) carved the *Journey of the Magi* and *Deposition* on the left portal.

Baroque gods and goddesses in the garden of the Palazzo Pfanner

of a king, removed from the cathedral façade, and a rare 12th-century Limoges casket, possibly created for a relic of St Thomas à Becket. The Croce dei Pisani, made by Vincenzo di Michele in 1411, is a sublime masterpiece of the goldsmith's art. It shows Christ on the Tree of Redemption, surrounded by angels, the Virgin, St John and the other Evangelists.

⛪ Palazzo Pfanner
🔵 *for restoration.*
The elegant Palazzo Pfanner, an imposing house built in 1667, has a beautiful outside staircase. It also boasts one of Tuscany's most delightful formal gardens. Laid out in the 18th century, the central avenue of the garden is lined with Baroque statues of the gods and goddesses of ancient Roman mythology. The garden can also be viewed while walking along the ramparts.

The house itself contains a collection of court costume of the 18th and 19th centuries. Many garments are made of silk, whose production accounted for much of Lucca's medieval wealth.

⛪ Ramparts
One of the pleasures of visiting Lucca is strolling along the ramparts – the magnificent city walls, whose tree-lined promenade offers some entrancing views of the city.

Work on the ramparts began around 1500, when advances in military technology made the old medieval defences ineffective. On their completion in 1645, the walls were some of the most advanced of their time. One of their most curious features was the open space that lay beyond them, and which survives to this day, cleared to prevent the enemy taking cover in trees and undergrowth. Ironically, the walls never actually had to be defended, and they were eventually converted into a public park in the early 19th century.

Part of the imposing 17th-century ramparts that encircle Lucca

Romanesque lion in the Museo Nazionale Guinigi

🔯 Santa Maria Forisportam
Piazza di Santa Maria Forisportam.
🔲 *daily.*
This church was built at the end of the 12th century, beyond the Roman walls of Lucca. Its name, Forisportam, means "outside the gate". The unfinished marble façade, in Pisan-Romanesque style, has blind arcading. Above the central portal is a relief of the *Coronation of the Virgin* (17th century). The interior was redesigned in the early 16th century, resulting in the nave and transepts being raised. The fourth altar of the south aisle contains a painting of *St Lucy*, and the north transept has an *Assumption*, both by Guercino (1591–1666).

🏛 Museo Nazionale di Villa Guinigi
Via della Quarquonia. 📞 0583-460 33. 🔲 *Tue–Sun.* 🎫
This massive Renaissance villa was built in 1418 for Paolo Guinigi, leading light of the powerful noble family who ruled Lucca in the early 15th century. A familiar landmark of the city is the battlemented tower, the Torre dei Guinigi, with oak trees growing at the top. It offers good views over the city and the Apuan Alps. The garden features traces of a Roman mosaic, together with a pride of Romanesque lions removed from the city's walls.

Inside, the museum's first floor is devoted to sculptures and archaeological displays. The highlights are works by Matteo Civitali, Jacopo della Quercia and fine Romanesque reliefs removed from several of Lucca's churches. Most of the paintings in the gallery on the floor above are by minor local artists, with the exception of two works by Fra Bartolomeo (c.1472–1517): *God the Father with Saints Catherine and Mary Magdalene* and the *Madonna della Misericordia*. The floor also has furnishings, church vestments and choir stalls from Lucca's cathedral, inlaid with marquetry views of the city carved in 1529.

Pisa ❼

FOR MUCH OF THE MIDDLE AGES, Pisa's powerful navy ensured its dominance of the western Mediterranean. Trading links with Spain and North Africa in the 12th century brought vast mercantile wealth and formed the basis of a scientific

Inlaid marble, Duomo façade

and cultural revolution that is still reflected in Pisa's splendid buildings – especially the Duomo, Baptistry and Campanile (Leaning Tower). Pisa's decline began in 1284, with its defeat by Genoa, and was hastened by the silting up of the harbour. The city fell to the Florentines in 1406, but suffered its worst crisis in 1944 when it fell victim to Allied bombing.

A detail from the Duomo pulpit

The circular Baptistry, a graceful counterpoint to the Duomo, was begun in 1152 along Romanesque lines, and finished a century later – after a delay caused by a shortage of money – in a more ornate Gothic style by Nicola and Giovanni Pisano. The former was responsible for the magnificent marble pulpit (1260) in the interior, carved with reliefs of the *Nativity*, the *Adoration of the Magi*, the *Presentation*, the *Crucifixion* and the *Last Judgment*. The pillars that support the pulpit feature statues of the Virtues. The inlaid marble font (1246) is by Guido da Como.

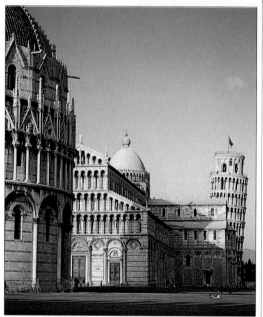

The Baptistry, Duomo and Leaning Tower in Pisa's Campo dei Miracoli

🏨 Leaning Tower
See p316.

🏛 Duomo and Baptistry
Piazza Duomo. **【** 050-56 05 47.
◯ *daily.*
Pisa's famous Leaning Tower is now the best known building in the Campo dei Miracoli (Field of Miracles). Originally, however, it was intended as a campanile to complement the Duomo, which was begun by Buscheto almost a century earlier in 1064. Today the Duomo stands as one of the finest Pisan-Romanesque buildings in Tuscany, its wonderful four-tiered façade a

medley of creamy colonnades and intricate blind arcades. Buscheto's tomb is in the left arch of the façade. Other important features of the exterior include the Portale di San Ranieri (leading to the south transept) and the bronze doors (1180), decorated with reliefs cast by Bonanno Pisano, the first architect of the Leaning Tower. Inside, the highlights are the carved pulpit (1302–11) by Giovanni Pisano, the *Tomb of Emperor Henry VII* (1315) by Tino da Camaino, and a mosaic of *Christ in Majesty* in the apse, completed by Cimabue in 1302.

🏛 Camposanto
Piazza dei Miracoli. **【** 050-56 05 47.
◯ *daily.*
The Camposanto – the "Holy Field", or cemetery – is the fourth element in the Campo dei Miracoli's lovely medieval ensemble. Begun in 1278 by Giovanni di Simone, the vast marble arcades of this long, rectangular building are said to enclose soil brought back from the Holy Land. Bombs in World War II all but destroyed its once famous frescoes, leaving only traces of scenes depicting *The Triumph of Death* (1360–80).

A fresco from the *Triumph of Death* cycle in the Camposanto

Santa Maria della Spina alongside the River Arno in Pisa

🏛 Museo dell'Opera del Duomo

Piazza Arcivescovado 6. **ℂ** *050-56 18 20.* **ℂ** *daily.* 🅿 &

Housed in the cathedral's 13th-century former Chapter House, this excellent modern museum displays exhibits removed over the years from the Duomo, Baptistry and Camposanto. Among the highlights is an imposing 10th-century hippogriff (half horse, half griffin). Cast in bronze by Moorish craftsmen, this statue was looted by Pisan adventurers during the wars against the Saracens. There are also works by both Nicola and Giovanni Pisano, notably Giovanni's ivory *Virgin and Child* (1300), carved for the Duomo's high altar. Other exhibits include paintings, Roman and Etruscan remains, and ecclesiastical treasures.

10th-century bronze hippogriff

🏛 Museo Nazionale di San Matteo

Lungarno Mediceo, Piazza San Matteo 1. **ℂ** *050-54 18 65.* **ℂ** *Tue–Sun.* 🅿

This museum is located on the banks of the Arno in San Matteo, an elegantly fronted medieval convent that also served as a prison in the 19th century. Much of the building has been closed for years, with the result that several of the rooms have no numbers and some of the exhibits are poorly labelled. Nevertheless, the museum presents a unique opportunity to examine the complete sweep of Pisan and Florentine art from the 12th to the 17th centuries.

The first rooms are devoted to sculpture and early Tuscan paintings. The best exhibits include a 14th-century polyptych by Francesco Traini of *Scenes from the Life of St Dominic*, Simone Martini's fine polyptych of *The Madonna and Saints* (1321), and a 14th-century statue of the *Madonna del Latte*, attributed to Andrea Pisano, another member of Pisa's talented school of medieval sculptors. The half-length statue, in gilded marble, shows Christ feeding at his mother's breast. In room 6 are some of the highlights of the museum, including Masaccio's *St Paul* (1426), Gentile da Fabriano's radiant 15th-century *Madonna of Humility*, and Donatello's reliquary bust of *San Rossore* (1424–7). Additional rooms contain paintings by Guido Reni, Benozzo Gozzoli, Rosso Fiorentino, and an important picture of *Christ* attributed to Fra Angelico (c.1395–1455).

🔒 Santa Maria della Spina

Lungarno Gambacorti. **ℂ** *050-53 24 74.* **ℂ** *by permission only.*

The roofline of this tiny church, located just beyond the Ponte Solferino, bristles with spiky Gothic pinnacles, miniature spires and niches sheltering statues of apostles and saints. The decoration reflects the history of the church, which was built between 1230 and 1323 to house a thorn *(spina)* from Christ's Crown of Thorns, the gift of a Pisan merchant. The church was once even closer to the Arno, but was rebuilt on the present site in 1871 to protect it from flooding.

🏛 Piazza dei Cavalieri

The huge building on the north side of this square is the Palazzo dei Cavalieri, home to one of Pisa University's most prestigious colleges: the Scuola Normale Superiore. Designed by Vasari in 1562, the building, which is covered in exuberant black and white *sgraffito* decoration (designs scratched into wet plaster), served as the headquarters of the Cavalieri di Santo Stefano, an order of knights created by Cosimo I in 1561. The equestrian statue outside depicts Cosimo I.

The Virgin and Child (1321) by Simone Martini in the Museo Nazionale

The Leaning Tower of Pisa

BEGUN IN 1173 on sandy silt subsoil, the Leaning Tower (Torre Pendente) started to tilt even before the third storey was finished in 1274. Despite the shallow foundations, construction continued and the structure was completed in 1350. The tower's apparent flouting of the laws of gravity has attracted many visitors over the centuries, including the Pisan scientist Galileo, who climbed to the top to conduct his famous experiments on the velocity of falling objects. Recently its tilt has increased alarmingly: the tower now leans in excess of 5 m (16.5 ft), and remains closed for restoration and underpinning.

Galileo Galilei (1564–1642)

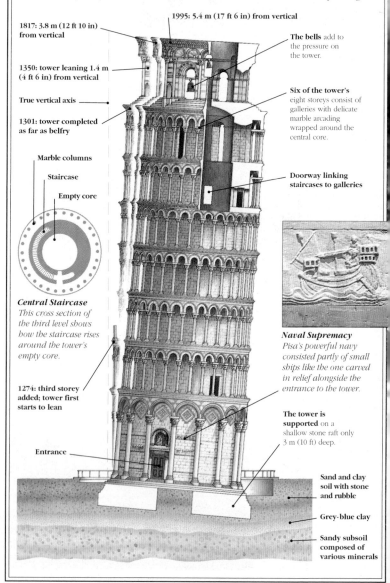

1995: 5.4 m (17 ft 6 in) from vertical

1817: 3.8 m (12 ft 10 in) from vertical

1350: tower leaning 1.4 m (4 ft 6 in) from vertical

True vertical axis

1301: tower completed as far as belfry

Marble columns

Staircase

Empty core

Central Staircase
This cross section of the third level shows how the staircase rises around the tower's empty core.

1274: third storey added; tower first starts to lean

Entrance

The bells add to the pressure on the tower.

Six of the tower's eight storeys consist of galleries with delicate marble arcading wrapped around the central core.

Doorway linking staircases to galleries

Naval Supremacy
Pisa's powerful navy consisted partly of small ships like the one carved in relief alongside the entrance to the tower.

The tower is supported on a shallow stone raft only 3 m (10 ft) deep.

Sand and clay soil with stone and rubble

Grey-blue clay

Sandy subsoil composed of various minerals

Vinci ⑧

Florence. 🏘 1,500. 🚌 🚇 Wed.

FAMOUS AS THE BIRTHPLACE of Leonardo da Vinci (1452–1519), this hilltop town celebrates the genius in the **Museo Leonardiano**, housed in the 13th-century castle. Among the displays are wooden models of Leonardo's machines and inventions, most of them based on drawings from his notebooks, shown alongside. These include a bicycle, his conception of a car, an armoured tank and even a machine-gun.

🏛 **Museo Leonardiano**
Castello dei Conti Guidi. ☎ 0571-560 55. ◐ daily. 📷

Detail of frieze (1514–25) by Giovanni della Robbia, Ospedale del Ceppo

Model bicycle based on designs by Leonardo, Museo Leonardiano

Pistoia ⑨

🏘 93,000. 🚆 🚌 🛈 Palazzo dei Vescovi, Piazza del Duomo (0573-216 22). 🛒 Wed & Sat.

PISTOIA'S CITIZENS were once known for violence and intrigue, a reputation grounded in the medieval disputes between the city's rival factions, the Bianchi and Neri (Whites and Blacks). Their favoured weapon was a tiny, locally made dagger known as a *pistola*. Long a centre of metalwork, everything from buses to mattress springs are now made here. In the centre, several fine historic buildings are preserved.

🏠 **Duomo**
Piazza del Duomo. ◐ daily.
Piazza del Duomo, Pistoia's main square, is dominated by the Duomo (San Zeno) and its bulky 12th-century campanile, originally built as a watchtower in the city walls. The interior of the Duomo is rich in funerary monuments. The finest of these, in the south aisle, is the tomb of Cino da Pistoia. He was a friend of Dante and fellow poet, and is depicted in a relief (1337) lecturing to a class of young boys.

Nearby is the chapel of St James and its extraordinary silver altar decorated with more than 600 statues and reliefs. Although the earliest of these dates from 1287, the altar was not completed until 1456. One of the craftsmen involved was Brunelleschi, who began his career as a silversmith before turning to architecture. Also in the Piazza del Duomo is the octagonal Baptistry, completed in 1359.

🏠 **Ospedale del Ceppo**
Piazza Giovanni XXIII.
This hospital and orphanage, founded in 1277, was named after the *ceppo* (hollowed-out tree trunk) that was used to collect donations for its work. The main façade features coloured terracotta panels (1514–25) by Giovanni della Robbia illustrating the *Seven Works of Mercy*. The portico is by Michelozzo.

The Pisan-Romanesque façade of Pistoia's Duomo (San Zeno)

🏠 **Cappella del Tau**
Corso Silvano Fedi 70.
◐ Mon–Sat am.
The Cappella del Tau (1360) is so called because the monks who built it wore on their cloaks the letter T (tau in Greek), symbolizing a crutch and their work with the sick and disabled. Inside there are frescoes by Niccolò di Tommaso on *The Creation* and the *Life of St Anthony Abbot* (1370). Two doors down the **Palazzo Tau** has work by Marino Marini, Pistoia's best-known 20th-century artist.

The Fall (1372) by Niccolò di Tommaso in the Cappella del Tau

🏠 **San Giovanni Fuorcivitas**
Via Cavour. ◐ daily.
Built in the 12th to 14th centuries, the striking church of San Giovanni Fuorcivitas (literally "St John Outside the City") once stood beyond the city walls. Its north flank is clad in banded marble and there is a Romanesque relief of the Last Supper over the portal. Inside, the holy water stoup, carved in marble with figures of the Virtues, is by Giovanni Pisano (1245–1320). A masterly pulpit, carved in 1270 with scenes from the New Testament, is by Guglielmo da Pisa. Both are among the finest works of this period, when artists were reviving the art of carving.

Prato ❿

Florence. 🏠 170,000. 🚃 🚌 ℹ️ *Via Cairoli 48 (0574-241 12).* 🗓️ *Mon.*

WHILE TEXTILE factories gird Prato's outskirts, the city's historic centre retains several important churches and museums. The **Duomo** (begun 1211) is flanked by the Pulpit of the Holy Girdle (1434–8), designed by Donatello and Michelozzo, used once a year to display a girdle, reputedly given to Thomas the Apostle before the Assumption of the Virgin. Inside the Duomo is a masterpiece by Fra Filippo Lippi, *The Life of John the Baptist* (1452–66), and a fresco cycle (1392–5) by Agnolo Gaddi describing how the Virgin's girdle reached Prato. The *Madonna del Ceppo* (15th century), also painted by Lippi, is kept in the **Museo Civico**.

Other sights include **Santa Maria delle Carceri** in Piazza delle Carceri, a Renaissance church designed by Giuliano da Sangallo; the **Castello dell' Imperatore**, a fortress built by Emperor Frederick II in 1237; and the **Museo del Tessuto**, which traces the history of Prato's textile industry.

🏛 **Museo Civico**
Palazzo Pretorio, Piazza del Comune.
📞 *0574-45 23 02 24.*
🕐 *Wed–Mon.* 🎟️
♣ **Castello dell'Imperatore**
Piazza delle Carceri. 🕐 *Wed–Mon.*
🏛 **Museo del Tessuto**
Palazzo Comunale. 📞 *0574-61 61.*
🕐 *by appt.*

Madonna del Ceppo by Fra Filippo Lippi in Prato's Museo Civico

Buontalenti's Villa di Artimino, or "Villa of a Hundred Chimneys"

Artimino ⓫

Prato. 🏠 400. 🚃

ASMALL FORTIFIED hamlet, Artimino is remarkable for the unspoiled Romanesque church of **San Leonardo**. Outside the walls lies the **Villa di Artimino**, designed by Buontalenti in 1594 for Grand Duke Ferdinando I. Also known as the "Villa of a Hundred Chimneys" – after the chimney pots crowding the roofline – it houses the **Museo Archeologico Etrusco**, a collection of archaeological exhibits.

ENVIRONS: For lovers of Pontormo's paintings, the church of **San Michele** in Carmignano, 5 km (3 miles) north of Artimino, contains *The Visitation* (1530). East of here lies the villa of **Poggio a Caiano**. Built in 1480 by Giuliano da Sangallo for Lorenzo de' Medici (see *p245*), it was the first Italian villa to be designed in the Renaissance style.

🏠 **Villa di Artimino**
Viale Papa Giovanni 23. **Villa** 📞 *055-879 20 40.* 🕐 *Tue am by appt.*
Museum 📞 *055-871 81 24.*
🕐 *Thu–Tue am.* 🎟️
🏠 **Poggio a Caiano**
Piazza Medici. 📞 *055-87 70 12.*
🕐 *Tue–Sun.* 🎟️ 🔵 📷

San Miniato ⓬

Pisa. 🏠 3,900. 🚃 ℹ️ *Piazza del Popolo 3 (0571-427 45).* 🗓️ *Tue.*

THIS HILLTOP TOWN manages to remain aloof from the vast industrial sprawl of the Arno valley. Its key building

is the semi-derelict Rocca (castle), built for Frederick II, German Holy Roman Emperor, in the 13th century. Close by stands the **Museo Diocesano**, which is home to a *Crucifixion* (c.1430) attributed to Filippo Lippi, a terracotta bust of Christ attributed to Verrocchio (1435–88), and the *Virgin of the Holy Girdle* by Andrea del Castagno (c.1417–57). Next door, the red-brick Roman-esque façade of the **Duomo** dates from the 12th century. Its strange inset majolica plates, evidence of trade with Spain or North Africa, probably represent the North Star and the constellations of Ursus Major and Minor (all three were key points of reference for early navigators).

🏛 **Museo Diocesano**
Piazza Duomo. 📞 *0571-41 82 71.*
🕐 *Mar–Oct: Tue–Sun; Nov–Feb: Sat & Sun.* 🎟️

Façade of the Duomo in San Miniato

Fiesole ⓭

Florence. 🏠 15,000. 🚃 ℹ️ *Piazza Mino da Fiesole 37 (055-59 87 20).* 🗓️ *Sat.*

FIESOLE STANDS IN rolling hilly countryside 8 km (5 miles) north of Florence. Idyllically situated among olive groves, it is a popular retreat from the city thanks to its hilltop position which attracts cool breezes. Founded in the 7th century BC, the original Etrus-can colony was a powerful force in central Italy, only

A view over the hills and rooftops of Fiesole from Via di San Francesco

surrendering its supremacy after the foundation of Florence (1st century BC).

The **Duomo** of San Romolo in Piazza Mino da Fiesole was begun in 1028. It has a massive bell tower and a bare Romanesque interior with columns topped with re-used Roman capitals. Behind the Duomo, an archaeological area contains the remains of a 1st-century BC **Roman theatre**, traces of **Etruscan walls** from the 4th century BC, and the **Museo Faesulanum**, with a collection of bronzes, ceramics and jewellery dating from the Bronze Age.

Via di San Francesco, a steep lane offering lovely views, leads to the Franciscan friary of **San Francesco** (14th century) and the interesting 9th-century church of **Sant'Alessandro**, with a Neo-Classical façade.

Via Vecchia Fiesolana leads to the little hamlet of **San Domenico**. Here the 15th-century church of the same name contains a painting of the *Madonna with Angels and Saints* (c.1430) by Fra Angelico, and the Chapter House contains a fresco of *The Crucifixion* (c.1430), also by him. Close by, on the Via della Badia dei Roccettini, stands the pretty Romanesque church of the **Badia Fiesolana** with its striped marble façade and interior of local grey sandstone, *pietra serena*.

🏛 **Museo Faesulanum**
Via Portigiani 1. 📞 055-594 77.
🕐 daily (Oct–Mar: Wed–Mon). 🈂

Arezzo ⑭

🏃 92,000. 🚍 🛈 Piazza della Repubblica (0575-37 76 78). 🛒 Sat.

A REZZO IS ONE of Tuscany's wealthiest cities, its prosperity based on a thriving jewellery industry. Although much of its medieval centre was destroyed during World War II, resulting in extensive rebuilding and many medieval alleys being replaced by broad avenues, the city preserves some outstanding sights: foremost are Piero della Francesca's famous frescoes in the church of **San Francesco** *(see pp320–21)*. Close to the church on Corso Italia, the main street, stands the **Pieve di Santa Maria**, which boasts one of the most ornate Romanesque façades in the region. To its rear stretches the steeply sloping **Piazza Grande**, flanked by an arcade (1573) designed by Vasari, and by

the **Palazzo della Fraternità dei Laici** (1377–1552). The latter features a *Madonna* relief by Bernardo Rossellino. The huge **Duomo** to the north is best known for its 16th-century stained glass and a small fresco of *Mary Magdalene* by Piero della Francesca (1416–92). The **Museo del Duomo** features three wooden crucifixes, dating from the 12th and 13th centuries, a bas relief of *The Annunciation* (1434) by Rossellino and paintings by Vasari. More works by Vasari can be seen in the **Casa di Vasari**, a house built by the artist in 1540. Still more frescoes by him are displayed in the **Museo d'Arte Medioevale e Moderna**, a museum that is famed for its excellent collection of majolica pottery.

The **Fortezza Medicea**, a ruined Medici castle built by Antonio da Sangallo during the 16th century, has fine views.

🏛 **Museo del Duomo**
Piazzetta del Duomo 13. 📞 0575-239 91. 🕐 Thu–Sat am. 🈂
🏠 **Casa di Vasari**
Via XX Settembre 55. 📞 0575-30 03 01. 🕐 daily.
🏛 **Museo d'Arte Medioevale e Moderna**
Via di San Lorentino 8. 📞 0575-30 03 01. 🕐 daily. 🈂
🏰 **Fortezza Medicea**
Parco il Prato. 📞 0575-37 76 66.
🕐 daily. 🈂

The monthly antiques market held in Arezzo's Piazza Grande

Arezzo: San Francesco

THE 13TH-CENTURY CHURCH of San Francesco houses one of Italy's greatest fresco cycles, the *Legend of the True Cross* (1452–66), the masterpiece of Piero della Francesca. The famous scenes, on the walls of the choir, describe the history of the Cross used to crucify Christ, from sprig to Tree of Knowledge, to its use as a bridge during the reigns of Solomon and the Queen of Sheba, and ultimately its discovery by Helena, mother of Constantine, the first Christian emperor.

A Group of Onlookers
These figures kneel in wonder while Heraclius returns the True Cross to Jerusalem.

Excavation of the Cross
The town, meant to be Jerusalem, gives a fair representation of 15th-century Arezzo.

The Cross returns to Jerusalem.

KEY TO FRESCOES

1 The Death of Adam; a sprig from the Tree of Knowledge is planted over his grave; **2** The Queen of Sheba visits Solomon and foresees that a bridge made from the Tree will be used to crucify the greatest king in the world; **3** Solomon, assuming he is the greatest king in the world, orders the bridge to be buried; **4** The Annunciation: Christ's death is foreshadowed in the panel's cruciform structure; **5** Constantine has a vision of the Cross and hears a voice saying "In this sign you shall conquer"; **6** Constantine defeats his rival Maxentius; **7** The Levite Judas is tortured and reveals the location of the True Cross; **8** Three crosses are dug up; Constantine's mother Helena recognizes the True Cross; **9** The Persian king Chosroes is defeated after stealing the Cross; **10** The True Cross is returned to Jerusalem.

The Defeat of Chosroes depicts the defeat of a Persian king who had stolen the Cross.

Judas reveals where the Cross is hidden.

Painted Crucifix
The 13th-century Crucifix forms the focal point of the fresco cycle. The figure at the foot of the Cross represents St Francis, to whom the church is dedicated.

The Death of Adam
Piero's vivid portrayal of Adam and Eve in old age shows an adept treatment of anatomy. He was one of the first Renaissance artists to paint nude figures.

The prophets appear to play no part in the narrative cycle; their presence may be for purely decorative reasons.

The buildings
in the fresco reflect the newly fashionable styles of Renaissance architecture.

The wood of the Cross is buried in a pit.

Constantine leads his cavalry into battle.

The Queen of Sheba recognizes the wood of the Cross.

Constantine dreams of the Cross on the eve of battle against rival emperor Maxentius.

Solomon's Handshake
The handshake between the Queen of Sheba and Solomon, King of Israel, portrays 15th-century hopes for a union between the Orthodox and Western churches.

Piero's *The Resurrection* (1463) in Sansepolcro

Sansepolcro ⑮

Arezzo. 🏠 *16,000.* 🚌 ℹ️ *Piazza Garibaldi 2 (0575-74 05 36).* 🚆 *Tue, Sat.*

SANSEPOLCRO IS the birthplace of Piero della Francesca (1410–92). The town's **Museo Civico** contains two of his masterpieces: *The Resurrection* (1463) and the *Madonna della Misericordia* (1462). It also has a 15th-century *Crucifixion* by Luca Signorelli. In the church of **San Lorenzo** on Via Santa Croce there is a *Deposition* in the Mannerist style by Rosso Fiorentino (1494–1541).

Another renowned painting by Piero della Francesca, the *Madonna del Parto* (1460), can be seen at Via Reglia 1 in Monterchi, 13 km (8 miles) southwest of Sansepolcro.

🏛 **Museo Civico**
Via Aggiunti 65. ℂ *0575-73 22 18.*
🔲 *daily.* ● *public hols.* 🖼

Cortona ⑯

Arezzo. 🏠 *23,000.* 🚆 🚌 ℹ️ *Via Nazionale 42 (0575-63 03 52).* 🚆 *Sat.*

CORTONA WAS FOUNDED by the Etruscans and apart from being one of the oldest hilltowns in Tuscany, it is also one of the most scenic. A major power in the Middle Ages, it was able to hold its own against Siena and Arezzo. Today it is a charming maze of old streets and medieval

buildings, like the **Palazzo Comunale** on Piazza Signorelli. The town's early history is traced in the **Museo dell'Accademia Etrusca**, which contains Etruscan artefacts and a wide variety of Egyptian and Roman remains. The small **Museo Diocesano** features several fine paintings, in particular a *Crucifixion* by the Renaissance artist Pietro Lorenzetti, a *Deposition* (1502) by Luca Signorelli, and a sublime *Annunciation* (c.1434) by Fra Angelico. Signorelli, born in Cortona, is buried in the church of **San Francesco** (built in 1245), which contains an *Annunciation* painted in Baroque style by Pietro da Cortona, another native artist. The other well-known church in Cortona is the **Madonna del Calcinaio** (1485), a gem of Renaissance architecture located on the southern outskirts of town.

The 13th-century Palazzo Comunale in Cortona

🏛 **Museo dell'Accademia Etrusca**
Palazzo Casali, Piazza Signorelli 9.
ℂ *0575-63 04 15.* 🔲 *Tue–Sun.* 🖼
🏛 **Museo Diocesano**
Piazza del Duomo 1. 🔲 *0575-628 30.* 🔲 *Tue–Sun.* 🖼

Chiusi ⑰

Siena. 🏠 *10,000.* 🚆 🚌 ℹ️ *Via Porsenna 73 (0578-22 76 67).* 🚆 *Tue*

CHIUSI IS NOW a largely modern town, but in the past it was one of the most powerful cities in the Etruscan league, reaching the height of its influence in the 7th and 6th centuries BC *(see p41).* Numerous Etruscan tombs lie dotted in the surrounding countryside, the source of the exhibits in the town's **Museo Nazionale Etrusco.** Founded in 1871, the museum is packed with cremation urns, vases decorated with black figures and Bucchero ware, burnished to resemble bronze.

The Romanesque **Duomo** in Piazza del Duomo incorporates recycled Roman pillars and capitals. The wall decorations in the nave, resembling frescoes, were painted by Arturo Viligiardi in 1887. There is a Roman mosaic underneath the high altar. Visits can be made to several Etruscan tombs under the town from the **Museo della Cattedrale**, a museum in the cloister of the Duomo that also features displays of Roman, Lombardic and medieval sculpture from the region.

🏛 **Museo Nazionale Etrusco**
Via Porsenna 17. ℂ *0578-201 77.*
🔲 *daily.* 🖼
🏛 **Museo della Cattedrale**
Piazza del Duomo. ℂ *0578-22 64 90.* 🔲 *daily.* 🖼

Etruscan frieze in the Museo Nazionale Etrusco in Chiusi

Pienza's Piazza Pio II, designed by Bernardo Rossellino (1459)

Montepulciano ⑱

Siena. 🏛 14,000. 🚌 🛈 Via Ricci 9 (0578-75 86 87). 🛒 Thu.

THIS IS ONE of Tuscany's highest hilltowns, its walls and fortifications offering broad views over Umbria and southern Tuscany, and the vineyards providing the Vino Nobile wine that has made its name famous. The streets are brimming with Renaissance palazzi. The steep main street, the Corso, climbs to the **Duomo** (1592–1630), the setting for one of the master-pieces of the Sienese School, the *Assumption* (1401) by Taddeo di Bartolo. The High Renaissance church, **Tempio di San Biagio** (1518–34), lies off the road to Pienza.

Pienza ⑲

Siena. 🏛 2,300. 🚌 🛈 Piazza Pio II (0578-74 85 02). 🛒 Fri.

PIENZA IS A delightful village whose intimate little centre was almost completely re-designed in the 15th century by Pope Pius II. Born as Aeneas Sylvius Piccolomini in 1405, when the village was known as Corsignano, he became a leading Humanist scholar and philosopher. Elected pope in 1458, Pius II decided to rebuild his birth-place a year later, renaming it Pienza in his own honour. The Florentine architect and sculptor, Bernardo Rossellino, was commissioned to build a cathedral, papal palace and town hall (all completed in the three years from 1459 to 1462), but the grander scheme for a planned model Renais-sance town was never realized. Some idea of what might have been, however, can still be gained from the **Palazzo Piccolomini**, the former papal palace, which continued to be inhabited by Pius's descendants until 1968. The rooms open to the public include Pius's bedroom and library, though the highlight of a visit is the superb panorama from the loggia and arcaded courtyard at the palace's rear.

Pleasant walks and more great views can be had from the village walls. The airy **Duomo** *(see p244)* next door contains six altarpieces of the *Madonna and Child*, each commissioned from the leading Sienese painters of the day. Rossellino was forced to build the Duomo on a cramped site with poor foundations, and cracks appeared in the building before it was even completed. Today the church's eastern end suffers from severe subsidence.

🏛 **Palazzo Piccolomini**
Piazza Pio II. 📞 0578-74 85 03. 🕐 Tue–Sun. 🎟

Montalcino ⑳

Siena. 🏛 5,100. 🚌 🛈 Costa del Municipio 8 (0577-84 93 31). 🛒 Fri.

HILLTOP MONTALCINO sits at the heart of vineyards that produce Brunello, one of Italy's finest red wines. A range of wines may be sampled in a wonderfully situated Enoteca (wine shop) in the **Fortezza**, a 14th-century fortress with impressive ramparts. The town's timeless streets are a pleasure to wander, but there is little to see apart from the **Palazzo Vescovile** (bishop's palace) which houses three museums containing paintings, sculptures and archaeological exhibits found in the area.

🏯 **Fortezza**
Piazzale della Fortezza. 📞 0577-84 92 11. **Enoteca** 🕐 mid-Jul–end Sep: daily; Oct–mid-Jul: Tue–Sun. 🎟 for ramparts.

🏛 **Palazzo Vescovile**
Via Spagni 4. 📞 0577-84 81 35.
Museo Civico, Museo Diocesano, Museo Archeologico 🕐 Tue–Sun. 🎟

The Tempio di San Biagio on the outskirts of Montepulciano

The landscape of the Crete Senesi

Crete Senesi ㉑

Siena. [FS] [bus] [i] *Corso Matteotti (0577-71 95 16).*

To the south of Siena and central Tuscany is the area known as the Crete Senesi, which is characterized by round clay hillocks eroded by heavy rain over the centuries. Dubbed the "Tuscan desert", it is almost completely barren. Cypress and pine trees, planted to provide windbreaks along roads and around isolated farm houses, are an important feature in this empty, primeval landscape. Shepherds tend flocks of sheep here; the milk is used to produce the strongly flavoured *pecorino* cheese that is popular throughout Tuscany.

Siena ㉒

See pp328–33.

Monteriggioni ㉓

Siena. [𝕸] *7,000.* [bus]

Monteriggioni is a gem of a medieval hilltop town. It was built in 1203 and ten years later became a garrison town. It is completely encircled by high walls with 14 heavily fortified towers, built to guard the northern borders of Siena's territory against invasion by Florentine armies.

Dante was sufficiently impressed to use Monteriggioni as a simile for the deepest abyss at the heart of his *Inferno*, which compares the town's "ring-shaped citadel. . . crowned with towers" with giants standing in a moat. The perfectly preserved walls are best viewed from the Colle di Val d'Elsa road. Within the walls, the sleepy town consists of a large piazza, a pretty Romanesque church (on the piazza), a few houses, a couple of craft shops, restaurants, and shops selling many of the locally produced Castello di Monteriggioni wines.

Environs: West of Monteriggioni by 3 km (2 miles) lies the former Cistercian Abbey of **Abbadia dell' Isola** (12th century). This Romanesque church was largely rebuilt in the 18th century, after the cupola fell apart. It contains frescoes by Taddeo di Bartolo and Vincenzo Tamagni and a Renaissance altarpiece.

San Gimignano ㉔

See pp334–5.

Volterra ㉕

Pisa. [𝕸] *13,000.* [bus] [i] *Via Giusto Turazza 2 (0588-861 50).* [🜨] *Sat.*

Like many Etruscan cities, Volterra is situated on a high plateau, offering fine views over the surrounding hills. In many places the ancient Etruscan walls still survive. The famous **Museo Guarnacci** contains one of the best collections of Etruscan artefacts in Italy. Of special interest is the group of over 600 Etruscan cinerary urns, made from alabaster or terracotta, many of which were gathered from local tombs.

The **Palazzo dei Priori**, the medieval seat of government on Piazza dei Priori, is the oldest of its kind in Tuscany. It was begun in 1208 and there are 14th-century frescoes inside. The Pisan-Romanesque **Duomo**, located on Piazza San Giovanni, has a fine 13th-century pulpit with sculptured panels.

Detail from the pulpit in Volterra's Duomo

Volterra's excellent art gallery and museum, the **Pinacoteca e Museo Civico**, features works by Florentine artists. Ghirlandaio's *Christ in Majesty* (1492) shows Christ hovering above an idealized Tuscan landscape. Luca Signorelli's *Madonna and Child with Saints* (1491) states his debt to Roman art through the reliefs on the base of the Virgin's throne. Painted in the same year, his *Annunciation* is a beautifully balanced composition. Another highlight is Rosso Fiorentino's Mannerist painting, *The Deposition* (1521).

The city is famous for its craftsmen who carve elaborate white statues and *objets d'art* from locally mined alabaster.

The beautifully preserved walls of Monteriggioni in central Tuscany

James Thin Ltd (Booksellers)
The Gyle, 35 Gyle Avenue
Edinburgh EH12 9JT
Tel. 0131-539-7757
VAT No. 271-4114-88
075130106X
SPAIN TRAVEL GUIDE   20.00
0751301051
ITALY TRAVEL GUIDE   20.00
                TOT: 40.00
ALL   CARDS AMT: 40.00
REC: 91379:081296:1033:015ALLY

   Thankyou for your custom
   Please keep hold of your
            receipt

The ruined abbey at San Galgano, surrounded by dense woodland

🏛 Museo Guarnacci
Via Don Minzoni 15. **📞** *0588-863 47.*
◯ *daily.* 🖼

🏛 Pinacoteca e Museo Civico
Via dei Sarti 1. **📞** *0588-875 80.*
◯ *daily.* 🖼

San Galgano **㉖**

Siena. **🚌** *from Siena.* **📞** *0577-75 10 44.* **Abbey & oratory** **◯** *daily.*

THE REMOTE Cistercian abbey at San Galgano lies in a superb setting. San Galgano (1148–81) was a brave but dissolute young knight who turned to God, renouncing the material world. When he tried to break his sword against a rock as a symbol of his rejection of war, it was swallowed by the stone. This he interpreted as a sign of God's approval. He built a hut on a hill above the abbey (the site of today's beehive-shaped chapel at **Montesiepi**, built c.1185). Here he later died a hermit. Pope Urban III declared him a saint and an example to Christian knights.

The abbey, begun in 1218, is Gothic in style, reflecting the French origins of the Cistercian monks who designed it. They avoided contact with the outside world and divided their lives between prayer and labour. Despite an emphasis on poverty, the monks became wealthy from the sale of wood, and by the middle of the 14th century the abbey was corruptly administered and gradually fell into decline.

In the late 14th century, the English mercenary Sir John Hawkwood sacked the abbey and by 1397 the abbot was its sole occupant. It was eventually dissolved in 1652.

St Galgano's sword stands embedded in a stone just inside the door of the circular **oratory**. The 14th-century stone walls of the side chapel are covered with worn frescoes showing scenes from Galgano's life by Ambrogio Lorenzetti (1344).

Massa Marittima **㉗**

Grosseto. **👥** *9,500.* **🚌** **ℹ** *Palazzo del Podestà, Piazza Garibaldi (0566-90 22 89).* **🛒** *Wed.*

SET IN THE Colline Metallifere (metal-bearing hills) where lead, copper and silver ores were mined as early as Etruscan times, Massa Marittima is far from being a grimy industrial town. Excellent examples of Romanesque architecture survive from the period when the town became an independent republic (1225–

1335). The Romanesque-Gothic **Duomo** in Piazza Garibaldi is dedicated to St Cerbone, a 6th-century saint whose story is sculpted in stone above the main portal. Inside the building, the *Maestà* is attributed to Duccio (c.1316).

The interesting **Museo della Miniera** (museum of mining) is located partially inside a former mine shaft and has exhibits that explain mining techniques, tools and locally found minerals.

The **Museo Archeologico**, housed in a 13th-century building, has material from Paleolithic to Roman times. There is also a picture gallery.

🏛 Museo della Miniera
Via Corridoni. **📞** *0566-90 22 89.*
◯ *Tue–Sun (Jul & Aug: daily).* 🖼

🏛 Museo Archeologico
Palazzo del Podestà, Piazza Garibaldi.
📞 *0566-90 22 89.* **◯** *Tue–Sun.* 🖼

View across the rooftops of Massa Marittima

Denuded hillocks of clay in the Crete Senesi area southeast of Siena ▷

Street-by-Street: Siena ㉒

Unicorn
Contrada

SIENA'S PRINCIPAL SIGHTS cluster in the maze of narrow streets and alleys around the fan-shaped Piazza del Campo. One of Europe's greatest medieval squares, the piazza sits at the heart of the city's 17 *contrade*, a series of parishes whose ancient rivalries are still acted out in the twice-yearly Palio *(see p331)*. Loyalty to the *contrada* of one's birth is fierce, and as you wander the streets you will see the parishes' animal symbols repeated on flags, plaques and carvings. Siena's hilly position also means that city walks offer delightful hidden corners and countless sudden views.

The Duomo dominating Siena's skyline

Via della Galluzza leads to the house of St Catherine.

The Baptistry has fine frescoes and a font with reliefs by Donatello, Jacopo della Quercia and Ghiberti.

★ Duomo
Striped black and white marble pillars, surmounted by a carved frieze of the popes, support the Duomo's vaulted ceiling, painted blue with gold stars to resemble the night sky.

Each tier of the Duomo's bell tower has one more window than the floor below.

Museo dell'Opera del Duomo
Duccio's Maestà, one of the greatest Sienese paintings, was paraded around Siena's streets on its completion in 1311, and influenced the city's painters for decades to come.

Bus station ↑

Railway station ↗

VIA D. GALLUZZA

PIAZZA INDIPENDENZA

VIA DI FONTEBRANDA

VIA DI DIACCETO

VIA DI CITTA

VIA FRANCIOSA

PIAZZA SAN GIOVANNI

VIA DEI PELLEGRINI

VIC. D. CAMPANE

VIA DEL FUSARI

VIA DEL POGGIO

VIA DI CITTA

PIAZZA DEL DUOMO

VIA DEL CAPITANO

KEY

– – –   Suggested route

| 0 metres | | 300 |
| 0 yards | | 300 |

Loggia della Mercanzia
Built in 1417, the arcade is where Siena's medieval merchants and money dealers carried out their business.

VISITORS' CHECKLIST

58,000. FS *Piazzale Rosselli.*
Piazza San Domenico.
Piazza del Campo 56 (0577-28 05 51). Wed. *Palio: 2 Jul, 16 Aug; Settimana Musicale Chigiana (Classical music concerts): Jul.*

The Logge del Papa, or Pope's colonnade, was built in honour of Pius II in 1462.

Tourist information

Drummer in Siena's Palio

🏛 Piazza del Campo

Italy's loveliest piazza occupies the site of the old Roman forum, and for much of Siena's early history was the city's principal marketplace. It began to assume its present shape in 1293, when the Council of Nine, Siena's ruling body at the time, began to acquire land with a view to creating a grand civic piazza. The red brick paving was begun in 1327 and completed in 1349, its distinctive nine segments designed to reflect the authority of the Council of Nine and to symbolize the protective folds of the Madonna's cloak. The piazza has been the focus of city life ever since, a setting for executions, bullfights and the twice-yearly drama of the Palio *(see p331)*, a festival centred around a bareback horse race. Cafés, restaurants and fine medieval palazzi now line the Campo's fringes, dominated by the **Palazzo Pubblico** (1297–1342) and **Torre del Mangia**, built in 1348 *(see p330)*. This imposing ensemble tends to overshadow the little **Fonte Gaia** on the piazza's northern edge. The fountain is a 19th-century copy of an original carved by Jacopo della Quercia in 1409–19. Its reliefs depict the *Virtues, Adam and Eve,* and the *Madonna and Child* (the originals are on the rear loggia of the Palazzo Pubblico). The fountain's water is still supplied by a 500-year-old aqueduct.

Fonte Gaia
These reliefs are 19th-century copies of originals by Jacopo della Quercia.

★ Palazzo Pubblico
The graceful Gothic town hall was completed in 1342. At 102 m (330 ft), the bell tower, Torre del Mangia, is the second highest medieval tower ever built in Italy.

STAR SIGHTS

★ Duomo

★ Palazzo Pubblico

The Piazza del Campo and Fonte Gaia from the Torre del Mangia

VIA BANCHI DI SOTTO
VIA DI PANTANETO
VIA MALIDINA
VIA DEL PORRIONE
PIAZZA DEL CAMPO
VIA DI SALICOTTO
PIAZZA DEL MERCATO
VIA DUPRE

Exploring Siena

O NCE A CAPITAL to rival Florence, Siena is still unspoilt and endowed with the grandeur of the age in which it was at its peak (1260–1348). The best place to begin an exploration of its historic centre is Piazza del Campo and the surrounding maze of medieval streets.

Lorenzetti's *Allegory of Good Government* (1338), Palazzo Pubblico

🏛 Palazzo Pubblico

Piazza del Campo 1. ☎ *0577-29 22 63.* **Museo Civico & Torre del Mangia** ◯ *daily (***Torre** ◯ *Nov–Mar).* 📷

Although it continues in its ancient role as Siena's town hall, the Palazzo Pubblico's medieval rooms, some decorated with paintings of the Sienese School, are open to the public. The **Museo Civico** is housed here. The main council chamber, or Sala del Mappamondo, is named after a map of the world painted by Ambrogio Lorenzetti in the early 14th century. One wall is covered by Simone Martini's recently restored fresco of the *Maestà* (1315), which depicts the Virgin in Majesty as the Queen of Heaven, attended by the Apostles, saints and angels. Opposite is a fresco (attributed to Simone Martini, but possibly later) of the mercenary *Guidoriccio da Fogliano* (1330). The walls of the chapel alongside are covered with frescoes of the *Life of the Virgin* (1407) by Taddeo di Bartolo, and the choir stalls

(1428) are decorated with wooden panels inlaid with biblical scenes. The Sala della Pace contains the famous *Allegory of Good and Bad Government*, a pair of frescoes by Ambrogio Lorenzetti, finished in 1338. They form one of the most important series of secular paintings from the Middle Ages. In the *Good Government* fresco civic life flourishes, while the *Bad Government* reveals rubbish-strewn streets and ruins.

The Sala del Risorgimento is covered with late 19th-century frescoes illustrating the events leading up to the unification of Italy under King Vittorio Emanuele II.

In the palace courtyard is the entrance to the magnificent **Torre del Mangia**, the palace's huge bell tower. Rising 102 m (330 ft), it is a prominent feature of Siena's skyline. Built by

the brothers Muccio and Francesco di Rinaldo between 1138 and 1148, it was named after the first bell-ringer, whose idleness led to the nickname *Mangiaguadagni* (literally "eat the profits"). There are 505 steps to the top of the tower, which has wonderful views of the Tuscan countryside.

🏛 Casa di Santa Caterina

Hotel Alma Domus, Via Camporegio 37. ☎ *0577-441 77.* ◯ *daily.*

Siena's patron saint, Catherine Benincasa (1347–80), was the daughter of a tradesman. At the age of eight she devoted herself to God and had many visions, as well as later receiving the stigmata (wounds of Christ). Like her namesake, St Catherine of Alexandria, she was believed to have been betrothed to the Christ child in a vision – a scene which inspired many artists. Her eloquence persuaded Pope Gregory XI to return the seat of the papacy to Rome in 1376, after 67 years of exile in Avignon. St Catherine died in Rome and was canonized in 1461.

Today Catherine's house is surrounded by chapels and cloisters. Among them is the Church of the Crucifixion, which was built in 1623 in her orchard to house the late 12th-century Crucifixion, in front of which she received the stigmata in 1375. The house is decorated with paintings of events from her life by artists including her contemporaries Francesco Vanni and Pietro Sorri.

Cloister of Casa di Santa Caterina, birthplace of Siena's patron saint

🏛 Palazzo Piccolomini

Via Banchi di Sotto 52. ▮ 0577-412 71. ○ Mon–Sat am.

Siena's most imposing private palazzo was built for the wealthy Piccolomini family in the 1460s by the Florentine architect and sculptor, Bernardo Rossellino. It now contains the Sienese state archives, account books and taxation documents dating back to the 13th century. Some of the leading artists of their day were employed to paint the wooden bindings used to enclose the tax and account records. The paintings, now on display in the Sala di Congresso, often show scenes of Siena itself, bristling with towers, or episodes from the city's past.

Other records include a will attributed to Boccaccio and the council's contract with Jacopo della Quercia for the Fonte Gaia (see p329).

A detail from Martini's *Blessed Agostino Novello* (c.1330)

🏛 Pinacoteca Nazionale

Via San Pietro 29. ▮ 0577-28 11 61. ○ Tue–Sun. 🖼 ♿

This fine gallery, which is housed in the 14th-century Palazzo Buonsignori, contains an unsurpassed collection of paintings by artists of the Sienese School. Arranged in chronological order, from the 13th century through to the Mannerist period (1520–1600), highlights include Duccio's *Madonna dei Francescani* (1285) and Simone Martini's masterpiece *The Blessed Agostino Novello and Four of His Miracles* (c.1330). Pietro Lorenzetti's *Two Views*, from the 14th century, are early examples of landscape painting, and Pietro da Domenico's *Adoration of the Shepherds* (1510) shows how the art of

The austere exterior of the church of San Domenico (begun 1226)

Siena remained visibly influenced by its Byzantine roots long after the naturalism of the Renaissance had reached across the rest of Europe.

🔒 San Domenico

Piazza San Domenico. ○ daily.

The preserved head of the city's patroness, St Catherine of Siena (1347–80), can be seen in a gilded tabernacle on the altar of a chapel dedicated to her in the huge, barn-like Gothic church of San Domenico (begun 1226). The chapel itself was built in 1460 for this purpose and is dominated by Sodoma's frescoes (1526), to the right and left of the altar, which show Catherine in states of religious fervour. The church has the only portrait of St Catherine considered authentic, painted by her friend Andrea Vanni.

THE SIENESE PALIO

The Palio is Tuscany's most celebrated festival and it occurs in the Campo each year on 2 July and 16 August. It is a bareback horse race first recorded in 1283, but it may have had its origins in Roman military training. The jockeys represent Siena's 17 *contrade* (districts); the horses are chosen by the drawing of lots and are blessed at the local *contrada* churches. Preceded by days **A *contrada* symbol** of colourful pageantry, costume processions and heavy betting, the races themselves last only 90 seconds each. Thousands of spectators crowd into the piazza to watch the race, and rivalry between competitors is intense. The winner is rewarded with a silk *palio* (banner). Festivities for the winners, and recriminations among the losers, can last for weeks.

The Sienese displaying their flag-throwing skills before the Palio

Siena: Duomo

A symbol of the Risen Christ on the façade

SIENA'S DUOMO (1136–1382) is one of Italy's greatest cathedrals, a spectacular mixture of sculpture, paintings and Pisan-influenced Romanesque-Gothic architecture. Had 14th-century plans to create a new nave come to fruition, the building would have become the largest church in Christendom. In the event the plan came to nothing, abandoned when the plague of 1348 virtually halved the city's population. Among the Duomo's treasures are sculptural masterpieces by Nicola Pisano, Donatello and Michelangelo, a fine inlaid pavement and a magnificent fresco cycle by Pinturicchio.

Baptismal Font
This Renaissance font by della Quercia and Donatello stands in the Baptistry.

Pulpit Panels
Carved in 1265–8 by Nicola Pisano, with help from Arnolfo di Cambio and his son Giovanni, the panels on the octagonal pulpit depict scenes from the Life of Christ.

In the nave, black and white marble pillars support the vault.

Chapel of St John the Baptist

The north aisle contains sculptures by Michelangelo of Saints Peter, Pius, Gregory and Paul (1501–4).

Inlaid Marble Floor
The Massacre of the Innocents *is one of 56 inlaid pavement scenes designed by many of Siena's leading artists between 1349 and 1547.*

Piccolomini Library
Pinturicchio's frescoes (1509) portray the life of the Piccolomini pope, Pius II. Here he presides at the betrothal of Frederick III to Eleonora of Portugal.

The **Museo dell'Opera del Duomo** occupies the side aisle of the unfinished nave, which was roofed over to house the museum.

The Campanile was added in 1313.

Archway leading to the Baptistry

Façade gives indication of planned size of nave

The unfinished nave, if completed, would have measured 50 m (162 ft) in length and 30 m (97 ft) in breadth.

Entrance to Duomo

The doors were built in 1284–97, the rest of the façade a century later.

Façade Statues
Many façade statues have been replaced by copies; the originals are in the Museo dell'Opera del Duomo.

VISITORS' CHECKLIST

Piazza del Duomo. 0577-473 21. Pollicino.
7:30am–7:30pm daily (Nov–Mar: 7:30am–1:30pm, 2:30–5pm daily). Piccolomini Library 9am–7:30pm (Nov–Mar: 10am–1pm, 2–5pm).

🏛 Museo dell'Opera del Duomo

Piazza del Duomo 8. 0577-28 30 48. daily. public hols.

Part of this museum is devoted to sculpture removed from the exterior of the Duomo, including a Renaissance tondo of a *Madonna and Child*, probably by Donatello, as well as several badly eroded Gothic statues by Giovanni Pisano and Jacopo della Quercia. The highlight is Duccio's huge *Maestà* (1308–11), one of the Sienese School's finest works. It depicts the Madonna and Child on one side, and scenes from the Life of Christ on the other. It was originally placed on the Duomo's high altar, where it replaced the striking *Madonna of the Large Eyes* (1220–30) by an anonymous Sienese painter, also in the museum.

Statues from the Duomo now on show in the Museo dell'Opera

🏰 Fortezza Medicea

Viale Maccari. **Fortezza** daily.
Enoteca 3pm–midnight.
Theatre Jun–Sep: daily.

This huge red-brick fortress was built for Cosimo I by Baldassarre Lanci in 1560, following Siena's defeat by the Florentines in the 1554–5 war. After an 18-month siege, during which more than 8,000 Sienese died, the town's banking and wool industries were suppressed and all major building work ended.

The fortress now houses an open-air theatre and the Enoteca Italica, a wine shop offering visitors the chance both to taste and to buy from a comprehensive list of quality wines from all over Italy.

Street-by-Street: San Gimignano ⓩ

THE THIRTEEN TOWERS that dominate San Gimignano's majestic skyline were built by rival noble families during the 12th and 13th centuries, when the town's position – on the main pilgrim route from northern Europe to Rome – brought it great prosperity. The plague of 1348, and later the diversion of the pilgrim route, led to its economic decline as well as its preservation. Street by street it remains mostly medieval. For a small town, San Gimignano is rich in works of art, good shops and restaurants.

San Gimignano's famous skyline, almost unchanged since the Middle Ages

Collegiata
This 11th-century church's interior is full of frescoes, including The Creation *(1367) by Bartolo di Fredi.*

Palazzo del Popolo
The council chamber of the town hall (1288–1323) features a large Maestà *(1317) by Lippo Memmi.*

The Annunciation by Ghirlandaio
This painting, completed in 1482, is located in a courtyard loggia alongside the Collegiata.

Sant'Agostino

Tourist information

VIA SAN MATTEO
VIA CAPASSI
VIA DIACCETO
PIAZZA NOMI
PIAZZA DEL DUOMO
PIAZZA DELLA CISTERNA
VIA DELLA COSTERELLA
VIA DI QUERCECCHIO
VIA BERIGNANO
VIA SAN GIOVANNI

Bus station

Via San Giovanni
is lined with shops selling local goods.

Among the Piazza del
Duomo's historic buildings
is the Palazzo Vecchio
del Podestà (1239),
whose tower is
probably the
town's oldest.

Piazza della Cisterna

*This square is
named after
the well at its
centre and
is the heart
of the old
town.*

L CASTELLO

NOCENTI

ANDORNELLA

The Museo
Civico provides
access to the tallest of the
town's 13 remaining towers.

KEY

— — — Suggested route

0 metres   250
0 yards   250

🏛 Museo Civico
Palazzo del Popolo, Piazza del
Duomo. ☎ 0577-94 03 40.
Museum & tower ◯ daily (Nov–
Mar: Tue–Sun). 🎫

Frescoes in the courtyard of
this museum feature the coats
of arms of city mayors and
magistrates, as well as a 14th-
century *Virgin and Child* by
Taddeo di Bartolo. The first
public room is the Sala di
Dante, where an inscription
recalls a visit by the poet in
1300. The walls are covered
with hunting scenes and a
huge *Maestà* fresco (1317) by
Lippo Memmi. The floor above
has an art collection, which
includes excellent works by
Pinturicchio, Bartolo di
Fredi, Benozzo Gozzoli
and Filippino Lippi. The
famous *Wedding Scene*
frescoes by Memmo di
Filippucci (early 14th
century) show a couple
sharing a bath and going
to bed – an unusual
record of life in 14th-
century Tuscany.

🏛 Collegiata
Piazza del
Duomo. ◯ daily.
This 12th-century
Romanesque church
contains a feast of
frescoes. In the
north aisle the
frescoes comprise
26 episodes from
the Old Testament
(1367) by Bartolo di Fredi.
The opposite wall features
scenes from the *Life of Christ*
(1333–41) by Lippo Memmi,
while at the back of the church

**Bartolo di Fredi's
Christ, Sant'Agostino**

**The ceiling of the Collegiata,
painted with gold stars**

there are scenes from the *Last
Judgment* painted by Taddeo
di Bartolo. Frescoes (1475) by
Ghirlandaio adorn both the
tiny Chapel of Santa Fina and
the nearby loggia.

🏛 Sant'Agostino
Piazza Sant'Agostino. ◯ daily.
Consecrated in 1298, this
church has a simple façade,
contrasting markedly with the
heavily decorated Rococo
interior (c.1740) by Vanvitelli.
Above the main altar is
the *Coronation of the
Virgin* by Piero del
Pollaiuolo, dated
1483. The choir is
entirely covered in
a cycle of frescoes
of *The Life of St
Augustine* (1465)
executed by the
Florentine artist
Benozzo Gozzoli.
In the Cappella di San
Bartolo, on the right of the
main entrance, is an elaborate
marble altar completed by
Benedetto da Maiano in 1495.

**Fresco from the early 14th-century *Wedding Scene* cycle by
Memmo di Filippucci in the Museo Civico**

Elba ㉘

Livorno. 🚶 29,000. 🚢 Portoferraio 🚌 ℹ️ Calata Italia 26 (0565-91 46 71). 🚌 Portoferraio: Fri.

ELBA'S MOST FAMOUS resident was Napoleon, who spent nine months here after the fall of Paris in 1814. Today the island is mainly populated by holidaymakers, who come by ferry from Piombino, 10 km (6 miles) away on the mainland. The main town is Portoferraio, with an old port and a modern seafront of hotels and fish restaurants.

The landscape of the island is varied. On the west coast, which tends to be a little quieter, there are sandy beaches suitable for all water sports. The east coast, centred on the town of Porto Azzurro, the island's second port, is more rugged, with high cliffs and stony beaches. Inland, olive groves and vineyards line hillsides, and vegetation covers the mountains. One of the best ways to see the interior is to take the road from Marciana Marina to the old medieval village of Marciana Alta. Close by, a minor road leads to a cable car that runs to Monte Capanne (1,018 m/3,300 ft), a magnificent viewpoint.

Marciana Marina on Elba

Sovana ㉙

Grosseto. 🚶 100.

SOVANA IS ONE of southern Tuscany's prettiest villages. Its single little street ends in Piazza del Pretorio, home to the ancient church of Santa

View over Pitigliano and the town's dramatic cliffs and caves

Maria, whose lovely interior contains frescoes and a 9th-century altar canopy. A lane beyond leads through olive groves to the Romanesque Duomo, filled with reliefs and carvings from an earlier church on the site. Tuscany's finest Etruscan tombs lie in the surrounding countryside, many of them clearly signed and easily visited from the village.

Maremma ㉛

Grosseto. ℹ️ Maremma Centro Visite, Alberese (0564-40 70 98). **Marginal Areas** 🚌 to entrances from Alberese. 🕐 7am–7pm daily. 🎫 🚫 **Inner Park Areas** 🚌 from Alberese to tour departure point. 🕐 7am–7pm daily. 🎫 only Jun–Sep: walking tours at 7am (4 hrs), 8am (3 hrs) & 4pm (3 hrs). 🚫

THE ETRUSCANS, followed by the Romans, were the first to cultivate the marshes and low hills of the Maremma. Following the collapse of the Roman Empire, however, the area fell prey to flooding and malaria, twin scourges that left it virtually uninhabited until the 18th century. The land has since been reclaimed, the irrigation canals unblocked and farming developed on the fertile soil. The stunning Parco Naturale della Maremma was set up in 1975 to preserve the area's native flora and fauna, and to prevent development on one of Italy's few pristine stretches of coastline. Entrance to much of the park is restricted to access on foot or by a park bus from Alberese. Other more marginal areas, however, such as the excellent beach at Marina di Alberese and the countryside around Talamone in the south, are easier to see.

Pitigliano ㉚

Grosseto. 🚶 4,400. 🚌 ℹ️ Via Roma 6 (0564-61 44 33). 🚌 Wed.

PITIGLIANO IS spectacularly situated high above the cave-riddled cliffs of the Lente valley. Its maze of tiny medieval streets includes a small Jewish ghetto, formed in the 17th century by Jews

Irrigated salt marsh   Trappola

Fiume Ombrone

Beaches

The Ombrone estuary is a mixture of pines, marsh and dunes and is home to birds such as the flamingo, sea eagle, roller and bee-eater.

KEY

═══ Roads

▭▭▭ Paths

▭▭▭ Canals and rivers

‒ ‒ Itineraries

| 0 kilometres | 2 |
| 0 miles | 1 |

fleeing from Catholic persecution. The **Palazzo Orsini** has its water supply brought in by an impressive aqueduct, built in 1545. It houses the **Museo Zuccarelli** with its small exhibition of work by artist Francesco Zuccarelli (1702–88), who lived locally. He also painted two of the altarpieces in the medieval **Duomo** in Piazza San Gregorio. The **Museo Etrusco** contains finds from ancient local settlements.

🏛 **Museo Zuccarelli**
Palazzo Orsini, Piazza della Fortezza Orsini 4. 📞 0564-61 55 68.
🕐 Mar–Jul: Tue–Sun; Aug: daily; Sep–Dec: Sat & Sun. ◪

🏛 **Museo Etrusco**
Piazza della Fortezza Orsini.
🕐 Tue–Sun.

Monte Argentario 32

Grosseto. 👥 13,000. 🚌 ℹ️ Corso Umberto 55, Porto Santo Stefano (0564-81 42 08). 🛒 Tue.

Monte Argentario was an island until the early 18th century, when the shallow waters separating it from the mainland began to silt up, creating two sandy spits of land, known as *tomboli*, which enclose the Orbetello lagoon. **Orbetello** itself, a lively and relatively unspoilt little town, was linked to the island in 1842, when a dyke was constructed from the mainland. The two harbour towns of **Porto Ercole** and **Porto Santo Stefano** are both up-market resorts, busy with visitors in

Porto Ercole, Monte Argentario

summer. Interior roads, however – notably the Strada Panoramica – offer more peaceful drives past rocky coves, cliffs and bays.

Entry tickets are sold at Alberese's park headquarters.

Spergolaia

Alberese 🅿️

Pratini

e di marino

Torre di Collelungo

Torre dell' Uccellina

San Rabano

🚉 **Stazione di Alberese**

Wild Boar
The most impressive of the Maremma's many wild animals is the indigenous wild boar, a smaller creature than the Eastern European boar found elsewhere in Tuscany.

San Rabano, a ruined Cistercian abbey (12th century), is close to the park's highest point.

Pine nuts for cooking are still collected from the park's woodlands.

The Uccellina Hills are crowned by old Spanish watchtowers, pinewoods and scented *macchia*.

Birds of prey, such as the hobby and peregrine, hunt in more remote parts of the park.

Unspoilt coastline

Marked Footpaths
Several gentle footpaths are marked around the park, but in practice you can wander almost at will among most of its dunes and pinewoods.

Rocca di Talamone

Stazione di Talamone 🚉

This fishing village is set against pretty countryside.

🅿️ Talamone

UMBRIA

LONG DISMISSED AS *Tuscany's "gentler sister"*, *Umbria has recently emerged from the shadow of its more famous western neighbour. Forming an expanse of gentle pastoral countryside and high mountain wilderness, the picturesque region has been dubbed the "Green Heart of Italy". Umbria is also well known for the beauty and profusion of its medieval hilltowns.*

The region was inhabited in the 8th century BC by the Umbrians, a peaceable farming tribe, and later colonized by the Etruscans and Romans. In the Middle Ages, the Lombards established a dukedom centred around Spoleto. By the 13th century much of the region was scattered with independent city-states, most of them eventually absorbed by the Papal States, where they remained until Italian unification in 1860.

Today the old towns are Umbria's chief glory. In Perugia, the region's capital, and the smaller centres of Gubbio, Montefalco and Todi, there are numerous Romanesque churches, civic palaces, vivid fresco cycles and endless medieval nooks and crannies. Spoleto, renowned for its summer arts festival, blends grandiose medieval monuments with Roman remains and some of Italy's oldest churches. The surrounding Vale of Spoleto is a chequerboard of agricultural countryside and fascinating traditional villages.

Assisi, the birthplace of St Francis, contains the Basilica di San Francesco, frescoed in part by Giotto. At Orvieto, magnificently situated on its volcanic crag, there are Etruscan remains and one of Italy's finest Romanesque-Gothic cathedrals.

Umbria's oak woods, ice-clear streams and rich soils yield many delicacies. Chief among these are trout and truffles, olive oils to rival those of Tuscany, prized lentils from Castelluccio, cured meats from Norcia and tangy mountain cheeses. A variety of well-regarded wines are produced from the vineyards of Torgiano and Montefalco.

A shop in Norcia selling a selection of Italy's finest hams, sausages and salamis

◁ A street scene in the ancient town of Todi

Exploring Umbria

ASSISI AND SPOLETO, Umbria's loveliest towns, are the most convenient and charming bases for exploring the region. Both these medieval gems are unmissable, as is the old centre of Perugia, the region's capital, and the alluring hilltowns of Gubbio, Spello, Montefalco and Todi. Umbria's landscapes are as compelling as its towns, from the eerie wastes of the Piano Grande and the mountain splendour of the Monti Sibillini national park (best reached from Norcia) to the gentler countryside of the Valnerina and the beach-fringed shores of Lake Trasimeno.

SIGHTS AT A GLANCE

SEE ALSO

Olive harvest in the Umbrian countryside near Orvieto

GETTING AROUND

Excellent road, rail and bus links exist in the region. The A1 from Florence passes Orvieto, which is linked to Todi by the N448. The N75 connects Perugia, Assisi and Spello, then the N3 continues to Trevi, Spoleto and Terni. Rome–Florence trains serve Orvieto, and Rome–Ancona trains serve Spoleto, with branch lines connecting Perugia, Spello and Assisi.

The hilltown of Castelluccio, east of Norcia, and the Monti Sibillini

A side street in the medieval town of Gubbio in northern Umbria

KEY

Motorway
Major road
Minor road
Scenic route
River
Viewpoint

0 kilometres   25

0 miles   15

Gubbio ●

Perugia. 🏛 *32,000.* FS 🚌 ℹ️ *Via Asidei 32 (075-922 06 93).* 🛒 *Tue.*

GUBBIO VIES with Assisi for the title of Umbria's most medieval town. A picture-perfect collection of twisting streets and terracotta-tiled houses, its beauty is enhanced by the forest-swathed slopes of the Apennines. Founded by the Umbrians in the 3rd century BC as Tota Ikuvina, it assumed greater prominence in the 1st century AD as the Roman colony, Eugubium. By the time it emerged as an independent commune in the 11th century, Gubbio had spread up the slopes of Monte Ingino. From 1387 to 1508 the town was ruled from Urbino by the Dukes of Montefeltro.

The 13th-century **Duomo** is distinguished by a wagon-vaulted ceiling whose arches curve gracefully to symbolize hands in prayer. Medieval Via dei Consoli leads to the 13th-century **Palazzo del Bargello** – a dour stone-faced building that once served as the headquarters of the chief of police. Also here is the **Fontana dei Matti** (Fountain of the Mad), named after the tradition that anyone who walks around it three times will go insane.

Macabre legends surround the walled-up **Porte della Morte** (Doors of Death) that can be seen in Via dei Consoli and elsewhere in the town. Reputedly used for the passage of coffins from houses, the doors, once tainted, were sealed and never used again. It is now thought their purpose was probably defensive.

Façade of the Palazzo dei Consoli in Gubbio

The interior of Perugia's San Pietro, rebuilt in the 15th century

In the lower town, the church of **San Francesco** (1259–82) is known for 17 faded frescoes showing scenes from the *Life of the Virgin*, painted between 1408 and 1413 by Ottaviano Nelli. Opposite is the **Tiratoio** (Weavers' Loggia). Wool was stretched out to dry in its shady arcade. West of here are the ruins of a 1st-century AD Roman amphitheatre.

🏛 Palazzo dei Consoli

Piazza della Signoria.
📞 *075- 927 42 98.*
🕐 *daily (Sun am).*
🔴 *1 Jan, 25 Dec.* 🎫

Dominating the skyline of Gubbio is this mighty civic palace, begun in 1332 by Gattapone. Its Salone dell'Arengo houses the Museo Civico, best known for the Eugubine Tablets (250–150 BC). Discovered in 1444, the seven bronze slabs are inscribed with Etruscan and Roman characters, probably a phonetic translation of prayers and rituals from the ancient Umbrian and Etruscan languages. Upstairs a small art gallery contains works by local painters.

One of the Eugubine Tablets in Gubbio

🏛 Palazzo Ducale

Via Ducale. 📞 *075-927 58 72.* 🕐 *daily.* 🔴 *1 Jan, 1 May, 25 Dec.* 🎫 ♿

Attributed to Francesco di Giorgio Martini, this palace was built in 1470 for the Montefeltro as a copy of the family home in Urbino (*see pp360–61*). It also has a Renaissance courtyard.

Assisi ●

See pp344–5.

Perugia ●

🏛 *160,000.* FS 🚌 ℹ️ *Piazza Matteotti 34 (075-572 33 27).* 🛒 *Sat.*

PERUGIA'S OLD CENTRE hinges around Corso Vannucci, named after the local painter Pietro Vannucci (Perugino). At its northern end lies Piazza IV Novembre, dominated by the **Fontana Maggiore**, a 13th-century fountain by Nicola and Giovanni Pisano.

To the rear rises Perugia's 15th-century **Duomo**, its entrance flanked by a statue of Pope Julius II (1555) and a pulpit built for Siena's San Bernardino (1425). The Cappella del Santo Anello inside contains the Virgin's "wedding ring", a weighty piece of agate said to change colour according to the character of the person wearing it. A pillar in the nave, festooned in votive offerings, holds a Renaissance painting of the *Madonna delle Grazie* by Gian Nicola di Paolo. The figure is credited with miraculous powers, and mothers bring newly baptized children to kneel before it. Buried in the transepts are Popes Urban IV and Martin IV.

Away from the Corso is the **Oratorio di San Bernardino** (1457–61) on Piazza San Francesco, with a colourful façade by Agostino di Duccio.

Beyond the old city walls on Borgo XX Giugno stands **San Pietro**, Perugia's most extravagantly decorated church. Founded in the 10th century and rebuilt in 1463, the best feature of the fine interior is the wooden choir (1526).

Piazza Giordano Bruno is home to **San Domenico** (1305–1632), Umbria's largest church, which is known for the Gothic tomb of Benedict XI (c.1304) and decoration by Agostino di Duccio.

🏛 Museo Archeologico Nazionale dell'Umbria

San Domenico, Piazza Giordano Bruno.
📞 075-572 71 41. ⭘ daily (Sun am).
⬤ 1 Jan, 1 May, 25 Dec. 🎫 📷
Housed in the cloisters of San Domenico, this museum exhibits prehistoric, Etruscan and Roman artefacts.

🏛 Palazzo dei Priori

Corso Vannucci. 📞 075-573 03 66. ⭘ daily.
⬤ 1 Jan, 1 May, 25 Dec.
🎫 ♿
The monumental walls and bristling crenellations of this redoubtable palace mark it as Umbria's finest public building *(see pp50–51)*. Among its finely decorated rooms is the Sala dei Notari (c.1295), the former lawyers' hall, which is vividly frescoed with scenes from the Old Testament – the work of a follower of Pietro Cavallini. The raised doorway is guarded by a pair of large bronzes made in 1274: a Guelph lion and a griffin, the medieval

Medieval street in Perugia

emblem of Perugia. The Sala di Udienza del Collegio della Mercanzia, built around 1390, was formerly used by the Merchants' Guild. This room is late Gothic in style, with exquisite panelling and 15th-century inlaid wood.

Also in the palace is the Collegio del Cambio, Perugia's former money exchange, which was begun in 1452. This room was used by the Bankers' Guild. Its walls are covered with superlative frescoes (1498–1500) by Perugino, works that are devoted to a mixture of Classical and religious scenes. A glum self-portrait scowls down from the centre of the left wall, while the hand of Perugino's pupil Raphael may be evident in some panels on the right wall.

Entrance of Palazzo dei Priori, Perugia

🏛 Galleria Nazionale dell'Umbria

Palazzo dei Priori, Corso Vannucci.
📞 075-572 03 16. ⭘ daily (Sun am).
⬤ 1 Jan, 1 May, 25 Dec. 🎫 ♿
Umbria's greatest collection of paintings is displayed here on the third floor of the palace. Most of the works are 13th- to 18th-century paintings by local artists, but the highlights are altarpieces by Piero della Francesca and Fra Angelico.

Lake Trasimeno ❹

Perugia. 🚉 🚌 Castiglione del Lago.
ℹ️ Piazza Mazzini 10, Castiglione del Lago (075-965 24 84).

EDGED WITH LOW HILLS and gentle farming country, this is Italy's fourth-largest lake. Its miles of placid water and reed-lined shores have a tranquil, melancholy beauty.

Drainage of the lake began under the Romans, but today the lake is gently drying up of its own accord. The town of **Castiglione del Lago**, jutting out on a fortified promontory, has an easy-going atmosphere and small sandy beaches. The 16th-century **castle** is used for summer concerts. The church of **Santa Maria Maddalena**, begun in 1836, has a fine *Madonna and Child* (c.1500) by Eusebio di San Giorgio.

Passignano sul Trasimeno has a bustling promenade and, like Castiglione, it offers boat trips to **Isola Maggiore**. The island's charming village is known for lace-making.

THE BATTLE OF LAKE TRASIMENO

In 217 BC the Romans suffered one of their worst ever military defeats on the shores of Lake Trasimeno. The Carthaginian general, Hannibal, lured the Romans (who were led by the consul Flaminius) into a masterful ambush close to present-day Ossaia (Place of Bones) and Sanguineto (Place of Blood).

19th-century engraving of General Hannibal

Some 16,000 centurions perished, hacked down on the lake's marshy fringes. Hannibal, by contrast, lost only 1,500 men. Today you can explore the battlefield, which includes over 100 mass graves found near Tuoro sul Trasimeno.

Colourful façade of Perugia's Oratorio di San Bernardino

Assisi: Basilica di San Francesco

THE BURIAL PLACE of St Francis, this basilica was begun in 1228, two years after the saint's death. Over the next century its Upper and Lower Churches were decorated by the foremost artists of their day, among them Cimabue, Simone Martini, Pietro Lorenzetti and Giotto, whose frescoes on the *Life of St Francis* are some of the most renowned in Italy. The basilica, which dominates Assisi, is one of the great Christian shrines and receives vast numbers of pilgrims throughout the year.

The campanile was built in 1239.

St Francis
Cimabue's simple painting (c.1280) captures the humility of the revered saint, who stood for poverty, chastity and obedience.

The choir (1501) features a 13th-century stone papal throne.

Faded paintings by Roman artists line the walls above Giotto's *Life of St Francis.*

Steps to the Treasury

★ Frescoes by Lorenzetti
The bold composition of Pietro Lorenzetti's fresco, entitled The Deposition *(1323), is based around the truncated Cross, focusing attention on the twisted figure of Christ.*

Lower Church
Side chapels were created here in the 13th century to accommodate the growing number of pilgrims.

The crypt contains the tomb of St Francis.

STAR FEATURES

★ Frescoes by Giotto

★ Frescoes by Lorenzetti

★ Cappella di San Martino

Upper Church
*The soaring Gothic lines of the
13th-century Upper Church
symbolized the heavenly
glory of St Francis. This style
also influenced later
Franciscan churches.*

The façade
and its rose
window are
early examples
of Italian
Gothic.

**Entrance
to Upper
Church**

**Entrance to
Lower Church**

★ **Frescoes by Giotto**
*The Ecstasy of St Francis is
one of 28 panels that make
up Giotto's cycle on the* Life
of St Francis *(c.1290–95).*

★ **Cappella di San Martino**
*The frescoes in this chapel
on the* Life of St Martin
*(1315) are by the Sienese
painter Simone Martini. This
panel shows the Death of the
Saint. Martini was also
responsible for the fine
stained glass in the chapel.*

Assisi ❷

Perugia. 🏠 *25,000.* FS ⛟ ℹ
Piazza del Comune 12 (075-81 25 34).
🗓 *Sat.*

THIS BEAUTIFUL medieval
town, with its geranium-
hung streets, lovely views and
fountain-splashed piazzas, is
heir to the legacy of St Francis
(c.1181–1226), who is buried in
the **Basilica di San Francesco**.
Piazza del Comune, Assisi's
main square, is dominated by
the columns of the **Tempio di
Minerva**, an almost perfectly
preserved Roman temple-front
from the Augustan age. The
Palazzo Comunale, opposite,
is home to the **Pinacoteca
Comunale**, an art gallery with
works by local medieval artists.
Down Corso Mazzini lies
the **Basilica di Santa Chiara**,
the burial place of St Clare –
Francis's companion and the
founder of the Poor Clares
(an order of nuns). One of its
chapels contains the crucifix
that is said to have bowed its
head and ordered Francis to
"Repair God's church". It came
from **San Damiano**, a sublime
church set amid olive groves
south of the Porta Nuova.
The **Duomo (San Rufino)**,
built during the 12th and 13th
centuries, has a superb Romanesque façade. Inside is a small
museum of paintings, and
there are archaeological
items in the crypt. From
the Duomo, Via Maria
delle Rose leads to the
Rocca Maggiore (rebuilt
in 1367), an evocative if
much-restored castle.
Thirteenth-century
San Pietro, on Piazza
San Pietro, is a simple
and carefully restored
Romanesque church.
The nearby **Oratorio
dei Pellegrini**, a 15th-
century pilgrims' hospice,
contains well-preserved
frescoes by Matteo da Gualdo.

🏛 **Pinacoteca Comunale**
Piazza del Comune. **(** 075-81 25 79.
◯ *daily.* ● *1 Jan, 25 Dec.* 🎫 ♿
🏛 **Duomo Museum & Crypt**
Piazza San Rufino. **(** 075-81 22 83.
◯ *Apr–Oct & 24 Dec–6 Jan: daily.* 🎫
🏛 **Oratorio dei Pellegrini**
Via San Francesco. **(** 075-81 22 67.
◯ *daily.* ● *religious & public hols.*

Giotto's fresco, *St Francis Appearing to the Friars at Arles* (c.1295), in the Basilica di San Francesco, Assisi ▷

Orvieto ❺

Terni. 🏛 22,000. FS 🚌 🛈 Piazza Duomo 24 (0763-417 72). 🗓 Thu & Sat.

ORVIETO IS MAGNIFICENT from any angle. Perched on a 300-m (984-ft) plateau, it looks down from its cliff-edged balcony over a vineyard-spotted plain. Visitors flood into the town to admire the **Duomo**, among the greatest of all Italy's Romanesque-Gothic cathedrals.

The tiny 13th-century church of **San Lorenzo in Arari** is at the end of Via Scalza. Its walls feature frescoes describing the martyrdom of St Lawrence, who was grilled to death. The altar is made from an Etruscan sacrificial slab. Via Malabranca leads to **San Giovenale** at Orvieto's western tip, a church that is beautifully and almost completely covered in detailed frescoes from the 15th and 16th centuries. It offers broad views over the surrounding countryside. **Sant'Andrea**, in Piazza della Repubblica, is distinguished by a curious 12-sided campanile, part of the original 12th-century building.

🏛 Museo dell' Opera del Duomo
Piazza Duomo. 📞 0763-424 77. ● for restoration until end 1996.
This interesting little museum contains an eclectic collection of treasures given to the Duomo. Among the highlights are paintings by Lorenzo Maitani (died 1330) and sculptures by Andrea Pisano (c.1270–1348).

🏛 Museo Archeologico Faina and Museo Civico
Piazza Duomo. 📞 0763-412 16. ● Tue–Sun. ● 1 Jan, 1 May, 25 Dec. 📷 📷 ♿
The first of these two museums has a well-known, low-key collection of Etruscan remains including many Greek vases

View into the Pozzo di San Patrizio in Orvieto

that were found in Etruscan tombs in the area. The Museo Civico contains ancient Greek artefacts, as well as Etruscan copies of Greek works.

🏛 Museo d'Arte Moderna "Emilio Greco"
Palazzo Soliano, Piazza Duomo. 📞 0763-446 05. ● Tue–Sun. ● 1 Jan, 25 Dec. 📷 ♿
This museum is devoted to the modern Sicilian sculptor, Emilio Greco, who made the bronze doors (1964–70) of the Duomo in Orvieto.

🏛 DUOMO OF ORVIETO
Piazza Duomo. 📞 0763-411 67. ● daily. ♿ 📷
Some 300 years in the building, Orvieto's Duomo (begun 1290), with its breathtaking façade, is one of Italy's greatest cathedrals. It was inspired by the Miracle of Bolsena in which real blood from a consecrated host supposedly fell on the altar cloth of a church in nearby Bolsena.

Carved choir stalls

The exterior is characterized by horizontal bands of white travertine and blue-grey basalt.

14th-century rose window by Orcagna

The reliquary of the Corporal contains the altar cloth from Bolsena.

Cappella del Corporale
This chapel contains Lippo Memmi's Madonna dei Raccomandati *(1320). There are also frescoes (1357–64) by Ugolino di Prete Ilario of the* Miracle of Bolsena *and* Miracles of the Sacrament.

Bronze doors by Emilio Greco (1964–70)

🏛 Pozzo di San Patrizio

Viale San Gallo. **0763-437 68.**
☐ *daily.* ● *1 Jan, 25 Dec.* 🏷

Orvieto's vast well was commissioned in 1527 by Pope Clement VII and designed by the Florentine architect Antonio da Sangallo to provide the town with a water supply in case of attack. Two 248-step staircases drop into its dank interior, cleverly arranged as a double helix (spiral) so as not to intersect. The 62-m (203-ft) shaft, built out of tufa blocks and bricks, took ten years to complete.

⋔ Necropoli del Crocifisso del Tufo

Viale Crispi. **0763-436 11.** ☐ *daily.*
● *1 Jan.* 🏷 ♿

This Etruscan necropolis from the 6th century BC has burial chambers built of blocks of tufa. Etruscan letters, which are thought to be the names of the deceased, are inscribed on the tombs.

Cappella Nuova
Luca Signorelli's great fresco cycle of the Last Judgment (1499–1504) features prominently in this chapel. Fra Angelico and Benozzo Gozzoli worked here before Signorelli.

The Façade
There are detailed carvings (c.1320–30) at the base of its four main pilasters. By Lorenzo Maitani, they depict scenes from the Old and New Testaments, including hell and damnation.

View of the hilltown of Todi in southern Umbria

Todi ❻

Perugia. 🏘 *17,000.* 🚉 🚌 🛈 *Via Ciuffelli 8 (075-894 38 67).* 🛒 *Sat.*

Looking down over the Tiber valley from its hilltop eyrie, Todi is one of the most strikingly situated of Umbria's famous hilltowns. An ancient Etruscan, and then Roman settlement, it still preserves an uncorrupted medieval air, with several tiny churches, three austere public palaces and many sleepy corners.

Most people are drawn here by the **Piazza del Popolo**, the main square, flanked by the lovely plain-faced **Duomo**. Built in the 13th century on the site of a Roman temple to Apollo, it has a dusky interior and one of Umbria's finest choirs (1521–30). Note Ferraù da Faenza's huge painting (1596) on the rear wall, a less than successful copy of Michelangelo's *Last Judgment*, and the altarpiece at the end of the right aisle by Giannicola di Paolo (a follower of Perugino).

Also flanking the piazza are the **Palazzo dei Priori** (1293–1337) and the linked **Palazzo del Capitano** (1290) and **Palazzo del Popolo** (1213). In the Palazzo del Capitano, distinguished by its redoubtable medieval interior, lies the **Museo Etrusco-Romano**. The museum contains a collection of local Etruscan and Roman artefacts. There are altarpieces and sacred objects in the **Pinacoteca Comunale**, also housed in the palace.

A few steps from the piazza rises **San Fortunato** (1292–1462), named after Todi's first bishop, with an outstanding florid Gothic doorway (1415–58). The church's airy interior is one of the finest of its kind in central Italy. The high vaulted plan is based on German Gothic "hall" churches and the "barn" churches of Tuscany, characterized by a low-pitched vault, polygonal apse and naves and aisles of equal height. The choir (1590) is superb, but the church's most famous work of art is a *Madonna and Child* (1432) by Masolino da Panicale (fourth chapel on the right). The crypt contains the tomb of Jacopone da Todi (c.1228–1306), a noted medieval poet and mystic.

To the right of the church are some shady gardens, from which a path (past the tiny castle) drops through the trees to emerge in front of **Santa Maria della Consolazione** (1508–1607), near the N79. One of central Italy's finest Renaissance churches, and based on a Greek cross, it may have been built to a plan by Bramante. The stark, chill interior is overshadowed by the harmonious exterior.

🏛 Museo Etrusco-Romano and Pinacoteca Comunale

Palazzi Comunali. **075-895 61.**
☐ *Tue–Sun.* ● *public hols.* 🏷 ♿

Santa Maria della Consolazione in Todi

Spoleto ❼

Perugia. 🏛 *38,000.* **FS** 🚌
ℹ *Piazza della Libertà 7 (0743-22 03 11).* 🛒 *Tue & Fri.*

Founded by the Umbrians, Spoleto became one of central Italy's most important Roman colonies, a prominence maintained by the Lombards, who in the 7th century made it the capital of one of their three Italian dukedoms. After a period as an independent city state, the town fell to the papacy in 1354.

Spoleto, within its wooded setting, is the loveliest of the Umbrian hilltowns. Its urbane atmosphere is enhanced by its superb monuments and by the Festival dei Due Mondi, one of Europe's leading arts festivals held annually in June and July.

At the southern end of Piazza del Mercato is the **Arco di Druso**, a 1st-century AD Roman arch. It is flanked by the church of **Sant'Ansano**, whose crypt is covered in frescoes that may date from the 6th century. Via Aurelio Saffi, at the piazza's northern end, leads to **Sant'Eufemia**. This utterly simple 10th-century Romanesque church is known for its matroneum (women's gallery), once used to segregate the congregation.

A short way beyond, the fan-shaped Piazza del Duomo opens out to reveal Spoleto's 12th-century **Duomo**, graced with one of the most elegant façades in Italy. Filling the apse of the Baroque interior is a great, newly-restored fresco cycle. The final work of Fra Lippo Lippi, from 1467–9, it describes episodes from the *Life of the Virgin*. The Cappella Erioli is adorned with Pinturicchio's unfinished *Madonna and Child* (1497).

The best of the exceptional churches in the lower town is 4th-century **San Salvatore**, located in the main cemetery, a spot suited to the church's eerie sense of antiquity. Nearby stands **San Ponziano**, fronted by a captivating three-tiered

Façade of San Pietro in Spoleto

Romanesque façade typical of Umbria. It has a 10th-century crypt, supported by odd little columns and decorated with Byzantine frescoes.

Romanesque **San Gregorio** in Piazza Garibaldi dates from 1069, but its cramped façade and stolid campanile incorporate fragments of Roman buildings. Inside is a raised presbytery and a lovely multi-columned crypt. Well-preserved patches of fresco dot the walls, interspersed with austere stone confessionals. Some 10,000 Christian martyrs are supposedly buried near the church. They were reputedly slaughtered in the town's Roman **amphitheatre**, traces of which can be seen in the barracks on Via del Anfiteatro.

🏛 **Ponte delle Torri**
This magnificent 14th-century aqueduct, the "bridge of towers", is 80 m (262 ft) high. Designed by Gattapone (from

Ponte delle Torri, Spoleto

ROMANESQUE CHURCHES IN UMBRIA

Umbria's church-building tradition had its roots in ancient Roman basilicas and in the chapels built over the shrines of its many saints and martyrs. The region's Romanesque façades are usually divided into three tiers, often with three rose windows arranged above a trio of arched portals. The three doors usually correspond to the interior's nave and two aisles, which derive from the simple barn-like plan of Roman basilicas. Inside, the presbytery is often raised in order to allow for the building of a crypt, which usually contained the relics of a saint or martyr. Many of the churches took centuries to build, or were repeatedly modified over time, often acquiring elements of Gothic, Baroque or Renaissance styles.

San Lorenzo di Arari *in Orvieto takes its name from an Etruscan altar (arari). This 14th-century church has a very simple façade (see p348).*

12th-century campanile

Renaissance portico

Spoleto's Duomo *(1198) has eight rose windows, a mosaic (1207) and a Renaissance portico (1491). The tower was built from old Roman remains.*

Gubbio), it is the town's single most famous monument. From the bridge, there are views of the bastions of the **Rocca Albornoz**, a huge papal fortress built in 1359–64, also by Gattapone. Unfortunately, the fortress is closed to the public. Across the bridge a path leads to the Strada di Monteluco and the church of **San Pietro**, which is renowned for the fascinating 12th-century carvings on its façade.

🏛 **Pinacoteca Comunale**
Palazzo Comunale, Piazza del Municipio. [0743-21 81. ○ Tue–Sun. ● 1 Jan, 25 Dec. 📷
Spoleto's art gallery has four beautifully appointed rooms with works by Perugino and his Spoletan protégé, Lo Spagna (c.1450–1528), including a painting of the Madonna and Child with Saints.

Montefalco ❽

Perugia. 🏘 4,900. 🚌 🛈 Mon.

MONTEFALCO, whose name (Falcon's Mount) draws inspiration from its lofty position and sweeping views, is the best of the fascinating villages in the Vale of Spoleto. Criss-crossed by streets almost too narrow for cars, it takes less than five minutes to walk through the village. Yet you might happily spend a morning here, most of it in the polished new **Museo Civico** housed in the former church

A panel from Gozzoli's fresco cycle (1452) in Montefalco's Museo Civico

of San Francesco. Its highlight is Benozzo Gozzoli's *Life of St Francis* (1452), a radiant fresco cycle that borrows heavily from Giotto's cycle in Assisi *(see pp344–7)*. Other painters represented here are Perugino, Tiberio d'Assisi and Nicolò Alunno, all leading medieval Umbrian artists.

The simple Gothic church of **Sant'Agostino** (begun 1279) on Corso Mameli is dotted with frescoes from the 14th–16th centuries. The church also contains three mummies.

In the main square local wines on sale include the rich, red Sagrantino di Montefalco. Just outside the town walls, the church of **Sant'Illuminata** is covered with charming frescoes, the work of the local 16th-century artist Francesco

Melanzio. About 2 km (1 mile) beyond, the prettily situated church of **San Fortunato** is decorated with frescoes by Gozzoli and Tiberio d'Assisi.

ENVIRONS: The village in the Vale of Spoleto with the most spectacular setting is **Trevi**. The churches of **San Martino** (16th century), on Passeggiata di San Martino, and **Madonna delle Lacrime** (1487–1522), south of Trevi on the road into the village, contain paintings by Perugino and Tiberio d'Assisi, among others.

🏛 **Museo Civico di San Francesco**
Via Ringhiera Umbra 9. [0742-37 95 98. ○ Apr–Sep: daily; Oct–Mar: Tue–Sun. ● 1 Jan, 25 Dec. 📷 ♿

The Duomo (1253) in Assisi is a fine example of the three-tiered façades found across central Italy (see p345). It has a pointed arch and a row of arcading.

Todi's Duomo was begun in the 12th century, but work on its windows and portals continued until the 17th century (see p349).

San Michele (c.1195) in Bevagna has a beautiful portal that combines both Romanesque and old Roman fragments (see p352).

Spello 9

Perugia. 🏛 8,000. FS 🚌
🛈 Piazza Matteotti 3 (0742-30
10 09). 🛒 Wed.

SPELLO IS ONE of the better
known villages in the Vale
of Spoleto. It is renowned for
a fresco cycle by Pinturicchio
in the Cappella Baglioni of
the church of **Santa Maria
Maggiore** (12th–13th century)
on Via Consolare. Executed
around 1500, the frescoes
depict scenes from the New
Testament. Towards the centre
of the village is the Gothic
church of **Sant'Andrea** (13th
century) on Via Cavour. This
road becomes Via Garibaldi,
which leads to **San Lorenzo**,
a Baroque gem of a church
dating from the 12th century.
Spello also boasts Roman
ruins from the age of Augustus:
the **Porta Consolare** at the
end of Via Consolare, and the
twin-towered **Porta Venere**
by Via Torri di Properzio.
The road to Assisi over
Monte Subasio offers stunning views from the top of
the mountain above Spello.

ENVIRONS: The least known
village in the Vale of Spoleto
is **Bevagna**. Like Spello, it
sprang to life as a way-station
on the Via Flaminia (the
Roman road that ran through
this part of Umbria). The
medieval Piazza Silvestri is
the setting for two
Romanesque
churches.

**The lofty peaks of the Monti
Sibillini in eastern Umbria**

San Silvestro (1195) is the
more atmospheric of the pair,
thanks to its shadowy interior
and ancient crypt, but **San
Michele** (late 12th century)
has an elegant portal, famed
for the little gargoyles on either
side. Both churches are the
work of Maestro Binello.

Monti Sibillini 10

Macerata. FS Spoleto. 🚌 Visso.
🛈 Largo Giovanni Battista Antinori 1,
Visso (0737-955 26).

RECENTLY AWARDED national
park status, the Monti
Sibillini in eastern Umbria
provide the region's wildest
and most spectacular scenery.
A range 40 km (25 miles) long,
the mountains form part of
the Apennines, a chain that
runs the length of the Italian
peninsula. **Monte
Vettore** is the
loftiest
point, and the peninsula's
third highest; it stands at
2,476 m (8,123 ft), a great
whale-backed peak close to
the cave of the mythical sybil
that gave the region its name.
Good maps and trails make
this a superb walking area,
while drivers can follow hair-
pin roads to some of Italy's
most magical landscapes.
Chief of these is the **Piano
Grande**, a huge upland plain
surrounded by a vast amphitheatre of mountains. Bare
but for flocks of sheep and
bedraggled haystacks, the plain
blazes with wild flowers in
spring and with lentils later in
the year. The only habitation
is **Castelluccio**, a beautiful,
neglected mountain village
now being restored. It can be
reached by road from Norcia
and Arquata del Tronto.

**Shop front in Norcia displaying
the town's varied meats**

Norcia 11

Perugia. 🏛 4,700. 🚌 🛈 Piazza
San Benedetto (0743-82 80 44).
🛒 Thu.

THE BIRTHPLACE of St
Benedict, Norcia is a
robust mountain town and an
excellent base for exploring
Valnerina and Monti Sibillini.
One of Italy's culinary capitals,
it is renowned for truffles and
some of the country's best
hams, sausages and salamis.
Norcia's main sights are in
Piazza San Benedetto. Occupying the eastern flank, the
church of **San Benedetto** has
a 14th-century portal adorned
with statues of Benedict and
his sister (Santa Scolastica).
Legend claims that the church
marks the site of Benedict's
birth – indeed there are the
remains of a 5th-century building in the crypt. However, the

Pinturicchio's *Annunciation* (c.1500) in Spello's Santa Maria Maggiore

The 8th-century monastery of San Pietro in Valle, set in the beautiful Valnerina

church was more likely to have been built over the site of an old Roman temple, since the forum of the Roman colony of Nursia once occupied this spot.

Left of the church stands the newly renovated **Palazzo Comunale**, a monument to the town's period as a free commune during the 13th and 14th centuries. On the opposite side of the square, still dominating the town, rises the **Castellina** (1554), a blunt papal fortress designed by Vignola to help impose order on an unruly mountain district. The **Duomo** (1560), to the left of the Castellina, has been ravaged by earthquakes over the centuries. Indeed, Norcia has been the victim of successive earthquakes and its houses are low and heavily buttressed with thick walls to protect them from further damage.

Piazza San Benedetto has enticing food shops, fronted by boars' heads, hams and strings of sausages. Nearby **Sant'Agostino** on Via Anicia features a range of good 16th-century frescoes. A little way beyond, the **Oratorio di Sant'Agostinaccio** in Piazza Palatina contains a superb 17th-century ceiling. Via Umberto shelters the **Edicola** (1354), a strange tabernacle believed to have been carved for a Holy Week procession.

Valnerina ⑫

Perugia. **FS** **🚌** *Spoleto.* **ℹ** *Piazza Garibaldi 1, Cascia (0743-714 01).*

THE VALNERINA (Little Valley of the River Nera) curves through a broad swathe of eastern Umbria, draining the mountains around Norcia and the Sibillini before emptying into the Tiber beyond Terni. It is edged with craggy, tree-covered slopes and dotted with countless upland villages and fortified hamlets.

The high spot is **San Pietro in Valle**, an idyllically situated monastery in the hills above the village of Colleponte. Founded in the 8th century, it is one of the few surviving memorials to the Lombards, whose central Italian duchy had its capital in Spoleto. The main body of the monastery church dates from this period, as does the high altar, an outstanding piece of Lombard work. The nave walls are covered in a wealth of 12th-century frescoes.

More popular than the monastery are the **Cascate delle Marmore** near Terni, among Europe's highest waterfalls at 165 m (541 ft). Created by the Romans during drainage work, their waters are now diverted to produce hydroelectric power on all but a few special days. You can view the falls from Marmore village or the N209.

🏠 San Pietro in Valle
Località Ferentillo, Terni. **☎** *0744-78 03 16.* **◯** *daily.*
🌊 Cascate delle Marmore
7 km (4 miles) along N209 Valnerina, Terni. **◯** *sporadically. Ask at tourist information.*

Piazza San Benedetto and the church of San Benedetto in Norcia

LE MARCHE

Tucked away *in a remote corner between the Adriatic Sea and the Apennine mountains, Le Marche (the Marches) is an enchanting rural patchwork of old towns, hill country and long, sandy beaches. In pre-Christian times the area was settled by the Piceni, a tribe eventually assimilated by the Romans.*

In the 4th century BC, exiles from Magna Graecia colonized much of the region. The most notable town was Ancona, also the northernmost point of Greek influence on the Italian peninsula. During the early Middle Ages the region marked the edge of the Holy Roman Empire, giving rise to its present name (*march* meant border area).

The region's historical peak was reached in the 15th century under Federico da Montefeltro, whose court at Urbino became one of Europe's leading cultural centres. Much of Urbino's former grandeur survives, particularly in Federico's magnificent Renaissance Palazzo Ducale, now home to a regional art collection. Ascoli Piceno is almost as enchanting as Urbino, its central Piazza del Popolo among the most evocative old squares in Italy. Smaller towns like San Leo and Urbania and the republic of San Marino also boast fine medieval monuments.

Today probably as many people come to Le Marche for its beaches and towns as for its hilly, unspoilt interior. Especially beautiful are the snowcapped peaks of the Monti Sibillini, situated in magnificent walking and skiing country.

Regional cuisine encompasses the truffles and robust cheeses of the mountains, tender hams and salamis, *olive ascolane* (olives stuffed with meat and herbs) and *brodetto*, fish soup made in several versions up and down the coast. Dry, white Verdicchio is the best known wine, although more unusual names, such as Bianchello del Metauro, are gaining in popularity.

A field of poppies and olive trees in the heart of Le Marche's countryside

◁ Medieval gates and ramparts surrounding the hilltop republic of San Marino

Exploring Le Marche

THE MEDIEVAL TOWNS of Urbino and Ascoli Piceno are the highlights of the region, but the rolling hills of the interior contain an abundance of smaller towns and all but undiscovered villages. San Leo, with its dramatic fortress, is one of the best. Most of the countryside is a pretty mixture of woods and remote hills, rising in the west to the majestic Monti Sibillini. Ancona and the attractive town of Pèsaro are the pivotal points of the vast coastline.

KEY

▰▰▰	Motorway
▰▰▰	Major road
▰▰▰	Minor road
▰▰▰	Scenic route
≈	River
☀	Viewpoint

Rolling countryside between Loreto and Ascoli Piceno

View of Ascoli Piceno, one of the prettiest towns in Le Marche

SIGHTS AT A GLANCE

The rocky reef near Portonovo on the Conero Peninsula

GETTING AROUND

The A14 provides easy access to the coastal resorts. Dual-carriageway spurs from the A14 lead to Urbino, Jesi and Ascoli Piceno, but north-south roads in the interior can be slow. Bus services are generally good, but in the interior can be infrequent. The railway service along the coast is excellent, with a good service through the heart of the region, though it can be slow.

A market scene in Fano

MAR ADRIATICO

SENIGALLIA

ANCONA ❾

CONERO PENINSULA ❿

LORETO ⓫

RECANATI

MACERATA

SEVERINO MARCHE

TOLENTINO

FERMO

SAN BENEDETTO DEL TRONTO

PARCO NAZIONALE DEI SIBILLINI

MONTE SIBILLA

ASCOLI PICENO ⓬

Teramo

0 kilometres   25

0 miles   10

SEE ALSO

• *Where to Stay* pp564–5

• *Where to Eat* pp597–8

The bell tower of the Duomo rising above the village of San Leo

San Leo ❶

Pèsaro. ℹ *Fortezza, Via Leopardi (0541-91 62 31).* 🚌 *from Rimini, change at Villanova.*

FEW CASTLES are as impressive as the great **fortress** that towers over the village of San Leo. Dante used this crag-top site as a model for the land-scapes of *Purgatorio*, while Machiavelli considered the citadel to be the finest piece of military architecture in Italy. Its rocky ramparts once contained the Mons Feretrius, a Roman temple dedicated to Jupiter.

An earlier Roman fortress on the site became a papal prison in the 18th century. Its most famous inmate was the larger-than-life Conte di Cagliostro. A swindler, womanizer, necro-mancer, quack and alchemist, Cagliostro was imprisoned for heresy in the 1790s. His cell was specially built so that its window faced the village's two churches. It is still visible, together with a small picture gallery, state rooms, and the majestic Renaissance ramparts, built by Francesco di Giorgio Martini for the dukes of Montefeltro in the 15th century.

The captivating village has a quaint cobbled square with a superb 9th-century **Pieve** (parish church). Built partly with stone from the ruined Mons Feretrius, the church was raised over the site of a 6th-century chapel.

Just behind lies the 12th-century **Duomo**, a fine Romanesque building with crumbling Corinthian capitals and stunted Roman columns from the Mons Feretrius. The lid of St Leo's sarcophagus is in the crypt. Ancient pagan carvings can be seen on the wall behind the altar.

♣ **Fortress**
Via Leopardi. 📞 *0541-91 62 31.*
🕐 *daily.*

San Marino ❷

🚌 *San Marino Città.* ℹ *Contrada Omagnano 20, San Marino (0549-88 24 00).*

EUROPE'S OLDEST republic, tiny San Marino was reputedly founded by St Marinus, a 4th-century monk and stonemason forced to flee the religious per-secution of the Emperor Diocletian. With him was St Leo, the founder of the nearby town of San Leo. Dramatically situated on the slopes of Monte Titano, the country has its own mint, stamps, football team – even its own 1,000-strong army.

There are no customs formalities in this small country, whose borders

Duty-free shop in San Marino

are just 12 km (7 miles) apart at the widest point. Sadly, the capital, also known as **San Marino**, is thronged with visitors for much of the year and its streets are clogged with souvenir stalls. Garibaldi, who sought shelter here after fleeing Venice in 1849, is honoured by a monument in Piazza Garibaldi. **Borgomaggiore**, the largest town, lies at the foot of Monte Titano, with a cable car to the capital above.

Pèsaro ❸

🏛 *91,000.* 🚆 🚌 ℹ *Via Mazzolari 4 (0721-693 41).* 🗓 *Tue & 1st Thu of month.*

Detail of the *Coronation of the Virgin* by Bellini (c.1470) in the Musei Civici

ONE OF THE ADRIATIC'S larger seaside resorts, Pèsaro has managed to retain a stylish air. Behind the promenade and the wall of white stucco hotels is a lively, attractive medieval area.

The art gallery of the **Musei Civici** contains Giovanni Bellini's sumptuous polyptych, the *Coronation of the Virgin* (c.1470). The museum also features Renaissance ceramics.

The **Museo Archeologico Oliveriano** presents historical displays from Roman remains to Iron Age artefacts from the necropolis of nearby Novilara.

The best of the town's churches is **Sant'Agostino** on Corso XI Settembre, remark-able for its superb choir stalls. Each is an intricate patchwork of inlaid landscapes and narrative scenes.

Pèsaro is also a point of musical pilgrimage. In 1792 the composer Gioachino Rossini was born here. His home, **Casa Rossini**, contains memorabilia, while his piano and some original manuscripts ie in the **Conservatorio Rossini**. His operas are performed in the **Teatro Rossini** n Piazza Lazzarini during the annual August music festival.

🏛 **Musei Civici**
Piazza Mosca 29. 🔲 0721-312 13.
🔘 Tue–Sun (Oct–Mar: am only). 🖼
🏛 **Museo Archeologico Oliveriano**
Via Mazza 97. 🔲 0721-333 44.
🔘 Mon–Sat am. 🌑 public hols. 🖼
🏛 **Casa Rossini**
Via Rossini 34. 🔲 0721-38 73 57.
🔘 Tue–Sun (Oct–Mar: am only). 🖼
🏛 **Conservatorio Rossini**
Piazza Olivieri 5. 🔲 0721-336 70.
🔘 Mon–Sat am. 🌑 public hols.

Fano ④

Pèsaro. 🏛 53,000. 🚊 🚌 🛳
🛈 Via Cesare Battisti 10 (0721-80 35 34). 🖼 Wed & Sat.

ANCIENT FANO stands out from the string of beach resorts south of Pèsaro, thanks to its fine old centre and historic monuments. Named after Fanum Fortunae, a pagan temple to the goddess Fortuna, it became the terminus of the Via Flaminia (an important consular road from Rome) and the largest Roman colony on the Adriatic coast. The **Arco d'Augusto** (AD 2), on Via Arco d'Augusto, is Fano's most significant ancient monument, having narrowly escaped destruction at the hands of Federico da Montefeltro in 1463. He destroyed its upper section while besieging the town as a papal *condottiere*.

The 16th-century **Fontana della Fortuna**, in Piazza XX Settembre, is dedicated to the goddess Fortuna. The large **Palazzo Malatesta** that rises up to its rear was built around 1420 and enlarged in 1544 for Fano's rulers, the Rimini-based Malatesta family. Inside are the small **Museo Civico** and the **Pinacoteca Malatestiana**, with works by Guercino, Guido Reni and the Venetian artist, Michele Giambono.

🏛 **Museo Civico and Pinacoteca Malatestiana**
Piazza XX Settembre. 🔲 0721-82 83 62. 🔘 Tue–Sun (Oct–Mar: Tue–Sun am). 🌑 1 Jan, Easter, 10 Jul, 25, 26 Dec. 🖼

Entrance to the Palazzo Ducale in Urbania

Urbino ⑤

See pp360–61.

Urbania ⑥

Pèsaro. 🏛 7,200. 🚌 🛈 Corso Vittorio Emanuele 27 (0722-31 72 11). 🖼 Thu.

URBANIA, WITH ITS elegant arcaded centre, takes its name from Pope Urban VIII (1623–44), who entertained the notion of converting the old medieval village known as Castel Durante into a model Renaissance town.

Its chief attraction is a monument from an earlier age, the huge **Palazzo Ducale**, built by the dukes of Montefeltro as one of several residential alternatives to the Palazzo Ducale in nearby Urbino. It was begun in the 13th century, and then rebuilt in the 15th and 16th centuries. Beautifully situated alongside the Metauro river, it houses a small art gallery, a modest museum, old maps and globes, and the remnants of Duke Federico's famous library.

🏛 **Palazzo Ducale**
Palazzo Ducale. 🔲 0722-31 99 85.
🔘 Tue–Sat (Oct–Mar: ask at library).
🌑 public hols. 🖼

Fontana della Fortuna in Fano

Urbino: Palazzo Ducale

I TALY'S MOST BEAUTIFUL Renaissance palace was built for Duke Federico da Montefeltro, the ruler of Urbino between 1444 and 1482, known for his prowess as a mercenary soldier. Federico was a man of the arts as well as a soldier, and his palace, with its library, paintings and refined architecture, is a monument to the high artistic and intellectual ideals of the Renaissance.

★ The Flagellation by Piero della Francesca
Dramatic perspective creates an unsettling effect in this 15th-century painting of the scourging of Christ.

Towers attributed to Laurana

The palace rising above Urbino

The simple east side of the palace was designed by Maso di Bartolomeo before 1460.

Cortile d'Onore
This early Renaissance courtyard was designed by the Dalmatian-born artist Luciano Laurana (1420–79).

M entra

The Libr
was one
Europe's
in its day

Ideal City
Attributed to Luciano Laurana, this 15th-century painting of an imaginary Renaissance city is notable for its measured perspective and lack of people.

VISITORS' CHECKLIST

Piazza Duca Federico. ☎ 0722-
27 60. 🚌 Piazza del Mercatale.
🕐 Jul–Sep: 9am–2pm Mon,
9am–7pm Tue–Sat, 9am–1pm
Sun; Oct–Jun: 9am–2pm Mon–
Sat, 9am–1pm Sun (last adm: 30
mins before closing). ● 1 Jan,
1 May, 25 Dec. 🎫 📷 ♿

★ **Studiolo**
*The former study of Federico
da Montefeltro is decorated with
intarsia (inlaid wood), some
of it designed by Botticelli.*

**Duke Federico by
Pedro Berruguete**
*The duke, shown
here with his son in
this 15th-century
painting, was always
portrayed in left
profile after an
injury to his face.*

**Hanging
garden**

The rooms in
this wing are
known as the
Appartamento
della Duchessa.

★ **La Muta by Raphael**
The Mute Woman *may be a
portrait of Maddalena Doni,
a Florentine noblewoman.*

STAR EXHIBITS

★ **The Flagellation by
Piero della Francesca**

★ **La Muta by Raphael**

★ **Studiolo**

Urbino ❺

Pèsaro. 👥 16,000. 🚌 ℹ *Via
Puccinotti 35 (0722-24 41).* 🛒 *Sat.*

AMID URBINO'S TANGLE of
medieval and Renaissance
streets stands the Neo-Classical
Duomo, on Piazza Federico,
built in 1789. Of special interest
is the painting of the *Last
Supper* by Federico Barocci
(c.1535–1612). The
Museo Diocesano
contains a collection
of ceramics, glass and
religious artefacts.
Urbino's famous son,
the painter Raphael
(1483–1520), lived in
the **Casa Natale di
Raffaello**. It has a
highly evocative
interior, especially the
kitchen and courtyard.
In Via Barocci stands
the medieval **Oratorio
di San Giuseppe**,
known for its *presepio*
(Christmas crib), and
the 14th-century
**Oratorio di San
Giovanni Battista**,
whose interior is
smothered in 15th-
century frescoes of the
Crucifixion and the *Life of John
the Baptist* by Giacomo and
Lorenzo Salimbeni.
The 15th-century **Fortezza
dell'Albornoz** on Viale Bruno
Buozzi is the defensive focus of
Urbino's surviving 16th-century
walls and bastions.

🏛 **Museo Diocesano**
Piazza Pascoli 2. ☎ 0722-28 50.
🕐 Mon–Sat (Oct–Mar: ask Duomo
custodian). 🎫 ♿
🏠 **Casa Natale di Raffaello**
Via di Raffaello 57. ☎ 0722-32 01 05.
🕐 daily (Sun am only). ● 1 Jan,
25 Dec. 🎫

**A street scene in the medieval
town of Urbino**

Fresh seafood and fishing boats in the harbour at Ancona

Grotte di Frasassi ❼

Ancona. 📞 0732-97 30 39. 🚌
🚆 San Vittore di Genga. 🕐 for guided tours only (1 hr 10 mins). 🔴 1 Jan, 4, 25 Dec. 🈳

SOME OF EUROPE's largest publicly accessible caverns lie in the cave network gouged out by the River Sentino south-west of Jesi. Of the vast network of 18 km (11 miles), an area of about 1,000 m (3,281 ft) is open to the public. The colossal **Grotta del Vento** is large enough to contain Milan cathedral – its ceiling extends to a height of 240 m (787 ft). This cavern has been used for a range of experiments, from sensory deprivation to an exploration of the social consequences of leaving a group of people alone in its depths for long periods.

Jesi ❽

Ancona. 👥 41,000. 🚆 🚌
🅸 Piazza della Repubblica 11 (0731-597 88). 🛍 Wed & Sat.

PERCHED ON A LONG, rocky ridge, Jesi lies in the heart of the verdant hill country where Verdicchio is produced. A crisp, white wine renowned for centuries, Verdicchio is bottled in unique containers – glass models of the terracotta amphorae once used to export the wine to ancient Greece. No wine is made in Jesi itself, but there are many vineyards in the surrounding countryside.

Housed in the town's 18th-century Palazzo Pianetti is the **Pinacoteca e Musei Civici**,

which contains fine late-period paintings by Lorenzo Lotto. Almost as alluring as the gallery's paintings, however, is the great central salon – an orgy of Rococo decoration that once formed the centrepiece of the Palazzo Pianetti. The nearby **Palazzo della Signoria** features an interesting little collection of archaeological finds, while beyond the old town's Renaissance walls stands the 14th-century church of **San Marco**, known for its collection of well-preserved Giottesque frescoes.

🏛 **Pinacoteca e Musei Civici**
Via XV Settembre. 📞 0731-53 83 43.
🕐 Tue–Sun. 🈳
🏛 **Palazzo della Signoria**
Piazza Colocci. 📞 0731-53 83 45.
🕐 Mon–Sat. 🔴 public hols.

Ancona ❾

👥 105,000. ✈ 🚆 🚌 🚢
🅸 Via Thaon de Revel 4 (071-349 38). 🛍 Tue & Fri.

THE CAPITAL OF LE MARCHE and its largest port, Ancona dates back to at least the 5th century BC, when it was settled by Greek exiles from Siracusa. Its name derives from *ankon* (Greek for elbow), a reference to the rocky spur that juts into the sea to form the town's fine natural harbour.

Heavy bombing during World War II, however, destroyed much of the medieval town. The 15th-century **Loggia dei Mercanti** (merchants' exchange) on Via della Loggia survives as a monument to the town's medieval heyday.

Just north of the loggia is the Romanesque church of **Santa Maria della Piazza**, with a lovely façade. The nearby **Pinacoteca Comunale F Podesti e Galleria d'Arte Moderna** includes canvases by Titian, Lorenzo Lotto and Carlo Crivelli, among others. In the **Museo Archeologico Nazionale delle Marche**, the town's best museum, there are displays of Greek, Gallic and Roman art and artefacts. The **Arco di Traiano**, by the harbour, was erected in AD 115 and is one of Italy's better preserved Roman arches.

An impressive cavern in the cave system of the Grotte di Frasassi

The beach at the village of Sirolo on the Conero Peninsula

🏛 Pinacoteca Comunale F Podesti e Galleria d'Arte Moderna

Via Pizzecolli 17. 📞 071-222 50 45.
☐ daily. ⬤ public hols. 🎫 🚻

🏛 Museo Archeologico Nazionale delle Marche

Palazzo Ferretti, Via Ferretti 6. 📞 071-207 53 90. ☐ daily (Oct–May: daily am). ⬤ 1 Jan, 25 Dec. 🎫 🚻

Conero Peninsula ⑩

Ancona. 🚉 🚌 Ancona.
🚌 from Ancona to Sirolo or Numana. 🛈 Via Thaon de Revel 4, Ancona (071-332 49).

THE BEAUTIFUL cliff-edged Conero Peninsula is the only natural feature to disturb the almost unbroken line of beaches along the coast of Le Marche. Easily accessible from Ancona to the north, it is a semi-wild area known for its scenery, its wines (notably Rosso del Conero) and for a collection of coves, beaches and picturesque little resorts.

The best of these resorts is **Portonovo**, above whose beach stands **Santa Maria di Portonovo**, a pretty 11th-century Romanesque church mentioned by Dante in Canto XXI of *Paradiso*. The villages of **Sirolo** and **Numana** are busier and more commercialized, but you can escape the summer crowds by hiking the flower-swathed slopes of Monte Conero, which stands at 572 m (1,877 ft), or by taking a boat trip to the smaller beaches beyond the resorts.

Loreto ⑪

Ancona. 🚶 11,000. 🚉 🚌 🛈 Via Solari 3 (071-97 02 76). 🛒 Fri.

LEGEND HAS IT that in 1294 the house of the Virgin Mary (**Santa Casa**) miraculously uprooted itself from the Holy Land and was brought by angels to a laurel grove *(loreto)* south of Ancona. Each year three million pilgrims visit the

Santa Casa in Loreto

Santa Casa in Loreto and its **Basilica**. Begun in 1468, the basilica was designed and built in part by Renaissance architects Bramante, Sansovino and Giuliano da Sangallo. Its paintings include works by Luca Signorelli. The **Museo-Pinacoteca** has 16th-century paintings by Lorenzo Lotto.

✝ Basilica and Santa Casa

Piazza Santuario. 📞 071-97 01 08.
☐ daily. 🚻

🏛 Museo-Pinacoteca

Palazzo Apostolico. 📞 071-97 77 59.
☐ Tue–Sun daily. 🎫

Ascoli Piceno ⑫

🚶 53,000. 🚌 🛈 Piazza del Popolo (0736-25 52 50). 🛒 Wed & Sat.

THIS ALLURING TOWN takes its name from the Piceni, a tribe eventually conquered by the Romans in 89 BC. The gridiron plan of Roman Asculum Picenum is visible in

the streets today, but it is the town's medieval heritage that attracts most visitors.

The enchanting **Piazza del Popolo** is dominated by the 13th-century **Palazzo dei Capitani del Popolo**, whose façade was designed by Cola dell'Amatrice, and the church of **San Francesco**, a large and faintly austere Gothic ensemble built between 1262 and 1549.

Via del Trivio leads north to a medieval district overlooking the River Tronto. Along Via Cairoli lies the 13th-century Dominican church of **San Pietro Martire**. Opposite is the church of **Santi Vincenzo e Anastasio** (11th century), with an ancient crypt built over a spring said to cure leprosy.

Around Piazza dell'Arringo is the 12th-century **Duomo**, spoiled by a Baroque overlay. Its Cappella del Sacramento contains a polyptych by the 15th-century painter, Carlo Crivelli. The **Pinacoteca Civica** has more works by Crivelli and by Guido Reni, Titian and Alemanno. The **Museo Archeologico** contains Roman, Piceni and Lombard artefacts.

🏛 Pinacoteca Civica

Palazzo Comunale, Piazza Arringo.
📞 0736-29 82 13. ☐ Mon–Sun.
⬤ public hols. 🎫 🚻

🏛 Museo Archeologico

Palazzo Panighi, Piazza Arringo.
📞 0736-25 35 62. ☐ Tue–Sun (Apr–Oct: Mon pm also). ⬤ 1 Jan, 1 May, 25 Dec. 🎫 🚻

A view of the medieval town of Ascoli Piceno

ROME AND LAZIO

Rome and Lazio at a Glance

THE FIRST SETTLEMENTS IN THE REGION can be traced back to the early Etruscan civilization in northern Lazio. Rome grew to rule a vast empire and, as the empire began to divide, the region became the centre of the Christian world. Artists and architects flocked to work for the popes and their families, notably in the Renaissance and Baroque periods when some magnificent architectural works were created. The legacy of this uninterrupted history can be seen all over the city and the surrounding area.

St Peter's, *with its majestic dome by Michelangelo, is a magnificent and sumptuous 16th-century basilica (see pp408–9).*

Piazza Navona, *flanked by cafés, contains three Baroque fountains, including the colossal Fontana dei Quattro Fiumi, one of Bernini's finest works* (see p389).

St Peter's

PIAZZA
NAVONA
(See pp386–9)

Fontana dei Quattro Fiumi

THE VATICAN
AND TRASTEVERE
(See pp404–19)

Santa Maria in Trastevere, *probably the first Christian church in Rome, holds some remarkable mosaics such as this detail from Cavallini's Life of the Virgin which dates from 1291* (see p418).

Santa Maria in Trastevere

LAZIO
(See pp444–55)

Cerveteri tombs

ROME
(See main map)

0 kilometres   15

0 miles   10

Cerveteri *is one of the many necropoli left by the Etruscan civilization in northern Lazio. The larger tumulus tombs often contained frescoes and utensils useful for the afterlife (see p450).*

◁ **Bernini's allegorical Fountain of the Four Rivers at the centre of Piazza Navona**

The Pantheon, *built between AD 118–125, is a marvel of Roman engineering with its huge dome hidden behind the Classical portico (see p394).*

SEE ALSO

• ***Where to Stay*** pp565–9

• ***Where to Eat*** pp599–602

NORTHEAST ROME
(See pp396–403)

Santa Maria Maggiore*'s richly decorated interior blends different architectural styles, such as this baldacchino from the 18th century (see p403).*

Santa Maria Maggiore

THE ANCIENT CENTRE
(See pp372–85)

Pantheon

Capitoline Museums

Colosseum

San Giovanni in Laterano

AVENTINE AND LATERAN
(See pp420–27)

San Giovanni in Laterano*, the Cathedral of Rome, incorporates the elaborate Corsini Chapel built in the 1730s (see p426).*

The Capitoline Museums *have held treasures of the Classical world since the Renaissance, including this colossal 4th century head of Constantine (see pp376–7).*

| 0 metres | | 750 |
| 0 yards | | 750 |

The Colosseum *was constructed in AD 80 by Emperor Vespasian. His aim was to gain popularity by staging deadly gladiatorial combats and wild animal fights for public viewing (see p383).*

Regional Food: Rome and Lazio

THE TRADITIONAL *cucina romanesca* has always relied on fresh seasonal produce from the nearby countryside bought in the local markets. Mushrooms, in autumn, and artichokes, in spring, are served in dozens of different ways, and the *misticanza*, a fresh mix of salad leaves including the peppery *rughetta* (rocket) and *puntarelle* (curly endive shoots), is also delicious when it is in season in the summer months. Many of the genuinely Roman dishes are highly seasoned with onions, garlic, rosemary, sage and bay leaves. The typical Roman meat dish, based on the so-called *quinto quarto* (fifth quarter) – head, tail, trotters and so on – is flavoured with olive oil, herbs, *pancetta* (bacon) and *guanciale* (pigs' cheek) and is a culinary delight. *Pecorino*, a tangy sheep's milk cheese, is often sprinkled onto dishes as seasoning and the blander *ricotta* is a filling for pizzas as well as the Roman dessert *torta di ricotta*.

Sage leaves

Supplì di Riso *are fried rice croquettes stuffed with mozzarella. They are typically Roman and make an excellent snack.*

Filetti di Baccalà, *deep-fried cod fillets which were originally a Jewish speciality, have become a feature of Roman cuisine.*

Batter-fried artichoke hearts

Batter-fried courgette flowers

An antipasto *starts the meal and is usually a selection of appetizers based on the vegetables that are in season. The vegetables may be fresh, grilled or preserved in aromatic oils or vinegar. Artichoke hearts and courgette flowers are excellent in spring, and are used in a variety of dishes, including the fritto misto,* a selection of local ingredients fried in batter.

Gnocchi alla Romana, *small potato or semolina dumplings, can be eaten with tomato sauce or just with butter.*

Risotto alla Romana *is a rice dish made with a sauce of liver, sweetbreads and Marsala, a fortified wine from Sicily.*

Bucatini all'Amatriciana *is hollow spaghetti-like pasta with bacon, tomatoes and onion sprinkled with pecorino cheese.*

Spaghetti alla Carbonara, *devised in Rome, is made with bacon, eggs, Parmesan cheese and, if desired, black pepper.*

Coda alla Vaccinara is a traditional Roman dish made from braised oxtail served with herbs and a tomato sauce.

Torta di Ricotta, a popular dessert from Rome, is a delicious cheesecake filled with ricotta, Marsala and lemon.

Saltimbocca alla Romana is a tasty dish of veal with ham and sage. It can also be served rolled and skewered.

Fave al Guanciale are young spring broad beans, simmered in olive oil with pigs' cheek (guanciale) and onion.

WHAT TO DRINK IN ROME AND LAZIO

Vines thrive in the warm climate and fertile land of Lazio, keeping up the wine-producing tradition that was started around the hills of Rome over 2,000 years ago by the ancient Romans. Today, wine is usually drunk with meals as a matter of course and the region offers abundant supplies of inexpensive dry white wine for the city's restaurants and cafés. Of local bottled white wines, Frascati is the best known, but Castelli Romani, Marino, Colli Albani and Velletri are very similar in style. All are made from one grape variety, the Trebbiano, though better quality versions contain a dash of Malvasia for perfume and flavour. Local red wine is rarer and most reds come from other parts of Italy. As well as the usual range of digestives and apéritifs, such as Campari, beer is also widely available and the popular Italian lager is Nastro Azzurro. Fruit juices are also good and bars squeeze fresh orange juice *(spremuta)*. Rome's drinking water, another debt to the ancient Romans, is particularly good, fresh and sweet, and in abundant supply.

Frascati, the best known local white

Torre Ercolana, one of the few red wines produced in Lazio, is made in small quantities and generally regarded as one of the region's best wines. It is made from both the local Cesanese grapes and the more robust Cabernet, and should be kept to age for at least five years.

Drinking water in Rome, unlike many other Mediterranean cities, is excellent. The city benefits from a constant supply of fresh drinking water, piped down from the hills through a system of pipes and aqueducts that has changed very little since ancient Roman times. At regular intervals throughout the city, ornate fountains pump delicious fresh water for general use as well as for drinking. Only if there is a sign saying acqua non potabile is the water not safe to drink.

One of Rome's many fresh water drinking fountains

Coffee is almost more important to Roman life than wine. Take espresso for a shot of neat strong black coffee at any time of the day, sit with a milky cappuccino for breakfast or mid-afternoon, or take a caffelatte in a glass for extra milk.

Espresso   **Cappuccino**   **Caffelatte**

Understanding Architecture in Rome and Lazio

THE ARCHITECTURE of Imperial Rome, a combination of Etruscan and Classical Greek styles, gradually developed new and uniquely Roman forms based on the arch, the vault and the dome. During the early Christian period simple, rectangular basilicas were built, forms which by the 12th century had been incorporated into the stark Romanesque style. The Renaissance, inspired by the example of Florence, saw a return to Classical ideals of simplicity and harmonious proportions, though it was to be in the flamboyance of the 17th-century Baroque that Rome once again found great architectural expression.

The extravagant Baroque style of the Fontana di Trevi, Rome

FROM ETRUSCAN TO CLASSICAL ROME

The Podium made the temple more prominent.

The arch became a feature of Roman architecture.

A portico was a porch with columns.

Reliefs were scavenged from earlier monuments.

Three naves divided the interior of the basilica.

***Etruscan temples**, based on Greek models, inspired early Roman architecture. A front portico was the only entrance.*

***The Arch of Constantine** (AD 315) is typical of triumphant Imperial Roman architecture (see p379). It stands at a colossal 25 m (82 ft).*

***Early Christian basilicas** (4th century) were based on a rectangular floorplan.*

FROM RENAISSANCE TO BAROQUE

Doric columns recall Classical architecture.

Bramante adopted the circular form of ancient temples.

Rustication, massive blocks divided by deep joints, was used for palazzi.

Ionic pilasters lend an air of elegance to the imposing upper storeys.

The elliptical staircase was a typical feature of Mannerist houses.

***The Tempietto** at San Pietro in Montorio, Rome (1502) is a model of Renaissance architecture: simple and perfectly proportioned (see p419).*

***Palazzo Farnese** at Caprarola, a pentagonal build- ing completed in 1575 (see p449), combines some Mannerist tricks of architecture with the strict geometric proportions characteristic of the Renaissance.*

WHERE TO SEE THE ARCHITECTURE

A walk through the back streets of the centre of Rome will reveal masterpieces of virtually every architectural age. The most ancient treasures are seven obelisks stolen from Egypt. One stands on the back of Bernini's elephant *(see p394)*. Highlights from Ancient Rome include triumphal arches and temples such as the Pantheon *(see p394)*. Romanesque elements survive in the church of San Clemente *(see p425)*, while the Renaissance finds expression in the dome of St Peter's *(see pp408–9)*. Magnificent Baroque treasures dot the entire city, in particular flamboyant fountains that adorn the squares. Outside the city the outstanding sights are the late Renaissance villas such as Caprarola *(see p449)*.

Part of Bernini's elephant supporting an ancient Egyptian obelisk

Coffering reduces the weight of the dome.

The oculus, a hole at the top of the dome, provides the only light.

The portico dates from an earlier temple.

The Pantheon (see p394) *is one of the cardinal buildings of late Roman architecture. Completed in AD 125, it reveals how the form of the Greek temple was elaborated upon to create a masterpiece of perfect proportions.*

Doric columns had straight capitals.

Corinthian capitals were decorated with acanthus leaves.

Ionic columns had scrolled capitals.

The orders *of Classical architecture were building styles based on ancient Greek models, identified by the column capitals.*

Columns around the altar draw attention away from the prominent lateral axis.

A concave portico reflects the oval body of the church.

Engaged pillars replace the flat pilasters of the Renaissance.

Deep recesses create complex effects of light and shade.

Two superimposed equilateral triangles form the complex hexagonal floorplan.

The oval floorplan *of the Baroque Sant'Andrea al Quirinale (see p401) makes ingenious use of restricted space.*

The Gesù *façade (1584) epitomizes Counter Reformation architecture and has been imitated throughout the Catholic world (see p393).*

Sant'Ivo alla Sapienza's *floorplan (1642) favoured grandiose design over Classical form (see p390).*

THE ANCIENT CENTRE

THE CAPITOL, the southern summit of the Capitoline Hill, was the symbolic centre of the Roman world and home to the city's three most important temples. These were dedicated to the god Jupiter Optimus Maximus, protector of Rome, Minerva, goddess of wisdom and war, and Juno Moneta, a guardian goddess. Below the Capitol lies the Forum, once the focus of political, social, legal and commercial life; the Imperial Fora, built when Rome's population grew; and the Colosseum, the centre of entertainment. Overlooking the Forum is the Palatine Hill, where Romulus is said to have founded Rome in the 8th century BC, and emperors lived for over 400 years.

Capitoline Wolf with Romulus and Remus

SIGHTS AT A GLANCE

Churches
Santa Maria in Aracoeli ❸

Museums and Galleries
Capitoline Museums pp376–7 ❶

Historic Piazzas
Piazza del Campidoglio ❷

Ancient Sites and Buildings
Arch of Constantine ❿

Colosseum ❾
Forum of Augustus ❺
Forum of Caesar ❼
Mamertine Prison ❻
Palatine pp384–5 ⓫
Roman Forum pp380–81 ❽
Trajan's Forum and Markets ❹

GETTING THERE
The Capitoline is in walking distance of Piazza Venezia, the hub of the city bus routes, while the Forum, Colosseum and Palatine are close to Metro Colosseo. Buses 81, 87 and 186 link Piazza Venezia and the Colosseum with Corso Rinascimento, in the heart of the *centro storico*.

0 metres 250
0 yards 250

KEY

Street-by-Street: The Capitoline Hill *pp374–5*

Ⓜ Metro station

◁ **View of the Colosseum rising behind the Forum**

Street-by-Street: The Capitoline Hill

THE CAPITOL, citadel of ancient Rome, was designed by Michelangelo in the 16th century. He was responsible for the trapezoid Piazza del Campidoglio as well as the Cordonata, the broad flight of steps leading up to it. The piazza is flanked by Palazzo Nuovo and Palazzo dei Conservatori, housing the Capitoline Museums, with their fine collections of sculpture and paintings. It is also well worth walking behind the museums to the Tarpeian Rock, for a fine view of the Forum lying below.

The Victor Emmanuel Monument was begun in 1885 and inaugurated in 1911 in honour of Victor Emmanuel II, the first king of unified Italy.

San Marco, dedicated to the patron saint of Venice, has splendid 9th-century mosaics in the apse.

PIAZZA VENEZIA

Palazzo Venezia, once the home of Mussolini, now holds a museum of fine and decorative arts. Exhibits include this medieval gilt and enamel angel.

The Aracoeli Staircase was completed in 1348 to commemorate the end of the plague.

VIA DEL TEATRO DI MARCELLO

The Cordonata is presided over by the colossal statues of Castor and Pollux.

★ Capitoline Museums
The collections of art and ancient sculpture include this statue of the Emperor Marcus Aurelius which used to stand in the centre of the piazza ❶

STAR SIGHT

★ Capitoline Museums

KEY

– – – Suggested route

| 0 metres | 75 |
| 0 yards | 75 |

Santa Maria in Aracoeli
The brick façade hides treasures such as this 15th-century fresco of the Funeral of San Bernardino *by Pinturicchio* ❸

LOCATOR MAP
See Rome Street Finder map 3

Palazzo Nuovo
was made into a public museum in 1734.

Palazzo Senatorio, the splendid Renaissance seat of the city government, is built on the ruins of the ancient Tabularium.

Piazza del Campidoglio
Michelangelo designed the geometric paving and the façades of the buildings ❷

Palazzo dei Conservatori

The Temple of Jupiter, represented on this coin, was dedicated to Jupiter Optimus Maximus, the most important of the Roman gods. He was believed to have the power to protect or destroy the city.

The Tarpeian Rock is a cliff from which traitors were believed to have been thrown to their death in ancient Rome.

Steps to the Capitoline

Capitoline Museums ❶

See pp376–7.

Piazza del Campidoglio ❷

Map 3 B5. 🚌 64, 65, 70, 75.

WHEN EMPEROR CHARLES V announced he was to visit Rome in 1536, Pope Paul III Farnese asked Michelangelo to give the Capitoline a face-lift. He redesigned the piazza, renovated the façades of its palaces and built a new stair-case, the Cordonata. This gently rising ramp is now crowned with the massive statues of Castor and Pollux.

Santa Maria in Aracoeli ❸

Piazza d'Aracoeli. **Map** 3 B5.
📞 06-679 81 55. 🚌 64, 65, 70, 75.
🕐 7am–noon, 3:30–6pm daily.

THIS CHURCH STANDS on the site of the Temple of Juno, and dates back at least to the 6th century. The church is famous today for its ornate gilded ceiling and a very fine series of frescoes by Pinturicchio, dating from the 1480s. They depict scenes from the life of San Bernardino of Siena. The miracle-working wooden *Santo Bambino* was an interesting attraction, but unfortunately it is still missing since being stolen in 1994.

The marble staircase and austere façade of Santa Maria in Aracoeli

Capitoline Museums: ❶
Palazzo Nuovo

A COLLECTION of Classical sculptures has been kept on the Capitoline Hill since Pope Sixtus IV donated a group of bronze sculptures to the city in 1471. Paintings as well as sculpture are now housed in two palaces designed by Michelangelo. The Palazzo Nuovo, first opened to the public in 1734 by Pope Clement XII, contains a fine selection of Greek and Roman sculptures.

LOCATOR MAP

Alexander Severus as Hunter
In this marble of the 3rd century AD, the emperor's pose is a pastiche of the mythical hero, Perseus, holding up the head of Medusa the Gorgon after he had killed her.

Discobolus
The twisted torso was part of a Greek statue of a discus thrower. An 18th-century sculptor turned him into a wounded warrior.

Mosaic of the Doves
This 1st-century AD naturalistic mosaic once decorated the floor of Hadrian's Villa at Tivoli (see p452).

Hall of the Philosophers
The hall contains Roman copies of portrait busts of Greek politicians, scientists and poets. These adorned the homes of wealthy Romans.

Courtyard

Main entrance

Stairs to ground floor

Stairs to first floor

Dying Galatian
Great compassion is conveyed in this Roman copy of a Greek work of the 3rd century BC.

KEY TO FLOORPLAN

☐ Ground floor
☐ First floor
☐ Second floor
☐ Non-exhibition space

Palazzo dei Conservatori

THE PALAZZO DEI CONSERVATORI was the seat of the city's magistrates during the late Middle Ages. Its frescoed halls are still used occasionally for political meetings and the ground floor houses the municipal registry office. While much of the palazzo is given over to sculpture, including fragments of a huge sculpture of Constantine, the art galleries on the second floor hold works by Veronese, Tintoretto, Caravaggio, Van Dyck and Titian.

VISITORS' CHECKLIST

Musei Capitolini, Piazza del Campidoglio. **Map** 3 B5.
06-67 10 20 71. 44, 64, 70, 110 & many other routes through Piazza Venezia.
9am–1:30pm Tue–Sat, 5–8pm Tue & Sat (Apr–Sep: 8–11pm Sat) 9am–1pm Sun (last adm: 30 mins before closing).
1 Jan, 29 Jun, 15 Aug, 25 Dec.
free last Sun of month.

St John the Baptist
Caravaggio's sensual portrait (1595–6) of the young saint caressing a sheep is a highly unorthodox image of Christ's forerunner.

Esquiline Venus
The 1st-century BC figure is thought by some scholars to be a portrait of Cleopatra.

Second-floor art gallery

Roman Garden

7

6

26

8

5

25

4

24 19

9

3

23

10

2

22

1

21

6

20

First floor

15

16

17

14

18

11

13

Courtyard

7

8

6

9

5

Stairs to first floor

1

11

10

2

3

4

The Rape of the Sabine Women
Pietro da Cortona glamorized the mass abduction of Sabine women by the Romans in this painting of 1629.

Spinario
This is a charming bronze sculpture from the 1st century BC of a boy trying to remove a thorn from his foot.

Stairs to ground floor

Main entrance

Trajan's Forum and Markets ❹

Map 3 B4. **Trajan's Forum**, Via dei Fori Imperiali. ● *to the public.* **Trajan's Markets**, Via IV Novembre. ◐ *9am–1pm Tue–Sat, 9am–12:30pm Sun (also Apr– Sep: 9am–6pm Thu & Sat).*

T RAJAN BEGAN to build his forum in AD 107 to commemorate his conquest of Dacia (present day Romania) after successful campaigns in AD 101–2 and 105–6. His new forum was the most ambitious yet, with a vast colonnaded open space centring on an equestrian statue of the emperor, a huge basilica, and two big libraries. Dominating the ruins today is **Trajan's Column**, which originally stood between the

Trajan's Column

two libraries. Spiralling up its 30 m (98 ft) high stem are minutely detailed scenes from the Dacian campaigns, beginning with the Romans preparing for war and ending with the Dacians being ousted from their homeland. The subtly modelled reliefs were designed to be seen from viewing platforms on the libraries, and are consequently difficult to interpret from ground level. If you want to examine the scenes in detail there are casts in the Museo della Civiltà Romana *(see p432).* The **market** complex, which is situated directly behind the forum, was begun slightly earlier. Like the forum it was probably designed by Apollodorus of Damascus, and was the

Via Biberatica, the main street through Trajan's Markets

ancient Roman equivalent of the modern shopping centre. There were around 150 shops selling everything from oriental silks and spices to fruit, fresh fish and flowers. It was also here that the *annone*, or corn dole, was distributed. This was a free ration of corn given to Roman men, a practice which was introduced in the Republic by politicians who wanted to buy votes and prevent unrest during periods of famine.

RECONSTRUCTION OF TRAJAN'S MARKETS

Cross vaulting

The Main Hall had 12 shops on two storeys. The corn ration was distributed from the upper floor.

Amphorae, used for storing wine and oil, were discovered on the upper corridor.

The terrace has a good view of Trajan's Forum.

Via Biberatica was probably lined with shops selling pepper and spices.

Staircase

The shops on the ground floor were cool, and probably sold vegetables, fruit and flowers.

Large hall with semi-domed ceiling

Forum of Augustus ❺

Piazza del Grillo 1. **Map** 3 B5.
🕻 06-679 00 48. 🚌 81, 85, 87, 186. ⬜ by appt only.

THE FORUM of Augustus, which once stretched from a high wall at the foot of sleazy Suburra to the edge of Caesar's Forum, was built to celebrate Augustus's victory in 41 BC over Brutus and Cassius, the assassins of Julius Caesar. As a consequence the temple in its centre was dedicated to Mars the Avenger. The temple, with its cracked steps and four Corinthian columns, is easily identified. Originally it had a statue of Mars that looked very like Augustus, but in case anyone failed to notice the resemblance, a colossal statue of the emperor himself was placed against the wall of the Suburra quarter.

19th-century engraving of the Mamertine Prison

Mamertine Prison ❻

Clivo Argentario 1. **Map** 3 B5.
🕻 06-679 29 02. 🚌 81, 85, 87, 186. ⬜ Apr–Sep: 9am–noon, 2:30–6pm daily; Oct–Mar: 9am–noon, 2–5pm daily. **Donation.** 📷

BELOW THE 16th-century church of San Giuseppe dei Falegnami is a dank dungeon in which, according to Christian legend, St Peter and St Paul were imprisoned. They are said to have caused

Podium of the Temple of Mars the Avenger, Forum of Augustus

a spring to bubble up into the cell, and to have used the water to baptize two prison guards. The prison was in an old cistern with access to the city's main sewer (the Cloaca Maxima). The lower cell was used for executions, and corpses were thrown into the sewer. However, the inmates, who received no food, often died of starvation.

Forum of Caesar ❼

Via del Carcere Tulliano. **Map** 3 B5.
🕻 06-67 10 30 65. 🚌 81, 85, 87, 186. ⬜ by appt only.

THE FIRST of Rome's Imperial fora was built by Julius Caesar to relieve congestion in the Roman Forum when Rome's population boomed. He spent a fortune – most of it booty from his recent conquest of Gaul – buying up and demolishing houses on the site. Pride of place went to a temple dedicated in 46 BC to Venus Genetrix (Venus the Ancestor) as Caesar claimed to be descended from the goddess. The temple contained statues of Caesar and Cleopatra as well as of Venus, but all that remains today is a platform and three Corinthian columns. The forum was once enclosed by a double colonnade, under which was sheltered a row of shops. However, this burnt down in AD 80 and was rebuilt by Domitian and Trajan. The latter also added the

Basilica Argentaria – which became an important financial exchange – as well as shops and a heated public lavatory.

Roman Forum ❽

See pp380–81.

Colosseum ❾

See p383.

Arch of Constantine ❿

Between Via di San Gregorio and Piazza del Colosseo. **Map** 7 A1.
🚌 81, 85, 87. 🚋 13. Ⓜ Colosseo.

THIS TRIUMPHAL ARCH is one of Imperial Rome's last monuments, built in AD 315, a few years before Constantine moved the capital of the Empire to Byzantium. It was built to celebrate Constantine's victory in AD 312 over his co-emperor Maxentius at the Battle of the Milvian Bridge. Constantine attributed the victory to a dream in which he was told to mark his men's shields with *chi-rho*, the first two Greek letters of Christ's name. Christian tradition prefers a more dramatic version in which the emperor has a vision of the Cross, mid-battle. There is, however, nothing Christian about the arch: most of the reliefs were taken from earlier pagan monuments.

Palatine ⓫

See pp384–5.

The north side of the Arch of Constantine

Roman Forum ⑧

IN THE EARLY REPUBLIC, the Forum was a chaotic place, with food stalls and brothels as well as temples and the Senate House. By the 2nd century BC it was decided that Rome required a more salubrious centre, and the food stores were replaced by business centres and law courts. The Forum remained the ceremonial centre of the city under the Empire, with emperors renovating old buildings and erecting new temples and monuments.

Arch of Septimius Severus
This triumphal arch was erected in AD 203, the 10th anniversary of Emperor Septimius Severus' accession.

The Temple of Antoninus and Faustina is now incorporated into the church of San Lorenzo in Miranda

Temple of Saturn

The Rostra was the orator's tribune from which speeches were made.

The Curia, or ancient Roman Senate House, has been reconstructed.

Basilica Julia
Named after Julius Caesar, who began its construction in 54 BC, this was the seat of the civil magistrates court.

Basilica Aemilia was a meeting hall for business and money exchange.

Temple of Vesta

Temple of Castor and Pollux
Although there has been a temple here since the 5th century BC, the columns and elaborate cornice date from AD 6 when the temple was rebuilt.

★ **House of the Vestal Virgins**
The priestesses who tended the sacred flame in the Temple of Vesta lived here. The house was a large rectangular building around a central garden.

0 metres   75
0 yards   75

★ **Basilica of Constantine**
The basilica's three vast barrel vaults are all that remain of the Forum's largest building. Like other basilicas, it was used for the administration of justice and conducting business.

The Temple of Romulus, now part of the church of Santi Cosma e Damiano which stands behind it, retains its original 4th-century bronze doors.

Arch of Titus
This arch was erected by Emperor Domitian in AD 81 to commemorate the sack of Jerusalem by his father Vespasian and brother Titus, 13 years earlier.

VIA DEI FORI IMPERIALI

VIA SACRA

Antiquarium Forense
This small museum contains finds from the Forum. Exhibits range from Iron Age burial urns to this frieze of Aeneas from the Basilica Aemilia.

The Temple of Venus and Rome was built in AD 135, and was largely designed by Hadrian.

VIA SACRA

Colosseum

Palatine

Santa Francesca Romana
The Romanesque bell tower of Santa Francesca Romana towers over one of a number of churches built among the ruins of the Forum.

THE VESTAL VIRGINS

The cult of Vesta, the goddess of fire, dates back to at least the 8th century BC. Romulus and Remus were allegedly born of the Vestal priestess Rhea and the god Mars. Six virgins kept the sacred flame of Vesta burning in her circular temple. The girls, who came from noble families, were selected when they were between six and ten years old, and served for 30 years. They had high status and financial security, but were buried alive if they lost their virginity and whipped by the high priest if the sacred flame died out. Although they were permitted to marry after finishing their service, few did so.

Honorary statue of a Vestal Virgin

Exploring the Roman Forum

To appreciate the layout of the Roman Forum before wandering through its confusing patchwork of ruined temples, triumphal arches and basilicas, it is best to view the whole area from the Capitoline Hill above. From there you can make out the more substantial ruins, and the course of the Via Sacra (Sacred Way), the route followed through the Forum by religious and triumphal processions making their way up to the Capitol to give thanks at the Temple of Jupiter *(see p375)*.

Corinthian columns of the Temple of Castor and Pollux

The Main Sights

The first building you come to on entering the Forum is the **Basilica Aemilia**. A rectangular hall built in 179 BC, it was a meeting place for moneylenders, businessmen and tax collectors. Although little more remains of it than a pastel marble pavement fringed with column stumps, you can still find splashes of verdigrised bronze, reputedly the remains of coins which melted when the Goths invaded Rome and burnt down the basilica in the 5th century.

Inside the Curia – the stark brick building next to the basilica – are the **Plutei of Trajan**, relief panels commissioned by either Trajan or Hadrian to decorate the Rostra, the public oratory platform. On one panel are piles of books holding tax records, which Trajan had destroyed in order to free citizens from debts. The **Arch of Septimius Severus** is the best preserved of the Forum's monuments. The marble relief panels depict the military triumphs of the emperor in Parthia (modern-day Iran and Iraq) and Arabia.

The **Temple of Saturn** was the focus of the annual Saturnalia celebrations, when, for up to a week in December, schools closed, slaves dined with their masters, presents were exchanged and a fair and market were held.

Soaring above the remains of the Basilica Julia are three delicately fluted columns and a finely carved slab of entablature taken from the **Temple of Castor and Pollux**. This striking relic is dedicated to the twin brothers of Helen of Troy, who were supposed to have appeared at the battle of Lake Regillus in 490 BC, aiding the Romans in their defeat of the Etruscans.

Restored section of Temple of Vesta

The elegant circular **Temple of Vesta** was one of ancient Rome's most sacred shrines and was dedicated to the goddess of the hearth. The flame, kept alive by the Vestal Virgins, symbolized the perpetuity of the state and its extinction prophesied doom for the city. The building was

partly reconstructed in 1930, but the circular form goes back to the Latin mud huts which originally occupied the site. Just behind is the **House of the Vestal Virgins**, the living quarters of the priestess and the Vestals. This enormous complex of 50 rooms was once annexed to the Temple. Best preserved are the rooms overlooking a pretty courtyard, ornamented with statues of Vestals, ponds of waterlilies and rose trees.

On the other side of the Forum lie the impressive remains of the **Basilica of Constantine**. It was begun in AD 306 by Maxentius, and is therefore also known as Basilica of Maxentius.

Constantine completed it after he defeated his rival at the battle of Milvio in AD 312. The stark remains of the huge arches and ceilings give an indication of the original scale and grandeur of the forum's public buildings. Three enormous coffered vaults remain, which originally measured up to 35 m (115 ft) and were faced with marble. The interior walls, which held niches for statues, were also covered with marble below and stucco above. Remains of a spiral staircase which once led to the roof can be found scattered on the ground.

The basilica's apse and hexagonal arches were often used as models by Renaissance architects striving to recreate a Classical symmetry and nobility in their work. They include Michelangelo, who allegedly studied the basilica's architecture when working on the dome of St Peter's.

Central courtyard of the House of the Vestal Virgins

Colosseum 🟑

Gladiator's shield

Rome's greatest amphitheatre was commissioned by Emperor Vespasian in AD 72. Deadly gladiatorial combats and wild animal fights were staged by emperors and wealthy citizens, largely to gain popularity. Slaughter was on a huge scale: at the inaugural games in AD 80, over 9,000 wild animals were killed. The Colosseum could hold up to 55,000 people, who were seated according to rank.

VISITORS' CHECKLIST

Piazza del Colosseo. **Map** 7 B1.
📞 06-700 42 61. 🚌 11, 27, 81, 110. 🚋 13. ◐ Apr–Sep: 9am–7pm Mon–Sat; Oct–Mar: 9am–3pm Thu–Mon, 9am–1pm Wed; 9am–1pm Sun all year.
● public hols. 🎫 for upper storey. 📷 ♿ limited.

Internal Corridors
These allowed the large and often unruly crowd to move freely and be seated quickly.

The Colossus of Nero
This gilt bronze statue from Nero's palace, over which the Colosseum was built, may have given the amphitheatre its name.

The Velarium, a huge sailcloth awning which sheltered spectators from the sun, was supported by poles on the upper storey.

Entry routes and stairs led to seats at the various levels. The emperor and consul had their own, separate entrances.

The arena floor covered a network of lifts and cages for wild animals.

Corinthian columns

Ionic columns

Doric columns

Entrances

Doric, Ionic and Corinthian Tiers
The tiers inspired many Renaissance architects, who also plundered the building, using its travertine to build palaces and part of St Peter's.

Roman Gladiators
These were originally soldiers in training. Their combat became a sport, and slaves, prisoners of war or criminals were forced to fight men or wild animals to the death.

Emperor Vespasian
He ordered the Colosseum to be built on the site of Nero's palace, to dissociate himself from the hated tyrant.

Palatine ⓫

THE PALATINE, once the residence of emperors and aristocrats, is the most pleasant of Rome's ancient sites. The ruins range from the simple house in which Augustus is thought to have lived, to the Domus Flavia and Domus Augustana, the public and private wings of a luxurious palace built by Domitian.

Statue of the Goddess Cybele

The Huts of Romulus, indicated by holes left by the supporting posts, were reputedly founded by Romulus in the 9th century BC.

Temple of Cybele, Goddess of fertility

The House of Augustus is thought to have been the public part of the emperor's modest home.

★ House of Livia
Many of the wall paintings have survived in the private quarters of the house where Augustus is believed to have lived with his wife Livia.

★ Domus Flavia
The courtyard of the Domus Flavia was lavishly paved with coloured marble. The Roman poets praised this villa as the most splendid.

Domus Augustana was the private home of the emperors.

STAR SIGHTS

★ Domus Flavia

★ House of Livia

Emperor Septimius Severus
During his reign (AD 193–211), he extended the Domus Augustana and built an impressive bath complex.

0 metres 75

0 yards 75

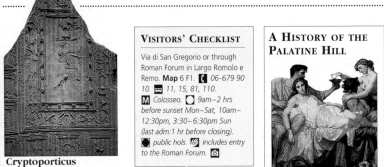

Cryptoporticus
This underground gallery, elaborately decorated with stuccoed walls, was built by Emperor Nero.

VISITORS' CHECKLIST

Via di San Gregorio or through Roman Forum in Largo Romolo e Remo. **Map** 6 F1. 06-679 90 10. 11, 15, 81, 110. Colosseo. 9am–2 hrs before sunset Mon–Sat, 10am–12:30pm, 3:30–6:30pm Sun (last adm:1 hr before closing). public hols. includes entry to the Roman Forum.

A HISTORY OF THE PALATINE HILL

Romans of the Decadence by Thomas Couture (1815–79)

The courtyard of the Domus Flavia was lined by Domitian with mirror-like marble, so he could spot would-be assassins.

The exedra of the stadium may have housed a balcony.

↗ **Forum entrance**

Stadium
Part of the Imperial palace, this enclosure may have been used by the emperors as a private garden.

The Palace of Septimius Severus
This extension of the Domus Augustana projected beyond the hillside, supported on giant arches.

The Founding of Rome
According to legend the twins Romulus and Remus were brought up on the Palatine by a wolf. Here Romulus, having killed his brother, is said to have founded the village that was destined to become Rome. Traces of mud huts dating back to the 8th century BC have been found on the hill, lending archaeological support to the legend.

The Republic
By the 1st century BC the Palatine was the most desirable address in Rome and home to the leading citizens of the Republic. Its residents, including the erotic poet Catullus and the orator Cicero, were notoriously indulgent, and their villas were magnificent dwellings with doors of ivory, floors of bronze and frescoed walls.

The Empire
Augustus was born on the Palatine in 63 BC, and lived there in a modest house after becoming emperor. The hill was therefore an obvious choice of abode for future emperors. Domitian's ambitious house, the Domus Flavia (1st century AD), and its private quarters, the Domus Augustana, remained the official residence of future emperors (who were referred to as *Augustus*) for more than 300 years.

AROUND PIAZZA NAVONA

Detail of an 18th-century street shrine

THE AREA around Piazza Navona, known as the *centro storico*, has been inhabited for at least 2,000 years. Piazza Navona stands above an ancient stadium; the Pantheon has been a temple since AD 27; and the Theatre of Marcellus in the Ghetto has been converted into exclusive flats. The area's heyday began in the 15th century, when the papacy returned to Rome. Throughout the Renaissance and Baroque eras princes, popes and cardinals settled here, as did the artists and artisans they commissioned to build and adorn lavish palaces, churches and fountains.

SIGHTS AT A GLANCE

Churches and Temples
Chiesa Nuova ⑥
Gesù ⑬
La Maddalena ⑳
San Luigi dei Francesi ③
Sant'Agostino ④
Santa Maria della Pace ⑤
Santa Maria sopra Minerva ⑮
Sant'Ignazio di Loyola ⑰
Sant'Ivo alla Sapienza ②

Museums and Galleries
Palazzo Doria Pamphilj ⑭

Ancient Sites and Buildings
Area Sacra di Largo Argentina ⑫
Pantheon ⑯

Historic Buildings
Palazzo della Cancelleria ⑦
Palazzo Farnese ⑨

Historic Piazzas and Areas
Campo de' Fiori ⑧
Ghetto and Tiber Island ⑪
Piazza Colonna ⑱
Piazza di Montecitorio ⑲
Piazza Navona ①

GETTING THERE

Corso Vittorio Emanuele II, Largo Argentina and Corso Rinascimento are main bus arteries, but only minibus 119 runs along the narrow streets of the *centro storico*.

KEY

▨ Street-by-Street: Around Piazza Navona *pp388–9*

▨ Street-by-Street: Around the Pantheon *pp392–3*

P Parking

| 0 metres | 250 |
| 0 yards | 250 |

◁ **Piazza Navona, with the Fontana del Moro (1653) and the 17th-century church of Sant'Agnese in Agone**

Street-by-Street: Around Piazza Navona

N O OTHER PIAZZA in Rome can rival the theatricality of Piazza Navona. The luxurious cafés are the social centre of the city, and day and night there is always something going on in the pedestrian area around the three flamboyant Baroque fountains. The Baroque is also represented in many of the area's churches. To discover an older Rome, walk along Via del Governo Vecchio to admire the façades of Renaissance buildings, browse in the fascinating antiques shops and lunch in one of the many trattorias.

The Torre dell'Orologio by Borromini (1648) formed part of the Oratorio dei Filippini.

Chiesa Nuova
This church was rebuilt in 1575 for the order founded by San Filippo Neri ⑥

The Vatican

VIA DEL CORALLO

VIA DEL GOVERNO VECCHIO

VIA DI PARIONE

At the Oratorio dei Filippini (1637) biblical stories were sung and the congregation responded with a chorus: the origin of the oratorio.

Via del Governo Vecchio preserves a large number of fine Renaissance houses.

CORSO VITTORIO EMANUELE II

PIAZZA DI PASQUINO

Santa Maria della Pace
This Renaissance church has frescoes of the Four Sibyls by Raphael and a refined courtyard by Bramante. The Baroque portico is by Pietro da Cortona ⑤

STAR SIGHTS

★ Piazza Navona

Pasquino is a 3rd-century BC Hellenistic statue of Menelaus. Romans have been hanging satirical verses at its feet since the 16th century.

Palazzo Braschi, a late 18th-century building designed by Cosimo Morelli, has a splendid balcony overlooking the piazza.

Fontana del Moro

Campo de' Fiori

Sant'Andrea della Valle, begun in 1591, has a flamboyant Baroque façade flanked by angels with outstretched wings by Ercole Ferrata. The church is the setting of the first act of Puccini's *Tosca*.

KEY

— — — Suggested route

0 metres   75

0 yards   75

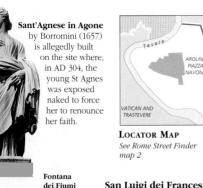

Sant'Agnese in Agone
by Borromini (1657)
is allegedly built
on the site where,
in AD 304, the
young St Agnes
was exposed
naked to force
her to renounce
her faith.

LOCATOR MAP
*See Rome Street Finder
map 2*

**Fontana
dei Fiumi**

San Luigi dei Francesi
*This church, which was
completed in 1589, is best
known for three paintings
by Caravaggio* ❸

Palazzo Madama,
the seat of the Italian
Senate, was originally built
for the Medici family in
the 16th century, on the
site of one of their banks.

Sant'Ivo alla Sapienza
*This tiny domed church is one
of Borromini's most original
creations. He worked on it
between 1642 and 1660* ❷

★ **Piazza Navona**
*The piazza is lined with palaces and
pavement cafés, and punctuated by
flamboyant Baroque fountains* ❶

**Largo
Argentina**

Piazza Navona ❶

Map 2 F3. 🚌 *46, 62, 64, 87.*

Rome's most beautiful
Baroque piazza follows
the shape of a 1st century AD
stadium built by Domitian,
which was used for athletic
contests (known as *agones*),
chariot races and other sports.
Traces of the stadium are still
visible below the church of
Sant'Agnese in Agone, which
is dedicated to a virgin
martyred on the site for
refusing to marry a pagan.

The piazza began to take
on its present appearance in
the 17th century, when Pope
Innocent X, whose family
palazzo was on the piazza,
commissioned a new
church, palace and
fountain. The fountain,
the Fontana dei Fiumi, is
Bernini's most magni-
ficent, with statues of the
four great rivers of the
world (the Nile, the Plate,
the Ganges and the
Danube) sitting on rocks
below an obelisk. Bernini
also designed the muscle-
bound Moor in the Fontana
del Moro, though the
present statue is a copy.
Until the 19th century, the
piazza was flooded in August
by stopping the fountain outlets. The rich would splash
around in carriages, while
street urchins paddled. Even
today the piazza remains the
social centre of the city.

**Symbolic figure of the River Nile
on Bernini's Fontana dei Fiumi**

Sant'Ivo alla Sapienza ❷

Corso del Rinascimento 40. **Map** 2 F4.
🚌 70, 81, 87, 90. ⭕ for mass
10am–noon Sun. ⬛ Jul–Aug. 📷 ♿

H IDDEN IN THE courtyard of
Palazzo della Sapienza,
seat of Rome's former
university, Sant'Ivo's spiral
belfry is nevertheless a distinctive landmark on Rome's
skyline. Built by Borromini
between 1642 and 1660,
the church is astonishingly
complex, an ingenious
combination of concave and
convex surfaces. The work
spanned the reigns of
three popes, and incorp-
orated in the design are
their emblems: Urban
VIII's bee, Innocent X's
dove and olive
branch and the
star and hills
(which resemble
a jelly mould) of
Alexander VII.

Spire of Sant'Ivo alla Sapienza

San Luigi dei Francesi ❸

Via della Scrofa. **Map** 2 F3. 📞 06-
683 38 18. 🚌 70, 87, 90, 186.
⭕ 8am–12:30pm, 4:30–6:30pm
daily. ⬛ Thu pm. 📷

T HE FRENCH NATIONAL church
in Rome, San Luigi is a
16th-century building, best
known for three magnificent
canvases by Caravaggio in the
Cerasi chapel. Painted between
1597 and 1602, these were
Caravaggio's first significant
religious works: *The Calling
of St Matthew*, the *Martyrdom
of St Matthew* and *St Matthew
and the Angel*. The first version

**Detail from Caravaggio's *The Calling of St
Matthew* (1597–1602) in San Luigi dei Francesi**

of this last painting was not
initially accepted because it
depicted the saint as a tired
old man with dirty feet.

Sant'Agostino ❹

Via della Scrofa 80. **Map** 2 F3.
📞 06-68 80 19 62. 🚌 81, 87, 90b,
492. ⭕ 8am–noon, 4:30–7:30pm
daily.

I N THE EARLY 16th century
the Renaissance church of
Sant'Agostino was frequented
by an elite circle of artists,
writers and courtesans.
Their patron, John Goritz,
commissioned a fresco of
Isaiah from Raphael (on
the third left-hand
pillar) and the marble
*Virgin, St Anne and
Child* below it from
Andrea Sansovino.
In 1520 Jacopo
Sansovino,
Andrea's pupil,
created the
*Madonna del
Parto* (Madonna of Childbirth)
at the back of the church, and
in 1605 Caravaggio painted the
Madonna dei Pellegrini,
showing the Virgin with two
rough-looking peasants.

Santa Maria della Pace ❺

Vicolo del Arco della Pace 5. **Map** 2
E3. 📞 06-686 11 56. 🚌 81, 87,
186, 492. ⭕ 10am–noon, 4–6pm
Tue–Sat, 9–11am Sun. 📷 ♿

D ESIGNED IN 1656 by Pietro
da Cortona, the pincer-like
façade of Santa Maria della
Pace embraces an intimate,
ivy-curtained piazza. The
church itself,
named by Pope
Sixtus IV to cele-
brate the peace
he hoped to bring
to Italy, dates from
the 1480s. The
refined cloister,
Bramante's first
work in Rome,
was added in
1504. Inside,
Raphael frescoed
four *Sibyls* for the
wealthy banker
Agostino Chigi.

Façade of the Chiesa Nuova

Chiesa Nuova ❻

Piazza della Chiesa Nuova. **Map** 2 E4.
📞 06-687 52 89. 🚌 46, 62, 64.
⭕ 8am–noon, 4:30–7pm daily. 📷 ♿

S AN FILIPPO NERI commissioned
this church in 1575 to
replace the dilapidated
medieval church his Order
had been given by Pope
Gregory XIII. Neri required
his followers to humble
themselves, and set aristocratic young men to work as
labourers on the church.
Against Neri's wishes, the
nave, dome and apse were
flamboyantly frescoed after
his death by Pietro da
Cortona. There are also three
paintings by Rubens around
the altar. The first versions
were rejected as being too
shiny, so Rubens repainted
them on slate, and put the
originals above his mother's
tomb in Grenoble, France.

Palazzo della Cancelleria ❼

Piazza della Cancelleria. **Map** 2 E4.
📞 06-69 82. 🚌 46, 62, 64, 492.
⭕ 4–8pm Mon–Sat with permit only.

A SUPREME EXAMPLE of the
confident delicacy of
early Renaissance architecture,
this palazzo was begun in
1485, allegedly financed by
the proceeds of a single
night's gambling. The gambler
was Raffaele Riario, a nephew
of Pope Sixtus I, who had
been made a cardinal at the
age of 17. In 1478 Riario had

been involved in the Pazzi conspiracy against the Medici, and when Giovanni de' Medici became Pope Leo XIII in 1513, he took belated revenge by seizing the Riario palace and turning it into the papal chancellery. The palace is rarely open, but concerts are held in its Doric courtyard, decorated with roses, the Riario family emblem.

Tiber Island, with Ponte Cestio, built in 46 BC, linking it to Trastevere

Campo de' Fiori ❽

Map 2 F4. 🚌 46, 62, 64, 492.

CAMPO DE' FIORI (field of Flora), was one of the liveliest and roughest areas of medieval and Renaissance Rome. Cardinals and nobles mingled with fishmongers and foreigners in the piazza's market; Caravaggio killed his opponent after losing a game of tennis on the square; and the goldsmith Cellini murdered a business rival nearby. Today, the area continues to be a hub of secular activity. The colourful market, trattorias and down-to-earth bars retain the original animated and raffish atmosphere.

In the Renaissance the piazza was surrounded by inns, many of which were owned by the 15th-century courtesan Vannozza Catanei, mistress of Pope Alexander VI.

The square was also a place of execution. The hooded statue in its centre is the philosopher Giordano Bruno, burnt at the stake for heresy on this spot in 1600 for suggesting the earth moved around the sun.

Palazzo Farnese ❾

Piazza Farnese. **Map** 2 E5. 🚌 46, 64, 87, 492. ⬤ to the public.

ORIGINALLY CONSTRUCTED for Cardinal Alessandro Farnese, who became Pope Paul III in 1534, this palazzo was started by Antonio da Sangallo the Younger, and continued after his death by Michelangelo, who created the cornice on the façade and the courtyard's third storey.

The palace, now the French Embassy, is closed to the public, but when the chandeliers are lit at night you may be able to glimpse the ceiling of the Galleria, an illusionistic masterpiece by Annibale Carracci (1597–1603) based on Ovid's *Metamorphoses*.

Palazzo Spada ❿

Piazza Capo di Ferro 13. **Map** 2 F5. 📞 06-686 11 58. 🚌 46, 64, 87, 492. ⬤ 9am–7pm Tue–Sat, 9am–1:30pm Sun. 🎫 📷

A STUCCO EXTRAVAGANZA studded with reliefs of illustrious Romans, ribbons and swags of flowers, Palazzo Spada was built in 1540, but bought in 1637 by Cardinal Bernardino Spada. A keen patron of the arts, he commissioned Borromini to create an illusionistic tunnel from the courtyard which appears four times longer than it is. The cardinal's superb art collection, which is now shown in the Galleria Spada, includes works by Dürer, Guercino, del Sarto and Artemisia Gentileschi.

Ghetto and Tiber Island ⓫

Map 3 A5. 🚌 44, 56, 60, 170.

FIRST BROUGHT to Rome as slaves by Pompey the Great, Jews were greatly appreciated for their financial and medical skills during the Roman Empire. Persecution began in the 16th century, when Pope Paul IV forced all Jews to live within a walled enclosure, an area later to form the hub of the present-day Ghetto. Today the district's main street, Via del Portico d'Ottavia, leads down to Rome's central synagogue, passing restaurants and shops selling Roman Jewish food.

Ponte Fabricio links the Ghetto with Tiber Island, a centre of healing since 293 BC when a Temple to Aesculapius was founded. The island is now home to a hospital.

Fruit stalls at Campo de' Fiori's lively morning market

Street-by-Street: Around the Pantheon

T HE MAZE OF NARROW STREETS around the Pantheon is a mixture of lively restaurants and cafés, and some of Rome's finest sights. This is also the city's financial and political district, home to Parliament, government offices and the stock exchange. The Pantheon itself, with its awe-inspiring domed interior, has long been a symbol of the city.

Sant'Ignazio di Loyola
This church has a superb illusionistic ceiling painted by Andrea Pozzo in 1685 ⓱

The Temple of Hadrian now forms the façade of the Stock Exchange.

★ **Palazzo Doria Pamphilj**
Among the masterpieces in the art gallery of this vast family palazzo is this Salomé by Titian painted in 1516 ⓮

Piazza della Minerva
centres on Bernini's outlandish sculpture of an elephant supporting an Egyptian obelisk.

★ **Pantheon**
The Pantheon, a temple to "all the gods", is Rome's best-preserved ancient building. It was built in the 1st century AD, probably to a design by Emperor Hadrian ⓰

Santa Maria sopra Minerva
This is one of Rome's few Gothic churches, with works by Michelangelo, Bernini and Filippino Lippi ⓯

KEY

--- --- Suggested route

LOCATOR MAP
*See Rome Street Finder
map 3*

Via della Gatta is overlooked
by this marble statue of a cat
(gatta) that gives the narrow
street its name.

The Pie' di Marmo,
an ancient marble
foot, is probably
part of a giant
statue from
the temple to
the Egyptian
goddess Isis.

Palazzo Altieri incorporates
the hovel of an old woman
who refused to allow it to be
demolished when this palace
was built in the 17th century.

Gesù
*Built in the late 16th
century, this Jesuit
church served as a model
for the Order's churches
throughout the world* ⓭

STAR SIGHTS

★ **Pantheon**

★ **Palazzo Doria
Pamphilj**

0 metres	75
0 yards	75

Area Sacra di Largo Argentina ⓬

Largo di Torre Argentina. **Map** 2 F5.
🚌 44, 46, 64, 90. ⬜ with permit
only (see p613).

Tʜᴇ ʀᴇᴍᴀɪɴs of four temples
were discovered in the
1920s at the centre of Largo
Argentina, now a busy bus
terminus and traffic junction.
They date from the era of the
Republic, and are among the
oldest to have been found in
Rome. For the purpose of
identification, they are known
as A, B, C and D. The oldest
(temple C) dates back to the
4th century BC. It was placed
on a high platform preceded
by an altar and is typical
of Italic temple plans as
opposed to the Greek
model. Temple A is from
the 3rd century BC, but in
medieval times the small
church of San Nicola was
built over its podium and the
remains of its two apses are
still visible. The column
stumps to the north belonged
to a great portico, known as
the Hecatostylum (portico
of 100 columns). In
Imperial times two
marble latrines were
built here – the remains
of one are visible
behind temple A.
Behind temples B and C,
near Via di Torre Argentina,
are the remains of a great
platform of tufa blocks. These
have been identified as part
of the Curia of Pompey, a
rectangular building where
the Senate met, and where
Julius Caesar was assassinated
by Brutus, Cassius and their
followers on 15 March 44 BC.

**Area Sacra, with the ruins of
circular temple B**

**Baroque *Triumph of Faith over
Heresy* by Pierre Legros in the Gesù**

Gesù ⓭

Piazza del Gesù. **Map** 3 A4. 📞 06-
678 63 41. 🚌 44, 64, 81, 90.
⬜ 6am–12:30pm, 4:30–7:30 pm
(Oct–Mar: 4–7pm) daily. 📷

Bᴜɪʟᴛ ʙᴇᴛᴡᴇᴇɴ 1568 and
1584, the Gesù was Rome's
first Jesuit church. The Jesuit
order was founded in Rome
in 1537 by a Basque soldier,
Ignatius Loyola, who became
a Christian after he was
wounded in battle. The order
was austere, intellectual and
heavily engaged in missionary
activity and religious wars.
The much-imitated design
of the Gesù typifies Counter
Reformation architecture, with
a large nave with side pulpits
for preaching to crowds, and
a main altar as the centrepiece
for the mass. The illusionistic
decoration on the nave ceiling
and dome was added by Il
Baciccia in the 17th century.
The nave depicts the
Triumph of the Name of Jesus
and its message is clear: faithful, Catholic worshippers will
be joyfully uplifted to heaven
while Protestants and other
heretics are flung into the fires
of hell. The message is reiter-
ated in the Cappella di
Sant'Ignazio, a rich display of
lapis lazuli, serpentine, silver
and gold. The Baroque marble
by Legros, *Triumph of Faith
over Heresy*, shows a female
"Religion" trampling on the
head of the serpent Heresy,
while in Théudon's *Barbarians
Adoring the Faith*, an angel
aims a vicious kick towards a
decrepit old barbarian couple
entangled with a snake.

Palazzo Doria Pamphilj

Piazza del Collegio Romano 1a.
Map 5 A4. ☏ 06-679 43 65. ⬜ 56, 60, 62, 64, 90. ⬜ 10am–1pm Tue, Fri, Sat & Sun. ⬛ public hols. 📷 ♿
🖼 by appt for private apartments.

PALAZZO DORIA PAMPHILJ is a vast edifice in the heart of Rome, the oldest parts dating from 1435. When the Pamphilj family took over in 1647 they built a new wing, a splendid chapel and a theatre.

The family art collection has over 400 paintings dating from the 15th–18th century, including a portrait of Pope Innocent X by Velázquez and works by Titian, Guercino, Caravaggio and Claude Lorrain. The opulent rooms of the private apartments retain many of their original furnishings, including Brussels and Gobelins tapestries, Murano chandeliers and a gilded crib.

Velázquez' Pope Innocent X (1650)

Santa Maria sopra Minerva

Piazza della Minerva 42. **Map** 4 F4.
☏ 06-679 39 26. ⬜ 56, 64, 81, 119. ⬜ 7am–noon, 4–7pm daily.

ONE OF ROME'S rare Gothic buildings, this church was built in the 13th century over what were thought to be the ruins of a Temple of Minerva. It was a stronghold of the Dominicans, who produced some of the Church's most infamous inquisitors, and who tried the scientist Galileo in the adjoining monastery.

Inside, the church has a superb collection of art and sculpture, ranging from 13th-century Cosmatesque tombs to

Interior of the Pantheon, burial place for Italian monarchs

a bust by Bernini. Highlights include Antoniazzo Romano's *Annunciation* featuring Cardinal Juan de Torquemada, uncle of the vicious Spanish Inquisitor, and the Carafa Chapel whose frescoes by Filippino Lippi have recently been restored.

In the Aldobrandini Chapel are the tombs of the 16th-century Medici popes, Leo X and his cousin Clement VII, and near the steps of the choir is a stocky *Risen Christ*, begun by Michelangelo.

The church also contains the tombs of many famous Italians, such as St Catherine of Siena who died in 1380 and Fra Angelico, the Dominican friar and painter, who died in 1455. Outside, Bernini's spectacular sculpture of an elephant holds an obelisk on its back.

Simple vaulted nave of Santa Maria sopra Minerva

Pantheon

Piazza della Rotonda. **Map** 3 F4.
☏ 06-68 30 02 30. ⬜ 64, 70, 75, 119. ⬜ 9am–6pm (Oct–Mar: 5pm) Mon–Sat, 9am–1pm Sun. ⬛ 15 Aug, 25, 26 Dec. 📷 ♿

THE PANTHEON, the Roman "temple of all the gods", is the most extraordinary and best preserved ancient building in Rome. The first temple on the site was a conventional rectangular affair erected by Agrippa between 27 and 25 BC; the present structure was built and possibly designed by Emperor Hadrian in AD 118.

The temple is fronted by a massive pedimented portico screening what appears to be a brick cylinder fused to a shallow dome. Only from the inside, however, can the true scale and beauty be appreciated: a vast hemispherical dome exactly equal in radius to the height of the cylinder giving perfectly harmonious proportions to the building. A circular opening, the *oculus*, lets in the only light.

In the 7th century Christians claimed to be plagued by demons as they passed by, and permission was given to make the Pantheon a church. Today it is lined with tombs, ranging from a restrained monument to Raphael to huge marble and porphyry sarcophagi holding the bodies of Italian monarchs.

Sant'Ignazio di Loyola ⑰

Piazza di Sant'Ignazio. **Map** 3 A4.
📞 06-679 44 06. 🚌 56, 60, 90.
119. ⏰ 7:30am–12:30pm,
4–7:15pm daily. 📷

THIS CHURCH WAS built by
Cardinal Ludovisi in 1626
in honour of St Ignatius of
Loyola, founder of the Society
of Jesus (Jesuits) and the man
who most embodied the zeal
of the Counter Reformation.
  Together with the Gesù *(see
p393)*, Sant'Ignazio forms the
nucleus of the Jesuit area of
Rome. It is one of the most
extravagant Baroque churches
and its vast interior is plated
with precious stones, marble,
stucco and gilt, creating a
thrilling sense of theatre. The
church has a Latin-cross plan,
with an apse and many side
chapels. A cupola was planned
but never built, as the nuns
from a nearby convent
objected that it would obscure
the view from their roof
garden. Instead the space was
filled by a perspective painting
of a dome on a flat disc.
  Even more striking is the
illusionistic ceiling created by
the Jesuit artist Andrea Pozzo
in 1685, a propagandist
extravaganza extolling the
success of Jesuit missionaries
throughout the world. Above
four women, representing
Asia, Europe, America and
Africa, lithe angels and
beautiful youths are sucked
into a heaven of fluffy clouds.

**Detail from the AD 180 Column of
Marcus Aurelius, Piazza Colonna**

Piazza Colonna ⑱

Map 3 A3. 🚌 56, 60, 85, 119.

HOME TO Palazzo Chigi,
official residence of the
prime minister, Piazza Colonna
is dominated by and named
after the majestic Column of
Marcus Aurelius. This was
erected after the death of
Marcus Aurelius in AD 180 to
commemorate his victories
over the barbarian tribes of
the Danube. It is clearly an
imitation of Trajan's Column
(see p378) with scenes from
the emperor's wars spiralling
in reliefs up the column. The
80-year lapse between the
two works produced a great
artistic change: the wars of
Marcus Aurelius are rendered
with simplified pictures in
stronger relief, sacrificing
Classical proportions for the
sake of clarity and immediacy.

Piazza di Montecitorio ⑲

Map 3 A3. 🚌 56, 60, 85, 119.

THE OBELISK in the centre of
Piazza Montecitorio
formed the spine of a giant
sundial brought back from
Heliopolis in Egypt by
Augustus. It vanished some
time in the 9th century, and
was rediscovered during the
reign of Julius II (1503–13)
lying under medieval houses.
  The piazza is dominated by
the rugged façade of Palazzo
di Montecitorio, designed by
Bernini and completed in
1697, after his death, by Carlo
Fontana. It has been the seat
of Italy's Chamber of Deputies
since the late 19th century.

La Maddalena's stuccoed façade

La Maddalena ⑳

Piazza della Maddalena. **Map** 3 A3.
📞 06-679 77 96. 🚌 70, 81, 85, 87,
492. ⏰ 7:30am–7pm daily. 📷

SITUATED IN a small piazza
near the Pantheon, the
Maddalena's Rococo façade,
built in 1735, epitomizes the
love of light and movement
of the late Baroque. The
façade has been lovingly
restored, despite the protests
of diehard Neo-Classicists
who dismissed its painted
stucco as icing sugar.
  The diminutive dimensions
of the church did not deter
17th- and 18th-century
decorators from filling the
interior with paintings and
ornaments from the floor to
the top of the elegant cupola.

Baroque illusionistic ceiling by Andrea Pozzo in Sant'Ignazio di Loyola

NORTHEAST ROME

THIS AREA stretches from the exclusive shopping streets around Piazza di Spagna, to the Esquiline Hill, once bourgeois, but now a poor, often seedy area full of early Christian churches. The Piazza di Spagna and Piazza del Popolo district grew up in the 16th century, when the increase in the influx of pilgrims

Lion fountain in Piazza del Popolo

was such that a road was built to channel them as quickly as possible to the Vatican. About the same time, the Quirinal Hill became the site of a papal palace. When Rome became capital of Italy in 1870, Via Veneto became a lavish residential area, and the Esquiline was covered with apartments for the new civil servants.

SIGHTS AT A GLANCE

Churches
Sant'Andrea al Quirinale ❼
San Carlo alle Quattro Fontane ❽
Santa Maria della Concezione ❿
Santa Maria Maggiore ⓯
Santa Maria del Popolo ❸
Santa Maria della Vittoria ⓫
San Pietro in Vincoli ⓮
Santa Prassede ⓭

Museums and Galleries
Museo Nazionale Romano ⓬
Palazzo Barberini ❾

Ancient Sites and Buildings
Ara Pacis ❹
Mausoleum of Augustus ❺

Historic Buildings
Villa Medici ❷

Piazzas and Fountains
Piazza di Spagna and the Spanish Steps ❶
Trevi Fountain ❻

GETTING THERE
Metro stations Repubblica, Barberini and Spagna (line A) cover the area between Termini and Piazza del Popolo. Buses 93 and 93b run from Termini to Santa Maria Maggiore and down Via Merulana.

KEY

Street-by-Street: Piazza di Spagna pp398–9

FS Railway station

M Metro station

P Parking

i Tourist information

— City walls

0 metres   250
0 yards   250

◁ **The Spanish Steps with their spring display of azaleas**

Street-by-Street: Piazza di Spagna

T HE NETWORK OF NARROW STREETS around Piazza di Spagna forms one of the most exclusive areas in Rome, drawing droves of tourists and Romans to the elegant shops around Via Condotti. The square and its nearby coffee houses have long attracted those who want to see and be seen. In the 18th century the area was full of hotels for frivolous aristocrats doing the Grand Tour, as well as artists, writers and composers, who took the city's history and culture more seriously.

Caffè Greco is an 18th-century café once frequented by writers and musicians such as Keats, Goethe, Byron, Liszt and Wagner.

Trinità dei Monti is a 16th-century church at the top of the Spanish Steps. There are fine views of Rome from the stairway.

Spagna

VIALE TRINITÀ DEI MONTI

Babington's Tea Rooms, founded by two English spinsters in 1896, still serves English teas.

PIAZZA DI SPAGNA

PIAZZA MIGNANELLI

★ Piazza di Spagna and the Spanish Steps
These have been at the heart of tourist's Rome since the 18th century ❶

VIA CONDOTTI

VIA DI PROPAGANDA

The Keats-Shelley Memorial House, where the poet Keats died in 1821, is now a museum honouring English Romantic poets.

The Colonna dell' Immacolata, erected in 1857, commemorates Pope Pius IX's doctrine of the Immaculate Conception.

The Collegio di Propaganda Fide, built for the Jesuits in 1662, has a superb façade designed by Francesco Borromini.

KEY

— — — Suggested route

0 metres   75

0 yards   75

LOCATOR MAP
See Rome Street Finder map 3

Sant'Andrea delle Fratte contains two angels by Bernini (1669) made for Ponte Sant'Angelo, which Pope Clement X thought too lovely to expose to the weather.

The Fontana della Barcaccia at the foot of the Spanish Steps

Piazza di Spagna and the Spanish Steps ❶

Map 3 A2. 🚌 119. Ⓜ *Spagna.*

SHAPED LIKE a crooked bow tie, and surrounded by muted, shuttered façades, Piazza di Spagna is crowded all day and (in summer) most of the night. The most famous square in Rome, it takes its name from the Palazzo di Spagna, built in the 17th century to house the Spanish Embassy to the Holy See.

The piazza has long been the haunt of foreign visitors and expatriates. In the 18th and 19th centuries the square stood at the heart of the city's main hotel district. Some of the travellers came in search of knowledge and inspiration, although most were more interested in collecting statues to adorn their family homes. When the Victorian novelist Charles Dickens visited, he reported that the Spanish Steps

were crowded with models dressed as Madonnas, saints and emperors, hoping to attract the attention of foreign artists.

The steps were built in the 1720s to link the square with the French church of Trinità dei Monti above. The French wanted to place a statue of Louis XIV at the top, but the pope objected, and it was not until the 1720s that the Italian architect Francesco de Sanctis produced the voluptuous Rococo design which satisfied both camps. The Fontana Barcaccia, sunk into the paving at the foot of the steps due to low water pressure, was designed by Bernini's less famous father, Pietro.

Villa Medici ❷

Accademia di Francia a Roma, Viale Trinità dei Monti 1. **Map** 3 B1.
📞 *06-679 83 81.* Ⓜ *Spagna.*
◯ for exhibitions. **Gardens** ◯
Mar–Jun & 6–25 Oct: 10am– 12:30pm daily. 📷 *only.*

SUPERBLY POSITIONED on the Pincio Hill, this 16th-century villa has retained the name that it assumed when Cardinal Ferdinando de' Medici bought it in 1576. It is now home to the French Academy, which was founded in 1666 to give artists the chance to study in Rome. From 1803 musicians were also allowed to study there: both Berlioz and Debussy were students.

The villa is only open for exhibitions, but the formal gardens, with a gorgeously frescoed pavilion, and copies of ancient statues, can be visited in certain months.

19th-century engraving of the inner façade of the Villa Medici

---

STAR SIGHT

★ **Piazza di Spagna and the Spanish Steps**

Pinturicchio's fresco of the *Delphic Sibyl* (1509) in Santa Maria del Popolo

Santa Maria del Popolo ❸

Piazza del Popolo 12. **Map** 2 F1.
📞 06-361 08 36. 🚌 90, 90b, 119, 495. Ⓜ Flaminio. ⏰ 7am–noon, 4–7pm daily. 📷

Santa Maria del Popolo was one of the first Renaissance churches in Rome, commissioned by Pope Sixtus IV della Rovere in 1472. Thanks to lavish endowments by Sixtus's descendants and other powerful families, it has become one of Rome's greatest stores of artistic treasures.

Shortly after Sixtus died in 1484, Pinturicchio and his pupils frescoed two chapels (first and third right) for the della Rovere family. On the altar of the first chapel there is a lovely *Adoration of the Child* that depicts a stable at the foot of a Classical column.

In 1503 Sixtus IV's nephew Giuliano became Pope Julius II and had Bramante build a new apse. Pinturicchio was called in again to paint its vaults with Sibyls and Apostles framed in an intricate tracery of freakish beasts.

In 1513 Raphael created the Chigi chapel (second left) for the wealthy banker Agostino Chigi. The design is an audacious Renaissance fusion of the sacred and profane; there are pyramid-like tombs and a ceiling mosaic of God holding the signs of the zodiac describing Chigi's horoscope. Raphael died before the chapel was finished and it was completed by Bernini who added the dynamic statues of Daniel and Habakkuk. In the Cerasi chapel, left of the altar, there are two realistic works painted by Caravaggio in 1601: the *Conversion of St Paul* and the *Crucifixion of St Peter*. The artist uses daringly exaggerated lighting effects and foreshortening techniques to intensify the dramatic effect.

Detail of the Ara Pacis frieze

Ara Pacis ❹

Via di Ripetta. **Map** 2 F2. 📞 06-67 10 24 75. 🚌 81, 90, 119, 926. ⏰ 9am–1.30pm Tue–Sat, 9am–1pm Sun; Apr–Sep: 2:30–6:30pm Tue & Sat. 📷

Painstakingly reconstructed over many years from scattered fragments, the exquisitely carved Ara Pacis (Altar of Peace) celebrates the peace created throughout the Mediterranean by Emperor Augustus. Commissioned by the Senate in 13 BC and completed four years later, the altar stands in a square enclosure of Carrara marble, carved with realistic reliefs of such high quality that experts think the craftsmen may have been Greek. The reliefs on the north and south walls depict a procession that took place on 4 July, 13 BC, in which the emperor's family can be identified, including Augustus's grandson, Lucius, the toddler clutching at the skirts of his mother, Antonia.

Mausoleum of Augustus ❺

Piazza Augusto Imperatore. **Map** 2 F2.
📞 06-67 10 38 19. 🚌 81, 90, 119, 926. ⏰ by written permission only from Comune di Roma, Ripartizione X, Piazza Campitelli 7. 📷

Now just a weedy mound ringed with cypresses and strewn with litter, this was once the most prestigious burial place in Rome. Augustus had the mausoleum built in 28 BC, the year before he became sole ruler, as a tomb for himself and his descendants. The circular building was 87 m (270 ft) in diameter with two obelisks (now in Piazza del Quirinale and Piazza dell' Esquilino) at the entrance. Inside were four concentric passageways linked by corridors where urns holding the ashes of the Imperial family were placed, including those of Augustus who died in AD 14.

Trevi Fountain ❻

Piazza di Trevi. **Map** 3 B3.

Nicola Salvi's theatrical design for Rome's largest and most famous fountain was completed in 1762. The central figures are Neptune, flanked by two Tritons, one trying to master an unruly

Rome's largest and most famous fountain, the Trevi

sea-horse, the other leading a quieter beast. These are intended to symbolize the two contrasting moods of the sea.

The site originally marked the terminal of the Aqua Virgo aqueduct, built by Augustus' right-hand man and son-in-law, Agrippa, in 19 BC to channel water to Rome's new bath complexes. One of the reliefs on the first storey shows a young girl, Trivia, after whom the fountain may have been named. She is said to have first shown the spring, 22 km (14 miles) from the city, to thirsty Roman soldiers.

The dome of San Carlo alle Quattro Fontane, by Borromini

Interior, Sant'Andrea al Quirinale

Sant'Andrea al Quirinale **7**

Via del Quirinale 29. **Map** 3 C3.
06-48 90 31 87. 56, 64, 70, 94. 10am–noon, 4–7pm Wed–Mon. Aug.

SANT'ANDREA was designed for the Jesuits by Bernini and executed by his assistants between 1658 and 1670. The site was wide but shallow, so Bernini took the radical step of pointing the long axis of his oval plan towards the sides, and leading the eye round to the altar by means of a strong horizontal cornice. At the altar he combined sculpture and painting to create a theatrical crucifixion of Sant'Andrea (St Andrew); the diagonally crucified saint on the altarpiece looks up at a stucco effigy of himself ascending to the lantern, where the Holy Spirit and cherubs await him in heaven.

San Carlo alle Quattro Fontane **8**

Via del Quirinale 23. **Map** 3 C3.
06-488 32 61. 52, 56, 62, 492. 9am–12:30pm, 4–6pm Mon–Fri, 9am–12:30pm Sat.

IN 1638, Borromini was commissioned by the Trinitarians to design a church and convent on a tiny cramped site at the Quattro Fontane crossroads. The church, so small that it is said it would fit inside one of the piers of St Peter's, is ingeniously designed, with bold fluid curves on both the façade and interior to give light and life to the diminutive building. One of the most cunning features is the dome, whose concealed windows, illusionistic coffering and tiny lantern are designed to make it look higher than it really is.

Palazzo Barberini **9**

Via delle Quattro Fontane 13. **Map** 3 C2. 06-481 45 91. 52, 58, 490, 495. Barberini. 9am–2pm Tue–Sat, 9am–1pm Sun & public hols.

WHEN MAFFEI BARBERINI became Pope Urban VIII in 1623, he decided to build a grand family palazzo. It now overlooks Piazza Barberini, where traffic hurtles around Bernini's Triton fountain, but was designed by Carlo Maderno as a typical country villa on the fringes of the city. Maderno died shortly after the foundations had been laid, and Bernini and Borromini took over.

The most dazzling room is the Gran Salone, with an illusionistic ceiling frescoed by Pietro da Cortona in 1633–9. The palazzo also houses part of the Galleria Nazionale d'Arte Antica with works by Filippo Lippi, Titian, Artemisia Gentileschi and Caravaggio. The most famous is a portrait of a courtesan, reputedly Raphael's lover, *La Fornarina*, said to be the daughter of a baker, although not painted by the artist himself.

Ceiling fresco detail in Palazzo Barberini (1633)

Santa Maria della Concezione **10**

Via Veneto 27. **Map** 3 C2. 06-487 11 85. 52, 56, 490, 495. Barberini. **Crypt** 9am–noon, 3–6pm daily.

BELOW THIS UNASSUMING church on Via Veneto is a crypt decked with the dismembered skeletons of 4,000 Capuchin monks. They form a macabre reminder of the transience of life, with vertebrae wired together to make sacred hearts and crowns of thorns, and, in one chapel, the poignant skeleton of a tiny Barberini princess.

Santa Maria della Vittoria ⑪

Via XX Settembre 17. **Map** 4 D2.
📞 06-482 61 90. 🚌 36, 37, 60, 61.
Ⓜ Repubblica. ⏰ 6:30am–noon,
4:30–6pm daily.

Santa Maria della Vittoria is an intimate Baroque church with a lavishly decorated, candlelit interior. Inside the Cornaro chapel (fourth left) is one of Bernini's most ambitious sculptures, the *Ecstasy of St Teresa* (1646). Visitors may be shocked or thrilled by the physical nature of St Teresa's ecstasy as she appears collapsed on a cloud with mouth half open and eyelids closed, struck by the arrow of a smiling angel. Ecclesiastical members, past and present, of the Venetian Cornaro family, who commissioned the chapel, sit in boxes as if in a theatre watching and discussing the scene played out in front of them.

Bernini's *Ecstasy of St Teresa* in Santa Maria della Vittoria

Museo Nazionale Romano ⑫

Viale Enrico de Nicola 79. **Map** 4 E2.
📞 06-488 05 30. **Collegio Massimo**,
Piazza Cinquecento. **Map** 4 E3.
📞 06-90 35 07. 🚌 57, 65, 170, 492.
Ⓜ Termini. ⏰ 9am–2pm Tue–Sat,
9am–1pm Sun & public hols. 📷 ♿

The museo nazionale occupies part of the Baths of Diocletian, once the largest baths in ancient Rome, as well as the 16th-century Carthusian monastery of Santa Maria degli Angeli, also built over the ruins of the baths.

Founded in 1889, the Museo Nazionale Romano was once one of the world's leading museums of Classical art. Most of the antiquities found in Rome since 1870, as well as important pre-existing collections, were housed here. After many years of disrepair, however, part of the collection has now been moved to the nearby Collegio Massimo, including many of the statues, sarcophagi, mosaics and detached frescoes. The original museum building in the Diocletian Baths still retains some mosaics and sculptures, most notably a Roman copy of the original Greek statue, the *Discus Thrower*. Most, however, is now dedicated to Roman inscriptions and writings, illustrating social, political and religious life in ancient Rome. There is also a cloister designed by Michelangelo as part of the Carthusian monastery and a 16th-century garden.

Santa Prassede ⑬

Via Santa Prassede 9a. **Map** 4 D5.
📞 06-488 24 56. 🚌 16, 93, 613.
Ⓜ Vittorio Emanuele. ⏰ 7:30am–
noon, 4–6:30pm daily. 📷 ♿

The church was founded by Pope Paschal II in the 9th century and decorated by artists from Byzantium with glittering mosaics, the most important in Rome. In the apse Christ stands between Santa Prassede and her sister, lavishly dressed as Byzantine empresses, among white-robed elders, spindly-legged lambs, feather-mop palms and bright red poppies. The Cappella di San Zeno is even lovelier, a jewel-box of a mausoleum, built by Pope Paschal for his mother, Theodora. Her square halo shows that she was still alive when the mosaic was created.

9th-century mosaic, Santa Prassede

San Pietro in Vincoli ⑭

Piazza di San Pietro in Vincoli. **Map** 4
D5. 📞 06-488 28 65. 🚌 11, 27,
81. Ⓜ Colosseo. ⏰ 7am–12:30pm,
3:30–7pm (Oct–Mar: 6pm) Mon–Sat,
8:45am–11:45am Sun. ♿

The church's name means St Peter in Chains; it is so called because it houses what are said to be the two chains with which Peter was shackled in the Mamertine Prison *(see p379).* According to tradition, one set of chains had been sent to Constantinople by Empress Eudoxia; when it was returned to Rome some years later it miraculously fused with its partner.

The chains are on display below the high altar, but San Pietro is now best known for the Tomb of Julius II, commissioned from Michelangelo by the pope in 1505. To the artist's chagrin, Julius soon became more interested in the building of a new St Peter's and the project was laid aside. After the pope died in 1513, Michelangelo resumed work on the tomb, but had only finished the statues of the *Dying Slaves* (now in Paris and Florence) and *Moses* when he was called away to paint the Sistine Chapel's *Last Judgment.* Cecil B de Mille apparently gave Charlton Heston the role of Moses in his film *The Ten Commandments* because he looked like Michelangelo's statue.

Michelangelo's *Moses* in San Pietro

Santa Maria Maggiore ⑮

A CONFIDENT BLEND of architectural styles, ranging from Early Christian to late Baroque, Santa Maria is also famous for its superb mosaics. Founded in about AD 420, it retains the original colonnaded triple nave, lined with panels of rare 5th-century mosaics. The Cosmatesque marble floor and bell tower are medieval, as are the spectacular mosaics on the triumphal arch and in the loggia. The lavish coffered ceiling is Renaissance; the façades, domes and chapels Baroque.

VISITORS' CHECKLIST

Piazza di Santa Maria Maggiore.
Map 4 E4. ☎ 06-48 31 95.
🚌 16, 70, 71, 93b. 🚊 14,
516. Ⓜ Cavour. ☐ 7am–7pm
daily (Oct–Mar: 6pm) (last adm:
15 mins before closing). ✝ 📷

Coronation of the Virgin
This is one of the wonderful 13th-century mosaics in the apse by Jacopo Torriti.

Bell tower

Tomb of Cardinal Rodriguez
This Gothic tomb, which dates from 1299, contains magnificent marblework by the Cosmati.

5th-century mosaics

18th-century façade by Ferdinando Fuga

13th-century mosaics

Cappella Paolina
Flaminio Ponzio, architect of the Villa Borghese, designed this sumptuous chapel in 1611 for Pope Paul V who is buried here.

Column in Piazza Santa Maria Maggiore
In 1611 a bronze of the Virgin and Child was added to this ancient marble column which came from the Basilica of Constantine.

Cappella Sistina
This chapel was built for Pope Sixtus V (1585–90) by Domenico Fontana and was opulently plated with ancient marble. It houses the pope's tomb.

THE VATICAN AND TRASTEVERE

ATICAN CITY, the world capital of Catholicism, is the world's smallest state. It occupies 43 ha (106 acres) within high walls watched over by the Vatican guard. It was the site where St Peter was martyred (c.AD 64) and buried, and it became the residence of the popes who succeeded him. The papal palaces, next to the great basilica of St Peter's, are home to the

Pope Urban VIII's coat of arms in St Peter's

Sistine Chapel and the eclectic collections of the Vatican Museums, as well as being the residence of the pope. Neighbouring Trastevere is quite different, a picturesque old quarter, whose inhabitants consider themselves to be the only true Romans. Sadly, the proletarian identity of the place is in danger of being destroyed by the proliferation of trendy restaurants, clubs and shops.

SIGHTS AT A GLANCE

GETTING THERE

The quickest way to the Vatican is by Metro Line A to Ottaviano, just north of Piazza San Pietro. The 64 bus links it with Termini and the 81 links it with the Colosseum. Trastevere is a short walk from Campo de' Fiori across Ponte Sisto. Bus 23 runs from the Vatican and the 75 from Termini.

Churches

San Francesco a Ripa ❾
San Pietro in Montorio and
   the Tempietto ❿
Santa Cecilia in Trastevere ❽
Santa Maria in Trastevere ❼
St Peter's pp408–9 ❷

Museums and Galleries

Palazzo Corsini and the
   Galleria Nazionale
   d'Arte Antica ❺
Vatican Museums pp410–17 ❸

Historic Buildings

Castel Sant'Angelo ❶
Villa Farnesina ❹

Parks and Gardens

Botanical Gardens ❻

KEY

▨	A Tour of the Vatican *pp406–7*
🅿	Parking
ℹ	Tourist information
—	City walls

0 metres   250
0 yards   250

◁ **View of St Peter's with the Ponte Sant'Angelo in the foreground**

A Tour of the Vatican

THE VATICAN, a sovereign state since February 1929, is ruled by the pope, Europe's only absolute monarch. About 500 people live here and, as well as accommodation for staff and ecclesiasts, the city has **Crucifix in** its own post office, banks, **the Vatican** currency, judicial system, radio station, shops and a daily newspaper, *l'Osservatore Romano.*

★ St Peter's
Most of the great architects of the Renaissance and Baroque had a hand in the design of the Basilica of St Peter's, the most famous church in Christendom (see pp408–9).

Vatican Radio broadcasts in 20 languages throughout the world from this tower, part of the 9th-century Leonine Wall.

★ Sistine Chapel
Michelangelo frescoed the ceiling with scenes from Genesis (1508–12), and the altar wall with the Last Judgment (1534–41). The chapel is used by cardinals when electing a new pope (see p414).

The Papal Audience Chamber

Information office

PIAZZA DEL SANT'UFFIZIO

★ Raphael Rooms
Raphael frescoed this suite in the early 16th century. Works like The School of Athens *established his reputation, to equal that of his contemporary Michelangelo* (see p417).

Piazza San Pietro
was laid out by Bernini between 1656 and 1667.

To Via della Conciliazione

PIA PL

This staircase up to the museums, designed in 1932 by Giuseppe Momo, is in the form of a double helix, consisting of two spirals: one to walk up and one to walk down.

Entrance to Vatican Museums

LOCATOR MAP
See Rome Street Finder map 1

★ **Vatican Museums**
This marble group of the Laocoön (AD 1) is one of many prestigious works of art in the Vatican (see p410).

The Cortile della Pigna is named after a bronze pine cone from an ancient fountain.

The Vatican Gardens, open for guided tours, make up a third of the Vatican's territory.

| 0 metres | 75 |
| 0 yards | 75 |

VIA DI PORTA ANGELICA

Castel Sant'Angelo ❶

Lungotevere Castello. **Map** 2 D3.
📞 06-687 50 36. 🚌 23, 64, 87, 280. Ⓜ Lepanto. 🕐 9am–2pm, Tue–Sat; 9am–1pm, 2–7pm Sun (Oct–Mar: 4:30pm). ● public hols.

THE MASSIVE FORTRESS of Castel Sant'Angelo takes its name from the vision of the angel by Pope Gregory the Great in the 6th century as he led a procession across the bridge, praying for the end of the plague.

The castle began life in AD 139 as the Emperor Hadrian's mausoleum. Since then it has had many roles: as a bridgehead in the Roman city wall, as a medieval citadel and prison, and as a place of safety for popes during times of political unrest. A corridor (built 1227) links it with the Vatican Palace, providing an escape route for the pope. From dank cells to fine apartments of Renaissance popes, the museums cover all aspects of the castle's history, including the Sala Paolina, with illusionistic frescoes (1544–7) by Pellegrino Tibaldi and Perin del Vaga and the Courtyard of Honour.

St Peter's ❷

See pp408–9.

Vatican Museums ❸

See pp410–17.

View of Castel Sant'Angelo from the Ponte Sant'Angelo

STAR SIGHTS

★ **St Peter's**

★ **Vatican Museums**

★ **Sistine Chapel**

★ **Raphael Rooms**

St Peter's ❷

CATHOLICISM'S most sacred shrine, the sumptuous, marble-caked basilica of St Peter's draws pilgrims and tourists from all over the world. It holds hundreds of precious works of art, some salvaged from the original 4th-century basilica built by Constantine, others commissioned from Renaissance and Baroque artists. The dominant tone is set by Bernini, who created the baldacchino twisting up below Michelangelo's huge dome. He also created the Cathedra in the apse, with four saints supporting a throne that contains fragments once thought to be relics of the chair from which St Peter delivered his first sermon.

Dome of St Peter's
The 136.5 m (448 ft) high dome, designed by Michelangelo, was not completed in his lifetime.

Baldacchino
Commissioned by Pope Urban VIII in 1624, Bernini's extravagant Baroque canopy stands above St Peter's tomb.

A staircase of 537 steps leads to the summit of the dome.

The church is 186 m (615 ft) long.

HISTORICAL PLAN OF THE BASILICA OF ST PETER'S

St Peter was buried in AD 64 in a necropolis near the site of his crucifixion in the Circus of Nero. In AD 324 Constantine constructed a basilica over the tomb. The old church was rebuilt in the 15th century, and throughout the 16th and 17th centuries various architects developed the existing structure. The new church was inaugurated in 1626.

KEY

- ◻ Circus of Nero
- ◻ Constantinian
- ◻ Renaissance
- ◻ Baroque

Entrance to Treasury and Sacristy

Stairs to the dome

The Papal Altar stands over the crypt where St Peter is reputedly buried.

Monument to Pope Alexander VII
Bernini's last work in St Peter's was finished in 1678 and shows the Chigi pope among the allegorical figures of Truth, Justice, Charity and Prudence.

The Grottoes
A fragment of this 13th-century mosaic by Giotto, salvaged from the old basilica, is now in the Grottoes, where many popes are buried.

Two minor cupolas by Vignola (1507–73)

The foot of St Peter by Arnolfo di Cambio, 13th century, has worn thin from the touch of pilgrims over the centuries.

Michelangelo's Pietà
Protected by glass since an attack in 1972, the Pietà was created in 1499 when Michelangelo was only 25.

VISITORS' CHECKLIST

Piazza San Pietro. **Map** 1 B3.
📞 06-69 88 44 66, 06-69 88 48 66. 🚌 32, 64, 98, 492. 🚋 19.
Ⓜ Ottaviano. **Basilica** ◐ Apr–Sep: 7am–7pm daily (mid-Oct–Mar: 6pm). 🚻 📷 ♿ 🎥
Treasury ◐ Apr–Sep: 9am–6pm (Oct–Mar: 5pm) daily.
Grottoes ◐ Apr–Sep: 7am–6pm (Oct–Mar: 5pm) daily.
Dome ◐ Apr–Sep: 8am–6pm (Oct–Mar: 5pm) daily. 🎥 **Papal audiences:** Usually 11am Wed in the Papal Audience Chamber, sometimes in Piazza San Pietro. Tickets (free) from the Prefecture of the Pontifical Household (north side of piazza) ◐ 9am–1pm Mon & Tue; or write to: Prefettura della Casa Pontificia, 00120 Città del Vaticano. The Pope also appears noon Sun to bless the crowd in Piazza San Pietro.

From this Library window, the pope blesses the faithful gathered in the piazza below.

Façade by Carlo Maderno (1614)

The Holy Door is used only by the pope.

Filarete Doors
These bronze doors from the old basilica were decorated with biblical reliefs by Filarete between 1439 and 1445.

Markings on the floor of the nave show how other churches compare in length.

Entrance

Atrium by Carlo Maderno

Piazza San Pietro
On religious festivals and special occasions such as canonizations, the pope blesses the crowds from a balcony.

Vatican Museums ❸

Home to the Sistine Chapel and Raphael Rooms as well as to one of the world's most important art collections, the Vatican Museums are housed in palaces originally built for Renaissance popes such as Julius II, Innocent VIII and Sixtus IV. Most of the later additions were made in the 18th century, when priceless works of art accumulated by earlier popes were first put on show.

Etruscan Museum
The Etruscan collection includes a woman's gold clasp (fibula) from the 7th-century BC Regolini-Galassi tomb at Cerveteri, north of Rome.

Gallery of Maps
The Siege of Malta *is one of 40 maps of the Church's territories, frescoed by the 16th-century cartographer Ignazio Danti on the gallery's walls.*

Gallery of the Candelabra

Raphael Rooms

This is a detail of the Expulsion of Heliodorus from the Temple, *one of many frescoes painted by Raphael and his pupils for Julius II's private apartments* (see p417).

Gallery of Tapestries

Stair down

Upper floor

Sistine Chapel *(see p414)*

Sala dei Chiaroscuri

Raphael Loggia

Borgia Apartment
Pinturicchio and his assistants frescoed these rooms for Alexander VI in 1492–95.

GALLERY GUIDE
The museum complex is vast: the Sistine Chapel is 20–30 minutes' walk from the entrance, so allow plenty of time. There is a strict one-way system, and it is best to be selective or choose one of four colour-coded itineraries, which vary from 90 minutes to a five-hour marathon.

Modern religious art on view here was sent to the popes by artists worldwide, such as Bacon, Ernst and Carrà.

Gregorian Profane Museum

Pio-Clementine Museum

The finest of the Vatican's Classical statues are on display here, like the Apollo Belvedere, a Roman copy in marble of a 4th-century BC Greek bronze.

Stairs up to Etruscan Museum

Entrance

VISITORS' CHECKLIST

Città del Vaticano (entrance in Viale Vaticano). **Map** 1 B2.
📞 06-69 88 33 33. 🚌 32, 64, 110, 492. 🚋 19. Ⓜ Ottaviano.
🕐 Apr–mid-Oct: 8:45am–4pm Mon–Fri, 8:45am–1pm Sat & last Sun of month; mid-Oct–Mar: 8:45am–1pm Mon–Sat & last Sun of month. ⬤ 1 & 6 Jan, 11 Feb, 19 Mar, 4 Apr, 12 May, 2 & 29 Jun, 15 Aug, 1 Nov, 8 & 26 Dec. Special permit required for Raphael Loggia, Vatican Library, Lapidary Gallery & Vatican Archives. 🎟 free last Sun of month. ♿ special routes.

Cortile Ottagonale

Lower floor

Braccio Nuovo

Chiaramonti Museum

Egyptian Museum
The collection of Egyptian artefacts includes this painted bas relief from a 2400 BC tomb. The museum was organized by Father Ungarelli, a 19th-century Egyptologist.

The Lapidary Gallery
contains inscriptions from pagan and Christian catacombs, but is closed to the public.

Pio-Christian Museum

Early Christianity adopted Classical images so that its doctrines could be more easily understood. This 4th-century statue of Christ as the Good Shepherd derives from the pastoral figure of the shepherd.

Pinacoteca

The Vatican's art gallery has 15th- to 19th-century works, and is particularly strong on the Renaissance. This unfinished painting of St Jerome by Leonardo da Vinci reveals his mastery of anatomy.

KEY TO FLOORPLAN

🟫	Egyptian and Assyrian art
⬜	Greek and Roman art
⬜	Etruscan art
⬜	Early Christian and medieval art
⬜	15th- to 19th-century art
⬜	Modern religious art
⬜	Lapidary Gallery
⬜	Non-exhibition space

Exploring the Vatican's Collections

THE VATICAN'S GREATEST TREASURES are its superlative
Greek and Roman antiquities, together with the magnificent artefacts excavated from Egyptian and Etruscan
tombs during the 19th century. Some of Italy's greatest
artists, such as Raphael, Michelangelo and Leonardo da
Vinci, are represented in the Pinacoteca (art gallery) and
parts of the former palaces, where they were employed
by popes to decorate sumptuous apartments and galleries.

**Head of an athlete in mosaic from
the Baths of Caracalla, AD 217**

EGYPTIAN AND ASSYRIAN ART

THE EGYPTIAN COLLECTION
contains finds from 19th-
and 20th-century excavations
in Egypt, as well as statues
that were brought to Rome
in Imperial times. There are
also Roman imitations of
Egyptian art from Hadrian's
Villa (see p452) and
from temples in Rome
devoted to Egyptian
gods and goddesses,
such as Isis and Serapis.

The genuine Egyptian
works, displayed on the
lower floor next to the
Pio-Clementine Mu-
seum, include statues,
mummies, mummy
cases and a Book of
the Dead. One of the
main treasures is a
colossal granite
13th-century statue
of Queen Mutuy,
the mother of
Rameses II, which
was found on the
site of the Horti Sallustiani
gardens near Via Veneto. Also
noteworthy are the head of a
statue of Mentuhotep IV (21st
century BC), the beautiful
mummy case of Queen
Hetep-heret-es, and the tomb
of Iri, who was the guardian
of the Pyramid of Cheops.
This dates back to the 22nd
century BC.

**Roman copy of the
Greek Doryphoros**

GREEK, ETRUSCAN AND ROMAN ART

THE GREATER PART of the
Vatican Museums is
dedicated to Greek and
Roman art. However, the
Etruscan Museum houses a
superb collection of Etruscan
(see p40) and pre-Roman
artefacts from Etruria and the
Greek colonies of southern
Italy. Here, the most famous
exhibits are the gold jewellery
and bronze throne, bed and
funeral cart, found in the 650
BC Regolini-Galassi tomb in
Cerveteri (see p450).

Prize Greek and Roman
pieces form the nucleus of the
Pio-Clementine Museum.
These include high-quality
Roman copies of 4th-
century BC Greek
statues, such as the
Apoxyomenos (an
athlete wiping his
body after a race) and
the Apollo del Belvedere.
The splendid Laocoön
(1st century AD), origin-
ally from Rhodes, was
found in 1506 in the
ruins of Nero's Golden
House. Works such as
these inspired Michel-
angelo and other
Renaissance artists.

The much smaller
Chiaramonti
Museum is lined
with ancient busts,
and its extension,
the Braccio Nuovo, has a 1st-
century BC statue of Augustus
from the villa of his wife Livia.
It is based on the Doryphoros
(spear-carrier) by the 5th-
century BC Greek sculptor
Polyclitus. There is also a
Roman copy of this on display
opposite. The Gregorian
Profane Museum, housed in a
new wing, follows the
evolution of Roman art from
reliance on Greek models to
a recognizably Roman style.

In this museum, original
Greek works include large
marble fragments from the
Parthenon in Athens. Among
the Roman pieces are two
reliefs, the Rilievi della
Cancelleria, commissioned
by Domitian in AD 81 to
glorify the military parades of
his father, Emperor Vespasian.
There are also fine Roman
floor mosaics, two from the
Baths of Caracalla (see p427),
and one, in the Round Room,
dated 3rd century AD, from
the Baths of Otricoli in Umbria.

In the Vatican Library is the
1st-century AD Aldobrandini
Wedding, a beautiful Roman
fresco depicting a bride being
prepared for her marriage.

Roman mosaic from the Baths of Otricoli, Umbria, in the Round Room

EARLY CHRISTIAN AND MEDIEVAL ART

T HE MAIN COLLECTION of early
Christian antiquities is in
the Pio-Christian Museum,
which contains inscriptions
and sculpture from catacombs
and early Christian basilicas.
The sculpture consists chiefly
of reliefs from sarcophagi,
though the most striking work
is a free-standing 4th-century
statue of the *Good Shepherd*.
The sculpture's chief interest
lies in the way it blends
Biblical episodes with pagan
mythology. The idealized
pastoral figure of the shepherd
became Christ himself, while
bearded philosophers turned
into the Apostles.

The first two rooms of the
Pinacoteca are dedicated to
late medieval art, mostly
wooden altarpieces painted in
tempera. The outstanding
work is Giotto's *Stefaneschi
Triptych* of about 1300 which
decorated the main altar of
the old St Peter's.

The Vatican Library has a
number of medieval treasures
including reliquaries, textiles,
enamels and icons.

Pietà (c.1471–4) by the Venetian artist Giovanni Bellini in the Pinacoteca

**Detail of Giotto's *Stefaneschi
Triptych* (1330) in the Pinacoteca**

15TH- TO 19TH-
CENTURY ART

M ANY RENAISSANCE popes
were connoisseurs of the
arts who considered it their
duty to sponsor the leading
painters, sculptors and
goldsmiths of the age. The
galleries around the Cortile
del Belvedere were decorated
by great artists between the
16th and the 19th centuries.

The Gallery of Tapestries is
hung with tapestries woven
in Brussels to designs by
students of Raphael. The
Apartment of Pope Pius V has
beautiful 15th-century Flemish
tapestries, and the Gallery of
Maps is frescoed with 16th-
century maps of ancient and
contemporary Italy.

Alongside the Raphael
Rooms *(see p417)* are the Room
of the Chiaroscuri and
Pope Nicholas V's
private chapel. This
was frescoed be-
tween 1447 and
1451 by Fra
Angelico. Also
worth seeing
is the Borgia
Apartment,
decorated in
the 1490s by
Pinturicchio

**Pinturicchio's *Adoration of the
Magi* (1490), Borgia Apartment**

and his pupils
for the Borgia
pope, Alexander VI. Another
set of fascinating frescoes can
be found in the Loggia of
Raphael, but a visit here
requires special permission.

The Pinacoteca has many
important Renaissance works.
Highlights from the 15th
century are a fine *Pietà* by
Giovanni Bellini, part of his
Coronation of the Virgin altarpiece in Pèsaro *(see p358)*; and
Leonardo da Vinci's unfinished
St Jerome, discovered, after
being long lost, in two halves.
One was being used as a
coffer lid in an antique shop,
the other as the seat of a stool
in a shoemaker's. Exceptional
pieces from the 16th
century include eight
tapestry cartoons, the
Transfiguration
and *Madonna
of Foligno* by
Raphael, in a
room devoted
to the artist; a
Deposition by
Caravaggio;
an altarpiece
by Titian;
and *St Helen*
by Veronese,
which shows the saint as a
gorgeously dressed aristocrat.

Sistine Chapel: The Ceiling

MICHELANGELO FRESCOED the ceiling for Pope Julius II between 1508 and 1512, working on specially designed scaffolding. The main panels, which chart the Creation of the World and Fall of Man, are surrounded by subjects from the Old and New Testaments – except for the Classical Sibyls who are said to have foreseen the birth of Christ. In the 1980s the ceiling was restored revealing colours of an unsuspected vibrancy.

Libyan Sibyl
The pagan prophetess reaches for the Book of Knowledge. Like most female figures Michelangelo painted, the beautiful Libyan Sibyl was probably modelled on a man.

Illusionistic architecture

KEY TO CEILING PANELS

☐ **GENESIS: 1** God Dividing Light from Darkness; **2** Creation of the Sun and Moon; **3** Separating Waters from Land; **4** Creation of Adam; **5** Creation of Eve; **6** Original Sin; **7** Sacrifice of Noah; **8** The Deluge; **9** Drunkenness of Noah.

☐ **ANCESTORS OF CHRIST: 10** Solomon with his Mother; **11** Parents of Jesse; **12** Rehoboam with Mother; **13** Asa with Parents; **14** Uzziah with Parents; **15** Hezekiah with Parents; **16** Zerubbabel with Parents; **17** Josiah with Parents.

☐ **PROPHETS: 18** Jonah; **19** Jeremiah; **20** Daniel; **21** Ezekiel; **22** Isaiah; **23** Joel; **24** Zechariah.

☐ **SIBYLS: 25** Libyan Sibyl; **26** Persian Sibyl; **27** Cumaean Sibyl; **28** Erythrean Sibyl; **29** Delphic Sibyl.

☐ **OLD TESTAMENT SCENES OF SALVATION: 30** Punishment of Haman; **31** Moses and the Brazen Serpent; **32** David and Goliath; **33** Judith and Holofernes.

Creation of the Sun and Moon
Michelangelo depicts God as a dynamic but terrifying figure commanding the sun to shed light on the earth.

Original Sin
This shows Adam and Eve tasting the forbidden fruit from the Tree of Knowledge, and their expulsion from Paradise. Michelangelo represents Satan as a snake with the body of a woman.

The Ignudi are athletic male nudes whose significance is uncertain.

The lunettes are devoted to frescoes of the ancestors of Christ, like Hezekiah.

RESTORATION OF THE SISTINE CEILING

The recent restorers of the Sistine Chapel used computers, photography and spectrum technology to analyse the fresco before cleaning began. They separated Michelangelo's work from that of later restorers and discovered that the restorers had attempted to clean the ceiling with materials ranging from bread to retsina wine. The new restoration revealed the familiarly

A restorer cleaning the Libyan Sibyl

dusky, eggshell-cracked figures to have creamy skins, lustrous hair and to be dressed in brightly-coloured, luscious robes: "a Benetton Michelangelo" mocked one critic, claiming that a layer of varnish which the artist had added to darken the colours had been removed. However, after examining the work, most experts agreed that the new colours probably matched those painted by Michelangelo.

Sistine Chapel: The Walls

THE MASSIVE WALLS of the Sistine Chapel, the main chapel in the Vatican Palace, were frescoed by some of the finest artists of the 15th and 16th centuries. The 12 paintings on the side walls, by artists including Perugino, Ghirlandaio, Botticelli and Signorelli, show parallel episodes from the life of Moses and of Christ. The decoration of the chapel walls was completed between 1534 and 1541 by Michelangelo, who added the great altar wall fresco, the *Last Judgment*.

KEY TO THE FRESCOES: ARTISTS AND SUBJECTS

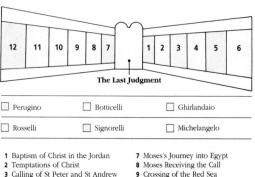

The Last Judgment

☐ Perugino   ☐ Botticelli   ☐ Ghirlandaio

☐ Rosselli   ☐ Signorelli   ☐ Michelangelo

1 Baptism of Christ in the Jordan
2 Temptations of Christ
3 Calling of St Peter and St Andrew
4 Sermon on the Mount
5 Handing over the Keys to St Peter
6 Last Supper
7 Moses's Journey into Egypt
8 Moses Receiving the Call
9 Crossing of the Red Sea
10 Adoration of the Golden Calf
11 Punishment of the Rebels
12 Last Days of Moses

THE LAST JUDGMENT BY MICHELANGELO

REVEALED IN 1993 after a year's restoration, the *Last Judgment* is considered to be the masterpiece of Michelangelo's mature years. It was commissioned by Pope Paul III Farnese, and required the removal of some earlier

Souls meeting the wrath of Christ in Michelangelo's *Last Judgment*

frescoes and two windows over the altar. A new wall was erected which slanted inwards to stop dust settling on it. Michelangelo worked alone on the fresco for seven years, until its completion in 1541.

The painting depicts the souls of the dead rising up to face the wrath of God, a subject that is rarely used for an altar decoration. The pope

chose it as a warning to Catholics to adhere to their faith in the turmoil of the Reformation. In fact the work conveys the artist's own tormented attitude to his faith. It offers neither the certainties of Christian orthodoxy, nor the ordered view of Classicism.

In a dynamic, emotional composition, the figures are caught in a vortex of motion. The dead are torn from their graves and hauled up to face Christ the Judge, whose athletic, muscular figure is the focus of all the painting's movement.

Christ shows little sympathy for the agitated saints around him, clutching the instruments of their martyrdom. Neither is any pity shown for the damned, hurled down to the demons in hell. Here Charon, pushing people off his boat into the depths of Hades, and the infernal judge Minos, are taken from Dante's *Inferno*. Minos has ass's ears, and is a portrait of courtier Biagio da Cesena, who had objected to the nude figures in the fresco. Michelangelo's self-portrait is on the skin held by the martyr St Bartholomew.

Raphael Rooms

POPE JULIUS II'S PRIVATE APARTMENTS were built above those of his hated predecessor, Alexander VI, who died in 1503. Julius was impressed with Raphael's work and chose him to redecorate the four rooms (stanze). Raphael and his pupils began in 1508, replacing works by better-known artists, including Raphael's teacher, Perugino. The new frescoes quickly established the young artist's reputation in Rome, but the project took 16 years to complete and he died before it was finished.

Detail from Raphael's The Mass of Bolsena (1512)

HALL OF CONSTANTINE

THE FRESCOES IN THIS ROOM were started in 1517 and completed in 1525, five years after Raphael's death, and are largely the work of the artist's pupils. The theme of the decoration is the triumph of Christianity over paganism, and the four major frescoes show scenes from the life of Constantine, the first Christian emperor. These include the Vision of the Cross and the emperor's victory over his rival, Maxentius, at The Battle of the Milvian Bridge, for which Raphael had provided a preparatory sketch.

ROOM OF HELIODORUS

RAPHAEL DECORATED this private antechamber between 1512 and 1514. The main frescoes all contain thinly veiled references to the protective powers of the papacy. The room's name refers to the fresco on the right, The Expulsion of Heliodorus from the Temple, showing Heliodorus felled by a horseman as he tries to rob the Temple in Jerusalem. It alludes to Pope Julius II's victory over foreign armies in Italy. The Mass of Bolsena on the left wall refers to a miracle that occurred in 1263, in which a priest who doubted the doctrine of the Holy Host was said to have seen blood issue from it at the moment of sacrifice.

ROOM OF THE SEGNATURA

COMPLETED BETWEEN 1508 and 1511, the frescoes here are the most harmonious in the series. The scheme followed by Raphael, dictated by Pope Julius II, reflected the Humanist belief that there could be perfect harmony between Classical culture and Christianity in the search for truth. The most famous work, The School of Athens, centres on the debate about truth between the Greek philosophers Plato and Aristotle. Raphael depicted some of his contemporaries as philosophers, including Leonardo da Vinci, Bramante and Michelangelo.

KEY TO FLOORPLAN

① Hall of Constantine
② Room of Heliodorus
③ Room of the Segnatura
④ Room of the Fire in the Borgo

ROOM OF THE FIRE IN THE BORGO

THIS WAS ORIGINALLY the dining room, but when the decoration was completed under Pope Leo X, it became a music room. All the frescoes exalt the reigning pope by depicting events in the lives of his 9th-century namesakes, Leo III and IV. The main frescoes were designed by Raphael, but finished by his assistants between 1514 and 1517. The most famous, The Fire in the Borgo, shows a miracle of 847, when Pope Leo IV put out a fire by making the sign of the cross. Raphael draws a parallel between this and the legendary flight of Aeneas from Troy, recounted by Virgil. Aeneas appears in the foreground, carrying his father Anchises on his back.

The School of Athens (1511) showing philosophers and scholars

Villa Farnesina ❹

Via della Lungara 230. **Map** 2 E5.
📞 06-68 80 17 67. 🚌 23, 65, 280.
🕐 9am–1pm Mon–Sat.

T HE FABULOUSLY WEALTHY
Sienese banker Agostino
Chigi commissioned this villa
in 1508 from his fellow
Sienese Baldassare Peruzzi.
Chigi's main home was across
the Tiber, and the villa was
designed purely for lavish
banquets. Artists, poets,
cardinals, princes and the
pope himself were entertained
here in magnificent style.
Chigi also used the villa for
sojourns with the courtesan
Imperia, who allegedly inspired one of the *Three Graces*
painted by Raphael in the
Loggia of Cupid and Psyche.

The simple, harmonious
design of the Farnesina, with
a central block and projecting
wings, made it one of the first
true villas of the Renaissance.
Peruzzi decorated some of
the interiors himself, such as
the Sala della Prospettiva
upstairs, in which the illusionistic frescoes create the
impression of looking out
over 16th-century Rome
through a marble colonnade.
Other frescoes, by Sebastiano
del Piombo and Raphael and
his pupils, illustrate Classical
myths, while the vault of the
main hall, the Sala di Galatea,
is adorned with astrological
scenes showing the position
of the stars at the time of
Chigi's birth. After his death
the business collapsed, and in
1577 the villa was sold off to
the Farnese family.

**Raphael's *Three Graces* in the
Villa Farnesina**

**Queen Christina of Sweden's
bedroom in the Palazzo Corsini**

Palazzo Corsini and the Galleria Nazionale d'Arte Antica ❺

Via della Lungara 10. **Map** 2 D5.
📞 06-68 80 23 23. 🚌 23, 41, 65,
280. 🕐 9am–1:30pm Tue–Sat,
9am–1pm Sun & public hols.

B UILT FOR CARDINAL DOMENICO
Riario in the late 15th
century, Palazzo Corsini has
numbered Bramante, Michelangelo, Erasmus, Queen
Christina of Sweden and
Napoleon's mother among its
guests. The original palazzo
was rebuilt by Ferdinando
Fuga in 1736, who designed
the façade so that it could be
seen from an angle, as Via
della Lungara is too narrow to
allow a full frontal view.

When the palazzo was
bought by the state in 1893,
the Corsini family donated
their collection of paintings,
which formed the core of the
national art collection, and
was soon augmented by other
bequests. The collection is now
split between Palazzo Barberini
and Palazzo Corsini. Although
the best works are in the
Barberini, there are fine paintings by Van Dyck, Rubens,
Murillo, Reni and Caravaggio,
notably an androgynous
St John the Baptist (c.1604) by
Caravaggio, and a *Salome*
(1638) by Reni. The strangest
work is a portrait of the rotund
Queen Christina as the goddess
Diana by J Van Egmont.

Botanical Gardens ❻

Largo Cristina di Svezia 24. **Map** 2 D5.
📞 06-686 41 93. 🚌 23, 65, 280.
🕐 9am–7pm (Oct–Mar: 6pm) Mon–
Sat, 10am–5pm Sun. 🌳 public hols.

S EQUOIAS, PALM TREES, orchids
and bromeliads are among
the 7,000 plants from all over
the world represented in the
Botanical Gardens (*Orto
Botanico*). Indigenous and
exotic species are grouped to
illustrate their botanical families and their adaptation to
different climates and eco-
systems. There are also some
curious plants like the ginkgo
that have survived almost
unchanged from earlier eras.

**Palm trees in the Botanical
Gardens, Trastevere**

Santa Maria in Trastevere ❼

Piazza Santa Maria in Trastevere.
Map 5 C1. 📞 06-581 48 02.
🚌 44, 56, 65, 170. 🕐 8am–1pm,
3–7pm daily.

S ANTA MARIA IN TRASTEVERE
was probably the first
Christian place of worship in
Rome, founded by Pope
Callixtus I in the 3rd century,
when emperors were still
pagan and Christianity a
minority cult. According to
legend, it was built on the
site where a fountain of oil
had miraculously sprung up
on the day that Christ was
born. The basilica became
the focus of devotion to the
Madonna, and although
today's church, and its
remarkable mosaics, date
largely from the 12th and
13th centuries, images of the

Apse mosaic of the *Coronation of the Virgin*, Santa Maria in Trastevere

Virgin continue to dominate. The façade mosaics probably date from the 12th century, and show Mary, Christ and ten lamp-bearing women. Inside in the apse is a stylized 12th-century *Coronation of the Virgin*, and below, a series of realistic scenes from the life of the Virgin by the 13th-century artist Pietro Cavallini. The oldest image of the Virgin is a 7th-century icon, the *Madonna di Clemenza*, which depicts her as a Byzantine empress flanked by a guard of angels. It sits above the altar in the Cappella Altemps.

Santa Cecilia in Trastevere ❽

Piazza di Santa Cecilia. **Map** 6 D2.
📞 06-589 92 89. 🚌 56, 60, 75, 710.
⭕ 10am–noon, 4–6pm daily.
Cavallini fresco ⭕ 10–11:30am
Tue & Thu.

ST CECILIA, aristocrat and patron saint of music, was martyred here in AD 230. After an unsuccessful attempt to suffocate her by locking her in the hot steam bath of her house for three days, she was beheaded. A church was built, possibly in the 4th century, on the site of the saint's house (still to be seen beneath the church, along with the remains of a Roman tannery). For a long time her body was lost, but it turned up again in the Catacombs of San Callisto (*see p432*). In the 9th century it was reburied here by Pope Paschal I, who rebuilt the church. A

fine apse mosaic survives from this period. The altar canopy by Arnolfo di Cambio and the fresco of *The Last Judgment* by Pietro Cavallini can be reached through the adjoining convent; they date from the 13th century, one of the few periods when Rome had a distinctive artistic style.

In front of the altar is a delicate statue of St Cecilia by Stefano Maderno, which is based on sketches made of her perfectly preserved relics when they were briefly disinterred in 1599.

San Francesco a Ripa ❾

Piazza San Francesco d'Assisi 88.
Map 6 D2. 📞 06-581 90 20. 🚌 44,
75, 170, 710. ⭕ 7am–noon, 4pm–
7pm daily. 📷 ♿

ST FRANCIS OF ASSISI lived here in a hospice when he visited Rome in 1219 and his stone pillow and crucifix are preserved in his cell. The church was built by a follower, a local nobleman called Rodolfo Anguillara, who is

portrayed on his tombstone wearing the Franciscan habit.

Entirely rebuilt in the 1680s by Cardinal Pallavicini, the church is rich in 17th- and 18th-century sculptures. Not to be missed in the Altieri chapel (fourth left, along the nave) is Bernini's exquisite late work, the *Ecstasy of Beata Ludovica Albertoni* (1674).

San Pietro in Montorio and the Tempietto ❿

Piazza San Pietro in Montorio 2.
Map 5 B1. 📞 06-581 39 40.
🚌 41, 44, 75, 710. ⭕ 9am–noon,
4–6:30pm daily. If closed, ring bell at
door to right of church. 📷

Bramante's circular Tempietto at San Pietro in Montorio

THE TEMPIETTO, a diminutive masterpiece of Renaissance architecture completed by Bramante in 1502, stands in the courtyard of San Pietro in Montorio. The name means "little temple" and its circular shape echoes early Christian *martyria*, chapels built on the site of a saint's martyrdom. This was erroneously thought to be the spot in Nero's Circus where St Peter was crucified. Bramante ringed the chapel with Doric columns, a Classical frieze and fine balustrade.

Bernini's *Ecstasy of Beata Ludovica Albertoni*, San Francesco a Ripa

AVENTINE AND LATERAN

THIS IS ONE of the greenest parts of the city, taking in the Celian and Aventine Hills, as well as the very congested area around San Giovanni in Laterano. The Celian, now scattered with churches, was a fashionable place to live in Imperial Rome. Some of the era's splendour is still apparent in the ruins of the Baths of Caracalla.

Mosaic fragment, Baths of Caracalla

Behind the Baths rises the Aventine Hill, a peaceful, leafy area, with the superb basilica of Santa Sabina, and lovely views across the river to Trastevere and St Peter's. In the valley below, cars and Vespas skim around the Circus Maximus, following the ancient charioteering track, while to the south lies Testaccio, a lively working-class district.

SIGHTS AT A GLANCE

Churches

San Clemente ❻
San Giovanni in Laterano ❼
Santa Maria in Cosmedin ❷
Santa Maria in Domnica ❸
Santi Quattro Coronati ❺
Santa Sabina ⓫
Santo Stefano Rotondo ❹

Ancient Sites and Buildings

Baths of Caracalla ❽
Temples of the Forum Boarium ❶

Monuments and Tombs

Protestant Cemetery ❿
Pyramid of Caius Cestius ❾

KEY

▨ Street by Street: Piazza della Bocca della Verità *pp422–3*

FS Railway station

M Metro station

P Parking

— City walls

GETTING THERE

Bus 95 runs from Piramide to Piazza della Bocca della Verità. The Celian is near Metro Colosseo and Circo Massimo; bus 94 climbs the Aventine; and bus 118 links the Baths of Caracalla with San Giovanni in Laterano.

0 metres 250
0 yards 250

◁ **Pines and orange trees in the Aventine's Parco Savelli, with the dome of St Peter's in the distance**

Street-by-Street: Piazza della Bocca della Verità

THE SITE OF ROME'S FIRST PORT and its busy cattle market, this is an odd little corner of the city, stretching from the heavily trafficked road running along the Tiber to the southern spur of the Capitoline Hill, a place of execution from ancient times until the Middle Ages. Although best known for the Bocca della Verità (Mouth of Truth) in Santa Maria in Cosmedin, which is supposed to snap shut on the hands of liars, there are many other sites in the area, notably two temples from the Republican era. In the 6th century the area became home to a Greek community who founded the churches of San Giorgio in Velabro and Santa Maria in Cosmedin.

The Casa dei Crescenzi, studded with ancient fragments, incorporates the ruins of a 10th-century tower built by the powerful Crescenzi family to guard the river Tiber.

Sant'Omobono stands on an archaeological site where finds date back to the 6th century.

★ **Temples of the Forum Boarium**
These two buildings are the best preserved of Rome's Republican temples ❶

Ponte Rotto, as this forlorn ruined arch in the Tiber is called, simply means "broken bridge". Built in the 2nd century BC, its original name was the Pons Aemilius.

The Fontana dei Tritoni, built by Carlo Bizzaccheri in 1715, shows the strong influence of Bernini.

★ **Santa Maria in Cosmedin**
The Bocca della Verità, *a medieval drain cover, is set into the portico* ❷

LUNGOTEVERE DEI PIERLEONI

TEVERE

PONTE PALATINO

VIA DI SAN GIOVANNI DECOLLATO

PIAZZA DELLA BOCCA DELLA VERITÀ

VIA DELLA GRE

KEY

– – –   Suggested route

0 metres   75
0 yards   75

San Giovanni Decollato belonged to a confraternity that encouraged condemned prisoners to repent.

Santa Maria della Consolazione was named after an image of the Virgin placed here in 1385 to give consolation to the condemned.

LOCATOR MAP
See Rome Street Finder map 6

San Teodoro is a circular church on the edge of the Palatine with exceptional 6th-century apse mosaics.

San Giorgio in Velabro, a 7th-century basilica, was damaged in an explosion in 1994, and is currently being repaired.

Arco degli Argentari

IA DEI FIENILI

VIA DI SAN TEODORO

The 4th-century Arch of Janus, a four-faced marble-plated arch at the edge of the Forum Boarium market, was an ideal place for merchants and customers to do business in the shade.

A DEI CERCHI

STAR SIGHTS

★ **Santa Maria in Cosmedin**

★ **Temples of the Forum Boarium**

Temples of the Forum Boarium ❶

Piazza della Bocca della Verità.
Map 6 E1. 🚌 *90, 92, 94, 95.*

THESE WONDERFULLY well-preserved Republican temples are at their best at moonlight, standing in their grassy enclave beside the Tiber sheltered by the umbrella pines. During the day, they look less romantic, stranded in a sea of traffic. They date from the 2nd century BC, and were saved from ruin by being consecrated as Christian churches in the Middle Ages by the Greek community then living in the area. The rectangular temple, formerly known as the Temple of Fortuna Virilis, was probably dedicated to Portunus, the god of rivers and ports. Set on a podium it has four Ionic travertine columns fluted at the front and 12 half-columns embedded in the tufa wall of the *cella* – the room that housed the image of the god. In the 9th century the Temple was converted into the church of Santa Maria Egiziaca, after a 5th-century prostitute who reformed and became a hermit.

The smaller circular Temple, which is made of solid marble and surrounded by 20 fluted columns, was dedicated to Hercules, though it was long believed to be a Temple of Vesta because of its similarity to the one in the Forum.

The Ionic façade of the Republican era Temple of Portunus

Apse mosaic from the 9th century of the Virgin and Child in Santa Maria in Domnica

Santa Maria in Cosmedin ❷

Piazza della Bocca della Verità. **Map** 6 E1. 06-678 14 19. 57, 90, 92. 9am–1pm, 2:30–7pm daily.

THIS BEAUTIFUL unadorned church was built in the 6th century on the site of the ancient city's food market. The elegant Romanesque bell tower and portico were added during the 12th century. In the 19th century a Baroque façade was removed and the church restored to its original simplicity. It contains many fine examples of Cosmati work, in particular the mosaic pavement, the raised choir, the bishop's throne, and the canopy over the main altar.

Set into the wall of the portico is the Bocca della Verità (Mouth of Truth), a grotesque slit-mouthed marble face, thought to have

The nave of Santa Maria in Cosmedin with its Cosmati floor

been an ancient drain cover. Medieval tradition had it that the jaws would snap shut on liars – a useful way of testing the faithfulness of spouses.

Santa Maria in Domnica ❸

Piazza della Navicella 12. **Map** 7 B2. 06-700 15 19. 15, 118, 673. 8:30am–noon, 3:30–7pm (Oct–Mar: 6pm) daily.

SANTA MARIA IN DOMNICA was probably founded in the 7th century, and renovated in the 9th century. By this time the Romans had lost the art of making mosaics, so Pope Paschal I imported mosaicists from Byzantium. They created an exquisite apse mosaic showing the Virgin, Child and angels in a delicate wind-stirred garden of paradise. Paschal I appears kneeling at the Virgin's feet wearing a square halo, indicating that he was alive when it was made.

In 1513 Andrea Sansovino added a portico decorated with lions' heads, a punning homage to Pope Leo X.

Santo Stefano Rotondo ❹

Via di Santo Stefano 7. **Map** 9 B2. 06-70 49 37 17. 15, 118, 673. 9am–1pm Tue–Sat.

SANTO STEFANO ROTONDO was built between 468 and 483 on a circular plan with four chapels jutting out in the shape of a cross. It has a

circular inner area surrounded by two concentric corridors. A third, outer corridor was demolished on the orders of Leon Battista Alberti in 1453. In the 16th century Niccolò Pomarancio, Antonio Tempesta and others covered the walls with 34 frescoes, gruesomely detailing the martyrdoms of saints by Roman emperors.

Cloister of Santi Quattro Coronati

Santi Quattro Coronati ❺

Via dei Santi Quattro Coronati 20. **Map** 7 C1. 06-73 53 21. 15, 85, 87, 118. 13, 30b. 9:30am–noon, 3:30–6pm (Oct–Mar: 9:30am–noon) Mon–Sat.

THIS FORTIFIED convent was built in the 4th century to house the relics of four Persian stonemasons, martyred after they refused to make a statue honouring the pagan god Aesculapius. It was rebuilt after invading Normans set fire to it in 1084.

Highlights are a delightful garden cloister and the Chapel of St Sylvester, where 12th-century frescoes recount the legend of Constantine's conversion to Christianity.

San Clemente ⑥

IN 1857 FATHER MULLOOLY, the Irish Dominican prior of San Clemente, began excavations beneath the existing 12th-century basilica. Directly underneath he and his successors discovered a 4th-century church, and below that a number of ancient Roman buildings. Both basilicas are dedicated to St Clement, the fourth pope. On the lowest level is a temple devoted to the cult of Mithras, a mystical all-male religion imported from Persia which rivalled Christianity for popularity.

VISITORS' CHECKLIST

Via di San Giovanni in Laterano.
Map 7 B1. 06-70 45 10 18.
81, 85, 186 to Via Labicana.
Colosseo. 13, 30.
9am–12:30pm, 3:30–6:30pm
(Oct–Mar: 6pm) daily. to
excavations.

Cappella di Santa Caterina
Recently restored frescoes by the 15th-century Florentine artist Masolino show scenes from the life of St Catherine of Alexandria.

Entrance

Apse Mosaic
The 12th-century Triumph of the Cross *includes finely detailed animals and acanthus leaves.*

Paschal Candlestick
This splendid 12th-century spiralling candlestick, striped with glittering multi-coloured mosaic, is the work of the Cosmati.

12th-century basilica

-century de

Piscina

Schola Cantorum

4th-century basilica

Temple of Mithras

Life of San Clemente
Faded frescoed episodes from the life of the fourth pope decorate the lower church. This one tells the story of a boy found alive in his tomb under the sea.

Triclinium
An altar to the god Mithras, showing him slaying a bull, stands in the dank triclinium, a room used for ritual banquets by cult members.

San Giovanni in Laterano ⁷

SAN GIOVANNI, the cathedral of Rome, was founded by Emperor Constantine in the early 4th century. It has been rebuilt several times, notably in 1646 when Borromini restyled the interior, but retains its original basilica form. Before the papacy moved to Avignon in 1309, the adjoining Lateran Palace was the official papal residence. The present structure dates from 1589, but older parts survive, like the Scala Santa (Holy Staircase) which Christ is said to have climbed at his trial.

VISITORS' CHECKLIST

Piazza di San Giovanni in Laterano.
Map 8 D2. 📞 06-69 88 64 33.
🚌 4, 15, 714, 715. 🚃 13.
Ⓜ San Giovanni. **Cathedral**
🕐 7am–6:45pm daily (Oct–Mar: 6pm). **Cloisters & Museum**
🕐 9am–6pm (Oct–Mar: 5pm) daily (last adm: 15 mins before closing). 🖼 📷 ⛪ ♿
Baptistry ⬤ for restoration.

Baptistry
Though much restored, the octagonal baptistry contains some beautiful 5th-century mosaics.

Apse

North façade

East Façade
The main entrance, on the east façade (1735), is adorned with statues of Christ and the Apostles.

Museum entrance

Lateran Palace

Papal Altar
The Gothic baldacchino, which rises over the papal altar, is decorated with 14th-century frescoes. Only the pope can celebrate mass here.

On Maundy Thursday the Pope, as Bishop of Rome, gives a blessing from the loggia of the city's main cathedral.

The Corsini Chapel
was built in the 1730s for Pope Clement XII Corsini, who lies buried in a porphyry tomb from the Pantheon.

Main entrance

Cloisters
Built by the Vassalletto family in about 1220, the cloisters are remarkable for their twisted columns and inlaid marble mosaics.

Boniface VIII Fresco
Possibly by Giotto, this fragment shows the pope announcing the Holy Year of 1300, which attracted around two million pilgrims.

Part of one of the gymnasia in the Baths of Caracalla

Baths of Caracalla ❽

Viale delle Terme di Caracalla 52.
Map 7 A3. 📞 06-575 86 26. 🚌 90,
160. ⏰ 9am–6pm (Oct–Mar: 5pm)
Tue–Sat, 9am–1pm Sun, Mon.
🌳 public hols. 🎟 📷 ♿
Concerts 📞 06-575 83 02.

Rearing up at the foot of the Aventine Hill are the monolithic red-brick ruins of the Baths of Caracalla. Begun by Emperor Septimius Severus in AD 206, and completed by his son Caracalla in AD 217, they remained in use until the 6th century, when the Goths sabotaged the city's aqueducts.

Going for a bath was one of the social events of the day in ancient Rome. Large complexes such as Caracalla, with a capacity for 1,500 bathers, were not simply places to get washed, but also offered an impressive array of facilities: art galleries, gymnasia, gardens, libraries, conference rooms, lecture rooms and shops selling food and drink.

A Roman bath was a long and complicated business, beginning with a form of Turkish bath, followed by a spell in the *calidarium*, a large hot room with pools of water to moisten the atmosphere. Then came the lukewarm *tepidarium*, followed by a visit to the large central meeting place known as the *frigidarium*, and finally a plunge into the *natatio*, an open-air swimming pool. For the rich, this was followed by a rub-down with scented woollen cloth.

Most of the rich marble decorations of the baths were scavenged by the Farnese family in the 16th century to adorn the rooms of Palazzo Farnese *(see p391)*. There are, however, statues and mosaics from the Baths in the Museo Nazionale Archeologico in Naples *(see pp474–5)* and in the Vatican's Gregorian Profane Museum *(see p412)*.

So dramatic is the setting, that until recently it was the regular venue for the open-air opera season in August.

Pyramid of Caius Cestius ❾

Piazzale Ostiense. **Map** 6 E4. 🚌 11,
23, 94. 🚋 13, 30b. Ⓜ Piramide.

Caius Cestius was a wealthy but unimportant 1st-century BC *praetor*, or senior magistrate. At the time, inspired by the Cleopatra scandals, there was a craze for all things Egyptian, and Caius decided to commission himself a pyramid as a tomb. Set into the Aurelian Wall near Porta San Paolo, it is built of brick and faced with white marble; according to an inscription, it took just 330 days to build in 12 BC.

The Pyramid of Caius Cestius on Piazzale Ostiense

Protestant Cemetery ❿

Via di Caio Cestio 6. **Map** 6 E4.
📞 06-574 11 41. 🚌 11, 23, 27, 94.
🚋 13, 30b. ⏰ 9am–6pm Apr–Sep
(Oct–Mar: 5pm) Tue–Sun. **Donation**.
📷 ♿

Non-catholics have been buried in this peaceful cemetery behind the Aurelian Wall since 1738. In the oldest part (on the left as you enter) is the grave of the poet John Keats, who died in 1821 in a house on Piazza di Spagna *(see p398)*. He wrote his own epitaph: "Here lies one whose name was writ in water". Not far away from here rest the ashes of Percy Bysshe Shelley, who drowned in 1822.

The interior of Santa Sabina

Santa Sabina ⓫

Piazza Pietro d'Illiria 1. **Map** 6 E4.
📞 06-574 35 73. 🚌 94. ⏰ 7am–
12:30pm, 3:30–6pm daily. 📷 ♿

High on the aventine stands a perfect early Christian basilica, founded by Peter of Illyria in AD 422 and later given to the Dominican order. It was restored to its original simplicity early this century. Light filters through 9th-century windows on to a wide nave framed by pale Corinthian columns. Above the main door is a blue and gold 5th-century mosaic inscription to Peter. In the side portico outside is a 5th-century panelled door carved with biblical scenes, notably, one of the oldest representations of the Crucifixion (top left-hand corner).

Further Afield

IT IS WELL WORTH making the effort to see some of Rome's outlying sights. Highlights are the Villa Giulia, home to a magnificent Etruscan museum, and the Museo Borghese on the splendid Villa Borghese estate, with its extraordinary collection of virtuoso statues by Bernini. Other sights range from ancient churches and catacombs, to the more modern suburb of EUR, a strange architectural medley begun by Mussolini in the 1930s.

KEY

▨	Central Rome
▢	Suburbs
═	Motorway
▬	Major road
═	Minor road
----	City walls

10 km = 6 miles

Villa Borghese ①

Map 3 B1. 🚌 *52, 53, 57, 95.* 🚊 *19, 19b, 30b.* ⭕ *dawn–sunset.*

THE VILLA AND ITS PARK were designed in 1605 for Cardinal Scipione Borghese, the sybaritic nephew of Pope Paul V. An extravagant patron of the arts, he amassed one of Europe's finest collections of paintings, statues and antiquities, many of which are still displayed in the villa which he built especially to house his antique sculptures.

The **park** was one of the first of its kind in Rome, its formal gardens divided by avenues and graced with statues. It contained 400 newly planted trees, garden sculpture by Bernini's father, Pietro, along with many ingenious fountains, "secret" flower gardens, enclosures of exotic animals and birds, and even a grotto with artificial rain. There was also a speaking robot and a trick chair, which trapped anyone who sat down in it. At first the grounds were open to the public, but after a visitor was shocked by Scipione's collection of erotic paintings, Paul V decided it was more prudent to keep the park private.

In 1773 work began on redesigning the park in the wilder, Romantic style made fashionable by landscape artists like Claude Lorrain and Poussin. Over the next few years mock-Classical temples, fountains and *casine* (summerhouses) were added. In 1902,

GIARDINO ZOOLOGICO

Zoo entrance, Villa Borghese

the park and villa were acquired by the state, and in 1911 the area was chosen as the site for the International Exhibition. Pavilions were built by many of the world's nations, the most impressive of which is the **British School at Rome** by Edwin Lutyens. In the same year a zoo was opened, now a depressing affair with small, cramped cages spread out over 17 hectares (42 acres). Today the estates of the Villa

British School at Rome in Villa Borghese, designed for the 1911 exhibition

Temple of Aesculapius, an 18th-century folly, in the Villa Borghese

Borghese, Villa Giulia and the Pincio gardens form one vast park, with the **Giardino del Lago** at its centre, named after an artificial boating lake. Its main entrance is marked by an 18th-century copy of the Arch of Septimius Severus, while on the lake's island is a fake Ionic temple to the Greek god of health, Aesculapius.

Dotted about the park are other picturesque follies, including a circular Temple of Diana between the Porta Pinciana, at the top of Via Veneto, and Piazza di Siena, a grassy amphitheatre which hosts Rome's international horse show in May. Its umbrella pines inspired the composer Ottorino Respighi to write *The Pines of Rome* (1924). The open-air opera season is also held in the park.

To the northwest of the park is the Galleria Nazionale d'Arte Moderna, which houses a large but somewhat uninspiring collection of 19th- and 20th-century paintings.

Museo Borghese ❷

Via Raimondo, Parco dei Daini, Villa Borghese. **Map** 2 F5. **⟁** 06-854 85 77. **⟁** 52, 53, 910. **○** 9am–7pm (Oct–Apr: 2pm) Tue–Sat, 9am–1pm Sun. **○** public hols. **⟁ ⟁**
Complesso San Michele Via San Michele. **⟁** 06-581 67 32.

SCIPIONE BORGHESE'S villa was designed in 1605 as a typical Roman country house, with its wings projecting into the surrounding gardens. It was built by Flaminio Ponzio,

Pope Paul V's architect, and was used by Scipione for entertaining guests and for displaying his impressive collection of paintings and sculpture. Between 1801 and 1809 Prince Camillo Borghese, husband to Napoleon's sister Pauline, sold many of the family paintings to his brother-in-law, and swapped 200 of Scipione's Classical statues for an estate in Piedmont. These statues are still in the Louvre and as a consequence the remaining antique Classical collection is perhaps less interesting. However, the hedonistic cardinal was an extravagant patron of the arts and the sculptures he commissioned from artists such as the young Bernini now rank among his most famous works.

The eight rooms of the ground floor are set around a central hall, the Salone. The most famous statue is one of Bernini's finest works, *Apollo and Daphne* (1624) in room 3, which shows the nymph Daphne with bay leaves sprouting from her outstretched fingers, roots growing from her toes and rough bark enfolding her smooth body, as she begins to metamorphose into a laurel tree to escape being abducted by the god Apollo.

Bernini's *Apollo and Daphne* (1624)

Detail of *Pluto and Persephone* by Bernini (1622), Museo Borghese

Abduction is the theme of *Pluto and Persephone*, also by Bernini, in room 4. Depicting Pluto, the god of the underworld, carrying Persephone off to be his bride, the sculpture is a virtuoso piece in which Bernini contrasts the taut musculature of Pluto with the soft yielding flesh of Persephone, whose thigh dimples in his iron grip.

The third famous Bernini piece, which dates from 1623, is *David* in room 2. The artist captures the tensed, grimacing youth the moment before he releases the stone that slew Goliath. It is said that Pope Urban VIII held a mirror up to Bernini so that the sculptor could model David's face on his own. In the next alcove is the Villa Borghese's most infamous work, a sculpture executed in 1805 by Canova of Pauline Borghese as *Venus Victrix* (Venus the Conqueror). The semi-naked Pauline reclining on a chaise longue shocked those who saw it and Pauline's husband kept the statue locked away, even denying Canova access.

The next room holds a selection of antiquities, notably a Roman copy of a plump *Bacchus* by the 4th century BC Greek sculptor Praxiteles, and fragments of a 3rd-century AD mosaic found on one of the Borghese estates in Torrenova, showing gladiators battling with wild animals.

The Galleria Borghese on the upper floor is currently closed for restoration, but the majority of works from this superb collection of Baroque and Renaissance paintings can be seen at the Complesso San Michele in Trastevere. It includes Raphael's masterpiece, the *Deposition*, various works by Caravaggio, the graceful *Danäe* by the 16th-century artist Correggio, as well as works by Pinturicchio, Barocci, Rubens and Titian.

Villa Giulia ③

THIS VILLA WAS BUILT in 1550 as a country retreat for Pope Julius III. Designed by Vignola and Ammannati, with contributions by Michelangelo and Vasari, it was intended for entertaining guests of the Vatican, such as Queen Christina of Sweden, rather than as a permanent home. The gardens were planted with 36,000 trees and peppered with pavilions and fountains, and the villa once housed an outstanding collection of statues: 160 boats filled with statues and ornaments were sent to the Vatican after the pope died in 1555.

Since 1889 the villa has been home to the Museo Nazionale Etrusco, an impressive collection of pre-Roman antiquities from central Italy.

Rooms 24–29 contain finds from the Ager Faliscus, an area between the Tiber and Lake Bracciano, in particular temples from Falerii Vetere, the principal Faliscan town.

Spiralled Faliscan Crater
Painted in the free style of the 4th century BC, this spiral handled vase was used to hold wines or oil. The Falisci were an Italic tribe influenced by the Etruscans.

Rooms 11–18, the Antiquarium collection, display domestic and votive objects and ceramics, including the Chigi vase from 6th-century BC Corinth.

Room 19 exhibits finds from the Castellani collection, including early 6th-century ceramics and bronzes.

Ficoroni Cist
Engraved and beautifully illustrated, this fine 4th-century BC bronze marriage coffer held mirrors and other body care implements

Replica Etruscan temple

Husband and Wife Sarcophagus
This 6th-century BC tomb from Cerveteri shows a deceased couple banqueting in the afterlife. Their tender expression bears witness to the skill of Etruscan artists.

Rooms 30–34 exhibit finds from various sites including the Temple of Diana at Nemi.

Rooms 1–10 are arranged by site, starting with Vulci (most importantly articles from the Warrior's Tomb) and including Bisenzio, Veio and Cerveteri.

Entrance

KEY TO FLOORPLAN

☐ Ground floor
☐ First floor
☐ Non-exhibition space

Apse mosaic in Sant'Agnese, showing the saint flanked by two popes

Sant'Agnese fuori le Mura ❹

Via Nomentana 349. ☎ 06-861 08 40. ▦ 36, 36b, 60, 137. ◯ 9am–noon, 4–6pm Mon & Wed–Sat, 4–6pm Sun & public hols. ▨ to catacombs. ◙ ✔

SANT'AGNESE FUORI LE MURA was built in the 4th century above the crypt of the 13-year-old martyr St Agnes, and although much altered it retains the form of the original basilica. According to legend it was founded by Constantine's daughter Constantia, who was cured from leprosy after sleeping beside Agnes's tomb.

In the 7th-century apse mosaic, St Agnes appears as a bejewelled Byzantine empress in a stole of gold and a violet robe. Tradition has it that she appeared like this eight days after her death holding a white lamb. On 21 January two lambs are blessed in the church and a vestment called a *pallium* is woven from their wool, to be given to a new archbishop.

Santa Costanza ❺

Via Nomentana 349. ☎ 06-861 08 40. ▦ 36, 36b, 60, 137. ◯ 9am–noon, 4–6pm Mon & Wed–Sat, 4–6pm Sun & public hols. ◙ ♿ ✔

THIS CIRCULAR church was built in the early 4th century as a mausoleum for Emperor Constantine's daughters, Constantia and Helena. The dome and its

drum are supported by an arcade that rests on 12 magnificent pairs of granite columns, while the encircling ambulatory has a barrel-vaulted ceiling decorated with the world's earliest surviving Christian mosaics. Dating from the 4th century, they are thought to have been copied from a secular Roman floor and include flowers, animals and birds. There is even a charming scene of a Roman grape-harvest, though the wine is said by Christians to represent Christ's blood.

In a niche on the far side of the church is a replica of Constantia's ornate porphyry sarcophagus, carved with cherubs crushing grapes. The original was moved to the Vatican Museums in 1790.

Circular interior of the 4th-century church of Santa Costanza

The sanctity of Constantia is somewhat debatable. Described by the historian Marcellinus as a fury incarnate, constantly goading her equally unpleasant husband, Hannibalianus, to violence, her canonization was probably the result of some confusion with a saintly nun of the same name.

Via Appia Antica ❻

▦ 118, 218.

Cypresses lining the Via Appia

THE FIRST PART of the Via Appia was built in 312 BC by Appius Claudius Caecus. In 190 BC, when it was extended to the ports of Taranto and Brindisi, the road became Rome's link with its empire in the East. It was the route taken by the funeral processions of the dictator Sulla (78 BC) and Emperor Augustus (AD 14), and it was along this road that St Paul was led as a prisoner to Rome in AD 56. The church of Domine Quo Vadis? marks the spot where St Peter is said to have met Christ when fleeing Rome.

The road is lined with ruined family tombs, decaying monuments, and collective burial places (*columbaria*). Beneath the fields on either side lies a maze of catacombs, including those of San Callisto and San Sebastiano.

Catacombs ❼

Via Appia Antica 110. 🚌 78, 118,
127. **San Callisto** ☎ 06-513 67 25.
🕐 8:30am–noon, 2:30–5:30pm
(Oct–Mar: 5pm) Thu–Tue. ⬤ public
hols. 🗺 🎫

IN BURYING THEIR DEAD in
underground cemeteries
outside the city walls, the
early Christians were simply
obeying the laws of the time.
They were not forced to use
them because of persecution,
as later popular myth has
suggested. Many saints were
buried there, and the catacombs later became shrines
and places of pilgrimage.

Today several catacombs
are open to the public. The
vast Catacombs of San Callisto,
hewn from volcanic tufa,
contain niches, or *loculi*, which
held two or three bodies, as
well as the burial places of
several early popes. Close by,
walls in the Catacombs of San
Sebastiano are covered in
graffiti invoking St Peter and
St Paul, whose remains may
once have been moved here.

**Engraving of Christian ceremony in
Catacombs of San Callisto (AD 50)**

EUR ❽

🚌 714, 717. Ⓜ EUR Fermi, EUR
Palasport. **Museo della Civiltà
Romana** ☎ 06-592 60 41. 🕐 9am–
1pm Tue–Sun & public hols, 4–7pm
Tue & Thu. 🗺

THE ESPOSIZIONE UNIVERSALE di
Roma (EUR), a suburb to
the south of the city, was
originally built for an international exhibition, a kind of
"Work Olympics", that was

**EUR's Palazzo della Civiltà del
Lavoro, the "Square Colosseum"**

planned for 1942, but never
took place because of the
outbreak of war. The architecture was intended to
glorify Fascism, and as a result
the bombastic style of the
buildings can look overblown
and rhetorical to modern
eyes. Of all the buildings the
best known is probably the
Palazzo della Civiltà del Lavoro
(the Palace of the Civilization
of Work), an unmistakable
landmark for people arriving
from Fiumicino airport.

The scheme was eventually
completed in the 1950s.
Despite the area's dubious
architecture, EUR has been a
planning success, and people
are still keen to live here. As
well as residential housing,
the vast marble halls along
the wide boulevards are also
home to a number of government offices and museums.
Best among the latter is the
Museo della Civiltà Romana,
famous for its casts of the
reliefs from the Column
of Trajan, and for a
large scale

model depicting 4th-century
Rome with all the buildings
which then stood within the
Aurelian walls. The south of
the suburb features a lake
and shady park, and the huge
domed Palazzo dello Sport,
built for the 1960 Olympics.

San Paolo fuori
le Mura ❾

Via Ostiense 186. 🚌 23, 93b, 170,
223. Ⓜ San Paolo. ☎ 06-541 03
41. 🕐 6:45am–7pm (Sep–Mar:
6pm) daily. 📷 ♿

TODAY'S CHURCH is a faithful
if somewhat soulless
reconstruction of the great
4th-century basilica destroyed
by fire in 1823. Only a few
fragments of the earlier church
survived, most notably the
cloister (1241), with its pairs
of colourful inlaid columns,
considered one of the most
beautiful in Rome.

Elsewhere, the church's
triumphal arch is decorated
on one side with heavily
restored 5th-century mosaics,
and on the other with mosaics
by Pietro Cavallini originally on
the façade. The equally fine
mosaics (1220) in the apse
represent the figures of Christ
with St Peter, St Andrew, St
Paul and St Luke.

The single most outstanding
work of art is the fine marble
canopy over the high altar, the
work of Arnolfo di Cambio
(1285), with the possible
assistance of Pietro Cavallini.
Below the altar is the *confessio*
where it is alleged St Paul
was once buried. To its right
is an impressive Paschal
candlestick dating from the
12th century by Nicolò di
Angelo and Pietro
Vassalletto.

19th-century mosaic on façade of San Paolo fuori le Mura

ROME STREET FINDER

MAP REFERENCES given with sights described in the Rome chapters relate to the maps on the following pages. Map references are also given for hotels *(see pp542–75)* and restaurant listings *(see pp578–609)* and for useful addresses in the *Travellers' Needs* and *Survival Guide* sections at the back of the book. The first figure in the map reference tells you which Street Finder map to turn to, and the letter and number which follow refer to the grid reference on that map. The small map below shows the area of Rome covered by each of the six maps and the corresponding map number is given in black. All the major sights are sketched out on the maps, and symbols, listed in the key below, are used to indicate the location of other important buildings.

The Vatican and Trastevere

Around Piazza Navona

Northeast Rome

The Ancient Centre

Aventine and Lateran

0 kilometres 2

0 miles 1

KEY AND SCALE FOR STREET FINDER PAGES

Major sight	**P** Parking	⊠ Post office
Place of interest	**i** Tourist information	═ Railway line
FS Railway station	Hospital with casualty unit	One-way street
M Metro station	Police station	— City walls
Bus terminus	**†** Church	0 metres 250
Tram terminus	**✡** Synagogue	0 yards 250

Rome Bus Routes

Buses in Rome are run by the ATAC bus company. Scores of orange buses cover the city from early morning until about midnight, but only the 119 runs through the historic centre.

KEY

57 — Bus route

4 — Start/end of bus route *(capolinea)*

▶ — Direction

■ — Major sight

Ⓜ — Metro station

FS — Railway station

\\ — Tunnel

LAZIO

....

L YING BETWEEN *the Apennines and the Tyrrhenian Sea, Lazio is a varied region of volcanic lakes, mountains, ravines, vineyards and olive groves. Before the rise of Rome, it was populated by the Etruscans and various Italic tribes, including the Latins, after whom the region is named. Besides rich archaeological sites, Lazio also offers skiing and swimming and watersports in the lakes and sea.*

Lazio was inhabited at least 60,000 years ago, although the first signs of a substantial civilization date back to the 10th century BC. By the 7th century BC a flourishing Etruscan and Sabine civilization based on trade and agriculture existed in the north, while the region's southern margins were colonized by the Latins, Volsci and Ernici. History mingles with myth in the writings of Virgil, who describes how Aeneas landed in Lazio where he married the daughter of the king of the Latins. Romulus and Remus (legendary founders of Rome) were descendants of this alliance.

With the rise of Rome as a power, the Etruscan and Latin peoples were, in time, overwhelmed and the focus of the region turned to the city of Rome. Great roads and aqueducts extended out of the city like spokes of a wheel, and wealthy patricians built lavish villas in the surrounding countryside. The early Middle Ages saw the rise of the Church's temporal power and, with the foundation of monasteries at Subiaco and Montecassino, Lazio became the cradle of western monasticism, and eventually part of the Papal States. In the 16th and 17th centuries, wealthy papal families competed with one another to build luxurious villas and gardens, hiring some of the best architects of the Renaissance and Baroque.

Throughout its history, however, Lazio has been eclipsed and neglected by Rome. The Pontine marshes were a malaria-ridden swamp until the 1920s, when Mussolini had them drained and brought new roads and agricultural improvements to the area.

Looking out over Caprarola during the early evening *passeggiata*

◁ Vignola's graceful Renaissance parterre gardens and fountains in Villa Lante, Viterbo

Exploring Lazio

Much of Lazio's landscape was formed by the eruption of four volcanoes which showered the area with lava. Lakes formed in the craters, and the soil, rendered fertile by the lava, nourished vines, olives, fruit and nut trees. The volcanic activity also left Lazio with hot springs, notably around Tivoli and Fiuggi. Rome dominates the area, dividing the wooded hills of the north from the reclaimed Pontine marshes in the south. Swimming and sailing are possible in lakes Bracciano, Bolsena and Albano, while Lazio's best beaches lie between Gaeta and Sabaudia in the Parco Nazionale del Circeo.

SIGHTS AT A GLANCE

SEE ALSO

• **Where to Stay** pp568–9

• **Where to Eat** pp601–2

The fertile Tolfa hills southwest of Lake Bracciano

KEY

▬▬	Motorway
▬▬	Major road
▬▬	Minor road
▬▬	Scenic route
≈	River
☀	Viewpoint

The old quarter overlooking the beach at Sperlonga

GETTING AROUND

Rome's two international airports at
Fiumicino and Ciampino serve the region.
The main motorways are the *Autostrada del
Sole* (A1) from Firenze–Roma and Roma–
Napoli, and the Roma–L'Aquila (A24). The
ring road *(raccordo anulare)* around Rome
connects the motorways and main roads.

The Lazio bus service, COTRAL, serves
all the main towns with changeover points
for the smaller locations in Rome and at
Latina, Frosinone, Viterbo and Rieti. Train
routes into the region from other Italian cities
are efficient, although within the region the
services are slower and less frequent.

Palestrina's terraces climbing up the hill

| 0 kilometres | 15 |
| 0 miles | 10 |

Carved loggia of the Palazzo Papale, Viterbo

Tuscania ❶

Viterbo. 🏛 7,500. 🚌 ℹ️ *Via Pozzo Bianco (0761-43 63 71).* 🛒 *Fri.*

Tuscania's trim walls and towers are visible from afar on the empty low-lying plains between Viterbo and Tarquinia. Although shaken by an earthquake in 1971, its medieval and Renaissance buildings have since been carefully re-constructed. Just outside the city walls, on the rocky Colle San Pietro, two remarkable churches dating from the Lombard-Romanesque period occupy the site of Tuscana, a major Etruscan centre conquered by Rome in 300 BC.

Santa Maria Maggiore, at the foot of the hill, has a typically Lombard-Romanesque asymmetric façade with blind arcades and a bold rose

Façade of San Pietro, Tuscania

window. Over the central door lies a simple marble Madonna and Child, framed by abstract motifs and biblical scenes. Inside, a rare 12th-century full immersion baptism font stands in the aisle. The Lombard-Romanesque church of **San Pietro**, on top of the hill, is a striking building of ochre-hued tufa and white marble details. It stands on a grassy piazza, along with two medieval towers and a bishop's palace. The façade features an intricately inlaid rose window flanked by strange reliefs, including three-headed bearded demons. The interior is true to its 8th-century form, with squat columns, toothed arches, capitals carved with stylized plants and a Cosmati floor. Below the church lies a strange mosque-like crypt.

Viterbo ❷

🏛 60,000. 🚆 🚌 ℹ️ *Piazza San Carluccio 5 (0761-30 47 95).* 🛒 *Sat.*

Viterbo was an important Etruscan centre before falling to the Romans in the 4th century BC. Its heyday, however, came in the 13th century when it briefly became the papal seat (1257–81). During World War II it was devastated, but the austere grey stone medieval core, still encircled by walls, and many of the town's churches, have been carefully restored.

In **San Pellegrino**, Viterbo's oldest and best preserved quarter, medieval houses with towers, arches and external staircases line narrow streets running between little piazzas decorated with fountains.

On Piazza San Lorenzo the 12th-century **Duomo** boasts an elegant black and white striped bell tower, a solemn 16th-century façade and a stark Romanesque interior. The adjacent 13th-century **Palazzo Papale**, with a finely carved loggia, was built for popes on their visits to the city.

The town's civic buildings border the main square, Piazza del Plebiscito. The most interesting is the 15th-century **Palazzo dei Priori**, frescoed inside by Baldassare Croce with scenes from the town's history and mythological past.

Outside the city walls, on Viale Capocci, the Romanesque **Santa Maria della Verità** has wonderful 15th-century frescoes by Lorenzo da Viterbo.

Villa Lante's small but splendid Renaissance gardens, considered Vignola's masterpiece

ENVIRONS: The **Villa Lante**, northeast of Viterbo, was begun in 1562 by Vignola for Cardinal Gambara. The main attractions are the outstanding Renaissance gardens and fountains. Be careful not to be a victim of a 16th-century practical joke: many of the fountains will sprinkle people without warning.

🏛 **Palazzo dei Priori**
Piazza Plebiscito. 📞 0761-34 07 29.
◐ Mon–Sat. ◑ public hols. ♿

🏛 **Villa Lante**
Bagnaia. 📞 0761-28 80 08.
◐ daily. ◑ 1 Jan, Easter, 25 Dec.
🎟 ♿ to gardens.

The main façade of the pentagonal Palazzo Farnese at Caprarola

Montefiascone ❸

Viterbo. 🚶 13,000. 🚆 🚌 ℹ Piazza Roma 8 (0761-82 66 72). 🔺 Wed.

Carved 11th-century capital in San Flaviano, Montefiascone

THIS PRETTY TOWN is perched on the edge of a defunct volcanic crater between the shores of Lake Bolsena, over which there are splendid views, and the Via Cassia. It is dominated by the octagonal bulk of its cathedral, **Santa Margherita**, whose dome, created in the 1670s by Carlo Fontana, is second only in size to St Peter's.

On the town's outskirts, along the Via Cassia towards Orvieto, lies **San Flaviano**, a lovely double-decker building with a 12th-century church oriented east over an 11th-century church pointing west. Inside are some fine 14th-century frescoes and freely carved capitals, thought to have been inspired by the traditions of Etruscan art.

ENVIRONS: The popular lakeside beach resort of **Bolsena**, 15 km (9 miles) north on Lake Bolsena, has a medieval castle, as well as boats to the islands of Bisentina and Martana.

Bomarzo ❹

Parco dei Mostri, Bomarzo. 📞 0761-92 40 29. 🚆 to Viterbo or Attigliano. 🚌 from Viterbo or Attigliano.
◐ 8am–1 hr before sunset. 🎟 ♿

THE SACRO BOSCO beneath the town of Bomarzo was created between 1522 and 1580 by Duke Vicino Orsini as a bizarre memorial to his late wife. Far from designing a meticulous Renaissance garden, Orsini embraced the artificiality and distortion of the Mannerist period by creating lop-sided buildings and sculpting huge boulders of stone into fantastic creatures and vast allegorical monsters.

One of the bizarre stone monsters in Bomarzo's Sacro Bosco

Caprarola ❺

Viterbo. 🚶 4,900. 🚌 ℹ Via Filippo Nicolai 2 (0761-64 73 47). 🔺 Tue.

PERHAPS THE GRANDEST of the country villas created during the 17th century by the wealthy families of Rome, **Palazzo Farnese** (see p370) is the focal point of the medieval village of Caprarola. Designed by Vignola, it was built between 1559 and 1575 and takes its star-shape from the foundations of a large pentagonal fortress designed by Antonio da Sangallo the Younger half a century earlier. On the main floor, reached by an elaborately stuccoed spiral staircase, the rooms were frescoed, largely by the Zuccari brothers in 1560, with scenes depicting heroic episodes from the life of Hercules and the Farnese family.

ENVIRONS: Created, according to legend, by the god Hercules ramming his club into the ground, **Lago di Vico**, 4 km (3 miles) west of Caprarola, in fact occupies the remnants of a volcanic crater. An idyllic enclave, the lake is encircled by the wooded slopes of the Cimini Hills (much of which is a nature reserve). A scenic road runs around the lake, and the best place for swimming is on the southeast shore.

🏛 **Palazzo Farnese**
Caprarola. 📞 0761-64 60 52.
◐ daily. ◑ 1 Jan, 1 May, 25 Dec. 🎟

Etruscan tumulus tombs from the necropolis at Cerveteri

Tarquinia **❻**

Viterbo. 🏛 *14,000*. **FS** 🚌
ℹ *Piazza Cavour (0766-85 63 84).*
🛒 *Wed.*

Ancient Tarquinia (Tarxuna) was one of Etruria's most important centres. It occupied a strategic position to the northeast of the present town, on a ridge dominating the coastal plain, until the 4th century BC when it fell to Rome.

Tarquinia itself is worth a wander for its crumbling medieval churches and spacious main square, though the main reason to visit is the **Museo Archeologico**, which has one of Italy's better collections of Etruscan finds. Relaxed, reclining statues of the deceased adorn the sarcophagi on the ground floor, but the star attraction, on the mezzanine, is a group of terracotta winged horses dating from the 4th century BC.

On a hilltop 2 km (1 mile) southeast of town are the frescoed tombs of the **necropolis** dug into the soft volcanic tufa. There are almost 6,000 tombs but only about 15 can be visited at a time. The frescoes that decorate them, designed to remind the dead of life, range from frenetic dancing figures in the Tomba delle Leonesse to the diners reclining in the Tomba dei Leopardi.

ℳ Museo Archeologico
Piazza Cavour. **☎** *0766-85 60 36.*
🕐 *Tue–Sun.* ● *public hols.*
🎟 *valid also for necropolis.* ♿

Cerveteri **❼**

Roma. 🏛 *30,000*. **FS** 🚌 **ℹ** *Piazza Risorgimento (06-995 18 58).* 🛒 *Fri.*

In the 6th century BC Cerveteri (ancient Kysry) was one of the most populated and culturally rich towns of the Mediterranean, trading with Greece and controlling a large area along the coast. The **necropolis**, a city of the dead 2 km (1 mile) outside town, is a network of streets lined with tombs dating from the 7th to the 1st century BC. Some of the larger tumulus tombs, like the Tomba degli Scudi e delle Sedie, are arranged like houses with rooms, doors and corridors. The Tomba dei Rilievi is decorated with plaster reliefs of tools, pets and mythological figures. Although the best finds from the necropolis are in museums such as the Vatican Museums, Villa Giulia and the British Museum in London, some can be seen in the small **Museo Nazionale Cerite** in the centre of town.

Environs: There are more traces of the Etruscans to be seen at **Norchia**, where the tombs are carved out of a rock face, and **Sutri**, whose amphitheatre is one of the few relics of the living Etruscans.

⋔ Necropolis
Via delle Necropoli. **☎** *06-994 00 01.*
🕐 *Tue–Sun.* ● *public hols.*
ℳ Museo Nazionale Cerite
Piazza Santa Maria. **☎** *06-994 13 54.*
🕐 *Tue–Sun.* ● *1 Jan, 1 May, 25 Dec.*

Lake Bracciano **❽**

Roma. **FS** 🚌 *Bracciano.* **ℹ** *Via Claudia 72, Bracciano (06-998 67 82).*

Medieval Anguillara on Lake Bracciano

Bracciano is a large lake famous for its fish, and popular for water sports and lakeside lunches.

Medieval **Anguillara**, to the south, is the prettiest of the lakeside towns with romantic views over the water. The main town, **Bracciano**, on the east shore, is dominated by the Orsini-Odescalchi fortress, a pentagonal 15th-century structure with frescoes by Antoniazzo Romano and other Tuscan and Umbrian artists.

♣ Castello Orsini-Odescalchi
Via del Castello. **☎** *06-99 80 43 48.*
🕐 *Tue–Sun.* 🎟

Dancers from the 4th-century BC frescoed Tomba del Triclinio in the Museo Archeologico, Tarquinia

Ostia Antica ❾

Viale dei Romagnoli 717, Ostia.
📞 06-565 00 22. Ⓜ Magliana on
line B then 🚆 to Ostia Antica.
🕐 9am–1 hr before sunset daily.
⬤ 1 Jan, 1 May, 25 Dec.

FOR OVER 600 years Ostia was
Rome's main port and a
busy commercial centre,
until the 5th century AD
when a combination of
malaria and competition
with the nearby port of
Portus brought the town
into decline. Silt from
the Tiber covered and
preserved its buildings
and it now lies 5 km
(3 miles) inland.

The ruins of Ostia
give a vivid idea of life in
Classical times. The main
thoroughfare, the **Decumanus
Maximus**, runs through the
Forum, which houses Ostia's
largest temple, the **Capitol**,
and past the restored **theatre**,
still used for open air concerts
in summer. The road is lined
with baths, shops and multi-
storey buildings divided into
apartments, maritime offices
and workshops. There is even
a **Thermopolium**, or bar, with
a marble counter and paintings
advertising food and drink.

**The building
material** for the
houses was
brick, left plain or
covered in mural
decoration.

**The internal
courtyard** has
remained a feature
of Italian housing.

**Ruins of shops and offices along
the Decumanus Maximus**

Balcony

Apartments
or single rooms
were rented out.

Shops
occupied the
ground floor
of the block.

The bar served
wine and snacks.

OSTIA APARTMENTS
Much of Ostia's population
lived in blocks of flats, such
as this building, based on the
Casa di Diana (2nd century AD).

Frascati and the Castelli Romani ❿

Roma. 🚆 🚌 Frascati. ℹ️ Piazza
Marconi 1, Frascati (06-942 03 31).
Villa Aldobrandini 🕐 with
permission from tourist office only.

THE ALBAN HILLS have long
been a country retreat for
Romans. In Classical times
they were scattered with villas;
in the Middle Ages with
fortified castles (hence the
name); and in the 16th and
17th centuries with luxurious
country residences and their
spectacular parks and gardens.
During World War II the
German defences were based
in the Alban hills and many
Castelli towns were severely
damaged by Allied bombs.
Nowadays, the 13 hilltop
towns are popular day-trip
destinations as well as being
famous for their white wine.

Frascati's central piazza is a
belvedere overlooked by the
Villa Aldobrandini, a majestic
17th-century building set in
a splendid park of secret
grottoes, fountains and statues.

The fortified Abbazia di San
Nilo in **Grottaferrata**, 3 km
(2 miles) south, was founded
in 1004 and contains some
lovely 17th-century frescoes by
Domenichino in the chapel.

Overlooking Lake Albano,
6 km (4 miles) south, **Castel
Gandolfo** is the site of the
pope's summer palace. When
in residence the pope addresses
the crowd from the balcony.

Gathered around a sturdy
9th-century castle, and famed
for its strawberries, **Nemi**, 10
km (6 miles) southeast, looks
down onto the glassy dark
blue waters of Lake Nemi.

The forested shores around the small, volcanic Lake Nemi

Tivoli, a favourite place to escape the heat of the Roman summer

Tivoli ⑪

Roma. 🏛 57,000. 🚉 🚌 🚶 *Largo Garibaldi (0774-212 49).* 🚲 *Wed.*

Hilltown Tivoli, now probably the most popular excursion from Rome, was once a favoured resort of the ancient Romans, attracted by its fresh water and sulphur springs, and beautiful countryside. The temples that once covered Tivoli's hilltop are still visible in places. Some are half buried in medieval buildings, others, such as the Temples of Sibyl and Vesta, inside the gardens of the Sibilla restaurant (on Via Sibilla), are relatively intact.

Splendours from around the world reproduced in Hadrian's Villa

The town's most famous sight is the **Villa d'Este**, a sumptuous country residence created in the 16th century by Pirro Ligorio for Cardinal Ippolito d'Este from the shell of a Benedictine monastery. It is known primarily for its gardens, steeply raked on terraces, and studded with spectacular, if somewhat faded and moss-hung, fountains. Although suffering from reduced water-pressure and polluted water due to centuries of neglect, the gardens give a vivid impression of the frivolous luxury enjoyed by the papal families. Highlights include the Viale delle Cento Fontane and the Fontana dell'Organo Idraulico, which, thanks to a hydraulic system, once played music. At the other end of town, the **Villa Gregoriana** is set in a lush wooded valley where paths wind down into a deep ravine.

ENVIRONS: About 5 km (3 miles) west of Tivoli are the ruins of **Hadrian's Villa**. Easily seen in conjunction with a visit to the town, this is one of the largest and most spectacular villas ever built in the Roman Empire (it once covered an area greater than the centre of Imperial Rome).

An inveterate traveller, Hadrian's aim in creating the villa was to reproduce some of the wonders he had seen around the world. The Stoa Poikile, for example, a walkway around a rectangular pool and garden, recalls the painted colonnade of the Stoic philosophers in Athens, while the Canopus evokes the grand sanctuary of Serapis in

Alexandria. There are also ruins of two bath complexes, a Latin and a Greek library, a Greek theatre, and a private study on a little island known as the Teatro Marittimo.

Today the rambling ruins, full of shady nooks and hidden corners, make a lovely place to relax, picnic or explore.

🏛 **Villa d'Este**
Piazza Trento. 📞 *0774-220 70.*
⬜ *daily.* ⬤ *1 May.* 🚫
🏛 **Villa Gregoriana**
Piazza Massimo. ⬜ *daily.* 🚫
⛪ **Hadrian's Villa**
Villa Adriana. 📞 *0774-53 02 03.*
⬜ *daily.* ⬤ *1 May.* 🚫 ♿

Palestrina ⑫

Roma. 🏛 16,000. 🚌 🚶 *Piazza Santa Maria degli Angeli (06-957 31 76).* 🚲 *Sat & 15th of the month.*

Mosaic fragment of Nile in flood, Archaeological Museum, Palestrina

Medieval Palestrina grew up over the terraces of a huge temple dedicated to the goddess Fortuna Primigenia, the mother of all gods. The temple, founded in the 8th century BC and rebuilt in the 2nd century BC by Sulla, housed one of the most important oracles of ancient times. The terraces of the sanctuary, littered with fragments of columns and porticoes, lead up to the curved **Palazzo Barberini**. Built over the site of a circular temple, it now houses the **Museo Nazionale Archeologico**, best known for a 1st-century BC mosaic, portraying the Nile in flood.

🏛 **Museo Nazionale Archeologico**
Via Barberini. 📞 *06-953 81 00.*
⬜ *daily.* ⬤ *1 Jan, 1 May.* 🚫

Subiaco ⑬

Roma. 🚶 9,000. 🚌 ❖ Via
Cadorna 59 (0774-82 20 13).
🚌 Sat.

I N THE 6th century, weary of
the decadence of Rome,
St Benedict left the city to
become a hermit in a cave
above Subiaco. Others joined
him, and eventually there were
12 monasteries in the area.

Only two now survive:
Santa Scolastica, dedicated
to Benedict's sister, is organized around three cloisters, one
Renaissance, one early Gothic
and the third Cosmatesque.
Higher up, the 12th-century
San Benedetto is a more
rewarding destination.
Overhanging a deep gorge, it
comprises two churches built
on top of each other. The
upper is decorated with 14th-
century Sienese frescoes; the
lower, built over several levels,
incorporates the original cave
where Benedict spent three
years after fleeing Rome.

🏛 **Santa Scolastica**
3 km (2 miles) E of Subiaco.
📞 0774-855 25. ◯ daily. 📷 ♿
🏛 **San Benedetto**
3 km (2 miles) E of Subiaco.
📞 0774-850 39. ◯ daily. 📷 ♿

Montecassino ⑭

Cassino. 📞 0776-31 15 29.
🚆 Cassino then bus. ◯ 8:30am–
noon, 3:30–6pm daily.

T HE ABBEY of Montecassino,
mother church of the
Benedictine order and a centre
of medieval art, was founded
in 529 by St Benedict over the
ruins of an ancient acropolis.
By the 8th century it was an
important centre of learning,
and by the 11th century had
become one of the richest
monasteries in Europe.

In 1944 it was a German
stronghold and a target for
Allied bombs. Most of the
complex was devastated,
including the lavish Baroque
church, but the walls remained
intact and the abbey withstood
for three months before falling
to the Allies. The adjoining war
cemeteries commemorate the
30,000 soldiers killed.

THE MONASTERIES OF LAZIO

**Rose
window,
Fossanova**

St Benedict founded the Abbey of Montecassino
around 529 and there wrote his famous Rule.
Based on the principles of prayer, study and
manual labour, this became the fundamental
monastic code of western Europe. The Cistercian
Order, an off-shoot of the Benedictines, came to
Italy from Burgundy in the 12th century. The
Cistercians were followers of St Bernard, whose creed was
based on austerity and self-sufficiency, qualities which were
reflected in the simple, early
Gothic architecture of their
monasteries. Their first abbey
was at Fossanova. Other
Cistercian abbeys in Lazio include Valvisciolo (northeast of
Sermoneta) and San Martino
in Cimino (near Lago di Vico).

The Abbey of Montecassino,
destroyed during World War II,
was rebuilt as a replica of its
17th-century predecessor.

The Abbey of San Benedetto,
Subiaco, was founded in the
11th century over St Benedict's
cave. A staircase carved in the
rock leads to the grotto where
he preached to shepherds.

The Abbey of Casamari,
14 km (8 miles) east of Frosinone,
was founded by Benedictine
monks in 1035 and banded
over to the Cistercians who
rebuilt it in 1203.

The abandoned medieval village of Ninfa, now a beautiful garden

Anagni ⓯

Frosinone. 🏛 19,000. FS 🚌
ℹ Piazza Innocenzo II (0775-72 78
52). 🚃 Wed.

ACCORDING TO LEGEND Saturn
founded five towns in
southeast Lazio, including
Anagni, Alatri and Arpino. This
area is now known as La
Ciociaria, from *ciocie*, the
bark clogs worn in the area
until about 20 years ago.

Before the Romans con-
quered this part of Lazio it was
inhabited by several different
tribes: the Volsci, the Sanniti,
and the Hernici. Little is known
of them, apart from the extraordinary walls with which they
protected their settlements. In
later years these were believed
to have been built by the
Cyclops, a mythical giant,
which gave them their present
name of Cyclopean walls.

Anagni was the most sacred
Hernician centre until its
destruction by the Romans in
306 BC. In the Middle Ages it
was the birthplace and family
seat of several popes, an era
from which many buildings
survive, most notably
Boniface VIII's 13th-century
mullion-windowed palace.

The beautiful Romanesque
Duomo, Santa Maria, built
over the ancient Hernician
acropolis, boasts a fine Cosmati
mosaic floor from the 13th

century as well as 14th-century
Sienese frescoes. The crypt of
San Magno is frescoed with
one of the most complete
surviving cycles of the 12th
and 13th centuries.

ENVIRONS: Alatri, perched on
an olive-covered slope 28 km
(17 miles) east of Anagni, was
an important Hernician town.
It preserves an impressive
double set of Cyclopean walls,
2 km (1 mile) long and 3 m
(10 ft) high, from its 7th-
century BC acropolis. In the
medieval town below the walls
is the Romanesque church of
Santa Maria Maggiore, greatly
restored in the 13th century.

Arpino, 40 km (25 miles)
east of Alatri, is a bustling
town with a medieval core,
and was the birthplace of the

An unusual pointed arch in the
Cyclopean walls at Arpino

Roman orator, Cicero. About
3 km (2 miles) above Arpino,
at the site of the ancient town
of Civitavecchia, is a tremendous stretch of Cyclopean
walls which includes a rare
gateway with a pointed arch.

Sermoneta and Ninfa ⓰

Latina. FS Latina Scalo. 🚌 from
Latina. ℹ Via Duca del Mare 19,
Latina (0773-69 54 04 17).
Ninfa ◯ Apr–Oct: 1st Sat & Sun of
the month; sporadically in May. 🌐

SERMONETA IS A LOVELY hilltop
town overlooking the
Pontine Plains, with narrow
cobbled streets winding
around medieval houses,
palaces and churches. The
Duomo has a fine 15th-
century panel by Benozzo
Gozzoli showing the Virgin
cradling Sermoneta in her
hands. At the top of the town
rises the moated fairy-tale
Castello Caetani, frescoed
with mythological scenes by a
pupil of Pinturicchio.

In the valley below lies the
romantic abandoned medieval
village of **Ninfa**, restored and
converted into lush botanical
gardens by the Caetani family
in 1921. Streams and waterfalls
punctuate the picturesque
garden laid out among the
crumbling buildings.

Terracina ⑰

Latina. 🏛 40,000. FS 🚌 ℹ Via Leopardi (0773-72 77 59). 🛋 Thu.

Roman terracina was an important commercial centre on the Via Appia (the Appian Way). Today it is a popular seaside resort, with a fascinating collage of medieval buildings and Roman ruins in its historic centre, perched on the slopes of the Ausonian Hills. The more modern part of town by the sea is full of restaurants, bars and hotels.

Bombing during World War II uncovered many of the town's ancient structures, notably a stretch of the Appian Way and the original paving of the Roman Forum in Piazza del Municipio. The 11th-century **Duomo** was built in the shell of a Roman temple, and is still entered by the temple's steps. The medieval portico is adorned with a lovely 12th-century mosaic and the interior preserves the 13th-century mosaic pavement. Next

Duomo at Terracina with original Roman steps

door, the modern town hall houses the **Museo Archeologico**, devoted to local Greek and Roman finds.

Three kilometres (2 miles) above the town are the podium and foundations that once supported the Temple of Jove Anxur, dating back to the 1st century BC. This huge arcaded platform is illuminated at night and offers vertiginous views of Terracina and its bay.

🏛 Museo Archeologico
Piazza Municipio. 📞 0773-70 22 20. ◯ Mon–Sat. ● public hols. 🈲

Sperlonga ⑱

Latina. 🏛 4,000. 🚌 ℹ Piazza della Rimembranza (0771-547 96). 🛋 Sat.

Sperlonga is a popular seaside resort surrounded by sandy beaches. The old town sits on a rocky promontory, a picturesque labyrinth of whitewashed buildings, narrow alleyways, piazzettas and balconies offering an occasional glimpse of the sea below. It is now full of bars, restaurants and boutiques. The modern part of town lies down on the seafront.

The area around Sperlonga was a favourite retreat for the ancient Romans during the hot summer months. They built villas along the coast, and converted the natural caves in the nearby cliffs into places to dine and relax. In 1957 archaeologists excavating the huge complex of Tiberius's luxury villa, 1 km (half a mile) on the southern outskirts of town, found some marvellous 2nd-century BC Hellenistic sculptures in a large cave open to the sea. These sculptures, representing

12th-century bell tower at Gaeta

incidents from Homer's *Odyssey*, are thought to be by the same artists from Rhodes (where the Emperor Tiberius once lived) who were responsible for the Laocoön *(see p407)*. They are displayed, along with other local finds, in the **Museo Archeologico Nazionale** which is part of the archaeological zone.

⋒ Zona Archeologica
Via Flacca. 📞 0771-540 28. ◯ daily. ● 1 Jan, 1 May, 25 Dec. 🈲

Gaeta ⑲

Latina. 🏛 22,000. 🚌 ℹ Piazza Traniello 19 (0771-46 27 67). 🛋 Wed.

According to virgil, Gaeta was named after Aeneas's wet nurse Caieta who was allegedly buried here. The town sits on the southern headland of the gulf of Gaeta, wedged under Monte Orlando. The historic centre is dominated by a mighty Aragonese castle and the pinnacles of mock-Gothic San Francesco. To the north, the modern quarter links Gaeta to the bay of Serapo, a popular and picturesque beach resort.

Gaeta's most beautiful feature is the **Duomo**'s elegant late Romanesque bell tower, its lofty summit topped by a roof of coloured ceramic tiles. On the seafront lies the tiny 10th-century church of **San Giovanni a Mare**, with faded frescoes, a hemispherical dome and a sloping floor to let the sea flow out after flooding.

Stretches of sandy beach along the coast between Gaeta and Terracina

SOUTHERN ITALY

Southern Italy at a Glance

VISITORS TO SOUTHERN ITALY are faced with a rich array of archaeological remains. Although those of the Romans at Pompei are high on everyone's list, Greek ruins litter Sicily and the southern coast and there are mysterious ancient structures in Sardinia. Naples, Puglia and Sicily are admired for their architecture, while across the south there are magnificent landscapes, abundant wildlife and endless opportunities for outdoor activities. The cuisine alone, with its eclectic heritage and diversity of tastes, provides the excuse to dawdle on the coast or in the rustic mountain villages.

Abruzz

Parco Nazic d'Abruzz

The Parco Nazionale d'Abruzzo, a vast unspoilt wilderness, is home to wolves, bears and many species of birds (see pp490–91).

Su Nuraxi

SARDINIA
(See pp528–35)

Su Nuraxi at Barumini, *built around 1500 BC, is the most celebrated of Sardinia's mysterious stone nuraghe sites* (see p533).

The cloister decoration *at Monreale cathedral is a legacy of Sicily's Arabic past, with elaborate columns adorned with fine mosaics and splendid sculpted capitals* (see pp514–5).

Monreale cathedral

Temple of (

Sicily's Valley of the Temples at Agrigento *contains some of the best ruins outside Greece. Mostly Doric in construction and style, they date from the 5th and 6th centuries BC* (see p520).

| 0 kilometres | 100 |
| 0 miles | 50 |

◁ **Vines and citrus trees growing along Campania's scenic Costiera Amalfitana (Amalfi Coast)**

The Museo Archeologico Nazionale in Naples is one of Italy's most important museums. It houses the treasures of Pompei, including sculptures, vases and everyday artefacts which provide a detailed glimpse of Roman life (see pp474–5).

ABRUZZO, MOLISE AND PUGLIA
(See pp484–497)

Molise

NAPLES
AND CAMPANIA
(See pp466–483)

Archeologico Nazionale

Pompei

Puglia

Basilicata

Santa Croce

Pompei's Roman ruins include streets, houses and an amphitheatre (see pp478–9).

BASILICATA
AND CALABRIA
(See pp498–505)

Calabria

The church of Santa Croce in Lecce is an excellent example of the exuberant Lecce Baroque style, from its elaborate rose window to the intricately carved capitals (see pp496–7).

Mount Etna

SICILY
(See pp506–527)

Mount Etna, one of the world's largest volcanoes, is still active, with lava erupting from fissures that dot its flanks. The nearby town of Catania has suffered repeatedly from volcanic damage (see p523).

Regional Food: Southern Italy

SOUTHERN ITALIAN FOOD is as varied as the landscape, each region having its own specialities. While pasta, for example, is eaten throughout Italy, nothing matches the handmade *orecchiette* of Puglia. Think of Naples, and wafer-thin pizza springs to mind. Sicilian food is both rustic and voluptuous. Across the south, the dishes are enlivened with seafood, fruity green olive oil and dry white wine and, together with fresh green vegetables and huge, bursting tomatoes, account for one of the most enviably healthy diets in Europe.

Dried chillies

Some of Italy's best olives *come from Puglia. Green and black olives may be served in piquant oil and garlic.*

Grilled swordfish

Squid   Anchovies

A dish of simply cooked seafood (frutti di mare) *may also contain mussels* (cozze), *oysters* (ostriche), *prawns* (gamberetti) *or octopus* (polpi) – *moistened with olive oil and a dash of lemon juice to enhance the flavours.*

Prawns

Roasted red pepper

Char-grilled courgette

Grilled tuna

Lobster   Mussels

Sliced vegetables *brushed with olive oil and lightly grilled are often served as an antipasto (appetizer).*

Pizza Napolitana *is a simple thin pizza topped with tomato, garlic, basil and anchovies.*

Marinated artichoke hearts

Char-grilled aubergine

Maccheroni con le sarde, *a Sicilian classic, contains sardines, fennel, raisins, pine nuts, breadcrumbs and saffron.*

Pesce spada *(swordfish steak), grilled or pan-fried with lemon and oregano, is a favourite in Campania, Puglia and Sicily.*

Agnello arrosto *(juicy roast lamb) is a Sardinian speciality, roasted on a spit or in casseroles with rosemary and thyme.*

Sicilian cassata is ice-cream made with ricotta cheese, candied fruit, pistachios, sugar and chocolate in a sponge cake.

Nougat is a sweet Sardinian speciality that can be made simply with nuts, or flavoured with chocolate.

Cannoli

Sicilian almond biscuits

Many biscuits and cakes are made in honour of a religious festival or saint's day. They might be deep-fried in oil, soaked in honey, encrusted with almonds or stuffed with ricotta, like the tube-shaped cannoli biscuits much favoured in Sicily.

TYPICAL SOUTHERN SEASONINGS

The food of the south is simple but often served with aromatic herbs like oregano, rosemary, basil, mint, sage and thyme, as well as garlic, capers, sundried tomatoes, anchovies and sardines.

Rosemary

Oregano   Capers

Sardines   Sundried tomatoes

SOUTHERN CHEESES

Cheese exists in almost infinite varieties. Creamy mozzarella di bufala, made with buffalo milk, is delicious eaten on its own. Scamorza, a similar spun cheese, is exceptional – especially from Basilicata. It is also smoked. Provolone, with a hard texture, can be mild or piquant, while ricotta, from sheep's milk, is creamy.

Provolone

Scamorza

Ricotta

Mozzarella

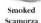

Smoked Scamorza

WINE

The south's sunny hillsides have produced wine since the Bronze Age. Puglia produces more wine than any other region in Italy, and Sicily boasts some of the south's finest wines. Good producers include Regaleali, Rapitalà, Corvo and Donnafugata. Marsala, a classic wine also from Sicily *(see p518)*, was devised in the 18th century and made famous by Admiral Nelson. De Bartoli is an excellent producer.

Sicilian white wine

Sweet Marsala

OLIVE OIL

Some of the finest olive oils *(olio di oliva)* in Italy come from the south. The words *extra vergine* (extra virgin) refer to the pure, unblended oil from the first pressings of the olives. A variation is chilli oil *(olio santo)*, soaked with red chilli peppers, resulting in a rich, spicy oil with a red hue.

Chilli oil (Olio santo)

Olive oil (Olio di oliva)

Understanding the Architecture of Southern Italy

THE ROMANESQUE STYLE of southern Italy owes much to the Normans, who in the 11th century brought from France both form and style in architecture and sculpture. In the southeast, the style has hefty Byzantine overtones; in Sicily it is characterized by strong traditional Islamic motifs and a love of rich colour, pattern and ornamentation. These elements surface later in Sicily's Baroque style and are allied to a dynamism that originates in the Baroque of

Baroque carving on Bagheria's Villa Palagonia

Rome – though in Sicily it is more vivacious. Neapolitan Baroque is more sophisticated and displays a greater interest in the creative use of space.

BYZANTINE AND ROMANESQUE FEATURES

Lateral towers

Interlacing arches

Multicoloured marble

Glass and plaster mosaics on gold

Rich ornamentation

Interlacing arches

***Cefalù**, begun in 1131 by Roger II, is one of Sicily's great Norman cathedrals (see p519). Its west front exhibits many northern Romanesque features, such as the massive towers.*

***Christ Pantocrator**, a Byzantine apse mosaic (c.1132), adorns the Cappella Palatina (see p510).*

***The east end** of the Norman cathedral of Monreale, founded in 1172 by William II, is built of multicoloured materials with interlacing arches (see pp514–15).*

BAROQUE FEATURES

Massive scale of stairway

Sweeping view down corridor

Bold statue of lion

Lifelike putti

Brilliant realism of drapery

***Caserta's Palazzo Reale**, a sumptuous royal palace begun by Charles III in 1752, is characterized by its monumental scale (see p480). The richly decorated interior is prefaced by several huge entrances and impressive staircases offering views. The enormous building was designed by Luigi Vanvitelli.*

***Giacomo Serpotta's** stucco reliefs (1517–27) in Palermo's Oratorio di Santa Zita illustrate Sicilians' love of exuberant decoration (see p513).*

WHERE TO SEE THE ARCHITECTURE

The best places to see Romanesque architecture are Puglia and the cathedral cities of northwestern Sicily. Puglia's best churches are those at Trani *(see p493)* and nearby Canosa, Molfetta and Bitonto; Ruvo di Puglia *(p494)*, San Leonardo di Siponto on the Gargano Peninsula and Martina Franca, near Alberobello. The Baroque style of the south is epitomized by the villas, palaces

The Duomo portal in Ruvo di Puglia

and churches of Naples and Sicily, and by the deeply encrusted ornamentation found on church façades in Lecce *(pp496–7)*, in Puglia. In Sicily, the Baroque of Palermo *(pp510–13)*, Bagheria *(p516)*, Noto, Modica and Ragusa *(p527)* and Siracusa *(pp526–7)* is well known. Less so are churches at Piazza Armerina *(p521)*, Trapani *(p516)*, Palazzolo Acreide, close to Siracusa, and Acireale, near Catania.

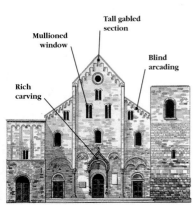

Mullioned window

Tall gabled section

Blind arcading

Rich carving

Bari's Basilica di San Nicola *(founded 1087) was the model for subsequent churches in Puglia (see p494). Based on Norman architecture, its façade is flanked by towers and divided vertically into three, reflecting the tripartite nature of its plan.*

Rose window

Half columns

Blind arcading

The façade of Troia cathedral *(1093–1125) owes its design to Pisan architecture and its rich ornamentation to Byzantine and Arab models (see pp492–3).*

Carved scroll

Protruding columns

Central bell tower

Stone-carved decoration

Three-tiered structure

Curved surface

The façade *of Siracusa's Duomo, begun in 1728 by Andrea Palma, is animated by broken or curved elements (see pp526–7).*

San Giorgio in Ragusa *(1744) has a façade by Gagliardi with layers of ornamentation culminating in the tower (see p527).*

Lecce's Chiesa del Rosario *(begun 1691) was built by Lo Zingarello of soft local sandstone in the Lecce Baroque style of profuse carving (see pp496–7).*

The Ancient Greeks in Southern Italy

SOME OF THE BEST ruins of the ancient Greek world are in Southern Italy. Syracuse, Selinunte, Segesta and Gela are among the better known Sicilian sites while those on the mainland include Croton, Locri and Paestum. Magna Graecia is the collective name given to these scattered colonies of ancient Greece, the earliest of which were founded in the Naples area in the 11th century BC. Many great figures of the age – including Pythagoras, Archimedes and Aeschylus – lived in these farflung settlements, and it was here that the ancient winemaker's art flourished. Artefacts from this age are exhibited in the excellent archaeological museums of Naples, Syracuse and Taranto.

KYME
Cuma

NEAPOLIS
Napoli

HERAKL
Ercolan

POSEIDONIA
Paestum

Ancient Herakleia (Herculaneum) was named after its patron deity, the mighty Hercules. It was buried by the eruption of Mount Vesuvius in AD 79 (see p479).

Poseidonia (today's Paestum), was the city of Poseidon, God of the Sea. Its ruins, dating from the 6th century BC, include the hulks of two well preserved Doric temples (see pp482–3).

Mount Etna was believed to be the forge of Hephaistos (Vulcan) – God of Fire – or the Cyclops, the one-eyed giant (see p523).

Tyndaris was one of the last Greek cities founded on Sicily.

LIPAR
Lipa

TYNDA
Tind

PANORMOS
Palermo

ERYX
Erice

EGESTA
Segesta

SOLUS
Soluto

HIMERA
Himera

Eryx, founder of the town, was the son of Aphrodite and Poseidon.

SELINUS
Selinunte

Valley of the Temples

HENNA
Enna

KA
Ca

MEGARA HYB
Me

The legendary founder of Agrigento was Daedalus, who created wings for himself and his son, Icarus, so they could fly.

AKRAGAS
Agrigento

GELA
Gela

Egesta (built 426–416 BC) was colonized by the Elymians who may have originated at Troy. Among the ruins of this town are a halfcompleted temple and a theatre (see p518). Ancient Greeks used theatres for plays and cultural entertainment rather than combat.

Gela was prosperous under the rule of Hippocrates in the 5th century BC.

Archeolo
Regic
Paolo

M

Simeto

Gela

Belice

Aeschylus, the dramatist, died in Gela in 456. Considered the father of Greek tragedy, his plays include Seven Against Thebes, Women of Aetna *and* Prometheus Bound.

0 kilometres   100

0 miles   50

Metapontion (Metapontum) was home to Pythagoras after his expulsion from Croton. Its ruins include Doric temples, the Tavole Palatine and a theatre *(see p503)*.

Taras was home to the philosopher and scientist, Archytas, and Aristoxenes, author of the earliest treatise on music.

GREECE AND ITS COLONIES

☐ *7th–5th century BC*

Museo Archeologico Nazionale

Museo Nazionale di Metaponto

Basento

METAPONTION •
Metaponto

SIRIS •
Nova Siri

• TARAS
Taranto

The Sybarites were famed for their luxurious lifestyle, hence the word "sybaritic". The wealth of Sybaris resulted from trade with the Etruscans.

Founded by Spartan Greeks (8th century BC), Taras was a rich and powerful city.

SYBARIS •
Sibari •

THURII
Thuri

KROTON
Crotone •

In about 540 BC, Croton became the chief school of Pythagoras's philosophy. Here the great thinker and mathematician remained for about 30 years until the government (which he supported) was overthrown, and he was expelled.

Locri Epizefiri was the first Greek city to have a written code of law.

• LOKROI
Locri Epizefiri

ANKLE-
ESSENE
essina

RHEGION
Reggio di Calabria

ni Naxos

Plato the philosopher visited Syracuse and advised the ruler, Dionysus II, how to govern.

The Straits of Messina vexed Odysseus, the hero of Homer's Odyssey. Here at the meeting of two seas the currents created a "whirlpool" – Charybdis – which posed a threat to safe entry of Messina (see p522). Another threat were the Sirens, who lured voyagers onto rocks with their singing. Odysseus is seen here tied to a mast, so he can hear their song, but resist its call.

OUSAI
a

The mathematician and inventor, Archimedes, was born in Syracuse c.287 BC. His inventions included the famous Archimedean screw, and various weapons to stave off the Romans (see pp526–7).

DEMETER AND PERSEPHONE

The complex web of Greek mythology was part of the daily life of the ancients. Enna was once the seat of the cult of Demeter, the earth goddess, and in 480 BC a temple was erected there in her honour. According to the legend, Persephone, the daughter of Demeter and Zeus, was abducted in the nearby fields by Hades who carried her off into the Underworld. Demeter then left Olympus and wandered the world searching in vain for her daughter. Discovering that Zeus had allowed the abduction to happen, Demeter put a blight on Sicily: it would remain barren until Persephone returned. Finally Hades allowed her return from the Underworld, but only for a few months of each year – from spring to autumn. Demeter, satisfied with the result, ensured that Sicily became the most fertile place on earth.

Sculpture of Persephone

NAPLES AND CAMPANIA

THE CAPITAL OF CAMPANIA, *Naples is one of the few European cities of the ancient world that has never been completely extinguished. Founded by Greeks, it was embellished and enlarged by the Romans and in subsequent centuries was the much-prized booty of foreign invaders and Imperialists – most prominently the Normans, Hohenstaufen, French and Spanish.*

Naples today is a chaotic yet spectacular, often crime-ridden metropolis that sprawls noisily and dirtily around the edge of the beautiful Bay of Naples. To one side is Mount Vesuvius; facing from the sea are the pretty islands of Capri, Ischia and Procida. Pompei and Herculaneum, lying in the shadow of the volcano that destroyed them, contain the most revealing Roman ruins in Italy.

For centuries Naples has dominated the Italian south – the *Mezzogiorno*, or land of the midday sun. The problems of poverty, crime and unemployment are magnified here, but there is also an attractive, rude ebullience.

The ancient history of Campania is associated with the Etruscans and the Greeks, whose gigantic ruins can be seen at Paestum. Next came a time of great prosperity under Roman leadership; archaeological evidence of this still exists at Benevento and Santa Maria Capua Vetere. The hinterland, with its rich, well-cultivated plains, is eclipsed by the Amalfi coastline with its breathtaking views and the dramatic seaboard of the Cilento. The mountainous interior, remote and unvisited, contains small towns that were settled by the Greeks, developed by the Romans and often abandoned in the wake of malaria and Saracen attacks.

A glimpse into the narrow streets of Naples' Quartieri Spagnoli (Spanish Quarter)

◁ The old fishing quarter on the island of Procida in the Bay of Naples

Exploring Naples and Campania

T HE MAIN CENTRE FROM WHICH to explore Campania is the anarchic
metropolis of Naples (Napoli). To the north, verdant plains
sweep down to Santa Maria Capua Vetere. To the
east is the lonely, mountainous province of
Benevento. Tragic, earthquake-ravaged
Avellino and its province lurk on a
plain beyond Vesuvius. The northern coastline is not as enticing as
the Roman ruins lining it at such
places as Cuma. The Costiera
Amalfitana, south of Naples, is
stunning. Beyond the tip of
the Sorrentine Peninsula
and along the Cilento
coast there is good
swimming, as on Capri,
Ischia and Procida in
the Gulf of Naples.

SIGHTS AT A GLANCE

Benevento **5**
Capri **9**
Caserta **4**
Costiera Amalfitana **6**
Ischia and Procida **10**
Naples (Napoli) pp470–77 **1**
Paestum **8**
Pompei pp478–9 **2**
Salerno **7**
Santa Maria Capua Vetere **3**

Typical Naples street viewed from Santa Maria Maggiore

KEY

▰▰ Motorway
➤➤ Major road
▰▰ Minor road
▰▰ Scenic route
〰 River
☀ Viewpoint

0 kilometres   25

0 miles   20

View of the Costiera Amalfitana from the hilltown of Ravello

GETTING AROUND

Northern Campania is easily accessible from Naples on the A1. The A16 heads east towards Puglia. Salerno and the Cilento can be reached on the A3. Branching off the A3, the N18 heads deep into the Cilento. To reach its coast, take the N267. The villages of the Costiera Amalfitana (Amalfi coast) lie along the scenic N145. The islands of Capri, Ischia and Procida are accessible by boat from Mergellina (the port of Naples), Sorrento, Positano, Amalfi and Salerno. Campania's main towns and important sights are linked by railway. The bus service is comprehensive, though infrequent in the interior of the Cilento.

SEE ALSO

- **Where to Stay** pp569–70

- **Where to Eat** pp602–4

Naples ❶

THE COMPACT CENTRE of Naples, filled with palaces, churches, convents and monasteries, revolves around just a few streets. From the Piazza del Plebiscito, Via Toledo (also called Via Roma) proceeds north towards Piazza Dante. To the east, narrow Via del Tribunale and Via San Biagio dei Librai penetrate the historic and noisy heart of the

San Gennaro, protector of Naples

View of the Bay of Naples and Mount Vesuvius

city, the *Spaccanapoli* (split Naples). South of Palazzo Reale is the Santa Lucia district. To the west is the port of Mergellina and overlooking the city is the Vomero district.

Exploring Northeast Naples

Many of the city's gems of art and architecture can be found here, including the Museo Archeologico Nazionale and its Roman treasures from Herculaneum and Pompei. The buildings provide a wide range of architectural styles from the French-Gothic of the Duomo to the Florentine-Renaissance style of the Porta Capuana.

Tomb of Ladislas, San Giovanni a Carbonara

including Marco and Andrea da Firenze's masterpiece, the Tomb of Ladislas, behind the church's high altar. Built to house the body of King Ladislas of Naples (1386–1414), who enlarged the church, the tomb is a three-storey confection of statues and arches topped by an equestrian figure.

🔓 San Giovanni a Carbonara

Via Carbonara 5. ☎ 081-29 58 73.
◻ daily.

A great and rare success story in the annals of Neapolitan building restoration, San Giovanni a Carbonara (built 1343) is now open again after suffering damage in 1943, long closure and pitiful neglect. Within are glorious medieval and Renaissance monuments,

🏛 Porta Capuana and Castel Capuano

Piazza Enrico de Nicola.

Between the Aragonese towers of the Capua Gate and facing a huge, noisy market is a rare southern sculpture in the Florentine-Renaissance manner. Created by Giuliano da Maiano (finished in 1490 by Luca Fancelli) as a defensive gate, the Porta Capuana is perhaps Italy's finest Renaissance gateway. The nearby Castel Capuano, begun by Norman King William I and completed by Frederick II, was used as a royal palace until 1540 when it became the Court of Justice. It has been renovated, and functions as a courthouse today.

The beautiful Renaissance gate of Porta Capuana

| 0 metres | 250 |
| 0 yards | 250 |

*Map labels:*

MUSEO DI CAPODIMONTE
CATACOMBE DI SAN GENNARO

PIAZZA CAVOUR
VIA LUCIANO
PIAZZA MUSEO NAZIONALE
VIA SANTA MARIA DI CONSTANTINOPOLI
VICO SANTO
VIA GAUDO
PISANI
VIA LUIGI DE CECCHO
VIA SAPIENZA
VIA ENRICO PESINA
VIA CONTE DI RUVO
VIA DEL SOLE
ATRI
VIA
PIAZZA DANTE
PIAZZA LUIGI MIRAGLIA
PIAZZA DOMENICO MAGGIORE
VIA DE SANCTIS
VIA TOLEDO
VIA BENEDETTO CROCE
PIAZZA DEL GESÙ NUOVO
POZZUOLI
VIA DOMENICO CAPITELLI
CALATA TRINITÀ MAGGIORE
VIA SANTA CHIARA
PIAZZA BANCHI NUOVI
PIAZZA MONTEOLIVETO
VIA MONTEOLIVETO
VIA DONNALBINA
PIAZZA CARITÀ
VIA
MUSEO NAZIONALE DI SAN MARTINO
CESARE BATTISTI
PIAZZA MATTEOTTI
VIA G SANFELICE
VIA ARMANDO DIAZ
VIA TOLEDO (ROMA)
VIA ROBERTO BRACCO
VIA M CERVANTES
RUA CATALANA
VIA AGOSTINO DEPRETIS
VILLA FLORIDIANA
PIAZZA MUNICIPIO
VIA SAN GIACOMO
VIA MEDINA
VICO D'AFFLITTO
EMILIO IMBRIANI
VIA SANTA BRIGIDA
VIA SANTA MATTIA
VIA SERGENTE MAGGIORE
VIA SAN CARLO
PIAZZA TRENTO E TRIESTE
AMMIRAGLIO
ACTON
VIA CHIAIA
MUSEO PRINCIPE DI ARAGONA PIGNATELLI CORTES
PIAZZA DEL PLEBISCITO
VIA CESARIO CONSOLE
CASTEL DELL'OVO
MERGELLINA

SIGHTS AT A GLANCE

KEY

M Metro

🚠 Funicular

ℹ Tourist information

✝ Church

Interior of the Duomo

�ⁿ Duomo

Via Duomo. **(** 081-44 90 97.
◯ daily. **●** 19 Sep.
Built between 1294 and
1323, the Duomo of San
Gennaro lies behind a
mostly 19th-century façade.
The nave is lined with
ancient columns, and there
is an interesting array of
monuments to past rulers,
together with paintings by
Lanfranco and Domenichino.
    The Duomo houses the
relics of San Gennaro, the
protector of Naples, who was
martyred in AD 305. The
ornate Cappella San Gennaro
contains his head, within a
silver-gilt bust, and phials of
his congealed blood, which
miraculously liquefies three
times annually. According to
tradition, if the blood should
fail to liquefy, the city will
have bad luck. The Cappella
Carafa, a Renaissance masterpiece built from 1497 to 1506,
contains the saint's tomb.
    Accessible from the Duomo's
north aisle is the Basilica di
Santa Restituta, founded in the
4th century on the site of a
former Temple of Apollo and
rebuilt in the 14th century. It
has ceiling paintings by Luca
Giordano (1632–1705). At the
end of the right aisle is the 5th-
century baptistry.

VISITORS' CHECKLIST

👥 1,200,000. **✈** Capodichino
4 km (2.5 miles) NW. **🚉** Napoli
Centrale, Piazza Garibaldi.
🚌 Piazza Garibaldi. **🚢** Stazione
Marittima, Molo Beverello &
Mergellina. **ℹ** Piazza del Gesù
Nuovo (081-551 27 01). **🗓** daily.
🎉 San Gennaro: 19 Sep.

�f Monte della Misericordia

Via Tribunali 253. **(** 081-44 69 73.
◯ Mon–Sat am. **♿**
The 17th-century octagonal
church belonging to this
charitable foundation houses
Caravaggio's huge *Seven Acts
of Mercy* (1607). Also here, in
the art gallery, is an important
collection of paintings, including works by Luca Giordano
and Mattia Preti.

�f Cappella Sansevero

Via Francesco de Sanctis 19. **(** 081-
551 84 70. **◯** Wed–Mon. **♿ ♿**
This small 16th-century
chapel is the burial sepulchre
of the Princes of Sangro di
Sansevero. It possesses both
Christian and Masonic symbolism, giving the chapel
an ironic character.
    Remarkable 18th-century
sculpture fills the chapel.
Antonio Corradini's ironic
Modesty is a voluptuous
female, carefully veiled. *The
Resurrection of the Prince*,
by an unknown artist, is
mirrored by that of Christ,
above the altar. Giuseppe
Sammartino's *The Dead
Christ* is an alabaster figure
beneath a marble veil, and
is a work of breathtaking
technical virtuosity.
    Eccentric Prince Raimondo,
an 18th-century alchemist, is
associated with the chapel.
He performed gruesome
experiments on human
bodies, for which he was
excommunicated. The results
of some of his experiments
can be seen in the crypt.

Sammartino's *The Dead Christ* (1753) in the Cappella Sansevero

Exploring Central Naples

THE PART OF SANTA LUCIA bordered by Via Duomo to the east, Via del Tribunale to the north, Via Toledo (Roma) to the west and the water to the south, is the old heart of Naples. Especially rich in 14th- and 15th-century churches, the area offers visitors an abundance of sights.

Interior of San Gregorio Armeno

♠ San Lorenzo Maggiore

Via Tribunali 316. **(** 081-45 49 48.
◯ daily. &
This mainly 14th-century Franciscan church (with an 18th-century façade) was built during the reign of Robert the Wise of Anjou. The storyteller Giovanni Boccaccio (1313–75) is said to have based the character Fiammetta on Maria, the daughter of King Robert, whom he saw here on Easter Eve, 1334. For Naples, San

Lorenzo Maggiore is a rare Gothic edifice. Its nave and the apse ambulatory have a magnificent period simplicity. The church houses some interesting medieval tombs, most notably the Gothic tomb of Catherine of Austria, who died in 1323, by a pupil of Giovanni Pisano. Excavations in the monastic cloister, where the lyric poet and scholar Petrarch (1304–74) once stayed, have revealed the remains of a Roman basilica. Greek and medieval excavations are also under way.

♠ San Gregorio Armeno

Via San Gregorio Armeno 1.
(081-552 01 86. ◯ daily.
Benedictine nuns still preside over this church. The convent attached to it earned a reputation for luxury since the nuns, traditionally from noble families, were accustomed to lavish living, which continued here.
   The sumptuous Baroque interior of the church sports frescoes by the prolific Luca Giordano. The cloister is a quiet haven in a

The simple Gothic interior of San Lorenzo Maggiore, looking down the nave to the apse

neighbourhood noisy with vendors of Neapolitan crib figures *(presepi)*, whose many workshops line the Via San Gregorio Armeno.

🏛 Museo Filangieri

Palazzo Cuomo, Via Duomo 288.
(081-20 31 75. ◯ Tue–Sun.
● 1 Jan. 🈯
The 15th-century Renaissance Palazzo Cuomo houses the Museo Filangieri. Founded in 1881, the original museum collections put together by Prince Gaetano Filangieri were destroyed during World War II. The new collection contains interesting and varied objects, including porcelain, embroidery, manuscripts, Italian and Spanish arms, objects from local archaeological excavations and paintings by such artists as Luca Giordano, Ribera and Mattia Preti.

♠ Sant'Angelo a Nilo

Piazzetta Nilo. **(** 081-551 62 27.
◯ daily.

Tomb of Cardinal Brancaccio, Sant'Angelo a Nilo

This 14th-century church contains a fine work of Renaissance sculpture: the Tomb of Cardinal Rinaldo Brancaccio. Designed by Michelozzo, it was sculpted in Pisa, and then shipped to Naples upon completion in 1428. Donatello reputedly carved the right-hand angel drawing back the curtain, the shallow relief *Assumption*, and the cardinal's head.

⛪ San Domenico Maggiore

Piazza San Domenico Maggiore.
☎ 081-551 70 06. ⏰ daily. ♿

This important Gothic church (1289–1324) contains some of the finest Renaissance monuments and sculpture in Naples. The tomb slab of John of Durazzo (died 1335), by Tino da Camaino, is in the south transept. In the sacristy are 18th-century ceiling frescoes by Solimena. The choir features a paschal candlestick (1585) supported by figures by da Camaino. The Cappellone del Crocifisso contains a medieval painting of the *Crucifixion* which supposedly spoke to St Thomas Aquinas. In the Chiesa Antica is the grand Brancaccio tomb by Jacopo della Pila (1492). Also of interest is the magnificent Cappella Saluzzo.

Detail of the embossed façade of Gesù Nuovo

⛪ Santa Chiara

Via Benedetto Croce. ☎ 081-552 62 80. ⏰ daily. ♿

This 14th-century church was badly bombed in World War II, but a reconstruction uncovered the original austere Provençal-Gothic structure. The most interesting monuments are the tombs of the Angevin monarchs. The tomb of Robert the Wise (died 1343) is by Giovanni and Pacio Bertini; that of Robert's son, Charles of Calabria (died 1328), is by Tino da

Camaino, and the tomb of Charles' wife, Mary of Valois (died 1331) is by da Camaino and his followers. Adjacent is a convent with a peaceful Angevin cloister designed by Vaccaro (1742) and adorned with splendid majolica tiles.

⛪ Gesù Nuovo

Piazza del Gesù Nuovo 2. ☎ 081-551 86 13. ⏰ daily. ⬤ 31 Jan, 16 Nov.

The 16th-century Jesuit church was constructed by Valeriano (and later Fanzago and Fuga) out of the Severini palace (15th century), of which only the curious embossed stone façade survives. The ebullient decoration of the interior (17th century) is fully in accordance with the needs of the Jesuits, who sought to attract the faithful through drama and direct appeal to the emotions. It is resplendent with coloured marble and huge paintings, including some by Ribera. In 1688 an earthquake destroyed Lanfranco's dome – the present one is 18th century.

⛪ Monteoliveto

Piazza Monteoliveto. ☎ 081-551 33 33. ⏰ daily.

Built in 1411 and restored after bomb damage from World War II, this church is a rich repository of Renaissance art.

Guido Mazzoni's *Pietà* (1492) in the church of Monteoliveto

Entering, past the tomb (1627) of Domenico Fontana (the architect who completed the dome of St Peter's in Rome after Michelangelo's death), the richness of the interior soon becomes clear.

The Cappella Mastrogiudice contains an *Annunciation* panel by Florentine sculptor Benedetto da Maiano (1489) and the Cappella Piccolomini contains Antonio Rossellino's monument (c.1475) to Maria d'Aragona (completed by da Maiano). The Cappella del Santo Sepolcro houses a vividly realistic *Pietà* by Guido Mazzoni (1492). Its eight terracotta figures are considered life-size portraits of the artist's contemporaries. The old Sacristy, frescoed by Vasari (1544), has inlaid stalls by Giovanni da Verona (1510).

Majolica tiles decorated with scenes of rural life in the cloisters of Santa Chiara

Naples: Museo Archeologico Nazionale

THIS MUSEUM IS ONE OF the world's most important. The building which houses it, a former military barracks, then university seat, was remodelled in 1790 to receive the treasures of Pompei and Herculaneum (see pp478–9). It also acquired the fabulous Farnese collections, containing Classical sculpture, which Charles of Bourbon inherited from his mother Elizabeth. The 1980 earthquake caused heavy damage to the collections while dust and chaos engulfed the rest. Restoration work has now revitalized the museum.

Sacrifice of Iphigenia
In this Pompeian fresco, Agamemnon's daughter, Iphigenia, is prepared to be sacrificed to Artemis, who saves her by taking a deer instead.

First floor

Roman Helmet
This handsome bronze gladiator's helmet was probably ornamental. It came from Herculaneum.

Bust of "Seneca"
This 1st-century BC Roman portrait head is said to represent Seneca the Elder (c.55 BC – AD 39). The bust was found in the Villa dei Papiri in Herculaneum.

Mezzanine

Ground floor

The building, begun in 1586, was once a barracks.

Mosaic Detail of Alexander
From Pompei's House of the Faun, an ancient mosaic depicts the Battle of Issus (333 BC) between Persian King Darius and Alexander the Great.

KEY TO FLOORPLAN

- ☐ Ground floor
- ☐ Mezzanine
- ☐ First floor
- ☐ Non-exhibition space

Blue Vase

Found in a tomb at Pompei, this glass vase is a fine example of the cameo-maker's art. Grape-gathering cupids are cut on to a superimposed white glass paste over the vase, creating a striking, complex design.

VISITORS' CHECKLIST

Piazza Museo Nazionale 19.
081-44 01 66. 185, 42.
M Piazza Cavour. Jun–Sep:
9am–7pm daily; Oct–May: 9am–
2pm Mon–Sat, 9am–1pm Sun
(last adm: 1 hr before closing).
1 Jan, 25 Dec.

Spring Fresco

From Stabiae comes the ancient fresco of "Spring", a delicate, dreamlike image of a robed girl gathering flowers. The colours remain soft and fresh.

Stairs down to Egyptian Collection

Farnese Bull

Excavated in the Baths of Caracalla (see p427) in Rome, this is the largest sculptural group (c.200 BC) to have survived from antiquity. It represents Amphion and Zethus tying Dirce to the horns of a bull.

GALLERY GUIDE

The ground floor contains the Farnese collections and sculpture from Herculaneum, Pompei and the Campanian cities. On the mezzanine level there are Pompeian mosaics. The first floor has domestic items, weapons, bronzes and murals from Pompei and Herculaneum. A lower ground floor level houses the Egyptian Collection. Be prepared for areas of the museum to be closed occasionally and without warning. Some will be opened on request, including coins and erotic art from Pompei.

Entrance

Farnese Hercules

An ancient Roman copy of a Greek original by Lysippus, this huge statue is the finest in the Farnese collections. Napoleon is said to have regretted leaving it when he removed his booty from Italy in 1797.

Exploring Southeast Naples

THE AREA SOUTH of Via A Diaz is home to Naples' castles and royal palace as well as the densely packed Spanish Quarter. On the outskirts of the old town are a number of museums in historic buildings.

♠ Castel Nuovo

Piazza Municipio. ☎ 081-551 03 64.
◻ Mon–Sat. ● some public hols. &
Museo Civico ◻ Mon–Sat. 🎫

Also known as the Maschio Angioino, this Angevin fortress was built for Charles of Anjou in 1279–82. However, apart from the squat towers and the Cappella Palatina (with Francesco Laurana's *Madonna* of 1474 above the portal), most of the structure is Aragonese.

The castle was once the main royal residence. In the Sala dei Baroni, Ferdinand I of Aragon brutally suppressed the ringleaders of the Baron's Revolt of 1486. The Aragonese were capable of acts of terror, but they were also inspired patrons of the arts.

The triumphal arch of the castle's entrance (begun 1454) is theirs. Commemorating Alfonso of Aragon's entry to Naples in 1443, this ingenious application of the ancient triumphal arch design was worked on, at least in part, by Laurana. The original bronze doors by Guillaume le Moine (1468) are kept in the Palazzo Reale. Part of the building houses the **Museo Civico**.

The colourful and compact Quartieri Spagnoli

♙ Quartieri Spagnoli

Via Toledo (Roma) to Via Chiaia.

The Spanish Quarter – the neighbourhood west of Via Toledo, sloping up to San Martino and Vomero – is one of the city's most densely populated areas. It was named after the Spanish troops who laid out its grid of narrow streets in the 17th century. This is where the archetypal Neapolitan scene comes to life, in which laundry hung above the streets crowds out the sun. This slum is lively by day, slightly sinister by night.

� Museo Nazionale di San Martino

Largo di San Martino 5. ☎ 081-578 17 69. ◻ Tue–Sun am. 🎫 &

High above Santa Lucia, the Baroque Certosa di San Martino, founded in the 14th century as a Carthusian monastery, has magnificent views of the Bay of Naples. It houses an excellent museum that features a variety of *presepi*, Christmas cribs of Neapolitan tradition. The cloister was completed in 1623–9 by Cosimo Fanzago (the creator of Neapolitan Baroque) to the 16th-century designs of Dosio. The church and choir are other remarkable examples of his virtuosity.

Next to the Certosa is Castel Sant'Elmo, which was built from 1329–43 and rebuilt in the 16th century, and offers stunning views over the bay.

� Museo Principe di Aragona Pignatelli Cortes

Riviera di Chiaia 200. ☎ 081-66 96 75. ◻ Tue–Sun. ● 1 Jan. 🎫

Lower down, in the Chiaia neighbourhood, the Neo-Classical Villa Pignatelli houses this museum and its interesting collection of porcelain, period furniture, paintings and sculpture.

The bold Castel Nuovo, with the triumphal arch entrance

🏛 Galleria Umberto I

Via Toledo. ☎ 081-797 23 03.
◯ daily am. ⬤ 1 Jan, Easter, 7–21 Aug, 25 Dec. ♿

Once a focus for fashionable Neapolitans, the arcades of the Galleria Umberto I were built in 1887 and rebuilt after World War II. Still handsome, though tatty, they face Italy's largest opera house: the **Teatro San Carlo**. Built for Charles of Bourbon in 1737, and later rebuilt, the magnificent interior has a luxurious auditorium that once aroused great envy in the courts of Europe.

Painting of *Lavinia Vecellio* (c.1540) by Titian in the Museo di Capodimonte

Magnificent glass-roofed interior of the Galleria Umberto I

🏛 Palazzo Reale

Piazza Plebiscito. **Museo** ☎ 081-41 38 88. ◯ Tue–Sun. ⬤ 1 Jan, 1 May, 25 Dec. ♿ **Biblioteca** ☎ 081-42 71 77. ◯ Mon–Sat. ⬤ public hols.

Begun by Domenico Fontana for the Spanish Viceroys in 1600, and expanded and embellished by subsequent residents, Naples' royal palace is a handsome edifice with great halls filled with furniture, tapestries, paintings and porcelain. The small private Teatro di Corte (1768) was built by Ferdinando Fuga. A large part of the building contains the

Biblioteca Nazionale. The exterior of the palace has been partly restored – note the 19th-century statues representing the dynasties of Naples. The huge Piazza del Plebiscito facing it has been cleaned up and cleared of traffic. The great colonnades sweep towards 19th-century **San Francesco di Paola**, modelled on Rome's Pantheon.

🏛 Villa Floridiana

Via Cimarosa 77. ☎ 081-578 84 18.
◯ Tue–Sat am. **Park** ◯ daily.
⬤ 1 Jan, 1 May, 25 Dec. ♿ 📷

Set in handsome gardens, this Neo-Classical villa houses the **Museo Nazionale della Ceramica Duca di Martina** which is famous for its collection of ceramics, including porcelain and majolica.

🏛 Museo di Capodimonte

Parco di Capodimonte. ☎ 081-744 13 07. ◯ daily. ♿

Begun in 1738 by the Bourbon king Charles III as a hunting lodge, the **Palazzo Reale di Capodimonte** houses this museum and its magnificent collections of Italian paintings. Included are works by Titian,

Botticelli, Perugino, Raphael and Sebastiano del Piombo, much of it originating in the Farnese family collections. There is also a gallery of 19th-century art, largely from southern Italy.

🏛 Catacombs of San Gennaro

Via di Capodimonte 16. ☎ 081-741 10 71. ◯ daily. ♿

These catacombs – the original burial place of San Gennaro – are located near the church of San Gennaro in Moenia. The small church was founded in the 8th century, and is adjoined by a 17th-century workhouse. Two tiers of catacombs dating from the 2nd century penetrate the tufa, and there are mosaics and early Christian frescoes. Further along the street, the Catacombs of San Gaudioso commemorate the 5th-century saint who founded a monastery on the spot. Above is the 17th-century church of Santa Maria della Sanità.

🏛 Castel dell'Ovo

Borgo Marinari. ◯ for exhibitions.

Away from the centre, Castel dell'Ovo occupies a small island facing, and joining, the Santa Lucia district – once the site of Naples' shellfish market. The castle was begun in 1154. Under the Normans and Hohenstaufen it was a royal residence, but today it belongs to the military.

Beneath its ramparts, tiny Porta Santa Lucia is filled with seafood restaurants, and the Via Partenope running past it is a lovely promenade that leads west to Mergellina.

The façade of the Palazzo Reale, Naples' royal palace

Pompei ❷

A<small>NCIENT POMPEI SPRAWLS</small> in a decrepit heap at the foot of Mount Vesuvius which erupted in AD 79, destroying the town. Stones and ash buried it, and it lay undiscovered until the 17th century. In 1748 excavation began, revealing a city frozen in time. All around, buildings have survived, often replete with paintings and sculpture. Graffiti is still on walls, streets are paved; the ghosts of that distant past are almost tangible on the site.

House of the Mysteries

★ House of the Vettii
This partly reconstructed patrician villa of the wealthy merchants, Aulus Vettius Conviva and Aulus Vettius Restitutus, contains frescoes (see pp44–5).

Forum Baths

★ House of the Faun
This famous villa of the wealthy patrician Casii is named after its bronze statuette. The mosaic Battle of Alexander, in the Museo Archeologico Nazionale in Naples, originated here.

0 metres   100

0 yards   100

Forum

Sacrarium of the Lares
Facing the Forum, and by the Temple of Vespasian, this building housed the statues of Pompei's guardian deities, the Lares Publici.

In the bakery
of Modesto, carbonized loaves of bread were found.

STAR SIGHTS

★ House of the Vettii

★ House of the Faun

Macellum
Pompei's market place was an important focus for the commercial activity of the town.

Last Days of Pompei
*Used as a backdrop for an
opera of the same name, this
dramatic 19th-century painting
by Sanquirico shows the people
of Pompei fleeing as Mount
Vesuvius erupts violently.*

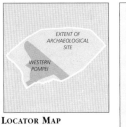

LOCATOR MAP

EXTENT OF
ARCHAEOLOGICAL
SITE

WESTERN
POMPEI

VISITORS' CHECKLIST

Piazza Esedra 5. **C** 081-861 10
51. **FS** Villa dei Misteri, Circumvesuviana Linea Napoli–Sorrento.
☐ Circumvesuviana from Piazza
Garibaldi, Napoli. **○** 9am–1 hr
before sunset (last adm: 1 hr
before closing). **●** 1 Jan, Easter
Mon, 1 May, 15 Aug, 25 Dec.

WESTERN POMPEI

This detailed western area
contains impressive Roman
ruins, some remarkably
intact. Parts of eastern
Pompei still await
excavation.

Palestra

**Teatro
Grande**

Via dell'Abbondanza
*This was one of the original
and most important roads
through ancient Pompei.
Many inns lined the route.*

VESUVIUS AND THE CAMPANIAN TOWNS

Nearly 2,000 years after
the eruption of Mount
Vesuvius, the Roman
towns in its shadow are
still being released from
the petrification that engulfed them. Both Pompei
and Stabiae (Castellam-
mare di Stabia), to the
southeast of
Naples and
the volcano,
were suffoc-
ated by hot ash
and volcanic
pumice-stone.
The roofs of the
buildings collapsed
under the weight
of the volcanic   **Pompeian vase in**
detritus. Fabrics,   **Museo Nazionale**
jewellery, food,   **Archeologico**
tools and utensils were
largely destroyed. To
the west, Herculaneum
(Ercolano) vanished
under a sea of mud.
A large number
of its buildings
have survived, their
roofs intact, and many
domestic items were
preserved by the mud. In
all, about 2,000 Pompeians
perished although few, if
any, of the residents of
Herculaneum died.

In AD 79 Pliny the Elder,
the Roman soldier, writer
and naturalist, was the
commander of a fleet
stationed off Misenum
(present-day Miseno, west
of Naples) and observed
the impending eruption
from afar. He related the
information to his nephew,
Pliny the Younger. Eager to
see this natural catastrophe
closer to hand, Pliny the
Elder proceeded to Stabiae,
but was overcome by

fumes and died. Pliny the
Elder's detailed account of
the first hours of that
eruption, described in
letters from his nephew to
Tacitus, has been referred
to ever since by scientists.

Much of our knowledge
of the daily lives of the
ancient Romans
derives from the
excavations of
both Pompei and
Herculaneum.
Most of the arte-
facts from them as
well as Stabiae have
been moved to the
Museo Archeo-
logico Nazionale in
Naples *(see pp474–
5)*, contributing to
one of the world's most
outstanding and fascinating
archaeological collections.

Mount Vesuvius has not
erupted since 1944, and
today interested visitors
are quite safe to reach it
by train or car. There is
so much to see at Pompei
that you will probably
need a day to explore it.

**Casts of a dying mother and
child in the museum in Naples**

Santa Maria Capua Vetere ❸

Caserta. 🏙 *34,000.* FS 🚇
🛈 *Via Albana (0823-79 95 89).*
🗓 *Thu & Sun.*

T HE BEST REASON to visit this
town is to see the ruined
Roman **amphitheatre** (1st
century AD), once Italy's
largest after the Colosseum
in Rome. Better preserved is
the series of tunnels beneath
it. The town itself occupies
the site of ancient Capua,
formerly an Etruscan city and
subsequently a flourishing
centre during the Roman
Empire. It was the scene of
the revolt of the gladiators,
led by Spartacus in 73 BC.
Nearby is a **Mithraeum**
(2nd–3rd century) with well-
preserved frescoes. Finds
from the archaeological sites
can be seen in the **Museo
Campano** in Capua.

♁ Amphitheatre
Piazza Adriano. 📞 *0823-79 88 64.*
◻ *daily.* ♿ 📷 *valid also for*
Mithraeum ◻ *daily.*
🏛 Museo Campano
Via Roma, Capua. 📞 *0823-96 14 02.*
◻ *Tue–Sun am.* ● *1 Jan, 25 Dec.* 📷

**Tunnels under the amphitheatre
in Santa Maria Capua Vetere**

Caserta ❹

🏙 *66,000.* FS 🚇 🛈 *Palazzo Reale
(0823-32 22 33).* 🗓 *Wed & Sat.*

M AGNIFICENTLY OPULENT, the
colossal **Palazzo Reale**,
likened in scale to Versailles,
dominates Caserta. Built for
the extravagant Bourbon
King Charles III, it boasts over
1,000 rooms, grand staircases

A fountain in the gardens of the Palazzo Reale at Caserta

and several richly adorned
royal apartments. The massive
construction was designed by
the architect Luigi Vanvitelli
and construction started in
1752. The vast surrounding
park is a showpiece in itself,
with fountains, ornamental
waterworks and statuary. The
scale is overwhelming.

ENVIRONS: The little medieval
town of **Caserta Vecchia**
lies 10 km (6 miles) to the
northeast. Its 12th-century
cathedral is a fine example of
southern Norman architecture.
San Leucio, 3 km (2 miles)
northwest of Caserta, is a
model town built by Ferdinand
IV. It remains the seat of a
silk industry, which was also
founded by the king.

🏯 Palazzo Reale
Viale Douhet. 📞 *0823-32 14 00.*
◻ *daily.* ● *1 Jan, 25 Dec.* 📷 ♿

Benevento ❺

🏙 *62,000.* FS 🚇 🛈 *Via Sala 31
(0824-254 24).* 🗓 *Fri & Sat.*

B ENEVENTO, set
in a lonely,
mountainous
province, is
home to one of
southern Italy's
most interesting
ancient Roman
monuments: the
Arch of Trajan
on Via Traiano.
The Roman city,
Beneventum, was
an important

centre. It stood at the end of
the first extension of the Via
Appia from Capua, and the
Arch was erected across the
old road in honour of Trajan.
Built from AD 114–166 of
Parian marble, it is extremely
well preserved. The relief
sculpture adorning it – scenes
from the life of Trajan and
mythological subjects – is in
excellent condition.

Elsewhere, evidence of the
Romans is to be found in the
ruined **Roman theatre**, built
during Hadrian's reign, and
in the **Museo del Sannio**,
which contains artefacts from
the region, from ancient
Greek finds to modern art.

During World War II, the
city stood directly in the way
of the Allied advance from
the south. It was heavily
bombed, hence its largely
modern appearance today.
The Duomo, a 13th-century
building reconstructed after
the war, has a sculpted façade
that, though badly damaged,
has since been restored. The
remains of its Byzantine
bronze doors are within.

**The ornate 2nd-century Roman arch in
Benevento, built to honour Trajan**

The town has centuries-old associations with pagan worship, and a liqueur called Strega (witch) is made here.

♫ Roman Theatre
Piazza Gaio Ponzio Telesino. ☐ Tue–Sun. ● public hols. 🈂 ♿

🏛 Museo del Sannio
Piazza Santa Sofia. ☎ 0824-218 18. ☐ Tue–Sun. ● public hols. 🈂 ♿

Costiera Amalfitana ➏

Salerno. 🚌 ⛴ Amalfi. 🛈 Corso Roma 19/21, Amalfi (089-87 11 07).

The small town of Atrani on the Costiera Amalfitana

THE MOST enchanting and most visited route in Campania is that skirting the southern flank of Sorrento's peninsula: the Costiera Amalfitana (Amalfi Coast). Among the popular pleasures here are dining on locally caught grilled fish and sipping icy Lacrima Christi from the vineyards on the slopes of Vesuvius, interspersed with beach-hopping and trips to coastal summits to admire the breathtaking views.

From **Sorrento**, a well developed holiday resort, the road winds down to **Positano**, a village clambering down a vertiginous slope to the sea. Expensive, it is nonetheless a good place to swim, or to catch the hydrofoil or ferry to Capri. Further on, **Praiano** is just as fashionable.

Amalfi is the coast's largest town. Its chief glory is a lovely 10th-century Duomo fronted by a rich, coloured façade (13th century). Amalfi was a maritime power before it was subdued in 1131 by King Roger of Naples. Its most illustrious citizens were buried in the 13th-century Chiostro del Paradiso, flanking the Duomo, a magnificent 9th-century structure facing the town from the top of a long flight of steps. The style is Lombard-Norman, though the cloisters have a Saracenic-inspired appearance. Amalfi is a tremendously popular resort.

Ravello has the best views on this coast. Poised on a shelf above Amalfi, the best vantage points are the gardens of Villa Cimbrone and Villa Rufolo. Views from the latter provided inspiration for Wagner's *Parsifal*. The 11th-century Duomo has entrance doors by Barisano da Trani (1179) and an ornate 13th-century ambo (pulpit) held aloft by six spiral columns. The chapel of San Pantaleone contains the blood of its 4th-century namesake which liquefies annually in May and August.

Further on, beyond **Atrani**, the ruins of a Roman villa at **Minori** serve as a reminder that this coastline has always been a popular holiday spot.

A breathtaking view of the steep village of Positano on the Costiera Amalfitana

Salerno **❼**

Salerno. **FS** 🚌 🚢 *Salerno.* **ℹ** *Piazza Ferrovia (089-23 14 32).*

SALERNO IS A BIG, busy port. Here the Allies landed in 1943, leaving in their wake a much bombed, ruinous city. Once famous for its School of Medicine (12th century), it is visited today for its **Duomo**, an 11th-century structure built on a 10th-century foundation. Its best feature is the Atrium, whose columns came from nearby Paestum. In the crypt is the Tomb of St Matthew, which was brought here in 954.

The **Museo Diocesano** is home to most of the cathedral treasures, including an 11th-century ivory altar-front called the Paliotto. Before wandering off down the bustling Corso Vittorio Emanuele, visit the **Museo Provinciale** for local archaeological finds.

ENVIRONS: The **Cilento** is a mountainous region south of Salerno with a remote interior and a lovely, quiet coastline that is only slightly more populous. Among the towns along the coast, **Agropoli** is a busy little seaside resort 42 km (25 miles) south of Salerno. Outside Castellammare di Velia, a further 28 km (17 miles) to the southeast, are the ruins of the Greek town of **Elea** (founded 6th century BC), once famous for its school of philosophy. It was much visited by the Romans – Cicero was here and Horace came on his doctor's orders to undergo a treatment of sea bathing.

The Temple of Hera I (left) and the Temple of Neptune at Paestum

Excavations have revealed a magnificent 4th-century Roman gateway: the Porta Rosa, Roman baths, the foundations of a temple and the remains of the ancient acropolis.

🏛 Museo Diocesano
Via Duomo. **ℹ** *089-23 35 68.*
⏰ *daily.*
🏛 Museo Provinciale
Via San Benedetto. **ℹ** *089-23 11 35.*
⏰ *Mon–Sat am.* ⏰ *1st & 3rd Mon of month.*

Capri **❾**

Napoli. 🚢 *Capri.* **ℹ** *Piazza Umberto I, Capri (081-837 06 86).* **Grotta Azzurra** 🚢 *from Marina Grande.* ⏰ *in calm sea.* **Certosa** *Via Certosa, Capri.* **ℹ** *081-837 62 18.* ⏰ *Tue–Sun am.* **⚦ Villa Jovis** *Via Tiberio.* ⏰ *daily.* 🔲

CAPRI'S ENDURING reputation as a sybaritic paradise is nearly eclipsed by its notoriety as a tourist trap. However, the great views are unmarred by the throng. The home of emperors, seat of monasteries, place of

Paestum **❽**

Zona Archeologica. **ℹ** *0828-81 10 16.* 🚌 *from Salerno.* **FS** *Paestum.* ⏰ *9am –1 hr before sunset daily.* **Museum** ⏰ *1st & 3rd Mon of month & some public hols.* 🔲 ⚦

THIS IS THE MOST important ancient Greek site south of Naples in Campania. The Greeks, who founded this city on the edge of the Piana del Sele in the 6th century BC,

exile, former haunt of goats and fishermen, its fortunes changed during the 19th century when English and German expatriates discovered its charms. Today it barely has a "low season"; farmers run little hotels, and fishermen rent pleasure boats. Capri has constant sunshine and enjoys a well-deserved reputation as a Garden of Eden.

The busy port of Salerno

The Grotta Azzurra, or the Blue Grotto, is a cave bathed in iridescent blue light which can be reached by tour boat from Marina Grande.

Anacapri is Capri's second town.

0 kilometres   1

0 miles   0.5

knew it as Poseidonia, the City of Poseidon. The Romans took and renamed it in 273 BC. It fell into decline and was abandoned in the 9th century due to malaria and a Saracen assault. It was rediscovered in the 18th century.

Today Paestum is visited for three massive surviving Doric temples in an excellent state of repair: the **Basilica** or **Temple of Hera I** (mid 6th century BC); the **Temple of Neptune** (5th century BC), the largest and most complete at Paestum; and the **Temple of Ceres**, thought to date between its two neighbours.

Excavations have revealed the remains of the ancient city, its public and religious buildings, roads and protective walls. A **museum** contains the extensive finds from the site, including tomb paintings, tomb treasures, some terracotta votive offerings, architectural fragments and sculpture.

A view from the highest point of Procida, called Terra Murata

Ischia and Procida ⑩

Napoli. 🚢 *Ischia Porto & Procida Porto.* 🛈 *Via Iasolino, Ischia (081-99 11 46). Via Roma, Procida (081-810 19 68).*

ISCHIA IS THE BIGGEST island in the Bay of Naples and, with its beach resorts, thermal springs, therapeutic sands and cheap hotels, it is nearly as

popular as its more glamorous neighbour, Capri. Ferries dock at **Ischia Porto**, the harbour and modern part of the main town, **Ischia**. **Ischia Ponte**, the older part, is a short walk away. The northern and the western shores are developed; the southern flank of the island is the quietest. Here, the village of **Sant'Angelo** is dominated by the hulk of a long-extinct volcano, **Monte Epomeo**, whose summit of 788 m (2,585 ft) offers terrific views back across the bay to Naples.

Procida is the odd one next to Ischia and Capri, and it is small – only 3.5 km (2 miles) long – and less visited by holiday crowds. Nevertheless, the swimming is good at **Chiaiolella** and, as at Ischia, there are inexpensive places to stay. The ramshackle main town, also called **Procida**, is home to the main ferry port – the **Marina Grande**.

There are views towards Vesuvius and the Bay of Naples from the north of the island.

Capri is the main town on the island.

Marina Grande
This is Capri's main port of call for ferries from Naples and other ports on the Tyrrhenian coast. An array of colourful houses overlooks the harbour.

I Faraglioni

Marina Piccola is reached by dramatic Via Krupp.

Villa Jovis
Covering an enormous area, this was the Imperial villa from which Tiberius ruled the Roman Empire during his final years.

Certosa di San Giacomo
Founded in 1371 on the site of one of Tiberius's villas, this Carthusian monastery was suppressed in 1808 and is now in part a school. The distant rocks are I Faraglioni.

ABRUZZO, MOLISE AND PUGLIA

P UGLIA IS THE "HEEL" *of the Italian boot, the Gargano Peninsula is its "spur" and Abruzzo and Molise together form the "ankle". Hugging the southeastern seaboard of Italy and looking towards the Balkans, the mountainous regions of Abruzzo and Molise, united until 1963, differ dramatically from Puglia, the richest of the three.*

Abruzzo and Molise are sparsely populated, quiet places where the wild landscape exerts a strong influence. Settled by various Apennine tribes in the Middle Bronze Age, the areas were later subdued by the Romans, united under the Normans in the 12th century and, thereafter, ruled by a succession of dynasties based in Naples. Abruzzo, dominated by the Apennines, is a brooding, introspective land of shepherds. Vertiginous drops preface the ascent to ramshackle hilltowns clinging to the sides of high mountains, semi-abandoned and poor. Molise is less dramatic, but life in both regions is primitive. Legends of witches persist, as do strange fertility rites and rituals celebrating the changing seasons.

Puglia's advantage over its poverty-stricken neighbours is that it is nearly all flat and highly fertile. It produces the largest amounts of olive oil and wine in Italy, and its big cities – Lecce, Bari and Taranto – are lively commercial centres.

The region experienced a long-lasting Greek influence, though the golden age of Puglia's past was under the rule of the Normans, followed by Frederick II who, between his return from Germany as emperor in 1220 and his death 30 years later, only spent four years away from here.

Puglia has glorious architecture, particularly in the churches and castles of the north. The curious *trulli* houses in central Puglia, the florid Baroque of Lecce and the Levantine atmosphere of its merchant cities complete the picture of an ancient land subject to more influences from outside the Italian peninsula than from within it.

Traditional dress worn in the town of Scanno in Abruzzo

◁ The curious *trulli* buildings found in central Puglia, particularly around Alberobello and Locorotondo

Exploring Abruzzo, Molise and Puglia

DOMINATED BY THE PROLIFIC Apennine mountain range, the hinterland of Abruzzo and Molise forms one of Italy's last wildernesses. At 2,912 m (9,554 ft), the highest peak is the Gran Sasso. Parts of Abruzzo are covered in endless tracts of forest. Molise is characterized by high plains, soft valleys and lonely peaks. The spectacular Gargano Peninsula in Puglia (Apulia) has a lovely seaboard. Reaching south is the fertile Tavoliere plain, and further south a series of upland plateaux (the Murge) descend towards the dry Salentine Peninsula and the Adriatic.

The exotic *trulli* houses in Alberobello in central Puglia

GETTING AROUND

Northern Abruzzo is well served by the A24 and A25, and the N17 traverses the interior of Abruzzo and Molise. The coastal highway (A14) heads south through Abruzzo and Molise into Puglia. Beyond Foggia, it joins the N16 to Taranto. Brindisi, the main port for Greece, is accessible from Bari or Taranto. The roads throughout are good. Train and bus services go to the major centres, with buses only to more remote parts.

The coast at Vieste on the beautiful Gargano Peninsula in Puglia

0 kilometres   50

0 miles   25

KEY

Motorway

Major road

Minor road

Scenic route

River

Viewpoint

SIGHTS AT A GLANCE

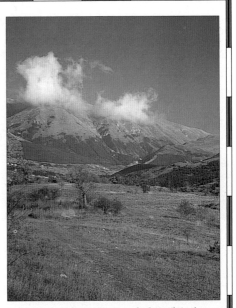

The high peaks of the Gran Sasso, north of L'Aquila in Abruzzo

Lecce's exuberant Baroque architecture, epitomized in Santa Croce's rose window

SEE ALSO

The pink and white stone façade of Santa Maria di Collemaggio in L'Aquila

L'Aquila ❶

🏛 64,000. 🚆 🚌 ℹ Via XX Settembre (0862-223 06). 🗓 daily.

Aᴮᴿᵁ�z�zo's capital lies at the foot of the **Gran Sasso**, the highest point of the Italian mainland south of the Alps (and good for skiing). Its ancient streets are peppered with churches and mansions. **Santa Giusta** (1257), off Via Santa Giusta, has a lovely rose window and a *Martyrdom of St Stephen* (1615) by Cavalier d'Arpino. **Santa Maria di Paganica** off Via Paganica has a 14th-century façade and a carved portal. The **Duomo** (1257) in Piazza del Duomo was rebuilt in the 18th century and subsequently enlarged.

The church of **Santa Maria di Collemaggio**, on Piazza di Collemaggio, is a massive structure with a façade of pink and white stone. It was built in the 13th century by Pietro dal Morrone, who later became Pope Celestine V. In the chapel to the right of the apse is the tomb of the founder who, in 1313, was canonized as St Peter Celestine.

San Bernardino, on Via di San Bernardino, houses the tomb (1505) of San Bernardino of Siena by Silvestro dell'Aquila. The church, built from 1454 to 1472, has a façade (1527) by Cola dell'Amatrice and an 18th-century carved ceiling by

Ferdinando Mosca. The second chapel in the south aisle has an altarpiece by Andrea della Robbia, the Renaissance artist.

The medieval **Fontanelle delle Novantanove Cannelle** at the end of Via San Iacopo is a fountain commemorating the 99 villages that Frederick II supposedly united when he founded L'Aquila in 1240.

The **Museo Nazionale d'Abruzzo**, in the 16th-century castle, contains the remains of a prehistoric elephant, Roman artefacts and religious works.

ENVIRONS: North of L'Aquila are the ruins of a **theatre** and **amphitheatre** of ancient **Amiternum**, a Sabine then Roman town, and the birthplace of Sallust (86–c.35 BC), the Roman historian and politician who helped to develop the monograph.

🏛 **Museo Nazionale d'Abruzzo**
Castello Cinquecentesco. 📞 0862-63 31. 🗓 daily. 🔴 1 Jan, Easter, 25 Dec. 🎫 ♿

Detail of Fontanelle delle Novantanove Cannelle in L'Aquila

Atri ❷

Teramo. 🏛 11,000. 🚌 🗓 Mon.

THE PRETTIEST in a series of small hilltowns in Abruzzo, Atri is a warren of stepped streets, alleys and passages bound by mostly brick and stone churches and houses. The 13th-century **Duomo**

occupies the site of a Roman bath; the crypt was once a swimming pool, and fragments of the original mosaic floor are visible in the apse. Also in the apse is Andrea Delito's great 15th-century fresco cycle, in which he combined landscape and architecture in a variety of religious scenes from the Old and New Testaments. The cloister has views of the 15th-century brick campanile.

ENVIRONS: South of Atri is the hilltown of **Penne**. Street by street it is remarkably homogeneous with its buildings of reddish brick, which give the town a warm glow. East of Atri, **Loreto Aprutino** is known for the *Last Judgment* fresco (14th century) in Santa Maria in Piano.

Detail from 15th-century fresco by Andrea Delito in Atri's Duomo

Sulmona ❸

L'Aquila. 🏛 24,000. 🚆 🚌 ℹ Corso Ovidio 208 (0864-532 76). 🗓 Wed & Sat.

THIS TOWN is famous as the home of both Ovid and *confetti* (sugared almonds). After a wedding ceremony in Abruzzo, the happy couple is pelted with *confetti* in an effort to see them on the road to good fortune. Sulmona is filled with ancient buildings, especially along medieval **Via dell'Ospedale**, imparting a beguiling atmosphere. The greatest treasure is the palace of the **Annunziata** on Corso Ovidio. Founded in 1320, the building combines Gothic and Renaissance styles. It houses the **Museo Civico** which contains local antiquities, paintings and the work of goldsmiths. The adjacent church of the **Annunziata**, with a robust Baroque façade, was rebuilt in the 18th century.

At the end of Viale Matteotti is the cathedral of **San Panfilo**, built over a Roman temple. **San Francesco della Scarpa**, in Piazza del Carmine, has a 13th-century portal. Winding past it to the **Fontana della Vecchia** (1474) is an aqueduct that once fuelled local industry.

ENVIRONS: East of Sulmona is the Maiella, a massif of 61 peaks and heavily forested valleys offering walking, bird-watching, climbing and skiing. To the west, Cocullo is the scene of the May Processione dei Serpari (Festival of Snakes) in which a statue of the patron saint, Domenico Abate, is draped with snakes and carried through the town. In the 11th century he is said to have freed the area from venomous snakes.

🏛 Museo Civico
Palazzo dell'Annunziata, Corso Ovidio.
📞 0864-21 02 16. **◯** Tue–Sun.

OVID, THE LATIN POET

Born in 43 BC, Ovid (Publius Ovidius Naso) was Sulmona's most illustrious son. Not much survives there to remind you of his presence, however, apart from a **Corso Ovidio**, a 20th-century statue of him in Piazza XX Settembre and, just outside the town, a ruin traditionally known as **Ovid's Villa**. Known as one of the greatest poets of Classical Rome, his subjects included love (*Ars Amatoria*) and mythology (*Metamorphoses*). In AD 8 he was banished into exile at the Black Sea, the far edge of the Roman Empire, after being implicated in a scandal of adultery with Julia, the granddaughter of Emperor Augustus (*see pp44–5*). Ovid continued to write of his hardships, and died in exile in AD 17.

Scanno ❹

L'Aquila. 🏠 2,400. 🚌 **ℹ** Piazza Santa Maria della Valle 12 (0864-743 17). ◉ Tue.

Precociously well-preserved, this medieval hilltown set in beautiful, wild countryside is one of Abruzzo's most popular attractions. There are alleys and narrow flights of steps, oddly-shaped courtyards into which small churches have been pressed, and ancient mansions in whose windows the women can be seen making lace or embroidering.

Traditional costume still worn in Scanno

In the shadow of Apennine peaks and beside lovely **Lago di Scanno**, the town is also a favoured halt on the way to the Parco Nazionale d'Abruzzo (*see pp490–91*). The summer months are the busiest, with a variety of amusements from riding, boating and camping by the lake, to the August classical music festival. During the January Festa di Sant'Antonio Abate, a large lasagna is cooked outside **Santa Maria della Valle**, built on the remains of a pagan temple. The food is doled out to whoever comes along first.

High Apennine peaks looming above the medieval hilltown of Scanno in Abruzzo

Parco Nazionale d'Abruzzo **⑤**

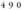

Iris

THIS VAST PARK with its rich landscape of high peaks, rivers, lakes and forests, is one of Europe's most important nature reserves. Until 1877 it formed part of a royal hunting reserve, but today it provides refuge for over 40 species of mammal, 30 types of reptile and 300 species of bird, including the golden eagle and white-backed woodpecker. Walkers can choose from an extensive network of paths, and there are opportunities for riding, skiing and canoeing, making the park popular with visitors.

Golden eagles
may be seen near
the Sangro
river.

PESCINA
AVEZZANO

N83

● Pescasseroli

MAI

● Opi

N83

CASSINO

N509

Sangro

Young Chamois
Dense forests of beech and maple hide the Apennine chamois. There are also red and roe deer in the park.

Forests of beech and black pine provide beautiful scenery.

Pescasseroli
At the heart of the park, this town is a major centre for information on the region. It has good tourist facilities, including a number of hotels, and ski facilities are nearby.

Marsican Brown Bear
Once hunted almost to extinction, the park now boasts between 80 and 100 brown bears.

Apennine Wolves
The park guarantees protection for the Apennine wolf, and about 30 wolves survive here. The chances of seeing one, however, are fairly remote.

VISITORS' CHECKLIST

L'Aquila. **FS** *Avezzano or Alfedena & then bus to Pescasseroli.* **bus** *Pescasseroli.* **i** *Viale Santa Lucia, 6, Pescasseroli (0863-91 07 15).*

Horse Riding
Pony trekking is an excellent way to explore more remote areas of the park.

The Camosciara is a spectacular area, home to many wild animals.

Lake Barrea
Created by the artificial damming of the River Sangro, this lake is surrounded by valleys and forests offering walking and pony trekking.

Dense Forests
Beech and maple forests, dotted with black hornbeam, ash, hawthorn, cherry, wild apple and pear, protect the once persecuted bears and wolves.

KEY

▬▬	Major road
▭▭	Minor road
▬ ▬	Walking path
✲	Viewpoint
i	Tourist information

0 kilometres 5

0 miles 5

Lanciano 6

Chieti. 🏠 *50,000.* **FS** **bus**
i *Piazza Plebiscito (0872-71 49 59).*
🕐 *Wed & Sat.*

GREAT CHUNKS of Lanciano's ancient nucleus are left in the Middle Ages. In the crumbling Civitanova quarter is the 13th-century church of **Santa Maria Maggiore**, with a magnificent 14th-century portal and a silver processional cross (1422) by Nicola da Guardiagrele. Also in this area are **Sant'Agostino** (14th century) and the now disused **San Biagio** (begun c.1059), near the 11th-century **Porta San Biagio** – a rare surviving town gate. The **Duomo**, with its 17th-century bell tower, is situated on top of the remains of a Roman bridge that dates from the period of Diocletian.

The Ripa Sacca (Jewish ghetto) was a busy commercial centre in the Middle Ages – the period of Lanciano's greatest prosperity. The hefty walls of the **Torri Montanara** were built then by the Aragonese as a bulwark against attack.

Isole Tremiti 7

Foggia. ⛴ *San Nicola.* **i** *Via Perrone 17, Foggia (0881-72 36 50).*

OF ALL ITALY'S coastal islands, these are the least visited by foreigners. **San Domino** is the largest of the group, with a sandy beach and coves. Here in AD 8, Julia, granddaughter of Augustus, was exiled for adultery and died in AD 28. The poet Ovid was supposedly involved *(see p489).*

San Nicola, the administrative centre of the group of islands, has an important 11th-century monument: **Santa Maria a Mare**. An abbey-fortress founded in the 8th century, it was turned into a prison late in the 18th century and ultimately became a place of detention for political prisoners, a role it kept until 1945.

Both islands are popular with Italians. The swimming is good, though the coastline of San Nicola is rocky.

The coast near Peschici on the Gargano Peninsula

Gargano Peninsula ⑧

Foggia. 🚉 🚌 ℹ️ *Corso Manfredi 26, Manfredonia (0884-58 19 98).*

A HIGH, ROCKY SPUR jutting into the Adriatic Sea, the Gargano is a dramatic wilderness dotted with coves and cliffs. Its coastal towns of **Rodi Garganico**, **Peschici**, **Vieste** and **Manfredonia** are popular with holidaymakers. To the east lies the **Foresta Umbra**, a vast woodland of beech, oak, yew and pine, and to the north the salt lakes of **Lesina** and **Varano**, havens for waterfowl.

Typical street scene in the town of Vieste on the Gargano Peninsula

Plunging through the Gargano is an old pilgrim route (N272) from **San Severo** in the west to the shrine at **Monte Sant' Angelo** in the east. The first stop is **San Marco in Lamis**, which is dominated by a huge 16th-century convent. Further along, **San Giovanni Rotondo** is a focus for pilgrims in search of a cure from Padre Pio (1887–1968), a miracle-worker who is buried here. The last stop is **Monte Sant'Angelo** with its grotto where in 490, according to tradition, the Archangel Michael appeared to the Bishop of Sipontum.

To the south of Manfredonia, beside the ruins of the ancient town of Siponto, is the oriental-inspired 12th-century church of **Santa Maria di Siponto**.

Lucera ⑨

Foggia. 🏠 *43,000.* 🚌 🖼️ *Wed.*

THIS WAS ONCE a prosperous Roman colony and, on the northeast edge of town, the ruins of a Roman **amphitheatre** survive. Lucera was rebuilt in the 13th century by Frederick II, who peopled it with 20,000 Muslims from Sicily. It became one of the strongest fortresses in southern Italy, and its **castle** is one of Puglia's most magnificent. Built by Frederick II in 1233, and enlarged by Charles I after 1269, its fortified wall of

900 m (2,953 ft) is interspersed with 24 towers. Of Frederick's original palace stronghold within, only the base and some vaulting remains.

In 1300 Charles II, who massacred most of Lucera's Muslim population, began the lovely **Duomo** on the site of their main mosque. It blends Gothic and Romanesque styles. The high, soaring nave is filled with frescoes and carvings.

The **Museo Civico Fiorelli** has displays of episodes from throughout Lucera's history.

🏛️ **Museo Civico Fiorelli**
Via de Nicastri 44. 📞 *0881-54 70 41.* 🕐 *Tue–Sun.* 📷

The remains of Lucera castle

Troia ⑩

Foggia. 🏠 *33,000.* 🚌 🖼️ *1st & 3rd Sat of month.*

FOUNDED IN 1017 as a Byzantine fortress against the Lombards, Troia fell to the Normans in 1066. Until Frederick II destroyed it in 1229, the town had been ruled by a succession of powerful bishops who were responsible for producing some of Puglia's most remarkable buildings, including Troia's **Duomo** *(see pp462–3).*

Begun in 1093 and constructed over the following 30 years, it exhibits an extraordinary diversity of styles. It successfully blends elements of Lombard, Saracenic and Byzantine style with that of the Pisan-Romanesque.

Elegant blind arcading distinguishes the Duomo's lower storey. The upper sections are characterized by powerfully carved sculpture – projecting lions and bulls. The upper façade displays a rose window with Saracenic-style detailing.

The main entrance, with bronze doors by Oderisio da Beneventano (1119), is dominated by carved capitals and an architrave, both Byzantine in style. Within the Duomo is a Romanesque pulpit (1169).

Trani ⓫

Lecce. 🏛 45,000. FS 🚌 ℹ *Piazza della Repubblica (0883-432 95).* 🗓 *Tue.*

The façade of Trani's Duomo

DURING THE MIDDLE AGES this small, lively whitewashed port bustled with mercantile activity and was filled with merchants and traders from Genoa, Amalfi, Pisa and Ravello. It reached its peak of prosperity under Frederick II.

Today it is visited for its Norman **Duomo** in Piazza Duomo, built mainly from 1159 to 1186 over an earlier church whose predecessor, the Ipogei di San Leucio, dates from the 6th century. It is dedicated to St Nicholas the Pilgrim, a little-remembered miracle-worker (died 1094) who was canonized as an act of rivalry against the town of Bari, which possessed the bones of another, more memorable St Nicholas. The Duomo's most notable external characteristics are its sculptures, particularly surrounding the rose window and the arched window below it, and the richly adorned entrance portal with bronze doors (1175–9) by Barisano da Trani. The vigour of the interior has recently been revealed following restoration.

Next to the Duomo is the **castle** (1233–49) that was founded by Frederick II. Rebuilt in the 14th and 15th centuries, it is a well-preserved edifice with one wall dropping sheer into the sea.

Elsewhere in Trani the 15th-century Gothic town house, the **Palazzo Caccetta** in Piazza Trieste, is a rare survival. Nearby, on Via Ognissanti, the 12th-century Romanesque church of the **Ognissanti**, the chapel of the Knights Templar erected in the courtyard of their hospital, is notable for its original portico.

Castel del Monte ⓬

Località Andria, Bari. ☐ *Apr–Sep: 9am–5pm Tue–Sat; Oct–Mar: 9am–1pm Tue–Sat.* ● *25 Dec.* 🗓 📷

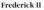
Frederick II

REMOTE IN THE endless plains near Ruvo di Puglia, Castel del Monte, begun in 1240, outclasses every other castle associated with Frederick II. It is also one of the most sophisticated secular buildings of the European Middle Ages. The emperor had broad intellectual interests, and he used his castles as hunting lodges where he could retire from the relentlessly itinerant court life with his falcons, books and correspondence. Inside there are two floors, each with eight lovely rib-vaulted rooms, some still lined with marble. This, and the marble mouldings on the entrance and the upper floor, as well as sophisticated lavatory arrangements, mark the castle as a palace.

Octagonal satellite tower

Graceful, arched windows

Thick and impenetrable walls

Octagonal courtyard

The main entrance portal is in the style of a Roman triumphal arch.

FLOORPLAN OF THE CASTLE
The building is a harmonious geometrical study with two storeys of eight rooms each. The reasons for such precise planning of this giant octagon remain a mystery to this day.

The castle standing alone on the summit of a low hill

Ruvo di Puglia ⑬

Bari. 🏚 24,000. 🚉 🚌 🚊 Sat.

Once celebrated for its vases, Ruvo di Puglia's ceramics industry, producing "Apulian" ware, flourished until the 2nd century BC. Using Archaic Corinthian and Attic models, the style was based on the striking red and black colours of the originals. An excellent overview can be seen in the **Museo Archeologico Nazionale Iatta**.

The 13th-century **Duomo** is a bold example of the Apulian-Romanesque style with a portal that blends Byzantine, Saracenic and Classical motifs.

🏛 Museo Archeologico Nazionale Iatta

Piazza Bovio 35. 📞 081-81 28 48. 🕐 daily. 🌑 1 Jan, 1 May, 25 Dec. 🚻

Bari ⑭

🏚 500,000. ✈ 🚉 🚌 🚢 🚆 Piazza Aldo Moro 33 (080-524 22 44). 🚊 daily.

Roman Barium was simply a commercial centre, but the city became the regional capital under the Saracens in 847, and was subsequently the seat of the *catapan*, the Byzantine governor of southern Italy. Under the Normans, to whom it fell in 1071, Bari became a centre of maritime significance rivalling Venice. Today it is Puglia's lively capital.

The **Basilica di San Nicola**, one of Puglia's first great Norman churches (begun 1087), was a model for others. Its plain exterior has a tall gabled section flanked by towers. The entrance portal is Apulian-Romanesque, with carving on the door jambs and arch in Arabic, Byzantine and Classical style.

Beyond the choir screen is a fine 12th-century altar canopy and an episcopal throne (c.11th century). The relics of St Nicholas – patron saint of Russia, children and sailors – are buried in the crypt.

The late 12th-century Apulian-Romanesque **Duomo** is based on San Nicola, with a dome and one surviving tower (the other tower collapsed during an earthquake in 1613). The Baroque portals on the entrance façade incorporate 12th-century doorways. The interior has been restored to its medieval simplicity. The canopy over the high altar, the pulpit and the episcopal throne are reconstructions from fragments of the originals. The sacristy, which was built as a baptistry, is known as the *Trulla*. The crypt houses the remains of San Sabino, Bari's original patron saint.

The city's **castle**, founded by Roger II, was adapted by Frederick II in 1233–9. In the vaulted hall is a collection of plaster casts of sculpture and architectural fragments from various Romanesque monuments in the region.

Portal detail of Ruvo di Puglia's Duomo

Sculpture at Bari castle

Bari castle, situated in the old district known as the Città Vecchia, where most of the town's sites are clustered

Alberobello ⑮

Bari. **FS** *to Alberobello & Ostuni.*
ℹ *Piazza del Popolo (080-72 19 16).*

I**N THE DRY**, almost arid landscape called the **Murge dei Trulli**, there is a profusion of olive groves, orchards, vineyards and *trulli*. Strange circular buildings with conical roofs and domed within, *trulli* are built from local limestone stacked without using mortar. The walls and openings are generally whitewashed, while the stone roof tiles are either bare or have religious or folk symbols painted onto them. Some have been converted into modern houses; others are farm buildings or storage barns. Their origins are obscure, though the name is traditionally applied to ancient round tombs found in the Roman countryside.

Alberobello is the *trulli* capital and, inevitably, a tourist haunt. Here the strange white buildings crowd the narrow streets, and there are *trulli* restaurants and shops, and even a *trulli* cathedral.

ENVIRONS: The whitewashed hilltown of **Locorotondo** is one of the region's prettiest places, although labyrinthine **Martina Franca** may be the most elegant, with streets enlivened by Rococo balconies. In late July or early August there is a music festival here, the Festivale della Valle d'Itria.

Whitewashed and sun-baked *trulli* in Alberobello

Taranto ⑯

▥ 245,000. **FS** ▤ **ℹ** *Corso Umberto 113 (099-459 34 03).*
▣ *Mon & Fri.*

L**ITTLE REMAINS OF** the ancient city of Taras, founded by Spartans in 708 BC. It enjoyed its greatest prosperity under the philosopher and scientist Archytas in the mid-4th century BC. The **Museo Archeologico Nazionale** has artefacts that shed light on much of the region's early history. Taranto suffered greatly due to heavy bombing in World War II and is garlanded by heavy industry, especially in the Borgo area. The picturesque **Città Vecchia**, an island dividing the Mare Grande from the Mare Piccolo, was the site of the Roman citadel of Tarentum. There is an ebullient fish market which still offers the shellfish for which the city was once famous. Here, too, is the **Duomo**. Founded in 1071, it has been the subject of subsequent rebuilding. The most interesting features include the catacomb-like crypt, with its sarcophagi and fragmented frescoes, and the antique marble columns of the nave. Behind it is the 11th-century **San Domenico Maggiore**, which later gained a high double-approach Baroque staircase. The huge **castle** built by Frederick of Aragon (18th century) covers the eastern corner of the Città Vecchia, with a swing bridge connecting it to the mainland.

Aphrodite in museum in Taranto

🏛 Museo Archeologico Nazionale
Corso Umberto 141. **☏** *099-459 04 11.* **◷** *daily (Nov–Mar: am only).* **◎** *1 Jan, Easter, 25 Dec.* **▨ ♿**

THE TARANTELLA

Italy's lively and graceful folk dance, the Tarantella, grew out of tarantism – the hysteria that appeared in 15th- to 17th-century Italy, and was prevalent in Taranto. Alleged victims of the tarantula spider's bite could supposedly cure themselves through frenzied dancing which sweated out the poison. The dance is characterized by light, quick steps and a "teasing" flirt. The strange ritual can be experienced annually on 28–29 June at the celebrations for the Feast of Saints Peter and Paul in Galatina. This remains the only place on the Salentine Peninsula where the phenomenon of tarantism has survived.

Street-by-Street: Lecce ⑰

**Façade detail,
Santa Croce**

Tʜɪꜱ ᴛᴏᴡɴ, tucked away on the Salentine Penin-sula, was the site of a Greek settlement. It became an important centre of the Roman Empire, and during the Middle Ages a strong tradition of scholarship was established. Much of the architecture is in the Lecce Baroque style, which flourished in the 17th century. Characterized by rich sculptural decoration, this style was possible due to the building material, *pietra di Lecce* – an easily carved stone. Giuseppe Zimbalo (lo Zingarello) was the greatest master of the style.

★ Palazzo Vescovile and Duomo
The bishop's palace (rebuilt in 1632), the adjoining Duomo by lo Zingarello (after 1659) and a seminary enclose the Piazza Duomo.

Chiesa del Rosario
Said to be the finest work by lo Zingarello (begun 1691), the exterior is ornate and idiosyncratic in its detail.

The Seminary once supplied the Vatican with *castrato* singers – eunuchs noted for their high voices.

Porta Rudiae
This 18th-century city gate leads to the suburbs and to the ruins of Roman Rudiae.

Chiesa del Carmine

Sᴛᴀʀ Sɪɢʜᴛꜱ

★ **Santa Croce**

★ **Palazzo Vescovile
and Duomo**

Kᴇʏ

– – –   Suggested route

0 metres	100
0 yards	100

★ **Santa Croce**
*Built from 1549 to 1679,
Gabriele Riccardi began
the façade and interior
and lo Zingarello
designed the imagin-
ative rose window
and pediment.*

**The 16th-century
Castello** is marooned
between ancient city and
modern suburbs. An inner
construction (12th century)
is enclosed by a later wall
built by Charles V.

**Detail of a 15th-century fresco in
Santa Caterina d'Alessandria**

Galatina ⑱

Lecce. 28,000. ▓ ▭ ▤ Thu.

AN IMPORTANT Greek colony
in the Middle Ages, this
town retains a distinctive
Greek flavour. It is the centre
of one of Puglia's chief wine-
producing regions, although
it is more famous for its lively
tarantella dance, performed
on 28–29 June *(see p495).*

The Apulian-Romanesque
church of **Santa Caterina
d'Alessandria** on Piazza Orsini
was built by Raimondello del
Balzo Orsini (begun 1384). This
lovely church contains early
15th-century frescoes with
scenes from the Old and New
Testaments that glorify the
Orsini, who were feudal lords.
Orsini's tomb is in the chancel.

VIA A GRANDI
VIALE XXV LUGLIO
VIA D'ARAGONA
LECCE

**Tourist
information**

**Church of
San Matteo**

Colonna di Sant'Oronzo
*St Oronzo was appointed
Bishop of Lecce by St Paul in
AD 57, and later martyred by
the Roman emperor Nero. This
bronze statue dates from 1739.*

ilway
tion

**A Roman
theatre** was
excavated
virtually intact
with its orches-
tra and seats.

Otranto ⑲

Lecce. 4,800. ▓ ▭ ▤ ▯ Via
Rondachi 8 (0836-80 14 36). ▤ Wed.

TODAY OTRANTO is a mere
shadow of its former self. It
was one of Republican Rome's
leading ports for trade with
Asia Minor and Greece, and
under the Byzantines was an
important toehold of the
Eastern Empire in Italy. In 1070
it fell to the Normans. Turks
attacked the town in
1480 and slaughtered
its inhabitants. The 800
survivors were promised
their lives if they
renounced Christianity,
but they all refused.

The Norman **Duomo**
(founded 1080) on Via
Duomo houses the
bones of the martyrs.
There is a 12th-century
mosaic floor and a fine
crypt. A **castle** (1485–98)
built by the Aragonese at the
centre of town, overlooking the
port, adds to Otranto's charm.

Roman Amphitheatre
*Excavated in 1938, only half of this
1st-century BC amphitheatre is visible.
The lower tier of seats has survived.*

BASILICATA AND CALABRIA

R EMOTE AND WILD, *Basilicata is one of the poorest regions in Italy. It is underdeveloped and undervisited, and so remains unspoilt. Neighbouring Calabria has been immortalized in the drawings of Edward Lear who, travelling through on a donkey in 1847, was transfixed by the "horror and magnificence" of its savage landscape.*

Today these regions are mutually distinct, but they share a common history and, along with Sicily and Puglia, were part of Magna Graecia. Ancient Metaponto in Basilicata was an important centre, as were Crotone and Locri Epizefiri in Calabria. Their ruins evoke a confident past.

After the Greeks came the Romans, followed by the Byzantines. The Cattolica at Stilo is a beautiful reminder of Byzantine rule. Then came eastern Christian Basilian monks, whose religious establishments make up a core of interesting monuments. Matera, for example, where the monks took refuge in caves, is a strange and fascinating place, decaying yet ebullient.

Many of the historic remains are Norman, but sporadic evidence of Hohenstaufen, Angevin, Aragonese and Spanish occupation also exists.

Centuries of rule by Naples led to the marginalization of Basilicata and Calabria. Nowadays Calabria has a terrifying reputation due to the *'ndrangheta*, the ferocious first cousin to the Mafia, whose activities are a constant menace. Banditry does still exist, but the sensible traveller should have little to fear.

Owing to emigration, Basilicata and Calabria are sparsely populated and have as much to offer in unspoilt countryside as in historic centres. The vast coastline boasts sandy beaches, while the interior features the rugged Aspromonte and Sila mountain ranges.

The remote landscape has kept change at bay. Isolated Pentedattilo, for example, preserves customs of Byzantine origin while around San Giorgio Albanese there live close-knit communities of Albanians, descended from 15th-century refugees.

Sparsely populated, rugged countryside surrounding Stilo in southern Calabria

◁ The silent Sassi district in Matera, where dwellings are scooped out of the rock

Exploring Basilicata and Calabria

MOSTLY UPLAND COUNTRY, Basilicata is scattered with Greek ruins (like those at Metaponto), medieval abbeys, Norman castles (such as Melfi's) and isolated hilltowns. Matera, its most interesting city, stands amid an arid lunar landscape of denuded valleys. Calabria is often described as the mountains between the seas. The lovely beaches and virgin landscape around Tropea and Maratea are popular with visitors. The Ionian coast's chief attractions are its Greek ruins, including Sybaris and Locri Epizefiri, and the hilltowns, like Gerace and Stilo, which eventually replaced them.

SIGHTS AT A GLANCE

Repairing nets in the town of Pizzo, northeast of Tropea

The picturesque hilltown of Rivello, north of Maratea in Basilicata

KEY

▬▬▬	Motorway
▬▬▬	Major road
▬▬▬	Minor road
▬▬	Scenic route
≋	River
❈	Viewpoint

0 kilometres   50

0 miles   25

The port of Maratea on the Tyrrhenian coast of Basilicata

GETTING AROUND

Calabria's Tyrrhenian coast is well served by the A3, a spur of which extends to Potenza in Basilicata. To reach the Ionian coast, it is best is to skirt the Aspromonte via the N106 from Reggio to Basilicata. Although the mountains can be crossed, namely on the N280 to Catanzaro, the roads are narrow and pass through isolated countryside. Much of Basilicata is even less accessible, and Matera is more easily reached from Puglia. There are airports at Reggio di Calabria, Lamezia (west of Catanzaro) and Brindisi (Puglia). Trains connect the bigger centres and country buses serve the small towns.

SEE ALSO

• *Where to Stay* p572

• *Where to Eat* p606

The countryside near Miglionico, south of Matera

The impressive castle at Melfi, showing evidence of both Angevin and later construction

Melfi ❶

Potenza. 🏛 *15,000.* FS 🚌
🍴 *Wed & Sat.*

ABROODING and now almost deserted medieval town, Melfi is crowned by the formidable **castle** where Pope Nicholas II conducted the investiture of Robert Guiscard in 1059, thus legitimizing the Normans in the south. Melfi subsequently became the Norman capital. Here, too, Frederick II proclaimed his *Constitutiones Augustales* (1231) which unified his kingdom as a state. The castle houses the **Museo Nazionale del Melfese**, with its collection of Byzantine jewellery.

The **Duomo**, off Via Vittorio Emanuele, was begun in 1155 by William the Bad but rebuilt in the 18th century. Only the campanile survives.

🏛 **Museo Nazionale del Melfese**
Castello di Melfi, Via Castello.
📞 *0972-23 87 26.* ⏰ *daily.*
⬤ *1 May, 25 Dec.* 🎫 🚻

Venosa ❷

Potenza. 🏛 *12,000.* FS 🚌 🛈 *Via Garibaldi 42 (open occasionally).*
🍴 *1st Sat & 3rd Thu of month.*

VENOSA WAS ONE of the most important Roman colonies around 290 BC, and remains of **baths** and an **amphitheatre** survive in the archaeological

zone along Via Vittorio Emanuele. It was also the birthplace of the Latin poet, Horace (65–8 BC), and the site where the Roman general Marcellus died at the hands of Hannibal in 208 BC. Marcellus' reputed **tomb** is in Via Melfi.

The **Duomo**, also on Via Vittorio Emanuele, and the huge **castle** in Piazza Umberto I date from the 16th century.

Occupying the site of a Roman temple is **La Trinità**, a partially ruined abbey complex formed by an older church, possibly early Christian (5th–6th century). It is backed by an unfinished 11th-century construction, in which Robert Guiscard (died 1085) was buried with his half-brothers and Alberada, his first wife. Only her tomb has survived.

Lagopesole ❸

Potenza. 📞 *0971-860 83.* FS *to Lagopesole Scalo then bus to town.*
⏰ *9am–noon, 3–7pm (Oct–Mar: 3:30–6pm) daily.* 🚻

RISING DRAMATICALLY on a hill with a village huddled at its feet, Lagopesole's **castle** is the most striking in Basilicata. Dating from 1242–50, it was the last castle Frederick II built and was used as a hunting lodge. There is interesting decoration, particularly the carved heads above the portal of the keep. One is said to be Frederick Barbarossa (the grandfather of Frederick II),

and the other is reputedly Barbarossa's wife, Beatrice. Inside, the royal apartments and chapel can be visited.

Matera ❹

🏛 *51,000.* FS 🚌 🛈 *Via de Viti de Marco 9 (0835-33 19 83).* 🍴 *Sat.*

The Sassi district of Matera

PERCHED ON THE EDGE of a deep ravine, this town consists of the bustling upper district and the silent lower **Sassi** (cave) district, divided into the Sasso Barisano and the more picturesque Sasso Caveoso. The people of Matera once lived here in dwellings scooped out of the rock. The two parts are odd neighbours, making Matera one of the most fascinating cities in southern Italy.

For the best overview, walk along the **Strada Panoramica dei Sassi** and look down into the caves. From the 8th to the

13th centuries, such caves probably provided refuge for monks from Eastern Anatolia. Many chapels, which were gouged out of the rock, were taken over in the 15th century by peasants. Subsequently, a cave-dwelling Matera evolved and by the 18th century some buildings fronting the caves had become fairly grand mansions and convents. By the 1950s and '60s the Sassi were overtaken by squalor and poverty, and the inhabitants were forcibly rehoused. Carlo Levi (1912–75) drew attention to their miserable living conditions in his book *Christ Stopped at Eboli*, comparing Sassi districts with Dante's *Inferno*. Today the warren of streets and steps amid the mostly empty Sassi are silent.

Of the 120 *chiese rupestri* (rock-cut churches) in the Sassi and the Agri district outside the town, **Santa Maria di Idris** in the Monte Errone area and **Santa Lucia alle Malve** in the Albanian quarter both contain 13th-century frescoes.

The **Museo Nazionale Ridola** provides a background to Matera and the Sassi. Many Neo-lithic trench villages, necropoli and other ancient sites have been discovered, and artefacts from them are displayed here.

The Apulian Romanesque **Duomo** (13th century) in Piazza Duomo has interesting sculpture and an anonymous 12th-century painting of the *Madonna della Bruna*, the patroness of Matera, who is celebrated on 2 July. Via Duomo leads toward **San Francesco d'Assisi** (13th century with Baroque overlay) which commemorates St Francis's visit to Matera in 1218. Other churches to visit are **San Domenico** and **San Giovanni Battista** on Via San Biagio (both 13th century), and the **Purgatorio** (1770) on Via Ridola.

🏛 **Museo Nazionale Ridola**
Via Ridola 24. 📞 0835-31 12 39.
◯ *daily.* 🚫

Church of San Francesco in Matera

Metaponto ❺

Zona Archeologica, Matera. 📞 0835-74 53 27. 🚌 🚆 *to Metaponto.*
◯ *9am–1 hr before sunset daily.*
● *1 Jan, Easter, 25 Dec.* 🚫 🚫

FOUNDED IN THE 7th century BC, ancient Metapontum was once the centre of a wealthy city-state with a philosophical tradition expounded by Pythagoras, who settled here after his expulsion from Croton. Its ruins include the **Tavole Palatine** (6th century BC) at the Bradano River bridge, and a Doric temple, probably dedicated to Hera, with 15 columns standing. The **Museo Nazionale di Metaponto** displays artefacts from the site. The ruins of a theatre and the Doric **Temple of Apollo Lycius** (6th century

BC) are in the **Archaeological Zone**. Further south, modern **Policoro** occupies the site of ancient Heraclea (founded 433 BC). Its **Museo Nazionale della Siritide** contains finds from this site and others.

🏛 **Museo Nazionale di Metaponto**
Metaponto Borgo. 📞 0835-74 53 27.
◯ *daily.* ● *public hols.* 🚫 *also valid for archaeological zone.* 🚫
🏛 **Museo Nazionale della Siritide**
Via Colombo 8, Policoro. 📞 0835-97 21 54. ◯ *daily.* ● *1 Jan, 1 May, 25 Dec.* 🚫 🚫

Maratea ❻

Potenza. 🚶 *5,000.* 🚆 🚌
🛈 *Piazza del Gesù 40 (0973-87 69 08).* 🏪 *1st & 3rd Sat of month.*

A TINY STRETCH of Basilicata meets the Tyrrhenian Sea in the Gulf of Policastro. This unblemished coast is home to Maratea. Its small port (Maratea Inferiore) is beneath the old centre (Maratea Superiore), which straddles the flank of a hill. From here the road climbs Monte Biagio to a summit with breathtaking views where a huge statue of the **Redeemer** stands.

ENVIRONS: Dramatically sited **Rivello**, 23 km (14 miles) to the north, once had a largely Greek population. Byzantine influences can be seen in the churches of **San Nicola dei Greci** and **Santa Barbara**.

The Tavole Palatine in Metaponto

The small port of Maratea Inferiore with fishing boats

A page from the precious *Codex Purpureus Rossanensis*

Rossano ❼

Cosenza. 🏛 *32,000.* FS ⛕
🛳 *2nd & 4th Fri of month.*

THIS HANDSOME hilltown was one of the main centres of Byzantine civilization in Calabria. It assumed power when Reggio di Calabria fell to the Saracens in the 9th, 10th and 11th centuries. The **Museo Diocesano** houses the *Codex Purpureus Rossanensis*, a rare 6th-century Greek Gospel with silver lettering and splendidly detailed miniatures.

The Baroque **cathedral** contains the *Madonna Acheropita* fresco, a much venerated Byzantine relic of the 8th or 9th century.

ENVIRONS: On a hilltop to the southeast of Rossano is the five-domed Greek church of **San Marco** (10th century). The 12th-century **Panaglia**, another Greek church, lies off Via Archivescovado. Both contain fragments of early frescoes.

Santa Maria del Patirion is magnificently adorned with coloured brickwork, tile and stone. It is situated on a hilltop 18 km (11 miles) to the west. It offers wonderful views over the Piana di Sibari (Plain of Sibari), the presumed location of the fabled city of Sybaris, which was destroyed in 510 BC. The church has remained virtually unaltered since it was built around 1095.

🏛 **Museo Diocesano**
Palazzo Arcivescovile. ☏ *0983-52 02 82.* ☐ *daily.* 📷

Tropea ❽

Vibo Valenzia. 🏛 *7,000.* FS ⛕
🛈 *Piazza Ercole.* 🛳 *Sat.*

ONE OF THE MOST picturesque towns on Calabria's largely built-up Tyrrhenian coast is Tropea, which offers superb views of the sea and beaches. The old town hangs on to a cliffside facing a large rock which was formerly an island. The rock is topped by **Santa Maria dell'Isola**, a former medieval Benedictine sanctuary. The **cathedral** at the end of Via Roma is of Norman origin, although it has been rebuilt several times. Inside is a 14th-century painting, the *Madonna di Romania*, by an unknown artist.

Casa Trampo (14th century) and **Palazzo Cesareo** (early 20th century) in Vicolo Manco are the most interesting of the small palaces in Tropea. The latter has a splendid balcony adorned with carvings.

Below the town are pretty beaches and a good choice of places to eat. Other seaside towns to visit are **Palmi** to the south, and **Pizzo** to the north.

Stilo ❾

Reggio di Calabria. 🏛 *3,000.* FS ⛕
🛳 *Tue.*

A SHORT DISTANCE from the coast, Stilo is a ramshackle and earthquake-damaged town clamped to the side of Monte Consolino. Standing on a ledge looking out over the arid countryside is the **Cattolica**, which has made Stilo a focus of dedicated pilgrimage for buffs of Byzantine architecture. Built in the 10th century by Basilian monks, the brick building with its terracotta-tiled roof is based on a Greek cross-in-a-square plan. Four antique, mis-matched marble columns divide the interior into nine quadrants. The capitals are placed at the base of the columns instead of on top, to indicate the triumph of Christianity over paganism. The frescoes within, discovered and restored in 1927, date from the 11th century.

The Cattolica dominates the town, but on Via Tommaso Campanella there is a medieval **Duomo** as well as the 17th-century ruins of the **Convent of San Domenico**, where the philosopher and Dominican friar Tommaso Campanella (1568–1639) lived. The church of **San Francesco**, built around 1400, has an ornate carved wooden altar and a lovely 16th-century painting of the *Madonna del Borgo* (unknown origin). The church of **San Giovanni** (11th century) in Bivongi, northwest of Stilo, although generally closed, is open during Easter week.

🛈 **Cattolica**
2 km (1 mile) above Stilo on Via Cattolica. ☐ *daily.* ♿

The beautiful and unspoilt coastline at Tropea

The distinctive five-domed Cattolica in Stilo

Gerace ⑩

Reggio di Calabria. 👥 3,000. 🚌

O CCUPYING an impregnable crag on the northeastern flank of the Aspromonte, this ancient place was founded by refugees from **Locri Epizefiri** who fled in the 9th century to escape Saracen attack. Its defensive character is reinforced by the medieval town walls and the remains of the once impregnable castle.

Apart from the slow pace of life here – where you are as likely to meet a flock of sheep in an alley as a Fiat 500 – the main attraction is Calabria's grandest **Duomo**. This massive structure indicates the significance of Gerace at least up to the time of the Normans. Constructed not later than the early 12th century, rebuilt in the 13th century and restored in the 18th century, the crypt is its chief treasure. Both crypt and church are simple, adorned by a series of antique coloured marble and granite columns probably stolen from the site of

ancient Locri Epizephyrii. At the end of Via Cavour is 12th-century **San Giovanello**, part Byzantine and part Norman. Nearby is the Gothic church of **San Francesco d'Assisi** which contains a Baroque marble altar (1615) and the Pisan-style tomb of Niccolò Ruffo (died 1372), a member of a prominent Calabrian family.

ENVIRONS: The vast site of **Locri Epizefiri**, the first Greek city to have a written code of law, was a well-known centre of the cult of Persephone. There are remains of **temples**, a **theatre** and Greek and Roman **tombs**. The **Museo** displays a ground plan of the site and a collection of votive statues, coins, inscriptions and sculptural fragments – evidence of Greek and Roman occupation of the site.

🏛 **Locri Epizefiri**
Southwest of Locri on the N106, Contrada Marasà. 📞 0964-39 00 23. ⬜ daily. **Museo** ⬜ daily. ⬛ 1, 6 Jan, 1 May, 25 Nov, 25 Dec.

Reggio di Calabria ⑪

👥 175,000. ✈ 🚆 FS 🚌 ⛴ 🛈 Corso Garibaldi 329 (0965-89 20 12). 🛒 Fri.

T HIS IS A TATTY CITY, but one reason to make a visit is to see the outstanding **Museo Nazionale della Magna Grecia**. The museum houses a fine collection of artefacts from ancient Rhegion – an important Greek city on the site of the present town – and from other Greek sites.

Chief among its treasures are the Greek bronzes, larger-than-life statues of warriors dredged from the sea off Riace Marina in 1972. Statue A (460 BC) is thought to be by Phidias, the Athenian sculptor and chief exponent of the idealizing, Classical style. If true, it is a rare survivor because his works, praised in the highest terms by ancient writers, were hitherto only known to us from Roman copies. Statue B (430 BC) has been attributed to the sculptor Polyclitus. It is possible that the statues originated from the Temple of Delphi, the Athenians' monument to the victory of Marathon.

🏛 **Museo Nazionale della Magna Grecia**
Piazza de Nava 26. 📞 0965-81 22 55. ⬜ Jun–Sep: daily except 1st & 3rd Mon of month; Oct–May: daily. ⬛ 1, 6 Jan, Easter, 15 Aug, 1 Nov, 25 Dec. 🎟

Riace Bronzes (6th and 5th century BC) in Reggio's Museo Nazionale

SICILY

O N A CROSSROADS *in the Mediterranean, part of Europe and Africa, yet belonging to neither, Sicily was tramped across by half the ancient civilized world. As conquerors came and went, they left behind a rich and varied cultural deposit. This has resulted in a quirky mixture in almost every aspect of the local vernacular from language, customs and cooking to art and, most notably, the diverse architecture of the island.*

During the 6th and 5th centuries BC, there cannot have been much difference between Athens and the Greek cities of Sicily. Their ruins are among the most spectacular of the ancient Greek world. The Romans took over in the 3rd century BC, followed by the Vandals, Ostrogoths and Byzantines. Not much that is tangible has survived from the days of the Arabs, who ruled from the 8th to 11th centuries, though Palermo's Vucciria is more souk than market. The Norman era, beginning in 1060, spawned brilliant artistic achievements, such as the cathedrals of Monreale and Cefalù, while the eclecticism of that period's architecture is best seen at Santi Pietro e Paolo outside Taormina.

The Sicilian Baroque of the 17th and 18th centuries is just as individual. The palaces and churches of Palermo, reflecting the elaborate ritual of the Spanish Viceregal court, tend towards extravagant display. At Noto, Ragusa, Modica, Siracusa and Catania the buildings are a useful vehicle for the Sicilians' love of ornamentation, itself a remnant from the island's early fling with the Arab world. The style is an expression of the nature of Sicilians, whose sense of pomp and pageantry is both magnificent and extreme.

Sicily is a curiosity, and the legacy of the past is redolent everywhere. The fact that it is an island has intensified the cultural impact of each successive occupier. They say that today there's less Italian blood in Sicilian veins than there is Phoenician, Greek, Arabic, Norman, Spanish or French. The resulting mixture – exotic, spicy and highly inflammable – has created a separate nation at the foot of Italy.

Detail of a 12th-century mosaic from the Palazzo dei Normanni in Palermo

◁ **The beautifully preserved Temple of Concord (c.430 BC) in the Valley of the Temples at Agrigento**

Exploring Sicily

The vast coastline of Sicily (Sicilia) provides many magnificent beaches, particularly at Taormina and the Golfo di Castellammare by Capo San Vito – part of a huge nature reserve. Sicily's varied interior is characterized by remote hilltowns and plains punctuated by mountain ranges known for spring flowers and wildlife. Among the most spectacular sights is Mount Etna, an active volcano whose lava flows over the centuries have left the land immensely fertile, supporting an abundance of walnut trees, citrus groves and vineyards.

Fishermen at work in their boats at Siracusa

The magnificent temple at Segesta

Sights at a Glance

0 kilometres   50

0 miles   25

Key

━━━ Motorway

━━━ Major road

━━━ Minor road

━━━ Scenic route

≈ River

✻ Viewpoint

SEE ALSO

• *Where to Stay* pp573–5

• *Where to Eat* pp607–8

ISOLE EOLIE
(LIPARI)

The Norman Duomo in Palermo

RENO

MESSINA
14

TINDARI
13

STRETTA DI
MESSINA

TROINA

NICOSIA

N120

15 TAORMINA

16
MOUNT ETNA

MAR IONIO

12 ENNA

PIAZZA ARMERINA
11

17
CATANIA

GOLFO DI
CATANIA

CALTAGIRONE

PANTALICA

18

GOLFO DI
AUGUSTA

SIRACUSA
19

GELA

LFO DI GELA

VITTORIA

PALAZZOLO
ACREIDE

COMISO

RAGUSA

20 NOTO

GOLFO DI
NOTO

GETTING
AROUND

The A19 connects
Palermo and Catania, the A18
links Catania and Messina and the
A20 (Palermo to Messina) is under construction. The west is accessible from Palermo
on the A29. Ferry routes run from Messina
to Reggio di Calabria, and from Palermo
to Genoa or Naples. Between the larger
towns, train services are efficient, but for
smaller towns the buses are better. Catania
and Palermo have international airports.

The scenic town of Cefalù, dominated by a huge rock

Palermo ①

Mosaic detail from Cappella Palatina

Nestling on the protective flank of Monte Pellegrino with Monte Alfano to the east, Palermo lies in a natural amphitheatre called the Conca d'Oro (Golden Shell). Against La Cala harbour, the setting is beautiful and the city, a mix of oriental and European, is without equal despite reduced circumstances. The architecture, ranging in style from Arabic to Norman, Baroque and Art Nouveau, is without comparison in Sicily, making this exotic city an exciting place to explore.

⛪ Gesù
Piazza Casa Professa. ⬜ *daily.*
In the poor, bomb-devastated Albergheria quarter, near the colourful market of Piazza Ballarò, lies this important Baroque church (1564–1633). Also known as the church of the Casa Professa, the interior is an excellent example of the virtuosity of Sicilian craftsmen in the treatment of marble carving and inlay. The oldest Jesuit church in Sicily, it was heavily restored after suffering extensive bomb damage in World War II.

Ruined cloister with the red domes of San Giovanni degli Eremiti behind

⛪ San Giovanni degli Eremiti
Via dei Benedettini. 🕾 091-651 50 19. ⬜ *daily.* 🈂
Reflecting Islamic architectural tradition with bulbous domes, corner arches and filigreed windows, this deconsecrated Norman church (1132–48) was built in the grounds of a mosque. Beyond church and mosque, a ruined cloister from a 13th-century monastery encloses a pretty garden.

⛪ Palazzo Reale
Piazza Indipendenza. 🕾 091-656 11 11. **Palazzo Reale** ⬜ *by appt only.* Contact Questura. 🕾 091-656 17 32 for permission. **Cappella Palatina** ⬜ *daily.* 🔴 *Easter, 25 Apr, 1 May, 25 Dec.* 🈂 🈳
Also called the Palazzo dei Normanni, this site has been the focus of power since the days of Byzantine rule and is now home to Sicily's regional government. The nucleus of the present building was constructed by the Arabs, but after the Norman conquest of the city (1072), it was enlarged and embellished for the Norman court. See the luxurious royal apartments, especially the Sala di Ruggero, and the splendid Cappella Palatina. Built by Roger II (1132–40), this dazzling chapel blends Byzantine, Islamic and Norman styles of craftsmanship. It is lavishly adorned with mosaics, as well as marble inlaid with gold, stone and glass. Next to the palace is the eccentrically decorated Porta Nuova (1535).

Sumptuous interior of the Cappella Palatina, Palazzo Reale

Duomo's exterior displaying a mixture of styles

VISITORS' CHECKLIST

🏠 730,000. ✈ Punta Raisi 32 km (20 miles) W. FS Stazione Centrale, Piazza Giulio Cesare. 🚌 Via Balsamo. 🚢 Stazione Marittima, Molo Vittorio Veneto. 🛈 Piazza Castelnuovo 34 (091-58 38 47). 🛒 daily. 🎉 U Festinu for the city's patron saint, Santa Rosalia: 10–15 Jul; Pilgrimage to grotto of Santa Rosalia: 4 Sep; Greek Orthodox celebrations in Martorana church: Easter.

⛪ Duomo

Via Vittorio Emanuele. ☎ 091-33 43 76. ⬜ daily. ♿ 🚫 for Treasury.

Founded in 1184 by the Arch-bishop of Palermo, the Duomo displays many architectural styles. The exterior shows the development of the Gothic style from the 13th–14th centuries.

porch are the remains of Emperor Frederick II; his wife, Constance of Aragon; his mother, Constance, daughter of Roger II (also entombed here); and his father, Henry VI. The Treasury houses the 12th-century Imperial Diadem of Constance of Aragon, which was removed from her tomb in the 18th century.

Fontana Pretorio with Santa Caterina in the background

The south porch (1453) is a masterpiece of the Catalan style, and at the apse end, sturdy Norman work can be seen through a decorative Islamic-inspired overlay. The dome is 18th century.

Within the much-altered interior are the tombs of Sicily's kings. Squeezed into an enclosure by the south

⛪ Santa Caterina

Piazza Bellini. ⬤ for restoration.

Although begun in 1566, most of the internal decoration of this unique church dates from the 17th and 18th centuries. A powerful example of the Palermitan Baroque, it over-whelms with colours, textures, sculpture and marble inlay. There are illusionistic ceiling frescoes (18th century) by Filippo Randazzo in the nave and Vito d'Anna in the dome.

The church is flanked by Piazza Pretorio, which is dominated by the monumental Mannerist Fontana Pretorio, erected here in 1544.

SIGHTS AT A GLANCE

Duomo ④
Gesù ③
La Magione ⑭
La Martorana ⑥
Museo Archeologico Regionale ⑩
Palazzo Abatellis and Galleria Regionale di Sicilia ⑬
Palazzo Reale ②
Oratorio del Rosario di San Domenico ⑧
Oratorio di San Lorenzo ⑫
Oratorio di Santa Zita ⑪
San Domenico ⑨
San Giovanni degli Eremiti ①
Santa Caterina ⑤
Villa Giulia ⑮
Vucciria ⑦

KEY

P Parking

⛪ Church

0 metres   250

0 yards   250

Exploring Palermo

EAST OF THE Quattro Canti, where Via Maqueda and Corso Vittorio Emanuele meet, the city is sprinkled with ornate palaces and more churches. Squeezed behind them are labyrinthine medieval quarters where ancient buildings with crumbling fabric still survive.

La Martorana
Piazza Bellini. ⚐ 091-616 16 92.
⚐ daily.
Also called Santa Maria dell'
Ammiraglio, this church was
built around 1140 by George
of Antioch, Roger II's admiral
and also an orthodox Greek
Christian. The design derives
from Norman and Islamic traditions with mosaics possibly
by Greek artisans. In the right
aisle, King Roger receives the
Imperial Diadem from Christ;
in the left aisle, George of
Antioch is portrayed.

A nearby convent, founded
by Eloisa Martorana in 1193,
was the site where the Sicilian
Parliament met in 1295 and
decided, in the wake of the
Sicilian Vespers, to hand the
crown of Sicily to Frederick of
Aragon. The church was presented to the convent in 1433.

**Mosaic of Christ with Four Angels
in the dome of La Martorana**

Vucciria
Via Roma. ⚐ daily.
Nowhere is Palermo's Arabic
past more apparent than in
this medieval casbah-style
market which burrows through
the ruinous Loggia district
below Via Roma. Merchants,
hawkers, shoppers and pickpockets crowd an area once
the haunt of artisans. The
alleys all around are named
after their professions, such
as silversmiths, dyers and
keymakers. This busy market,
the largest in Palermo, offers
the usual market ware from
daily objects to junk, as well
as a wide selection of fresh
fruit, vegetables and fish.

**Stuccoed interior of the Oratorio
del Rosario di San Domenico**

Oratorio del Rosario di
San Domenico
Via Bambinai 2. ⚐ for restoration.
The interior of this tiny chapel,
which was built in the 16th
century, displays elegant
Baroque decoration by the
master of stucco, Giacomo
Serpotta. Created around
1720–30, this was his latest
and possibly his finest work.
Serpotta's technical virtuosity,
not to mention the sensory
indulgence and whimsical
fantasy in evidence here, are
remarkable. The altarpiece is
the famous *Madonna of the*
Rosary (1624–8) by Anthony
Van Dyck, and there are wall
paintings by Luca Giordano
and Pietro Novelli.

San Domenico
Piazza San Domenico. ⚐ 091-58
48 72. ⚐ daily. **Museo del**
Risorgimento ⚐ 091-58 27 74.
⚐ Mon, Wed, Fri am. ● Jul & Aug.
Although the present building
was begun in 1640, there has
been a Dominican church on
the site since the 14th century.
The architect responsible for
the exuberant church façade
(1726) and square in front
(1724) was Tommaso Maria
Napoli, one of the masters
of Sicilian Baroque.

Within, the most interesting
feature is Antonello Gagini's
bas-relief of *Santa Caterina*
(1528) in the third chapel on
the left. Next to the church is
the 14th-century cloister, part
of the original monastery
which gives access to the
Museo del Risorgimento.

Museo Archeologico
Regionale
Via Bara all'Olivella 24.
⚐ 091-662 02 20. ⚐ daily.
Housed in a former monastery
of the Filippini, Sicily's most
important museum contains
sculpture, architectural fragments and artefacts, including
ceramics, glassware, bronzes,
jewellery, terracottas and
weapons. The collection is
taken from the island's great
Phoenician, Greek and Roman
sites of antiquity – Tindari,
Termini Imerese, Agrigento,
Siracusa, Selinunte and Mozia.
The highlights are sculptures
from the friezes of the ancient
Greek temples at Selinunte.

Palermo's noisy, bustling Vucciria market east of Via Roma

Oratorio di Santa Zita

Via Valverde 3. 091-32 27 79.
daily.
This small chapel is dedicated
to the Virgin of the Rosary
after her miraculous interven-
tion at the Battle of Lepanto
(see pp54–5). The stucco
relief decoration, again, is the
work of Giacomo Serpotta
(after 1688): the panel on the
rear wall depicts the battle,
and other reliefs show scenes
from the New Testament, all
portrayed with extravagant
realism. The neighbouring
16th-century church of Santa
Zita, from which the oratory
takes its name, is filled with
sculptures by Antonello
Gagini (1517–27).

Ornate interior of the Oratorio di Santa Zita

Oratorio di San Lorenzo

Via Immacolatella 5. for restoration.
Lining the walls of this tiny
oratory are incredible stucco
scenes from the lives of St
Francis and St Lawrence, and
allegorical figures and putti by
Giacomo Serpotta (1699–1706).
These remarkable, expressive
works exhibit the virtuosity of
their creator in the handling
of his medium. Caravaggio's
*Nativity with St Francis and
St Lawrence* (1609) graced the
space above the altar until it
was stolen in 1969. The oratory
lies hidden next to the church
of San Francesco d'Assisi (13th
century), which is brimming
with excellent sculpture. The
undoubted highlight of the
church is the triumphal arch
(1468) by Francesco Laurana
and Pietro da Bonitate in the
Cappella Mastrantonio.

The Palazzina Cinese (c.1799) set in the Parco della Favorita

Palazzo Abatellis and Galleria Regionale di Sicilia

Via Alloro 4. 091-616 43 17.
daily am (Tue & Fri pm
also).
Matteo Carnelivari built
this palace combining
elements of Spanish
late-Gothic and Italian
Renaissance styles in the
15th century. It is home
to the Galleria Regionale
di Sicilia, which houses
Antonello da Messina's
Annunciation (1473),
Francesco Laurana's
marble head of Eleanor
of Aragon (15th century),
and sculptures by the
Gagini. Nearby, the 15th-
century church of Santa
Maria degli Angeli (or La
Gancia) contains works
by Antonello Gagini
and Giacomo Serpotta.

Annunciation (1473) by da Messina
in the Galleria Regionale di Sicilia

La Magione

Via Magione. 091-617 05 96.
daily.
Badly damaged in World
War II, later restorations have
revealed the ancient structure
of this church. It was founded
in 1150 by Matteo d'Aiello,
Roger II's chancellor. With its
simple, tall nave flanked by
fine Gothic columns, La
Magione is a major feature of
any tour of Norman Sicily.

Villa Giulia

Via Abramo Lincoln. daily. Orto
Botanico 091-616 24 72. daily
(Sat & Sun am only). public hols.
The formal gardens of the villa
were established in the 18th
century. Once, with their
statues and fountains, they
were an exotic evocation of
the antique world; the writer
Goethe thought they were
"wonderful". Nowadays, both
the tropical flora and sense of
faded grandeur make them a
delightful setting for walks.
In the adjacent Orto Botanico
(botanical gardens) there are
magnificent tropical plants. In
Léon Dufourny's Neo-Classical
Gymnasium (1789), plant
specimens can be examined.

Parco della Favorita

Entrance on Piazza Leoni & Piazza
Generale Cascino. daily. Museo
Etnografico Siciliano Pitré, Via Duca
degli Abruzzi. 091-671 10 60.
Sat–Thu am. public hols.
This park, laid out as a hunting
ground in 1799 by Bourbon
King Ferdinand IV, was surrounded by summer villas of
the aristocracy. One of these,
the Palazzina Cinese (c.1799),
was built in a Chinese style for
the King's wife, Maria Carolina,
the sister of Marie Antoinette.
  The Museo Etnografico
Siciliano Pitré, in the stables
of the Palazzina Cinese, has
an outstanding collection of
objects from Sicilian life.

Monreale ❷

Capital from cloister column

Magnificently adorned, and with a splendid view of the Conca d'Oro, the cathedral at Monreale is one of the great sights of Norman Sicily. Founded in 1172 by the Norman King William II, it was given to a monastery of the Benedictine Order. The interior of the cathedral glitters with mosaics carried out by Sicilian and Byzantine artists – the inspiration of a king who wanted to rival the power of the Archbishop of Palermo. Like Cefalù, and later Palermo, it was to serve as a royal sepulchre.

★ **Christ Pantocrator**
The cathedral's Latin-cross plan focuses on the imposing mosaic of the all-powerful Christ (12th–13th century).

Nave and aisles separated by Roman columns

Magnificent gilded wood ceiling

Apse Exterior
With their rich multi-coloured ornamentation in tufa and marble, the three apses represent the apogee of Norman decoration.

Entrance to Cappella del Crocifisso and Treasury

Original Cosmati floor in choir

The royal tomb of William II, in white marble, flanks the porphyry tomb of William I in the corner of the transept.

Barisano da Trani's bronze door (1179) on the north side is shielded by a portico designed by Gian Domenico and Fazio Gagini (1547–69).

★ **Mosaic Cycle**
Completed in 1182, the rich mosaics show scenes from the Old Testament (nave), Teachings of Christ (aisles, choir and transepts), and the Gospels (side apses). The story of Noah's Ark is depicted here.

★ **Cloisters**
A masterpiece of Norman artistic expression from the time of William II, the columns – plain, carved or inlaid with richly lustred tiles – support elaborate capitals from which spring Saracenic-style arches.

VISITORS' CHECKLIST

Piazza Vittorio Emanuele. 🚌 809, 8/9 & many others going W. **Church** ☎ 091-640 24 24. ◯ 8:30am–noon, 3:30–6:30pm daily. ✝ 📷 📹 **Cloister** ☎ 091-640 44 03. ◯ Apr–Sep: 9am–7pm Mon–Fri, 9am–12:30pm Sat & Sun; Oct–Mar: 9am–1pm Mon–Fri (also: 3–5pm Mon & Thu), 9am–12:30pm Sat & Sun. 📷 📹

The south wall and cloisters survive as elements from the Benedictine monastery.

Small Oriental-inspired fountain

Column Detail
Craftsmen from Campania, Puglia, Lombardy and Sicily worked on the cloister columns. The detail here shows Adam and Eve.

The 18th-century porch is flanked by two squat towers.

Bronze Door Panel
Bonanno da Pisa's fine bronze door (1185), signed by him, depicts 42 scenes from the Bible set within elaborate borders. The lion and griffin are symbols of the Norman kingdom.

STAR FEATURES

★ **Cloisters**

★ **Mosaic Cycle**

★ **Christ Pantocrator**

Bagheria ❸

Palermo. 🏠 *40,000.* FS 🚌
🛈 *Comune di Bagheria, Via
Mattarella (091-94 34 82).* 🛥 *Wed.*

Today Bagheria is almost a
suburb of Palermo, though
open countryside with olive
and orange groves once
separated them. In the 17th
century Giuseppe Branciforte,
Prince of Butera, built a
summer retreat there, starting
a fashion that was quickly
followed by other Palermitan
aristocrats. The town's core is
sprinkled with their Baroque
and Neo-Classical villas.

The **Villa Palagonia** was
designed in 1705 by the
architect Tommaso Maria
Napoli for Ferdinando
Gravina, the Prince
of Palagonia. It has
remarkable architectural
qualities: a complex
open-air staircase leads
to the first floor, and
the principal rooms,
all with unusual shapes,
are arranged around a
curved axis. A later prince
adorned the perimeter wall
with the grotesque stone
monsters which amused the
18th-century traveller Patrick

**Stone figure on
Villa Palagonia**

Brydone, and horrified Goethe,
who also travelled here and
called this the "Palagonian
madhouse". Across
the piazza are **Villa
Valguarnera** (begun
in 1713 by Napoli), set
in its own park, and
Villa Trabia (mid-18th
century), but neither is
open to the public.
Villa Cattolica (18th
century) houses a
modern art gallery.

🏛 **Villa Palagonia**
Piazza Garibaldi. 📞 *0336-89 95 51.*
🕐 *daily.*
🏛 **Villa Cattolica**
Via Consolare. 📞 *091-94 33 52.*
🕐 *Tue–Sun.*

Open-air staircase of the eccentric Villa Palagonia in Bagheria

Fishing and pleasure boats moored in the harbour of Trapani

Trapani ❹

🏠 *73,000.* FS 🚌 ⛴ ✈ 🛈 *Piazza
Saturno (0923-290 00).* 🛥 *Thu.*

Old Trapani occupies a
narrow peninsula. The
best buildings in this gutsy,
lively quarter are the churches,
in particular the **Cathedral
of San Lorenzo** (1635) and
the **Chiesa del Collegio dei
Gesuiti** (c.1614–40). The
façades of both, and that of
the **Municipio** (17th century)
on Corso Vittorio Emanuele,
display magnificently the
curious ebullience of west
Sicilian Baroque architecture.

The 17th-century **Purgatorio**
on Via San Francesco d'Assisi
contains 18th-century *Misteri* –
realistic, life-sized wooden
statues used annually in the
Good Friday procession. **Santa
Maria del Gesù** on Via Sant'
Agostino should be visited for
the *Madonna degli Angeli* by
Andrea della Robbia (1435–
1525) and Antonello Gagini's
canopy (1521). In the Jewish
quarter, west of Via XXX
Gennaio, the **Palazzo della
Giudecca** (16th century) has a
strangely textured façade.

The **Museo Nazionale
Pepoli** has a comprehensive
collection of local antiquities.
Of greatest interest are the
coral objects and the Christmas
crib figures *(presepi)*, modern
versions of which are made
here. Next to the museum, the
Santuario dell'Annunziata
contains the *Madonna di
Trapani*, a statue revered by
fishermen and sailors for its
legendary miraculous powers.

🏛 **Museo Nazionale Pepoli**
Via Conte Agostino Pepoli.
📞 *0923-55 32 69.* 🕐 *Tue–Sun.*

Erice ❺

Trapani. 👥 *29,000.* 🚌 ℹ️ *Viale Conte Pepoli 11 (0923-86 93 88).* 🗓️ *Mon.*

Poised on a crag overlooking Trapani, Erice was once the seat of the cult of the fertility goddess Venus Erycina. Her temple stood on the present site of the Norman **castle**, beyond the **Villa Balio** public gardens. The ancient town of Eryx was renamed Gebel-Hamed by the Arabs and then it became Monte San Giuliano under the Normans. It was not until 1934 that Mussolini adopted the present name.

Erice is medieval throughout. The **Duomo** (14th century) has a 15th-century porch and an earlier battlemented campanile used as a watchtower by the Aragonese. Inside is a lovely *Madonna and Child* (c.1469), attributed to either Francesco Laurana or Domenico Gagini. Deconsecrated 13th-century **San Giovanni Battista** on Viale Nunzio Nasi is home to Antonello Gagini's *St John the Evangelist* (1531) and Antonino Gagini's *St John the Baptist* (1539). **San Cataldo**, a plain 14th-century building on Via San Cataldo, contains a holy water stoup from the workshop of Domenico Gagini (c.1474). The **Biblioteca-Museo Comunale Cordici** houses Antonello Gagini's *Annunciation* (1525) and a variety of Classical remains.

🏛️ Biblioteca-Museo Comunale Cordici
Piazza Umberto I. 📞 *0923-86 92 58.* ⬜ *Mon–Sat am.* ⬛ *public hols.*

A typical medieval street in the small hilltown of Erice

SICILIAN ISLANDS

Surrounding Sicily are several island groups. The Isole Eolie or Lipari (Aeolian Islands), to which Panaria, Lipari, Vulcano and Stromboli belong, are a mass of extinct, or nearly extinct, volcanoes poking out of the sea off the coast of Milazzo. The Isole Egadi (Egadi Islands), off the coast of Trapani, have a distinctly Arabic flavour. They include Favignana, Levanzo (which has Palaeolithic and Neolithic paintings and drawings), and Marettimo – the smallest and most unspoilt. Ustica, renowned for its marine life and popular among divers, lies north of Palermo. To the south are the remarkably tourist-free Isole Pelagie (Pelagic Islands) – Lampedusa and Linosa, which are North African in character. Remote Pantelleria lies closer to Tunisia than to Sicily.

Part of the Isole Pelagie, *Lampedusa was once owned by the family of Giuseppe Tomasi di Lampedusa, author of* The Leopard, *Sicily's most famous novel. The island has clean water and great beaches.*

Favignana, *the largest and most populous of the Isole Egadi, is the scene of the traditional tuna slaughter – la mattanza. This takes place, as it has for centuries, in May. These fishermen are bringing in the nets following the slaughter.*

The biggest and most popular *of the Isole Eolie is Lipari, which offers a pretty port and a good range of hotels, bars and restaurants. Nearby Vulcano, smelling of sulphur, provides hot mud-baths and fine black beaches.*

USTICA

ISOLE EOLIE (LIPARI)

ISOLE EGADI

Palermo

SICILY

PANTELLERIA

ISOLE PELAGIE

0 kilometres 100
0 miles 50

Marsala

Trapani. 🏛 *80,000.* FS 🚌 ⛴ 🛈 *Via Garibaldi 45 (0923-71 40 97).* 🚉 *Tue.*

THE PORT OF MARSALA is the home of a thick, strong wine which has been in production here since the 18th century. In 1798 Admiral Nelson ordered vast quantities of it following the Battle of the Nile. Its early manufacture was presided over by three British families living in Sicily. One of the old warehouses where the wine was produced is now the **Museo Archeologico di Baglio Anselmi**, housing important Phoenician artefacts.

Among other important attractions are the ruins of **Lilybaeum**, an outpost of the Phoenician Empire, founded in 396 BC. It was peopled by the survivors of the massacre by Dionysius I of Siracusa at Mozia (ancient Motya) – the island used by the Phoenicians as a commercial centre. Best of all are the unique reconstructed remains of a Punic ship thought to have been active in the First Punic War (263–241 BC). The **Museo di Mozia** in the Whitaker villa contains a remarkable early 5th-century BC statue of a Greek youth.

The excavations here are important; what we know of the Phoenicians today comes mostly from the Bible, and from Mozia. The **Duomo**, begun in the 17th century, was built on the site of an earlier church; both were dedicated to Marsala's patron saint, Thomas Becket of Canterbury. Its interior is full of sculptural works by members of the Gagini family – Antonio, Domenico, Antonino and Antonello. The small **Museo degli Arazzi**, behind the Duomo, contains several magnificent 16th-century Brussels tapestries, woven from fine wool and silk.

🏛 **Museo Archeologico di Baglio Anselmi**
Via Lungomare. 📞 *0923-95 25 35.* ◯ *daily.* &

🏛 **Museo degli Arazzi**
Via Garappa. 📞 *0923-71 29 03.* ◯ *Tue–Sun.* ♿

🏛 **Museo di Mozia**
Isola di Mozia. 📞 *0923-71 25 98.* ◯ *daily am.* ♿ & 📷

Statue of a Greek youth in Museo di Mozia

Segesta

Trapani. 🚌 *from Trapani & Palermo.* ◯ *9am–1 hr before sunset.*

ACCORDING TO LEGEND, the ancient town of Segesta – still largely unexcavated – was founded by Trojan followers of Aeneas. It presents one of the most spectacular sights on the island: a massive unfinished **temple** stranded on a remote hillside. Its construction was started between 426 and 416 BC, and it was left incomplete following the devastation of Selinunte by the Carthaginians in 409 BC. Archaeologists regard the temple as a good example of "work in progress". Nearby, close to the summit of Monte Barbaro, the ruins of an ancient theatre (3rd century BC) can be visited. Summer concerts are now held here.

Selinunte

Trapani. 📞 *0924-462 77.* FS *Castelvetrano then bus.* ◯ *9am–1 hr before sunset. Ticket office closes at 7pm.* ♿

FOUNDED IN 651 BC, Selinunte became one of the great cities of Magna Graecia – the part of southern Italy that was colonized by ancient Greece – and its toppled ruins are among Sicily's most important historic sites. Its ancient name, Selinus, derives from the wild celery that still grows here. The city was an important port, and its wall defences can still be seen around the Acropolis. The Carthaginians, under Hannibal, completely destroyed the city in 409 BC in a battle famous for its epic and spectacularly savage proportions.

While the city itself has virtually disappeared, eight of its temples are distinguishable, particularly the so-called **Eastern Temples** (E, F and G). Of these, the columns of huge Doric **Temple E** (490–480 BC) have been partially re-erected. **Temple F** (c.560–540 BC) is in ruins. **Temple G** (late 6th century BC), which had 17 massive side columns, was one of the greatest Greek temples ever built.

Higher on the Acropolis lie the remains of **Temples A, B, C, D** and **O**. Metope sculpture from **Temple C** (early 6th century), originally located on the frieze between the triglyphs, can be seen in the Museo Archeologico Regionale in Palermo *(see p512)*, along with ceramics, jewellery and other artefacts excavated here. A small **museum** on site houses less important finds, as does one in Castelvetrano, 14 km (8.5 miles) north of Selinunte. The ancient city is still being excavated; its **North Gate** entrance is well preserved and further north there is also a **necropolis**.

The spectacularly situated, unfinished Doric temple at Segesta

Cefalù ❾

Palermo. 🏛 *14,000.* **FS** 🚌 **ℹ** *Corso Ruggero 77 (0921-210 50).* 🛒 *Sat.*

THIS PRETTY, unspoilt seaside town with good beaches and numerous hotels and restaurants, is dominated by a huge rock – once the site of a Temple of Diana – and by one of the finest Norman cathedrals in Sicily. Begun in 1131 by Roger II, the **Duomo** was intended as the principal religious seat in Sicily. Though it failed to fulfil this function, the building's magnificence has never been eclipsed. Its splendid mosaics (1148), which feature a huge image of Christ Pantocrator in the apse, are remarkable and often celebrated as purely Byzantine works of art on Sicilian soil.

The **Museo Mandralisca** houses a fine *Portrait of a Man* (c.1465) by Antonello da Messina and an interesting collection of artefacts that includes coins, ceramics, vases, minerals and shells.

🏛 **Museo Mandralisca**
Via Mandralisca. **☎** *0921-215 47.* ⚪ *daily; Sun & public hols am only.* 📷

The lavish apse of Cefalù's Duomo

Agrigento ❿

🏛 *57,000.* **FS** 🚌 🚢 **ℹ** *Via Empedocle 73 (0922-203 91).* 🛒 *Fri.*

MODERN AGRIGENTO occupies the site of Akragas, an important city of the ancient Greek world. Founded by Daedalus, according to legend, it was famed for the luxurious lifestyle of its inhabitants, and was a great power and rival to

The twin-towered façade of the Norman Duomo in Cefalù

Siracusa. In 406 BC it fell to the Carthaginians, who sacked and burned it following the flight of its citizens and soldiers.

The historic core of the city, with its narrow medieval streets, focuses on the Via Atenea. **Santo Spirito** (13th century) houses stuccoes by Giacomo Serpotta (1695). **Santa Maria dei Greci** was built on the remains of a 5th-century BC temple – see the flattened columns in the nave. The **Duomo**, founded in the 14th century and altered in the 16th and 17th centuries, exhibits a unique mixture of Arab, Norman and Catalan detailing.

ENVIRONS: The chief reason to visit Agrigento nowadays is to see the archaeological zone known as the Valley of the Temples *(see p520).* The **Museo Regionale Archeologico** houses an interesting display of artefacts from the temples and the city, including an outstanding collection of vases, coins and Greek and Roman sculpture.

🏛 **Museo Regionale Archeologico**
Contrada San Nicola, Viale Panoramica. **☎** *0922-290 08.* ⚪ *daily am.* ♿

THE MAFIA

An international organization founded in Sicily, the Mafia (meaning hostility to law) developed against a background of a cruel State, exploitative nobility and severe poverty. By the late 19th century it had become a criminal organization thriving on property speculation and drug trafficking. Since the "singing" of Tommaso Buscetta and the capture of Toto Riina, the Mafia has been on the defensive against a State that has doubled its efforts against it. Although violence is common, it is not aimed at tourists. Indeed, Sicilians on the whole are known for their hospitality.

Mafia assassination depicted in this scene from the film *The Godfather Part III* (1990)

Valley of the Temples

STRADDLING A LOW RIDGE to the south of Agrigento, the Valley of the Temples (Valle dei Templi) ranks among the most impressive complexes of ancient Greek buildings outside Greece. Its Doric temples, dating from the 5th century BC, were destroyed in part by Carthaginian attack in 406 BC. In the 6th century pious Christians, believing the temples to be pagan, wreaked further havoc on them, as did subsequent earthquakes. The extraordinary ruins in this archaeological zone can be covered in a day, though crowd-free early morning and evening visits are recommended.

Temple of Hephaistos ①
Apart from a couple of incomplete columns still standing, very little remains of this temple, built c.430 BC. It is also called the Temple of Vulcan.

Sanctuary of the Chthonic Divinities ②
At this group of shrines, the forces of nature were worshipped.

Telamone from the Temple of Olympian Zeus

San Biagio

Rock Sanctuary of Demeter →

(see p519)
Museo Regionale Archeologico •
San Nicola

Via dei Templi

• Hellenistic and Roman Quarter

Strada Panoramica

Temple of Herakles ⑥
This is the oldest temple in the valley (late 6th century BC).

Via dei Templi

• Catacombs

P

Via Sacra

Temple of Asklepios

N115

Temple of Olympian Zeus ④
Begun c.480 BC, this was the biggest Doric temple ever built. Unfinished at the time of the Carthaginian attack, it is now a toppled ruin. Giant figures known as telamones were used in its construction.

Temple of Juno ⑧
Built around 450 BC, this temple still has many intact columns.

Tomb of Theron ⑤
Here are the ruins of a Roman tomb (1st century AD).

Temple of Castor and Pollux ③
This is an incorrect assemblage of pieces from other buildings, erected in the 19th century. Modern Agrigento (see p519) is in the background.

KEY

`– –` Suggested route

P Parking

`—` Ancient walls

| 0 metres | 500 |
| 0 yards | 500 |

Temple of Concord ⑦
This beautifully preserved temple (c.430 BC) was converted into a Christian church in the 6th century and thus saved from destruction.

Piazza Armerina ⓫

Enna. 🚶 22,000. 🚌 ℹ️ *Via Cavour 15 (0935-68 02 01).* 🛒 *Thu.*

THIS ACTIVE, ebullient provincial town is half medieval and half Baroque. The 17th-century **Duomo**, at its highest point, is the most interesting of the Baroque buildings.

In August, the lively *Palio dei Normanni* festival attracts many visitors, but the main reason to visit Piazza Armerina is to see the early 4th-century mosaics in the **Villa Romana del Casale**, 5 km (3 miles) southwest of the town.

It is thought that this huge, once sumptuous villa with its public halls, private quarters, baths and courtyards, belonged to Maximianus Herculeus, Diocletian's co-emperor, from AD 286 to 305. His son and successor, Maxentius, probably continued its decoration, with Constantine taking over on Maxentius's death in 312.

Although little remains of the building fabric, the floors are decorated with some of the finest surviving mosaics from Roman antiquity. The hunting, mythological, and domestic scenes, and exotic landscapes, all exhibit astonishingly realistic attention to detail.

🏛 **Villa Romana del Casale**
Contrada Paratore. 📞 *0935-68 00 36.* 🕐 *daily.* 💷

Roman mosaic depicting athletic girls from the Villa Romana del Casale

Enna ⓬

🚶 28,000. 🚈 🚌 ℹ️ *Piazza Colaianni 6 (0935-261 19).* 🛒 *Tue.*

IMPREGNABLE on a crag above a fertile landscape where Persephone, mythological daughter of Demeter, once played, Sicily's highest town has been coveted by successive invaders since its earliest days. The venerated seat of the Cult of Demeter (Patroness of Fertility) was at Enna. Her temple stood on the **Rocca Cerere**, not far from the huge **Castello di Lombardia** (13th century) built by Frederick II.

Most of Enna's sights are clustered at the core of the old town among the warren of ancient streets that open out of the Via Roma. The church of **San Francesco** has a 16th-century tower. **Piazza Crispi**, with its fine views to nearby Calascibetta, is dominated by a copy of Bernini's *Rape of Persephone*. The 14th-century **Duomo**, altered and adorned in later centuries, contains parts of Demeter's temple.

The **Museo Alessi** houses the Cathedral Treasury and an interesting coin collection. The **Museo Varisano** has exhibits on the area's history, from Neolithic to Roman. Away from the centre, the octagonal **Torre di Federico II** (13th century) is a former watchtower.

ENVIRONS: The ancient hill-town of **Nicosia**, northeast of Enna, was damaged in the 1967 earthquake, but still contains a smattering of churches. San Nicola, built in the 14th century and subsequently haphazardly readorned, has a magnificent, carved entrance portal. Inside there is a much venerated wooden crucifix (17th century) by Fra Umile di Petralia. Santa Maria Maggiore houses a 16th-century marble polyptych by Antonello Gagini and a throne reputedly used by Charles V in 1535. Further east is **Troina**. It was captured in 1062 by the Normans, whose work survives in the Chiesa Matrice. Southeast of Enna, **Vizzini** commands fine views of the countryside.

🏛 **Museo Alessi**
Via Roma. 📞 *0935-240 72.* 🕐 *Tue–Sun.* 💷
🏛 **Museo Varisano**
Piazza Mazzini. 📞 *0935-50 03 31.* 🕐 *Tue–Sun.*

A view from the hills overlooking Vizzini, southeast of Enna

Taormina's magnificently situated Greek theatre, with Mount Etna in the distance

Tindari ⓭

Messina. ⎮ 0941-36 90 23.
🚆 Patti or Oliveri then bus.
🕓 9am–1 hr before sunset daily. ♿

POISED ON THE EDGE of a cliff overlooking the Golfo di Patti are the ruins of **Tyndaris**, almost the last Greek city to have been founded in Sicily (395 BC) and strategically important to this coast. Apart from the city walls, the ruins are mostly Roman, including the huge **basilica**, **theatre** and houses. An **antiquarium** houses artefacts from the site.

Tindari is better known for its shrine to a Byzantine icon, the **Black Madonna** on Piazzale Belvedere.

Messina ⓮

🏙 275,000. 🚆 🚌 ⛴ 🚢 🛈 Piazza
Cairoli 45 (090-293 52 92). 🛒 daily.

NO SICILIAN CITY has suffered more than Messina, the victim of earthquakes and the bombs of World War II. The **Museo Regionale** houses treasures from many of the buildings no longer standing. **Santissima Annunziata dei Catalani** in Piazza Catalani displays the typical eclecticism of 12th-century Norman

architecture, with rich decoration. It surpasses the **Duomo** (begun 1160) which, despite faithful rebuilding after the war, is a ghost of its former self.

Outside, GA Montorsoli's **Fontana d'Orione** (1547) is the finest fountain of its kind from 16th-century Sicily. His **Fontana di Nettuno** (1557) celebrates Messina's foundation and position in the world as a principal commercial port.

🏛 Museo Regionale
Via della Libertà 465. ⎮ 090-36 12 92.
🕓 daily am (Tue, Thu, Sat pm also). 🌀

Antonello da Messina's *Madonna and Child* (1473), Museo Regionale

Taormina ⓯

Messina. 🏙 10,000. 🚆 🚌
🛈 Palazzo Corvaja, Piazza Santa Caterina (0942-232 43). 🛒 Wed.

SPLENDIDLY SITUATED, Taormina is Sicily's window on the modern world. It is a delight to visit; filled with a wide range of restaurants and hotels, with sandy beaches far below.

The most illustrious relic of the past is the **theatre**. Begun in the 3rd century BC by the Greeks, it was subsequently rebuilt by the Romans. Among other Classical remains are the ruins of the **odeon** (for musical performances) and the **naumachia** (an artificial lake for mock-battles). On Piazza Vittorio Emanuele (site of the Roman Forum), **Palazzo Corvaia** (14th century) was built using stone from a temple that once stood here. The 13th-century **Duomo** (renovated in 1636) is a fortress-like building.

ENVIRONS: South of Taormina at **Capo Schisò** are the ruins of ancient **Naxos**. Up the coast in the Val d'Agro is the church of **Santi Pietro e Paolo d'Agro**, part Norman, Arab and Byzantine. **Savoca** boasts the **Chiesa Madre** (13th century) and **catacombs** beneath the Cappuccini monastery.

Mount Etna ⑯

Catania. 🚉 to Linguaglossa or
Randazzo; Circumetnea railway from
Catania to Riposto. 🚌 to Nicolosi.
🛈 Piazza Vittorio Emanuele 32,
Nicolosi (095-91 44 88).

ONE OF THE WORLD's largest
active volcanoes, Mount
Etna was thought by the
ancients to have been the
forge of Vulcan (god of fire).
The authorities are constantly
on the lookout for violent
eruptions – like those that
devastated Catania repeatedly
in the past. To view it in
comfort, the Circumetnea
railway runs around the base
from Catania to Riposto.

Catania ⑰

🏛 365,000. ✈ 🚉 🚌 🛈 Largo
Paisiello 5 (095-31 21 24). 🛒 Mon–Sat
(general); Sun (antique & bric-a-brac).

HAVING BEEN DECIMATED by
the earthquake of 1693,
Catania was comprehensively
rebuilt, and today contains

The façade of Catania's Duomo

some of Sicily's most imaginative Baroque buildings. From
Piazza del Duomo, distinguished by a lava elephant
(Catania's symbol) carrying an
Egyptian obelisk, there is a
dramatic vista to Mount Etna.
In 1736 the Norman **Duomo**
was given a new façade by
Vaccarini, who also worked on
the **Municipio** (finished 1741).
A vigorous plasticity of form
is his hallmark – see the
façade of **Sant'Agata** (1748),
and the designs of **Collegio**

Cutelli, probably built by
a pupil around 1779, and
Palazzo Valle (c.1740–50).

Carrying on the Vaccarini
tradition is Stefano Ittar's
San Placido (around 1768).
The frenzied stone carving on
the **Palazzo Biscari** (early
18th century) is exceeded by
Antonino Amato's unrestrained
decoration of both the vast
Benedictine **convent** (1704)
and the adjacent huge church
of **San Niccolò** (1730).

On Via Vittorio Emanuele is
the **Museo Belliniano**, birthplace of composer Vincenzo
Bellini (1801–35), and the
Teatro Romano (21 BC), built
from lava. **Verga's House**, the
former home of the great
Sicilian novelist Giovanni Verga
(1840–1922), is on Via Sant'
Anna. Via Crociferi is home
to 18th-century churches **San
Francesco Borgia**, **San
Benedetto** and **San Giuliano**,
whose interior is Vaccarini's
masterpiece (1760). Further
along Via Crociferi, the church
of **Santo Carcere** contains the
prison of St Agatha, who was
martyred in AD 253.

INFLUENCES ON TRADITIONAL SICILIAN CUISINE

Sicily has one of Italy's
most varied cuisines. The
island's unique location –
marooned between North
Africa, Europe and the
eastern Mediterranean –
and the invaders it attracted,
are responsible for this.
The earliest Western cook-
book, the now lost *Art of
Cooking* (5th century BC),
was written by Mithaecus,
a Siracusan Greek. Sicily's
fertility attracted Greek
colonists, who exported
oil, wheat, honey, cheese,
fruit and vegetables to their
homeland. To the Romans,
Sicily was merely a bread-
basket. The Arabs, however,
introduced oranges, lemons,
aubergines and sugar cane.
Their love of sweet con-

An impressive selection of olives displayed in a Palermo market stall

fections provided the inspiration for *granita*, a form of
flavoured ice. The Sicilians
love to claim an Arabic origin
for their ice cream, but the
Greeks and Romans had
created an earlier
version by chilling
their wine with snow
from Mount Etna.
Traditionally, the
peasants existed on a
subsistence diet while

the aristocracy enjoyed
extravagant fare, and one of
the peculiarities of Sicilian
food today is that it can be
both frugal and handsomely
ornate. All of the usual
Italian dishes are available,
but more interesting are
the variations using local
ingredients like swordfish,
sardines, ricotta cheese, red
chillies, aubergines, capers,
olives and almond paste.

Marzipan fruits made from almond paste

Overlooking the beach at Mazzarò near Taormina ▷

Shorefront in Siracusa, one of the most beautiful cities of the ancient Greek world

Pantalica ⑱

Siracusa. **[** 0923-95 36 95. **🚍** from
Siracusa to Sortino then 5 km (3 miles)
walk to entrance or bus from Siracusa
to Ferla then 10 km (6 miles) walk to
entrance. **Necropolis** ◯ 7am–sunset
(Oct–Mar: 6pm). **[&]**

R EMOTE IN THE desolate
Monti Iblei and over-
looking the River Anapo is
the prehistoric **necropolis** of
Pantalica – today a pleasant
place to walk and picnic. The
dead of a large, unexcavated
village (which was occupied
from 13th–8th century BC)
were buried here in deep,
cave-like tombs cut into the
rock. More than 5,000 of
these tombs were arranged in
tiers with a single flat stone
sealing each opening.
   The inhabitants of Pantalica
are thought to have come
from coastal **Thapsos**, which
was abandoned after raids by
warlike tribes from mainland
Italy. The site was re-inhabited
in the Byzantine period when
some tombs were made into

**Rock-cut tombs in the prehistoric
necropolis of Pantalica**

cave dwellings and chapels.
Artefacts from the necropolis
are displayed in Siracusa's
Museo Archeologico Regionale.

Siracusa ⑲

🏛 125,000. **FS 🚍 ⛴** Via San
Sebastiano 43 (0931-677 10). **🅰** Wed.

Interior of Duomo in Siracusa

S IRACUSA (SYRACUSE) was one
of the most important cities
of the ancient Greek world,
and the most beautiful according to Cicero, the Roman
consul. The peninsula **Ortigia**
is the self-contained hub of
the old city. On the mainland,
Achradina, **Tyche** and
Neapolis have been occupied
almost without a break since
the expansion of the city in
480 BC. These were the years
of Gelon, tyrant of Gela,
when Siracusa was enriched
with new temples, theatres
and dockyards. The city was
a powerful force until 211 BC,
when it fell to the Romans in

a battle that also killed the
mathematician Archimedes,
its most famous inhabitant.
   The highlight of Ortigia is
the extraordinary **Duomo**,
begun in 1728 by architect
Andrea Palma. Its Baroque
façade masks the **Temple of
Athena** (5th century BC),
which has been absorbed
into the Duomo. Facing the
Ponte Nuovo are the ruins of
Sicily's earliest Doric temple,
the **Temple of Apollo**, which
had monolithic columns.
   Across from the Duomo is
the **Palazzo Beneventano
del Bosco** (1778–88), a bold
example of Siracusan Baroque,
as is **Santa Lucia alla Badia**
(1695–1703). In the Municipio
a small museum records the
history of Ionic temples, and
the coin collection of the
Galleria Numismatica records
Siracusa's past wealth. The
delightful **Fonte Aretusa** is
frequently referred to by
Classical writers as the point
where Aretusa emerged from
the ground, having been
changed into a spring by
Artemis to help her escape
her lover Alpheus.
   At Ortigia's furthest point
is the **Castello Maniace**,
built by Frederick II around
1239. Here too is the **Museo
Regionale d'Arte Medioevale
e Moderna**, with sculpture
and paintings including
the *Burial of St Lucy* (1608)
by Caravaggio.
   The painting comes from
the church of **Santa Lucia** in
the Achradina quarter. This
area was flattened during

World War II, but the church survived the bombs. It is mostly 17th century with a Norman campanile, and occupies the site where St Lucy, patron saint of Siracusa, was martyred in AD 304. Achradina is now the centre of modern Siracusa.

To the north, in Tyche, is the **Museo Archeologico Regionale Paolo Orsi**, with its important collection of artefacts from the Paleolithic to the Byzantine era, taken from southeastern sites in Sicily. Included are vases, coins, bronzes, votive objects, busts, sculpture and fragments from Siracusan temples.

The Neapolis quarter and its **Parco Archeologico** feature the Teatro Romano, the Altar of Hieron II and the spectacular Teatro Greco, carved from the hillside. Beyond the Nymphaeum is the 2nd-century AD Roman amphitheatre and the stone quarries – the Latomia del Paradiso. It is thought that 7,000 Athenians were incarcerated here and left to die after their calamitous defeat in 413 BC, in a battle described by Thucydides as "the greatest action in Hellenic history".

ENVIRONS: At **Epipolae**, 8 km (5 miles) north of Neapolis is the **Castle of Euryalus** – the most important ancient Greek fortification to have survived.

🏛 **Museo Regionale d'Arte Medioevale e Moderna**
Palazzo Bellomo, Via Capodieci 16.
📞 0931-653 43. 🕐 daily am.
🏛 **Museo Archeologico Regionale Paolo Orsi**
Viale Teocrito 66. 📞 0931-46 40 22.
🕐 Tue–Sun am.

Noto ⓴

Siracusa. 🏠 21,000. 🚉 🚌
🛈 Piazza XVI Maggio (0931-83 67
44). 🗓 Mon & 1st & 3rd Tue of
the month.

NOTO WAS BUILT from scratch in the early 18th century to replace Noto Antica, which was devastated by an earth-quake in 1693. The town was comprehensively designed in Baroque style, using the local white tufa, a limestone which

The façade of the Duomo in Noto rises above a huge staircase

has turned a lovely honey-brown colour from the sun. It is now one of the most enchanting towns in Sicily.

The twin-towered **Duomo** (completed 1770s), which dominates Noto, is attributed to the important architect Rosario Gagliardi. He also designed the eccentric tower façade of the seminary of **San Salvatore** (18th century) in Piazza Municipio, the convex façade of **San Domenico** (around 1732) in Piazza XVI Maggio and the oval interior of **Santa Chiara** (1730) on

Corso Vittorio Emanuele. The magnificent **Palazzo Trigona** (1781) stands on Via Cavour behind the Duomo. The **Palazzo Villadorata** (1730s) on Via Nicolaci is set off by a splendid façade festooned with elaborate stone carvings. At the north end of Via Nicolaci, the **Monastery of Montevergine** has a striking curved façade. Gagliardi's church of the **Crocifisso** (1728) stands on the town's summit, containing a sculpture of the Madonna by Francesco Laurana (1471). The **Municipio** (1740s), facing the Duomo, has a fine "billowing" ground floor design.

ENVIRONS: The earthquake of 1693 also devastated the towns of **Modica**, around 30 km (19 miles) to the west, and **Ragusa**, a short distance further. Like Noto, they were rebuilt in the region's rich, vital Baroque style. Gagliardi was at work in both places, on Modica's **San Giorgio** (early 18th century), on Ragusa's **San Giorgio** (begun around 1746, and one of his masterpieces), and on **San Giuseppe** (mid-18th century).

Boisterous carving on the façade of the Palazzo Villadorata in Noto

SARDINIA

···

I N HIS TRAVELOGUE, Sea and Sardinia, *DH Lawrence wrote that Sardinia was "left outside of time and history". Indeed, the march of time has been slow here, and traditions from ancient Europe have survived – the legacy of invasion by Phoenicians, Carthaginians, Romans, Arabs, Byzantines, Spanish, Savoyards and Italians.*

These traditions are displayed in Sardinia's many festivals – some soberly Christian, others with pagan roots. Several different dialects and languages are spoken in Sardinia. Catalan can be heard in Alghero, and on the island of San Pietro, there is a Ligurian dialect. Even remnants of Phoenician and Etruscan survive. In the south, the traditional influences are Arab and Spanish, while pure native strains of people and language survive in the Gennargentu mountains. Peopled by shepherds in isolated communities, this region is so impenetrable that invaders have never bothered it.

Of particular interest are the prehistoric *nuraghe* castles, villages, temples and tombs which litter the countryside – most notably around Barumini, north of Cagliari, and in the

Valle dei Nuraghe, south of Sassari. The *nuraghe* were built by a people whose origins constitute one of the Mediterranean's great mysteries. In Cagliari, the capital of Sardinia, there is a museum with an excellent archaeological collection that offers insight into this enigmatic people.

Sassari, Oristano, Alghero and Olbia are all centres of areas marked by their individuality. Some remarkable Pisan-Romanesque churches are located around Sassari and here too dialects reveal close links with the languages of Tuscany. Olbia is a boom town made rich by tourism and the proximity of the jet-setting Costa Smeralda. Sober Nuoro with its province in the shadow of the Gennargentu mountains, by contrast, has little in common with the Sardinia of tourist brochures.

Relaxing during the day in the tiny resort of Carloforte on the Isola di San Pietro, next to Sant'Antioco

◁ **The Bay of Simius east of Cagliari in the southeast corner of Sardinia**

Exploring Sardinia

THIS ISLAND, called Sardegna in Italian, is characterized by an interior of dramatic, rolling uplands covered in *macchia* – grassland mingled with myrtle, wild thyme, prickly pears and dwarf oaks – and a coastline of beguiling, translucent sea, isolated coves, long sandy beaches and caves. The Gennargentu mountains, with the highest peak at 1,834 m (6,017 ft), shield a nearly impenetrable area of rural villages. In the northeast, mountains fall away dramatically to the Costa Smeralda, Sardinia's most exclusive coastal area. Further south, the shoreline around the Golfo di Orosei is completely unspoilt. Around Oristano in the west the land is flat, leading to the plain of Campidano where the island's corn, fruit and vegetables grow.

Prehistoric nuraghic remains at Su Nuraxi near Barumini

SIGHTS AT A GLANCE

Alghero **3**
Bosa **4**
Cagliari **9**
Cala Gonone **6**
Costa Smeralda **1**
Nuoro **5**
Oristano **7**
Sant'Antioco **8**
Sassari **2**

A typical scene of clothes hanging out to dry in Alghero

SEE ALSO

- *Where to Stay* p575
- *Where to Eat* p609

0 kilometres   50

0 miles   25

Waves lapping at the rocks on Isola di San Pietro, northwest of Sant'Antioco

KEY

▬▬	Major road
▭▭	Minor road
▭▭	Scenic route
≈	River
❀	Viewpoint

Southernmost reach of the Gennargentu mountains

GETTING AROUND

Ferries from a wide range of ports on the Italian mainland dock at Cagliari, Olbia and Porto Torres. International charter flights use the domestic airports at Cagliari, Olbia and Alghero. The island is neatly cut by the N131. It skirts the Gennargentu mountains, which are accessible only by tortuously winding passes. Branches of the N131 reach Olbia and Nuoro. Express bus and excellent, fast train services connect the major cities, while slower, daily bus services and narrow-gauge trains operate between the smaller towns.

The extravagantly beautiful, *macchia*-scented Costa Smeralda

Costa Smeralda ➊

Sassari. **FS** 🚆 *Olbia.* 🚌 *Porto
Cervo.* ℹ️ *Via Catello Piro 1, Olbia
(0789-214 53).*

THE FORMERLY WILD, lonely
Costa Smeralda, stretching
from the Golfo di Cugnana to
the Golfo di Arzachena, was
developed at the end of the
1950s by a consortium of
magnates, including the Aga
Khan, into one of the world's
most lucrative holiday resorts.
Its pristine appearance is now
strictly controlled.

In **Porto Cervo**, the main
town, boutiques jostle with
nightclubs, fine restaurants and
luxury hotels. It caters for the
seriously rich – billionaires,
crowned heads and pop stars.

ENVIRONS: If this leaves you
cold, head north to rural **Baia
Sardinia** and **Cannigione**.
From **Palau** ferries leave for
La Maddalena and **Isola
Caprera**, the home of
Garibaldi and the **Museo
Nazionale Garibaldino**.

🏛 **Museo Nazionale
Garibaldino**
Frazione Caprera, Maddalena.
📞 *0789-72 71 62.* ⬜ *daily am.*
⬤ *1 Jan, 1 May, 25 Dec.* 🎫 🚫

Sassari ➋

🏙 *120,000.* 🚶 **FS** 🚌 ℹ️ *Viale
Caprera 36 (079-29 95 44).* ⬤ *Mon.*

FOUNDED BY GENOESE and
Pisan merchants early in
the 13th century, Sassari is
known for its spectacular

Cavalcata Sarda festival on
Ascension Day. There is a
raucous, tight, church-filled
medieval quarter around the
Duomo (11th century
with later, mostly
Baroque, additions),
and to the north is
the handsome **Fonte
Rosello**, a huge late-
Renaissance fountain.
The **Museo Archeo-
logico Nazionale
"GA Sanna"** is a
good starting point
from which to begin
an investigation
into the region's
nuraghic history.

ENVIRONS: To the
southeast along the
N131 is the Pisan-
Romanesque church
of **Santissima Trinità di
Saccargia** (1116), which
contains the only extant cycle
of 13th-century frescoes in
Sardinia. Further on is the
church of **San Michele di
Salvenero**
(12th century),
and at **Ardara**
the basalt-built
Romanesque
**Santa Maria
del Regno**,
or "Black
Cathedral".

🏛 **Museo
Archeologico
Nazionale
"GA Sanna"**
Via Roma 64.
📞 *079-27 22 03.*
⬜ *daily am (also:
pm 2nd Wed of
month).* 🎫

*Façade of Santissima
Trinità di Saccargia*

Alghero ➌

Sassari. 🏙 *41,000.* 🚶 **FS** 🚌 🚢
ℹ️ *Piazza Porta Terra 9 (079-97 90 54).*
⬤ *Wed.*

FOUNDED ON A PENINSULA
facing the Bay of Alghero
early in the 12th century, and
taken from the Genoese
Dorias by the Aragonese in
1353, Alghero was peopled
by settlers from Barcelona
and Valencia. Its original
occupants – Ligurians and
Sardinians – were expelled
with such thoroughness that
today the Catalan language
and culture is enjoying a
revival and the look of old
Alghero is consistently Spanish.

Filled with labyrinthine alleys
and cobbled streets, the lively
port of old Alghero is flanked
by battlemented walls and
defensive towers on all but
the landward section. Facing
the Giardino Pubblico is the
massive 16th-century **Torre di
Porta Terra**, also known as
the Jewish Tower after
its builders. Around
the periphery of the
old town are more
towers, including
**Torre dell'Espero
Reial** and **Torre
San Giacomo**
on Lungomare
Colombo, and
**Torre della
Maddalena** on
Piazza Porta Terra.
The 16th-century **Duomo** at
the bottom of Via Umberto is
predominantly Catalan-Gothic
with an Aragonese portal.
Off Via Carlo Alberto, **San
Francesco** (14th century)

A typical house in Alghero

The waterfront at Bosa

has a delightful cloister and octagonal campanile which towers over Alghero, and Baroque **San Michele** has a bright, handsome tiled dome. In Via Principe Umberto is the **Casa Doria**, the house where the pre-Hispanic rulers of Alghero lived. It has a beautiful Renaissance portal and Gothic-arched window.

ENVIRONS: Boat or car trips can be made to the spectacular **Grotta di Nettuno** around the point of Capo Caccia, a deep natural cave, or the nearby **Grotta Verde**.

Bosa ❹

Nuoro. 🏚 8,500. 🚉 🚌 🚶 *Corso Vittorio Emanuele 59 (0785-37 61 07).* 🗓 *Tue.*

BOSA IS A SMALL, picturesque seaside town at the mouth of Sardinia's only navigable river, the Temo. The historic **Sa Costa** district struggles up the side of a low hill capped by the **Castello di Serravalle**, built in 1122 by the Malaspina family. The narrow passages and alleys here have changed little since the Middle Ages. By the Temo are **Sas Conzas** – the former dyers' houses and workshops.

Languishing on the riverside, the **Sa Piatta** district is more cosmopolitan than the rest of Bosa. It houses the Aragonese-Gothic **Duomo** (15th century) and Romanesque **San Pietro** (11th century), with a Gothic façade added by Cistercian monks in the 13th century.

NURAGHE IN SARDINIA

The dominant feature of Sardinia is the 7,000 or so *nuraghe* dotted around the island. Dating from 1500 to 400 BC, these strange, truncated cone structures were built without any bonding from huge basalt blocks taken from extinct volcanoes. Almost nothing is known about the identity of the nuraghic people. They must have been well organized and possessed remarkable engineering skills, judging by their buildings, but appear to have left no written word. The mystery of these enigmatic people has plagued Sardinians for centuries.

The individual nuraghe *are fairly small. A few were fortresses, equipped with wells and other defensive features.*

Su Nuraxi at Barumini (*above*), *Serra Orrios, near Dorgali, and Santu Antine at Torralba are among the most important* nuraghe *complexes. Houses, temples, tombs, and even a theatre have been identified.*

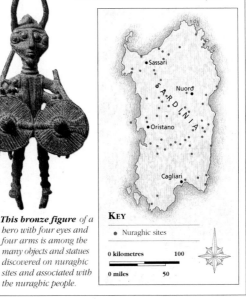

This bronze figure *of a hero with four eyes and four arms is among the many objects and statues discovered on nuraghic sites and associated with the nuraghic people.*

KEY

• Nuraghic sites

0 kilometres   100

0 miles   50

Nobel Prize-winning novelist Grazia Deledda from Nuoro

Nuoro ❺

🏃 38,000. �f🆂 🚌 ℹ️ *Piazza d'Italia 19 (0784-300 83).* 🍴 *Fri & Sat.*

THIS TOWN, in a spectacular setting beneath the gaze of Monte Ortobene and the dramatic Sopramonte, has been the home of some of Sardinia's most important men and women of letters. Among these literary figures is Grazia Deledda, who won the Nobel Prize for Literature in 1926 in recognition of her understanding portrayal of the power and passions in the primitive communities around her. A comprehensive collection of ethnic items, such as traditional Sardinian costumes and jewellery, can be seen in the excellent **Museo della Vita e delle Tradizioni Popolari Sarde**. Attending the *Sagra del Redentore* festival is the best way to witness the region's dancing and dialects.

ENVIRONS: Nuoro is on the edge of the Barbagia region, which has isolated villages of shepherds who have never experienced the hand of any overlord, so impenetrable are the **Gennargentu** mountains. This region was known to the Romans as Barbaria, an area they were never able to subdue. Traces of the traditional lawlessness of the Barbagia can be seen in **Orgosolo**, with its wall murals calling for Sardinia's independence. Rival clans were locked in bloody vendetta for almost 50 years, and the deeds of native bandits form part of local folklore.

In **Mamoiada**'s *Feast of the Mamuthones*, men in sinister masks and traditional costume perform a ritual dance ending with a symbolic "killing" of a scapegoat. The passion and fervour of the event is indicative of the survival of a fierce folkloric tradition and deep resistance to change.

🏛 **Museo della Vita e delle Tradizioni Popolari Sarde**
Via Mereu 56. 📞 *0784-314 26.*
🕐 *Apr–Oct: daily; Nov–Mar: Tue–Sun am.* 📷

Cala Gonone ❻

Nuoro. 🏃 800. 🚌 ℹ️ *Via Lamarmore 189, Dorgali (0784-962 43).* 🍴 *daily.* 🚤 *to grottoes (Apr–mid-Oct).* 📞 *0784-933 05.*

EAST OF NUORO, squeezed between the sea and the base of high mountains, is the hamlet of Cala Gonone – a bustling seaside resort and fishing port, with magnificent beaches. Along the unspoilt coast are the isolated coves of **Cala di Luna** and **Cala Sisine** as well as deep natural caves, including the famous **Grotta del Bue Marino** which is adorned with weird rock formations. The area around Cala Gonone is good for walking and hiking, especially down to Cala Sinisi, and the road from Dorgali to Baunei and Tortoli is spectacular.

Oristano ❼

Cagliari. 🏃 32,000. 🚆🆂 🚌 ℹ️ *Via Cagliari 278 (0783-741 91).* 🍴 *Tue & Fri.*

Ruins of Tharros near Oristano

THE PROVINCE of Oristano corresponds roughly with historical Arborea, over which Eleonora ruled *(see opposite)*. She is commemorated by an 18th-century statue in **Piazza Eleonora**. On Corso Vittorio Emanuele is the 16th-century **Casa di Eleonora**, and nearby the **Antiquarium Arborense**, which has Neolithic, nuraghic, Punic and Roman artefacts. The **Torre di San Cristoforo** (1291) in Piazza Roma once formed part of Oristano's fortifications. The **Duomo** (13th century) was later rebuilt in the Baroque style. More interesting are the churches of **Santa Chiara** (1343) on Via Garibaldi and 14th-century **San Martino** on Via Cagliari.

ENVIRONS: The 12th-century Pisan-Romanesque **Cathedral** at Santa Giusta has interior columns probably taken from

Entrance to the Grotta del Bue Marino, south of Cala Gonone

The tiny resort of Carloforte, the capital of Isola di San Pietro

Tharros, an 8th-century BC Punic settlement whose extensive ruins lie 20 km (12 miles) west of Oristano on the Sinis peninsula.

🏛 **Antiquarium Arborense**
Via Parpaglia 37. 📞 *0783-79 12 62.*
⏱ *Tue–Sun.* 🌐 ♿

Sant'Antioco ❽

Cagliari. 🚊 🚌 ℹ *Piazza Repubblica (0781-820 31).*

THE MAIN TOWN on this unspoilt island is **Sant' Antioco**. It was a Phoenician port known as Sulcis and an important Roman base. Proof of almost continual occupation is clear at the **catacombs**, a Phoenician burial place later used by Christians, under the 12th-century basilica of **Sant' Antioco Martire**. The **Antiquarium** contains Phoenician artefacts. The Punic **Tophet** (sanctuary of the goddess Tanit) and the **necropolis** are nearby. The small **Isola di San Pietro** can be reached by ferry from Calasetta.

♠ **Catacombs**
Piazza Parrocchia.
📞 *0781-830 44.*
⏱ *daily.* 📷 *only.*
● *Easter, 15 Aug, 25 Dec.* 🌐
🏛 **Antiquarium**
Via Regina Margherita.
📞 *0781-835 90.*
⏱ *daily.* ● *1 Jan, Easter, 8, 25 & 26 Dec.* 🌐

Cagliari ❾

🏙 *220,000.* ✈ 🚊 🚌 ⛴
ℹ *Piazza Matteotti 9 (070-66 92 55).*
🛒 *daily; also Sun (flea) and second Sun of month (antiques).*

THE CAPITAL of Sardinia, this site was occupied by the Phoenicians, Carthaginians and Romans, and extensive ruins of the Phoenician city of Nora lie to the southwest of Cagliari. A 2nd-century **amphitheatre** survives from the Roman era, cut from rock. The best indication of the town's earlier history is to be found in the **Cittadella dei Musei**. Fashioned from the former royal arsenal, it houses several museums including the **Museo Nazionale Archeologico**. The nuraghic items are the most interesting in the collection, especially the bronze votive statuettes. Also in the Cittadella dei Musei is the **Pinacoteca**, an art gallery.

The 6th-century church of San Saturnino in Cagliari, built on a Greek-cross plan

The compact old core of Cagliari has an appealing North African character. In the high **Castello** district, the Romans and, much later, Pisans built defences. The gracious **Bastione San Remy** on Piazza Costituzione offers magnificent views over the city and surrounding countryside. The **Duomo** is a 20th-century rehash of a Romanesque building. Flanking the entrance are two 12th-century pulpits originally destined for the cathedral in Pisa.

Nearby is the Pisan tower **Torre San Pancrazio** (14th century). From the partially-ruined **Torre dell'Elefante** on Via dell'Università to the port lies the **Marina** quarter, which expanded from the old town in the 16th to 17th centuries. In Piazza San Cosimo, the 6th-century church of **San Saturnino** is a rare monument to Byzantine occupation.

♠ **Amphitheatre**
Viale Sant'Ignazio. ⏱ *daily.*
🏛 **Cittadella dei Musei**
Piazza Arsenale. **Museo Nazionale Archeologico** 📞 *070-65 59 11.*
Pinacoteca 📞 *070-67 01 57.*
⏱ *daily.* ● *1 Jan, 1 May, 25 Dec.* 🌐 ♿

ELEONORA OF ARBOREA

A champion against rule from abroad, Eleonora was governing *giudicessa* (judge) of Arborea, one of four administrative divisions of Sardinia, from 1383–1404. Her marriage to Brancaleone Doria consolidated Genoese interests in Sardinia. She rallied the island to keep out Spanish invaders who tried to claim land that had been given to the Aragonese King James II. Her greatest legacy was the completion of the codifying of laws begun by her father. Written in Sardinian, they called for community of property in marriage and the right of women to seek redress from rape.

TRAVELLERS'
NEEDS

WHERE TO STAY

PEOPLE COME FROM all over the world to visit Italy and the majority of Italians choose to spend their holidays there as well, particularly in the mountains or by the sea. This means that there is a dazzling range of accommodation options on offer, from splendid hotels in old palazzi and historic residences, to simple family-run *pensioni* and hostels. Those who want self-catering accommodation are

Sign for a 3-star hotel

also well served with everything from stately, isolated villas in Tuscany to purpose-built holiday flats in, or near, busy seaside resorts. Italian hotels are notorious for being expensive and short of services but you can nevertheless find excellent value in all price ranges. The hotels listed on pages 542–75 have been selected from every price category as among the best value in each area for style, comfort or location.

The Gritti Palace, one of Venice's historic palazzi *(see p544)*

GRADINGS

HOTELS IN ITALY are graded with one to five stars. Grading depends on facilities offered rather than atmosphere and each region awards stars according to slightly different criteria. Sometimes a hotel has a lower rating than it deserves. This may be because the local tourist office hasn't upgraded it yet or the hotel itself has opted to stay in a lower category to avoid higher taxes.

ALBERGHI

ALBERGO IS ITALIAN for hotel but the term tends to refer to the upper categories. Room sizes vary considerably: in city centres even expensive hotels can have far smaller rooms than their counterparts in other countries, whereas outside the city your room may be more like a small suite. In general, *alberghi* will have private showers in all rooms and the more luxurious have baths.

In city centres you may come across the sign *albergo diurno*. This is a day hotel without accommodation but with bathroom, showers, hairdressing, drying and other cleaning facilities you may need when travelling. Day hotels are usually situated at or near the main railway station.

PENSIONI

ALTHOUGH THE TERM *pensione* is no longer in official use it still describes one and two star hotels, most of which are small and family run. On the whole you'll meet immaculate standards of cleanliness and

Street sign showing the direction and location of hotels

friendly, helpful service with basic, although perfectly functional, rooms. However, as *pensioni* are often in old buildings, historic charm may be paid for with noisy, erratic plumbing and dark rooms. Many do not have public rooms other than a sparsely furnished breakfast room. Most will offer at least some rooms with a private shower although rarely a bath. If you intend being out late, check that you'll be able to get back into the *pensione*. Not all of them have night porters after midnight or 1am but most will at least be able to provide a key to the main door.

If you are planning to stay in a *pensione* in winter, check that it has central heating. Not all of them do and, even in the south, temperatures are low from November to February.

A *locanda* was traditionally an inn, offering cheap food and a place to sleep for the traveller. The word is still in use, particularly in central and northern Italy, but is now synonymous with *pensione* and may be more of an affectation for the benefit of the tourist.

CHAIN HOTELS

THERE ARE VARIOUS Italian chain hotels at the upper end of the market, as well as the big internationals. **Ciga** hotels have a turn-of-the-century opulence and include some of the oldest hotels in Italy; **Jolly** are more akin to the international luxury chains and **Agip**, aligned with the Forte group, offers uniform

◁ **Popular café in Piazza Navona, Rome**

Romantic Hotel Villa Pagoda in Nervi, Genova *(see p555)*

motels. **Relais et Châteaux** run charming hotels in historic castles, villas and monasteries with facilities to match.

MEALS AND FACILITIES

ITALIAN HOTELS TEND to guarantee fewer special facilities than those in many other countries. In spite of the warm summers, for example, air-conditioning is rare in all but five-star hotels, as is 24-hour room service.

Some hotels may insist on full board *(pensione completa)* or half board *(mezza pensione)* in peak season. However, avoid this if you can: unless it's very isolated, there will almost certainly be a good range of places to eat nearby. Many *pensioni* (particularly in high season) may insist on your taking their breakfast which will probably consist of coffee and biscuits or brioches with butter and jam. Once again, try to avoid this as breakfast at a local bar is an enjoyable Italian institution.

For a double room, stipulate whether you want twin beds *(letti singoli)* or a double bed *(matrimoniale)*. Bathrooms in all but the most expensive hotels will tend to have showers rather than baths so state your preference (you may be charged more for a bath).

CHILDREN

ITALIANS ACCEPT CHILDREN as an ordinary part of life and, although there may not be many special facilities, they are always welcome. Some of the cheaper hotels may not be able to provide cots. However,

virtually all hotels, from the simplest to the most grand, will put a small bed or two into a double room for families travelling together. The price of this is usually an extra 30–40 per cent of the double room rate per bed. Most of the large hotels will also offer a regular babysitting service.

PRICES

HOTELS IN ITALY are not cheap, although prices vary between places and seasons. Prices, which include tax and service and are quoted per room, start at around L60,000 for a double room without a bath-room, and can rise to at least L90,000 with a bath, even for a very basic hotel. A single room will cost about two-thirds of a double. Around L200,000 will get you something comfortable and often picturesque, although not particularly luxurious. For L400,000 and upwards you

Hotel Sant'Anselmo's garden, Rome *(see p565)*

can expect a good range of facilities, a pleasant or central location and often a lot of local or historic charm. Hotels in the major cities and resorts are likely to be more expensive.

By law hotels have to display their rates in every bedroom. Variation between high and low season can be 100 per cent or more in resorts.

Also, beware of extras: the mini-bar can be extortionate as can charges for parking, laundry or phoning directly from your hotel bedroom.

BOOKING

BOOK AS SOON AS possible, particularly if you have special requests such as a room with a view, off the street or with a bath. Two months should be ample, but during the high season popular hotels can be fully booked six months in advance. August is very busy at beach resorts and February at mountain resorts. The same goes for cities and towns depending on their particular cultural calendars *(see pp62–5)*.

You will be asked for a deposit when you book; this can usually be paid for by credit card (even in places that do not accept credit cards for final payment); otherwise by Eurocheque or international money order.

Under Italian law the hotel must issue you with a receipt *(ricevuta fiscale)* for final payment which you must keep until you leave Italy.

Mirrored entrance hall of the hotel Campo de' Fiori in Rome *(see p565)*

Vaulted central entrance of **Hotel Porta Rossa** in Florence *(see p557)*

CHECKING IN AND OUT

WHEN YOU ARRIVE at the hotel the management will take your passport to fulfil its legal obligation of registering you with the police. This is a mere formality and you should get your passport back within an hour or two.

Checking-out time is usually before noon, although this might be earlier in small hotels. The room must be vacated but most places will allow you to leave luggage in the reception to be collected later on in the day.

Albergo al Sole, Venice (see p544)

SELF-CATERING AND AGRITURISMO

IF YOU INTEND to be based in one area, self-catering accommodation often enjoys marvellous locations and is generally of a high standard.

Across rural Italy there are more than 2,000 farms, villas and mountain chalets offering reasonably priced self-catering or hotel-style accommodation as part of the **Agriturismo** scheme. Facilities range from those of a first-class hotel in beautifully kept villas or ancient castles to basic rooms with the family on a working farm. Some have excellent restaurants which serve farm and local produce, others can arrange riding, fishing or other activity holidays *(see p624)*. There may be a minimum stay requirement, especially in peak season. The booklets *Guida dell'Ospitalità Rurale* or *Vacanze e Natura* can be found in the central office in Rome or the regional offices. Other self-catering options can be arranged through specialized agencies such as **Italian Chapters**, **Tailor-Made Tours**, **Vacanze in Italia** and **The Magic of Italy** before you leave for Italy, but again, make sure you book in advance; they can be booked up for months.

There are also so-called *residence*, found in the **ENIT** accommodation lists. These are halfway between a hotel and self-catering flats and often offer cooking facilities and some sort of restaurant service.

For stays of several months or more, accommodation agencies for apartments in the city centre as well as the surrounding countryside can be found under *Immobiliari* in the *Pagine Gialle* (Yellow Pages).

BUDGET ACCOMMODATION

AS WELL AS THE International Youth Hostel Association (**AIG** in Italy), tourist offices in the major cities have lists of privately-run hostels. Prices, at around L15,000 per person per night, are considerably less than even the cheapest *pensioni* but accommodation is in single-sex dormitories and washing facilities may be overstretched. A room in a private house is another cheap option, offering often small but clean rooms, probably vacated by now grown-up children.

The **Centro Turistico Studentesco** can help students find rooms in university accommodation across Italy. This is not limited to students taking courses, particularly in the summer when resident students are on holiday.

A peaceful alternative is to stay in one of a number of convents and monasteries with guest accommodation. The rooms are clean, although often rather sparse and they are generally in a quiet corner off the road or behind cloister walls. However, strict rules may be a price to pay: most have early curfews and many will not admit members of the opposite sex even when with their spouses. There is no central agency dealing with these but they are included in the **ENIT** accommodation lists for each region.

A suitcase boat carrying visitors' luggage to a hotel in Venice

MOUNTAIN REFUGES AND CAMPSITES

BASIC ACCOMMODATION in huts and refuges is available in mountainous areas where there is hill-walking and hiking. Most of these huts are owned and run by the **Club Alpino Italiano** whose offices are in Rome.

Campsites abound in the mountains and around the coastal regions. Many of them offer basic accommodation in family-sized cabins *(bungalow)* as well as spaces for tents,

The highest refuge in the Valsesia alps, Rifugio Francesco Pastore

caravans and trailers, with basic facilities such as water, electricity and washing. There is usually a restaurant and, especially in campsites by the sea, there may also be sports facilities such as swimming pools, boat and water sports equipment hire and tennis courts. The **Touring Club Italiano** publishes a full list in *Campeggi e Villaggi Turistici in Italia* (L35,000), as does **Federcampeggio**.

DISABLED TRAVELLERS

FEW HOTELS IN ITALY have special facilities for disabled travellers. Those that do are indicated with the appropriate

Villa San Michele, a former monastery in Fiesole, Tuscany *(see p559)*

symbol in the hotels listings on pages 542–75. In many cases, however, hotels without special facilities will do all they can to accommodate people in wheelchairs by giving them downstairs rooms (when available) and help with lifts or stairs.

FURTHER INFORMATION

THE ITALIAN STATE TOURIST office (**ENIT**) has accommodation lists for every region. They are reprinted annually but may not be updated and prices may have changed. Rooms can also be booked at the local **APT** (Azienda Provinciale per il Turismo).

DIRECTORY

GENERAL

ENIT (Ente Nazionale Italiano per il Turismo)
Via Marghera 2–6,
00185 Rome.
(06-497 11.
FAX 06-446 99 07.

Italian State Tourist Board
1 Princes Street,
London W1R 8AY.
(0171-408 12 54.
FAX 0171-493 66 95.

CHAIN HOTELS

Ciga Hotels
Piazza della Repubblica 32,
20124 Milano.
(02-626 61.
FAX 02-670 05 71.

Forteagip
Via Fabio Filzi 28,

20124 Milano.
(02-66 98 18 81.
FAX 02-670 06 96.

Jolly Hotels
Via Bellini 6, Valdagno
36078, Vicenza.
(0445-41 00 00.
FAX 0445-41 14 72.

Relais et Châteaux
7 Cork Street,
London W1X 2AB.
(0171-287 09 87.
FAX 0171-487 02 41.

SELF-CATERING

Agriturismo
Corso Vittorio Emanuele II
89, 00185 Rome.
(06-685 23 42.
FAX 06-685 24 24.

Italian Chapters
102 St John's
Wood Terrace,
London NW8 6PL.
(0171-722 95 60.
FAX 0171-722 91 40.

Vacanze in Italia
Bignor, near Pulborough,
West Sussex RH20 1QD.
(01798-86 94 26.
FAX 01798-86 93 43.

Tailor-Made Tours
22 Church Rise,
London SE23 2UD.
(0181-291 97 36.
FAX 0181-699 42 37.

The Magic of Italy
227 Shepherd's Bush Road,
London W6 7AS.
(0181-748 49 99.
FAX 0181-748 63 81.

MOUNTAIN REFUGES AND CAMPSITES

Club Alpino Italiano
Piazza Sant'Andrea 300,
Rome.
(06-68 61 01 11.
FAX 06-68 80 34 24.

Touring Club Italiano
Corso Italia 10,
20122 Milano.
(02-852 61.
FAX 02-852 63 62.

Federcampeggio
Via Vittorio Emanuele 11,
50041 Calenzano, Firenze.
(055-88 23 91.
FAX 055-882 59 18.

BUDGET ACCOMMODATION

Centro Turistico Studentesco
Via Nazionale 66,
00184 Rome.
(06-467 91.
FAX 06-467 92 05.

AIG (Associazione Italiana Alberghi per la Gioventù)
Via Cavour 44,
00184 Rome.
(06-487 11 52.
FAX 06-488 04 92.

Choosing a Hotel

THE HOTELS in this guide have been selected from a wide price range for their good value or exceptional location, comfort and style. The chart highlights some of the factors which may influence your choice and gives a brief description of each hotel. Entries are listed by price category within the towns, with colour-coded thumb tabs to indicate the regions covered on each page.

VENICE

	NUMBER OF ROOMS	RESTAURANT	SWIMMING POOL	GARDEN OR TERRACE
CANNAREGIO: *Guerrini* ⓁⓁ Calle delle Procuratie, 265. **Map** 2 D4. 041-71 53 33. FAX 041-71 51 14. Just off the Lista di Spagna and reached through a pretty archway. The rooms are simple and quiet in spite of this being a busy area.	32			
CANNAREGIO: *Abbazia* ⓁⓁⓁ Calle Priuli, 66–68. **Map** 3 A4. 041-71 73 33. FAX 041-71 79 49. Quietly situated just off the lively Lista di Spagna area. The rooms are large and comfortable, and drinks are served in the delightful garden.	36			■
CANNAREGIO: *Continental* ⓁⓁⓁ Lista di Spagna, 166. **Map** 2 D4. 041-71 51 22. FAX 041-524 24 32. A large, well-equipped, modern hotel. Some rooms overlook the Grand Canal, while others are quieter with views of a tree-shaded square.	93	■		
CANNAREGIO: *Giorgione* ⓁⓁⓁ Santi Apostoli, 4587. **Map** 3 B5. 041-522 58 10. FAX 041-523 90 92. Well-situated for the Rialto area. This is a recently refurbished hotel in a delightful colour-washed building with a spacious reception area.	70			■
CASTELLO: *Paganelli* ⓁⓁ Riva degli Schiavoni, 4182. **Map** 8 D2. 041-522 43 24. FAX 041-523 92 67. Excellent views of St Mark's Basin from cosy old-fashioned rooms; those situated in the *dipendenza* (annexe) are less attractive but quieter.	22			
CASTELLO: *Pensione Bucintoro* ⓁⓁ Riva San Biagio, 2135. **Map** 8 F3. 041-522 32 40. FAX 041-523 52 24. A simple, old family pensione along the Riva. It is very peaceful and has lovely views as well as a busy restaurant popular with locals.	28	■		
CASTELLO: *Pensione Wildner* ⓁⓁⓁ Riva degli Schiavoni, 4161. **Map** 8 D2. 041-522 74 63. FAX 041-526 56 15. A family-run hotel with simple yet immaculate rooms offering stunning views across to San Giorgio Maggiore. There is also a small bar.	16	■		
CASTELLO: *Scandinavia* ⓁⓁⓁ Campo Santa Maria Formosa, 5243. **Map** 7 Ç1. 041-522 36 07. FAX 041-523 52 32. Set on one of Venice's prettiest squares, the Scandinavia has good-sized bed-rooms, a spacious reception area and welcoming management.	34	■		
CASTELLO: *Danieli* ⓁⓁⓁⓁⓁ Riva degli Schiavoni, 4196. **Map** 8 D2. 041-522 64 80. FAX 041-520 02 08. This luxurious hotel was the palace of the Dandolo family and has strong literary and musical connections. Service is impeccable.	233	■		■
CASTELLO: *Londra Palace* ⓁⓁⓁⓁⓁ Riva degli Schiavoni, 4171. **Map** 8 D2. 041-520 05 33. FAX 041-522 50 32. A lovely stone-faced hotel, the comfortable bedrooms are very traditional, and are decorated with antique furniture. The best ones are on the lagoon. Tchaikovsky composed his Fourth Symphony here in 1877.	54	■		
DORSODURO: *Montin* Ⓛ Fondamenta Eremite, 1147. **Map** 6 D3. 041-522 71 51. FAX 041-520 02 55. These few rooms above one of Venice's best restaurants (*see p578*) are full of charm and character. Book well ahead of your visit.	7	■		
DORSODURO: *Agli Alboretti* ⓁⓁ Rio Terrà Antonio Foscarini, 884. **Map** 6 E4. 041-523 00 58. FAX 041-521 01 58. A great favourite with English and American visitors, this modern hotel has a cosy wood panelled reception area and a warm atmosphere. The pergola is enchanting, and the best rooms look onto the interior gardens.	25	■		■

		Number of Rooms	Restaurant	Swimming Pool	Garden or Terrace

Price categories for a standard double room for one night, including tax and service charges but not including breakfast:
Ⓛ under L100,000
ⓁⓁ L100 – 200,000
ⓁⓁⓁ L200 – 300,000
ⓁⓁⓁⓁ L300 – 400,000
ⓁⓁⓁⓁⓁ over L400,000.

RESTAURANT
A restaurant within the hotel sometimes reserved for residents.
SWIMMING POOL
Hotel swimming pools are usually quite small and are outdoors unless otherwise stated.
GARDEN OR TERRACE
A garden, courtyard or terrace belonging to the hotel, often providing tables for eating outside.
CREDIT CARDS
The major credit cards Visa, MasterCard (Access) and American Express are accepted in hotels with the credit card symbol.

Hotel	Price	Rooms	Rest.	Pool	Garden
DORSODURO: *American* Fondamenta Bragadin, 628. **Map** 6 E4. ☎ 041-520 47 33. **FAX** 041-520 40 48. A comfortable hotel tucked away beside a small canal near the Accademia. The rooms are well-appointed and the management is friendly.	ⓁⓁⓁ	29			
DORSODURO: *Pensione Accademia Villa Maravegie* Fondamenta Bollani, 1058. **Map** 6 E3. ☎ 041-521 01 88. **FAX** 041-523 91 52. This elegant 17th-century villa just off the Grand Canal was once the Russian Embassy. Rooms are slightly shabby but furnished with antiques. Service is of a high standard. Book in advance; guests come from around the world.	ⓁⓁⓁ	27			■
GIUDECCA: *Casa Frollo* Fondamenta Zitelle, 50. **Map** 7 B5. ☎ 041-522 27 23. **FAX** 041-520 62 03. Housed in a 17th-century palazzo with views towards San Marco, the bedrooms are simple and the public areas are full of antiques, paintings and flowers.	ⓁⓁ	26			■
GIUDECCA: *Cipriani* Giudecca 10. ☎ 041-520 77 44. **FAX** 041-520 39 30. One of the most luxurious and famous hotels in the world. The rooms are decorated with taste and opulence, each one in a different style.	ⓁⓁⓁⓁⓁ	104	■	●	■
LIDO DI VENEZIA: *Villa Parco* Via Rodi 1. ☎ 041-526 00 15. **FAX** 041-526 76 20. A family-run hotel set in its own garden only a few minutes from the sea, this is ideal for travellers with children. Rooms are modern and pleasant and the hotel is in a quiet location near the summer casino.	ⓁⓁⓁ	23			■
LIDO DI VENEZIA: *Excelsior Palace* Lungomare Marconi 41. ☎ 041-526 02 01. **FAX** 041-526 72 76. A flamboyantly Moorish exterior (even the beach huts are styled like Arabian tents), the service and comfort of the interior are equally splendid.	ⓁⓁⓁⓁ	197	■	●	■
LIDO DI VENEZIA: *Hotel des Bains* Lungomare Marconi 17. ☎ 041-526 59 21. **FAX** 041-526 01 13. This was the setting for Luchino Visconti's film *Death in Venice* and it was here that Thomas Mann wrote the original novel. Reception rooms are in Art Deco style, bedrooms are spacious and service superb.	ⓁⓁⓁⓁ	191	■	●	■
SAN MARCO: *Ai Due Mori* Calle Larga San Marco, 658. **Map** 7 B2. ☎ 041-520 48 17. This friendly little pensione has only a few rooms with bathrooms, but it is clean and characterful and offers good value. Some rooms have superb views.	Ⓛ	11			
SAN MARCO: *Al Gambero* Calle dei Fabbri, 4687. **Map** 7 B2. ☎ 041-522 43 84. **FAX** 041-520 04 31. Situated on one of Venice's main shopping streets, close to the piazza. The Gambero has simple rooms, several with views over the canal.	Ⓛ	30			
SAN MARCO: *La Fenice et des Artistes* Campiello Fenice, 1936. **Map** 7 A2. ☎ 041-523 23 33. **FAX** 041-520 37 21. A pretty hotel that is popular with artists and performers at the nearby theatre. It is made up of two houses joined together by a small patio. Rooms are comfortable and furnished with antiques; ask for one with a terrace.	ⓁⓁⓁ	68			■
SAN MARCO: *Flora* Calle Larga XXII Marzo, 2283a. **Map** 7 A3. ☎ 041-520 58 44. **FAX** 041-522 82 17. A charming and quiet hotel on a secluded alley near Piazza San Marco. During the summer breakfast is served in the flower-filled garden.	ⓁⓁⓁ	44			■
SAN MARCO: *San Moisè* Piscina San Moisè, 2058. **Map** 7 A3. ☎ 041-520 37 55. **FAX** 041-521 06 70. Set on a placid back canal, the San Moisè is wonderfully quiet yet very central. Rooms are decorated in traditional Venetian style with antiques.	ⓁⓁⓁ	16			

For key to symbols see back flap

		Number of Rooms	Restaurant	Swimming Pool	Garden or Terrace

Price categories for a standard double room for one night, including tax and service charges but not including breakfast:
Ⓛ under L100,000
ⓁⓁ L100 – 200,000
ⓁⓁⓁ L200 – 300,000
ⓁⓁⓁⓁ L300 – 400,000
ⓁⓁⓁⓁⓁ over L400,000.

RESTAURANT
A restaurant within the hotel sometimes reserved for residents.

SWIMMING POOL
Hotel swimming pools are usually quite small and are outdoors unless otherwise stated.

GARDEN OR TERRACE
A garden, courtyard or terrace belonging to the hotel, often providing tables for eating outside.

CREDIT CARDS
The major credit cards Visa, MasterCard (Access) and American Express are accepted in hotels with the credit card symbol.

		Number of Rooms	Restaurant	Swimming Pool	Garden or Terrace
SAN MARCO: *San Stefano* ⓁⓁⓁ Campo Santo Stefano, 2957. **Map** 6 F3. ☎ 041-520 01 66. **FAX** 041-522 44 60. This tall narrow hotel has good views over the Santo Stefano quarter. Traditional furnishings, but some rooms are cramped. Shut in winter. 🖨 TV 🌳		11			
SAN MARCO: *Bauer Grünwald and Grand* ⓁⓁⓁⓁⓁ Campo San Moisè, 1459. **Map** 8 D2. ☎ 041-520 70 22. **FAX** 041-520 75 57. A luxury hotel set in a beautifully-restored 13th-century palazzo overlooking the Grand Canal. Some rooms are in a less attractive modern wing. 🖨 🌳		210	■		
SAN MARCO: *Gritti Palace* ⓁⓁⓁⓁⓁ Santa Maria del Giglio, 2467. **Map** 6 F3. ☎ 041-79 46 11. **FAX** 520 09 42. An elegant, sumptuous hotel housed in the 15th-century palazzo that once belonged to the Gritti family. Rooms are superb and it is charmingly old-fashioned. Ernest Hemingway stayed here while in Venice. 🖨 TV 🌳		93	■		■
SAN MARCO: *Monaco and Grand Canal* ⓁⓁⓁⓁⓁ Calle Vallaresso, 1325. **Map** 7 B3. ☎ 041-520 02 11. **FAX** 041-520 05 01. An elegant hotel in an 18th-century palazzo overlooking the Grand Canal. Public rooms are intimate and bedrooms are beautifully decorated. 🖨 TV 🌳		74	■		■
SAN POLO: *Alex* Ⓛ Rio Terrà Frari, 2606. **Map** 6 E1. ☎ 041-523 13 41. A slightly scruffy family-run hotel that does, however, offer excellent value for its price and is located in a good position near the Frari. 🖨		12			
SAN POLO: *Hotel Marconi* ⓁⓁⓁ Riva del Vin, 729. **Map** 7 A1. ☎ 041-522 20 68. **FAX** 041-522 97 00. A refurbished 16th-century palazzo with opulently Venetian reception rooms. Bedrooms are plainer, but some have views of the Grand Canal. 🖨 TV ▤ 🌳		26			
SANTA CROCE: *Falier* ⓁⓁ Salizzada San Pantalon, 130. **Map** 5 C1. ☎ 041-522 88 82. **FAX** 041-71 08 82. On the edge of the student district, the reasonably priced Falier is away from the main hotel area of Venice. It has recently been restored. 🖨 🌳		19			
SANTA CROCE: *Al Sole* ⓁⓁⓁ Fondamenta Minotta, 136. **Map** 5 C1. ☎ 041-71 08 44. **FAX** 041-71 43 98. This 14th-century building is conveniently situated in a quiet corner near the station. It has pleasant rooms and a marble-floored reception area. 🖨 ▤ 🌳		80	■		■
TORCELLO: *Locanda Cipriani* ⓁⓁⓁⓁⓁ Piazza Santa Fosca 29. ☎ 041-73 01 50. **FAX** 041-73 54 33. A perfect place to stay away from the crowds. Be sure to sample the cuisine, especially the fish; meals are served in the garden or gallery. The impeccable service and comfort make it essential that you book in advance. 🖨 TV ▤ 🌳		5	■		■

THE VENETO AND FRIULI

		Number of Rooms	Restaurant	Swimming Pool	Garden or Terrace
BARDOLINO: *Kriss International* ⓁⓁ Lungolago Cipriani 3, 37011. ☎ 045-621 24 33. **FAX** 045-721 02 42. A modern hotel, attractively placed on a promontory jutting into the lake with balconies in every room. Train travellers are met at the station. 🖨 TV ▤ 🌳 P		33	■		■
BASSANO DEL GRAPPA: *Victoria* Ⓛ Viale Diaz 33, 36061. ☎ 0424-50 36 20. **FAX** 0424-50 31 30. Just outside the city walls, this pleasant hotel has comfortable rooms. It is a busy hotel that can be noisy but is well placed for sightseeing. 🖨 TV P		23			■
BASSANO DEL GRAPPA: *Belvedere* ⓁⓁ Piazzale G Giardino 14, 36061. ☎ 0424-52 98 45. **FAX** 0424-52 98 49. Set on one of Bassano's main squares, this busy hotel is the best equipped in the area. Rooms are comfortable (if noisy) and service is good. 🖨 TV 🌳 P		91	■		

BELLUNO: *Astor* — Ⓛ Ⓛ — 32
Piazza dei Martiri 26e, 32100. **(** 0437-94 20 94. **FAX** 0437-94 24 93.
Centrally situated, this hotel is popular with skiers in winter. The rooms are
well-designed and comfortable, offering good value for money. 🖼 TV 🗎

CHIOGGIA: *Grande Italia* — Ⓛ — 43
Piazza Vigo 1, 30015. **(** 041-40 05 15. **FAX** 041-40 05 15.
This unpretentious old-fashioned hotel, at the head of the main street, has
comfortable rooms and is well-situated for boats running to Venice. 🖼 🗎 P

CIVIDALE DEL FRIULI: *Locanda al Castello* — Ⓛ — 10
Via del Castello 20, 33043. **(** 0432-73 32 42. **FAX** 0432-70 09 01.
An attractive historic building, this was once a castle and a Jesuit monastery
before becoming a welcoming friendly hotel with wonderful views. 🖼 TV 🗎

CONEGLIANO: *Canon d'Oro* — Ⓛ Ⓛ — 35
Via XX Settembre 129, 31015. **(** 0438-342 46. **FAX** 0438-342 46.
On the main street of the town, this hotel offers solid comfort and a warm
welcome. Relax in the lovely garden with a glass of Prosecco. 🖼 TV 🗎 🗎 P

CORTINA D'AMPEZZO: *Corona* — Ⓛ Ⓛ Ⓛ — 38
Via Val di Sotto 12, 32043. **(** 0436-32 51. **FAX** 0436-86 73 39.
One of Cortina's stylish hotels ideal for both winter and summer. The rooms
are pretty and comfortable and public areas are pleasantly furnished. 🖼 TV 🗎

CORTINA D'AMPEZZO: *Menardi* — Ⓛ Ⓛ Ⓛ — 53
Via Majon 110, 32043. **(** 0436-24 00. **FAX** 0436-86 21 83.
The Menardi family have run this hotel since 1900. Originally a farmhouse, it
is furnished with antiques and has a welcoming atmosphere. 🖼 TV 🗎

GARDA: *Biseti* — Ⓛ Ⓛ Ⓛ — 90
Corso Italia 34, 37016. **(** 045-725 57 66. **FAX** 045-725 59 27.
Well-placed near the town centre and the lake. Many rooms in this modern
holiday hotel have their own balcony and there is a private beach. 🖼 🗎 P

GARDA: *Locanda San Vigilio* — Ⓛ Ⓛ Ⓛ Ⓛ — 7
San Vigilio, 37016. **(** 045-725 66 88. **FAX** 045-725 65 51.
One of the loveliest, most exclusive hotels on Lake Garda. Comfort and
service live up to all expectations and there is a private beach. 🖼 TV 🗎 P

GRADO: *Grand Hotel Astoria* — Ⓛ Ⓛ Ⓛ — 121
Largo San Grisogono 2, 34073. **(** 0431-835 50. **FAX** 0431-833 55.
The Astoria is a modern hotel with good facilities including baby-sitting, a
leisure club and indoor pool. Half the rooms are mini-suites. 🖼 TV 🗎 🗎 P

MALCESINE: *Excelsior Bay* — Ⓛ Ⓛ — 64
Lungolago 13, 37018. **(** 045-740 03 80. **FAX** 045-740 16 75.
The Excelsior offers good-value rates in this hotel-rich town. It is situated
next to the lake and is close to all the town's amenities. 🖼 🗎 P

MALCESINE: *Sailing Center Hotel* — Ⓛ Ⓛ Ⓛ — 32
Località Molini Campagnola 3, 37018. **(** 045-740 00 55. **FAX** 045-740 03 92.
A modern hotel just outside town, away from the crowds. Rooms are cool
and pleasant, and there is a tennis court and private beach. 🖼 TV P

PADUA: *Donatello* — Ⓛ Ⓛ — 49
Via del Santo 102, 35123. **(** 049-875 06 34. **FAX** 049-875 08 29.
A modern hotel in an old building with big comfortable bedrooms, named after
the sculptor of the equestrian statue of Gattamelata in the square. 🖼 TV 🗎 P

PADUA: *Grande Italia* — Ⓛ Ⓛ — 64
Corso del Popolo 81, 35160. **(** 049-65 08 77. **FAX** 049-875 08 50.
Close to the city's main sights, the rooms are slightly shabby but comfortable
and offer good value. The rooms towards the back are quieter. 🖼 🗎

PADUA: *Leon Bianco* — Ⓛ Ⓛ — 22
Piazzetta Pedrocchi 12, 35160. **(** 049-875 08 14. **FAX** 049-875 61 84.
A centrally situated hotel overlooking the Caffè Pedrocchi. Rooms are small
but staff are friendly and welcoming. Book well in advance. 🖼 TV 🗎 P

PADUA: *Augustus Terme* — Ⓛ Ⓛ Ⓛ — 132
Viale Stazione 150, Montegrotto Terme 35036. **(** 049-79 32 00. **FAX** 049-79 35 18.
One of the best hotels at Montegrotto Terme, this is a big, functional and
comfortable hotel. It has tennis courts and hot thermal springs. 🖼 TV 🗎 P

Price categories for a standard double room for one night, including tax and service charges but not including breakfast:
Ⓛ under L100,000
ⓁⓁ L100–200,000
ⓁⓁⓁ L200–300,000
ⓁⓁⓁⓁ L300–400,000
ⓁⓁⓁⓁⓁ over L400,000.

RESTAURANT
A restaurant within the hotel sometimes reserved for residents.
SWIMMING POOL
Hotel swimming pools are usually quite small and are outdoors unless otherwise stated.
GARDEN OR TERRACE
A garden, courtyard or terrace belonging to the hotel, often providing tables for eating outside.
CREDIT CARDS
The major credit cards Visa, MasterCard (Access) and American Express are accepted in hotels with the credit card symbol.

		NUMBER OF ROOMS	RESTAURANT	SWIMMING POOL	GARDEN OR TERRACE
PESCHIERA DEL GARDA: *Peschiera* Ⓛ		30	■	●	■
Via Parini 4, 37010. █ *045-755 05 26.* **FAX** *045-755 04 44.* This modern hotel, built in the local architectural style, is set in its own grounds, with lofty, cool bedrooms. It is five minutes from the A4 motorway, or the friendly staff will collect train travellers from the station. �car 🅟					
PORDENONE: *Palace Hotel Moderno* ⓁⓁ		111	■		
Viale Martelli 1, 33170. █ *0434-282 15.* **FAX** *0434-52 03 15.* A comfortable, recently refurbished traditional hotel with a good range of facilities in all bedrooms. It is centrally located close to the station. The restaurant specializes in traditional cuisine, particularly fish dishes. 🚗 📺 🅟					
SAN FLORIANO DEL COLLIO: *Romantik Golf Hotel* ⓁⓁⓁ		15		●	■
Via Oslavia 2, 34070. █ *0481-88 40 51.* **FAX** *0481-88 40 52.* A lovely 18th-century building furnished with antiques and set in its own well-kept grounds with a nine-hole golf course and tennis courts. 🚗 📺 🅟					
TORRI DEL BENACO: *Hotel Gardesana* ⓁⓁ		34	■		■
Piazza Calderini 20, 37010. █ *045-722 54 11.* **FAX** *045-722 57 71.* The 15th-century harbourmaster's house overlooking Lake Garda has been converted into a friendly, comfortable hotel. Ask for a room on the third floor; they are quieter and have wonderful views of the lake. 🚗 📺 ▤ 🅟					
TREVISO: *Ca' del Galletto* ⓁⓁⓁ		58	■		■
Via Santa Bona Vecchia 30, 31100. █ *0422-43 25 50.* **FAX** *0422-43 25 10.* Set in its own grounds and only ten minutes' walk from the city walls, this efficiently-run hotel has good-sized modern bedrooms. 🚗 🅟					
TRIESTE: *Jolly* ⓁⓁⓁ		174	■		
Corso Cavour 7, 34132. █ *040-760 00 55.* **FAX** *040-36 26 99.* A modern hotel aiming at business as well as holiday clientele. The well-equipped rooms are spacious if slightly impersonally decorated. 🚗 🅟					
TRIESTE: *Hotel Duchi d'Aosta* ⓁⓁⓁⓁ		48	■		
Piazza Unità d'Italia 2, 34121. █ *040-760 00 11.* **FAX** *040-36 60 92.* A palace from a bygone era, this hotel has enormous rooms fitted with modern conveniences. It is set in the old part of town, near the fort. 🚗 📺 ▤					
UDINE: *Quo Vadis* Ⓛ		26			■
Piazzale Cella 28, 33100. █ *0432-210 91.* **FAX** *0432-210 92.* A comfortable hotel on a tranquil tree-lined street. The decor is mixed (some rooms have rather fussy wallpaper) but there are plenty of plants. 🚗 📺 🅟					
VERONA: *Giulietta e Romeo* ⓁⓁ		29			
Vicolo Tre Marchetti 3, 37121. █ *045-800 35 54.* **FAX** *045-801 08 62.* Situated in a quiet street just behind the Arena, the bedrooms are spacious and comfortable with modern furnishings. Breakfast is served in the bar. 🚗 ▤					
VERONA: *Il Torcolo* ⓁⓁⓁ		19			■
Vicolo Listone 3, 37121. █ *045-800 75 12.* **FAX** *045-800 40 58.* This friendly hotel is close to the Arena and is popular during the opera season. It has a breakfast terrace, and some pretty and traditional rooms. 🚗 📺					
VERONA: *Colomba d'Oro* ⓁⓁⓁ		29			
Via Carlo Cattaneo 10, 37121. █ *045-59 53 00.* **FAX** *045-59 49 74.* An old stone building in a quiet pedestrian street near the Arena. Rooms are rather plain and functional but it is conveniently placed. 🚗 📺 ▤ 🅟					
VERONA: *Due Torri Hotel Baglioni* ⓁⓁⓁⓁⓁ		91	■		
Piazza Sant'Anastasia 4, 37121. █ *045-59 50 44.* **FAX** *045-800 41 30.* Right in the heart of medieval Verona, this is one of Italy's most eccentric hotels. The huge bedrooms are each decorated and furnished in the style of a different era. Many of the walls and ceilings are frescoed. 🚗 📺 🅟					

VICENZA: *Casa San Raffaele*   Ⓛ | 24
Viale X Giugno 10, 36100. ☎ *0444-54 57 67.* **FAX** *0444-54 22 59.*
A tranquil hotel with excellent views set on the slopes of Monte Berico. The
comfortable rooms make this one of the best budget choices in the area. 🛏

VICENZA: *Castello*   ⓁⓁ | 18
Contrà Piazza del Castello 24, 36100. ☎ *0444-32 35 85.* **FAX** *0444-32 35 83.*
Very near the cathedral, this is also an excellent choice for train
travellers. Rooms are pleasant and the location is fairly quiet. 🛏 🗐

VICENZA: *Campo Marzo*   ⓁⓁⓁ | 35
Via Roma 21, 36100. ☎ *0444-54 57 00.* **FAX** *0444-320 49.*
A stylish hotel with good facilities near the city centre. Bedrooms are
large, light and well furnished, and the location is peaceful. 🛏 📺 🗐 🅿

TRENTINO - ALTO ADIGE

BOLZANO (BOZEN): *Asterix*   ⓁⓁ | 24
Piazza Mazzini 35, 39100. ☎ *0471-27 33 01.* **FAX** *0471-26 00 21.*
Set in the newer part of central Bolzano, the Asterix is a simple but quite
comfortable town hotel which is excellent value for money. 🛏 📺 🗐 🅿

BOLZANO (BOZEN): *Luna-Mondschein*   ⓁⓁ | 73
Via Piave 15, 39100. ☎ *0471-97 56 42.* **FAX** *0471-97 55 77.*
One of the oldest hotels in Bolzano, the Luna-Mondschein dates from 1798,
although the buildings have been much added to since then. It is set near the
town centre with a pleasant garden allowing for summer dining. 🛏 🗐 🅿

BOLZANO (BOZEN): *Castel Guncina*   ⓁⓁⓁ | 18
Via Miramonti 9, Guncina 39100. ☎ *0471-28 57 42.* **FAX** *0471-26 63 45.*
Set in its own attractive grounds on a hill surrounded by trees and vineyards.
Some bedrooms have wonderful views, others are rather small. 🛏 📺 🗐 🅿

BRESSANONE (BRIXEN): *Dominik*   ⓁⓁⓁ | 29
Via Terzo di Sotto 13, 39042. ☎ *0472-83 01 44.* **FAX** *0472-83 65 54.*
One of the luxurious Relais et Châteaux group, the Dominik is attractively
furnished with antiques, although the buildings themselves date from the 1970s.
It is peacefully set near the River Rienza and the Rapp gardens. 🛏 📺 🗐 🅿

BRESSANONE (BRIXEN): *Elefante*   ⓁⓁⓁ | 44
Via Rio Bianco 4, 39042. ☎ *0472-83 27 50.* **FAX** *0472-83 65 79.*
A smart, traditional hotel that dates from the 16th century and, while offering
all modern comforts, has retained a strong historical atmosphere. 🛏 📺 🗐 🅿

BRUNICO (BRUNECK): *Andreas Hofer*   ⓁⓁ | 54
Via Campo Tures 1, 39031. ☎ *0474-55 14 69.* **FAX** *0474-55 12 83.*
A welcoming family-run chalet hotel which has been fitted out with wood
panelling and wooden Alpine-style furniture. The Andreas Hofer is quietly
set in its own garden and some of the rooms have balconies. 🛏 📺 🗐 🅿

CALDARO (KALTERN): *Leuchtenburg*   ⓁⓁ | 19
Campi al Lago 100, 39052. ☎ *0471-96 00 93.* **FAX** *0471-96 00 93.*
Set in a beautiful 16th-century farmhouse surrounded by vineyards. Some of
the simple bedrooms are furnished with traditional painted furniture. 🛏 🅿

CANAZEI: *Park Hotel Faloria*   ⓁⓁ | 36
Via Pareda 103, 38032. ☎ *0462-611 18.* **FAX** *0462-627 15.*
Surrounded by its own well-kept gardens, this friendly hotel is managed by its
owners. Some bedrooms have balconies overlooking the grounds. 🛏 📺 🗐 🅿

CASTELROTTO (KASTELRUTH): *Cavallino d'Oro*   ⓁⓁ | 23
Piazza Kraus, 39040. ☎ *0471-70 63 37.* **FAX** *0471-70 71 72.*
This charming hotel is set in a pretty village 26 km (16 miles) from Bolzano,
where traditional costume is still worn. The rooms are well-kept. 🛏 📺 🗐 🅿

CAVALESE: *Fiemme.*   ⓁⓁ | 15
Via Cavazzal 27, 38033. ☎ *0462-34 17 20.* **FAX** *0462-23 11 51.*
A modern hotel in a peaceful setting with good views, conveniently close
to both the town centre and the station. It also has a sauna. 🛏 🗐 🅿

COLFOSCO: *Cappella*   ⓁⓁⓁ | 40
Strada Pecei 17, 39030. ☎ *0471-83 61 83.* **FAX** *0471-83 65 61.*
A chalet in the Dolomites, opened by the present owner's grandfather. The
pioneer spirit lives on and the hotel has now opened an art gallery. 🛏 📺 🗐 🅿

| | | **Price categories** info | **NUMBER OF ROOMS** | **RESTAURANT** | **SWIMMING POOL** | **GARDEN OR TERRACE** |

Price categories for a standard double room for one night, including tax and service charges but not including breakfast:
Ⓛ under L100,000
ⓁⓁ L100–200,000
ⓁⓁⓁ L200–300,000
ⓁⓁⓁⓁ L300–400,000
ⓁⓁⓁⓁⓁ over L400,000

RESTAURANT
A restaurant within the hotel sometimes reserved for residents.
SWIMMING POOL
Hotel swimming pools are usually quite small and are outdoors unless otherwise stated.
GARDEN OR TERRACE
A garden, courtyard or terrace belonging to the hotel, often providing tables for eating outside.
CREDIT CARDS
The major credit cards Visa, MasterCard (Access) and American Express are accepted in hotels with the credit card symbol.

	Price	Number of Rooms	Restaurant	Swimming Pool	Garden or Terrace
FIE ALLO SCILIAR: *Turm* Piazza della Chiesa 9, 39050. ☎ 0471-72 50 14. FAX 0471-72 54 74. The owner's art collection, displayed on the hotel walls, is one of the main attractions at this friendly Alpine hotel with cosy bars and two pools.	ⓁⓁⓁ	23	▦	●	▦
MADONNA DI CAMPIGLIO: *Grifone* Via Vallesinella 7, 38084. ☎ 0465-420 02. FAX 0465-405 40. A modern wooden chalet set near the lake in the Madonna di Campiglio ski resort. Although rather ordinarily decorated and furnished, it offers an excellent range of facilities ideal for winter sports holidays.	ⓁⓁⓁ	38	▦		▦
MALLES VENOSTA (MALS IM VINSCHGAU): *Garberhof* Via Nazionale 25, 39024. ☎ 0473-83 13 99. FAX 0473-83 19 50. A modern chalet-style hotel with extensive panoramic terraces. It is surrounded by meadows and has a good range of sports and leisure facilities.	ⓁⓁ	29	▦	●	▦
MERANO (MERAN): *Castel Rundegg* Via Scena 2, 39012. ☎ 0473-23 41 00. FAX 0473-23 72 00. A fairy-tale whitewashed castle, parts of which date from the 12th century, set in pretty gardens. Inside, the romantic atmosphere continues with traditional wood furniture, beamed ceilings and parquet floors.	ⓁⓁⓁ	30	▦	●	▦
MERANO (MERAN): *Castel Schloss Labers* Via Labers 25, 39012. ☎ 0473-23 44 84. FAX 0473-23 41 46. A romantic castle is the setting for this high-class country hotel. There are wonderful views over the surrounding vineyards and woods.	ⓁⓁⓁ	32	▦	●	▦
MERANO (MERAN): *Der Punthof* Via Steinach 25, 39022. ☎ 0473-44 85 53. FAX 0473-44 99 19. Set in peaceful and attractive gardens, this farmhouse dates back to the Middle Ages. Inside, wooden floors and ceilings match the Alpine furniture.	ⓁⓁⓁ	12	▦	●	▦
MERANO (MERAN): *Villa Mozart* Via San Marco 26, 39012. ☎ 0473-23 06 30. FAX 0473-21 13 55. A charming, pagoda-like villa houses this Art Nouveau hotel where everything (even the cutlery) matches. A delightfully fresh and peaceful place.	ⓁⓁⓁ	9	▦	●	▦
ORTISEI (SANKT ULRICH): *Hell* Via Promenade 3, 39046. ☎ 0471-79 67 85. FAX 0471-79 81 96. A pleasant hotel that is open for the skiing season and during the summer. It has a sauna and a gym, and is set in a peaceful part of town.	ⓁⓁⓁ	25	▦		▦
PERGINE VALSUGANA: *Castel Pergine* Via al Castello 10, 38057. ☎ 0461-53 11 58. FAX 0461-53 11 58. Set in a 13th-century castle with exquisite views over the countryside. The interior is simply decorated and has traditional wooden furnishings.	ⓁⓁ	21	▦		▦
RASUN ANTERSELVA (RASEN ANTHOLZ): *Ansitz Heufler* Rasun di Sopra 37, 39030. ☎ 0474-49 62 88. FAX 0474-49 81 99. In the historic centre of town close to the main monuments, this beautifully decorated 16th-century castle has large rooms and a pleasant garden.	ⓁⓁ	8	▦		▦
RIVA DEL GARDA: *Europa* Piazza Catena 9, 38066. ☎ 0464-55 54 33. FAX 0464-52 17 77. A turn-of-the-century colour-washed building right next to the lake and near the bustling town centre. Many of the simply furnished bedrooms have views over the lake. Guests may be expected to take half-board in the summer.	ⓁⓁ	63	▦		
RIVA DEL GARDA: *Lido Palace* Viale Carducci 10, 38066. ☎ 0464-55 26 64. FAX 0464-55 19 57. An immaculately run hotel in a spacious country villa set in its own well-kept grounds on the outskirts of Riva del Garda. Rooms on the first floor are particularly spacious and the leisure facilities include a tennis court.	ⓁⓁⓁ	63	▦	●	▦

SAN PAOLO (ST PAULS): *Schloss Korb* ⓁⓁ | 65
Via Castel d'Appiano 5, Missiano 39050. 📞 0471-63 60 00. FAX 0471-63 60 33.
Partly set in a 13th-century castle, this simply decorated and prettily furnished
hotel also has a more modern annexe, and tennis courts for residents. ⌂ TV P

TIRES (TIERS): *Stefaner* ⓁⓁ | 15
San Cipriano 88d, 39050. 📞 0471-64 21 75. FAX 0471-64 21 75.
A friendly chalet hotel on the edge of the western Dolomites. Bedrooms are
light, spacious and simple. Balconies are decked with flowers. ⌂ P

TRENTO: *Accademia* ⓁⓁⓁ | 43
Vicolo Colico 4–6, 38100. 📞 0461-23 36 00. FAX 0461-23 01 74.
Set in a well-restored medieval building right in the historic centre of
Trento. The interior of this relaxing hotel, although essentially modern,
retains many original features. The restaurant is also very good. ⌂ TV 🖿

VIPITENO (STERZING): *Aquila Nera* ⓁⓁ | 36
Piazza Città 1, 39049. 📞 0472-76 40 64. FAX 0472-76 65 22.
A comfortable hotel for winter sports or summer walking holidays with many
leisure facilities including a sauna, gym and a famous restaurant. ⌂ TV 🖿 P

LOMBARDY

BELLAGIO: *La Pergola* Ⓛ | 13
Piazza del Porto 4, 22021. 📞 031-95 02 63.
An attractive hotel tucked away to the south of Lake Como, charmingly
furnished in an old-fashioned style with a rustic and friendly atmosphere. 🖿

BELLAGIO: *Florence* ⓁⓁ | 38
Piazza Mazzini 46, 22021. 📞 031-95 03 42. FAX 031-95 17 22.
This friendly hotel has a bar, and its rooms overlook the lively port of Lake
Como. The hotel has plenty of charm, and tastefully furnished rooms. ⌂ TV 🖿

BERGAMO: *Città dei Mille* ⓁⓁ | 40
Via Autostrada 3c, 24126. 📞 035-31 74 00. FAX 035-31 73 85.
Well placed for motorway travellers from Milan, the Città dei Mille is an
unexceptional but satisfactory hotel on the outskirts of Bergamo. ⌂ TV 🖿 P

BRESCIA: *Park Hotel Ca' Noa* ⓁⓁ | 80
Via Tiumplina 66, 25127. 📞 030-39 87 64. FAX 030-39 87 64.
A beautiful modern hotel set in its own grounds with tasteful and bright
decor, large, spacious public rooms and excellent service. ⌂ TV 🖿 P

BORMIO: *Palace* ⓁⓁⓁ | 80
Via Milano 54, 23032. 📞 0342-90 31 31. FAX 0342-90 33 66.
A recently-built hotel with a wide range of business and leisure facilities that
include a gym, sunbeds, a discotheque and a piano bar. ⌂ TV 🖿 P

CAPRIATE SAN GERVASIO: *Vigneto* ⓁⓁ | 12
Via del Porto 5, 24042. 📞 02-90 93 93 51. FAX 02-909 01 79.
A pleasant villa hotel set in its own grounds; in summer dinner is served on
the riverside terrace. A convenient stopover near the motorway. ⌂ TV 🖿 P

CERVESINA: *Castello di San Gaudenzio* ⓁⓁⓁ | 45
Via Mulino 1, Frazione San Gaudenzio 27050. 📞 0383-33 31. FAX 0383-33 34 09.
A wonderful, almost kitsch hotel in a building with parts dating from the
15th century. Furnishings are from a variety of periods; some are French
18th century, others are heavier and more 16th-century baronial. ⌂ TV 🖿 P

COLOGNE FRANCIACORTA: *Cappuccini* ⓁⓁⓁ | 13
Via Cappuccini 54, 25033. 📞 030-715 72 54. FAX 030-715 72 57.
A converted convent (built in 1569), which has been restored. Long hallways
and white rooms create a pleasant monastic atmosphere. ⌂ TV 🖿 🖿

COMO: *Villa Semplicitas* ⓁⓁ | 14
San Fedele d'Intelvi, 22010. 📞 031-83 11 32.
A homely hotel with lots of character and pleasant rooms. Set in a charming
19th-century villa with wonderful views of the lakes and mountains. ⌂ P

CREMONA: *Continental* ⓁⓁ | 57
Piazza della Libertà 26, 26100. 📞 0372-43 41 41. FAX 0372-43 41 41.
This luxurious hotel has been owned and run by the Ghiraldi family since 1920
and is excellently situated for Cremona's main places of interest. Rooms are
comfortable and the restaurant is one of the best in the city. ⌂ TV 🖿 🖿 P

<table>
<tr><td colspan="2">

Price categories for a standard double room for one night, including tax and service charges but not including breakfast:
Ⓛ under L100,000
ⓁⓁ L100 – 200,000
ⓁⓁⓁ L200 – 300,000
ⓁⓁⓁⓁ L300 – 400,000
ⓁⓁⓁⓁⓁ over L400,000.

</td></tr>
</table>

RESTAURANT
A restaurant within the hotel sometimes reserved for residents.

SWIMMING POOL
Hotel swimming pools are usually quite small and are outdoors unless otherwise stated.

GARDEN OR TERRACE
A garden, courtyard or terrace belonging to the hotel, often providing tables for eating outside.

CREDIT CARDS
The major credit cards Visa, MasterCard (Access) and American Express are accepted in hotels with the credit card symbol.

	Price	NUMBER OF ROOMS	RESTAURANT	SWIMMING POOL	GARDEN OR TERRACE
CREMONA: *Duomo* Via Gonfalonieri 13, 26100. 〖 0372-352 42. FAX 0372-45 83 92. Unsurprisingly, given its name, this hotel is right next to the cathedral in Cremona's historic centre. Some of the rooms have good views. 🛏 📺 🍽 🖼	ⓁⓁ	23			
DESENZANO DEL GARDA: *Piroscafo* Via Porto Vecchio 11, 25015. 〖 030-914 11 28. FAX 030-991 25 86. An attractive old hotel, well placed for all the town's amenities. Bedrooms at the front have balconies overlooking the busy old port. 🛏 📺 🖼	Ⓛ	32	■		
GARDONE RIVIERA: *Villa Fiordaliso* Corso Zanardelli 132, 25083. 〖 0365-201 58. FAX 0365-29 00 11. This beautiful, eclectic villa overlooking Lake Garda has comfortable rooms. It was once the private residence of Clara Petacci, Mussolini's lover. 🛏 🖼 P	ⓁⓁⓁ	6	■		■
GARDONE RIVIERA: *Villa Del Sogno* Via Zanardelli 107, 25083. 〖 0365-29 01 81. FAX 0365-29 02 30. A turn-of-the-century villa set in beautiful gardens and furnished with antiques of various periods. All rooms are spacious and light and it's a good choice for those seeking luxurious tranquillity. 🛏 📺 🖼 P	ⓁⓁⓁⓁ	33	■	●	■
GARGNANO: *Baia d'Oro* Via Gamberera 13, 25084. 〖 0365-711 71. FAX 0365-725 68. Right on the shore of Lake Garda, this is a friendly family-run hotel. Rooms are bright, welcoming and pretty and the restaurant specializes in fish. 🛏 🖼 P	ⓁⓁ	12	■		■
LIMONE SUL GARDA: *Capo Reamol* Via IV Novembre 92, 25010. 〖 0365-95 40 40. FAX 0365-95 42 62. A stunning location on the edge of the lake below the main road. Rooms are spacious and all have their own terrace. Sports and leisure facilities are excellent for families and include private beach, gym and jacuzzi. 🛏 📺 🖼 P	ⓁⓁⓁⓁ	50	■	●	■
LIVIGNO: *Camana Veglia* Via Ostaria 107, 23030. 〖 0342-99 63 10. FAX 0342-97 04 38. Set in a typical chalet that dates from the beginning of the century. The interior is wood-panelled and furnished in Alpine style. 🛏 📺 🖼 P	Ⓛ	15	■		■
MANTOVA: *Broletto* Via Accademia 1, 46100. 〖 0376-32 67 84. FAX 0376-22 12 97. A small, immaculate hotel in a renovated 16th-century town house. Rooms are bright with attractive modern furnishings and polished marble floors. 🛏 📺 🖼	ⓁⓁ	16			
MANTOVA: *San Lorenzo* Piazza Concordia 14, 46100. 〖 0376-22 05 00. FAX 0376-32 71 94. A modern hotel in the centre of Mantova with excellent views from the terrace. Rooms are sumptuous and some have antique furniture. 🛏 📺 🖼 P	ⓁⓁⓁ	41			■
MILAN: *Antica Locanda Solferino* Via Castelfidardo 2, 20121. 〖 02-657 01 29. FAX 02-657 13 61. Excellent value at this surprisingly rustic old inn. Bedrooms are small but nicely decorated with old furniture, paintings and flowery wallpaper. There is also an informal bistro next door to the hotel. Book in advance. 🛏 📺 🖼	ⓁⓁ	11			
MILAN: *London* Via Rovello 3, 20121. 〖 02-72 02 01 66. FAX 02-805 70 37. Half of the rooms in this pleasant modern hotel look out over Via Rovello which, in spite of being in the centre of Milan, is relatively quiet. 📺 🖼	ⓁⓁ	29			
MILAN: *Cavour* Via Fatebenefratelli 21, 20121. 〖 02-657 20 51. FAX 02-659 22 63. Very well placed for Milan's main sights, this modern city hotel has good-sized, comfortable rooms and unobtrusive furnishings. The management are friendly and there is a pleasant bar and an attractive spiral staircase. 🛏 📺 🖼 P	ⓁⓁⓁ	113	■		

MILAN: *Zurigo* ⓁⓁⓁ   42
Corso Italia 11a, 20122. 02-72 02 22 60. FAX 02-72 00 00 13.
A modern, innovative hotel whose central location appeals to both business and holiday travellers. Guests can borrow bicycles for sightseeing. 🖫 TV 🗐 P

MILAN: *Pierre Milano* ⓁⓁⓁⓁ   49
Via de Amicis 32, 20123. 02-72 00 05 81. FAX 02-805 21 57.
A very luxurious hotel that blends traditional and modern styles in its interior design and furnishings. The restaurant is one of the best in Milan. 🖫 TV 🗐 P

PAVIA: *Moderno* ⓁⓁ   54
Viale Vittorio Emanuele 41, 27100. 0382-30 34 01. FAX 0382-252 25.
Set in a restored palazzo, the Moderno is a calm, well-run establishment with a welcoming atmosphere and comfortable rooms. 🖫 TV 🗐 P

RANCO: *Sole* ⓁⓁⓁ   8
Piazza Venezia 5, 21020. 0331-97 65 07. FAX 0331-97 66 20.
The restaurant is the highlight of the Sole which has been in the same family for five generations. The few rooms are in newly built suites and some have lovely views over Lake Maggiore (these do cost slightly more). 🖫 TV 🗐 P

RIVA DI SOLTO: *Miranda da Oreste* Ⓛ   22
Via Cornello 8, 24060. 035-98 60 21. FAX 035-98 60 21.
A family-run pensione offering simple, modern accommodation. The restaurant serves good local cuisine on a terrace with views of Lake Iseo. 🖫 🗐 P

SABBIONETA: *Al Duca* Ⓛ   10
Via della Stamperia 18, 46018. 0375-524 74. FAX 0375-524 74.
A plain but comfortable family-run pensione in a much-converted Renaissance palazzo, located in the historic centre. Prices are very reasonable. 🖫 🗐

SALÒ: *Romantik Hotel Laurin* ⓁⓁⓁ   38
Viale Landi 9, 25087. 0365-220 22. FAX 0365-223 82.
A family hotel in a pretty lakeside villa on a sheltered bay. Spacious bedrooms and a happy atmosphere, as well as a beach and tennis courts. 🖫 🗐

SIRMIONE SUL GARDA: *Villa Cortine Palace Hotel* ⓁⓁⓁⓁ   55
Via Grotte 6, 25019. 030-91 60 21. FAX 030-91 63 90.
Huge, frescoed rooms furnished with antiques in this luxurious and tranquil hotel set in a Classical villa. Excellent service and comfort. 🖫 TV 🗐 P

TREMEZZO: *San Giorgio* ⓁⓁ   26
Via Regina 81, Località Lenno 22016. 0344-404 15. FAX 0344-415 91.
Set in its own large garden on the shores of Lake Como, the San Giorgio is a traditional lakeside hotel with elegant terraces and public rooms. Ask for a room with a balcony for wonderful views of the lake. 🖫 🗐 P

VALSOLDA: *Stella d'Italia* ⓁⓁ   35
Piazza Roma 1, San Mamete 22010. 0344-681 39. FAX 0344-687 29.
An exquisite setting with a shady terrace right on the edge of Lake Lugano. Rooms have lake views and are prettily decorated with floral prints and bright bedspreads. Guests can use the lakeside lido and the hotel library. 🖫 🗐 P

VARENNA: *Hotel du Lac* ⓁⓁⓁ   18
Via del Prestino 4, 22050. 0341-83 02 38. FAX 0341-83 10 81.
There are wonderful views from this delightfully peaceful hotel overlooking Lake Como. Furnishings are simple but comfortable and modern. 🖫 TV 🗐 P

VALLE D'AOSTA AND PIEDMONT

ALESSANDRIA: *Domus* ⓁⓁ   27
Via Castellani 12, 15100. 0131-433 05. FAX 0131-23 20 19.
Very centrally located and close to the station, the Domus is however quiet and peaceful inside. All the rooms have double beds. 🖫 TV 🗐 🗐 P

AOSTA: *Milleluci* ⓁⓁ   12
Località Porossan Roppoz 15, 11100. 0165-23 52 78. FAX 0165-23 52 84.
An old farmhouse, carefully and attractively restored, is the setting for this pleasant hotel. The lounge has a wonderful open fireplace. 🖫 TV 🗐 P

AOSTA: *Valle d'Aosta* ⓁⓁⓁ   104
Corso Ivrea 146, 11100. 0165-418 45. FAX 0165-23 66 60.
Behind a rather forbidding modern façade lurks a very comfortable hotel. Most of the bedrooms have been elegantly restored. 🖫 TV 🗐 P

Price categories for a standard double room for one night, including tax and service charges but not including breakfast: Ⓛ under L100,000 ⓁⓁ L100–200,000 ⓁⓁⓁ L200–300,000 ⓁⓁⓁⓁ L300–400,000 ⓁⓁⓁⓁⓁ over L400,000.	**RESTAURANT** A restaurant within the hotel sometimes reserved for residents. **SWIMMING POOL** Hotel swimming pools are usually quite small and are outdoors unless otherwise stated. **GARDEN OR TERRACE** A garden, courtyard or terrace belonging to the hotel, often providing tables for eating outside. **CREDIT CARDS** The major credit cards Visa, MasterCard (Access) and American Express are accepted in hotels with the credit card symbol.		

	NUMBER OF ROOMS	RESTAURANT	SWIMMING POOL	GARDEN OR TERRACE
ARONA: *Giardino* ⓁⓁ Corso Repubblica 1, 28041. 【 0322-459 94. **FAX** 0322-24 94 01. A friendly, comfortable lakeside hotel. A large terrace offers spectacular views over Lake Maggiore and bedrooms are tastefully furnished. 🖥 TV 🖼	56	■		■
ASTI: *Aleramo* ⓁⓁ Via Emanuele Filiberto 13, 14100. 【 0141-59 56 61. **FAX** 0141-300 39. A slick, modern hotel in the centre of town and close to the station. Rooms have a good range of facilities, including hairdriers and safes. 🖥 TV 🖼 P	42			
ASTI: *Lis* ⓁⓁ Viale Fratelli Roselli 10, 14100. 【 0141-59 50 51. **FAX** 0141-35 38 45. Centrally but peacefully located opposite the town's public gardens and close to the historic centre. Rooms are modern and well-equipped. 🖥 TV 🗐 🖼 P	29			
ASTI: *Salera* ⓁⓁ Via Monsignor Marello 19, 14100. 【 0141-41 01 69. **FAX** 0141-41 03 72. A modern, comfortable hotel well placed for the motorway. Rooms are simply but attractively furnished and all are equipped with mini-bar. 🖥 TV 🗐 🖼 P	50	■		
BREUIL-CERVINIA: *Les Neiges d'Antan* ⓁⓁ Frazione Cret-Perrères, 11021. 【 0166-94 87 75. **FAX** 0166-94 88 52. A delightful mountain chalet hotel attached to one of the best restaurants in the area. Both are run by the friendly and enthusiastic Bich family. Inside it's all clean white walls and original wooden beams. 🖥 TV 🖼 P	28	■		■
BREUIL-CERVINIA: *Hermitage* ⓁⓁⓁⓁ Strada Cristallo, 11021. 【 0166-94 89 98. **FAX** 0166-94 90 32. Those looking for luxury and charm will find it here. This well-equipped modern hotel has bright and flower-filled rooms. 🖥 TV 🖼 P	36	■	●	■
CANNERO RIVIERA: *Cannero* ⓁⓁ Lungo Lago 2, 28051. 【 0323-78 80 46 (Nov–Mar: 0323-78 81 13). **FAX** 0323-78 80 48. The hotel, set in a former monastery, has been in the same family for four generations and, although modernized, it has retained the atmosphere of other times. It also has tennis courts and a good restaurant. 🖥 🖼 P	40	■	●	■
CANNOBIO: *Pironi* ⓁⓁ Via Marconi 35, 28052. 【 0323-706 24. **FAX** 0323-72 31 84. Housed in a 15th-century palazzo in a pedestrianized zone in the historic centre, the hotel retains many original features such as the inner courtyard. Bedrooms are comfortable with views over the lake or old town. 🖥 🖼 P	12			
CHAMPOLUC: *Villa Anna Maria* Ⓛ Via Croues 5, 11020. 【 0125-30 71 28. **FAX** 0125-30 79 84. A simple country hotel in a 1920s chalet-style house with lots of wood panelling. The restaurant offers simple but excellent food. TV 🖼 P	20	■		
COGNE: *Bellevue* ⓁⓁⓁ Rue Grand Paradis, 11012. 【 0165-748 25. **FAX** 0165-74 91 92. This is a beautifully situated hotel surrounded by meadows and with excellent views of the Gran Paradiso. Guests are expected to take half-board. 🖥 🖼 P	33	■	●	■
COURMAYEUR: *La Grange* ⓁⓁ Strada la Brenva 1, Entreves 11013. 【 0165-86 97 33. **FAX** 0165-86 97 44. A restructured barn, which has been in the same family since the 14th century, is the setting for this clean, bright Alpine hotel. Furnishings are new but based on traditional designs, and the atmosphere is cosy and homely. 🖥 TV 🖼 P	23			■
COURMAYEUR: *Palace Bron* ⓁⓁⓁ Via Plan Gorret 41, 11013. 【 0165-84 67 42. **FAX** 0165-84 40 15. An elegant family-run hotel that is furnished in the style of a smart home. Most of the rooms have balconies with wonderful views. 🖥 TV 🖼 P	27	■		■

COURMAYEUR: *Gallia Gran Baita*   Ⓛ Ⓛ Ⓛ | 53
Strada Larzey Courmayeur, 11013. 【 *0165-84 40 40.* FAX *0165-84 48 05.*
A modern, luxury hotel catering to the upmarket skier; it has saunas, a
fitness centre, beauty parlour and free transport to the slopes. 🛏 TV 🏊 P

CUNEO: *Smeraldo*   Ⓛ | 21
Corso Nizza 27, 12100. 【 *0171-69 63 67.* FAX *0171-69 80 76.*
A reasonably priced hotel located on one of the main roads of central Cuneo;
the historic centre is easily reached by bus or on foot. 🛏 TV 🏊 P

DOMODOSSOLA: *Corona*   Ⓛ Ⓛ | 32
Via Marconi 8, 28037. 【 *0324-24 21 14.* FAX *0324-248 42.*
Set in the centre of town, the Corona combines tradition with modern
convenience. The restaurant offers a range of local cuisine. 🛏 TV 🍽 🏊 P

IVREA: *Castello San Giuseppe*   Ⓛ Ⓛ | 17
Località Castello San Giuseppe, 10010. 【 *0125-42 43 70.* FAX *0125-64 12 78.*
Originally a convent, this pretty, peaceful hotel has a lovely garden. The
simple rooms are attractively furnished in traditional style. 🛏 TV 🏊 P

LAKE MAGGIORE: *Verbano*   Ⓛ Ⓛ | 12
Via Ugo Ara 1, Isola dei Pescatori 28049. 【 *0323-304 08.* FAX *0323-331 29.*
A rambling villa is the setting for this friendly hotel with views over the lake.
All of the prettily decorated bedrooms have their own balcony. 🛏 🏊

NOVARA: *Italia*   Ⓛ Ⓛ | 64
Via Paolo Solaroli 8, 28100. 【 *0321-39 93 16.* FAX *0321-39 93 10.*
Located in the centre of Novara next to the cathedral, the Italia is comfortable
and well-run. The hotel's restaurant is also very good. 🛏 TV 🍽 🏊 P

NOVARA: *Maya*   Ⓛ Ⓛ | 94
Via Boggiani 54, 28100. 【 *0321-45 08 10.* FAX *0321-45 27 86.*
The modern Maya hotel is pleasantly and comfortably decorated. The
popular restaurant holds dinner dances on Saturday nights. 🛏 TV 🏊 P

ORTA SAN GIULIO: *La Bussola*   Ⓛ Ⓛ | 16
Orta San Giulio, 28016. 【 *0322-91 19 13.* FAX *0322-91 19 34.*
The hotel is a traditional villa set in a pretty flower-filled garden with views
over the lake. Guests are expected to take half-board in summer. 🛏 🏊

ORTA SAN GIULIO: *Leon d'Oro*   Ⓛ Ⓛ | 32
Piazza Motta 42, 28016. 【 *0322-902 54.* FAX *0322-903 03.*
Beautifully located on the shores of Lake Orta, the bedrooms have functional,
if rather bland, decor and some have balconies with views. 🛏 🏊 P

ORTA SAN GIULIO: *Orta*   Ⓛ Ⓛ | 35
Orta San Giulio, 28016. 【 *0322-902 53.* FAX *0322-90 56 46.*
Set on the main piazza of Orta San Giulio, the hotel terrace overlooks the lake.
It has a pleasant old-fashioned atmosphere and spacious rooms. 🛏 🏊 P

PONT-SAINT-MARTIN: *Ponte Romano*   Ⓛ | 13
Piazza IV Novembre 14, 11026. 【 *0125-80 43 29.* FAX *0125-80 71 08.*
Attractively located next to an ancient Roman bridge, this small, comfortable
family-run hotel is conveniently close to the centre of town. 🛏 TV 🏊

SAN GIORGIO MONFERRATO: *Castello San Giorgio*   Ⓛ Ⓛ Ⓛ | 11
Via Cavalli d'Olivola 3, 15020. 【 *0142-80 62 03.* FAX *0142-80 65 05.*
An elegant, refined hotel with an excellent restaurant in a pretty castle set
in its own grounds 6 km (4 miles) from Casale Monferrato. 🛏 TV 🏊 P

SAUZE D'OULX: *Il Capricorno*   Ⓛ Ⓛ Ⓛ | 8
Case Sparse 21, Le Clotes 10050. 【 *0122-85 02 73.* FAX *0122-85 04 97.*
Set on the wooded hills above the village, this is a delightfully traditional
chalet hotel with traditional wooden beams and furniture. 🛏 TV 🏊 P

SESTRIERE: *Principe di Piemonte*   Ⓛ Ⓛ Ⓛ | 94
Via Sauze di Cesana, 10058. 【 *0122-79 41.* FAX *0122-75 54 11.*
This was once the grand hotel of Sestriere and it is still plush and extremely
comfortable. It has everything you will need from sauna to shops. 🛏 TV 🏊

SUSA: *Napoleon*   Ⓛ Ⓛ | 62
Via Mazzini 44, 10059. 【 *0122-62 28 55.* FAX *0122-319 00.*
The Napoleon is a modern, clean hotel that has always been run by
the same family. It is well placed in the town centre. 🛏 TV 🏊 P

For key to symbols see back flap

Price categories for a standard double room for one night, including tax and service charges but not including breakfast:
Ⓛ under L100,000
ⓁⓁ L100 – 200,000
ⓁⓁⓁ L200 – 300,000
ⓁⓁⓁⓁ L300 – 400,000
ⓁⓁⓁⓁⓁ over L400,000.

RESTAURANT
A restaurant within the hotel sometimes reserved for residents.
SWIMMING POOL
Hotel swimming pools are usually quite small and are outdoors unless otherwise stated.
GARDEN OR TERRACE
A garden, courtyard or terrace belonging to the hotel, often providing tables for eating outside.
CREDIT CARDS
The major credit cards Visa, MasterCard (Access) and American Express are accepted in hotels with the credit card symbol.

		NUMBER OF ROOMS	RESTAURANT	SWIMMING POOL	GARDEN OR TERRACE
TURIN: *Conte Biancamano* Corso Vittorio Emanuele II 73, 10128. 011-562 32 81. FAX 011-562 37 89. A centrally placed family-run hotel whose public rooms are decorated with paintings and chandeliers. Bedrooms are light and spacious. 📶 TV 🗝 P	ⓁⓁ	25			
TURIN: *Due Mondi* Via Saluzzo 3, 10125. 011-669 89 81. FAX 011-669 93 83. This reasonably priced hotel is well-positioned for exploring the town. Rooms are modern and well-equipped with mini-bars and safe. 📶 TV ▤ 🗝	ⓁⓁ	40			
TURIN: *Genova e Stazione* Via Sacchi 14b, 10128. 011-562 94 00. FAX 011-562 98 96. Well placed in the city centre, close to the station. Bedrooms are decorated in a mixture of styles including Art Deco and 18th century. 📶 TV 🗝 P	ⓁⓁ	59			
TURIN: *Victoria* Via Nino Costa 4, 10123. 011-561 19 09. FAX 011-561 18 06. The comfortable, pretty rooms in this modern hotel combine function with innovative decor; choose the Egyptian or New Orleans rooms. 📶 TV 🗝	ⓁⓁ	98	■		
TURIN: *Turin Palace* Via Sacchi 8, 10128. 011-562 55 11. FAX 011-561 21 87. Dating from 1872, Turin's smartest hotel has an impressive array of modern facilities. The sumptuous rooms are furnished with antiques. 📶 TV 🗝 P	ⓁⓁⓁ	125	■		
TURIN: *Villa Sassi-El Toulà* Strada al Traforo del Pino 47, 10132. 011-898 05 56. FAX 011-898 00 95. Set in a beautiful 17th-century villa, this luxurious hotel just outside Turin still has many original features such as marble floors and candelabra. 📶 TV 🗝 P	ⓁⓁⓁⓁ	17	■		■
VARALLO SESIA: *Vecchio Albergo Sacro Monte* Regione Sacro Monte 14, 13019. 0163-542 54. FAX 0163-511 89. A peaceful hotel in a restored 16th-century building at the entrance to the Sacro Monte. Many of the original features have been retained. 📶 TV 🗝 P	ⓁⓁ	24	■		■
LIGURIA					
CAMOGLI: *Cenobio dei Dogi* Via Cuneo 34, 16032. 0185-77 00 41. FAX 0185-77 27 96. A vast luxurious hotel that offers everything you would expect for the price. It has tennis courts, panoramic terraces and its own beach. 📶 TV 🗝 P	ⓁⓁⓁⓁⓁ	110	■	●	■
FINALE LIGURE: *Punta Est* Via Aurelia 1, 17024. 019-60 06 11. FAX 019-60 06 11. An 18th-century villa overlooking the sea is the setting for this elegant hotel. The interior is spacious and furnished with antiques while the terraces and gardens offer some wonderful views. Half-board is normally offered. 📶 🗝 P	ⓁⓁⓁ	41	■	●	■
GARLENDA: *La Meridiana* Via ai Castelli, 17033. 0182-58 02 71. FAX 0182-58 01 50. This elegant country villa hotel with comfortable rooms is set in peaceful gardens. Guests come here to play golf at the course next door and the hotel offers tennis, bikes and a sauna. Mini-apartments are also available. 📶 TV 🗝	ⓁⓁⓁⓁ	34	■	●	■
GENOA: *Best Western Hotel Metropoli* Piazza Fontane Marose, 16123. 010-28 41 41. FAX 010-28 18 16. Conveniently placed for both business and sightseeing, the hotel offers tastefully decorated rooms equipped with mini-bars and hairdriers. 📶 TV 🗝 P	ⓁⓁ	48			
GENOA: *Nuovo Astoria* Piazza Brignole 4, 16122. 010-87 33 16. FAX 010-831 72 26. A simple, no frills, modern hotel in the centre of Genoa, very close to the station and a short walk from the city's main sights. 📶 TV 🗝 P	ⓁⓁ	69			

MELE: *Fado 78* Ⓛ 8
Via Fado 82, 16010. ☎ 010-63 18 02.
This is a modest but comfortable hotel in a modernized 19th-century
house set in its own pretty garden with good views. 🖼 📺 🅿

MONTEROSSO AL MARE: *Porto Roca* ⓁⓁⓁ 43
Via Corone 1, 19016. ☎ 0187-81 75 02. FAX 0187-81 76 92.
Set on a cliff overlooking the sea in a charming village in the Cinque Terre,
the decor in this hotel is a congenial combination of different styles. 🖼 📺 🎖

NERVI: *Villa Pagoda* ⓁⓁⓁ 18
Via Capolungo 15, 16167. ☎ 010-372 61 61. FAX 010-32 12 18.
A splendidly romantic early 19th-century villa set in spectacular gardens.
Rooms are large and the decor is bright and clean. 🖼 📺 🎖 🅿

RAPALLO: *Stella* Ⓛ 27
Via Aurelia Ponente 10, 16035. ☎ 0185-503 67. FAX 0185-27 28 37.
A tall, thin, pink villa with good views of the sea from the roof terrace.
The decor is a little stark but the owners are friendly and welcoming. 🎖 🅿

PORTOFINO: *Eden* ⓁⓁⓁ 9
Via Dritto 18, 16034. ☎ 0185-26 90 91. FAX 0185-26 90 47.
Conveniently located just behind the piazza of the pretty harbour, the Eden is
set in an attractive garden. Bedrooms are simple but well-equipped. 🖼 📺 🎖

PORTOVENERE: *Genio* ⓁⓁ 7
Piazza Bastreri 8, 19025. ☎ 0187-79 06 11. FAX 0187-79 06 11.
A delightful hotel built into the walls of the medieval castle in 1924. Rooms
are simple, but it is one of the best value hotels in the area. 🖼 📺 🎖

SAN FRUTTUOSO: *Albergo da Giovanni* Ⓛ 7
Via San Fruttuoso 10, Camogli 15032. ☎ 0185-77 00 47.
Usually only a day-trip destination from Camogli, this very basic beach house
is an opportunity to stay in this wonderfully secluded inlet overnight.

SAN REMO: *Royal* ⓁⓁⓁⓁⓁ 149
Corso Imperatrice 80, 18038. ☎ 0184-53 91. FAX 0184-66 14 45.
A traditional deluxe seaside hotel that has been owned by the same family
since 1872. The comfortable bedrooms are decorated with delicate floral
patterns and there is a range of sports and leisure facilities. 🖼 📺 ▤ 🎖 🅿

SESTRI LEVANTE: *Grand Hotel dei Castelli* ⓁⓁⓁⓁ 30
Penisola 26, 16039. ☎ 0185-48 72 20. FAX 0185-447 67.
Set in spectacular gardens rising from the sea, this converted castle is decorated
with mosaics and Moorish columns. The service is very cordial. 🖼 📺 🎖 🅿

EMILIA-ROMAGNA

BOLOGNA: *Commercianti* ⓁⓁⓁ 35
Via de Pignattari 11, 40124. ☎ 051-23 30 52. FAX 051-22 47 33.
This was Bologna's first town hall in the 12th century and some of its medieval
features have been retained; some bedrooms are in the tower. 🖼 📺 ▤ 🎖 🅿

BOLOGNA: *Orologio* ⓁⓁⓁ 31
Via IV Novembre 10, 40123. ☎ 051-23 12 53. FAX 051-26 05 52.
Set in the medieval historic centre, nearly all of the rooms in this quiet town
hotel have exceptional views over Piazza Maggiore. 🖼 📺 ▤ 🎖 🅿

BOLOGNA: *Corona d'Oro 1890* ⓁⓁⓁⓁ 35
Via Oberdan 12, 40126. ☎ 051-23 64 56. FAX 051-26 26 79.
Parts of the building date back to the 14th century and there has been a hotel
here for more than 100 years. Today it has a turn-of-the-century elegance,
with Art Nouveau friezes combined with all mod-cons. 🖼 📺 ▤ 🎖 🅿

BUSSETO: *I Due Foscari* ⓁⓁ 20
Piazza Carlo Rossi 15, 43011. ☎ 0524-922 05. FAX 0524-916 25.
Kitschly decorated and furnished in Hollywood medieval style with mock
Gothic windows and wood beams, this hotel is popular with film stars who
come here especially for the annual opera season in June and July. 🖼 📺 🎖 🅿

CASTELFRANCO: *Villa Gaidello Club* ⓁⓁ 3
Via Gaidello 18, 41013. ☎ 059-92 68 06. FAX 059-92 66 20.
The "club" consists of just three pleasantly furnished suites in a lovely 18th-
century farmhouse set amid peaceful grounds with a lake. 🖼 📺 🎖 🅿

Price categories for a standard double room for one night, including tax and service charges but not including breakfast:
Ⓛ under L100,000
ⓁⓁ L100–200,000
ⓁⓁⓁ L200–300,000
ⓁⓁⓁⓁ L300–400,000
ⓁⓁⓁⓁⓁ over L400,000.

RESTAURANT
A restaurant within the hotel sometimes reserved for residents.
SWIMMING POOL
Hotel swimming pools are usually quite small and are outdoors unless otherwise stated.
GARDEN OR TERRACE
A garden, courtyard or terrace belonging to the hotel, often providing tables for eating outside.
CREDIT CARDS
The major credit cards Visa, MasterCard (Access) and American Express are accepted in hotels with the credit card symbol.

	NUMBER OF ROOMS	RESTAURANT	SWIMMING POOL	GARDEN OR TERRACE
CESENATICO: *Miramare* ⓁⓁ	30	■	●	■
FAENZA: *Vittoria* ⓁⓁ	46	■		
FERRARA: *Ripagrande* ⓁⓁⓁ	40	■		■
FERRARA: *Duchessa Isabella* ⓁⓁⓁⓁⓁ	27	■		
FIDENZA: *Astoria* Ⓛ	30			
MARINA DI RAVENNA: *Bermuda* ⓁⓁ	23	■		■
MODENA: *La Torre* Ⓛ	26			
MODENA: *Central Park* ⓁⓁⓁ	48			■
PARMA: *Torino* ⓁⓁ	33			■
PARMA: *Grand Hotel Baglioni* ⓁⓁⓁⓁ	169	■		
PIACENZA: *Florida* ⓁⓁ	65			■
PORTICO DI ROMAGNA: *Al Vecchio Convento* ⓁⓁ	15	■		

CESENATICO: *Miramare*
Viale Carducci 2, 47042. **(** 0547-800 06. **FAX** 0547-847 85.
Excellently placed for both beach fans and for those who want to explore the surrounding countryside, the Miramare has a good range of sports and leisure facilities and hosts an important local tennis training ground. 🛏 TV 🖥 P

FAENZA: *Vittoria*
Corso Garibaldi 23, 48018. **(** 0546-215 08. **FAX** 0546-291 36.
The hotel, in the historic centre and close to the station, is Art Nouveau in style and has frescoes in the hall and some of the bedrooms. 🛏 TV 🖥 P

FERRARA: *Ripagrande*
Via Ripagrande 21, 44100. **(** 0532-76 52 50. **FAX** 0532-76 43 77.
A very attractively restored Renaissance palace is the setting for this smart, well-run hotel. Rooms are light and many are furnished with antiques; those with balconies have lovely views over Ferrara. 🛏 TV 🖥 P

FERRARA: *Duchessa Isabella*
Via Palestro 70, 44100. **(** 0532-20 21 21. **FAX** 0532-20 26 38.
A splendid hotel set in a 15th-century palazzo in the centre of Ferrara, named after Isabella d'Este who was famous for her parties. Impeccable service and luxurious bedrooms that look out onto a garden full of birds. 🛏 TV 🖥 P

FIDENZA: *Astoria*
Via Gandolfi 5, 43036. **(** 0524-52 43 14. **FAX** 0524-52 72 63.
A good value hotel in the historic centre of town, situated close to the Duomo and main square. There are family rooms with three or four beds. 🛏 🖥 P

MARINA DI RAVENNA: *Bermuda*
Viale della Pace 363, 48023. **(** 0544-53 05 60. **FAX** 0544-53 16 43.
Set in the pine woods near the beach 10 km (6 miles) from Ravenna, this modern family-run hotel is basic but clean and welcoming. 🛏 TV 🖥

MODENA: *La Torre*
Via Cervetta 5, 41100. **(** 059-22 26 15. **FAX** 059-21 63 16.
A short walk from the historic centre's main tourist sights, this friendly hotel is decorated in Art Nouveau style and the rooms are clean and bright. TV 🖥 P

MODENA: *Central Park*
Via Carlo Sigonio 50, 41100. **(** 059-22 58 58. **FAX** 059-22 51 41.
A well-equipped hotel near the centre of Modena and easily reached from the motorway. There is a babysitting service on request. 🛏 TV 🖥 P

PARMA: *Torino*
Via Angelo Mazza 7, 43100. **(** 0521-28 10 46. **FAX** 0521-23 07 25.
A restuctured former convent, the Torino has been in the same family for three generations and offers peaceful accommodation in the heart of Parma. Bedrooms and public rooms are furnished with Art Nouveau artefacts. 🛏 TV 🖥 P

PARMA: *Grand Hotel Baglioni*
Viale Piacenza 12c, 43100. **(** 0521-29 29 29. **FAX** 0521-29 28 28.
A modern hotel in the centre of Parma, this may not be the most personal of hotels, but it does have a full range of facilities on offer. 🛏 TV 🖥 P

PIACENZA: *Florida*
Via Cristoforo Colombo 29, 29100. **(** 0523-59 26 00. **FAX** 0523-59 26 72.
A reasonably priced pensione located just outside the historic centre and within easy reach of the train station. 🛏 TV 🖥 P

PORTICO DI ROMAGNA: *Al Vecchio Convento*
Via Roma 7, 47010. **(** 0543-96 70 53. **FAX** 0543-96 70 53.
An exquisite hotel, tastefully furnished with simple antiques and white linen, all combining to create an impression of space and tranquillity. 🛏 TV 🖥

RAVENNA: *Argentario* ⓁⓁ 30
Via di Roma 45, 48100. 【 *0544-355 55.* FAX *0544-351 47.*
Well situated in the heart of Ravenna, close to its main monuments and the
public gardens, this is a well-equipped hotel with attractive rooms. 🔲 TV 🔲

RAVENNA: *Bisanzio* ⓁⓁ 38
Via Salara, 48100. 【 *0544-21 71 11.* FAX *0544-325 39.*
A faded façade hides a welcoming, modern interior overlooking a pretty
garden, conveniently located in the centre of Ravenna. 🔲 TV 🔲 🔲 P

REGGIO NELL'EMILIA: *Hotel Posta* ⓁⓁⓁ 43
Piazza del Monte 2, 42100. 【 *0522-43 29 44.* FAX *0522-45 26 02.*
Located in the historic centre, this comfortable hotel has very original decor. An
austere medieval façade hides an embellished Rococo interior. 🔲 TV 🔲 P

RIMINI: *Rosabianca* ⓁⓁ 52
Viale Tripoli 195, 47037. 【 *0541-39 06 66.* FAX *0541-39 06 66.*
A modern, recently renovated hotel close to both the beach and the historic
centre of Rimini. Guests can make use of the private beach huts. 🔲 TV 🔲

RIMINI: *Grand Hotel* ⓁⓁⓁⓁ 120
Via Ramuscio 1, 47037. 【 *0541-560 00.* FAX *0541-568 66.*
Conveniently situated near the seafront, the port and the station, this large, well-
equipped, smart hotel has tennis courts and its own beach. 🔲 TV 🔲 🔲 P

SANTARCANGELO DI ROMAGNA: *Hotel della Porta* ⓁⓁ 22
Via Andrea Costa 85, 47038. 【 *0541-62 21 52.* FAX *0541-62 21 68.*
Set a few miles out of Rimini in a region steeped in references to Dante's
Divine Comedy (see pp30–31), this hotel is divided into two houses. Ornate
frescoes and antique furniture decorate some of the rooms. 🔲 TV 🔲 🔲 & P

SASSO MARCONI: *Locanda dei Sogni* ⓁⓁ 5
Via Pieve del Pino 54, 40037. 【 *051-84 70 28.* FAX *051-39 83 88.*
The restaurant is the main attraction at this peaceful and friendly modern
country villa, beautifully set off in its well-maintained grounds. 🔲 🔲 P

FLORENCE

FLORENCE: *Hotel Locanda Orchidea* Ⓛ 7
Borgo degli Albizi 11, 50122. **Map** 2 D5 (6 F3). 【 *055-248 03 46.*
A family-run hotel in a 12th-century building. The rooms, although
comfortable and cosy, are basic and do show some signs of wear.

FLORENCE: *Pensione Maxim* Ⓛ 23
Via de' Medici 4, 50123. **Map** 6 D2. 【 *055-21 74 74.* FAX *055-28 37 29.*
Stairs lead up from a side street to the reception. Some of the bedrooms in
this third-floor hotel look on to the pedestrianized Via dei Calzaiuoli. 🔲 🔲

FLORENCE: *Ariele* ⓁⓁ 39
2 km (1 mile) W, Via Magenta 11, 50123. **Map** 1 A4. 【 *055-21 15 09.* FAX *055-26 85 21.*
Located on a residential side street, the lounge in this homely hotel is
furnished with antiques. Bedrooms are spacious but austere. 🔲 TV 🔲 P

FLORENCE: *Hotel Porta Rossa* ⓁⓁ 70
Via Porta Rossa 19, 50100. **Map** 3 C1 (5 C3). 【 *055-28 75 51.* FAX *055-28 21 79.*
Italy's second-oldest hotel, it dates from 1386 and has a warm and welcoming
atmosphere. The huge bedrooms are airy and pleasantly decorated and the
vaulted entrance hall is furnished with fine leather suites. 🔲 TV 🔲

FLORENCE: *Hotel Silla* ⓁⓁ 35
Via dei Renai 5, 50125. **Map** 4 D2 (6 E5). 【 *055-234 28 88.* FAX *055-234 14 37.*
This 16th-century hotel is approached through an elegant courtyard with
a grand staircase. There is a pretty terrace giving views of the Arno. 🔲 🔲

FLORENCE: *Splendor* ⓁⓁ 31
Via San Gallo 30, 50129. **Map** 2 D4. 【 *055-48 34 27.* FAX *055-46 12 76.*
A family hotel with dark red decor and frescoed, stuccoed ceilings that give
it the impression of a grand mansion. It shows some signs of wear. 🔲 TV 🔲

FLORENCE: *Hotel Aprile* ⓁⓁⓁ 29
Via della Scala 6, 50123. **Map** 1 B4 (5 A1). 【 *055-21 62 37.* FAX *055-28 09 47.*
The façade still has traces of 16th-century paintings representing the *Triumph
of David*. Other parts of this scene are displayed in the reception area. There
is an old-fashioned tearoom as well as the courtyard garden. 🔲 🔲

Price categories for a standard double room for one night, including tax and service charges but not including breakfast: Ⓛ under L100,000 ⓁⓁ L100–200,000 ⓁⓁⓁ L200–300,000 ⓁⓁⓁⓁ L300–400,000 ⓁⓁⓁⓁⓁ over L400,000.	**RESTAURANT** A restaurant within the hotel sometimes reserved for residents. **SWIMMING POOL** Hotel swimming pools are usually quite small and are outdoors unless otherwise stated. **GARDEN OR TERRACE** A garden, courtyard or terrace belonging to the hotel, often providing tables for eating outside. **CREDIT CARDS** The major credit cards Visa, MasterCard (Access) and American Express are accepted in hotels with the credit card symbol.		

		NUMBER OF ROOMS	RESTAURANT	SWIMMING POOL	GARDEN OR TERRACE
FLORENCE: *Hotel Hermitage* Vicolo Marzio 1, 50122. **Map** 6 D4. ☎ 055-28 72 16. ℻ 055-21 22 08. Spectacular views from the more expensive upper-storey rooms of this medieval building a few yards from the Ponte Vecchio. This small hotel has comfortable rooms, each one decorated in a different style. 🛏 🌿	ⓁⓁⓁ	29			
FLORENCE: *Hotel Loggiato dei Serviti* Piazza della SS Annunziata 3, 50122. **Map** 2 D4. ☎ 055-28 95 92. ℻ 055-28 95 95. Built in 1527, the reception areas in this hotel near the Spedale degli Innocenti have vaulted ceilings and a bar area flanked by stone columns. 🛏 📺 🌿	ⓁⓁⓁ	29			
FLORENCE: *Hotel Tornabuoni Beacci* Via de' Tornabuoni 3, 50123. **Map** 1 C5 (5 C2). ☎ 055-26 83 77. ℻ 055-28 35 94. This former palazzo is situated on a busy central street. Wide carpeted hallways lead to lounge areas furnished with antiques and tapestries. Bedrooms are luxurious with beds piled high with pillows. 🛏 📺 🌿	ⓁⓁⓁ	28	▣		
FLORENCE: *Hotel Villa Belvedere* Via Benedetto Castelli 3, 50124. **Map** 3 A5. ☎ 055-22 25 01. ℻ 055-22 31 63. A spacious 1930s villa set in landscaped grounds near the Boboli Gardens. The first-floor terraces have good views of the garden. 🛏 📺 🌿	ⓁⓁⓁ	25		●	▣
FLORENCE: *Hotel Villa Liberty* Viale Michelangelo 40, 50125. **Map** 4 F3. ☎ 055-68 38 19. ℻ 055-681 25 95. This turn-of-the-century villa lies on a tree-lined street in the southeast of town. Curving steps lead into a homely, old-fashioned interior. 🛏 ▤ 🌿 🅿	ⓁⓁⓁ	16			
FLORENCE: *Morandi alla Crocetta* Via Laura 50, 50121. **Map** 2 E4. ☎ 055-234 47 47. ℻ 055-248 09 54. A lovely former convent run by an Englishwoman who has lived here since the 1920s. The interior is decorated with antique rugs and plants. 🛏 📺 ▤ 🌿	ⓁⓁⓁ	9			
FLORENCE: *Pensione Annalena* Via Romana 34, 50125. **Map** 3 A3. ☎ 055-22 24 02. ℻ 055-22 24 03. A 15th-century hotel with spacious, simply but attractively decorated bedrooms. The public areas are all contained in one great hall. 🛏 📺 🌿	ⓁⓁⓁ	20			
FLORENCE: *Hotel J and J* Via di Mezzo 20, 50121. **Map** 2 E5. ☎ 055-24 09 51. ℻ 055-24 02 82. This pretty, peaceful hotel is set in a former 16th-century monastery and has windows set between old stone arches and frescoed ceilings. 🛏 📺 🌿	ⓁⓁⓁⓁ	19			
FLORENCE: *Hotel Monna Lisa* Borgo Pinti 27, 50121. **Map** 2 E5. ☎ 055-247 97 51. ℻ 055-247 97 55. An impressive stone courtyard leads into this Renaissance palazzo. Some of the bedrooms are huge, with old furniture and high ceilings. 🛏 📺 🌿 🅿	ⓁⓁⓁⓁ	30			
FLORENCE: *Rivoli* Via della Scala 33, 50123. **Map** 1 A4 (5 A1). ☎ 055-28 28 53. ℻ 055-29 40 41. The weathered façade gives a clue to the age of this 15th-century hotel. It is generally spacious, cool and decorated to a high standard, combining both modern and Classical styles with unfussy elegance. 🛏 📺 ▤ 🌿	ⓁⓁⓁⓁ	65			
FLORENCE: *Villa Carlotta* Via Michele di Lando 3, 50125. **Map** 3 B4. ☎ 055-233 61 51. ℻ 055-233 61 47. This gracious 19th-century building, hidden in a remote, secluded area, is an attractive, homely villa decorated in Neo-Classical style. 🛏 📺 ▤ 🌿	ⓁⓁⓁⓁ	27	▣	●	▣
FLORENCE: *Grand Hotel Villa Cora* Viale Machiavelli 18, 50125. **Map** 3 A3. ☎ 055-229 84 51. ℻ 055-22 90 86. A stunning Renaissance building with balustraded terraces segregated by Classical pillars and tall windows. Inside, the reception rooms are decorated with frescoed ceilings and varnished wooden floors. 🛏 📺 ▤ 🌿 🅿	ⓁⓁⓁⓁⓁ	48	▣	●	

FLORENCE: *Hotel Brunelleschi* ⓁⓁⓁⓁ 96
Piazza Santa Elisabetta 3, 50122. **Map** 6 D2. 055-56 20 68. **FAX** 055-21 96 53.
This unique hotel was built inside a Byzantine tower and the adjoining buildings. It is wonderfully atmospheric, with a small Byzantine museum collection and stunning views over Florence from the roof terrace.

FLORENCE: *Hotel Continental* ⓁⓁⓁⓁ 48
Lungarno degli Acciaiuoli 2, 50123. **Map** 3 C1 (5 C4). 055-28 23 92. **FAX** 055-28 31 39.
In a prime location near the Ponte Vecchio, the hotel's bar and top-floor suites overlook the river. The walls are decorated with a marble effect.

FLORENCE: *Hotel Excelsior* ⓁⓁⓁⓁⓁ 177
Piazza d'Ognissanti 3, 50123. **Map** 1 B5 (5 A2). 055-26 42 01. **FAX** 055-21 02 78.
Occupying two houses rebuilt in 1815, the hotel is decorated with gracious marble floors and stained glass with lovely views over the Arno.

FLORENCE: *Hotel Helvetia e Bristol* ⓁⓁⓁⓁ 52
Via de' Pescioni 2, 50123. **Map** 1 C5 (5 C2). 055-28 78 14. **FAX** 055-28 83 53.
A luxurious 18th-century hotel a few steps from the Duomo, with antiques, a domed, stained glass ceiling and a splendid wood and marble bar.

FLORENCE: *Hotel Regency* ⓁⓁⓁⓁ 34
Piazza Massimo d'Azeglio 3, 50121. **Map** 2 F5. 055-24 52 47. **FAX** 055-234 67 35.
Behind the modest exterior of a Florentine town house lies a grand, Classical-style reception area and bar with wood-panelling decor.

FLORENCE: *Torre di Bellosguardo* ⓁⓁⓁⓁ 16
Via de' Michelozzi 2, 50124. **Map** 5 B5. 055-229 81 45. **FAX** 055-22 90 08.
A long, sweeping road leads to this 14th-century tower and adjoining 16th-century villa. Inside, colossal wooden doors lead to huge rooms, filled with antiques and Persian rugs. There are spectacular views over Florence.

FLORENCE: *Villa La Massa* ⓁⓁⓁⓁ 42
Via la Massa 24, Candeli 50012. 055-651 01 01. **FAX** 055-651 01 09.
On a riverside setting 6 km (4 miles) northeast of Florence, this luxurious 17th-century hotel has elegant rooms with antique furniture.

TUSCANY

AREZZO: *Castello di Gargonza* ⓁⓁ 7
Gargonza, Monte San Savino, 52048. 0575-84 70 21. **FAX** 0575-84 70 54.
A sweeping tree-lined driveway curves around the walls of this castle guest-house, which also has 18 self-catering apartments. The views are magnificent and weekly services are held in the pretty frescoed chapel.

CORTONA: *Hotel San Luca* ⓁⓁ 56
Piazzale Garibaldi 1, 52044. 0575-63 04 60. **FAX** 0575-63 01 05.
This hillside hotel has simple bedrooms, but the comfortable reception rooms offer good panoramas over the surrounding valleys.

CORTONA: *Hotel San Michele* ⓁⓁ 37
Via Guelfa 15, 52044. 0575-60 43 48. **FAX** 0575-63 01 47.
A beautifully restored Renaissance palazzo on a narrow street. A maze of corridors leads to comfortable bedrooms and a superb attic suite.

CASTELLINA IN CHIANTI: *Tenuta di Ricavo* ⓁⓁⓁⓁ 23
Località Ricavo, 53011. 0577-74 02 21. **FAX** 0577-74 10 14.
A charming hotel occupying the entire hamlet and furnished with a mixture of antiques and rustic furniture. Many rooms are in old country houses.

ELBA: *Capo Sud* ⓁⓁ 42
Località Lacona, 57037. 0565-96 40 21. **FAX** 0565-96 42 63.
A village-like resort with excellent bay views. The rooms are housed in a complex of villas and the restaurant serves produce from its orchard.

FIESOLE: *Hotel Villa Bonelli* ⓁⓁ 20
Via F Poeti 1, 50014. 055-595 13. **FAX** 055-59 89 42.
This simple, friendly hotel is pleasantly furnished and has excellent views of Florence. Guests have to take half-board in summer.

FIESOLE: *Villa San Michele* ⓁⓁⓁⓁ 36
Via Doccia 4, 50014. 055-594 51. **FAX** 055-59 87 34.
Allegedly designed by Michelangelo, the beautiful monastery has extensive grounds and beautiful panoramas over the city from the loggia.

Price categories for a standard double room for one night, including tax and service charges but not including breakfast:
Ⓛ under L100,000
ⓁⓁ L100–200,000
ⓁⓁⓁ L200–300,000
ⓁⓁⓁⓁ L300–400,000
ⓁⓁⓁⓁⓁ over L400,000.

RESTAURANT
A restaurant within the hotel sometimes reserved for residents.
SWIMMING POOL
Hotel swimming pools are usually quite small and are outdoors unless otherwise stated.
GARDEN OR TERRACE
A garden, courtyard or terrace belonging to the hotel, often providing tables for eating outside.
CREDIT CARDS
The major credit cards Visa, MasterCard (Access) and American Express are accepted in hotels with the credit card symbol.

		Number of Rooms	Restaurant	Swimming Pool	Garden or Terrace
GAIOLE IN CHIANTI: *Castello di Spaltenna* ⓁⓁⓁ Via Spaltenna 13, 53013. ☏ *0577-74 94 83.* FAX *0577-74 92 69.* A beautiful, fortified former monastery with spacious rooms overlooking a courtyard; some rooms have jacuzzis. The restaurant is excellent. 🖼		21	■	●	■
GIGLIO PORTO: *Castello Monticello* ⓁⓁ Via Provinciale, 58013. ☏ *0564-80 92 52.* FAX *0564-80 94 73.* A castle hotel, it was originally built on this pretty island as a private house. It sits on a hill, and there are superb views from the bedrooms. 🖼 TV 🖼 P		29	■		■
LUCCA: *Piccolo Hotel Puccini* ⓁⓁ Via di Poggio 9, 55100. ☏ *0583-554 21.* FAX *0583-534 87.* Housed in a lovely old stone building, this smart, small hotel has an attractive bar that overlooks the pretty narrow street outside. 🖼		14			
LUCCA: *Hotel Universo* ⓁⓁⓁ Piazza del Giglio 1, 55100. ☏ *0583-49 36 78.* FAX *0583-95 48 54.* This big, but slightly worn hotel was built in the 19th century. It has large and comfortable bedrooms, some with pleasant views on to the quiet square. The big luxurious bathrooms are an added attraction. 🖼 TV 🖼		60	■		
LUCCA: *Hotel Principessa Elisa* ⓁⓁⓁⓁⓁ Via Nuova per Pisa 1952, 55050. ☏ *0583-37 97 37.* FAX *0583-37 90 19.* There is a peaceful and luxurious atmosphere in this stately home that imitates 18th-century Parisian style. Bedrooms are beautifully decorated with antiques and there are two elegant drawing rooms. 🖼 TV 🖼		10	■	●	■
MONTERIGGIONI: *Albergo Casalta* Ⓛ Località Strove, 53035. ☏ *0577-30 10 02.* FAX *0577-30 10 02.* Housed in a 1,000-year-old building, a central hearth in the reception adds to the warm and welcoming atmosphere. The restaurant is also very elegant. 🖼		11	■		
PISA: *Royal Victoria Hotel* ⓁⓁ Lungarno Pacinotti 12, 56126. ☏ *050-94 01 11.* FAX *050-94 01 80.* A dignified hotel built in the 19th century. It retains several original features, including exquisite trompe l'oeil drapery and wood panelled doors. 🖼 🖼 P		48			
PISA: *Hotel d'Azeglio* ⓁⓁⓁ Piazza Vittorio Emanuele II 18b, 56125. ☏ *050-50 03 10.* FAX *050-280 17.* Excellent views over Pisa from the 7th-floor breakfast room of this modern hotel. Windows look over Pisa to the mountains beyond. 🖼 TV 🖼 P		29			
PISTOIA: *Albergo Patria* ⓁⓁ Via Crispi 8, 51100. ☏ *0573-251 87.* FAX *0573-36 81 68.* An ancient hotel with a dark, modern interior and 1970s bedrooms. It is on a pretty street in the centre of Pistoia, well placed for sightseeing. Upper bedrooms have excellent views of the Romanesque Duomo. 🖼 🖼		28	■		
PISTOIA: *Hotel Piccolo Ritz* ⓁⓁ Via Vannucci 67, 51100. ☏ *0573-267 75.* FAX *0573-277 98.* Near the station in the historic centre of Pistoia, this small hotel lives up to its name and has a pleasant, frescoed café-style bar. 🖼 TV 🖼		21			
PORTO ERCOLE: *Il Pellicano* ⓁⓁⓁⓁⓁ Località Cala dei Santi, 58018. ☏ *0564-83 38 01.* FAX *0564-83 34 18.* Luxurious and exclusive with its own rocky beach, this old-style Tuscan villa is covered with vines and has wonderful views from the terraces descending to the sea. Rooms are elegantly furnished with antiques. 🖼 TV 🗐 🖼 P		37	■	●	■
RADDA IN CHIANTI: *Villa Miranda* ⓁⓁ Siena 53017. ☏ *0577-73 80 21.* FAX *0577-73 86 68.* Run by the same family since the original building (the Post House) was built in 1842. Bedrooms have beamed ceilings and brass bedsteads. 🖼 🖼		42	■	●	■

San Gimignano: *Hotel Belvedere* ⓁⓁ 12
Via Dante 14, 53037. 0577-94 05 39. FAX 0577-94 03 27.
A pretty terracotta villa set in a cypress-filled garden with hammocks.
Light, modern bedrooms are painted in soothing pastel shades.

San Gimignano: *Hotel Leon Bianco* ⓁⓁ 25
Piazza della Cisterna 13, 53037. 0577-94 12 94. FAX 0577-94 21 23.
Airy rooms with pleasant views and terracotta floors typify this former
palazzo. Parts of the original stone wall can still be seen.

San Gimignano: *Villa San Paolo* ⓁⓁⓁ 18
Strada per Certaldo, 53037. 0577-95 51 00. FAX 0577-95 51 13.
An attractive hillside villa set in terraced gardens with tennis courts.
Inside there are pretty bedrooms and intimate lounges.

San Miniato: *Hotel Miravalle* ⓁⓁ 20
Piazza Castello 3, 56027. 0571-41 80 75. FAX 0571-41 96 81.
The Miravalle is perched on a 10th-century castle wall, adjoining what
remains of the castle tower. The interior is somewhat worn but rooms are
comfortable and have splendid views, especially from the restaurant.

Siena: *Hotel Chiusarelli* ⓁⓁ 50
Viale Curtatone 15, 53100. 0577-28 05 62. FAX 0577-27 11 77.
A pretty villa that still looks slightly the worse for wear in spite of its recent
restoration. The pleasant garden is filled with palm trees.

Siena: *Santa Caterina* ⓁⓁ 19
Via Enea Silvio Piccolomini 7, 53100. 0577-22 11 05. FAX 0577-27 10 87.
The comfortable rooms overlook the marvellous flower garden which has
charming views of the red roofs of Siena. The Santa Caterina, situated near
the Porta Romana, was once a privately owned villa.

Siena: *Villa Patrizia* ⓁⓁⓁⓁ 33
Via Fiorentina 58, 53100. 0577-504 31. FAX 0577-504 31.
A rambling old villa on the city's northern outskirts. The bedrooms, all of which
look out onto the gardens, are simply furnished but comfortable.

Siena: *Villa Scacciapensieri* ⓁⓁⓁⓁ 33
Via di Scacciapensieri 10, 53100. 0577-414 41. FAX 0577-27 08 54.
Set in attractive grounds, this villa features an old-fashioned lounge with a huge
stone fireplace. The spacious bedrooms have views of Siena.

Siena: *Hotel Certosa di Maggiano* ⓁⓁⓁⓁⓁ 17
Via Certosa 82, 53100. 0577-28 81 80. FAX 0577-28 81 89.
A former Carthusian monastery built in 1314 and turned into an exclusive,
peaceful retreat. The rooms are adorned with antique paintings.

Sinalunga: *Locanda L'Amorosa* ⓁⓁⓁⓁ 17
L'Amorosa, 53048. 0577-67 94 97. FAX 0577-67 82 16.
An enchanting stone and pink terracotta building is the setting for this beautiful
inn. The luxurious bedrooms are quiet and comfortable.

Viareggio: *Hotel President* ⓁⓁⓁ 37
Viale Carducci 5, 55049. 0584-96 27 12. FAX 0584-96 36 58.
A smart seaside hotel with attractively refurbished and comfortable bedrooms.
There are excellent sea views from the roof-top restaurant.

Volterra: *Albergo Villa Nencini* Ⓛ 14
Borgo Santo Stefano 55, 56048. 0588-863 86. FAX 0588-806 01.
A stone country hotel set in a park a few minutes from the town. Cool, light
bedrooms, a smart breakfast room, basement trattoria and terrace.

UMBRIA

Assisi: *Country House* Ⓛ 9
Via San Pietro Campagna 178, Località Valecchie, 06081. 075-81 61 55.
FAX 075-81 63 63.
A convenient 700 m (half a mile) from the centre of Assisi, this 1920s villa is set
amid peaceful countryside. Rooms are furnished with antiques.

Assisi: *Dei Priori* ⓁⓁ 34
Corso Mazzini 15, 06081. 075-81 22 37. FAX 075-81 68 04.
Set in a 17th-century building in the historic centre, the bedrooms are
pretty and fresh and there is a lovely vaulted dining room.

For key to symbols see back flap

Price categories for a standard double room for one night, including tax and service charges but not including breakfast:
Ⓛ under L100,000
ⓁⓁ L100 – 200,000
ⓁⓁⓁ L200 – 300,000
ⓁⓁⓁⓁ L300 – 400,000
ⓁⓁⓁⓁⓁ over L400,000.

RESTAURANT
A restaurant within the hotel sometimes reserved for residents.
SWIMMING POOL
Hotel swimming pools are usually quite small and are outdoors unless otherwise stated.
GARDEN OR TERRACE
A garden, courtyard or terrace belonging to the hotel, often providing tables for eating outside.
CREDIT CARDS
The major credit cards Visa, MasterCard (Access) and American Express are accepted in hotels with the credit card symbol.

		NUMBER OF ROOMS	RESTAURANT	SWIMMING POOL	GARDEN OR TERRACE
ASSISI: *Umbra* Via degli Archi 6, 06081. 075-81 22 40. FAX 075-81 36 53. A friendly hotel in an atmospheric back street in the historic centre. Furnishings are comfortable and there is a charming terrace for outside dining.	ⓁⓁ	25	■		■
ASSISI: *Romantik Hotel Le Silve* Località Armenzano di Assisi, 06081. 075-801 90 00. FAX 075-801 90 05. Set in its own grounds about 12 km (7 miles) from Assisi, the Romantik has wonderful views of the Tuscan hills as well as an excellent range of sports and leisure facilities. Apartments are also available in the grounds.	ⓁⓁⓁ	13	■	●	■
CAMPELLO SUL CLITUNNO: *Il Vecchio Molino* Via del Tempio 34, Località Pissignano 06042. 0743-52 11 22. FAX 0743-27 50 97. Set in a converted mill on an island in the river, the bedrooms are spacious and comfortable. A Roman temple can be seen from the garden.	ⓁⓁ	13			■
CASTIGLIONE DEL LAGO: *Miralago* Piazza Mazzini 6, 06061. 075-95 11 57. FAX 075-95 19 24. Set in the centre of this town on the shores of Lake Trasimeno, the Miralago is a small hotel run by a family from Kenya who extend a friendly welcome to all guests. Fresh fish from the lake is served in the restaurant.	ⓁⓁ	19	■		■
FONTIGNANO: *Villa di Monte Solare* Via Montali 7, Colle San Paolo 06007. 075-83 23 76. FAX 075-835 54 62. A beautiful 18th-century villa set in its own grounds with many original features such as terracotta floors, period furniture and frescoes. Colle San Paolo is 25 km (15 miles) from Perugia through beautiful Umbrian landscape.	ⓁⓁ	15	■	●	■
GUBBIO: *Oderisi-Balestrieri* Via Mazzatinti 2/12, 06024. 075-922 06 62. FAX 075-922 06 63. A hotel in the medieval town centre; the rooms are pleasantly furnished with modern, wooden beams, bedsteads and tables.	Ⓛ	35			■
GUBBIO: *Bosone Palace* Via XX Settembre 22, 06024. 075-922 06 88. FAX 075-922 05 52. Set in the Palazzo Raffaelli, one of the oldest palazzi in the historic centre, the Bosone has a mixture of bedrooms from the spectacular to the ordinary. All of them, however, have a wonderfully historic atmosphere.	ⓁⓁ	30			■
GUBBIO: *Villa Montegranelli* Località Monteluiano, 06024. 075-922 01 85. FAX 075-927 33 72. An elegant country villa about 4 km (2 miles) from Gubbio with attractive bedrooms and a highly recommended restaurant (see p596).	ⓁⓁ	21	■		■
LAKE TRASIMENO: *Hotel da Sauro* Isola Maggiore, 06060. 075-82 61 68. FAX 075-82 51 30. A basic hotel with friendly staff in an exceptional location. Isola Maggiore remains fairly isolated making this a quiet and simple retreat.	Ⓛ	12	■		
MONTEFALCO: *Ringhiera Umbra* Via G Mameli 20, 06036. 0742-37 91 66. FAX 0742-37 91 66. A simple yet immaculately kept hotel in a historic building in the centre of Montefalco. The reasonably priced restaurant is in a vaulted room.	Ⓛ	13	■		
MONTEFALCO: *Villa Pambuffetti* Via della Vittoria 20, 06036. 0742-37 94 17. FAX 0742-37 92 45. The spacious and comfortable bedrooms in this hotel are all different. The tower room has wonderful views of the surrounding country.	ⓁⓁⓁⓁ	15	■	●	
NORCIA: *Garden* Viale XX Settembre 2b, 06046. 0743-81 66 87. FAX 0743-81 66 87. A simple hotel close to the centre of Norcia, with basic but comfortable rooms. The Garden is a good base from which to explore the city.	ⓁⓁ	44	■		

ORVIETO: *Villa Ciconia* Ⓛ Ⓛ 10
Via dei Tigli 69, 05019. ☎ 0763-929 82. ⒻⒶⓍ 0763-906 77.
Set in lovely grounds a short distance out of Orvieto, this 16th-century country
house makes a peaceful base from which to explore Umbria. 🖼 📺 📧 🅿

ORVIETO: *Virgilio* Ⓛ Ⓛ 15
Piazza Duomo 5–6, 05018. ☎ 0763-418 82. ⒻⒶⓍ 0763-437 97.
Located in central Orvieto, this simple hotel was converted by the owner from
what was once his home. Some rooms have views of the cathedral. 🖼 📧

ORVIETO: *La Badia* Ⓛ Ⓛ Ⓛ 26
Località la Badia 8, 05019. ☎ 0763-903 59. ⒻⒶⓍ 0763-927 96.
Housed in a spectacular former monastery, parts of which date back to the
12th century, modern comfort is combined with medieval splendour. 🖼 📧 🅿

PERUGIA: *Lo Spedalicchio* Ⓛ Ⓛ 25
Piazza Bruno Buozzi 3, Ospedalicchio 06080. ☎ 075-801 03 23. ⒻⒶⓍ 075-801 03 23.
Built within the walls of a 14th-century fortress, the rooms are simply but
comfortably decorated in keeping with the style of the building. 🖼 📺 📧 🅿

PERUGIA: *Locanda della Posta* Ⓛ Ⓛ Ⓛ 39
Corso Vannucci 97, 06100. ☎ 075-572 89 25. ⒻⒶⓍ 075-572 24 13.
This elegant 200-year-old hotel is housed in a charming old palazzo on
the pedestrianized main street of the historic centre. 🖼 📺 ▤ 📧 🅿

PERUGIA: *Brufani* Ⓛ Ⓛ Ⓛ Ⓛ 24
Piazza Italia 12, 06100. ☎ 075-573 25 41. ⒻⒶⓍ 075-572 02 10.
Opened in 1884, the public rooms of this exclusive hotel were painted by Lillis,
the German interior designer. The views are spectacular. 🖼 📺 📧 🅿

SPELLO: *La Bastiglia* Ⓛ Ⓛ 22
Piazza Vallegloria 7, 06038. ☎ 0742-65 12 77. ⒻⒶⓍ 0742-65 12 77.
An adapted old mill is the setting for this airy, homely hotel whose extensive
terraces give excellent views over the surrounding countryside. 🖼 📺 📧 🅿

SPELLO: *Palazzo Bocci* Ⓛ Ⓛ Ⓛ 23
Via Cavour 17, 06038. ☎ 0742-30 10 21. ⒻⒶⓍ 0742-30 14 64.
Set in a much restored 14th-century palazzo in the centre of Spello, this
hotel combines modern convenience with traditional charm. 🖼 📺 📧 🅿

SPOLETO: *Aurora* Ⓛ Ⓛ 15
Via Apollinare 3, 06049. ☎ 0743-22 03 15. ⒻⒶⓍ 0743-22 18 85.
A good value hotel in the historic centre. It is connected to the Apollinare
restaurant and (unusually for this price) all rooms have mini-bars. 🖼 📺 📧 🅿

SPOLETO: *Charleston* Ⓛ Ⓛ 18
Piazza Collicola 10, 06049. ☎ 0743-22 00 52. ⒻⒶⓍ 0743-22 20 10.
A 17th-century building in the centre of Spoleto. The modern and traditional
furnishings in this hotel create an uncluttered yet homely feel. 🖼 📺 📧 🅿

SPOLETO: *Clarici* Ⓛ Ⓛ 24
Piazza della Vittoria 32, 06049. ☎ 0743-22 33 11. ⒻⒶⓍ 0743-22 20 10.
Run by the same family as the Charleston, the Clarici is not quite as
charming but still offers excellent value in central Spoleto. 🖼 📺 📧 🅿

SPOLETO: *Gattapone* Ⓛ Ⓛ Ⓛ 14
Via del Ponte 6, 06049. ☎ 0743-22 34 47. ⒻⒶⓍ 0743-22 34 48.
A smart hotel, built on the highest point of the town, five minutes' walk
from the centre with excellent views of the Ponte delle Torri. 🖼 📺 📧 🅿

TODI: *Bramante* Ⓛ Ⓛ Ⓛ 43
Via Orvietana 48, 06059. ☎ 075-894 83 81. ⒻⒶⓍ 075-894 80 74.
Although rebuilt, parts of the 13th-century convent remain and the simple
furnishings of this quiet hotel add to the peaceful atmosphere. 🖼 📺 ▤ 📧 🅿

TODI: *Hotel Fonte Cesia* Ⓛ Ⓛ Ⓛ 32
Via Lorenzo Leonj 3, 06059. ☎ 075-894 37 37. ⒻⒶⓍ 075-894 46 77.
A beautiful 17th-century palazzo is the setting for this elegant and intimate
hotel that combines traditional charm with all modern comforts. 🖼 📺 📧

TORGIANO: *Le Tre Vaselle* Ⓛ Ⓛ Ⓛ 72
Via G Garibaldi 48, 06089. ☎ 075-988 04 47. ⒻⒶⓍ 075-988 02 14.
Set in a 17th-century country house, the hotel has retained its terracotta floor
tiles and beamed ceilings and is furnished with rural antiques. 🖼 📺 📧 🅿

For key to symbols see back flap

Price categories for a standard double room for one night, including tax and service charges but not including breakfast:
Ⓛ under L100,000
ⓁⓁ L100–200,000
ⓁⓁⓁ L200–300,000
ⓁⓁⓁⓁ L300–400,000
ⓁⓁⓁⓁⓁ over L400,000.

RESTAURANT
A restaurant within the hotel sometimes reserved for residents.
SWIMMING POOL
Hotel swimming pools are usually quite small and are outdoors unless otherwise stated.
GARDEN OR TERRACE
A garden, courtyard or terrace belonging to the hotel, often providing tables for eating outside.
CREDIT CARDS
The major credit cards Visa, MasterCard (Access) and American Express are accepted in hotels with the credit card symbol.

LE MARCHE

		NUMBER OF ROOMS	RESTAURANT	SWIMMING POOL	GARDEN OR TERRACE
ANCONA: *Emilia* Poggio di Portonovo, 60020. ☎ 071-80 11 45. FAX 071-80 13 30. A refined hotel with bright and pretty interior decorations. As well as hosting concerts for the Ancona Jazz festival in its elegant garden, the Emilia organizes an annual art prize and has a collection of contemporary art. 🛏 TV ▤ ✉ P	ⓁⓁ	33	■	●	■
AQUAVIVA PICENA: *Hotel O'Viv* Via Marziale 43, 63030. ☎ 0735-76 46 49. FAX 0735-76 50 54. Set in an attractive palazzo in the medieval town centre, the bedrooms in this traditional hotel are spacious with wonderful views from the terrace. 🛏 TV ✉	Ⓛ	12			
FANO: *Corallo* Via Leonardo da Vinci 3, 61032. ☎ 0721-80 42 00. FAX 0721-80 36 37. Built on the seafront, the furnishings in the Corallo are functional but there is a good range of services. The restaurant specializes in fish. 🛏 TV ▤ ✉ P	Ⓛ	27	■		
FANO: *Elisabeth Due* Piazzale Amendola 2, 61032. ☎ 0721-82 31 46. FAX 0721-82 31 47. Within an anonymous modern exterior lies a slickly furnished, comfortable beach hotel with wood panelling and squashy sofas. 🛏 TV ✉ P	ⓁⓁ	32	■		
FANO: *Grand Hotel Elisabeth* Viale Carducci, 61032. ☎ 0721-80 42 41. FAX 0721-80 42 42. Well positioned for both beach and town, the interior of this modern block is more comfortable and attractive than the exterior would suggest. 🛏 TV ✉ P	ⓁⓁ	37	■		■
FOLIGNANO: *Villa Pigna* Viale Assisi 33, 63040. ☎ 0736-49 18 68. FAX 0736-49 18 68. A modern, efficiently-run hotel in the centre of town. The public rooms are attractive and the bedrooms, if unexceptional, are satisfactory. 🛏 TV ✉ P	ⓁⓁ	54	■		
JESI: *Federico II* Via Ancona 100, 60035. ☎ 0731-21 10 79. FAX 0731-572 21. A slick post-modern hotel offering a massive range of facilities: indoor pool, gym, and a conference centre. A little impersonal, but comfortable. 🛏 TV ✉ P	ⓁⓁⓁ	76	■	●	■
MONTECASSIANO: *Villa Quiete* Località Vallecascia, 62010. ☎ 0733-59 95 59. FAX 0733-59 95 59. A country villa hotel set in its own beautiful gardens. Some of the pretty rooms have antique furnishings. There are also two suites. 🛏 TV ✉ P	ⓁⓁ	36	■		■
PESARO: *Villa Serena* Via San Nicola 6–3, 61100. ☎ 0721-552 11. FAX 0721-559 27. This 17th-century mansion, set in its own well-kept grounds, is a very comfortable, friendly hotel where no two rooms are alike. 🛏 TV ✉	ⓁⓁ	9	■	●	■
PESARO: *Vittoria* Via A Vespucci 2, Piazzale Libertà 2, 61100. ☎ 0721-343 43. FAX 0721-652 04. The Vittoria is a perfect combination of old-fashioned charm and modern convenience. It has a good range of facilities and is close to the sea. 🛏 TV ✉	ⓁⓁⓁ	30	■	●	■
PORTONOVO: *Fortino Napoleonico* Via Poggio 166, 60020. ☎ 071-80 14 50. FAX 071-80 14 54. Built to protect the coast from marauding English during the Napoleonic wars, the fortress has been comfortably restored with tasteful decor and antiques, and has its own beach. Now even the English are welcome. 🛏 TV ✉ P	ⓁⓁⓁ	30	■		■
SAN BENEDETTO DEL TRONTO: *Sabbia D'Oro* Viale Marconi 46, 63039. ☎ 0735-819 11. FAX 0735-819 67. A modern beach hotel in this busy, fashionable resort. Rooms are well-designed and comfortable, and all have mini-bar and safe. 🛏 TV ▤ ✉ P	ⓁⓁ	63	■	●	■

SAN LEO: *Castello* Ⓛ 14
Piazza d'Alighieri 12, 61018. ☏ 0541-91 62 14. ℻ 0541-92 69 26.
Housed in a restored 16th-century town building in the town centre, the white tiles and light colours in the interior create an airy atmosphere. 🛏 📺 ✉

SAN MARINO: *Panoramic* Ⓛ 27
Via Voltone 89, 47031. ☏ 0549-99 14 36. ℻ 0549-99 03 56.
A family-run hotel in a tranquil part of this independent republic in the middle of Italy. The Panoramic is particularly proud of its restaurant. 🛏 📺 ✉ 🅿

SIROLO: *Monte Conero* ⓁⓁ 48
Via Monteconero 26, 60020. ☏ 071-933 05 92. ℻ 071-933 03 65.
Splendid sea views from this hotel in an 11th-century monastery with a Romanesque church. Rooms are bright and have their own balconies. Guests are expected to take half or full board during July and August. 🛏 ✉ 🅿

URBINO: *Due Querce* Ⓛ 13
Via della Stazione 35, 61029. ☏ 0722-25 09.
A friendly and welcoming hotel conveniently placed near the historic centre of town. Rooms are basic but some have views of the surrounding plain. 🅿

URBINO: *Locanda la Brombolona* Ⓛ 12
Località Sant'Andrea in Primicilio 22, 61029. ☏ 0722-535 01. ℻ 0722-535 01.
Pleasantly located in the rolling hills above Urbino, this charming little hotel makes a peaceful rural base from which to explore the surroundings. Inside it is simply furnished and rooms have views over the countryside. 🛏 🅿

URBINO: *Bonconte* ⓁⓁⓁ 23
Via delle Mura 28, 61029. ☏ 0722-24 63. ℻ 0722-47 82.
A recently refurbished old villa; furnishings include some antiques among the more modern suites. The bright rooms are well-equipped. 🛏 📺 ▤ ✉

ROME

AVENTINE: *Aventino* ⓁⓁ 23
Via San Domenico 10, 00153. **Map** 6 E3. ☏ 06-574 51 74. ℻ 06-578 36 04.
A modest hotel with large but fairly simple rooms. However, the lush garden location and the stained glass in the breakfast room are gorgeous. 🛏 ✉

AVENTINE: *Sant'Anselmo* ⓁⓁ 46
Piazza Sant'Anselmo 2, 00153. **Map** 6 E3. ☏ 06-574 51 74. ℻ 06-578 36 04.
A pretty villa on the peaceful Aventine within walking distance of the Colosseum. It has a secluded garden and some of the prettily decorated rooms are furnished with antique and hand-painted furniture. 🛏 📺 ✉

AVENTINE: *Domus Aventino* ⓁⓁⓁ 26
Via di Santa Prisca 11b, 00153. **Map** 6 E3. ☏ 06-57 30 00 04. ℻ 06-57 30 00 44.
Situated in a 14th-century convent at the foot of the Aventine Hill, the hotel offers large, simply decorated rooms, most of them with balconies. 🛏 📺 ✉ 🅿

CAMPO DE' FIORI: *Piccolo* Ⓛ 15
Via dei Chiavari 32, 00186. **Map** 2 F4. ☏ 06-68 80 25 60.
A cool, serene family-run hotel with clean, simple rooms and a TV in the breakfast room. It is one of the cheapest hotels in the area. ✉

CAMPO DE' FIORI: *Campo de' Fiori* ⓁⓁ 27
Via dei Biscione 6, 00186. **Map** 2 F4. ☏ 06-687 48 86. ℻ 06-687 60 03.
The small bedrooms are prettily decorated, some with beams or ceiling paintings. A roof garden on the sixth floor gives vertiginous views. ✉

CAMPO DE' FIORI: *Lunetta* ⓁⓁ 36
Piazza del Paradiso 68, 00186. **Map** 2 F4. ☏ 06-686 10 80. ℻ 06-689 20 28.
A well-maintained hotel with neat, clean rooms, on a tiny crumbling piazza near Campo de' Fiori. Popular with young groups of musicians and students.

CAMPO DE' FIORI: *Teatro di Pompeo* ⓁⓁⓁ 13
Largo del Pallaro 8, 00186. **Map** 2 F4. ☏ 06-68 30 01 70, 687 25 66. ℻ 06-68 80 55 31.
A small courteously run hotel whose basement breakfast room is in the ruins of Pompey the Great's theatre. Bedrooms have beamed ceilings. 🛏 📺 ✉

FORUM: *Forum* ⓁⓁⓁⓁ 76
Via Tor de' Conti 25, 00184. **Map** 3 C5. ☏ 06-679 24 46. ℻ 06-678 64 79.
An old-fashioned hotel with wood-panelled public rooms and a sunny roof-terrace restaurant with views over the archaeological zone. 🛏 📺 ▤ ✉

Price categories for a standard
double room for one night,
including tax and service charges
but not including breakfast:
Ⓛ under L100,000
ⓁⓁ L100 – 200,000
ⓁⓁⓁ L200 – 300,000
ⓁⓁⓁⓁ L300 – 400,000
ⓁⓁⓁⓁⓁ over L400,000.

RESTAURANT
A restaurant within the hotel sometimes reserved for residents.
SWIMMING POOL
Hotel swimming pools are usually quite small and are outdoors
unless otherwise stated.
GARDEN OR TERRACE
A garden, courtyard or terrace belonging to the hotel, often
providing tables for eating outside.
CREDIT CARDS
The major credit cards Visa, MasterCard (Access) and American
Express are accepted in hotels with the credit card symbol.

	NUMBER OF ROOMS	RESTAURANT	SWIMMING POOL	GARDEN OR TERRACE
PANTHEON: *Abruzzi* ⓁⓁ Piazza della Rotonda 69, 00186. **Map** 2 F4. ☏ 06-679 20 21. Terracotta-tiled floors in an ochre-coloured palazzo overlooking the Pantheon. The Abruzzi provides clean, simple but pleasant rooms without breakfast.	25			
PANTHEON: *Santa Chiara* ⓁⓁⓁ Via di Santa Chiara 21, 00186. **Map** 2 F4. ☏ 06-687 29 79. FAX 06-687 31 44. A conveniently located hotel with cool, marble reception area and well-furnished bedrooms. Rooms facing the street can be noisy. 📶 📺 ▤ 🔖	97			
PANTHEON: *Holiday Inn Crowne Plaza Minerva* ⓁⓁⓁⓁ Piazza della Minerva 69, 00186. **Map** 3 A4. ☏ 06-69 94 18 88. FAX 06-679 41 65. The interior, with its semi-translucent Venetian glass and marble, was designed by post-modern architect, Paolo Portoghesi and the bedrooms are spacious and bright. The roof terrace commands magnificent views. 📶 📺 ▤ 🔖	134	■		■
PANTHEON: *Nazionale* ⓁⓁⓁⓁ Piazza di Montecitorio 131, 00186. **Map** 3 A3. ☏ 06-69 50 01. FAX 06-678 66 77. Opposite the Chamber of Deputies, the Nazionale's comfortable and sometimes huge rooms are furnished with British and Italian antiques. The hotel is popular with business travellers and well-heeled tourists. 📶 📺 🔖	86	■		
PANTHEON: *Sole al Pantheon* ⓁⓁⓁⓁ Piazza della Rotonda 63, 00186. **Map** 2 F4. ☏ 06-678 04 41. FAX 06-69 94 06 89. A historic hotel dating from 1467. Some of its beautiful modernized rooms have painted panelled ceilings and magical views of the Pantheon. 📶 📺 🔖	29			
PIAZZA NAVONA: *Navona* ⓁⓁ Via dei Sediari 8, 00186. **Map** 2 F4. ☏ 06-686 42 03. FAX 06-68 80 38 02. Book well in advance for this superbly located, good value hotel run by the owner's friendly Australian son-in-law. Rooms are basic but satisfactory. 📶	21			
PIAZZA NAVONA: *Due Torri* ⓁⓁⓁ Vicolo del Leonetto 23–25, 00186. **Map** 2 F3. ☏ 06-687 69 83. FAX 06-686 54 42. An amiable hotel tucked into an alleyway in the artisans' district. Rooms vary in size and style. Public rooms have a country house feel. 📶 📺 ▤ 🔖	26			■
PIAZZA NAVONA: *Raphael* ⓁⓁⓁⓁ Largo Febo 2, 00186. **Map** 2 F3. ☏ 06-68 28 31. FAX 06-687 89 93. An ivy-clad luxury hotel whose reception is full of antique statues and modern sculpture. It has a restaurant and elegantly furnished bedrooms. 📶 📺 ▤ 🔖	63	■		
PIAZZA DI SPAGNA: *Jonella* Ⓛ Via della Croce 41, 00187. **Map** 3 A2. ☏ 06-679 79 66. FAX 06-446 23 68. The low prices and location on one of the main shopping streets of the Piazza di Spagna area make this simple pensione well worth considering.	5			
PIAZZA DI SPAGNA: *Margutta* ⓁⓁ Via Laurina 34, 00187. **Map** 3 A1. ☏ 06-679 84 40, 322 36 74. FAX 06-320 03 95. Pretty rooms on a quiet street. Book in advance if you want one of the three attic rooms that share a roof terrace. Public rooms are airy and bright. 📶 🔖	21			
PIAZZA DI SPAGNA: *Condotti* ⓁⓁⓁ Via Mario de' Fiori 37, 00187. **Map** 3 A2. ☏ 06-679 47 69. FAX 06-679 04 57. A comfortable, welcoming hotel in the heart of the designer shopping district. Rooms are medium to large and well decorated. One room has its own small terrace and three others share one. 📶 📺 ▤ 🔖	17			
PIAZZA DI SPAGNA: *Gregoriana* ⓁⓁⓁ Via Gregoriana 18, 00187. **Map** 3 B2. ☏ 06-679 42 69. FAX 06-678 42 58. This stylish hotel, popular with writers and artists in the 19th century, has an interesting variety of decoration, including some unusual leopard-spotted wallpaper. Bedrooms, however, are flowery and fresh. 📶 📺 ▤ 🅿	19			

PIAZZA DI SPAGNA: *Homs*   ⓁⓁⓁ   50
Via della Vite 71–72, 00187. **Map** 3 A2. 📞 06-679 29 76. 🆔 06-678 04 82.
Clean, pleasant rooms on one of the area's quieter, less pretentious shopping
streets. The breakfast room opens onto a pleasant terrace. 🔧 🗳 🅿

PIAZZA DI SPAGNA: *Scalinata di Spagna*   ⓁⓁⓁ   15
Piazza Trinità dei Monti 17, 00187. **Map** 3 B2. 📞 06-679 30 06. 🆔 06-69 94 05 98.
A convivial hotel in a small 18th-century villa at the top of the Spanish Steps.
The rooms that open onto the terrace have exquisite views. 🔧 📺 ☰ 🗳 🅿

PIAZZA DI SPAGNA: *Hassler*   ⓁⓁⓁⓁⓁ   100
Piazza Trinità dei Monti 6, 00187. **Map** 3 B2. 📞 06-678 26 51. 🆔 06-678 99 91.
Venetian glass chandeliers and wood-panelled bathrooms retain the air of a
more extravagant era. Magnificent views from the roof-terrace. 🔧 📺 ☰ 🗳 🅿

QUIRINAL: *Grand*   ⓁⓁⓁⓁ   170
Via VE Orlando 3, 00185. **Map** 4 D2. 📞 06-47 09. 🆔 06-474 73 07.
One of the smartest hotels in Rome, with spectacular turn-of-the-century decor
and impressive facilities, including a sauna and a hairdresser. 🔧 ☰ 📺 🗳

TERMINI: *Katty*   Ⓛ   11
Via Palestro 35, 00185. **Map** 4 E1. 📞 06-444 12 16. 🆔 06-444 13 11.
The Katty has clean, basic rooms with an occasional piece of antique furniture.
It is extremely popular with British and American students, so book early.

TERMINI: *Mari*   Ⓛ   13
Via Palestro 55, 00185. **Map** 4 E1. 📞 06-446 21 37. 🆔 06-482 83 13.
A friendly hotel run by three women. It has clean pleasant rooms with no frills.
Guests can be accommodated at a nearby pensione when this one is full. 🗳

TERMINI: *Canada*   ⓁⓁ   70
Via Vicenza 58, 00185. **Map** 4 F2. 📞 06-445 77 70. 🆔 06-445 07 49.
A good, mid-range hotel behind Termini station, which has a pleasant lounge-bar
with attractive cane seats and squashy sofas. Courteous service. 🔧 📺 🗳

TRASTEVERE: *Manara*   Ⓛ   6
Via Manara 25, 00153. **Map** 5 C1. 📞 06-581 47 13.
This is one of the few hotels in Trastevere and lies just off the main market
square. Its clean and simple rooms make it an excellent budget choice.

VATICAN: *Alimandi*   ⓁⓁ   32
Via Tunisi 8, 00192. **Map** 3 D1. 📞 06-39 72 39 48. 🆔 06-39 72 39 43.
A simple pensione near the entrance to the Vatican museums. It has a large
terrace where you can have barbecues if you ask in advance. 🔧 🗳 🅿

VATICAN: *Colombus*   ⓁⓁⓁ   100
Via della Conciliazione 33, 00193. **Map** 1 C3. 📞 06-686 54 35. 🆔 06-686 48 74.
Occupying a former monastery near St Peter's Square, the hotel's function
room is in the old refectory and has retained its original frescoes. 🔧 📺 🗳 🅿

VIA VENETO: *Merano*   ⓁⓁ   30
Via Veneto 155, 00187. **Map** 3 C1. 📞 06-482 17 96. 🆔 06-482 18 10.
The best feature of this slightly over-priced but very friendly hotel in a
19th-century palazzo is its sunny, parquet-floored breakfast room. 🔧 🗳

VIA VENETO: *Alexandra*   ⓁⓁⓁ   45
Via Veneto 18, 00187. **Map** 3 C1. 📞 06-488 19 43, 488 19 44. 🆔 06-487 18 04.
A good value hotel on this expensive street, the Alexandra has a pleasant
breakfast room and each bedroom has been decorated differently. 🔧 📺 🗳 🅿

VIA VENETO: *Residenza*   ⓁⓁⓁ   29
Via Emilia 22–24, 00187. **Map** 3 C1. 📞 06-488 07 89. 🆔 06-48 57 21.
An elegant, courteously-run hotel in a quiet villa, with stylish public rooms,
comfortable bedrooms and a delightful canopied terrace. 🔧 📺 ☰ 🗳 🅿

VIA VENETO: *Excelsior*   ⓁⓁⓁⓁⓁ   327
Via Veneto 125, 00187. **Map** 3 C1. 📞 06-47 08. 🆔 06-482 62 05.
This extravagant hotel has sumptuous public rooms with marble floors and
brocade furnishings. Bedrooms are elegant and spacious. 🔧 📺 ☰ 🗳 🅿

VIA VENETO: *Imperiale*   ⓁⓁⓁⓁ   95
Via Veneto 24, 00187. **Map** 3 C1. 📞 06-482 63 51. 🆔 06-482 63 51.
Friendly staff make for a relaxed atmosphere in this reasonably priced
hotel with well decorated bedrooms and marble bathrooms. 🔧 📺 ☰ 🗳

For key to symbols see back flap

	NUMBER OF ROOMS	RESTAURANT	SWIMMING POOL	GARDEN OR TERRACE

Price categories for a standard double room for one night, including tax and service charges but not including breakfast:
ⓛ under L100,000
ⓛⓛ L100 – 200,000
ⓛⓛⓛ L200 – 300,000
ⓛⓛⓛⓛ L300 – 400,000
ⓛⓛⓛⓛⓛ over L400,000.

RESTAURANT
A restaurant within the hotel sometimes reserved for residents.
SWIMMING POOL
Hotel swimming pools are usually quite small and are outdoors unless otherwise stated.
GARDEN OR TERRACE
A garden, courtyard or terrace belonging to the hotel, often providing tables for eating outside.
CREDIT CARDS
The major credit cards Visa, MasterCard (Access) and American Express are accepted in hotels with the credit card symbol.

		Rooms	Rest.	Pool	Garden
VILLA BORGHESE: *Villa Borghese* ⓛⓛⓛ Via Pinciana 31, 00198. 🄲 06-841 41 00. FAX 06-841 41 00. This pleasant hotel has the atmosphere of a private home rather than a hotel. Rooms are small but comfortable and are tastefully decorated. 🖥 TV 🗐		31			▓
VILLA BORGHESE: *Lord Byron* ⓛⓛⓛⓛⓛ Via Notaris 5, 00197. 🄲 06-361 30 41. FAX 06-322 04 05. A small, refined hotel housed in a former monastery in the Parioli district, the Lord Byron has lavishly decorated public rooms. 🖥 TV 🗏 🗐 P		37	▓		▓

LAZIO

		Rooms	Rest.	Pool	Garden
ANAGNI: *Villa La Floridiana* ⓛⓛ Via Casilina, km 63,700, 03012. 🄲 0775-76 99 60. FAX 0775-76 78 46. A beautiful medieval village is the setting for this charming villa with a traditional faded pink façade, green shutters and large, comfortable rooms. 🖥 TV 🗐 P		9	▓		
BAGNI DI TIVOLI: *Grand Hotel Duca d'Este* ⓛⓛⓛ Via Tiburtina Valeria 330, 00011. 🄲 0774-3883. FAX 0774-38 81 01. A modern well-equipped hotel near Tivoli and Villa Adriana and within easy reach of Rome by road or rail. Suites have satellite TV and jacuzzis. 🖥 TV 🗏 🗐		184	▓		▓
BRACCIANO: *Casina del Lago* ⓛⓛ Via del Lago 11, 00062. 🄲 06-99 80 54 75. In a beautiful lakeside setting, this small, simple hotel affords some wonderful views and has its own tennis courts. Bedrooms are basic but satisfactory. 🖥 P		10			
FORMIA: *Castello Miramare* ⓛⓛ Via Balze di Pagnano, 04023. 🄲 0771-70 01 38. FAX 0771-70 01 38. The castle was built in 1910 on a hill in the centre of Formia with fine views over the sea. Spacious bedrooms are decorated in Spanish style. 🖥 TV 🗐 P		10	▓		▓
GROTTAFERRATA: *Villa Fiorio* ⓛⓛ Viale Dusmet 42, 00046. 🄲 06-945 92 76. FAX 06-941 34 82. Built as a summer residence at the turn of the century, this pretty villa, which retains some original frescoes, has large, cool and quiet rooms. 🖥 TV 🗐		20	▓	●	▓
ISOLA DI PONZA: *Cernia* ⓛⓛⓛ Via Panoramica, Chiaia di Luna 04027. 🄲 0771-804 12. FAX 0771-80 99 54. A beautiful setting for this modern but stylish hotel with a dense garden. Wicker furniture and rocking chairs create a friendly atmosphere. 🖥 TV 🗏 🗐 P		60	▓	●	▓
LADISPOLI: *La Posta Vecchia* ⓛⓛⓛⓛⓛ Località Palo Laziale, 00055. 🄲 06-994 95 01. FAX 06-994 95 07. A magnificent 17th-century villa on the sea, it was restored by John Paul Getty as his Italian residence and is now one of Italy's most luxurious hotels. All rooms are exquisitely and individually decorated with antiques. 🖥 TV 🗐 P		12	▓	●	▓
PALESTRINA: *Stella* ⓛ Piazzale della Liberazione 3, 00036. 🄲 06-953 81 72. FAX 06-957 33 60. A friendly, peaceful hotel in the historic centre of Palestrina close to the town's sights and with an excellent restaurant. 🖥 TV 🗐 P		28	▓		▓
SAN FELICE CIRCEO: *Punta Rossa* ⓛⓛⓛⓛ Via delle Batterie 37, 04017. 🄲 0773-54 80 85. FAX 0773-54 80 75. A charming hotel set in a garden that leads down to the sea. Rooms are in various buildings, all have terraces and sea views and there is a covered sea-water swimming pool as well as a second pool by the sea. 🖥 TV 🗐 P		37	▓	●	▓
SUBIACO: *Livata* ⓛⓛ Località Monte Livata, 00028. 🄲 0774-82 60 31. FAX 0774-82 60 33. A good choice if you're visiting the monastery of San Benedetto, the Livata is a friendly country hotel with tennis courts and attractive gardens. 🖥 🗐 P		84	▓		

TARQUINIA LIDO: *La Torraccia*   ⓁⓁ   18
Viale Mediterraneo 45, 01010. **☎** 0766-86 43 75. **FAX** 0766-86 42 96.
A modern, comfortable hotel set in pinewoods 200 m (656 ft) from the
sea. All rooms have a terrace and there is a private beach. 🛏 📺 ▤ 🗐 🅿

VITERBO: *Balletti Palace*   ⓁⓁ   105
Via Molini 8, 01100. **☎** 0761-34 47 77. **FAX** 0761-34 47 77.
A modern hotel set in Viterbo's historic centre with elegant bedrooms and
suites. There is no restaurant but the Grenier Café serves light meals. 🛏 📺 🗐 🅿

VITERBO: *Balletti Park*   ⓁⓁⓁ   136
Via Umbria 2, San Martino al Cimino 01030. **☎** 0761-37 71. **☎** 0761-37 94 96.
A modern hotel set in its own extensive gardens. There are sports facilities
and a health centre as well as some independent apartments. 🛏 📺 🗐 🅿

NAPLES AND CAMPANIA

AMALFI: *Cappuccini Convento*   ⓁⓁⓁ   54
Via Annunziatella 46, 84011. **☎** 089-87 18 77. **FAX** 089-87 18 86.
Balanced on a cliff above Amalfi, this exquisitely restored 12th-century
monastery has spectacular views over the sea and antiques in the bedrooms. There are occasional recitals in the converted cloisters. 🛏 🗐 🅿

AMALFI: *Luna Convento*   ⓁⓁⓁ   45
Via Comite 33, 84011. **☎** 089-87 10 02. **FAX** 089-87 13 33.
This tastefully furnished 13th-century monastery overlooking the sea makes a
luxurious, peaceful base from which to explore the countryside. 🛏 📺 🗐 🅿

BAIA DOMIZIA: *Hotel della Baia*   ⓁⓁ   56
Via dell'Erica, 81030. **☎** 0823-72 13 44. **FAX** 0823-72 15 56.
A charming, friendly hotel run by three sisters with its own private beach.
The pretty bedrooms are comfortable and all have sea views. 🛏 🗐 🅿

BENEVENTO: *Grand Hotel Italiano*   ⓁⓁ   71
Viale Principe di Napoli 137, 82100. **☎** 0824-241 11. **FAX** 0824-217 58.
The Italiano family are justly proud of the hotel's reputation for courtesy
and good service. Public areas are spacious and elegant. 🛏 📺 🗐

CAPRI: *Villa Sarah*   ⓁⓁⓁ   20
Via Tiberio 3a, 80073. **☎** 081-837 78 17. **FAX** 081-837 72 15.
A peaceful family-run villa hotel set among the island's vineyards. Rooms
are clean and pretty and home produce is served for breakfast. 🛏 🗐

CAPRI: *Punta Tragara*   ⓁⓁⓁⓁ   47
Via Tragara 57, 80073. **☎** 081-837 08 44. **FAX** 081-837 77 90.
A sumptuous hotel built into a cliff over the sea, designed by Le Corbusier,
with all the comforts of a luxury residence. No children under 12. 🛏 📺 ▤ 🗐

CASERTA: *Europa*   ⓁⓁⓁ   60
Via Roma 29, 81100. **☎** 0823-32 54 00. **FAX** 0823-24 51 11.
A smart modern hotel conveniently placed in central Caserta. The Europa also
has several mini-apartments with cooking facilities for longer stays. 🛏 📺 🗐 🅿

ISCHIA: *Il Monastero*   ⓁⓁ   22
Castello Aragonese 3, Ischia Ponte 80070. **☎** 081-99 24 35.
A charming, simple pensione set in a converted monastery overlooking the
town of Ischia. The walls are hung with paintings and furniture is plain
but attractive. Guests are expected to take half-board in summer. 🛏

ISCHIA: *La Villarosa*   ⓁⓁⓁ   33
Via Giacinto Gigante 5, Porto d'Ischia 80070. **☎** 081-99 13 16. **FAX** 081-99 24 25.
An enchanting, elegant hotel set in a beautiful tropical garden. Many of the
discreetly charming rooms have balconies filled with bougainvilleas. 🛏 🗐

NAPLES: *Rex*   ⓁⓁ   38
Via Palepoli 12, 80132. **☎** 081-764 93 89. **FAX** 081-764 92 27.
A friendly, family hotel on the seafront of Naples, well placed for theatres and
beaches. Public rooms are elegantly furnished with wicker chairs. 🛏 📺 🗐 🅿

NAPLES: *Britannique*   ⓁⓁⓁ   86
Corso Vittorio Emanuele 133, 80121. **☎** 081-761 41 45. **FAX** 081-66 04 57.
A smart, modern hotel in the centre of Naples. Bedrooms are attractively
decorated and there are spectacular views from the roof terrace. Some
suites with cooking facilities are available for longer stays. 🛏 📺 🗐 🅿

For key to symbols see back flap

		Price categories for a standard double room for one night, including tax and service charges but not including breakfast: Ⓛ under L100,000 ⓁⓁ L100 – 200,000 ⓁⓁⓁ L200 – 300,000 ⓁⓁⓁⓁ L300 – 400,000 ⓁⓁⓁⓁⓁ over L400,000.	**RESTAURANT** A restaurant within the hotel sometimes reserved for residents. **SWIMMING POOL** Hotel swimming pools are usually quite small and are outdoors unless otherwise stated. **GARDEN OR TERRACE** A garden, courtyard or terrace belonging to the hotel, often providing tables for eating outside. **CREDIT CARDS** The major credit cards Visa, MasterCard (Access) and American Express are accepted in hotels with the credit card symbol.	NUMBER OF ROOMS	RESTAURANT	SWIMMING POOL	GARDEN OR TERRACE

NAPLES: *Paradiso* ⓁⓁⓁ Via Catullo 11, 80122. 📞 081-761 41 61. FAX 081-761 34 49. An elegant hotel set in a residential area of Naples, with good views of the bay and Vesuvius from its terrace restaurant and from some bedrooms. It is ten minutes' walk from the pier for hydrofoils to Capri and Ischia. 🔲 TV 🔲 🔲 P	74	■		■
NAPLES: *Grande Albergo Vesuvio* ⓁⓁⓁⓁⓁ Via Partenope 45, 80121. 📞 081-764 00 44. FAX 081-589 03 80. Founded in 1882, the Grande Hotel overlooks the marina in central Naples. It is well decorated and furnished with marble bathrooms and antiques, and includes a "baby" room with a rocking horse, mobiles and toys. 🔲 TV 🔲 P	167	■		■
PAESTUM: *Le Palme* ⓁⓁ Via Sterpinia 33, 4063. 📞 0828-85 10 25. FAX 0828-85 15 07. A pleasant, peaceful seaside hotel with tennis courts and its own beach. Rooms are comfortable and the hotel is set in attractive grounds. 🔲 🔲 P	50	■	●	■
POSITANO: *L'Ancora* ⓁⓁ Via Colombo 36, 84017. 📞 089-87 53 18. FAX 089-81 17 84. Excellent value in expensive Positano from this modern, central hotel with sea views. The good-sized bedrooms are comfortable. 🔲 TV 🔲 P	18			■
POSITANO: *Palazzo Murat* ⓁⓁⓁ Via dei Mulini 23, 84017. 📞 089-87 51 77. FAX 089-81 14 19. A pretty 18th-century palazzo in central Positano, near the cathedral. Rooms have traditional wooden furniture, and some have balconies. 🔲 TV 🔲 🔲	30			■
RAVELLO: *Graal* ⓁⓁ Via della Repubblica 8, 84010. 📞 089-85 72 22. FAX 089-85 75 51. The hotel has a wonderful swimming pool with attractive views over Ravello. The restaurant serves good local specialities. 🔲 🔲 P	35	■	●	■
RAVELLO: *Palumbo* ⓁⓁⓁⓁⓁ Via San Giovanni del Toro 28, 84010. 📞 089-85 72 44. FAX 089-85 81 33. This 12th-century palazzo has been run as a hotel by the same family for more than 100 years. Furnishings are elegant and there are antiques in some bedrooms. Rooms in the modern annexe are cheaper. 🔲 TV 🔲 🔲 P	24	■		■
SALERNO: *Fiorenza* ⓁⓁ Via Trento 145, 84100. 📞 089-33 88 00. FAX 089-33 88 00. A 1960s hotel overlooking the sea on the outskirts of Salerno. All the rooms are modern and have private safes, mini-bars and satellite TV. 🔲 TV 🔲 🔲 P	30			■
SAPRI: *Mediterraneo* Ⓛ Via Verdi, 84073. 📞 0973-39 17 74. FAX 0973-39 11 57. Excellent value at this comfortable, no frills hotel built right next to the rocky beach with garden and terrace overlooking the sea. 🔲 P	20	■		■
SAPRI: *Tirreno* Ⓛ Corso Italia 73, 84073. 📞 0973-39 10 06. FAX 0973-39 11 57. A good value pensione facing the sea. Inside it is airy and light and bedrooms have their own balconies. The restaurant serves local specialities. 🔲 P	47	■		
SORRENTO: *Bellevue Syrene* ⓁⓁⓁ Piazza della Vittoria 5, 80067. 📞 081-878 10 24. FAX 081-878 39 63. A typical grand beach hotel, now slightly faded. It is perched on the cliffs with a lift to take guests down to the beach. Sumptuous bedrooms. 🔲 TV 🔲	74	■		■
SORRENTO: *Grand Hotel Cocumella* ⓁⓁⓁⓁ Via Cocumella 7, 80065. 📞 081-878 29 33. FAX 081-878 37 12. Opulent elegance from another era characterizes this peaceful hotel on the Amalfi coast set in fragrant and peaceful gardens. The sea is nearby and the hotel sailing boat will take guests to Capri for the day. 🔲 TV 🔲 🔲 P	60	■	●	■

ABRUZZO, MOLISE AND PUGLIA

ALBEROBELLO: *Colle del Sole* Ⓛ 24
Via Indipendenza 63, 70011. █ 080-72 18 14. **FAX** 080-72 13 70.
A comfortable, modern hotel with a balcony for every bedroom. Art and
photo exhibitions are sometimes arranged in the restaurant. 🖼 TV 🗲 **P**

ALBEROBELLO: *Dei Trulli* ⓁⓁⓁ 30
Via Cadore 32, 70011. █ 080-932 35 55. **FAX** 080-932 35 60.
The hotel is set in a mini-village of *trulli (see p495)*. Furnishings are simple,
even stark, but the grounds are pleasant. Half-board in summer. 🖼 TV 🗲 **P**

BARI: *Boston* ⓁⓁ 70
Via Piccinni 155, 70122. █ 080-521 66 33. **FAX** 080-524 68 02.
A modern hotel near the historic centre of Bari. Furnishings are stylish and
functional and there is much dark wood panelling. Half-board. 🖼 TV 🗲 **P**

GARGANO PENINSULA: *Seggio* ⓁⓁ 28
Via Vesta 7, Vieste 71019. █ 0884-70 81 23. **FAX** 0884-70 87 27.
Perched on a small cliff over its own private bay, this restored 17th-century
building was the original town hall. Bedrooms are simple. 🖼 TV 🗲 **P**

ISOLE TREMITI: *Kyrie* ⓁⓁⓁ 64
San Domino, 71040. █ 0882-66 32 32. **FAX** 0882-66 34 15.
The largest and best-equipped of the Tremiti hotels. It is in the pinewoods
next to the sea and, as well as conventional rooms, has some mini-
apartments for longer stays. Open from June to September only. 🖼 🗲

L'AQUILA: *Castello di Balsorano* ⓁⓁ 10
Piazza Piccolomini 10, 67100. █ 0863-95 12 36. **FAX** 0863-95 05 84.
A former manor is the setting for this tranquil hotel with dark woodwork and
low beds. Some secret passageways create a medieval atmosphere. 🖼 🗲 **P**

L'AQUILA: *Grand Hotel e del Parco* ⓁⓁ 36
Corso Federico II 74, 67100. █ 0862-41 32 48. **FAX** 0862-659 38.
A comfortable, modern hotel in the centre of L'Aquila within easy reach
of the ski-slopes and hiking trails of the Gran Sasso. The hotel also has a
health centre, complete with saunas and Turkish baths. 🖼 TV 🗲 **P**

LECCE: *Grand* ⓁⓁ 70
Viale Oronzo Quarta 28, 73100. █ 0832-30 94 05. **FAX** 0832-30 98 91.
This Art Nouveau villa was converted into an elegant hotel in the 1930s.
Although some of the rooms are rather shabby, it is still charming. 🖼 TV 🗲 **P**

MARINA DI LESINA: *Maddalena Club* ⓁⓁ 80
Via Saturno 82, 71010. █ 0882-950 76. **FAX** 0882-954 34.
A modern beach hotel with a range of sports and leisure facilities, including
a private beach. The restaurant serves a variety of local fish dishes. 🖼 🗲 **P**

MONOPOLI: *Il Melograno* ⓁⓁⓁⓁⓁ 37
Contrada Torricella 345, 70043. █ 080-690 90 30. **FAX** 080-74 79 08.
A luxurious oasis of tranquillity in a peaceful, verdant corner of Puglia.
The sumptuous interior of this restored 16th-century residence is furnished
with antiques, and there are tennis courts and a private beach. 🖼 TV 🗲 **P**

OTRANTO: *Albania* Ⓛ 10
Via San Francesco di Paola 10, 73028. █ 0836-80 11 83.
A small, simple, family hotel ideally situated just outside the walls of old
Otranto, near the port and within a short walk of the beach. 🖼 TV 🎜 🗲 **P**

RUVO DI PUGLIA: *Talos* Ⓛ 18
Via Aldo Moro 12, 70037. █ 080-81 16 45.
A simple, modern hotel that is good value for travellers on a budget. It is
well placed for exploring the surrounding countryside. 🖼 TV 🗲 **P**

RUVO DI PUGLIA: *Pineta* ⓁⓁ 15
Via Carlo Marx 5, 70037. █ 080-81 15 78. **FAX** 080-81 15 78.
A modern hotel set in peaceful grounds on the outskirts of town. Furnishings
are basic but the rooms are bright and there are good views. 🖼 TV 🗲 **P**

SCANNO: *Mille Pini* ⓁⓁ 21
Via Pescara 2, 67038. █ 0864-743 87.
A friendly, good value chalet hotel at the foot of Monte Rotondo chairlift.
Facilities are simple and rustic but comfortable and there is a restaurant. 🖼 **P**

<table>
<tr><td colspan="2">

Price categories for a standard double room for one night, including tax and service charges but not including breakfast:
Ⓛ under L100,000
ⓁⓁ L100 – 200,000
ⓁⓁⓁ L200 – 300,000
ⓁⓁⓁⓁ L300 – 400,000
ⓁⓁⓁⓁⓁ over L400,000.
</td><td colspan="2">

RESTAURANT
A restaurant within the hotel sometimes reserved for residents.
SWIMMING POOL
Hotel swimming pools are usually quite small and are outdoors unless otherwise stated.
GARDEN OR TERRACE
A garden, courtyard or terrace belonging to the hotel, often providing tables for eating outside.
CREDIT CARDS
The major credit cards Visa, MasterCard (Access) and American Express are accepted in hotels with the credit card symbol.
</td></tr>
</table>

			NUMBER OF ROOMS	RESTAURANT	SWIMMING POOL	GARDEN OR TERRACE
SULMONA: *Italia* Piazza Salvatore Tommasi 3, 67039. ☎ 0864-523 08. A charming ivy-covered town house in a quiet square. Furnishings vary from modern utility to antique, giving a lived-in feeling to this friendly hotel. 🛏 P	Ⓛ		27			
TARANTO: *Plaza* Via d'Aquino 46, 74100. ☎ 099-459 07 75. FAX 099-459 06 75. A big, city hotel that is very well placed in the newer part of Taranto near the major sights. Both business and holiday guests are catered for. 🛏 TV 🗑	ⓁⓁ		112	■		

BASILICATA AND CALABRIA

			NUMBER OF ROOMS	RESTAURANT	SWIMMING POOL	GARDEN OR TERRACE
ACQUAFREDDA MARATEA: *Villa Cheta Elite* Via Timpone 46, 85041. ☎ 0973-87 81 34. FAX 0973-87 81 35. An elegant, Liberty-style villa with stunning views over a picturesque bay. The comfortable rooms are attractively furnished in traditional southern Italian style and staff and service are friendly and polite. 🛏 🗑 P	ⓁⓁ		20	■		■
COSENZA: *Royal* Via Molinella 24e, 87100. ☎ 0984-41 21 65. FAX 0984-41 17 77. One of the best modern hotels in Cosenza, conveniently located in the centre of town, not far from the station. 🛏 TV ▤ 🗑 ♿ P	ⓁⓁ		44	■		■
MATERA: *De Nicola* Via Nazionale 158, 75100. ☎ 0835-38 51 11. FAX 0835-38 51 13. A large modern hotel in central Matera close to the station and easily accessible from the motorway. Bedrooms are functional. 🛏 ▤ 🗑 P	ⓁⓁ		119	■		
METAPONTO LIDO: *Turismo* Viale delle Ninfe 5, 75010. ☎ 0835-74 19 18. FAX 0835-74 19 17. A functional, if unexceptional, seaside hotel with its own beach and bar. The restaurant has outside tables for summer dining. 🛏 🗑 P	ⓁⓁ		61	■		■
PARGHELIA: *Baia Paraelios* Località Fornaci, 88035 (nr Tropea). ☎ 0963-60 03 00. FAX 0963-60 00 74. A little village of 72 bungalows each with terrace and sitting room, with superb views over the beach and sea. The restaurant is on a beach terrace. 🛏 🗑 P	ⓁⓁⓁ		72	■	●	■
REGGIO DI CALABRIA: *Grand Hotel Excelsior* Via Vittorio Veneto 66, 89121. ☎ 0965-81 22 11. FAX 0965-89 30 84. This hotel has some of the best facilities in southern Italy. Situated in the centre of town, it appeals to business as well as holiday visitors. 🛏 TV 🗑 P	ⓁⓁⓁ		84	■		■
ROSSANO SCALO: *Murano* Viale Mediterraneo 2, 87068. ☎ 0983-51 17 88. FAX 0983-53 00 88. Set in its own grounds over the sea, the Murano has a private beach and rooms with sea views. There is a piano bar and an outside pizzeria as well as a traditional restaurant serving Calabrian specialities. 🛏 🗑 P	Ⓛ		37	■		■
STILO: *San Giorgio* Via Citarelli 8, 89049. ☎ 0964-77 50 47. FAX 0964-77 50 47. Set in the heart of Stilo, this comfortable hotel is located in a restored 17th-century palazzo and furnished with some 18th-century antiques. 🛏 🗑	Ⓛ		24	■	●	■
TROPEA: *La Pineta* Via Marina 150, 88038. ☎ 0963-617 00. FAX 0963-622 65. This typical resort hotel is open only from June to September. The decor is fairly ordinary but La Pineta does have tennis courts. 🛏 ▤ 🗑 P	ⓁⓁ		59	■		■
VENOSA: *Il Guiscardo* Via Accademia dei Rinascenti 106, 85029. ☎ 0972-323 62. FAX 0972-329 16. There are wonderful views from the terrace over the red roofs of Venosa's historic centre. Bedrooms are elegant and public rooms spacious. 🛏 TV 🗑 P	Ⓛ		36	■		■

SICILY

AGRIGENTO: *Colleverde Park Hotel* ⓁⓁ 48
Via dei Templi, 92100. **(** 0922-295 55. **FAX** 0922-290 12.
A peaceful modern hotel in the Valley of the Temples, with stunning views.
The facilities include safes in the bedrooms and a gym.

AGRIGENTO: *Jolly Hotel dei Templi* ⓁⓁⓁ 146
Parco Angeli, Villaggio Mose 92100. **(** 0922-60 61 44. **FAX** 0922-60 66 85.
One of the modern, efficient Jolly chain, this large, well equipped hotel lies
just outside Agrigento. Rooms are comfortably furnished.

AGRIGENTO: *Villa Athena* ⓁⓁⓁ 40
Via Panoramica dei Templi 33, 92100. **(** 0922-59 62 88. **FAX** 0922-40 21 80.
Set in an 18th-century villa just outside Agrigento. The decor is modern but
the gardens are exquisite, with views of the Temple of Concord.

CATANIA: *Excelsior Grand Hotel* ⓁⓁⓁ 164
Piazza Giovanni Verga 39, 95129. **(** 095-53 70 71. **FAX** 095-53 70 15.
Its anonymous modern block exterior hides a more attractive interior with
marble and wood floors and comfortable furnishings. Its central location and
excellent restaurant makes it popular with business travellers.

CATANIA: *Nettuno* ⓁⓁⓁ 80
Viale Ruggero di Lauria 121, 95127. **(** 095-712 52 52. **FAX** 095-49 80 66.
One of the well-equipped, modern Turisthotels chain. The Nettuno is
near the sea and has views of Mount Etna.

CEFALÙ: *Riva del Sole* ⓁⓁⓁ 28
Viale Lungomare Cefalù 25, 90015. **(** 0921-212 30. **FAX** 0921-219 84.
A hotel on the seafront with good views. Bedrooms are basic but there is a
terrace for sunbathing and a shadier internal courtyard with tables.

ENNA: *Sicilia* ⓁⓁ 80
Piazza Colaianni 7, 94100. **(** 0935-50 08 50. **FAX** 0935-50 04 88.
A comfortable well-run hotel in central Enna, well placed for the town's main
tourist attractions. Some of the rooms have excellent views.

ISOLE EGADI: *Egadi* ⓁⓁ 12
Via Colombo 17, Favignana 0923. **(** 0923-92 12 32. **FAX** 0923-92 12 32.
A small, friendly pensione attached to one of the best restaurants on the island.
Favignana is famous for its tuna which comes from the local fisheries.

ISOLE EOLIE: *Pensione Villa Diana* ⓁⓁ 12
Via Diana Tufo, Lipari 98055. **(** 090-981 14 03. **FAX** 090-981 14 03.
A comfortable family hotel with antiques in some rooms, and spacious
gardens and terraces. The hotel is open from April to October.

ISOLE EOLIE: *La Sciara Residence* ⓁⓁⓁ 62
Via Soldato Cincotta, Isola Stromboli 98050. **(** 090-98 60 05. **FAX** 090-98 62 84.
A splendid garden full of bougainvilleas is the setting for this spacious
and comfortable hotel. Mini-apartments are also available.

ISOLE EOLIE: *Raya* ⓁⓁⓁ 32
Via San Pietro, Isola Panarea 98050. **(** 090-98 30 13. **FAX** 090-98 31 03.
This modern, fashionable hotel consists of pink and white houses on terraces
descending to the sea. The restaurant and bar overlook the port.

ERICE: *Elimo* ⓁⓁ 21
Via Vittorio Emanuele 75, 91016. **(** 0923-86 93 77. **FAX** 0923-86 92 52.
This 18th-century villa retains several original features including traditional
Sicilian wall, ceiling and floor tiles. The hotel is located in the centre of
Erice and has spectacular views as far as the Egadi Islands.

ERICE: *Ermione* ⓁⓁ 48
Via Pineta Comunale 43, 91016. **(** 0923-86 91 38. **FAX** 0923-86 95 87.
Beautifully set amid pine trees close to the centre of Erice with spectacular
views over Trapani to the Egadi islands. Bedrooms are tastefully decorated
and comfortable, and there is an interesting Sicilian tiled bar.

ERICE: *Moderno* ⓁⓁ 41
Via Vittorio Emanuele 63, 91016. **(** 0923-86 93 00. **FAX** 0923-86 91 39.
A family-run hotel that has some attractively old-fashioned bedrooms as well
as some more modern ones. Excellent views from the terrace.

For key to symbols see back flap

Price categories for a standard double room for one night, including tax and service charges but not including breakfast:
- Ⓛ under L100,000
- ⓁⓁ L100 – 200,000
- ⓁⓁⓁ L200 – 300,000
- ⓁⓁⓁⓁ L300 – 400,000
- ⓁⓁⓁⓁⓁ over L400,000.

RESTAURANT
A restaurant within the hotel sometimes reserved for residents.

SWIMMING POOL
Hotel swimming pools are usually quite small and are outdoors unless otherwise stated.

GARDEN OR TERRACE
A garden, courtyard or terrace belonging to the hotel, often providing tables for eating outside.

CREDIT CARDS
The major credit cards Visa, MasterCard (Access) and American Express are accepted in hotels with the credit card symbol.

	Price	Number of Rooms	Restaurant	Swimming Pool	Garden or Terrace
GIARDINI-NAXOS: *Arathena Rocks*	ⓁⓁ	53	■	●	■
MARSALA: *President*	ⓁⓁ	84	■	●	■
MESSINA: *Paradis*	ⓁⓁ	92	■		■
PALERMO: *Orientale*	Ⓛ	21			
PALERMO: *Splendid Hotel La Torre*	ⓁⓁ	179	■	●	■
PALERMO: *Grand Hotel Villa Igiea*	ⓁⓁⓁⓁ	117	■	●	■
SCIACCA: *Grand Hotel delle Terme*	ⓁⓁ	72	■	●	■
SIRACUSA: *Gran Bretagna*	Ⓛ	12	■		
SIRACUSA: *Grand Hotel Villa Politi*	ⓁⓁ	95	■	●	■
TAORMINA: *Romantik Villa Ducale*	ⓁⓁⓁ	10			■
TAORMINA: *Villa Belvedere*	ⓁⓁⓁ	47		●	■
TAORMINA: *San Domenico Palace*	ⓁⓁⓁⓁⓁ	111	■	●	■

GIARDINI-NAXOS: *Arathena Rocks* — Ⓛ Ⓛ
Via Calcide Eubea 55, 98035. 【 0942-513 49. FAX 0942-516 90.
A friendly hotel near the beach and slightly out of this busy resort. Rooms are bright and airy with views over the sea or the hotel gardens. 📶 🈂 P

MARSALA: *President* — Ⓛ Ⓛ
Via Nino Bixio 1, 91025. 【 0923-99 93 33. FAX 0923-99 91 15.
About 1 km (half a mile) from the centre of town this modern, comfortable hotel serves Sicilian and international cuisine in the restaurant. 📶 TV ▤ 🈂 P

MESSINA: *Paradis* — Ⓛ Ⓛ
Via Consolare Pompea 441, 98168. 【 090-31 06 82. FAX 090-31 20 43.
About 3 km (2 miles) out of central Messina, the Paradis has good views and an excellent restaurant. Rooms are basic but satisfactory. 📶 TV 🈂 P

PALERMO: *Orientale* — Ⓛ
Via Maqueda 26, 90134. 【 091-616 57 27.
A budget alternative in the historic centre of Palermo with simple rooms, the Orientale is conveniently located close to the railway station.

PALERMO: *Splendid Hotel La Torre* — Ⓛ Ⓛ
Via Piano Gallo 11, Mondello 90151. 【 091-45 02 22. FAX 091-45 00 33.
A big, traditional seaside hotel, set on a promontory with its own private beach. Some bedrooms have their own balcony with sea views. 📶 TV 🈂 P

PALERMO: *Grand Hotel Villa Igiea* — Ⓛ Ⓛ Ⓛ Ⓛ
Salita Belmonte 43, 90142. 【 091-54 37 44. FAX 091-54 76 54.
An exquisite hotel dating from the beginning of the century with Art Nouveau stained glass and wall paintings. It's set by the sea in gardens with their own ancient ruins. An elegant cocktail bar opens onto the terrace. 📶 TV 🈂 P

SCIACCA: *Grand Hotel delle Terme* — Ⓛ Ⓛ
Viale Nuove Terme 1, 92019. 【 0925-231 33. FAX 0925-217 46.
A spa hotel with access (for an extra charge) to the local mineral springs that were used by the Phoenicians more than 2,000 years ago. Many of the clientele come for various cures. TV in bedrooms on request. 📶 🈂 P

SIRACUSA: *Gran Bretagna* — Ⓛ
Via Savoia 21, 96100. 【 0931-687 65. FAX 0931-687 65.
A small, friendly, family-run hotel with comfortable rooms. The restaurant has special family menus and serves Sicilian and Italian specialities. 🈂

SIRACUSA: *Grand Hotel Villa Politi* — Ⓛ Ⓛ
Via Maria Politi Laudien 2, 96100. 【 0931-41 21 21. FAX 0931-360 61.
A slightly shabby old-fashioned hotel whose vast reception rooms belong to another era. The hotel dates from the turn of the century. 📶 TV ▤ 🈂 P

TAORMINA: *Romantik Villa Ducale* — Ⓛ Ⓛ Ⓛ
Via Leonardo da Vinci 60, 98039. 【 0942-281 53. FAX 0942-281 54.
This elegant villa is now a comfortable hotel. The rooms are all different, furnished with antiques and with excellent views of Etna and the sea. The library has books on the region for guests to browse through. 📶 TV ▤ 🈂 P

TAORMINA: *Villa Belvedere* — Ⓛ Ⓛ Ⓛ
Via Bagnoli Croci 79, 98039. 【 0942-237 91. FAX 0942-62 58 30.
A very comfortable, family hotel in the centre of Taormina. Some rooms have sea views and balconies. Light meals are served by the pool. 📶 🈂 P

TAORMINA: *San Domenico Palace* — Ⓛ Ⓛ Ⓛ Ⓛ Ⓛ
Piazza San Domenico 5, 98039. 【 0942-237 01. FAX 0942-62 55 06.
A peaceful, 15th-century monastery restored and furnished with genuine antiques. This is one of the most luxurious hotels in Sicily and it has a beautiful formal garden as well as an elegant swimming pool. 📶 TV ▤ 🈂 P

TRAPANI: *Astoria Park* Ⓛ Ⓛ 93
Lungomare Dante Alighieri, 91100. 🄲 *0923-56 24 00.* **FAX** *0923-56 74 22.*
A modern hotel on the seafront with all you need for a beach holiday (tennis,
discotheque). A good base from which to explore the region. �̈ 📺 ▤ 🗹 🅿

TRAPANI: *Vittoria* Ⓛ Ⓛ 65
Via Francesco Crispi 4, 91100. 🄲 *0923-87 30 44.* **FAX** *0923-298 70.*
Very conveniently placed in the centre of Trapani, this modern functional
hotel has very simple, well-designed furnishings. �̈ 📺 ▤ 🗹

SARDINIA

ALGHERO: *Villa las Tronas* Ⓛ Ⓛ Ⓛ 29
Lungomare Valencia 1, 07041. 🄲 *079-98 18 18.* **FAX** *079-98 10 44.*
A mustard-coloured villa on a promontory is the setting for this comfortable,
elegantly decorated hotel. Public rooms are full of gilt and 18th-century
French-style furniture; bedrooms are simpler but pretty. �̈ 📺 ▤ 🗹 🅿

CAGLIARI: *Italia* Ⓛ Ⓛ 113
Via Sardegna 31, 09124. 🄲 *070-66 05 10.* **FAX** *070-65 02 40.*
Housed in two much-restored palazzi in central Cagliari, this slightly shabby
hotel is a convenient base from which to explore the countryside. �̈ 📺 🗹

CAGLIARI: *Sardegna* Ⓛ Ⓛ 90
Via Lunigiana 50, 09122. 🄲 *070-28 62 45.* **FAX** *070-29 04 69.*
A modern hotel close to the town centre and 2 km (1 mile) from the
airport. The rooms are comfortably but simply decorated. �̈ ▤ 🗹 🅿

ISOLA DI SANT'ANTIOCO: *Club Ibisco Farm* Ⓛ Ⓛ Ⓛ 8
Capo Sperone, 09017. 🄲 *0781-80 90 21.* **FAX** *0781-80 90 18.*
Set in extensive, untamed grounds, this old farmhouse has wonderful views of
the sea, and good sports facilities. Minimum one week full board. �̈ 🗹 🅿

ISOLA DI SAN PIETRO: *Hotel Paola e Primo Maggio* Ⓛ 21
Tacca Rossa, Carloforte, 09014. 🄲 *0781-85 00 98.* **FAX** *0781-85 01 04.*
A modern pensione overlooking the sea with lovely views and charging
very reasonable prices. There is a shady terrace for outside dining. �̈ 🗹

NUORO: *Grazia Deledda* Ⓛ Ⓛ 72
Via Lamarmora 175, 08100. 🄲 *0784-312 57.* **FAX** *0784-322 58.*
A well-equipped modern hotel in a central position with an American-style
bar. The restaurant serves Sardinian and Italian specialities. �̈ 📺 ▤ 🗹 🅿

OLIENA: *Su Gologone* Ⓛ Ⓛ 67
Località Su Gologone, 08025. 🄲 *0784-28 75 12.* **FAX** *0784-28 76 68.*
A rambling villa in the mountainous Barbagia region is the setting for this
delightfully peaceful hotel which offers a good range of sports. �̈ 📺 🗹 🅿

ORISTANO: *Mistral* Ⓛ Ⓛ 48
Via Martiri di Belfiore, 09170. 🄲 *0783-21 25 05.* **FAX** *0783-21 00 58.*
A well-equipped hotel in the historic centre of Oristano, the functional
Mistral hotel also offers facilities for small conferences. �̈ 📺 🗹 🅿

PORTO CERVO: *Capriccioli* Ⓛ Ⓛ Ⓛ 50
Località Capriccioli, 07020. 🄲 *0789-960 04.* **FAX** *0789-964 22.*
One of the best value hotels on the expensive Costa Smeralda. This family-run
hotel is close to the beach and has an excellent restaurant. �̈ 📺 ▤ 🗹 🅿

PORTO CERVO: *Balocco* Ⓛ Ⓛ Ⓛ Ⓛ 35
Località Liscia di Vacca, 07020. 🄲 *0789-915 55.* **FAX** *0789-915 10.*
An attractive, airy hotel surrounded by palm-filled grounds and terraces for
every room. It offers comparatively good value for the fashionable Costa
Smeralda, but beware: prices double for the summer season. �̈ 📺 ▤ 🗹 🅿

PORTO ROTONDO: *Sporting* Ⓛ Ⓛ Ⓛ Ⓛ 27
Porto Rotondo, 07026. 🄲 *0789-340 05.* **FAX** *0789-343 83.*
An oasis of comfort that is one of the most expensive and luxurious hotels
in the exclusive Costa Smeralda region. It has its own beach and tranquil
grounds and bedrooms have flower-filled terraces. Half-board. �̈ 📺 ▤ 🗹 🅿

SASSARI: *Leonardo da Vinci* Ⓛ Ⓛ 112
Via Roma 79, 07100. 🄲 *079-28 07 44.* **FAX** *079-28 07 44.*
A large, comfortable hotel a few minutes' walk from the city centre. Furnishings
are functional but there is a sense of space and tranquillity. �̈ 📺 🗹 🅿

WHERE TO EAT

Waiter at Alberto Ciarla *(see p601)*

OOD IS A serious subject in Italy. The Italians are justly proud of their fine cuisine and wines and many sociable hours are spent around the table. One of the great pleasures of travelling in Italy is exploring regional variations in pasta, breads and cheeses. Whether it is spinach-filled *tortelloni* from the north or stuffed sweet red peppers from the south, restaurants will rarely serve anything other than Italian specialities. You don't have to head to the most expensive places for good food; a simple trattoria, which has to answer to the local clientele, will often serve much better fare than the nearby international restaurant. However, whether it's a crowded osteria or a terrace with sea views, this introduction gives a few practical tips on types of restaurants, ordering and service to help you enjoy eating out in Italy.

TYPES OF RESTAURANTS AND SNACK BARS

TRADITIONALLY a trattoria and an osteria were cheaper and more popular alternatives to the smarter ristorante. These days, however, the terms are interchangeable and high cost is not always indicative of memorably delicious food.

A pizzeria is usually a cheap place to eat (as little as L15,000 with beer) and many serve pasta, meat and fish dishes as well as pizzas. Pizzerie are often open in the evening only, especially those with wood-fired ovens *(forno a legna)*.

A birreria is another cheap option, serving pasta and snacks such as sausages and hamburgers. An enoteca, or vineria, is in fact a place to taste wine, however, as Italians will rarely drink without eating, there will normally be a range of light dishes on offer as well as a superb selection of wines. Prices vary and tend not to be cheap for the quantities served.

El Gato restaurant, Chioggia, famous for its fish *(see p580)*

At lunch time and in the early evening rosticcerie sell roast chicken, slices of pizza *(pizza al taglio)* and other snacks to take away. Pizza al taglio, with various different toppings, can also be bought straight from the baker. Bars have filled rolls *(panini)* and sandwiches *(tramezzini)* and some have a *tavola calda* counter with hot dishes for under L10,000.

Stop at a *gelateria* for ice cream, with a sometimes mesmerizing choice of different flavours, or a *pasticceria* for one of a dazzling variety of sweet and savoury pastries, cakes and biscuits.

EATING HOURS

LUNCH IS generally served between 1pm and 2:30pm and, particularly in the south, all other activity stops between these hours. Dinner is at about 8pm and goes on until 11pm or later (in the south eating hours tend to be later). It is not unusual to see tables still full from lunch at 4pm or diners sipping *digestivi* well after midnight.

RESERVATIONS

GOOD RESTAURANTS in Italy are likely to be popular, so reserve a table if you can. Otherwise, get there early to avoid having to queue. Many restaurants close for a few weeks in either winter or the summer holiday season so phone first if in doubt.

THE MENU

ITALIAN MEALS consist of at least three or four courses and restaurants generally expect you to eat at least two. The *antipasto* (starter), is followed by the *primo*, of pasta, rice or soup. The *secondo* is the main meat or fish course with vegetables or salad (as *contorni*). Fruit, cheese or dessert follow, with coffee and a *digestivo* such as *grappa* or a bitter *amaro* to finish the meal. Menus usually change with the season to make use of the best and freshest local produce and the day's specials may be recited to you by the waiter rather than written down.

Villa Crespi in Piedmont, inspired by the Arabian Nights *(see p587)*

Persevere, if you don't immediately understand, using the
menu decoders explained at
the beginning of each section.

VEGETARIANS

W HILE FEW PLACES advertise
specifically vegetarian
meals, you're unlikely to have
much trouble choosing from an
Italian menu. Many pasta and
antipasto dishes use no meat
at all and for a main course
you can ask for a selection of
vegetables from the *contorni.*
Vegetarians eat particularly
well in spring when the first
new vegetables come into the
markets, and in autumn when
wild mushrooms abound.

WINE AND DRINKS

M ANY REGIONS have their
own *aperitivo* for before
the meal and a *digestivo* for
afterwards. Universal alternatives are *prosecco* (dry fizzy
white wine) or an *analcolico*
(non-alcoholic) aperitif and
grappa as a digestive. House
wine (red or white) will be a
simple local wine served by
the litre or fraction thereof
and will generally be perfectly
palatable. In addition, all but
the cheapest places have a
range of other local and
regional wines specially
selected to accompany the
food on the menu. For this
reason, it is unusual to come
across many non-Italian wines.
Tap water *(acqua del
rubinetto)* is always drinkable
and often very good, but Italy
has a massive range of mineral
waters. Fizzy ones *(frizzante)*
may contain carbon dioxide

The 11th-century Badia a Coltibuono in Gaiole in Chianti *(see p594)*

while *naturale* can mean still
or naturally sparkling. The
popular *Ferrarelle* lies somewhere between the two. If
you particularly want a still
water ask for *non gassata.*

PAYING

T AX AND SERVICE are included
in the menu prices but it
is normal to leave a small tip
(from L2,000 to L10,000).
Take note of the cover charge
(coperto): an unavoidable
extra which basically covers
bread (whether you eat it or
not) and is charged per person.
Credit cards are not always
accepted in Italy, particularly
in smaller towns, and it is
wise to check before you eat.

DRESS

I TALIANS GENERALLY tend to
look smart but don't neces-
sarily expect visitors to do the
same. In most places you
won't be expected to dress
particularly smartly; however,
very scruffy or dirty clothes
are unlikely to get you good
or particularly friendly service.

CHILDREN

C HILDREN ARE welcome in all
but the smartest establishments and throughout Italy
restaurants are likely to be
filled with extensive Italian
families for Sunday lunch.
Facilities such as high-chairs
or special menus are rare, but
most places will provide
cushions and small portions.

Roman trattoria, Sora Lella, on
Tiber Island *(see p599)*

SMOKING

S MOKING IS POPULAR in Italy
and it is common for
people to light up between
courses or while others are
still eating. Be warned: non-
smoking sections are rare and
if somebody else's cigarette is
bothering you, you are the
one who will have to move.

WHEELCHAIR ACCESS

F EW RESTAURANTS have special
facilities for people in
wheelchairs, but let them know
you are coming in advance so
they can reserve a suitable
table and be ready to help if
necessary when you arrive.

La Marinella restaurant overlooking the Amalfi coast *(see p603)*

Choosing a Restaurant

THE RESTAURANTS in this guide have been selected across a wide range of price categories for their good value, exceptional food and interesting location. This chart lists the restaurants by region, starting with Venice. The thumb tabs on the side of the page use the same colour-coding as the corresponding regional chapter in the main section of the guide. *Buon appetito!*

	FIXED-PRICE MENU	GOOD WINE LIST	FORMAL DRESS	OUTDOOR TABLES

VENICE

BURANO: *Al Pescatore* ⓁⓁⓁ
Via Galuppi, 371. 【 041-73 06 50.
A welcoming restaurant whose menu includes lobster and tagliolini (flat pasta) with cuttlefish. In winter the menu includes excellent game. The extensive wine list offers foreign as well as Italian wines. ● *Wed.* ☙

		■		■

BURANO: *Da Romano* ⓁⓁⓁ
Piazza Galuppi, 221. 【 041-73 00 30.
A pretty restaurant founded in the 1800s, now run by the original owner's descendant. Excellent fish at very good prices. ● *Tue.* ☙

				■

CANNAREGIO: *Osteria al Bacco* ⓁⓁ
Fondamenta delle Cappuccine, 3054. **Map** 2 D2. 【 041-71 74 93.
A rustic restaurant with a pretty shaded courtyard. The menu serves mainly fish and includes spaghetti with black cuttlefish-ink sauce. ● *Mon.* ☙

CANNAREGIO: *Vini Da Gigio* ⓁⓁ
Fondamenta San Felice, 3628a. **Map** 3 A4. 【 041-528 51 40.
A cosy restaurant serving traditional Venetian cuisine with a difference. The risotto of nettles and prawns is particularly recommended. ● *Mon.* ☙

		■		

CANNAREGIO: *Fiaschetteria Toscana* ⓁⓁⓁ
San Crisostomo, 5719. **Map** 3 B5. 【 041-528 52 81.
The Busatto family offer many Venetian dishes such as warm salad of lagoon fish, eels and turbot with black butter and capers. ● *Tue.* ☙

		■		■

CASTELLO: *Da Remigio* ⓁⓁ
Salizzada dei Greci, 3416. **Map** 8 D2. 【 041-523 00 89.
A lively local fish restaurant where Venetians outnumber visitors: booking is advisable. The food is robust and straightforward. ● *Mon eve, Tue.* ☙ ▤

CASTELLO: *Arcimboldo* ⓁⓁⓁ
Calle dei Furlani, 3219. **Map** 8 D1. 【 041-528 65 69.
Named after the 16th-century painter who used vegetables and fruit to create portraits of people. The food is similarly innovative today; try sea bass with tomatoes or marinated salmon with citrus fruit and herbs. ● *Tue.* ☙

		■		

CASTELLO: *Corte Sconta* ⓁⓁⓁ
Calle del Pestrin, 3886. **Map** 7 A3. 【 041-522 70 24.
This simple eating house has become one of the city's top restaurants. The fish and the home-made pasta are both superb. ● *Sun, Mon.* ☙

		■		■

DORSODURO: *Ai Gondolieri* ⓁⓁ
San Vio, 366. **Map** 6 F4. 【 041-528 63 96.
Housed in a sympathetically restored old inn, friendly hosts offer good regional specialities including sformati (soufflé) flavoured with wild herbs. ● *Tue.* ☙

		■		

DORSODURO: *Taverna San Trovaso* ⓁⓁ
Fondamenta Priuli, 1016. **Map** 6 E3. 【 041-520 37 03.
A cheerful, bustling restaurant between the Accademia and the Zattere. The cooking is straightforward and includes pizzas. ● *Mon.* ☙

DORSODURO: *Locanda Montin* ⓁⓁⓁ
Fondamenta Eremite, 1147. **Map** 6 D3. 【 041-522 71 51.
A famous restaurant with artistic and literary connections. Food and service can vary in quality but there is a lively atmosphere. ● *Tue eve, Wed.* ☙

				■

GIUDECCA: *Do Mori* ⓁⓁ
Fondamenta Sant'Eufemia, 588. 【 041-522 54 52.
This rustic restaurant right on the waterfront, run by the ex-chef of Harry's Bar, serves good, homely Venetian cooking at a reasonable price. ● *Sun.* ☙

Average prices for a three-course meal for one, including a half-bottle of house wine, tax and service:
Ⓛ up to L35,000
ⓁⓁ L35–55,000
ⓁⓁⓁ L55–75,000
ⓁⓁⓁⓁ L75–100,000
ⓁⓁⓁⓁⓁ over L100,000.

FIXED-PRICE MENU
A fixed-price menu on offer, usually with three courses.

GOOD WINE LIST
Denotes a wide range of good quality wines.

FORMAL DRESS
Some restaurants require men to wear a jacket and tie.

OUTDOOR TABLES
Tables for eating outdoors, often with a good view.

CREDIT CARDS
The symbol shows that major credit cards are accepted.

	Price	Fixed-Price Menu	Good Wine List	Formal Dress	Outdoor Tables
GIUDECCA: *Harry's Dolci*	ⓁⓁⓁ				▪
MAZZORBO: *Antica Trattoria alla Maddalena*	Ⓛ				▪
SAN MARCO: *Al Conte Pescaor*	ⓁⓁⓁ				▪
SAN MARCO: *Da Arturo*	ⓁⓁⓁ		▪		
SAN MARCO: *Da Raffaele*	ⓁⓁⓁ				▪
SAN MARCO: *Antico Martini*	ⓁⓁⓁⓁ		▪		▪
SAN MARCO: *La Caravella*	ⓁⓁⓁⓁ		▪		▪
SAN MARCO: *Harry's Bar*	ⓁⓁⓁⓁⓁ		▪		
SAN POLO: *Da Silvio*	Ⓛ				▪
SAN POLO: *Antica Trattoria Posta Vecchia*	ⓁⓁⓁ				▪
SAN POLO: *Da Fiore*	ⓁⓁⓁ		▪		
TORCELLO: *Locanda Cipriani*	ⓁⓁⓁⓁ		▪		▪

GIUDECCA: *Harry's Dolci*
Fondamenta San Biagio, Sant'Eufemia 773. **Map** 6 D5. 041-522 48 44.
Originally a bar and tea-room, this is now a restaurant serving similar food to Harry's Bar in San Marco. Try carpaccio (marinated, sliced raw beef), the pasta and beans, and the delicious house chocolate cake. ● *Tue.*

MAZZORBO: *Antica Trattoria alla Maddalena*
Mazzorbo 7c. 041-73 01 51.
This modest restaurant, popular with the locals, acts as a local bar as well as an eating house. It has a tranquil atmosphere, however, and the wild duck served with polenta is famous throughout the area. ● *Thu.*

SAN MARCO: *Al Conte Pescaor*
Piscina San Zulian, 544. **Map** 7 B1. 041-522 14 83.
A little restaurant with a superb fish menu. The clientele are mainly local people, which guarantees the high quality of the food. ● *Sun.*

SAN MARCO: *Da Arturo*
Calle degli Assassini, 3656. **Map** 7 A2. 041-528 69 74.
This wood-panelled restaurant must be the only place in Venice that doesn't serve fish. Vegetarian antipasti include aubergines in a pickle sauce. ● *Sun.*

SAN MARCO: *Da Raffaele*
Fondamenta delle Ostreghe, 2347. **Map** 7 A3. 041-523 23 17.
A romantic setting in which to eat regional dishes. Try the granseola (spider crab), risotto di scampi and rombo (turbot) alla Raffaele. ● *Thu.*

SAN MARCO: *Antico Martini*
Campo San Fantin, 1983. **Map** 7 A2. 041-522 41 21.
Overlooking the Fenice theatre, this smart restaurant serves until 1am. The cooking is creative: try the duck with black truffles. ● *Tue, Wed lunch.*

SAN MARCO: *La Caravella*
Calle Largo XXII Marzo, 2396. **Map** 7 A3. 041-520 89 01.
Now the only restaurant in the Hotel Saturnia, this has a beautiful setting with a waterside terrace by the Grand Canal. The food is outstanding with imaginative dishes including lobster soup and scampi in champagne.

SAN MARCO: *Harry's Bar*
Calle Vallaresso, 1323. **Map** 7 B3. 041-528 57 77.
People come here because it's so famous. The wine list and cocktails are good but the food is not particularly exciting for the price. ● *Oct–Apr: Mon.*

SAN POLO: *Da Silvio*
Calle San Pantalon, 3748. **Map** 6 D2. 041-520 58 33.
A genuine local restaurant with a lovely garden for summer eating. The menu has no surprises but the food is all fresh and home-made. ● *Sun.*

SAN POLO: *Antica Trattoria Posta Vecchia*
Rialto Pescheria, 1608. **Map** 3 A5. 041-72 18 22.
This stylish restaurant near the fish market claims to be the oldest in Venice. Dishes include home-made ravioli as well as lovely desserts. ● *Tue.*

SAN POLO: *Da Fiore*
Calle del Scaleter 2202a. **Map** 3 B5. 041-72 13 08.
Fish specialities include a wonderful seafood antipasto, grilled fish and fritto misto (mixed fish in batter). Try the house white wine. ● *Sun, Mon.*

TORCELLO: *Locanda Cipriani*
Piazza Santa Fosca 29. **Map** 2 F4. 041-73 01 50.
Transformed from a fishermen's inn in the 1930s, dishes include fritto misto (batter-fried fish and vegetables) and a risotto with vegetables from the pretty kitchen garden. A launch collects diners from Piazza San Marco. ● *Tue.*

	FIXED-PRICE MENU	GOOD WINE LIST	FORMAL DRESS	OUTDOOR TABLES

Average prices for a three-course meal for one, including a half-bottle of house wine, tax and service:
Ⓛ up to L35,000
ⓁⓁ L35–55,000
ⓁⓁⓁ L55–75,000
ⓁⓁⓁⓁ L75–100,000
ⓁⓁⓁⓁⓁ over L100,000.

FIXED-PRICE MENU
A fixed-price menu on offer, usually with three courses.
GOOD WINE LIST
Denotes a wide range of good quality wines.
FORMAL DRESS
Some restaurants require men to wear a jacket and tie.
OUTDOOR TABLES
Tables for eating outdoors, often with a good view.
CREDIT CARDS
The symbol shows that major credit cards are accepted.

THE VENETO AND FRIULI

		FIXED-PRICE MENU	GOOD WINE LIST	FORMAL DRESS	OUTDOOR TABLES
ASOLO: *Villa Cipriani* ⓁⓁⓁⓁ Via Canova 298, 31011. ☎ 0423-95 21 66. Set in one of the grand hotels of the Veneto. Local ingredients are used in the creative cuisine with dishes such as veal medallions with asparagus. 🗺			▦	●	▦
BELLUNO: *Terracotta* Ⓛ Borgo Garibaldi 61. ☎ 0437-94 26 44. A family-run restaurant serving exotic Thai dishes as well as the speciality: Tagliatelle "Terracotta" with oregano, white sauce and tomatoes. ● *Sat lunch, Sun.*			▦		
CAORLE: *Duilio* ⓁⓁ Via Strada Nuova 19, 30021. ☎ 0421-810 87. A spacious restaurant where the fish-based regional cuisine is given a creative slant. Try the turbot poached in champagne. ● *Oct–Apr: Mon.* 🗺			▦	●	▦
CASTELFRANCO: *Barbesin* ⓁⓁ Via Montebelluna 41, 31033. ☎ 0423-49 04 46. A restaurant serving regional specialities, including risotto with porcini mushrooms and duck breast with rosemary. ● *Wed eve, Thu.* 🗺		●	▦		
CHIOGGIA: *El Gato* ⓁⓁⓁ Campiello Sant'Andrea 653, 30015. ☎ 041-40 18 06. Classic cooking based on seafood in an elegant, slightly restrained setting. Cuttlefish is served in a special Chioggia way with polenta. ● *Mon.* 🗺			▦		▦
CIVIDALE DEL FRIULI: *Zorutti* ⓁⓁ Borgo di Ponte 9, 33043. ☎ 0432-73 11 00. A family-run restaurant with a well-deserved reputation for good, regional cuisine served in generous portions. The house speciality is buzera, a local speciality of spaghetti with seafood, giant prawns or lobster. ● *Mon.* 🗺			▦		▦
CONEGLIANO: *Al Salisà* ⓁⓁ Via XX Settembre 2, 31015. ☎ 0438-242 88. An elegant restaurant set in an old house with a pretty veranda for outside eating. Interesting dishes include home-made fettuccine with radicchio and chicken liver sauce, and turbot wrapped in spinach. ● *Tue eve, Wed.* 🗺			▦		▦
DOLO: *Alla Posta* ⓁⓁⓁⓁ Via Ca' Tron 33, 30031. ☎ 041-41 07 40. This superb restaurant in an old Venetian posthouse prepares regional specialities with fresh ingredients and well-blended flavours. ● *Mon.* 🗺		●	▦		▦
GORIZIA: *Nanut* Ⓛ Via Trieste 118, 34170. ☎ 0481-205 95. A long-established trattoria in the industrial zone. It serves good local food; gnocchi, market vegetables, meats and fish on Friday. ● *Sat, Sun.*					
GRADO: *Trattoria de Toni* ⓁⓁ Piazza Duca d'Aosta 37, 34073. ☎ 0431-801 04. A traditional trattoria in the historic centre, the house speciality is boreto al Gradese, a fish stew cooked in oil and vinegar. ● *Oct–Apr: Wed.* 🗺 ♿			▦		
LAKE GARDA: *Antica Locanda Mincio* ⓁⓁⓁ Via Michelangelo 12, Valeggio sul Mincio 37067. ☎ 045-795 00 59. Once a staging post, this is now a delightful restaurant with frescoed walls and open fireplaces serving good regional food. ● *Wed eve, Thu.* 🗺			▦		▦
LAKE GARDA: *Locanda San Vigilio Regina* ⓁⓁⓁⓁ Punta San Vigilio, Garda 37016. ☎ 045-725 66 88. This excellent restaurant overlooking Lake Garda has an antipasto buffet and an astounding range of fish and seafood dishes. ● *Tue; Nov–Mar.* 🗺			▦		▦

ODERZO: *Gambrinus Parco* ⓁⓁⓁ
Località Gambrinus 22, San Polo di Piave 31020. 📞 *0422-85 50 43*.
Traditional regional cuisine that includes delicious freshwater prawns
(gamberi) alla Gambrinus and sturgeon cooked with coarse salt. ⬤ *Mon.* 🅖

PADUA: *La Braseria* Ⓛ
Via N Tommaseo 48, 35100. 📞 *049-876 09 07*.
A friendly restaurant with straightforward cooking. Penne with porcini
mushrooms and the speck (smoked bacon) are recommended. ⬤ *Sun.* 🅖

PADUA: *Osteria L'Anfora* Ⓛ
Via dei Soncin 13, 35122. 📞 *049-65 66 29*.
Traditional Veneto cuisine, with elements originally brought by Renaissance
merchants from far afield, is served in a lively atmosphere. ⬤ *Sun, Mon lunch.*

PADUA: *Dotto* ⓁⓁ
Via Soncin 9, 35100. 📞 *049-875 14 90*.
A 1920s-style restaurant with traditional seasonal food. Try the home-made
pasta, the baccalà (salt cod) and the tasty desserts. ⬤ *Sun eve, Mon.* 🅖

PADUA: *Belle Parti* ⓁⓁⓁ
Via Belle Parti 11, 35139. 📞 *049-875 18 22*.
This is one of the stars of Paduan cuisine. Long-forgotten dishes are served
such as chilled tomato soup with melon and prawns. ⬤ *Sun, Mon lunch.* 🅖

PADUA: *San Clemente* ⓁⓁⓁⓁ
Corso Vittorio Emanuele II 142, 35123. 📞 *049-880 31 80*.
Set in a villa attributed to Palladio, the excellent food and service match the
elegant ambience. Try the pigeon with stuffed pear. ⬤ *Sun, Mon lunch.* 🅖

PIEVE DI CADORE: *La Pausa* ⓁⓁ
Località Col Contras, 32044. 📞 *0435-300 80*.
A small restaurant in magnificent surroundings offering a range of game and
local specialities of smoked hams and meats. ⬤ *Oct–Apr: Sun eve, Mon.* 🅖

PORDENONE: *Vecia Osteria del Moro* ⓁⓁ
Via Castello 2, 33170. 📞 *0434-286 58*.
A refined restaurant set in a beautifully-restored 13th-century convent. Daily
specials include rabbit with polenta. ⬤ *Sun (Jul–mid-Aug: Sat, Sun).* 🅖

ROVIGO: *Tre Pini* ⓁⓁ
Viale Porta Po 68, 45100. 📞 *0425-42 11 11*.
Set in a pretty villa with a garden. Specialities include onion tart, eels
cooked with herbs, wild duck and vegetarian dishes. ⬤ *Sun.* 🅖

TREVISO: *Osteria Snack Bassanello* Ⓛ
Viale Cairoli 133, 31100. 📞 *0422-26 06 23*.
Excellent local cuisine is served in this popular osteria. In season, radicchio
(endive) is used in numerous ways including the digestive, grappa. ⬤ *Mon.*

TREVISO: *Toni del Spin* Ⓛ
Via Inferiore 7, 31100. 📞 *0422-54 38 29*.
A homely restaurant serving regional fare. House specialities include
pasta and fagioli (beans), baked tripe and tiramisù. ⬤ *Sun, Mon lunch.* 🅖

TREVISO: *Agnoletti* ⓁⓁ
Via della Vittoria 190, 31040. 📞 *0422-77 60 09*.
A pretty hillside location in a lovely garden north of Treviso. Seasonal
antipasti followed by gnocchi are particularly recommended. ⬤ *Mon, Tue.*

TREVISO: *Ristorante alle Beccherie* ⓁⓁⓁ
Piazza Ancillotto 10, 31100. 📞 *0422-54 08 71*.
Housed in a lovely building reminiscent of Venetian splendour. The guinea
fowl in pepper sauce is a particular delicacy. ⬤ *Sun eve, Mon.* 🅖

TOLMEZZO: *Roma* ⓁⓁⓁⓁ
Piazza XX Settembre 14, 33028. 📞 *0433-20 81*.
Stupendous food that is the result of careful research into old local recipes.
Try polenta with cheese and truffles or goose liver. ⬤ *Sun eve, Mon.* 🅖

UDINE: *Al Passeggio* ⓁⓁ
Viale Volontari della Libertà 49, 33100. 📞 *0432-462 16*.
A well thought-out menu, including delights like lasagne with asparagus
and courgettes, and chocolate fondue of fruits. ⬤ *Sun, Mon lunch.* 🅖

<table>
<tr><td>

Average prices for a three-course meal for one, including a half-bottle of house wine, tax and service:
Ⓛ up to L35,000
ⓁⓁ L35–55,000
ⓁⓁⓁ L55–75,000
ⓁⓁⓁⓁ L75–100,000
ⓁⓁⓁⓁⓁ over L100,000.

</td><td>

FIXED-PRICE MENU
A fixed-price menu on offer, usually with three courses.
GOOD WINE LIST
Denotes a wide range of good quality wines.
FORMAL DRESS
Some restaurants require men to wear a jacket and tie.
OUTDOOR TABLES
Tables for eating outdoors, often with a good view.
CREDIT CARDS
The symbol shows that major credit cards are accepted.

</td></tr>
</table>

		FIXED-PRICE MENU	GOOD WINE LIST	FORMAL DRESS	OUTDOOR TABLES
VERONA: *Al Bersagliere* Via dietro Pallone 1, 37100. (045-800 48 24. Traditional Veronese food in an old wood-lined dining room. Dishes include mixed boiled meats and polenta with wild mushrooms. ● *Sun.* 🗲	Ⓛ	●	■		■
VERONA: *Baba-jaga* Via Cabalao 11, 37030. (045-745 02 22. Black-truffle risotto and linguine with sturgeon, tomatoes and leeks are a good choice in the Soave wine-producing area. ● *Sun eve, Mon.* 🗲	ⓁⓁ		■		■
VERONA: *Arche* Via Arche Scaligere 6, 37100. (045-800 74 15. A long-established fish restaurant serving seafood soup with lentils and a wonderful warm lobster salad with basil and rocket. ● *Sun, Mon lunch.* 🗲	ⓁⓁⓁⓁ	●	■		
VERONA: *Il Desco* Via dietro San Sebastiano 5–7, 37100. (045-59 53 58. One of Italy's best restaurants, set in a harmonious 16th-century palazzo. Imaginative dishes include veal with ginger and lobster risotto. ● *Sun.* 🗲	ⓁⓁⓁⓁ	●	■		
VICENZA: *Al Torresan* Via Zabarella 1, Breganze 36042. (0445-87 32 60. In the autumn the locals flock here for the wild mushroom dishes. The cooking is hearty and is complemented by local wines. ● *Thu.* 🗲	ⓁⓁ				■
VICENZA: *Antica Trattoria Tre Visi* Contrà Porti 6, 36100. (0444-32 48 68. The building, in the historic centre, dates from 1483. Diners can see into the kitchen where the excellent local dishes are prepared. ● *Sun eve, Mon.* 🗲	ⓁⓁ		■		
VICENZA: *Taverna Aeolia* Piazza Conte da Schio 1, 36023. (0444-55 50 36. Housed in an elegant villa with a beautiful frescoed ceiling, the speciality of the chef-patron is roasted lamb with sesame seeds. ● *Tue.* 🗲	ⓁⓁ	●	■		■
VICENZA: *Trattoria Isetta* Via Pederiva 96, 36040. (0444-88 99 92. Regional food, with the emphasis on grilled meats and good puddings, in Galdino Glanesin's restaurant in the Berici hills. ● *Tue eve, Wed.* 🗲	ⓁⓁ		■		
VICENZA: *Cinzia e Valerio* Piazzetta Porta Padova 65–67, 36100. (0444-50 52 13. A stylish restaurant within the city walls, serving nothing but fish. Dishes include marinated raw salmon, prawn risotto, lobster and clams. ● *Mon.* 🗲	ⓁⓁⓁⓁ	●	■		

TRENTINO-ALTO ADIGE

BOLZANO (BOZEN): *Domino* Piazza Walther 3, 39100. (0471-98 16 10. This town centre wine bar is a good stop for a delicious lunchtime snack or a glass of wine in the evening before it closes at 8pm. ● *Sun.*	Ⓛ				■
BOLZANO (BOZEN): *Amadè* Vicolo Ca' de Bezzi 8, 39100. (0471-97 12 78. Set in part of a restored late-medieval mill complex, the best of seasonal, local ingredients are used for innovative dishes with a traditional flavour. Try air-dried venison with redcurrant sauce, and white wine soup. ● *Sun.* 🗲	ⓁⓁⓁ	●			
BRESSANONE (BRIXEN): *Oste Scuro* Vicolo Duomo 3, 39042. (0472-83 53 43. One of the oldest buildings in the historic centre, it has been an inn since the early 18th century. Today it specializes in creative cuisine such as kid in butter, and roast rabbit with bacon and mushrooms. ● *Sun eve, Mon.* 🗲 ♿	ⓁⓁ				■

BRESSANONE (BRIXEN): *Fink*   ⓁⓁⓁ
Via Portici Minori 4, 39042. [0472-83 48 83.
Popular with locals who come to sample the immaculately prepared dishes
such as black polenta or potato soup. ● *Tue eve, Wed.* 🥗 ⚡ ♿

BRUNICO (BRUNECK): *Oberraut*   ⓁⓁ
Via Ameto 1, 39031. [0474-55 99 77.
Set in the middle of woods, this Tyrolean-style restaurant specializes in local
game and seasonal dishes. There is a tantalizing dessert list. ● *Thu.* 🥗 ♿

CARZANO: *Le Rose*   ⓁⓁ
Via XVIII Settembre 35, 38050. [0461-76 61 77.
This popular Valsugana restaurant concentrates on fish and seasonal
produce. Try the tortelli of oysters with courgette flowers. ● *Mon.* 🥗

CAVALESE: *Al Cantuccio*   ⓁⓁ
Via Unterberger 14, 38033. [0462-34 01 40.
A popular restaurant with specialities such as sauerkraut and bean soup,
marinated venison and pear strudel. Booking is advisable. ● *Mon, Tue.* 🥗 ♿

CIVEZZANO: *Maso Cantanghel*   ⓁⓁ
Via della Madonnina 33, Località Forte 38045. [0461-85 87 14.
An excellent restaurant just outside Trento. Food is simple yet delicious;
sausages, garden-grown vegetables and home-made pasta. ● *Sat, Sun.* 🥗

LEVICO TERME: *Boivin*   Ⓛ
Via Garibaldi 9, 38056. [0461-70 16 70.
This excellent trattoria is one of the best places to taste authentic, local cuisine;
booking is essential. Only open evenings and for Sunday lunch. ● *Mon.* 🥗

MADONNA DI CAMPIGLIO: *Hermitage*   ⓁⓁ
Via Castelletto Inferiore 69, 38084. [0465-415 58.
Set in a private park at the foot of the Dolomites, the Hermitage serves imagin-
atively regional cuisine, with fresh-flavoured, tasty dishes. ● *Easter–Jun.* 🥗 ⚡

MALLES VENOSTA (MALS IM VINSCHGAU): *Greif*   ⓁⓁ
Via Generale Vedross 40a, 39024. [0473-83 11 89.
The enterprising chef creates Tyrolean dishes using organically grown produce.
They have a vegetarian menu and use wholewheat pasta. ● *Mon.* 🥗 ⚡ ♿

MALLES VENOSTA (MALS IM VINSCHGAU): *Weisses Kreuz*   ⓁⓁ
Località Burgusio 82, 39024. [0473-83 13 07.
This excellent value restaurant serves traditional fare such as gnocchi agli spinaci
and knödel (dumplings), as well as pork with gorgonzola. ● *Thu, Fri lunch.* 🥗 ♿

MERANO (MERAN): *Sissi*   ⓁⓁⓁ
Via Plankenstein 5, 39012. [0473-25 10 62.
A 19th-century building close to the town centre, the Sissi offers a seasonal
menu combining traditional and modern dishes. ● *Mon.* 🥗 ♿

MERANO (MERAN): *Andrea*   ⓁⓁⓁⓁ
Via Galilei 44, 39012. [0473-23 74 00.
Set in the town centre, its walls hung with the works of acclaimed artists.
The cuisine is an interesting mix of new ideas and local tradition. ● *Mon.* 🥗

MOENA: *Malga Panna*   ⓁⓁⓁ
Via Costalunga 29, 38035. [0462-57 34 89.
Mushrooms and game are served at this romantic restaurant in a rustic setting
about 1 km (half a mile) from the centre of Moena. ● *Oct–Apr: Mon.* 🥗 ♿

RENON (RITTEN): *Patscheiderhof*   Ⓛ
Località Signato 178, 39050. [0471-36 52 67.
About 10 km (6 miles) northeast of Bolzano, this traditional trattoria serves
barley soup, stuffed rabbit and other regional delights. ● *Tue, Wed lunch.*

ROVERETO: *Novecento*   ⓁⓁⓁ
Corso Rosmini 82d, 38068. [0464-43 52 22.
A refined restaurant, part of a hotel in the middle of Rovereto, serving some
carefully prepared local dishes and home-made pasta. ● *Sun.* 🥗 ⚡

ROVERETO: *Al Borgo*   ⓁⓁⓁⓁ
Via Garibaldi 13, 38068. [0464-43 63 00.
Situated in the historic centre of the town, Al Borgo's variety of excellent
dishes use a great range of choice, fresh ingredients. ● *Sun eve, Mon.* 🥗

Average prices for a three-course meal for one, including a half-bottle of house wine, tax and service:
Ⓛ up to L35,000
ⓁⓁ L35–55,000
ⓁⓁⓁ L55–75,000
ⓁⓁⓁⓁ L75–100,000.
ⓁⓁⓁⓁⓁ over L100,000.

FIXED-PRICE MENU
A fixed-price menu on offer, usually with three courses.
GOOD WINE LIST
Denotes a wide range of good quality wines.
FORMAL DRESS
Some restaurants require men to wear a jacket and tie.
OUTDOOR TABLES
Tables for eating outdoors, often with a good view.
CREDIT CARDS
The symbol shows that major credit cards are accepted.

	Price	FIXED-PRICE MENU	GOOD WINE LIST	FORMAL DRESS	OUTDOOR TABLES
TONADICO: *Baita del Vecio* Località Domadoi Passo Cereda, 38054. (0439-76 20 58. An unpretentious hotel restaurant offering carefully prepared dishes with home-made pasta, seasonal mushrooms and local cheeses. ● Mon.	Ⓛ				■
TRENTO: *Al Castello* Via Val Gola 2–4, Località Ravina 38040. (0461-92 33 33. This family-run restaurant concentrates on good basics, including home-made pasta, gnocchi of potato, ricotta, turnip and meat. ● Sun eve, Mon.	ⓁⓁ		■		■
TRENTO: *Port'Aquila* Via Cervara 66, 38100. (0461-23 86 96. An excellent family-run trattoria in an atmospheric position just beneath the old gate, the Port'Aquila has a menu of traditional fare. ● Sun.	ⓁⓁ		■		
TRENTO: *A le Due Spade* Via Don Rizzi 11, 38100. (0461-23 43 43. A welcoming cellar restaurant near the Duomo, serving traditional Trentino cuisine, including freshwater fish dishes. ● Sun, Mon lunch.	ⓁⓁⓁ	●	■		
VIPITENO (STERZING): *Kronen Keller* Città Vecchia 31, 39049. (0472-76 64 99. A wine bar in the Krone hotel's cellar where light meals such as speck (smoked ham), cheese and bruschetta are served with drinks. ● Wed.	Ⓛ		■		
VIPITENO (STERZING): *Pretzhof* Località Tulve, 39040. (0472-76 44 55. Karl and Ulli Mair run this peaceful country inn, using fresh produce from their own farm to concoct Tyrolean specialities. ● Mon, Tue.	ⓁⓁ				■

LOMBARDY

	Price	FIXED-PRICE MENU	GOOD WINE LIST	FORMAL DRESS	OUTDOOR TABLES
BELLAGIO: *Silvio* Via Carcano 12, 22021. (031-95 03 22. Silvio and his son Cristian catch much of the lake fish which is used for patés, pasta sauces, ravioli and risottos. There is a relaxed atmosphere in this lovely restaurant and hotel with beautiful lakeside views. ● Jan, Feb.	Ⓛ	●			■
BERGAMO: *Vineria Cozzi* Via Colleoni 22, 24129. (035-23 88 36. An attractive, old wine shop decorated in 19th-century style, the Cozzi has a spectacular list of wines and a range of light dishes and cheeses to accompany them. Try polenta with baccalà (salt cod), a house speciality. ● Wed.	Ⓛ		■		■
BERGAMO: *Taverna del Colleoni dell'Angelo* Piazza Vecchia 7, 24129. (035-23 25 96. An elegant taverna with a medieval atmosphere. Specialities include pasta with squid, prawns with light polenta and delicious desserts. ● Mon.	ⓁⓁⓁ	●	■		■
BORMIO: *Taula* Via Dante 6, 23032. (0342-90 47 71. A lovely restaurant in a refurbished 17th-century barn. It serves local cuisine with a good range of antipasti based on dried and cured meats. ● Tue.	ⓁⓁ				
BRESCIA: *Trattoria Mezzeria* Via Trieste 66, 25121. (030-403 06. A busy trattoria serving home-made potato or squash gnocchi, followed by traditional main dishes such as boiled chicken and carpaccio. ● Sun.	ⓁⓁ		■		
CASTELVECCANA: *Sant'Antonio* Località Sant'Antonio, 21010. (0332-54 84 42. This restaurant is set in a delightful 10th-century village with beautiful views of Lake Maggiore. Tasty trattoria favourites are served. ● Sept–Oct: Mon–Fri.	Ⓛ				■

COMO: *Sant'Anna 1907* Ⓛ Ⓛ Ⓛ
Via Turati 3, 22100. 031-50 52 66.
Run by the Fontana family for three generations. The traditional dishes include fish risotto and veal in an olive crust. ● *Fri, Sat lunch.* 🅴 🅶

CREMONA: *Porta Mosa* Ⓛ Ⓛ
Via Santa Maria in Betlem 11, 26100. 0372-41 18 03.
A refined trattoria with excellent wines and good, simple dishes, such as ravioli, onion soup and polenta with seasonal sauces. ● *Sun.* 🅴

CREMONA: *Aquila Nera* Ⓛ Ⓛ Ⓛ
Via Sicardo 3, 26100. 0372-256 46.
An elegant restaurant serving carefully prepared dishes, including goose liver with grapes and pine nuts, and mustard fricassée. ● *Sun eve, Mon.* 🅴

GARGNANO DEL GARDA: *La Tortuga* Ⓛ Ⓛ Ⓛ Ⓛ
Porticciolo di Gargnano, 25084. 0365-712 51.
A charming lakeside location for light imaginative cuisine. Lake fish is cooked with care; try the coregone with tomatoes and capers. ● *Mon eve, Tue.* 🅴

LAKE COMO: *Locanda dell'Isola Comacina* Ⓛ Ⓛ Ⓛ Ⓛ
Isola Comacina, 22010. 0344-550 83.
Set by the water's edge on an otherwise uninhabited island. A wonderful five-course set menu is served, which is full of unexpected delights. ● *Tue.*

LECCO: *Casa di Lucia* Ⓛ Ⓛ
Via Lucia 27, Località Acquate 22053. 0341-49 45 94.
Simple fare such as salami, bresaola (cured beef), rabbit and the traditional pasta e fagioli is served with good local and national wines. ● *Mon; Aug.* 🅶

MANERBA DEL GARDA: *Capriccio* Ⓛ Ⓛ
Piazza San Bernardo 6, 25080. 0365-55 11 24.
Excellent lake views from this restaurant that uses the local fish and olive oil. Desserts include a delicate muscat-grape jelly with peach sauce. ● *Tue eve.* 🅴

MANTOVA: *Ai Ranari* Ⓛ
Via Trieste 11, 46100. 0376-32 84 31.
A simple trattoria with no frills. Dishes are Mantuan and include pumpkin tortelli with butter sauce and meat polenta for the first course. ● *Mon.* 🅴

MANTOVA: *L'Ochina Bianca* Ⓛ Ⓛ
Via Finzi 2, 46100. 0376-32 37 00.
A simple restaurant serving some of the less well-known local specialities such as smoked pork with courgettes in vinegar. ● *Mon, Tue lunch.* 🅴

MANTOVA: *Trattoria dei Martini* Ⓛ Ⓛ Ⓛ
Piazza Carlo d'Arco 1, 46100. 0376-32 71 01.
A gracious restaurant where good Mantuan cuisine is accompanied by excellent wines. Try rabbit with pine nuts and grape sauce. ● *Mon, Tue.* 🅴

MILAN: *Geppo* Ⓛ
Viale GB Morgagni 37, 20124. 02-29 51 48 62.
Original pizzas include an "Indian" one with curry, tomato, gorgonzola and rocket, and another with prosciutto and melon. ● *Sun.*

MILAN: *La Capanna* Ⓛ Ⓛ
Via Donatello 9, 20131. 02-29 40 08 84.
Don't be put off by the plain appearance, the food, based on Tuscan cuisine, is exceptional; fresh pasta and home-made puddings. ● *Mon eve, Sat.* 🅴

MILAN: *Lucca* Ⓛ Ⓛ
Via Castaldi 33, 20100. 02-29 52 66 68.
A venue for business lunches and a popular place for dinner, the cuisine is Mediterranean in style. There is also a bistro. ● *Mon, Sat lunch.* 🅴

MILAN: *Trattoria Pagni* Ⓛ Ⓛ Ⓛ
Via Orti 7, 20122. 02-55 01 12 67.
A rustic restaurant serving Tuscan cuisine, using flavoursome ingredients such as salami, wild mushrooms and fresh herbs. ● *Sat eve, Sun.* 🅴

MILAN: *Aimo e Nadia* Ⓛ Ⓛ Ⓛ Ⓛ
Via Montecuccoli 6, 20147. 02-41 68 86.
A small, chic restaurant which is famed for its delicious, imaginative dishes, such as stuffed courgette flowers. ● *Sat lunch, Sun.* 🅴

	FIXED-PRICE MENU	GOOD WINE LIST	FORMAL DRESS	OUTDOOR TABLES
Average prices for a three-course meal for one, including a half-bottle of house wine, tax and service: Ⓛ up to L35,000 ⓁⓁ L35–55,000 ⓁⓁⓁ L55–75,000 ⓁⓁⓁⓁ L75–100,000 ⓁⓁⓁⓁⓁ over L100,000.	**FIXED-PRICE MENU** A fixed-price menu on offer, usually with three courses. **GOOD WINE LIST** Denotes a wide range of good quality wines. **FORMAL DRESS** Some restaurants require men to wear a jacket and tie. **OUTDOOR TABLES** Tables for eating outdoors, often with a good view. **CREDIT CARDS** The symbol shows that major credit cards are accepted.			

		FIXED-PRICE MENU	GOOD WINE LIST	FORMAL DRESS	OUTDOOR TABLES
MONTE ISOLA: *La Foresta*	ⓁⓁ				▦
Località Peschiera Maraglio, 25050. 030-988 62 10. The owner's brother catches the lake fish that form the basis of the menu, making this a mecca for lovers of freshwater fish. ● *Wed.* 🗗					
PAVIA: *Locanda Vecchia Pavia*	ⓁⓁⓁ		▦		
Via Cardinal Riboldi 2, 27100. 0382-30 41 32. A calm place to eat in the centre of Pavia. Frothy desserts follow creative dishes that bring a light touch to local specialities. ● *Mon, Wed lunch.* 🗗 ♿					
PAVIA: *Vecchio Mulino*	ⓁⓁⓁ	●	▦		▦
Via al Monumento 5, Certosa di Pavia 27012. 0382-92 58 94. A famous restaurant in a restructured old mill outside Pavia. Pavian traditions with some modern flair, such as excellent risottos. ● *Sun eve, Mon.* 🗗					
SALÒ: *Alla Campagnola*	ⓁⓁ	●	▦		▦
Via Brunati 11, 25087. 0365-221 53. A mother and son team offer interesting traditional recipes including pasta stuffed with pumpkin or aubergine. ● *Mon, Tue lunch.* 🗗					
VALLE D'AOSTA AND PIEDMONT					
ACQUI TERME: *La Schiavia*	ⓁⓁⓁ		▦		
Vicolo della Schiavia 1, 15011. 0144-559 39. An elegant restaurant on the ground floor of a 17th-century palazzo. Cuisine is regional including a delicious mix of vegetables and fish. ● *Sun.* 🗗					
ALBA: *Porta San Martino*	ⓁⓁ		▦		
Via Einaudi 5, 12051. 0173-36 23 35. Excellent value for money at this refined restaurant with good service and a menu of Piedmontese and Albese specialities: vitello tonnato (veal with a sauce of tuna and capers) and fillet steak with rosemary. ● *Mon.* 🗗					
ALESSANDRIA: *Il Grappolo*	ⓁⓁⓁ	●	▦		▦
Via Casale 28, 15100. 0131-25 32 17. Piedmontese cuisine with a few borrowed touches. Try the gnocchi with rosemary, artichoke risotto and swordfish pancakes. ● *Mon eve, Tue.* 🗗 ♿					
AOSTA: *Grotta Azzurra*	ⓁⓁ		▦		
Via Croix de Ville 97, 11100. 0165-26 24 74. This good pizzeria also serves excellent fish, pasta and risotto. Try the seafood salad, risotto or fish soup as a first course. ● *Wed.* 🗗					
AOSTA: *Le Foyer*	ⓁⓁ	●			
Corso Ivrea 146, 11100. 0165-321 36. Popular with locals, this suburban trattoria serves excellent fish including salmon carpaccio, risotto of prawns, and rocket and courgette flan. 🗗 ♿					
AOSTA: *Vecchia Aosta*	ⓁⓁ	●	▦		▦
Piazza Porta Pretoria 4c, 11100. 0165-36 11 86. Set into the old Roman wall, the Vecchia Aosta offers typical regional dishes such as vegetable terrines and ravioli with lobster sauce. ● *Wed.* 🗗 ▨ ♿					
ASTI: *Gener Neuv*	ⓁⓁⓁ	●	▦		
Lungotanaro 4, 14100. 0141-55 72 70. A peacefully rustic restaurant about 1 km (half a mile) from the town centre. The Gener Neuv serves carefully and deliciously prepared local dishes and the family who run it give attentive service. ● *Sun eve, Mon.* 🗗 ▨					
BRA: *Osteria Boccondivino*	ⓁⓁ		▦		
Via Mendicita Istruita 14, 12042. 0172-42 56 74. An informal restaurant with Piedmontese cuisine. Try stuffed veal and panna cotta (crème brûlée), and truffle dishes in autumn. ● *Sun, Mon lunch.* 🗗					

BREUIL-CERVINIA: *Les Neiges d'Antan* ⓁⓁⓁ
Frazione Cret de Perrères, 11021. █ *0166-94 87 75.*
Elegantly rustic, this restaurant has beautiful mountain views and serves
carefully prepared rich mountain fare. ● *May, Jun, Oct, Nov.* 🅰 ⚡

CANNOBIO: *Del Lago* ⓁⓁⓁⓁ
Via Nazionale 2, Località Carmine Inferiore 28052. █ *0323-705 95.*
A lovely lakeside restaurant where the imaginative cuisine combines
sometimes surprising flavours to great effect. ● *Tue, Wed lunch.* 🅰

CASALE MONFERRATO: *La Torre* ⓁⓁⓁ
Via Diego Garoglio 3, 15033. █ *0142-702 95.*
An elegant restaurant with panoramic views near the town centre. Cuisine is
innovative and includes risotto of peppers and gorgonzola. ● *Wed.* 🅰 ♿

COGNE: *Lou Ressignon* ⓁⓁ
Rue Mines de Cogne 22, 11012. █ *0165-740 34.*
A 17th-century inn where an open fireplace creates an old-world feeling. Rustic
cuisine with regional salamis, polenta and breads. ● *Mon eve, Tue.* 🅰 ♿

COSTIGLIOLE D'ASTI: *Collavini* ⓁⓁ
Via Asti-Nizza 84, 14055. █ *0141-96 64 40.*
A comfortable atmosphere, where good service and carefully prepared simple
food combine to make the Collavini a popular restaurant. ● *Tue eve, Wed.* 🅰

COURMAYEUR: *Pierre Alexis 1877* ⓁⓁ
Via Marconi 54, 11013. █ *0165-84 35 17.*
A converted barn in the historic centre with dishes based on local traditions;
beef in four sauces and pappardelle (pasta) alla Pierre Alexis. ● *Mon.* 🅰

CUNEO: *Osteria della Chiocciola* ⓁⓁ
Via Fossano 1, 12100. █ *0171-662 77.*
An excellent restaurant where seasonal fare is combined with the appropriate
wines. Winter has full-bodied reds to go with truffles and risottos. ● *Sun.* 🅰

DOMODOSSOLA: *Piemonte da Sciolla* ⓁⓁ
Piazza Convenzione 5, 28037. █ *0324-24 26 33.*
Immaculately prepared regional specialities such as gnocchi with rye and
chestnuts, set in a historic building in the town centre. 🅰 ⚡

FEISOGLIO: *Piemonte da Renato* ⓁⓁ
Via Firenze 19, 12050. █ *0173-83 11 16.*
A family atmosphere at this trattoria serving seasonal specialities, especially
dishes with white and black truffles. Booking is advisable. ● *Dec–Easter.* ♿

IVREA: *La Trattoria* Ⓛ
Via Aosta 47, 10015. █ *0125-489 98.*
A bright restaurant where the food is simple and based on regional
cuisine. Specials of the day are the chef's own innovations. ● *Sun.* 🅰

MONCUCCO TORINESE: *Trattoria del Freisa* ⓁⓁ
Via Mosso 6, 14024. █ *011-987 47 65.*
A traditional country trattoria, open only in the evenings during the week,
with immaculately prepared regional specialities and local wines. ● *Tue, Wed.*

NOVARA: *La Famiglia* ⓁⓁ
Via P Solaroli 8, 28100. █ *0321-39 95 29.*
A small, peaceful restaurant, its walls painted with frescoes of Lake
Maggiore. The cuisine specializes in fresh fish and risottos. ● *Fri.* 🅰 ♿

NOVARA: *Osteria del Laghetto* ⓁⓁⓁⓁ
Case Sparse 11, Veveri 28100. █ *0321-62 15 79.*
Set in a park, the flower-filled Laghetto specializes in dishes using fresh
fish, mushrooms and truffles. Booking is advisable. ● *Sat lunch, Sun.* 🅰 ♿

ORTA SAN GIULIO: *Villa Crespi* ⓁⓁⓁⓁ
Via Generale Fava 8–10, 28016. █ *0322-91 19 02.*
The exotic decor is based on the Arabian Nights. The cuisine is equally
well thought-out and uses seasonal truffles and foie gras (liver pâté). 🅰 ♿

SAINT VINCENT: *Batezar* ⓁⓁⓁⓁ
Via Marconi 1, 11027. █ *0165-51 31 64.*
An excellent restaurant serving classic cuisine with special touches (ravioli
with lobster sauce, pheasant in polenta crust). ● *Wed, Mon–Fri lunch.* 🅰

Average prices for a three-course meal for one, including a half-bottle of house wine, tax and service:
Ⓛ up to L35,000
ⓁⓁ L35 – 55,000
ⓁⓁⓁ L55 – 75,000
ⓁⓁⓁⓁ L75 – 100,000
ⓁⓁⓁⓁⓁ over L100,000.

FIXED-PRICE MENU
A fixed-price menu on offer, usually with three courses.
GOOD WINE LIST
Denotes a wide range of good quality wines.
FORMAL DRESS
Some restaurants require men to wear a jacket and tie.
OUTDOOR TABLES
Tables for eating outdoors, often with a good view.
CREDIT CARDS
The symbol shows that major credit cards are accepted.

	FIXED-PRICE MENU	GOOD WINE LIST	FORMAL DRESS	OUTDOOR TABLES
SAN SECONDO DI PINEROLO: *La Ciau* ⓁⓁ Via Castello di Miradolo 2, 10060. 0121-50 06 11. Much care and some innovation go into the preparation of regional dishes. Try the stuffed gnocchi and the home-baked bread. ● *Wed.* 🅔		▨		▨
SORISO: *Al Soriso* ⓁⓁⓁⓁⓁ Via Roma 18, 28016. 0322-98 32 28. One of the most highly acclaimed restaurants in Italy. The excellent cuisine makes creative use of what's in season locally and draws on a wide range of traditions from Italy and abroad for inspiration. ● *Mon, Tue lunch.* 🅔 🗲		▨		
TURIN: *Vincenzo Nebiolo* Ⓛ Via Priocco 10, 10152. 011-436 81 68. Piedmontese specialities from a menu that changes daily. Try the anchovy dishes accompanied by the owner's own wines. Open for lunch only. ● *Sun.*	●			
TURIN: *Birilli* ⓁⓁ Strada Val San Martino 6, 10131. 011-819 05 67. A friendly, cheerful restaurant opened in 1991 as part of a family-run chain whose first branch opened in Los Angeles in 1929. Simple reliable dishes include meats and the house pasta Birilli alla Birilli. ● *Sun.* 🅔 ♿				▨
TURIN: *Dai Saletta* ⓁⓁ Via Belfiore 37, 10125. 011-668 78 67. A warm, friendly atmosphere in central Turin. House specialities include meat braised in Barolo wine, and a fluffy zabaglione. ● *Sun.* 🅔		▨		
TURIN: *Porto di Savona* ⓁⓁ Piazza Veneto 2, 10100. 011-817 35 00. A friendly, slightly Bohemian restaurant in an 18th-century building in central Turin. The regional cuisine includes such dishes as gnocchi with gorgonzola and meats braised in Barolo wine. ● *Mon, Tue lunch.* 🅔		▨		
TURIN: *Neuv Caval 'd Brôns* ⓁⓁⓁⓁ Piazza San Carlo 151, 10123. 011-562 74 83. An elegant, spacious restaurant offering excellent food from a range of cuisine including vegetarian dishes. Specialities include the renowned mint and chocolate pudding San Vittorio. ● *Sat lunch, Sun.* 🅔 🗲	●	▨	●	
VARALLO SESIA: *Osteria del Muntisel* ⓁⓁ Via Fiume 1, 13019. 0163-521 55. A small, refined restaurant in the middle of a public garden. The menu makes much use of smoked fish, salami, cheese and soups. ● *Mon, Tue.*	●			
VERBANIA PALLANZA: *Milano* ⓁⓁⓁⓁ Corso Zanitello 2, 28048. 0323-55 68 16. Close to the town centre, the Milano has lake views and a romantic interior. Dishes include tagliolini with lake fish and home-made pasta. ● *Tue.* 🅔				▨
VERCELLI: *Il Giardinetto* ⓁⓁ Via Luigi Sereno 8, 13100. 0161-25 72 30. The restaurant of an elegant villa hotel, it specializes in cuisine with truffles and mushrooms in season. Try the risotto Mediterraneo. ● *Mon.* 🅔 ♿		▨		▨
VERCELLI: *Il Paiolo* ⓁⓁ Corso Garibaldi 72, 13100. 0161-25 05 77. A country trattoria in the historic centre, it specializes in local cuisine. The Vercellese risotto is particularly recommended. ● *Thu.* 🅔 ♿				
VILLARFOCCHIARDO: *La Giaconera* ⓁⓁⓁ Via Antica di Francia 1, 10050. 011-964 50 00. This elegantly restored staging inn makes good use of seasonal ingredients such as truffles. There is often a pianist in the evenings. ● *Mon.* 🅔 ♿	●	▨		

LIGURIA

CAMOGLI: *La Cucina di Nonna Nina*   ⓁⓁ
Via Franco Molfino 126, San Rocco di Camogli 16032. ☎ *0185-77 38 35.*
"If you're in a hurry" says the menu, "relax; our food is prepared according
to traditional methods." The atmosphere is friendly and there are wonderful
views of the Golfo Paradiso. The cuisine is mainly Ligurian. ● *Wed.*

CAMOGLI: *Rosa*   ⓁⓁⓁ
Largo Casabona 11, 16032. ☎ *0185-77 34 11.*
Set in a pretty villa on the Golfo Paradiso, the menu offers exquisitely prepared
fish such as taglierini in sugo di triglie (pasta with red mullet). ● *Tue.* ▣

CERVO: *San Giorgio*   ⓁⓁⓁⓁ
Via Volta 19, 18010. ☎ *0183-40 01 75.*
Booking is absolutely essential at this popular spot for regional cuisine with
a different twist. The dishes are mainly fresh fish and seafood; the branzino (sea
bass) with rosemary and beans is exceptional. ● *Mon eve, Tue.*

DOLCEACQUA: *Gastone*   ⓁⓁ
Piazza Garibaldi 2, 18035. ☎ *0184-20 65 77.*
Home-made pasta and regional meat dishes are two of the attractions
at this elegant restaurant in the historic centre. ● *Mon eve, Tue.* ▣ ♿

GENOA: *Do' Colla*   ⓁⓁ
Via alla Chiesa di Murta 10, Località Bolzaneto. ☎ *010-40 05 79.*
It's worth heading the few kilometres out of Genoa to taste the exquisite
home-style Ligurian cooking of this simple trattoria. ● *Sun eve, Mon.*

GENOA: *Capun Pascia*   ⓁⓁⓁ
Via Boccadasse 19, 16146. ☎ *010-376 07 37.*
A small menu of perfectly executed, mainly fish-based dishes that are
specialities of the house. Try tartare of salmon to start with. ● *Tue.*

LEVANTO: *Araldo*   ⓁⓁ
Via Jacopo 24, 19015. ☎ *0187-80 72 53.*
The menu changes every month but is always based on regional produce. The
dining room is attractively decorated with trompe l'oeil drapes. ● *Tue.* ▣

MANAROLA: *Marina Piccola*   ⓁⓁⓁ
Via Discovolo 38, 19010. ☎ *0187-92 01 03.*
There are wonderful sea views from this restaurant whose menu of regional
specialities includes seafood antipasti, pesto and grilled fish. ● *Thu.* ▣ ♿

NERVI: *Astor*   ⓁⓁ
Viale delle Palme 16, 16167. ☎ *010-372 83 25.*
This hotel restaurant offers a good selection of dishes including pesto, fish
and the local pasta dish (pansoti) with wild herbs and nut sauce. ▣ ♿

PORTOFINO: *Puny*   ⓁⓁⓁ
Piazza Martiri Olivetta 5, 16034. ☎ *0185-26 90 37.*
A spectacular view of the bay of Portofino spreads out before you as you
enjoy well-prepared dishes accompanied by crisp Ligurian wines. ● *Thu.*

PORTOVENERE: *Taverna del Corsaro*   ⓁⓁⓁⓁ
Calata Doria 102, 19025. ☎ *0187-79 06 22.*
Reinterpreted regional recipes form the basis of the exclusively fish menu. Set
on the tip of the Portovenere Peninsula with views over the sea. ● *Tue.* ▣

RAPALLO: *Roccabruna*   ⓁⓁⓁ
Via Sotto la Croce 6, Località Savagna 16035. ☎ *0185-26 14 00.*
Set on a pretty terrace away from the crowds on the seafront, this restaurant
simply serves the menu of the day, from the antipasti to the wines. ● *Mon.* ▣

SAN REMO: *Paolo e Barbara*   ⓁⓁⓁⓁ
Via Roma 47, 18038. ☎ *0184-53 16 53.*
A small, refined place to eat where the cuisine is based on Ligurian
and Mediterranean specialities, especially fish and seafood. ▣

VERNAZZA: *Gambero Rosso*   ⓁⓁⓁ
Piazza Marconi 7, 19018. ☎ *0187-81 22 65.*
Rice with lemon and prawns, roast anchovies, gamberoni in pigiama (deep-
fried prawns) and pansoti *(see p174)* with cocoa and thyme are only some of
the imaginatively interpreted Ligurian dishes here. ● *Nov–Apr: Mon.* ▣ ♿

	FIXED-PRICE MENU	GOOD WINE LIST	FORMAL DRESS	OUTDOOR TABLES

Average prices for a three-course meal for one, including a half-bottle of house wine, tax and service:
Ⓛ up to L35,000
ⓁⓁ L35–55,000
ⓁⓁⓁ L55–75,000
ⓁⓁⓁⓁ L75–100,000
ⓁⓁⓁⓁⓁ over L100,000.

FIXED-PRICE MENU
A fixed-price menu on offer, usually with three courses.
GOOD WINE LIST
Denotes a wide range of good quality wines.
FORMAL DRESS
Some restaurants require men to wear a jacket and tie.
OUTDOOR TABLES
Tables for eating outdoors, often with a good view.
CREDIT CARDS
The symbol shows that major credit cards are accepted.

EMILIA-ROMAGNA

BOLOGNA: *Lamma*　　　　　　Ⓛ
Via dei Giudei 4, 40100. 【 051-26 83 62.
A central trattoria with no-frills standard fare, such as bean, tuna and onion salad, pasta with beans, tripe, grilled vegetables and tiramisù. ● *Sun.* 🗲

BOLOGNA: *Antica Trattoria del Cacciatore*　　ⓁⓁⓁ
Via Caduti di Casteldebole 25, 40132. 【 051-56 42 03.
A country inn near the airport. The menu is a mix of local and international dishes with home-made bread, game and truffles. ● *Sun eve, Mon.* 🖧 🗲
(good wine list ■, outdoor tables ■)

BOLOGNA: *Pappagallo*　　　　ⓁⓁⓁⓁ
Piazza Mercanzia 3c, 40125. 【 051-23 28 07.
Housed in a 14th-century palazzo in the historic centre, this elegant restuarant serves Bolognese dishes; tortellini and lasagna. ● *Sun.* 🗲
(good wine list ■)

CASTELL'ARQUATO: *Maps*　　　ⓁⓁⓁ
Piazza Europa 3, 29014. 【 0523-80 44 11.
In a restructured medieval mill in the historic centre, fish is the mainstay of the menu that changes according to what's available each day. ● *Tue.* 🗲
(good wine list ■)

COMACCHIO: *La Pace*　　　ⓁⓁ
Via Fogli 21, 44022. 【 0533-812 85.
A peaceful spot where you can also stay the night. The menu is almost entirely fish, particularly eels cooked in every imaginable way. ● *Fri.*

FAENZA: *Le Volte*　　　ⓁⓁ
Corso Mazzini 54, 48018. 【 0546-66 16 00.
Housed in an atmospheric building in the historic centre. The food is delicious with a strong Pugliese influence. Try medallions of chicken in balsamic vinegar, cannolini (pasta) with crispy vegetables and lamb with thyme. ● *Sun.* 🗲
(good wine list ■)

FERRARA: *La Sgarbata*　　　ⓁⓁ
Via Sgarbata 84, 44100. 【 0532-71 21 10.
An unpretentious country trattoria on the outskirts of Ferrara which serves Ferrarese specialities as well as rich and tasty pizzas. ● *Wed.*
(outdoor tables ■)

FERRARA: *Quel Fantastico Giovedì*　　ⓁⓁ
Via Castelnuovo 9, 44100. 【 0532-76 05 70.
A bright little restaurant whose varied national and international menu, which changes every week, includes Japanese-style sashimi. ● *Wed.* 🗲 🖃 🖧
(fixed-price menu ●, good wine list ■)

FIDENZA: *Del Duomo*　　　ⓁⓁ
Via Micheli 27, 43036. 【 0524-52 42 68.
Near the 12th-century cathedral, the menu includes home-made spaghetti with mushrooms, steak with vinegar and tripe alla parmigiana. ● *Mon.* 🗲

GORO: *Ferrari*　　　ⓁⓁⓁ
Via Antonio Brugnoli 240–4, 44020. 【 0533-99 64 48.
Next to the fish market, the menu changes every day to make use of the best of the day's catch; the menu is, not surprisingly, almost entirely fish. ● *Wed.*
(fixed-price menu ●)

MODENA: *Al Boschetto*　　　Ⓛ
Via Due Canali Nord 202, 41100. 【 059-25 17 59.
A rustic restaurant set in a vast park that allows for outside dining in summer. In winter, instead, there is an open fire. Specialities include tortellini in chicken broth, ragù sauce and spit-roasted meats. ● *Sun eve, Wed.* 🗲 🖃
(fixed-price menu ●, outdoor tables ■)

MODENA: *Fini*　　　ⓁⓁⓁ
Piazzetta San Francesco, 41100. 【 059-22 33 14.
A mainstay of local cuisine with exquisitely prepared dishes; lasagna di maccheroni with delicious desserts (zuppa inglese – trifle). ● *Mon, Tue.* 🗲
(good wine list ■)

Parma: *Aldo*   Ⓛ Ⓛ
Piazzale Inzani 15, 43100. 📞 0521-20 60 01.
A relaxed trattoria serving traditional classics with interesting touches:
smoked roast beef, and guinea fowl with orange sauce. ● *Sun eve, Mon.* 🗐

Parma: *Le Viole*   Ⓛ Ⓛ
Strada Nuova 60a, Località Castelnuovo Golese 43031. 📞 0521-60 10 00.
A delightful place to eat offering a successful mix of modern ideas and
tradition. Antipasti include a sausage flan with porcini mushroom sauce,
but the desserts are probably the pièce de resistance. ● *Wed, Thu lunch.* 🗐

Piacenza: *Da Faccini*   Ⓛ
San Antonio di Castell'Arquato 10, 29014. 📞 0523-89 63 40.
Pasta and game are the highlights in this rustic trattoria. Try gnocchi with
carrots, duck and truffle ravioli and rabbit with mustard. ● *Wed.* 🗐 ♿

Piacenza: *Antica Osteria del Teatro*   Ⓛ Ⓛ Ⓛ Ⓛ
Via Verdi 16, 29100. 📞 0523-32 37 77.
An excellent wine list accompanies a menu of imaginative dishes prepared
with immense flair from the best of local produce. The setting, in a 15th-
century palazzo in the historic centre, is also pleasant. ● *Sun eve, Mon.* 🗐

Ravenna: *Trattoria Capannetti*   Ⓛ Ⓛ
Vicolo Capannetti 21, 48100. 📞 0544-666 81.
Creative, regional home-made cuisine that changes with the season.
It's a peaceful restaurant in the historic centre. ● *Sun eve, Mon.* 🗐 ♿

Ravenna: *Tre Spade*   Ⓛ Ⓛ
Via Faentina 136, 48100. 📞 0544-50 05 22.
Set in a 19th-century villa in a park. The chef's specialities include tortelli
with duck sauce and lamb with aromatic herbs. ● *Sun eve, Mon.* 🗐 🗲 ♿

Rimini: *Europa di Piero e Gilberto*   Ⓛ Ⓛ
Via Roma 51, 47037. 📞 0541-287 51.
Fish forms the basis of the menu here, with dishes including salad of warm
fish with radicchio, seafood spaghetti and grilled Adriatic sole. ● *Sun.* 🗐 ♿

Rimini: *Il Melograno*   Ⓛ Ⓛ Ⓛ
Viale Vespucci 16, 47037. 📞 0541-522 55.
The restaurant of the Imperiale Hotel serves mainly fish (turbot in a potato
crust, red mullet with rosemary) as well as delicious grilled meats. 🗐 🗲

FLORENCE

Florence: *Acquacotta*   Ⓛ
Via de' Pilastri 51r, 50124. **Map** 2 E5. 📞 055-24 29 07.
A cheap, three-roomed restaurant named after a Florentine vegetable soup.
Grilled meats and other Tuscan specialities are also featured. ● *Tue eve, Wed.*

Florence: *La Maremmana*   Ⓛ
Via de' Macci 77r, 50100. **Map** 4 E1. 📞 055-24 12 26.
A basic trattoria with traditional fare, off the main tourist circuit and close to
Santa Croce. The fixed-price menu is particularly recommended. ● *Sun.* 🗐

Florence: *Le Mossacce*   Ⓛ
Via del Pronconsolo 55r, 50122. **Map** 2 D5 (6 E2). 📞 055-29 43 61.
Don't be put off by the multilingual menus, the paper tablecloths and the
chaos; the 100-year-old Mossacce serves robust Tuscan food. ● *Sat, Sun.* 🗐

Florence: *Palle D'Oro*   Ⓛ
Via Sant'Antonino 43r, 50123. **Map** 1 C5 (5 C1). 📞 055-28 83 83.
Sparse, simple, spotlessly clean trattoria. The food is basic but cooked well
and there is a very good take-away sandwich bar at the front. ● *Sun.* 🗐

Florence: *Trattoria Mario*   Ⓛ
Via Rosina 2r, 50123. **Map** 1 C4. 📞 055-21 85 50.
A popular lunchtime trattoria catering to students and market traders. Specials
change daily; on Friday there is fish and on Thursday, gnocchi. ● *eves, Sun.*

Florence: *Buca dell'Orafo*   Ⓛ Ⓛ
Volta de' Girolami 28r, 50122. **Map** 6 D4. 📞 055-21 36 19.
A friendly hole-in-the-wall that is a long-time favourite with Florentines.
The homely cooking is based on home-made pasta, and daily specials include
the typically Tuscan pasta and fagioli (beans) on Saturday. ● *Sun, Mon.*

For key to symbols see back flap

	FIXED-PRICE MENU	GOOD WINE LIST	FORMAL DRESS	OUTDOOR TABLES

Average prices for a three-course meal for one, including a half-bottle of house wine, tax and service:
ⓛ up to L35,000
ⓛⓛ L35–55,000
ⓛⓛⓛ L55–75,000
ⓛⓛⓛⓛ L75–100,000
ⓛⓛⓛⓛⓛ over L100,000.

FIXED-PRICE MENU
A fixed-price menu on offer, usually with three courses.
GOOD WINE LIST
Denotes a wide range of good quality wines.
FORMAL DRESS
Some restaurants require men to wear a jacket and tie.
OUTDOOR TABLES
Tables for eating outdoors, often with a good view.
CREDIT CARDS
The symbol shows that major credit cards are accepted.

FLORENCE: *Buca Mario* — ⓛⓛ
Piazza degli Ottaviani 16r, 50100. **Map** 1 B5. **(** 055-21 41 79.
A crowded restaurant where it is normal to book or queue for a table. Enjoy the home-made pasta and grilled meats at good prices. ● *Wed, Thu lunch.* ▱

FLORENCE: *Cafaggi* — ⓛⓛ
Via Guelfa 35r, 50123. **Map** 1 C4. **(** 055-29 49 89.
This classic Tuscan trattoria serves oil and wines from the family farm. Crostini (toasts), zuppa di farro and involtini are particularly good. ● *Sun.* ▱
— *GOOD WINE LIST: ●*

FLORENCE: *Da Pennello* — ⓛⓛ
Via Dante Alighieri 4r, 50100. **Map** 4 D1. **(** 055-29 48 48.
Book well ahead or risk a long wait for a table. This popular restaurant is famous for its extensive antipasti, a meal in themselves. ● *Sun eve, Mon.*
— *GOOD WINE LIST: ●*

FLORENCE: *Dino* — ⓛⓛ
Via Ghibellina 51r, 50122. **Map** 4 D1 (6 E3). **(** 055-24 14 52.
A well-regarded restaurant in a beautiful 14th-century palazzo. It has one of the best wine lists in Florence and a menu of adventurous dishes such as pasta with herbs and pork fillets baked in paper. ● *Sun eve, Mon.* ▱
— *GOOD WINE LIST: ▪*

FLORENCE: *Paoli* — ⓛⓛ
Via dei Tavolini 12r, 50100. **Map** 6 D3 (4 D1). **(** 055-21 62 15.
A spectacular setting: the dining room is a vaulted hall smothered in medieval frescoes. The food does not quite live up to the surroundings. ● *Tue.* ▱

FLORENCE: *San Zanobi* — ⓛⓛ
Via San Zanobi 33r, 50100. **Map** 1 C4. **(** 055-47 52 86.
Delicate, inventive food served in a sedate, refined dining room. The dishes, based on a Florentine theme, are light and well presented. ● *Mon.* ▱

FLORENCE: *Trattoria Angiolino* — ⓛⓛ
Via di Santo Spirito 36r, 50125. **Map** 3 B1. **(** 055-239 89 76.
An attractive restaurant with a typically Florentine, bustling atmosphere. The food and service are sometimes inconsistent but can be excellent. In winter an iron stove in the middle of the restaurant is lit. ● *Sun eve, Mon.* ▱
— *GOOD WINE LIST: ▪*

FLORENCE: *Trattoria Zà Zà* — ⓛⓛ
Piazza del Mercato Centrale 26r, 50123. **Map** 1 C4. **(** 055-21 54 11.
A canteen-like restaurant that is always packed. The food is Tuscan. Excellent soups include ribollita (vegetable), and passata di fagioli (bean purée). ▱

FLORENCE: *Alle Murate* — ⓛⓛⓛ
Via Ghibellina 52r, 50122. **Map** 4 D1. **(** 055-24 06 18.
An increasingly popular trattoria, the young female chef cooks delicate specialities such as prawn ravioli and combines Italian staples with more far-flung Mediterranean cuisines. Light and interesting desserts. ● *Mon.* ▱
— *GOOD WINE LIST: ▪*

FLORENCE: *Cibreo* — ⓛⓛⓛ
Via Andrea del Verrocchio 8r, 50122. **Map** 4 E1. **(** 055-234 11 00.
Superbly prepared Tuscan food in an informal atmosphere. There is no pasta, but specialities include tripe and kidneys. For the squeamish there are some delicious non-offal alternatives such as duck stuffed with sultanas. ● *Mon.* ▱
— *GOOD WINE LIST: ▪   OUTDOOR TABLES: ▪*

FLORENCE: *Da Ganino* — ⓛⓛⓛ
Piazza dei Cimatori 4r, 50100. **Map** 6 D3. **(** 055-21 41 25.
A small, friendly restaurant popular with locals, da Ganino offers all the basics of local fare, including ravioli with butter and sage. ● *Sun.* ▱
— *OUTDOOR TABLES: ▪*

FLORENCE: *Il Francescano* — ⓛⓛⓛ
Via di San Giuseppe 26, 50120. **Map** 4 E1. **(** 055-24 16 05.
A smartly fitted restaurant of wood, marble and objets d'art. A young clientele enjoys artichoke tarts, soups and meat dishes. ● *Oct–Apr: Wed.*
— *GOOD WINE LIST: ▪*

FLORENCE: *I Quattro Amici* ⓁⓁⓁ
Via degli Orti Oricellari 29, 50100. **Map** 1 A5. ☎ *055-21 54 13.*
Four friends with many years in the business created this fish restaurant.
The interior is cool and spartan but the fish, which comes from Porto
Santo Stefano, is good enough to have won a Michelin star. ● *Sun.* ▨

FLORENCE: *La Taverna del Bronzino* ⓁⓁⓁ
Via delle Ruote 27r, 50129. **Map** 2 D3. ☎ *055-49 52 20.*
Named after the Florentine painter who had connections with the 15th-century
palazzo which houses this restaurant. Finest quality cooking. ● *Sun.* ▨

FLORENCE: *Le Fonticine* ⓁⓁⓁ
Via Nazionale 79r, 50123. **Map** 1 C4. ☎ *055-28 21 06.*
A long-established restaurant serving Tuscan food with a refined twist. The
meat is of the highest quality and the pasta is home-made. ● *Sun, Mon.* ▨

FLORENCE: *Enoteca Pinchiorri* ⓁⓁⓁⓁⓁ
Via Ghibellina 87, 50122. **Map** 1 A4 (5 A1). ☎ *055-24 27 77.*
Often described as Italy's best restaurant with the finest wine cellar in Europe,
the Pinchiorri is on the ground floor of a 15th-century palazzo. Cuisine is a
mix of Tuscan and French-inspired cucina nuova. ● *Sun, Mon, Wed lunch.* ▨

FLORENCE: *Sabatini* ⓁⓁⓁⓁⓁ
Via Panzani 9a, 50123. **Map** 1 C5 (5 C1). ☎ *055-28 28 02.*
Once Florence's best restaurant, the cuisine (Italian and international) is
sometimes excellent and the ambience and service are good. ● *Mon.* ▨

TUSCANY

AREZZO: *Buca di San Francesco* ⓁⓁ
Via San Francesco 1, 52100. ☎ *0575-232 71.*
The medieval atmosphere and position alongside the church of Piero della
Francesca's fresco cycle make this an obvious choice. ● *Mon eve, Tue.* ▨ ▤

ARTIMINO: *Da Delfina* ⓁⓁⓁ
Via della Chiesa 1, 50041. ☎ *055-871 80 74.*
A lovely restaurant outside a walled medieval village. Game is a speciality,
as is pork with fennel and black Tuscan cabbage. ● *Sun eve, Mon.*

BAGNI DI LUCCA: *Locanda Maiola* ⓁⓁ
Via della Controneria, 55022. ☎ *0583-862 96.*
A beautiful trattoria serving excellent regional specialities, such as fritto
misto (fried lamb), pastas with ragù sauce and hazelnut fritters. ● *Tue.* ▨

CAPALBIO: *Da Maria* ⓁⓁ
Via Comunale 3, 58011. ☎ *0564-89 60 14.*
Holidaying politicians from Rome sit down with locals to enjoy soundly cooked
Maremma specialities like wild boar and pasta with truffles. ● *Oct–Apr: Tue.* ▨

CASTELNUOVO BERARDENGA: *La Bottega del Trenta* ⓁⓁⓁ
Via Santa Caterina 2, Villa a Sesta 53019. ☎ *0577-35 92 26.*
A tasteful restaurant serving adventurous cooking including duck breast
with wild fennel and delicious desserts. ● *Tue, Wed, Mon–Sat lunch.*

COLLE DI VAL D'ELSA: *L'Antica Trattoria* ⓁⓁⓁ
Piazza Arnolfo 23, 53034. ☎ *0577-92 37 47.*
A homely, family-run restaurant dedicated to traditional regional cuisine.
The setting is medieval and the service lively and attentive. ● *Tue.* ▨

CORTONA: *La Loggetta* ⓁⓁ
Piazza Pescheria 3, 54044. ☎ *0575-63 05 75.*
Set in a quaint medieval loggia, the atmosphere is cool and sedate and the
home-made cannelloni stuffed with spinach and ricotta, delicious. ● *Mon.* ▨

ELBA: *Publius* ⓁⓁ
Piazza XX Settembre, Poggio di Marciana 57030. ☎ *0565-992 08.*
A pleasant trattoria with the best wine cellar on Elba. In addition to fish,
you can eat wild mushrooms, game and wild boar. ● *Nov–Mar: Mon.* ▨

GAIOLE IN CHIANTI: *Badia a Coltibuono* ⓁⓁⓁ
Badia a Coltibuono, 53013. ☎ *0577-74 94 24.*
An 11th-century abbey at the heart of a vineyard whose oils and wines are
used in the restaurant. The menu includes spit-roasted meats and delicious
desserts. Tours of the estate are on offer for wine tasters. ● *Mon.* ♿

Average prices for a three-course meal for one, including a half-bottle of house wine, tax and service:
Ⓛ up to L35,000
ⓁⓁ L35–55,000
ⓁⓁⓁ L55–75,000
ⓁⓁⓁⓁ L75–100,000
ⓁⓁⓁⓁⓁ over L100,000.

FIXED-PRICE MENU
A fixed-price menu on offer, usually with three courses.
GOOD WINE LIST
Denotes a wide range of good quality wines.
FORMAL DRESS
Some restaurants require men to wear a jacket and tie.
OUTDOOR TABLES
Tables for eating outdoors, often with a good view.
CREDIT CARDS
The symbol shows that major credit cards are accepted.

	FIXED-PRICE MENU	GOOD WINE LIST	FORMAL DRESS	OUTDOOR TABLES
LIVORNO: *La Chiave* ⓁⓁⓁ Scale delle Cantine 52, 57100. 📞 0586-88 86 09. Refined and elegant dining from a menu that includes traditional Tuscan meat and fish cuisine and is changed every fortnight. ● *Wed.* 🃏				
LUCCA: *Buca di Sant'Antonio* ⓁⓁ Via della Cervia 3, 55100. 📞 0583-558 81. This is Lucca's most famous restaurant of traditional rustic cooking. Although it is not as good as it was, it has a good range of dishes. ● *Sun eve, Mon.* 🃏				
MASSA MARITTIMA: *Bracali* ⓁⓁ Frazione Ghirlanda, 58024. 📞 0566-90 20 63. Mouth-watering Maremma cooking in a family restaurant; thinly sliced wild boar, pigeon with honey and guinea fowl with white grapes. ● *Tue.* 🃏				
MOGGIONA: *Il Cedro* ⓁⓁ Via di Camaldoli 20, 52010. 📞 0575-55 60 80. Venison, wild boar and fried vegetables are among some of the excellently cooked specialities of Il Cedro. This good-value restaurant stands in a wonderful setting that overlooks forests and mountains. ● *Oct–Apr: Mon.*				
MONTALCINO: *Taverna dei Barbi* ⓁⓁ Località Podernovi, 53024. 📞 0577-84 93 57. Superb country cooking, served with Brunello wines, in a renowned restaurant that also has wonderful views over the surrounding hills. ● *Tue eve, Wed.*		▦		
MONTECATINI TERME: *Pier Angelo* ⓁⓁⓁⓁ Viale IV Novembre 99, 51016. 📞 0572-77 15 52. An acclaimed restaurant in an Art Nouveau villa serves unique nouvelle cuisine dishes prepared and served with an innovative flair. ● *Sun eve, Mon.* 🃏				
MONTEPULCIANO: *Il Marzocco* ⓁⓁ Piazza Savonarola 18, 53045. 📞 0578-75 72 62. Part of a 19th-century hotel, this is a pleasant family-run restaurant that offers well-presented food in unpretentious surroundings. ● *Wed.* 🃏				
MONTERIGGIONI: *Il Pozzo* ⓁⓁⓁ Piazza Roma 23, 53035. 📞 0577-30 41 27. A stone-walled restaurant in the charming medieval village of Monteriggioni. The Tuscan food is simple and enthusiastically prepared, and the home-made desserts are well-known in the surrounding region. ● *Sun eve, Mon.* 🃏				
ORBETELLO: *Osteria del Lupacante* ⓁⓁ Corso Italia 103, 58015. 📞 0564-86 76 18. The cooking concentrates on fish and seafood specialities with some touches of adventure; look out for mussels in Marsala sauce, risotto with prawns and pine nuts and sole with almonds and onions. ● *Oct–Apr: Tue.* 🃏				
PESCIA: *Cecco* ⓁⓁ Via Francesca Forti 94–96, 51017. 📞 0572-47 79 55. A friendly local restaurant where the food is often outstanding. Try the local Pescia asparagus, and cioncia (the house main course). ● *Mon.* 🃏		▦		▦
PIENZA: *Da Falco* ⓁⓁ Piazza Dante Alighieri 7, 53026. 📞 0578-74 85 51. A friendly local restaurant with excellent antipasti and a magnificent choice of primi and secondi from a menu of local specialities. ● *Fri.* 🃏	●			▦
PISA: *Al Ristoro dei Vecchi Macelli* ⓁⓁⓁ Via Volturno 49, 56126. 📞 050-204 24. Innovative dishes in a pleasant, intimate restaurant that serves light Tuscan food with an adventurous twist. Fish, seafood and game specialities are delicately prepared and the desserts are a delight. ● *Sun lunch, Wed.* 🃏		▦		

Porto Ercole: *Bacco in Toscana* ⓁⓁⓁ
Via San Paolo 6, 58018. **℄** *0564-83 30 78.*
An intimate restaurant that serves an array of excellent seafood dishes;
scampi with lemon and spaghetti alle vongole (clams). ● *Wed.* 🍴

Porto Santo Stefano: *La Bussola* ⓁⓁ
Piazza Fucchinetti 11, 58019. **℄** *0564-81 42 25.*
Adventurous primi include some excellent seafood pastas as well as simpler
grilled fish. The views from the terrace are really spectacular. ● *Wed.* 🍴

Prato: *Il Piraña* ⓁⓁⓁⓁ
Via Valentini 110, 50047. **℄** *0574-257 46.*
Rated as one of the best fish and seafood restaurants in Tuscany; don't be
put off by its setting or over-precious modern interior. ● *Sat lunch, Sun.* 🍴

San Gimignano: *Le Terrazze* ⓁⓁ
Albergo la Cisterna, Piazza della Cisterna 24, 53037. **℄** *0577-94 03 28.*
Set on a terrace with views over the rolling hills of southern Tuscany, one
of the dining rooms is medieval and forms part of a 13th-century palazzo.
Good for regional specialities with some novelties. ● *Tue, Wed lunch.* 🍴 ▤

Sansepolcro: *Paola e Marco Mercati* ⓁⓁⓁ ●
Via Palmiro Togliatti 68, 52037. **℄** *0575-73 50 51.*
A new restaurant whose dishes include Tuscan black cabbage cooked with
white truffles, vegetable ravioli, roast pigeon and gnocchi. ● *Sun.* 🍴

Saturnia: *I Due Cippi da Michele* ⓁⓁ
Piazza Vittorio Veneto 26a, 58050. **℄** *0564-60 10 74.*
One of the region's most popular restaurants, it is a touchstone for Maremma
cuisine and its traditional offerings are unbeatably good value. ● *Tue.* 🍴

Siena: *Al Marsili* ⓁⓁ
Via del Castoro 3, 53100. **℄** *0577-471 54.*
Perhaps not as delicious as it once was, the food at Al Marsili, long
regarded as one of the best restaurants in Siena, is still good. ● *Mon.* 🍴 ▤

Siena: *Osteria le Logge* ⓁⓁⓁ
Via del Porrione 33, 53100. **℄** *0577-480 13.*
Siena's prettiest restaurant, with dark wood and marble interior. Home-
produced oils and Montalcino wines accompany dishes that include
guinea fowl, duck and fennel, and rabbit with capers. ● *Sun.* 🍴

Sovana: *Taverna Etrusca* ⓁⓁ ●
Piazza del Pretorio 16, 58010. **℄** *0564-61 61 83.*
A small restaurant with a beautifully presented medieval dining area. The
carefully produced cuisine is Tuscan with sophisticated touches. ● *Mon.* 🍴

Viareggio: *Romano* ⓁⓁⓁ ● ■
Via Mazzini 120, 55049. **℄** *0584-313 82.*
This is one of Tuscany's best fish and seafood restaurants. The service is
courteous and friendly and the wines are well-priced. ● *Mon.* 🍴

UMBRIA

Amelia: *Anita* ⓁⓁ
Via Roma 31, 05022. **℄** *0744-98 21 46.*
This simple restaurant offers no-frills local food, such as crostini (fried bread),
meat kebabs, pasta with porcini mushrooms and wild boar. ● *Mon.* 🍴

Assisi: *Medioevo* ⓁⓁⓁ
Via Arco dei Priori 4b, 06081. **℄** *075-81 30 68.*
This elegant restaurant in old Assisi has a delightful vaulted dining room
dating from the Middle Ages. Pastas are home-made (try them with black
truffles in season). Meats are cooked to traditional recipes. ● *Wed; Jan, Jul.* 🍴

Assisi: *San Francesco* ⓁⓁⓁ
Via San Francesco 52, 06081. **℄** *075-81 23 29.*
A carefully chosen menu includes carpaccio of porcini mushrooms (raw,
thinly sliced), stuffed goose and fillet steak with truffles. ● *Wed.* 🍴

Città di Castello: *Amici Miei* Ⓛ ●
Via del Monte 2, 06012. **℄** *075-855 99 04.*
Set in the storerooms of a 16th-century palazzo in the historic centre, the
menu is based on regional cuisine with a few inspired touches. ● *Wed.* 🍴

	FIXED-PRICE MENU	GOOD WINE LIST	FORMAL DRESS	OUTDOOR TABLES
Average prices for a three-course meal for one, including a half-bottle of house wine, tax and service: Ⓛ up to L35,000 ⒧Ⓛ L35–55,000 ⒧⒧Ⓛ L55–75,000 ⒧⒧⒧Ⓛ L75–100,000 ⒧⒧⒧⒧Ⓛ over L100,000.	**FIXED-PRICE MENU** A fixed-price menu on offer, usually with three courses. **GOOD WINE LIST** Denotes a wide range of good quality wines. **FORMAL DRESS** Some restaurants require men to wear a jacket and tie. **OUTDOOR TABLES** Tables for eating outdoors, often with a good view. **CREDIT CARDS** The symbol shows that major credit cards are accepted.			

CITTÀ DI CASTELLO: *Il Bersaglio* ⒧Ⓛ Via Vittorio Emanuele Orlando 14, 06012. 📞 *075-855 55 34.* A traditional Umbrian restaurant with specialities including gnocchetti (little gnocchi) with truffles and almond dessert with coffee cream. ● *Wed.* 🔲 ⚡	●	▨		
CAMPELLO SUL CLITUNNO: *Le Casaline* ⒧Ⓛ Poreta di Spoleto, 06042. 📞 *0743-52 11 13.* An oasis of calm in a restored 18th-century mill in the countryside. Try the gnocchi stuffed with mushrooms, wild boar alla cacciatora (in wine and tomato sauce) and the selection of salamis. ● *Mon.* 🔲 ♿	●			▨
CAMPELLO SUL CLITUNNO: *Trattoria Pettino* ⒧Ⓛ Frazione Pettino 31, 06042. 📞 *0743-27 60 21.* Set in the middle of the mountains in an old restored house. The bruschetta and the plethora of dishes with truffles are delicious. ● *Tue.* ♿				▨
FOLIGNO: *Villa Roncalli* ⒧⒧Ⓛ Via Roma 25, 06034. 📞 *0742-39 10 91.* A charming country inn set in its own garden 1 km (half a mile) from Foligno. Regional specialities are well prepared using fresh ingredients. ● *Mon.* 🔲		▨		
GUBBIO: *Alcatraz* Ⓛ Località Santa Cristina, 06020. 📞 *075-92 00 52.* An Agriturist centre about 25 km (15 miles) southwest of Gubbio, the simple, rustic food is produced on the farm, including the olive oil, pastas and wines.				▨
GUBBIO: *Villa Montegranelli* ⒧Ⓛ Località Monteluiano, 06024. 📞 *075-922 01 85.* Set in an 18th-century villa with an elegantly rural atmosphere. Exquisitely made specialities include crostini (toasts) with porcini mushroom terrine and chestnut flour pancakes with melted cheese and ricotta. 🔲 ⚡	●	▨		
MAGIONE: *Associazione Agrituristica Montemelino* Ⓛ Località Montemelino, 06063. 📞 *075-84 36 06.* Another of the simple, reliable Agriturist restaurants. This one serves its own lake fish and, in season, ravioli of porcini mushrooms. ● *Oct–Apr: Mon.*				
NARNI: *Monte del Grano 1696* ⒧⒧Ⓛ Strada Guadamello 128, Località San Vito 05030. 📞 *0744-74 91 43.* Much care goes into creating a pleasant atmosphere in which to sample excellent regional dishes, often with creative flourishes. ● *Mon.* 🔲	●	▨		▨
NORCIA: *Dal Francese* ⒧Ⓛ Via Riguardati 16, 06046. 📞 *0743-81 62 90.* A country-style trattoria in the centre of Norcia. It offers regional specialities such as a truffle-based menu-degustazione in season. ● *Oct–Apr: Fri.* 🔲 ♿				
ORVIETO: *La Volpe e L'Uva* Ⓛ Via Ripa Corsica 1, 05018. 📞 *0763-416 12.* A popular trattoria in the centre of Orvieto offering a large variety of regional dishes that change with the season at very reasonable prices. ● *Mon.* 🔲		▨		
ORVIETO: *I Sette Consoli* ⒧Ⓛ Piazza Sant'Angelo 1a, 05018. 📞 *0763-439 11.* A comfortable, friendly restaurant with a garden for summer dining. Try baccalà (salt cod) marinated in apple vinegar with potato salad, stuffed rabbit, bean soup with fennel, and crostini with smoked ricotta. ● *Wed.* 🔲 ♿	●	▨		▨
PASSIGNANO SUL TRASIMENO: *Cacciatori da Luciano* ⒧⒧⒧Ⓛ Lungolago A Pompii 11, 06065. 📞 *075-82 72 10.* The menu is based on sea fish, including scampi salad, fish carpaccio (raw, thinly sliced fish), risotto of different types of prawn and shrimp and grilled sole. Some of the desserts are made with forest fruits. ● *Oct–Apr: Wed.* 🔲		▨		

PERUGIA: *Aladino* ⒧⒧

Via delle Prome 11, 06100. **C** *075-572 09 38.*
In the historic centre, the Aladino offers wonderful cuisine with emphasis
on Sardinian specialities. Desserts are home-made. ● *lunch daily; Mon.*

PERUGIA: *Gio Arte e Vini* ⒧⒧

Via Ruggero d'Andreotto 19, 06124. **C** *075-573 11 00.*
Famous for its spectacular selection of wines and well-chosen regional
dishes with special touches. The Umbrian minestrone and the trecciola
di agnello (lamb) are particularly good. ● *Sun eve, Mon lunch.*

PERUGIA: *Osteria del Bartolo* ⒧⒧⒧

Via Bartolo 30, 06122. **C** *075-573 15 61.*
An elegant restaurant that is one of the mainstays of the Perugian eating
tradition. Many items, like the bread and butter, are home-made. ● *Sun.*

SPOLETO: *Il Tartufo* ⒧⒧

Piazza Garibaldi 24, 06049. **C** *0743-402 36.*
The floor of one of the dining rooms is ancient Roman. Well-tried regional
specialities, including, not surprisingly, truffles, as well as other delights
such as barley soup and duck in Sagrantino wine sauce. ● *Wed.*

TERNI: *Da Carlino* ⒧

Via Piemonte 1, 05100. **C** *0744-42 01 63.*
Robust rustic food, such as crostini with local salami, tagliatelle with truffles
or duck sauce, roasted lamb, and bean involtini (bean parcels). ● *Mon.*

TERNI: *Gulliver* ⒧⒧⒧

Via Sant'Alo 10, 05100. **C** *0744-42 52 25.*
A delightful restaurant run by a group of young people. Local ingredients
are chosen for creative dishes such as fresh salmon ravioli and orecchiette
(ear-shaped pasta) with asparagus and white truffles. ● *Sun, Wed.*

TODI: *La Mulinella* ⒧

Località Pontenaia, 06059. **C** *075-894 82 35.*
In the countryside about 2 km (1 mile) from Todi serving simple, reliable
dishes. Tagliatelle al profumo di bosco is recommended. ● *Wed.*

TODI: *Lucaroni* ⒧⒧

Strada Rosceto-Soprano 25, Località Casella 06059. **C** *075-88 73 70.*
Regional fish, meat and game (including hare, duck and lamb with truffles).
Puddings, such as crema with warm chocolate, are also good. ● *Tue.*

TREVI: *La Taverna del Pescatore* ⒧⒧

Via della Chiesa Tonda 50, 06039. **C** *0742-78 09 20.*
The freshest of local produce is combined and cooked in simple yet exquisite
recipes and the atmosphere is relaxed with attentive service. ● *Wed.*

LE MARCHE

ANCONA: *La Moretta* ⒧⒧⒧

Piazza Plebiscito 52, 60124. **C** *071-20 23 17.*
A lovely traditional restaurant serving excellent local dishes; polenta with
calamari and truffles, and lamb with artichokes and almonds. ● *Sun.*

ANCONA: *Passetto* ⒧⒧⒧

Piazza IV Novembre 1, 60124. **C** *071-332 14.*
Outside eating with splendid views onto the sea in the summer. The meat
dishes are good but it is the fish and seafood that excel here. ● *Wed.*

FABRIANO: *Il Convivio* ⒧⒧⒧

Via P Mattarella 62, 60044. **C** *0732-45 74.*
The restaurant is above a birreria and serves excellent imaginative seasonal
cuisine such as pigeon with a sauce of port and truffles. ● *Mon.*

FANO: *Darpetti Quinta* ⒧

Viale Adriatico 42, 61032. **C** *0721-80 80 43.*
An excellent, basic trattoria where the daily menu consists of simple but
delicious cuisine, such as some light pasta sauces and tasty grills. ● *Sun.*

FANO: *Ristorantino da Giulio* ⒧⒧

Viale Adriatico 100, 61032. **C** *0721-80 56 80.*
A calm restaurant opposite the beach. The cuisine is basically regional, with
the chef's personal touches. Fish antipasti are especially good. ● *Tue.*

Average prices for a three-course meal for one, including a half-bottle of house wine, tax and service:
Ⓛ up to L35,000
ⒽⓁ L35–55,000
ⓁⓁⓁ L55–75,000
ⓁⓁⓁⓁ L75–100,000
ⓁⓁⓁⓁⓁ over L100,000.

FIXED-PRICE MENU
A fixed-price menu on offer, usually with three courses.
GOOD WINE LIST
Denotes a wide range of good quality wines.
FORMAL DRESS
Some restaurants require men to wear a jacket and tie.
OUTDOOR TABLES
Tables for eating outdoors, often with a good view.
CREDIT CARDS
The symbol shows that major credit cards are accepted.

	FIXED-PRICE MENU	GOOD WINE LIST	FORMAL DRESS	OUTDOOR TABLES

JESI: *Ensalada* ⓁⓁ
Via San Marcello 86, 60035. 【 .0731-574 87.
The chef has exacting standards for selecting only the best quality fish which is prepared with utmost care. Antipasti and primi are mainly fish based and the cuisine is light and flavourful. ● Mon. ▣

	●			▪

JESI: *Tana Liberatutti* ⓁⓁ
Piazza B Pontelli 1, 60035. 【 0731-592 37.
A dignified restaurant where simple dishes are prepared with care. Try marinated veal or crostini of forest mushrooms for antipasti. ● Sun. ▣

				▪

LORETO: *Andreina* ⓁⓁ
Via Buffolareggia 14, 60025. 【 071-97 01 24.
A mother and daughter team prepare traditional cuisine with home-made pasta, chicken, rabbit and game, followed by tempting desserts. ● Tue. ▣

		▪		

MACERATA: *Da Secondo* ⓁⓁ
Via Pescheria Vecchia 26–28, 62100. 【 0733-26 09 12.
Regional cuisine; vincisgrassi (local lasagna) alla Macerata and frittura mista (batter-fried fish and vegetables) are highly recommended. ● Mon. ▣ ⚡ ⓓ

	●			▪

NUMANA: *La Costarella* ⓁⓁⓁ
Via IV Novembre 35, 60026. 【 071-736 02 97.
Booking is advisable in this specialist fish restaurant; pasta with black cuttlefish ink and fried fish with courgette flowers. ● Oct–Apr: Mon.

PESARO: *Daniela e Umberto il Rifugio del Gabbiano* ⓁⓁⓁ
Strada Panoramica San Bartolo, Località Santa Marina Alta 61100. 【 0721-27 98 44.
Pèsaro traditional dishes are presented with flair. Fish is the mainstay of the menu; try pasta in squid ink, fish ravioli and baked fish. ● Mon. ▣

		▪		

PESARO: *Da Teresa* ⓁⓁⓁ
Viale Trieste 180, 61100. 【 0721-302 22.
A gracious restaurant offering imaginatively prepared dishes strongly based on local cuisine. As well as exquisite fish and seafood there are a few meat dishes and some delightful desserts to follow. ● Sun eve, Mon. ▣ ▤ ⓓ

	●	▪		

PESARO: *Da Alceo* ⓁⓁⓁⓁ
Via Panoramica Ardizio 101, 61100. 【 0721-513 60.
A famous fish restaurant with a spectacular panoramic terrace serving gnocchi with shellfish, and risotto. Desserts are home-made and tasty. ● Mon. ▣

		▪		▪

SENIGALLIA: *Uliassi* ⓁⓁ
Via Banchina di Levante 6, 60020. 【 071-654 63.
Run by a brother and sister, this is a friendly restaurant offering a high standard of cuisine. Try the speciality pasta with clams, mussels and saffron. ● Tue. ▣

				▪

SIROLO: *Rocco* ⓁⓁ
Via Torrione 1, 60020. 【 071-933 05 58.
Open during the summer evenings only, Rocco serves delicious (mainly fish) dishes such as gnocchi with clams, fried mixed fish and vegetables and sea bass with a sauce of lettuce and balsamic vinegar. ● Tue. ▣

				▪

URBANIA: *Big Ben* ⓁⓁ
Corso Vittorio Emanuele 61, 61049. 【 0722-31 97 95.
In the historic centre of town, Big Ben's specialities include tagliolini (pasta) with truffles and cicciarchiata (specially prepared dessert). ● Wed. ▣ ⚡

				▪

URBINO: *Vecchia Urbino* ⓁⓁⓁ
Via del Vasari 3–5, 61029. 【 0722-44 47.
A country restaurant with views over the historic centre, serving simply prepared traditional rustic dishes from the region, including vincisgrassi, the local lasagna, rabbit, and lamb with herbs. ● Oct–Apr: Tue. ▣ ⓓ

		▪		

ROME

AVENTINE: *Pierilli a Testaccio* ⓁⓁ
Via Marmorata 39, 00153. **Map** 6 E3. **☎** 06-574 24 15.
An archetypal noisy Roman trattoria serving a regular clientele with robust,
traditional fare that includes artichokes and rigatoni alla pajata. ● *Wed.* &

AVENTINE: *Checchino dal 1887* ⓁⓁⓁ
Via di Monte Testaccio 30, 00153. **Map** 6 D4. **☎** 06-574 63 18.
Roman cuisine served at old convent tables under vaulted ceilings with
an open fire in winter. ● *Oct–May: Mon, Sun eve; Jun–Sep: Mon eve, Sun.* ⊟ &

CAMPO DE' FIORI: *Al Pompiere* ⓁⓁ
Via Santa Maria dei Calderari 38, 00186. **Map** 2 F5. **☎** 06-686 83 77.
In the heart of the Jewish ghetto, on the first floor of the Palazzo Cenci
Bolognetti with frescoed, beamed ceilings. The food is classically Roman,
including fried courgette flowers and rigatoni con la pajata. ● *Sun.* ⊟

CAMPO DE' FIORI: *Le Maschere* ⓁⓁ
Via Monte della Farina 29, 00186. **Map** 2 F5. **☎** 06-687 94 44.
A tiled hall opens onto a rustic indoor terrace with a pleasant country
feel. The house wine and the fiery food are Calabrian. ● *Mon.* ⊟

CAMPO DE' FIORI: *Taverna Giulia* ⓁⓁ
Vicolo dell'Oro 23, 00186. **Map** 2 D3. **☎** 06-686 97 68.
The food is Ligurian with salmon and mozzarella canapés and baccalà alla
genovese. The atmosphere is quiet and the service discreet. ● *Sun.* ⊟ &

CAMPO DE' FIORI: *Il Drappo* ⓁⓁⓁ
Vicolo del Malpasso 9, 00186. **Map** 2 E4. **☎** 06-687 73 65.
An intimate restaurant with ceiling drapes and candlelight, serving Sardinian
cuisine; seada (sweet cheese-filled ravioli) and mirtillo liqueur. ● *Sun.* ⊟ &

CAMPO DE' FIORI: *Sora Lella* ⓁⓁⓁ
Via Ponte Quattro Capi 16, 00186. **Map** 6 E1. **☎** 06-686 16 01.
Named after the Roman actress who founded it and now run by the son.
Local cuisine served in an exquisite location on Tiber Island. ● *Sun.* ⊟

CAMPO DE' FIORI: *Camponeschi* ⓁⓁⓁⓁ
Piazza Farnese 50, 00186. **Map** 2 E5. **☎** 06-687 49 27.
Modern and regional Italian cooking, and refined French specialities, served in
a sumptuous interior on one of the most beautiful piazzas in Rome. ● *Sun.* ⊟

ESQUILINE: *Trattoria Monti* ⓁⓁ
Via di San Vito 13a, 00185. **Map** 4 E4. **☎** 06-446 65 73.
Delicate dishes from the Marches are prepared by Franca Camerucci whose
husband, Mario, is an attentive waiter and sommelier. Specialities include
tacchino all'aceto balsamico (turkey with balsamic vinegar). ● *Tue.* ⊟

ESQUILINE: *Agata e Romeo* ⓁⓁⓁⓁ
Via Carlo Alberto 45, 00185. **Map** 4 E4. **☎** 06-446 61 15.
Agata cooks predominantly Roman and southern Italian fare while Romeo
serves. Tables are well-spaced and the atmosphere is tranquil. ● *Sun.* ⊟ &

JANICULUM: *Al Tocco* ⓁⓁⓁ
Via San Pancrazio 1, Piazzale Aurelio 7, 00152. **Map** 5 A1. **☎** 06-581 52 74.
A 15th-century, ivy-clad restaurant with a homely atmosphere. The cuisine
is from the Tuscan Maremma; rustic soups, fish and grills. ● *Mon.* ⊟ ⊟ &

LATERAN: *Alfredo a Via Gabi* ⓁⓁ
Via Gabi 36, 00183. **Map** 8 E3. **☎** 06-77 20 67 92.
A spacious trattoria with cheerful service and ample portions. Try porcini
mushrooms, straccetti all'ortica (meat in nettle sauce) and panna cotta. ● *Tue.*

PANTHEON: *Da Gino* ⓁⓁ
Vicolo Rosini 4, 00186. **Map** 3 A3. **☎** 06-687 34 34.
An ancient, traditional Roman trattoria full of journalists, politicians
and the initiated. Daily dishes include gnocchi and ossobuco and
baccalà as well as some classic sturdy soups. ● *Sun.* &

PANTHEON: *Sangallo* ⓁⓁⓁ
Vicolo della Vaccarella 11a, 00186. **Map** 2 F3. **☎** 06-686 55 49.
Small, elegant bistro specializing in regional fish dishes and a huge array of
antipasti, including many types of cured meat and seafood. ● *Sun.* ⊟ &

<table>
<tr><td>
Average prices for a three-course meal for one, including a half-bottle of house wine, tax and service:
Ⓛ up to L35,000
ⓁⓁ L35–55,000
ⓁⓁⓁ L55–75,000
ⓁⓁⓁⓁ L75–100,000
ⓁⓁⓁⓁⓁ over L100,000.
</td></tr>
</table>

Fixed-Price Menu
A fixed-price menu on offer, usually with three courses.

Good Wine List
Denotes a wide range of good quality wines.

Formal Dress
Some restaurants require men to wear a jacket and tie.

Outdoor Tables
Tables for eating outdoors, often with a good view.

Credit Cards
The symbol shows that major credit cards are accepted.

	Fixed-Price Menu	Good Wine List	Formal Dress	Outdoor Tables
Pantheon: *El Toulà* ⓁⓁⓁⓁⓁ Via della Lupa 29b, 00186. **Map** 2 F3. ☎ 06-687 34 98. One of the most exclusive and traditional restaurants in Rome. The cuisine is mainly Venetian, the service is excellent and the wines are superb. ● *Sun.* ⬛	●	▨	●	
Piazza Navona: *La Taverna* ⓁⓁ Via del Banco di Santo Spirito 58, 00186. **Map** 2 D3. ☎ 06-686 41 16. A crowded Roman trattoria with a family atmosphere. The rigatoni all'amatriciana is a speciality as are the traditional gnocchi, baccalà (salt cod) and tripe on Thursday, Friday and Saturday respectively. ● *Mon.* ⬛ ♿	●			▨
Piazza Navona: *Papà Giovanni* ⓁⓁⓁⓁ Via del Sediari 4, 00186. **Map** 2 F4. ☎ 06-686 53 08. Giovanni's son now runs this restaurant with an excellent cellar. New, lighter Roman cuisine is served alongside heartier traditional dishes. ● *Sun.* ⬛ ⚡		▨		
Piazza di Spagna: *Birreria Viennese* Ⓛ Via della Croce 21, 00187. **Map** 3 A2. ☎ 06-679 55 69. Traditional beers and Austrian specialities have been served in this long and crowded room for more than 60 years. In the atmospheric setting, try the sausages, goulash, sauerkraut or the Wienerschnitzel. ● *Wed.* ⬛ ♿	●			
Piazza di Spagna: *Mario alla Vite* Ⓛ Via della Vite 55, 00187. **Map** 3 A2. ☎ 06-678 38 18. Simple, honest Tuscan fare. The service can be haphazard but the ribollita, fagioli al fiasco (beans), steaks and desserts make up for it. ● *Sun.* ⬛				▨
Piazza di Spagna: *Al 34* ⓁⓁ Via Mario de' Fiori 34, 00187. **Map** 3 A2. ☎ 06-679 50 91. The perfect setting for a comfortable chat or a romantic tête-à-tête. The extensive menu offers mostly southern Italian cuisine. ● *Mon.* ⬛ ♿				▨
Piazza di Spagna: *Porto di Ripetta* ⓁⓁⓁ Via di Ripetta 250, 00187. **Map** 2 F2. ☎ 06-361 23 76. A friendly restaurant serving wonderful dishes with fish and seafood brought in daily. Try the giant prawns with artichokes or fish soup. ● *Sun.* ⬛	●	▨	●	
Quirinal: *Al Moro* ⓁⓁ Vicolo delle Bollette, 00185. **Map** 3 B3. ☎ 06-678 34 95. A reliable choice for traditional Roman cooking in this noisy and crowded trattoria. Fresh local ingredients are used to make dishes such as bucatini all'amatriciana and spaghetti alla Moro (a version of carbonara). ● *Sun.* ♿				
Quirinal: *Colline Emiliane* ⓁⓁ Via degli Avignonesi 22, 00187. **Map** 3 C3. ☎ 06-481 75 38. A small, family trattoria serving specialities from Emilia-Romagna; home-made pasta, salami, boiled meats and salsa verde (parsley, onion and anchovy sauce) and a choice of Emilian and Romagnoli wines. ● *Fri.* ♿		▨		
Quirinal: *Il Posto Accanto* ⓁⓁⓁ Via del Boschetto 36a, 00184. **Map** 3 C4. ☎ 06-474 30 02. This elegant family-run restaurant owes its success to a carefully chosen menu based on home-made pasta, fish and meat. ● *Sun.* ⬛ ♿				
Termini: *Gemma alla Lupa* Ⓛ Via Marghera 39, 00185. **Map** 4 F3. ☎ 06-49 12 30. A typical, modest Roman trattoria serving real Roman cuisine in a bustling atmosphere. Excellent value with speedy service. ● *Sun.* ♿	●			▨
Trastevere: *Da Lucia* Ⓛ Vicolo del Mattonato 2b, 00153. **Map** 5 C1. ☎ 06-580 36 01. A popular, crowded trattoria serving basic Roman cuisine. Try the pasta e ceci and the spaghetti alla grici (pecorino, pancetta and pepper). ● *Mon.* ♿				▨

TRASTEVERE: *Da Paris*
Piazza San Calisto 7a, 00153. **Map** 5 C1. **[** 06-581 53 78.
A Roman-Jewish restaurant popular with locals. Home-made pasta and
traditional dishes include minestra di arzilla (skate), tripe and exquisite
fritto misto (batter-fried fish) with vegetables. ● *Sun eve, Mon.* ▣

Ⓛ Ⓛ Ⓛ

TRASTEVERE: *Peccati di Gola*
Piazza dei Ponziani 7a, 00153. **Map** 6 E1. **[** 06-581 45 29.
Calabrian fish cuisine is interpreted for modern tastes in this ivy-clad piazza.
There is a great selection of seafood, risotti and fish. ● *lunch, Mon.* ▣ ⬧

Ⓛ Ⓛ Ⓛ

TRASTEVERE: *Romolo nel Giardino della Fornarina*
Via Porta Settimiana 8, 00153. **Map** 2 E5. **[** 06-581 82 84.
La Fornarina was Raphael's mistress and this is said to have been her home. In
summer the Roman food is served in the courtyard. ● *Mon, Aug.* ▣ ⬧

Ⓛ Ⓛ Ⓛ

TRASTEVERE: *Alberto Ciarla*
Piazza San Cosimato 40, 00153. **Map** 5 C1. **[** 06-581 86 68.
This is the place for fish. Based on the day's fish from the market, traditional
blends with modern. The decor is elegant and dramatic. ● *lunch, Sun.* ▣ ⚡

Ⓛ Ⓛ Ⓛ Ⓛ

VATICAN: *Tavola d'Oro*
Via Marianna Dionigi 37, 00193. **Map** 2 E2. **[** 06-321 26 01.
Simple, family atmosphere in a small, noisy room where excellent Sicilian
fare is prepared. Portions are generous; try swordfish, aubergine purée,
pasta con sarde (sardines), or involtini (meat parcels). ● *Sun.* ⚡

Ⓛ

VIA VENETO: *Cantina Cantarini*
Piazza Sallustio 12, 00187. **Map** 4 D1. **[** 06-48 55 28.
A popular local trattoria with friendly service. Meat is served from Monday
to Thursday lunchtime and fish is served for the rest of the week. ● *Sun.* ▣

Ⓛ Ⓛ

VIA VENETO: *Giovanni*
Via Marche 64, 00187. **Map** 3 C1. **[** 06-482 18 34.
A crowded restaurant popular with locals. Traditional food from Lazio and the
Marches, including fresh fish, pasta and ossobuco. ● *Fri eve, Sat.* ▣

Ⓛ Ⓛ Ⓛ

VIA VENETO: *Tullio*
Via San Nicola da Tolentino 26, 00187. **Map** 3 C2. **[** 06-481 85 64.
A genuine Tuscan restaurant frequented by an enthusiastic crowd. Typical
dishes include porcini mushrooms in numerous ways. ● *Sun, Aug.* ▣ ⬧

Ⓛ Ⓛ Ⓛ

VIA VENETO: *George's*
Via Marche 7, 00187. **Map** 3 C1. **[** 06-42 08 45 75.
A survivor from the Dolce Vita era with a nostalgic air of luxurious elegance.
Service is impeccable and there is a tempting selection of dishes. ● *Sun.* ▣

Ⓛ Ⓛ Ⓛ Ⓛ Ⓛ

VILLA BORGHESE: *Al Ceppo*
Via Panama 2, 00198. **[** 06-841 96 96.
Run by two sisters who serve a strictly seasonal menu of traditional dishes
with flashes of inspiration in a hospitable atmosphere. ● *Mon.* ▣ ⬧

Ⓛ Ⓛ

VILLA BORGHESE: *Relais le Jardin dell'Hotel Lord Byron*
Via Giuseppe de Notaris 5, 00198. **[** 06-322 45 41.
High prices are matched by impeccable service and haute cuisine at its best.
Inspired cooking draws on tradition with delicious mixtures of fruit, herbs
and vegetables combined with top-quality meats and fish. ▣ ⚡

Ⓛ Ⓛ Ⓛ Ⓛ Ⓛ

LAZIO

ALATRI: *La Rosetta*
Via del Duomo 35, 03011. **[** 0775-43 45 68.
A quiet restaurant near the 6th-century BC acropolis. Try the maccheroni alla
ciociaria (a wine, herb, bacon and meat sauce). ● *Oct–Apr: Tue.* ▣ ⚡ ⬧

Ⓛ

CERVETERI: *Da Fiore*
Località Procoio di Ceri, 00052. **[** 06-99 20 42 50.
A simple country trattoria: specialities include home-cooked pastas with ragù,
rabbit and grilled meats. The bruschette and pizzas are also good. ● *Tue.*

Ⓛ

FRASCATI: *Enoteca Frascati*
Via Armando Diaz 42, 00044. **[** 06-941 74 49.
A good range of light dishes accompany the more than 400 wines in this
enoteca: Smoked fish, soups and carpaccio (thin slices) of duck. ● *Sun.* ▣

Ⓛ Ⓛ

		FIXED-PRICE MENU	GOOD WINE LIST	FORMAL DRESS	OUTDOOR TABLES

Average prices for a three-course meal for one, including a half-bottle of house wine, tax and service:
Ⓛ up to L35,000
ⓁⓁ L35–55,000
ⓁⓁⓁ L55–75,000
ⓁⓁⓁⓁ L75–100,000
ⓁⓁⓁⓁⓁ over L100,000.

FIXED-PRICE MENU
A fixed-price menu on offer, usually with three courses.
GOOD WINE LIST
Denotes a wide range of good quality wines.
FORMAL DRESS
Some restaurants require men to wear a jacket and tie.
OUTDOOR TABLES
Tables for eating outdoors, often with a good view.
CREDIT CARDS
The symbol shows that major credit cards are accepted.

	FIXED-PRICE MENU	GOOD WINE LIST	FORMAL DRESS	OUTDOOR TABLES
GAETA: *La Cianciola* Ⓛ Vicolo 2 Buonomo 16, 04024. 📞 0771-46 61 90. A charming trattoria hidden up a little alley into which tables are tightly packed. Try the pasta with aubergines and shellfish. ● *Oct–Apr: Mon.* 🗎				▓
NETTUNO: *Sangallo* ⓁⓁⓁ Via Sangallo, 04024. 📞 06-980 44 79. Set in a charming medieval village, this trattoria serves simple local fare based mainly on seafood. The pizzas are also good. ● *Oct–Apr: Thu.* 🗎		▓		
OSTIA ANTICA: *Il Monumento* ⓁⓁ Piazza Umberto I 18, 00119. 📞 06-565 00 21. A fish-based menu; the house speciality, spaghetti monumento, is served with seafood sauce. The home-made ragù is also good. ● *Mon.* 🗎 ⓺				▓
PALESTRINA: *Il Palestrina* ⓁⓁⓁ Via E Toti 4, 00036. 📞 06-953 46 15. Well-prepared, light dishes that are a little different from traditional cuisine. Marinated swordfish and coffee dessert (zuppone). ● *Mon.* 🗎				
SPERLONGA: *La Bisaccia* ⓁⓁ Via Romita 25, 04029. 📞 0771-545 76. Linguine with wild asparagus and prawns is a highlight of this restaurant that also makes use of local fish for soups and grills. ● *Oct–Apr: Tue.* 🗎 ⓺		▓		▓
TERRACINA: *Da Baffone* ⓁⓁ Via Appia, km 104, 04029. 📞 0773-72 60 07. This popular restaurant along the beautiful beach of Terracina is a peaceful place to sample some good local fish dishes. ● *Oct–Apr: Tue.* 🗎 ⓺		▓		▓
TIVOLI: *Villa Esedra* ⓁⓁ Via di Villa Adriana 51, Località Villa Adriana 00011. 📞 0774-53 47 16. Typical menu with imaginative antipasti such as fish salad and carpaccio of smoked cheese. In the evening there are also pizzas. ● *Oct–Apr: Tue.* 🗎				▓
TREVIGNANO: *Ristorante Il Palazzetto* ⓁⓁ Via Vittorio Emanuele III 20, 00069. 📞 06-999 92 54. A little restaurant with views over Lake Bracciano. The excellent menu makes good use of lake fish, including eel terrine, ravioli al persico (perch) and delicious king prawns in cognac. Desserts are home-made. ● *Wed.* 🗎 ⓺	●	▓		▓
TUSCANIA: *Al Gallo* ⓁⓁⓁ Via del Gallo 22, 01017. 📞 0761-44 33 88. An unusual interpretation of regional dishes has created an exceptionally good menu. Warm atmosphere and charming service. ● *Mon.* 🗎 ⓺	●	▓		
VITERBO: *Porta Romana* Ⓛ Via della Bontà 12, 01100. 📞 0761-30 71 18. A simple trattoria where a wide range of classic dishes are immaculately prepared. In the winter, try pignataccia, a Viterbo speciality of mixed veal, beef and pork cooked in the oven with celery, carrots and potatoes. ● *Sun.*				

NAPLES AND CAMPANIA

	FIXED-PRICE MENU	GOOD WINE LIST	FORMAL DRESS	OUTDOOR TABLES
AGROPOLI: *'U Saracino* ⓁⓁⓁ Via Trentova, 84043. 📞 0974-82 40 63. Fresh seafood and fish dishes are the speciality here; prawns with grated artichokes, pasta and beans with seafood, and fish pancakes. ● *Tue.* 🗎				▓
AMALFI: *La Marinella* Ⓛ Via Lungomare dei Cavalieri di San Giovanni di Gerusalemme 1, 84011. 📞 089-87 10 43. A lively, friendly restaurant overlooking the the Amalfi coast. Much fish is served as well as the traditional local specialities. ● *Oct–Apr: Fri; Jan–Feb.* 🗎	●			

AMALFI: *Da Gemma* ⓁⓁ
Via Fra' Gerardo Sasso 10, 84011. 〖 089-87 13 45.
This welcoming restaurant has an essentially sea based menu. Try the "chocolate aubergine", a speciality of Salerno, for dessert. ● *Nov–Jan: Wed.* 🗐

BENEVENTO: *Pina e Gino* Ⓛ
Viale dell'Università, 82100. 〖 0824-438 38.
In the heart of the historic centre; try cardone (a type of thistle), sfoglia al forno (meat baked in a parcel) and orecchiette (pasta) with broccoli. ● *Sun.* 🗐 ♿

CAPRI: *La Savardina da Eduardo* Ⓛ
Via Lo Capo 8, 80073. 〖 081-837 63 00.
This is reputedly the best restaurant in Capri, with orange trees, sea views and tastily prepared regional specialities, such as home-made ravioli. 🗐

CAPRI: *Quisi del Grand Hotel Quisisana* ⓁⓁⓁⓁ
Via Camerelle 2, 80073. 〖 081-837 07 88.
The atmosphere is elegant and the food is delightful. Try the succulent roast duck with peaches and hot apple pie with calvados. ● *Nov–Mar.* 🗐

CASERTA: *La Brace* ⓁⓁⓁ
Piazza Madonna delle Grazie 9, Località Vaccheria 81020. 〖 0823-30 19 22.
An old-fashioned country inn in a village outside Caserta. Try bruschetta and risotto with porcini mushrooms. ● *Tue.* 🗐 ✄ ♿

ISCHIA: *La Tavernetta* Ⓛ
Via Sant'Angelo 77, Località Serrara Fontana 80070. 〖 081-99 92 51.
You can relax in this peaceful corner for breakfast, lunch, supper or a snack of pasta with Mediterranean sauces, salads, or fried fish. ● *Oct–Apr: Wed.*

ISCHIA: *Da Peppina di Renato* ⓁⓁ
Via Bocca 23, Località Forio 80070. 〖 081-99 83 12.
Basic, traditional fare served in this simple trattoria; pasta e fagioli, soups and bruschette and pizzas cooked in a wood oven. ● *Dec–Mar: Wed.*

FAICCHIO: *La Campagnola* Ⓛ
Via San Nicola, Località Massa 82100. 〖 0824-81 40 81.
Set in a village 38 km (23 miles) northwest of Benevento, serving simple, tasty cuisine. Try torciglioni alle melanzane (pasta with aubergines). ● *Wed.*

NAPLES: *Al Canterbury* ⓁⓁ
Via Ascensione a Chiaia 6, 80122. 〖 081-41 35 84.
Good food and a pleasant atmosphere. Try marinated salmon, aubergine parmigiana and mascarpone sprinkled with chocolate powder. ● *Sun.* 🗐

NAPLES: *California* ⓁⓁ
Via San Lucia 101, 80132. 〖 081-764 97 52.
Well-presented stalwarts are on offer such as spaghetti alla carbonara and bucatini amatriciana as well as American-style sandwiches. ● *Sun.* 🗐 ✄ ♿

NAPLES: *Il Pozzo Arcigola Slow Food* ⓁⓁ
Via F Magnoni 18b, 80132. 〖 081-66 83 33.
An attractive setting in a 17th-century building in the gardens of an old monastery. Food is traditional and makes use of local produce. ● *Sun.* 🗐

NAPLES: *La Chiacchierata* ⓁⓁ
Piazzetta Matilde Serao 37, 80100. 〖 081-41 14 65.
A traditional trattoria popular with the locals. Among Neapolitan specialities are orecchiette (ear-shaped pasta) with chick peas, and octopus. ● *Sun.* 🗐

NAPLES: *La Cantinella* ⓁⓁⓁⓁ
Via Cuma 42, 80132. 〖 081-764 86 84.
One of Naples' most famous restaurants, with an astounding reputation for its carefully and successfully prepared regional cuisine. ● *Sun.* 🗐 ✄

NERANO: *Taverna del Capitano* ⓁⓁ
Piazza delle Sirene 10, 80068. 〖 081-808 10 28.
A refined restaurant on the beach serving regional specialities with some creative touches; try grilled fish with mint sauce. ● *Oct–Apr: Mon; Jan.* 🗐 ✄

PAESTUM: *La Pergola* ⓁⓁ
Via Nazionale 1, Capaccio Scala 84040. 〖 0828-72 33 77.
Innovative regional cuisine that makes use of seasonal specialities in a rustic restaurant 3 km (2 miles) from the ruins of Paestum. ● *Mon.* 🗐

	FIXED-PRICE MENU	GOOD WINE LIST	FORMAL DRESS	OUTDOOR TABLES

Average prices for a three-course meal for one, including a half-bottle of house wine, tax and service:
Ⓛ up to L35,000
ⓁⓁ L35–55,000
ⓁⓁⓁ L55–75,000
ⓁⓁⓁⓁ L75–100,000
ⓁⓁⓁⓁⓁ over L100,000.

FIXED-PRICE MENU
A fixed-price menu on offer, usually with three courses.
GOOD WINE LIST
Denotes a wide range of good quality wines.
FORMAL DRESS
Some restaurants require men to wear a jacket and tie.
OUTDOOR TABLES
Tables for eating outdoors, often with a good view.
CREDIT CARDS
The symbol shows that major credit cards are accepted.

		FIXED-PRICE MENU	GOOD WINE LIST	FORMAL DRESS	OUTDOOR TABLES
POMPEII: *Il Principe* Piazza Bartolo Longo 8, 80045. 【 081-850 55 66. An airy, refined restaurant close to the excavations. Fish-based cuisine served such as fish-filled ravioli and turbot with vegetables. ● *Mon.* 🗲 ⚡ ♿	ⓁⓁⓁ	●	■		■
POSITANO: *Da Adolfo* Località Laurito, 84017. 【 089-87 50 22. A boat leaves Positano harbour every half hour for this charming, rustic trattoria serving spaghetti with clams or courgettes with grilled mozzarella.	Ⓛ				■
POSITANO: *La Sponda* Via C Colombo 30, 84017. 【 089-87 50 66. A sumptuous restaurant where guests are treated like family friends and offered a tempting range of modern (as well as traditional) dishes. 🗲	ⓁⓁⓁⓁⓁ	●	■		■
SALERNO: *Pizzeria Vicolo della Neve* Vicolo della Neve 24, 84100. 【 089-22 57 05. A pizzeria in the historic centre also serving a range of dishes such as pasta and fagioli, baccalà casserole and sausages with broccoli. ● *Wed.* 🗲	Ⓛ				
SALERNO: *Al Cenacolo* Piazza Alfano I 4, 84100. 【 089-23 88 18. Dedicated cuisine with a menu that changes daily to make good use of local ingredients. The pasta and bread are home-made. ● *Sun eve, Mon.* 🗲	ⓁⓁ				
SANT'AGATA SUI DUE GOLFI: *Don Alfonso 1890* Piazza Sant'Agata 11, 80064. 【 081-878 00 26. Set in elegant gardens, dishes include leg of lamb with Mediterranean herbs and a delicious rumbaba with zabaglione. ● *Oct–Jun: Mon, Tue.* 🗲 ⚡ ♿	ⓁⓁⓁⓁⓁ	●	■		
SICIGNANO DEGLI ALBURNI: *La Taverna* Via Nazionale, Frazione Scorzo 84029. 【 0828-97 80 50. An 18th-century country inn, near Salerno. The regional cuisine includes salamis, bean and chick pea soups and grilled meats. ● *Wed.* 🗲	Ⓛ				
SORRENTO: *Antico Frantoio* Via Cala 5, Località Casarlano 80067. 【 081-878 58 45. A great variety of dishes for all courses, made from local ingredients. Try the corn bread and the beer brewed at the next-door birreria. 🗲	ⓁⓁ				■

ABRUZZO, MOLISE AND PUGLIA

		FIXED-PRICE MENU	GOOD WINE LIST	FORMAL DRESS	OUTDOOR TABLES
ALBEROBELLO: *Il Poeta Contadino* Via Indipendenza 27, 70011. 【 080-72 19 17. An elegant restaurant where the excellent service matches the high standard of both food and wine. The cuisine makes imaginative use of fresh local ingredients, offering both fish and meat dishes. ● *Oct–Jun: Mon.* 🗲	ⓁⓁ	●	■		
ATRI: *Campana d'Oro* Piazza Duomo 23, 64032. 【 085-87 01 77. A traditional, welcoming trattoria with good, simple cuisine. Try the excellent cheeses and salami and the home-made pastas and desserts. ● *Wed.* 🗲	ⓁⓁ				
BARI: *Kilimangiaro* Lungomare Starita 64, 70122. 【 080-534 76 10. A homely trattoria and pizzeria on the seafront. Specialities include orecchiette (ear-shaped pasta) with rucola (rocket) and meat kebabs. ● *Wed.* 🗲 ♿	ⓁⓁ				■
BARI: *Murat* Via Lombardi 13, 70122. 【 080-521 65 51. An elegant restaurant on the top floor of the Palace Hotel with views over the historic centre of Bari. The cuisine is mainly Pugliese and Mediterranean with orecchiette (ear-shaped pasta) and seafood. ● *Sun.* 🗲 ⚡	ⓁⓁ	●	■		■

ISOLE TREMITI: *Al Gabbiano* ⓁⓁ
San Domino, 71040. 📞 0882-66 34 10.
The food here is based on the best fish from the sea. Try fresh fish roasted in a case of salt and the fish soup from Le Marche. 🍽

L'AQUILA: *Ernesto* ⓁⓁ
Piazza Palazzo 22, 67100. 📞 0862-210 94.
A peaceful, sophisticated place to eat. The menu is a tasty, creative mix of different inspirations and there is a wine bar attached. ● *Sun, Mon.* 🍽 ♿

LECCE: *Taverna di Carlo V* ⓁⓁ
Via G Palmieri 46, 73100. 📞 0832-24 88 18.
The appearance is of a 16th-century inn. Inside it is homely, simple and offers very well-prepared traditional specialities. ● *Sun eve, Mon.* 🍽 ♿

LECCE: *Barbablu* ⓁⓁⓁ
Via Umberto 7, 73100. 📞 0832-24 11 83.
An old palazzo in the historic centre is the perfect setting for imaginative and delicious dishes that use only fresh local ingredients. ● *Mon.* 🍽

LOCOROTONDO: *Centro Storico* ⓁⓁ
Via Eroi di Dogali 6, 70010. 📞 080-931 54 73.
Hidden among the winding streets of the historic centre, this little trattoria offers some excellent Pugliese cuisine often with creative touches. 🍽

OTRANTO: *Vecchia Otranto* ⓁⓁⓁ
Corso Garibaldi 96, 73028. 📞 0836-80 15 75.
Good marine and other regional specialities in this traditional trattoria include pasta with sea urchin and pepper sauce. ● *Oct–Jan: Mon.* 🍽 ♿

OVINDOLI: *Il Pozzo* Ⓛ
Via dell'Alpino, 67046. 📞 0863-71 01 91.
Wonderful mountain setting for this atmospheric restaurant in the historic centre of town. Local specialities are served. ● *Oct–Apr: Wed.* 🍽

PORTO CESAREO: *L'Angolo di Beppe* ⓁⓁⓁ
Via Zanella 24, 73050. 📞 0833-56 53 05.
A cosy atmosphere and elegant decor with a large open fire in winter. The cuisine mixes local and international traditions. ● *Sep–Jun: Mon.* 🍽 ♿

ROCCA DI MEZZO: *La Fiorita* Ⓛ
Piazza Principe di Piemonte 3, 67048. 📞 0862-91 74 67.
Efficient, friendly service in this family-run trattoria where the food is based on local products from the Abruzzi mountains. ● *Oct–Jun: Tue.* 🍽 ♿

SULMONA: *Rigoletto* ⓁⓁ
Via Stazione Introacqua 46, 67039. 📞 0864-555 29.
A short walk from the centre of town, reliable home-made pastas are served with beans, ravioli of scamorza (cheese), rabbit and truffles. ● *Tue.* 🍽 ♿

TARANTO: *Al Faro* ⓁⓁ
Via Galeso 126, 74100. 📞 099-471 44 44.
The menu is exclusively marine, using locally caught fish and seafood for antipasti, risotti and grills. Ignore the unattractive exterior. ● *Sun.* 🍽 ♿

TARANTO: *Le Vecchie Cantine* ⓁⓁⓁ
Via Girasoli 23, Frazione Lama 74020. 📞 099-777 25 89.
Set in restored storerooms just outside Taranto. A tasty fish and seafood menu, such as carpaccio of swordfish and fusilli with sardines. ● *Wed.* 🍽

TRANI: *Torrente Antico* ⓁⓁⓁⓁ
Via Fusco, 70059. 📞 0883-479 11.
Exquisite, lightly prepared dishes based on traditional regional cuisine with modern touches. The wine list is also extensive. ● *Sun eve, Mon.* 🍽

VIESTE: *Il Trabucco dell'Hotel Pizzomunno* ⓁⓁⓁⓁ
Spiaggia di Pizzomunno, 71019. 📞 0884-70 73 21.
Surrounded by gardens and very close to the sea. The cuisine has some creative touches and the dishes are light and tasty. ● *Nov–Mar.* 🍽 ⚡

VILLETTA BARREA: *Trattoria del Pescatore* Ⓛ
Via Virgilio 175, 67030. 📞 0864-891 52.
A simple, family-run trattoria in the Abruzzo National Park. Regional dishes include trout and home-made chitarrini (pasta cut like guitar strings). 🍽 ⚡

Average prices for a three-course meal for one, including a half-bottle of house wine, tax and service:
Ⓛ up to L35,000
ⓁⓁ L35–55,000
ⓁⓁⓁ L55–75,000
ⓁⓁⓁⓁ L75–100,000
ⓁⓁⓁⓁⓁ over L100,000.

FIXED-PRICE MENU
A fixed-price menu on offer, usually with three courses.
GOOD WINE LIST
Denotes a wide range of good quality wines.
FORMAL DRESS
Some restaurants require men to wear a jacket and tie.
OUTDOOR TABLES
Tables for eating outdoors, often with a good view.
CREDIT CARDS
The symbol shows that major credit cards are accepted.

BASILICATA AND CALABRIA

	Price	FIXED-PRICE MENU	GOOD WINE LIST	FORMAL DRESS	OUTDOOR TABLES
BIVONGI: *Vecchia Miniera* Contrada Perrocalli, 89040. ☎ 0964-73 18 69. Unusual cuisine such as pasta with sugo di capra (goat sauce), a favourite ancient Roman dish, in this village just outside Stilo. ● *Jul–Aug.* ⛱	Ⓛ				■
MARATEA: *Taverna Rovita* Via Rovita 13, 85046. ☎ 0973-87 65 88. An elegant country restaurant with white walls and tiled floors serving regional cuisine. Try the risotto of asparagus and venison. ● *Oct–Apr: Tue.* ▣ ⛱	ⓁⓁ		■		■
MATERA: *Al Casino del Diavolo* Via La Martella, 75100. ☎ 0835-26 19 86. Excellent Matera fare at this elegant, traditional restaurant just outside the town. Try orecchiette (ear-shaped pasta) with rape (sharp tasting greens). ● *Mon.*	ⓁⓁ				■
MATERA: *Il Terrazzino* Vicolo San Giuseppe 7, 75100. ☎ 0835-33 25 03. In the Sassi district *(see p502)*, the restaurant has a panoramic terrace. Try soups of grains and chick peas, or grilled lamb involtini (lamb parcels). ● *Tue.* ▣	ⓁⓁ				■
MATERA: *Venusio* Via Lussemborgo 2, Borgo Venusio 75100. ☎ 0835-25 90 81. An elegant restaurant 6 km (4 miles) south of Matera. Specialities include fish baked in a bread case, truffles and hot antipasti. ● *Mon.* ▣ ⛱ ♿	ⓁⓁⓁ		■		■
MELFI: *Vaddone* Corso da Sant'Abruzzese, 85025. ☎ 0972-243 23. A well-known trattoria serving delicious soups of pulses, and grilled meats. Prices perhaps a little high for such simple fare. ● *Sun eve, Mon.*	ⓁⓁ				■
POTENZA: *Fuori le Mura* Via IV Novembre, 85100. ☎ 0971-254 09. A big trattoria and pizzeria offering regional specialities. One of Potenza's oldest restaurants, it is now run by a cooperative of former employees. ● *Mon.* ▣	Ⓛ				
REGGIO DI CALABRIA: *Villeggianti* Via Eremo-Condera 31, 89125. ☎ 0965-250 21. A Reggio Calabrian institution where good simple fare is well prepared and served alla famiglia. Try spaghetti with broccoli or rich, spicy sausages. ● *Mon.*	Ⓛ				■
ROSSANO: *Arca* Corso da Cultura Centrale ENEL, 87068. ☎ 0983-56 53 79. Very good use is made of the simplest and freshest of local ingredients to create delicious typical dishes with a few new ideas. ▣ ♿	Ⓛ				■
SCILLA: *La Grotta Azzurra* Via Marina, 89058. ☎ 0965-75 48 89. A wonderful setting on the beach where, according to legend, Ulysses came ashore. This basic trattoria serves mainly fish. ● *Oct–Apr: Mon.* ▣ ♿	ⓁⓁ				■
TROPEA: *Pimm's* Largo Migliarese 2, 88038. ☎ 0963-66 61 05. A beautiful setting in the historic centre. Simple, local fare, well prepared and pleasantly served. Start with seafood crostini or smoked swordfish then try pasta with sea urchins and stuffed, grilled squid. ● *Oct–Apr: Mon.* ▣	ⓁⓁ				
VENOSA: *Taverna Ducale* Piazza Municipio 2, 85029. ☎ 0972-355 35. The 15th-century building sets the scene for a cuisine based on rediscovered ancient dishes such as preferito di Orazio (the favourite of the Latin poet) and triticum (a mixture of pulses and vegetables). ● *Fri.* ▣ ⛱ ♿	ⓁⓁ	■			

SICILY

AGRIGENTO: *Kalos* ⓁⓁ
Piazza San Calogero, 92100. 【 0922-263 89.
A bright restaurant with original and well-prepared cuisine. Try pasta with pistachio and gorgonzola, grilled fish and cassata of ricotta. ● *Sun.* 🗗

AGRIGENTO: *Le Caprice* ⓁⓁ
Via Panoramica dei Templi, 92100. 【 0922-264 69.
A good restaurant in an exquisite setting in the Valley of the Temples. Regional cuisine is carefully prepared; the antipasti buffet is a speciality. 🗗 ♿

AGRIGENTO: *Trattoria del Pescatore* ⓁⓁⓁ
Via Lungomare 20, Località Lido di San Leone 92100. 【 0922-41 43 42.
The chef chooses the fish daily and uses it, sometimes raw, in simple but delicious dishes with oil and lemon juice. The pasta speciality is spaghetti with swordfish, aubergine and basil. ● *Nov–Apr: Wed.* 🗗 ♿

BAGHERIA: *Don Ciccio de Figlio* Ⓛ
Via del Cavaliere 78, 90011. 【 091-93 24 42.
This town-centre trattoria concentrates on regional specialities. Look out for maccheroncino with sardines, broccoli, tuna and other sauces. ● *Sun, Wed.* ▤

CATANIA: *I Vicere* ⓁⓁ
Via Litteri 59, 95129. 【 095-711 66 06.
Outside dining on a terrace with spectacular views. Good food, particularly the succulent pork fillet in mandarin sauce. ● *Oct–Apr: lunch; Mon.* 🗗 🗲 ♿

CEFALÙ: *L'Antica Corte* ⓁⓁ
Cortile Pepe 7, 90015. 【 0921-232 28.
A trattoria in an old courtyard in the historic centre, the cuisine is local with influences from almost-forgotten old Sicilian recipes. ● *Thu.* 🗗

ENNA: *Ariston* ⓁⓁ
Via Roma 353, 94100. 【 0935-260 38.
In the heart of Enna, with a selection of fish dishes as well as meat specialities, such as stuffed lamb, or bean and pea soup and frittata (omelette). ● *Sun.* 🗗

ERICE: *Cortile di Venere* ⓁⓁ
Via Sales 38, 91016. 【 0923-86 93 62.
A delightful restaurant in an attractive 17th-century building with good views. The menu is basically Sicilian and Mediterranean. ● *Oct–Apr: Wed.* 🗗

ERICE: *Monte San Giuliano* ⓁⓁ
Via San Rocco 7, 91016. 【 0923-86 95 95.
Located in the centre of town, the menu is based on Sicilian traditions and includes fresh pasta with sardines, and couscous with fish. ● *Mon.* 🗗

ISOLE EOLIE: *Filippino* ⓁⓁ
Piazza del Municipio, Lipari 98055. 【 090-981 10 02.
An essentially Sicilian, sea-based menu includes swordfish, home-made maccheroni and some excellent cassata Siciliana. ● *Nov–Apr: Mon.* 🗗 🗲 ♿

MARSALA: *Delfino* Ⓛ
Via Lungomare Mediterraneo 672, 91025. 【 0923-99 81 88.
Three lovely rooms all with views over either the sea or the garden. Try the sunflower spaghetti or pasta with eel sauce. ● *Nov–Apr: Tue.* 🗗 🗲 ♿

MARSALA: *Mothia* Ⓛ
Contrada Ettore Inversa 13, 91016. 【 0923-74 52 55.
Simple, delicious cooking with home-made bread, pasta, rich desserts and cakes. The lobster soup is particularly recommended. ● *Nov–Apr: Wed.* 🗗 ♿

PALERMO: *Simpaty* ⓁⓁ
Via Piano Gallo 18, Località Mondello 90151. 【 091-45 44 70.
The dining room has good views over the popular bay of Mondello and the menu is almost exclusively fish. Try ricci (little sea urchins) – served as antipasto or as a pasta sauce - octopus and squid. ● *Thu.* 🗗 ♿

PALERMO: *Temptation* ⓁⓁ
Via Torretta 94, Località Sferracavallo 90148. 【 091-691 11 04.
Sferracavallo is a lively part of Palermo. This trattoria offers an all-inclusive menu of beautifully prepared seafood antipasti, home-made pastas and secondi using ingredients caught that day or the night before. ● *Thu.*

For key to symbols see back flap

	FIXED-PRICE MENU	GOOD WINE LIST	FORMAL DRESS	OUTDOOR TABLES

Average prices for a three-course meal for one, including a half-bottle of house wine, tax and service:
Ⓛ up to L35,000
ⓁⓁ L35–55,000
ⓁⓁⓁ L55–75,000
ⓁⓁⓁⓁ L75–100,000
ⓁⓁⓁⓁⓁ over L100,000.

FIXED-PRICE MENU
A fixed-price menu on offer, usually with three courses.
GOOD WINE LIST
Denotes a wide range of good quality wines.
FORMAL DRESS
Some restaurants require men to wear a jacket and tie.
OUTDOOR TABLES
Tables for eating outdoors, often with a good view.
CREDIT CARDS
The symbol shows that major credit cards are accepted.

PALERMO: *La Scuderia* ⓁⓁ
Viale del Fante 9, 90146. 【 091-52 03 23.
Set in the Parco della Favorita, this elegant restaurant sticks to traditional Sicilian cuisine that is carefully and deliciously prepared. ● *Sun.* ▤ ▤

RAGUSA: *La Ciotola* ⓁⓁ
Via Archimede 23, 9710. 【 0932-22 89 44.
An elegant, modern restaurant in the city centre serving well-prepared specialities such as maccheroncini with aubergines, and much fish. ● *Mon.* ▤

SCIACCA: *Hostaria del Vicolo* ⓁⓁ
Vicolo Sammaritano 10, 92019. 【 0925-230 71.
A quiet restaurant in the historic centre. The menu is essentially Sicilian with dishes such as tagliatelle with prawns, aubergine and bottarga (tuna eggs), sole cooked in the Sciacca way and tasty desserts. ● *Sun, Mon eve.* ▤

SELINUNTE: *Lido Azzurro* ⓁⓁ
Via Marco Polo 51, Località Marinella 91020. 【 0924-462 11.
A bustling trattoria with views of the top of the acropolis from the terrace. There's a wide range of buffet-style antipasti, as well as fettuccine with tuna eggs among the primi and grilled fish for secondi. ● *Nov–Apr: Mon.*

SIRACUSA: *Minerva* Ⓛ
Piazza Duomo 20, 96100. 【 0931-694 04.
A pizzeria right in the historic centre, with a wide and imaginative range of pizzas on offer. Tables are outside in the cathedral square. ● *Mon.* ▤

SIRACUSA: *La Foglia* ⓁⓁ
Via Capodieci 29, 96100. 【 0931-662 33.
Vegetables and pulses are the mainstay of the menu at this restaurant in the historic centre. Try fresh pasta with vegetables or fish and the soups. ▤ ▤

SIRACUSA: *Jonico 'a Rutta 'e Ciauli* ⓁⓁ
Riviera Dionisio il Grande 194, 96100. 【 0931-655 40.
The menu is Sicilian with several innovative interpretations of traditional favourites. The attractive, bright dining room has walls which are covered with Sicilian ceramics and some old, agricultural artefacts. ● *Tue.* ▤ ▤

TAORMINA: *Pizzeria Vecchia Taormina* Ⓛ
Vicolo Ebrei 3, 98039.
A traditional pizzeria in the old Jewish quarter of Taormina. There's a massive range of Sicilian-style pizzas and delicious antipasti. ● *Wed.* ▤

TAORMINA: *Al Duomo* ⓁⓁ
Vicolo Ebrei 11, 98039. 【 0942-62 56 56.
A traditional Sicilian restaurant in the historic centre. Dishes include pasta with breadcrumbs, fish, lamb and delicious involtini (parcels) of swordfish. ▤

TAORMINA: *La Giara* ⓁⓁⓁ
Vicolo La Floresta 1, 98039. 【 0942-233 60.
A pretty restaurant with beautiful views over the bay of Taormina. Try ravioli with aubergine and wild fennel involtini (parcels). ● *Nov–Mar: Mon.* ▤

TRAPANI: *Da Peppe* ⓁⓁ
Via Spalti 50, 91100. 【 0923-282 46.
Trapani specialities served as well as house dishes established over the years. The mainstay is fish, including locally caught tuna. ● *Nov–Mar: Sat.* ▤

TRAPANI: *P&G* ⓁⓁ
Via Spalti 1, 91100. 【 0923-54 77 01.
This restaurant has become an institution in Trapani where Mediterranean food, including couscous, is served at its best. During the annual tuna mattanza, fresh tuna is served in a huge variety of ways. ● *Sun.* ▤ ▤

SARDINIA

ALGHERO: *Al Tuguri* ⒧⒧
Via Maiorca 113, 07041. █ 079-97 67 72.
A pretty restaurant in a 15th-century building in the historic centre with an interesting menu of well-prepared Mediterranean specialities. ● *Sun.* 🄴 ⚡

ALGHERO: *La Lepanto* ⒧⒧⒧⒧
Via Carlo Alberto 135, 07041. █ 079-97 91 16.
Regional dishes, such as bottarga (tuna roe) and lobster and other creative dishes: warm octopus, and scampi with pecorino. ● *Nov–Apr: Mon.* 🄴 ♿

BOSA: *Mannu* ⒧⒧⒧
Viale Alghero, 08013. █ 0785-37 53 06.
A smart, modern restaurant offering extremely good local fish specialities; Bosa is famous for fresh lobster, which is served here in a celery sauce. 🄴

CAGLIARI: *Nuovo Saint Pierre* ⒧⒧
Via Coghinas 13, 09122. █ 070-27 15 78.
Traditional dishes include wild boar with lentils, wild asparagus risotto, lamb with artichokes and stuffed beef. Fish is served in summer. ● *Sun.* 🄴

CAGLIARI: *Dal Corsaro* ⒧⒧⒧⒧
Viale Regina Margherita 28, 09124. █ 070-66 43 18.
Good service and a pleasant atmosphere in which to enjoy carefully prepared regional dishes (onion ravioli), original creations (tagliatelle with courgettes and clams) and some rediscovered Cagliari classics. ● *Sun.* 🄴

CALASETTE: *Da Pasqualino* ⒧⒧
Via Roma 99, 09011. █ 0781-884 73.
Delicious local fish-based specialities are served in this simple and relaxed trattoria, including bottarga (tuna roe) and lobster. ● *Oct–May: Tue.* 🄴 ▤

NUORO: *Canne al Vento* ⒧⒧
Viale Repubblica 66, 08100. █ 0784-20 17 62.
Dishes on offer at this regional restaurant include roast meats, excellent cheeses, octopus salad and a hot sebalda (honey dessert). ● *Sun.* 🄴

OLBIA: *Bacchus* ⒧⒧
Via Gabriele D'Annunzio 2nd floor, 07026. █ 0789-216 12.
An elegant restaurant with views of the sea. Creative cooking with regional undertones includes fish, lamb with artichokes, and crab. ● *Sun.* 🄴 ⚡ ♿

OLIENA: *CK* ⒧⒧
Via ML King 24, 08025. █ 0784-28 80 24.
Typical local specialities in this family-run restaurant include game and herbs and maharrones hurriaos (fresh cheese gnocchi). ● *Mon.* 🄴 ▤ ♿

ORISTANO: *Faro* ⒧⒧⒧
Via Bellini 25, 09170. █ 0783-700 02.
One of Sardinia's best restaurants, serving regional dishes based on what is fresh in the market that day, particularly fish and seafood. ● *Sun.* 🄴 ▤ ♿

PORTO CERVO: *Gianni Pedrinelli* ⒧⒧⒧⒧
Bivio Pevero, 07020. █ 0789-924 36.
The menu is regional serving much fish. Try the house speciality, a typically Sardinian dish, Porcettu allo Spiedo (pork on the spit). ● *Nov–Feb.* 🄴

PORTO ROTONDO: *Da Giovannino* ⒧⒧⒧⒧
Piazza Quadra, 07026. █ 0789-352 80.
Popular with Italian politicos and media types, who dine on expensive but exquisitely prepared (and attentively served) Mediterranean specialities, which are accompanied by superbly chosen wines. ● *Nov–Apr: Mon.* 🄴 ⚡

PORTOSCUSO: *La Ghinghetta* ⒧⒧⒧⒧
Via Cavour 26, 09010. █ 0781-50 81 43.
Set in a charming fishing village, the almost exclusively fish-based menu adds a different twist to local specialities. ● *Sun; Oct–Apr.* 🄴 ▤ ⚡

SASSARI: *Florian* ⒧⒧
Via Bellieni 27, 07100. █ 079-23 62 51.
The menu here offers the very best of sea and land regional specialities according to the season: there are mushrooms in autumn, seafood in summer and appropriate vegetables all year round. ● *Sun.* 🄴 ♿

PRACTICAL INFORMATION

ASK ANY ITALIAN and they will almost certainly tell you that Italy is the most beautiful country in the world. They may not be far wrong. However, the charm and allure of Italy may help to veil some of her numerous practical problems. Getting information is rarely straightforward; public

ENTE NAZIONALE
ITALIANO PER IL TURISMO
Tourist board logo

offices and banks are nearly always crippled by long queues and bureaucracy, and the postal service is renowned for its inefficiency. This section, together with some forward planning and a little patience, should help you cope with some of Italy's idiosyncrasies.

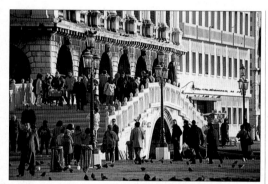

Tourists crossing the Ponte della Paglia in Venice *(see p105)*

VISAS AND PERMESSO DI SOGGIORNO

EUROPEAN UNION nationals and citizens of the US, Canada, Australia and New Zealand do not need visas for stays of up to three months. All visitors are required to present a full passport on entry and, officially, need to declare their presence to the Italian police within eight days of arrival. If you are staying in a hotel or campsite, this will be done for you, otherwise contact the local *Questura* (police station).

Anyone wishing to stay in Italy for more than three months (eight days for non-EU citizens) will have to wade through complicated Italian bureaucracy to obtain a *permesso di soggiorno* (permit to stay). You can apply for a permit at any main police station, *Questura di Provincia*. Depending on your motive for staying, you must apply for either a permit to work *(lavoro)* or a permit to study *(studio)*. For each permit you will need to submit a written application *(domanda)*, passport-style photographs

and photocopies of your passport. If you are looking for work, these items need to be accompanied by proof of your future employment in Italy or some other means of financial support.

If you are applying for a study permit, it is necessary to obtain a letter from the relevant school or university giving details of your course. This then has to be sent to the Italian consulate in your country of origin to obtain an official covering letter, or declaration. You will also need some form of guarantee that your medical bills will be paid should you become ill or have an accident. A comprehensive insurance policy *(see p616)* would be sufficient.

WHEN TO VISIT

ITALY'S TOWNS and historic sites are extremely popular attractions and it is worth considering this when planning your trip. Rome, Florence and Venice are all crowded from spring to October and it is advisable to book a hotel well in advance. In August the cities are generally slightly

less busy, abandoned by their inhabitants in the summer heat. At Easter, Rome is overrun by pilgrims and tourists, and in February, Venice triples its population during Carnevale *(see p65)*. Seaside resorts fill up over the months of July and August, whereas June and September can be equally hot and far less crowded. The seas and beaches are notably cleaner at the beginning of summer. December to March is the time of year for skiing, although the first snow often falls as early as November. Most sights are open all year, except on some public holidays *(see p65)* and often two Mondays each month *(see p614)*.

Rome's renowned Tazza d'Oro café, an ideal rest stop after sightseeing

SEASONAL DIFFERENCES

THE NORTHERN PART of Italy is generally more temperate than the south, which has a Mediterranean climate. June to September is hot and in peak summer, also humid. Summer storms can be quite dramatic, but often only last a few hours. Spring and autumn are ideal for visiting cities; temperatures are mild. Winter can be bitterly cold, especially in the north. *The Climate of Italy* on pages 68–9 takes a detailed look at the country's regional weather.

◁ **The beautiful Piazza del Campo in Siena, meeting place for visitors and locals**

**Unacceptable dress in church:
both sexes are required to
cover torsos and upper arms**

ETIQUETTE AND TIPPING

PEOPLE IN ITALY ARE, on the whole, friendly towards foreign visitors. On entering a shop or bar it is customary to greet people with a general *buon giorno* (good morning) or *buona sera* (good evening), and the same applies when leaving. They will also try to be helpful when asked directions in the street. If your Italian is slight, *scusi* followed by the name of the place you wish to go to will often suffice. *Grazie* (thank you) is always replied to with *prego* (not at all).

Tipping in restaurants is expected when the 15 per cent service is not included. However, as much as 15 per cent would be considered generous and a tip is often not expected at all in family-run restaurants. Taxi drivers and hotel porters expect a few thousand lire if they have been helpful. You could simply round the bill up to the nearest L5,000.

Italians are very dress conscious and unusual or risqué clothes do get noticed. Strict dress codes are enforced in many places of worship, where your torso and upper arms must be covered; shorts and skirts must reach below the knee.

DUTY-FREE GOODS AND CUSTOMS INFORMATION

RESIDENTS OF THE EU can bring duty-free goods into Italy for their own use: 800 cigarettes, 200 cigars, 400 cigarillos, 1 kg of smoking tobacco, 10 litres of spirits, 90 litres of wine and 110 litres of beer. Duty-free limits for non-EU citizens are much stricter: 400 cigarettes, 100 cigars, 200 cigarillos or 500 grams of smoking tobacco, 1 litre of spirits or 2 litres of wine and 50 grams of perfume. To find out what you can take back from Italy to a non-EU country, contact that particular country's customs department.

TAX EXEMPTION

VALUE ADDED TAX (known as IVA in Italy) ranges from 12–35 per cent, depending on the item. Non-European Union citizens can obtain an IVA refund for each purchase over L650,000, but be prepared for a long process. It is easier to get a refund if you shop where you see the "Euro Free Tax" sign. After showing your passport to the shop assistant and completing a form, the IVA will be deducted from your bill. The alternative is to present a customs officer with your purchases on your departure from Italy along with the relevant receipts. He or she will stamp the receipts which you then send back to the vendor. A refund will eventually be posted to you.

**The clock of San Giacomo di
Rialto in Venice (see p93)**

ITALIAN TIME

ITALY IS ONE HOUR ahead of Greenwich Mean Time (GMT). The clocks are put forward one hour in March and back in September. For example: London is one hour behind Italy; Sydney is ten hours ahead; while Ottawa is six hours behind.

ELECTRICAL ADAPTORS

THE VOLTAGE IN ITALY is 220 volts, with two-pin round-pronged plugs. For European appliances, the plug can simply be changed over, whereas US equipment will need an adaptor. Italian plugs come in many different sizes, without any apparent special purpose, and you can buy adaptors or even just swap plugs. It is worth buying travel plugs before you leave as they are difficult to find in Italy. Most hotels with three or more stars have hairdriers and shaving points in all bedrooms, but check the voltage first, to be safe.

Standard Italian plug

BOOKING TICKETS

THEATRES IN ITALY do not generally take bookings over the telephone – you have to visit the box office in person. However, there are agencies, such as **Box Office** and **Cangrande**, that will book tickets for you (for a fee). Opera tickets are sold months in advance, with just a few held back until two days before the performance. Tickets for rock and jazz concerts are also sold at some record shops whose names appear on the publicity posters.

TOURIST INFORMATION

THE NATIONAL tourist board, ENIT, has branches in capital cities worldwide and offers general information on Italy. For more specific requests, contact the local tourist offices. The addresses and telephone numbers are listed under each town or city, directly under the title, and they are plotted on the town and city maps. An EPT *(Ente Provinciale di Turismo)* has information on its town and surrounding province, whereas an APT *(Azienda di Promozione Turistica)* deals exclusively with individual towns. Both offices help with practical information such as hotel bookings and tours. They also provide free maps and guidebooks in various languages. The EPT and APT can refer you to local tour guides and advise on trips and excursions. Small towns will have a *Pro Loco*, a tourist office run by the local administration, which is sometimes open only during the tourist season. It is usually located in the town hall *(comune)*, or occasionally in someone's private residence.

TOURS

MANY TOUR COMPANIES organize coach trips, with English-speaking guides, that include all the main tourist attractions in Italy. American Express offices in Rome,

A guided group tour through the streets of Florence

A student relaxing in the sun in Gaiole in Chianti

Florence, Venice and Milan organize local trips and **CIT** offers coach tours that go all over the country. If you are looking for something a little more personal and off the beaten track, check the local pages of national newspapers for tour groups or organizations. Local tourist boards will also be able to advise you. Always employ official guides and be sure to establish the fee in advance. For information on various specialist holidays, turn to pages 624–5.

Sign for tourist information

SIGHTSEEING PERMITS

TO VISIT CERTAIN SITES in Rome, such as the Vatican library, you need a written permit, which can be obtained from:

Comune di Roma Ripartizione X
Piazza Campitelli 7, Rome. **Map** 3 A5.
[C] 06-67 10 30 64.
[FAX] 06-67 10 31 18.

SIGHTSEEING OPENING HOURS

ITALIAN MUSEUMS are gradually conforming to new regulations, particularly in the north, opening from 9am–7pm daily, except for two Mondays each month. In winter, however, many of them revert to 9am–2pm Tuesday to Saturday, and 9am–12:30pm on Sunday. Privately run and smaller museums have their own times, so it is advisable to phone in advance. Archaeological sites are generally open from 9am until one hour before

sunset, Tuesday to Sunday. Churches are usually open from around 7am–12:30pm and 4–7pm. However, they often prefer not to let tourists in during services, so Sunday is not the best day to visit.

Daytime sightseeing on a tranquil canal in Venice

ADMISSION CHARGES

SIGHTSEEING FEES generally range from about L2,000 to L12,000 (but churches are usually free). Reductions for students are not always offered but many state-run museums and archaeological sites allow free entry for EU residents under 18 and over 60 years of age. Large groups are often entitled to a discount as well. If reductions are available, you will need to show a valid piece of identification, such as a student card or passport.

STUDENT INFORMATION

THE NATIONAL STUDENT travel organization, **CTS** (Centro Turistico Studentesco), has branches throughout Italy and the rest of Europe. They issue the International Student Identity Card (ISIC) and the Youth International Educational Exchange Card (YIEE). Both can be used, in conjunction with a passport, for discounts at museums and other tourist attractions. The ISIC card also gives access to a 24-hour

telephone helpline that provides general advice and information. As well as issuing youth cards, CTS offers cut-price car hire and will organize holidays and courses. For details

ISIC card

about youth hostels, contact the **Associazione Italiana Alberghi per la Gioventù** (the Italian YHA), as long as you are a current member.

TRAVELLING WITH CHILDREN

ON THE WHOLE, Italians love children, to an extent that sometimes seems over-indulgent. Most trattorias and pizzerias welcome them and there are no rules excluding children from bars. Hotels also welcome children, but smaller establishments usually have limited facilities. Some of the more up-market hotels may offer a babysitting service. It is a common sight to see children playing outside fairly late at night, especially in summer. Most towns have playgrounds and many have summer funfairs. For young swimmers, the calm Mediterranean is ideal.

Fascinated child feeding pigeons at Piazza Navona, Rome

DISABLED TRAVELLERS

PUBLIC AWARENESS of the needs of the disabled is low, but improving. Some towns now have buses for the disabled and ramps and lifts are slowly being added to museums and some churches. **Associazione Nazionale Andicappati** (with offices all over Italy) provides information on hotels, services and general assistance.

A mechanically operated wheelchair ramp across a bridge

RELIGIOUS SERVICES

ALMOST 85 PER CENT of the population is Catholic. Sunday mass is celebrated throughout the country, while in the principal churches services are also held during the week. In major cities some churches, such as the church of San Silvestro (Piazza San Silvestro) in Rome, offer services and confession in English. For some visitors, a trip to Rome will include an audience with the pope (*p409*).

Although Italy is predominantly Catholic, all the main religious beliefs are represented. For details contact the main centres in Rome.

CONVERSION CHART

Imperial to Metric
1 inch = 2.54 centimetres
1 foot = 30 centimetres
1 mile = 1.6 kilometres
1 ounce = 28 grams
1 pound = 454 grams
1 pint = 0.57 litre
1 gallon = 4.6 litres

Metric to Imperial
1 centimetre = 0.4 inch
1 metre = 3 feet 3 inches
1 kilometre = 0.6 mile
1 gram = 0.04 ounce
1 kilogram = 2.2 pounds
1 litre = 1.8 pints

DIRECTORY

TRAVEL ASSOCIATIONS

Associazione Italiana Alberghi per la Gioventù
Via Cavour 44 (3rd floor), Rome.
Map 3 C5. *06-487 11 52.*

Associazione Nazionale Andicappati
Via Tommaso Fortifiocca 100,
Rome. *06-781 07 72.*

CIT
Piazza della Repubblica 64, Rome.
Map 4 D3.
06-72 28 93 50.

CTS
Presidenza Nazionale
Via Nazionale 66, Rome.
Map 4 D3. *06-467 91.*

TOURIST OFFICES

ENIT UK
1 Princes Street, London
W1R 8AY. *0171-408 1254.*

ENIT Rome
Via Marghera 2. **Map** 4 F3.
06-497 11.

APT Florence
Via Cavour 1r. **Map** 2 D4.
055-29 08 32.

APT Siena
Piazza del Campo 56.
0577-28 05 51.

APT Venice
Castello 4421. **Map** 3 B5.
041-522 63 56.

RELIGIOUS ORGANIZATIONS

Catholic
Ufficio Informazioni Vaticano,
Piazza San Pietro, Vaticano,
Rome. **Map** 1 B3.
050-68 56 54.

Jewish
Unione delle Comunità Ebraiche
Italiane,
Lungotevere Sanzio 9, Rome.
Map 6 D1.
06-580 36 70.

Mosque
Centro Islamico Culturale d'Italia,
Viale della Moschea, Rome.
06-808 22 58.

Personal Security and Health

ALTHOUGH ITALY IS GENERALLY a safe place for visitors, it is wise to keep a watchful eye on your personal belongings, especially in the larger towns and cities. There is a conspicuous police presence throughout the country, and in the event of an emergency or crime, any of the police officers described in this section will be able to assist you and tell you where to go to report an incident. If you fall ill, pharmacies are a good first stop where medically trained staff can give advice or tell you where to find further help. In an emergency, the Casualty Department *(Pronto Soccorso)* of any hospital will treat you.

Commissariato di Polizia – a police station

Police car

Green Cross ambulance in Venice

Roman fire engine

PERSONAL PROPERTY

PETTY THEFT such as pickpocketing, bag snatching and car theft is rife. In the event of a theft you must report it within 24 hours to the nearest *questura* or *commissariato* (police station).

Avoid leaving anything visible in an unattended car, including a car radio. If you have to leave luggage in a car, find a hotel that has private parking. When making a purchase, always check your change and do not keep wallets in back pockets, especially on buses and in other crowded places. "Bum bags" and money belts are a favourite target for pickpockets, so try to keep them hidden. When walking, hold bags and cameras on the inside of the pavement so as not to tempt motorized snatchers and do not show expensive cameras and video equipment in areas off tourist routes. The safest way to carry large sums of money is to use travellers' cheques or Eurocheques. Try to keep your receipts and Eurocheque card separately, together with a photocopy of vital documents, in case of loss or theft. It is also advisable to get comprehensive travel insurance that covers theft of personal possessions in addition to covering cancellation/delay of flights, loss/damage of luggage, money and other valuables, as well as personal liability and accidents. If you do need to make an insurance claim for stolen or lost property, you must get a copy of the report *(denuncia)* from the police station when you report the incident. In case of lost passports, go to your embassy or consulate; for lost travellers' cheques, contact the issuing company's nearest office.

LEGAL ASSISTANCE

A COMPREHENSIVE insurance package should include cover for legal assistance and advice. If you do not have insurance cover, contact your embassy as soon as possible after an incident, such as an accident, occurs. The embassy can offer advice and should provide you with a list of English- and Italian-speaking lawyers who are knowledgeable about both the Italian and English legal systems.

PERSONAL SECURITY

ALTHOUGH PETTY CRIME in the cities is frequent, violent crime in Italy is rare. However, it is common for people to raise their voices aggressively during an argument. Usually, remaining calm and being polite will help to defuse the situation. Always be wary of unofficial tour guides, taxi drivers or strangers who wish to assist you or advise you on accommodation, restaurants or shops as they may expect money in return.

WOMEN TRAVELLERS

WOMEN TRAVELLING on their own in Italy are likely to meet with a lot of attention. Although this is often more of an irritation than a danger, it is best to keep away from lonely, unlit streets and areas

A team of *carabinieri* in traffic police uniform

near railway stations at night. Walking quickly and purposefully is a good way to avoid any unwanted attention. The staff at hotels and restaurants generally treat their single female guests and customers with extra care and attention.

THE POLICE

THERE ARE SEVERAL different police forces in Italy and each one fulfils a particular role. The state police, *la polizia*, wear blue uniforms and drive blue cars. They deal with most crimes. The *carabinieri* are militarily trained and wear dark blue and black uniforms with red striped trousers. These officers deal with a variety of offences from organized crime to speeding and can also conduct random security checks. The *guardia di finanza* are the financial police force (the fraud squad), and wear grey uniforms with yellow striped trousers. The *vigili urbani*, or the municipal traffic police, wear blue and white uniforms in winter and white during the summer. Even though they are not official police officers, the *vigili urbani* can issue heavy fines for traffic and parking offences. They can usually be spotted patrolling the streets, enforcing laws or directing traffic. Officers from any of the forces will be able to help.

Municipal policeman

INTERPRETERS

INDEPENDENT INTERPRETERS and translators often advertise their services in newspapers and foreign-language bookshops. You will find agencies listed in the Yellow Pages *(Pagine Gialle)* and the AITI *(Associazione Italiana di Traduttori e Interpreti)* has a list of qualified translators and interpreters. In an emergency, your embassy will be able to provide an interpreter.

Outside a Florentine pharmacy with a red cross sign

MEDICAL TREATMENT

EMERGENCY MEDICAL care in Italy is free for all EU citizens. The E111 form, which is available from main post offices throughout the UK, covers emergencies only; private medical insurance is needed for all other types of treatment. The E111 comes with a booklet that contains general health advice and information about how to claim free medical treatment when travelling abroad. In order for the form to be valid, it has to be completed in full and stamped at a post office in the UK before your journey. Non-EU citizens should try to arrive in Italy with comprehensive private medical insurance to cover all eventualities. If you do need emergency treatment, go to the *Pronto Soccorso* (Casualty Department) of the nearest hospital.

No inoculations are needed for Italy, but mosquito repellent is advisable in summer. Repelling creams and sprays can be found in pharmacies, and electrical devices can be bought which burn tablets.

EMERGENCY SUPPLIES

VARIOUS MEDICAL products, including homeopathic medicines, are available in any pharmacy *(farmacia)*, but a prescription is often required. Thanks to a night rota *(servizio notturno)*, there is always a pharmacy open in all cities and most towns.

DIRECTORY

EMBASSIES AND CONSULATES

Australia
Via Alessandria 215, Rome.
Map 4 E1.
[06-85 27 21.

Canada
Via G B De Rossi, Rome.
[06-841 53 41.

United Kingdom
Via XX Settembre 80a, Rome.
Map 4 D2.
[06-482 54 41.

EMERGENCY NUMBERS

General Emergency
[113.
Police (Carabinieri)
[112.
Fire Service
[115.
Medical Emergencies
[118.

Those that are open at night are listed in the local pages of daily newspapers and on all pharmacy doors.

Tabacchi (tobacco) shops are a good source of many useful supplies and are easily recognized by their "T" signs (see below). Apart from tobacco, cigarettes and matches, you can buy razors and batteries, bus and metro tickets, telephone cards and tokens *(gettoni)*. At some, you can also purchase postage stamps and get parcels weighed and costed.

A Tabacchi shop, with its characteristic white "T" sign

Banking and Local Currency

Eurocheque logo

VIRTUALLY ALL ITALIAN HOTELS, many shops, large restaurants and petrol stations now accept major credit cards and Eurocheques. Only in the more off-the-beaten-track locations will you have difficulties without Italian lire. When you pay with credit cards, you may be asked to show identification. Currency can be changed in the often crowded banks, but service is not always fast. All banks will cash travellers' cheques and cashpoint machines *(bancomat)* will accept Eurocheque cards with a pin number. Some machines also accept MasterCard (Access), Visa and American Express cards. Although banks often have the best exchange rates, bureaux de change and foreign exchange machines can be more convenient.

Electronic exchange machine

Cash dispenser which also accepts Visa and MasterCard (Access)

CHANGING MONEY

BANKING HOURS are somewhat restrictive and can also be slightly erratic so it is safest to acquire some local currency before you arrive in Italy. Exchange rates will vary from place to place.

Once you arrive, the most convenient way to change money is to use the electronic exchange machines, which are located at all major airports, train stations and banks. The machines have multilingual instructions and the exchange rate is clearly displayed on the screen. You simply feed in up to ten notes of the same foreign currency and you will receive lire in return.

Bureaux de change can be found in all main towns. Although they are easier to use, they tend to have higher exchange rates and charge more commission than banks.

EUROCHEQUES

EUROCHEQUE CARDS can be used in any cashpoint machine that displays the Eurocheque logo. They can also be used as direct payment for a wide variety of goods and services. Most upmarket shops, hotels and restaurants in the popular tourist areas will accept Eurocheques, but it would be worthwhile asking before trying to use them. Alternatively, you can cash the cheques at any bank that displays the Eurocheque logo. A Eurocheque card guarantees cheques up to L300,000.

REGIONAL DIFFERENCES IN COST OF LIVING

THE NORTH is generally more expensive than the south, but there are many exceptions. Restaurants and hotels off the beaten track are usually better value, and buying locally made produce is cost effective if you avoid obvious tourist traps.

Metal-detecting security doors found at most banks

BANKING HOURS

BANKS ARE USUALLY open between 8:30am and 1:30pm, Monday to Friday. Most also open for an hour in the afternoon, from about 1:30pm to 2:30pm or 2:30pm until 3:30pm, depending on the bank. All banks close at weekends and for public holidays, and they also close early the day before a major holiday. Bureaux de change are often open all day, and in some places, also late at night.

USING BANKS

FOR SECURITY PURPOSES, most banks have electronic double doors with metal detectors, allowing one person in at a time. Metal objects and bags should first be deposited in lockers situated in the foyer. Press the button to open the outer door, then wait for it to close behind you. The inner door then opens automatically. Do not be alarmed by the heavily armed guards that patrol most banks in Italy.

Changing money at a bank can at times be a frustrating process, as it can involve endless form-filling and queuing. First you have to go to the window that displays the *cambio* sign and then you will have to go to the *cassa* to obtain your Italian money. If in doubt, ask someone in order to avoid waiting in the wrong queue.

If you need to have money sent to you in Italy, banks at home can telex money to an Italian bank, but it takes about a week. American Express, Thomas Cook and Western Union all provide swifter money transfer services, with a charge to the sender.

CURRENCY

Italy's currency is the *lira* (plural *lire*) and is usually written as L or, confusingly, £. Lira means pound, so the English pound is referred to as the *lira sterlina*. Initially, the thousands of units of currency may seem confusing, but the distinctive colours of the notes make distinguishing between them easy. From time to time, however, familiar coins and notes are redesigned or even discontinued, although plans to alter the basic unit have not yet been implemented. You will find that the last three noughts are usually ignored in spoken Italian: *cinquanta* will usually mean L50,000 and not, as you may think, L50. Shop and bar owners are not keen to accept high-value notes for small purchases, so try to get some small denomination notes when changing money. Always keep some coins reserved for telephones, tips and the coin-operated lights that illuminate works of art in churches and cathedrals.

Bank Notes

All bank notes are issued by the Banca d'Italia. Each denomination is a different colour and carries a portrait of a historic person, such as Caravaggio on the L100,000 note. As a further aid to identification, the denominations above L2,000 increase in size according to their value. The lira itself is never subdivided.

1,000 lire

2,000 lire

5,000 lire

10,000 lire

50,000 lire

100,000 lire

Coins

Coins, shown here at actual size, are in denominations of L500, L200, L100 and L50. Old L100 and L50 coins are still in use and there are L10 and L20 coins of minute value. Telephone gettoni are worth L200.

50 lire (new)   100 lire (new)   500 lire

50 lire (old)   100 lire (old)   200 lire   *Gettone* (200 lire)

Communications

ALTHOUGH THE ITALIAN POSTAL service is known for being particularly slow, Italy's other forms of communication, at least in the cities, are more efficient. Fax machines, courier services and telephones are the most popular means of communication. Foreign-language newspapers and magazines are available in all cities and most large towns. Although there are both state-run and privately owned television stations, only satellite television and radio stations broadcast foreign-language programmes.

Telephone company logo

PUBLIC TELEPHONES

THE ITALIAN NATIONAL telephone company changed its name from SIP to Telecom Italia in 1994, but both names are still in use. Coin-operated telephones are becoming a rarity in favour of the new card-operated machines. Although many of the new telephones will take both cards and coins, some only accept a Telecom credit card. You can buy phone cards (*carta* or *scheda telefonica*) from bars, newspaper kiosks and *tabacchi*. The latest

Telephone sign

public telephones have instructions in four languages (Italian, English, French and German). To select a language, push the top right-hand button.

Coin telephones, usually located in bars and restaurants, accept L100, L200, L500 and *gettone* coins (the old phone tokens worth L200). A local call costs L200. When making long-distance or international calls have at least L2,000 in change at hand. If you don't put enough coins in to start with, you will be disconnected and lose your money. An easier alternative is to look for a *telefono a*

scatti, or metered phone. Ask the bar or restaurant owner if you can phone and the call will be metered. You then pay when you have finished.

Main towns have telephone offices (*Telefoni*) where you are assigned a booth and pay after your calls. No premium is charged for this service.

Using one of the new public telephone or *interurbani*

USING A COIN AND CARD TELEPHONE

1 Lift the receiver and wait for the dialling tone.

3 The display shows how much credit is left.

4 Dial the number and wait to be connected.

5 If you still have credit and want to make a second call, press the "follow-on call" button.

6 If your telephone card is about to expire, place a new one in the telephone card slot. When the old card expires, it will feed through automatically.

2 If you use coins or *gettoni* insert them in the slot at the top. The slot for telephone cards is lower down.

7 After your call is finished, unused coins or *gettoni* are returned from the left-hand slot. Cards are returned from the slot on the right.

Telephone cards have values of L5,000 or L10,000.

To use a card, break off the marked corner and insert, arrow first.

L200   L500

L100   *Gettone*

DIRECTORY

For operator-assisted calls from a public phone, insert L200 which will be returned after the call.

To calculate the cost of a call from a private phone, dial * 40 # before and after the call and the number of units will be read to you. Off-peak rates apply from 10pm–8am and all day Sunday.

USEFUL NUMBERS

Directory Enquiries
📞 *12*.

International Directory Enquiries
📞 *176*.

Italcable
📞 *17 90* (for reverse charge and calling card calls).

British Operator
📞 *172 00 44*.

American Operators
📞 *172 15 98* (AT&T).
📞 *172 10 11* (MCI).
📞 *172 10 22* (Sprint).

Australian Operators
📞 *172 10 61* (Telstra).
📞 *172 11 61* (Optus).

COUNTRY CODES

To call Italy from these countries dial the code and then the number.

📞 *00 39 – UK*
📞 *0 1139 – US & Canada*
📞 *00 39 – Ireland*
📞 *00 1139 – Australia*

TV AND RADIO

TELEVISION CHANNELS in Italy include the state-owned RAI (Uno, Due and Tre) and Fininvest (Retequattro, Canale Cinque and Italia Uno). There are also many local channels. Most foreign programmes are dubbed into Italian, although satellite channels, such as Sky, CNN and RTL, show news and sports programmes in a variety of languages. There are three national radio stations and hundreds of local stations. The BBC World Service is on 15.070MHz (short wave) in the mornings and 648KHz (medium wave) at night.

NEWSPAPERS

THE MAIN NATIONAL daily newspapers are *La Stampa*, *Il Corriere della Sera* and *La Repubblica*. Papers with the most detailed news of Italy's major cities include *Il Mattino* for Naples, *Il Messaggero* for Rome and *Il Giornale* for Milan. All newspapers have local pages and listings for cinemas, theatres and main concerts. In Rome and Milan, *La Repubblica* publishes "what's on and where to go" supplements called *TrovaRoma* and *TrovaMilano*. Florence's *Firenze Spettacolo* and Rome's *RomaC'è* are weekly entertainment listings magazines. Foreign papers, such as the *International Guardian*, *International Herald Tribune* and *USA Today*, arrive in the main cities at or shortly after midday.

Newspaper stall selling national and international publications

POST OFFICE

POST OFFICES AND also some tobacconists weigh and price letters and sell stamps. Local post offices open from 8:25am–1:50pm weekdays, and from 8:25am–12 noon on Saturday. Main post offices are open from 8:25am–7pm

City letters Other destinations

Italian post box

Post Office sign

non-stop. The Vatican City and the state of San Marino have their own postal system and stamps. Letters and postcards destined for Europe cost the same as post within Italy. The red post boxes (blue in the Vatican) usually have two slots labelled *per la città* (for the city only) and *tutte le altre destinazioni* (for all other destinations). Italian post is renowned for its unreliability and letters can take from four days to two weeks to arrive.

For a faster service, send letters express *(espresso)*. More reliable are recorded delivery *(raccomandata)* and recorded delivery with an arrival receipt *(raccomandata con ricevuta di ritorno)*. However, anything of value should be sent by insured post *(assicurata)*.

For urgent communications, try state couriers *Posta celere* and *Cai post*, which are based at all main post offices. They guarantee delivery within 24–72 hours and are far cheaper than private couriers. Main post offices also provide telegram, telex and fax services. The fax service, however, is not available for certain countries. Post offices also provide a *fermo posta* service (poste restante) for a small collection fee. Send letters to the central post office, c/o Fermo Posta. You will need to show some identification when collecting the letters.

REGIONS OF ITALY

ITALY CONSISTS OF 20 regions that are divided into provinces. Each province has a *capoluogo* (an administrative capital) and a *sigla*, the initials of the capital. For example, FI stands for the *capoluogo* of Florence *(Firenze)*. The *sigla* appears on car licence plates registered before 1994 and denotes the origins of the vehicle owner. The code can also be used to address letters, appearing after the town name.

Shopping

ITALY IS KNOWN FOR ITS QUALITY designer goods, ranging from chic clothing and sleek cars to stylish household items. There is a strong tradition of craftsmanship, often from family-run businesses, and there are numerous markets selling regional specialities. Apart from the town markets, it is not a country for bargains, but the joys of window shopping will offer plenty of compensation.

Fresh vegetables on display at a Florentine market stall

OPENING HOURS

OPENING TIMES for shops are usually 8am–1pm and around 3:30–8pm, Tuesday to Saturday and Monday afternoons. However, shopkeepers are increasingly working to more flexible hours. There are not that many large department stores, but most large towns will have a Standa, Upim and perhaps a Coin or Rinascente. These stores are often open non-stop *(orario continuato)* from 9am–8pm, Monday to Saturday. Boutiques generally open later; music and bookshops sometimes stay open after 8pm and on Sundays.

FOOD SHOPS

EVEN THOUGH there are super-markets throughout Italy, the specialist shops, although more expensive, are still the most interesting way to shop. A *forno* has the best bread and a *macellaio* has the finest meat (go to a *norceria* for pork products). Vegetables are freshest from market stalls or the *fruttivendolo*. You can buy cakes at the *pasticceria*, milk at the *latteria*, and pasta, ham, cheese and general foods at the often impressively stocked *alimentari*. Here you can also buy wine, but for a wider choice, head for the *enoteca*, *vineria* or *vinaio*, where you can sometimes taste the wine before purchasing.

MARKETS

ALL TOWNS HAVE regional markets that take place each week. Large towns will have several small daily markets followed by a weekly flea market, usually held on a Sunday. In this guide the main market days are listed under each town. Traders set up at 5am and start to clear away at about 1:30pm. Food is sold by the *etto* (100 grams) and the *chilo* (kilo) *(see p615)*, or in numbers (two onions, etc). Food stalls selling seasonal products generally have fresher and less expensive produce than the shops. Bargaining is not usually done when buying food, but it is worth asking for a discount *(sconto)* for clothes and other items.

SEASONAL PRODUCE

TO MAKE THE MOST of Italian food, try to buy and eat what is in season. Grapes and mushrooms are best in autumn, whereas spring is the season for asparagus, straw-berries and Roman artichokes. In winter, vegetables such as cauliflower and broccoli are at their best, as are lemons from Amalfi and Sicilian blood oranges. Summer is the time for plums, pears and cherries, as well as courgettes, auber-gines, tomatoes and melon.

CLOTHES AND DESIGNER SHOPS

ITALY IS RENOWNED worldwide for its fashion industry. Milan is the fashion capital and Via Monte Napoleone, in the city centre, is lined with the most famous of the designer boutiques. All large towns will have a selection of designer shops, usually situated near each other. Less ex-pensive clothes are available in markets and many high-street shops, where the styles tend to be

Protective bag with designer label

Souvenir shop in Ostuni, near Brindisi, Puglia

more conventional and classical. Sales, called *saldi*, are held during summer and winter. Second-hand shops are often quite expensive, but the quality and condition of the clothes can be very good. Larger markets will have stalls piled high with clothes priced between L1,000 and L10,000. Rummage through and you will often find bargains. Many markets sell fake Rayban sunglasses, Lacoste T-shirts and Levi's jeans. Some shops have signs that read *ingresso libero*, meaning "browsers welcome", but do not be surprised if a sales assistant assails you as soon as you walk in.

An elegant designer clothes boutique in Treviso

Colourful shop display of leather handbags in Florence

JEWELLERY AND ANTIQUE SHOPS

GLITZY GOLD JEWELLERY is very popular in Italy and every *gioielleria* (jewellery shop) will have a wide selection. For more unusual items, try the *bigiotteria* or artisan shops (*oreficeria*). Antique stores like *Antichità* and *Antiquariato* sell furniture and ornaments of varying quality and prices. You will rarely find bargains in Italy, except perhaps at the *Fiere dell'Antiquariato* (antique fairs), held throughout the year all over the country.

INTERIOR DESIGN AND HOUSEHOLD WARES

INTERIOR DESIGN is another Italian sector where top names demand extravagant prices, with many shops concentrating on modern, high-tech styles.

There are household shops in cities and towns throughout the country. Italian kitchenware is particularly striking, with its stainless steel and copper pots, pans and utensils. For the lowest prices, avoid the tourist shops and, if possible, buy directly from the manufacturer. Less expensive items include the characteristic brown espresso and cappuccino cups sold in all markets.

REGIONAL SPECIALITIES

MANY OF ITALY'S regional specialities are world famous: Parma ham, Chianti wine, olive oil and grappa. Regional sweets including the Sienese *panforte* and Sicilian marzipan are also well-known, as are cheeses such as gorgonzola from Lombardy and Parmesan from Emilia-Romagna. Traditional crafts are still practised in Italy and range from delicate lacework and glassware in the Veneto to leatherwork, jewellery and marbled paper in Florence. Italian ceramics include elaborate Tuscan pottery, hand-painted dishes around Amalfi and De Simone's stylized designer plates from Sicily.

Display of decorative glazed pottery from Tuscany

SIZE CHART
For Australian sizes follow the British and American conversions.

Women's dresses, coats and skirts

Italian	38	40	42	44	46	48	50
British	8	10	12	14	16	18	20
American	6	8	10	12	14	16	18

Women's shoes

Italian	36	37	38	39	40	41
British	3	4	5	6	7	8
American	5	6	7	8	9	10

Men's suits

Italian	44	46	48	50	52	54	56	58 (size)
British	34	36	38	40	42	44	46	48 (inches)
American	34	36	38	40	42	44	46	48 (inches)

Men's shirts (collar size)

Italian	36	38	39	41	42	43	44	45 (cm)
British	14	15	15½	16	16½	17	17½	18 (inches)
American	14	15	15½	16	16½	17	17½	18 (inches)

Men's shoes

Italian	39	40	41	42	43	44	45	46
British	6	7	7½	8	9	10	11	12
American	7	7½	8	8½	9½	10½	11	11½

Specialist Holidays and Outdoor Activities

**Exploring the country-
side on horseback**

ITALY OFFERS AN AMAZING variety of cultural, sporting and leisure activities. However, many schools and groups require annual membership and short-term activities are often expensive and difficult to find. Information on current leisure and sporting events in a specific region is available from the tourist office listed for each town in this guide. For details on annual festivals, see *Italy Through the Year* on pages 62–5. The following suggestions include some of the most popular as well as some more unusual pursuits.

**Cycling on the tree-lined flatlands
of the Po Delta**

WALKING, CYCLING AND HORSERIDING

SOME ITALIAN BRANCHES of the **World Wide Fund for Nature (WWF)** organize walks and treks. **Club Alpino Italiano (CAI)** runs trekking and climbing excursions and the **Italian Birds Protection League (LIPU)** arranges nature walks and bird-watching trips. The military *IGM* maps are the most detailed but unfortunately are only available from specialist map shops.

Cycling is a national sport despite the country's mountainous landscape. The Po Delta, however, has miles of flat and stunningly beautiful cycling areas. Travel bookshops stock publications with suggested cycling routes.

Many riding schools organize trips and outings, even on a daily basis, which are also advertised in the local press. For general information, contact the **Federazione Italiana di Sport Equestre**.

MOUNTAIN SPORTS

THE MOST WELL-EQUIPPED and famous ski resorts are in the Dolomites. Smaller and less expensive resorts, however, are in the Apennines and in Sicily.

Package ski holidays, arranged from outside Italy, offer the best deals. The **Federazione Arrampicata Sportiva Italiana** has a list of mountain climbing schools that organize climbs for people at all levels.

**Ski lift near the desolate Falzarego
Pass, in the heart of the Dolomites**

ARCHAEOLOGICAL DIGS

THE BRITISH MONTHLY magazine *Archaeology Abroad*, available in the UK, gives a comprehensive list of archaeology groups and digs worldwide. In Italy, the **Gruppo Archeologico Romano** runs two-week digs in various regions. There are summer and winter digs, for both adults and children. The group has contacts with local archaeological organizations as well.

ITALIAN LANGUAGE AND CULTURE

FOR A WIDE SELECTION of material on courses and schools in Italy, contact the Italian consulate in your home country. The **Società Dante Alighieri** provides courses in the Italian language, history of art, literature and culture. There are both full- and part-time courses available, for every level. Language schools abound in Italy's main cities and are advertised in the Yellow Pages *(Pagine Gialle)* or foreign language bookshops and newspapers. For young students, **Intercultura** will organize weekly, monthly and year-long exchanges including language courses, accommodation with Italian families and enrolment in Italian schools.

Group hiking tour in the Dolomites of Trentino-Alto Adige *(see p78)*

A *Tasting Italy* **cookery lesson in Sicily**

In recent years, cooking holidays run by English-speaking experts in Italian cooking have become very popular. **Tasting Italy**, for example, does wine tours and week-long courses in Italian cuisine, and provides beautiful private accommodation. The course locations include the Veneto, Sicily, Tuscany and Piedmont. Wine-tasting tours are organized by local tourist boards. The Università per Stranieri in Perugia runs courses on Italian culture, history and cooking.

WATER SPORTS

MOST LAKES AND many seaside resorts rent out sailing boats, canoes and windsurfing equipment. Lessons and courses are organized by clubs, which usually require membership. For a list of authorized associations contact the **Federazione Italiana di Canoa e Kayak** and the **Federazione Italiana di Vela**. Weekend and weekly sailing holidays and courses are featured in the magazine *Avventure nel Mondo* and most travel agents have a selection of sailing holidays.

Swimming pools are expensive in Italy and many do not accept people on a daily basis. You often have to pay a membership fee and a monthly tariff. Some of the luxurious hotels open their pools to the public in summer, but at pricy rates. Water parks are popular and provide pools, slides, wave machines and games. Before diving into any lakes or rivers (and even the sea near main towns) it is best to check that the water is not polluted. The **Federazione Italiana di**

Attività Subacquee runs underwater diving courses, and can give information on all local centres.

AIR SPORTS

THERE ARE SCHOOLS nationwide that offer hang-gliding and flying courses, but the minimum duration of each course is one month. For information and a list of schools contact the **Aeroclub Italiano**. You must be licensed before you can fly and all crafts must be registered with the Aeroclub.

OTHER SPORTS

GOLF IS A POPULAR sport in Italy and there are plenty of courses to choose from. Home membership and handicap are often required for daily access to a club. Italian tennis clubs usually operate on a membership basis, unless you are invited as a member's guest. The national **Federazione Italiana di Tennis** has a list of all the tennis clubs in Italy. Football is an Italian obsession and you will see friendly, noisy games in action in every park, beach or open space. It is possible to rent five-a-side courts at most sports centres, but for a more relaxed game you can get a group of friends together or join in with other people.

Sailing in Italy, a popular leisure activity and competitive sport

TRAVEL INFORMATION

Alitalia aircraft

ITALY HAS TRANSPORT SYSTEMS of varying efficiency, from the modern road, bus and rail networks of the north to the slower and more antiquated systems of the south. Numerous airlines operate flights to several of the country's major airports, while within Italy itself the national carrier Alitalia, and several smaller companies, provide an extensive network of internal flights.

Connections by road to the rest of Europe are good, though Alpine roads can be adversely affected by the weather. Motorways and other roads within the country are generally good, but can be busy at weekends and peak periods. Italy also has an efficient system of ferries connecting Sicily, Sardinia and many of the smaller off-shore islands. Many of these are car ferries, and are busy in summer.

Arriving by Air

ROME'S LEONARDO DA VINCI (Fiumicino) and Milan's Malpensa are the key airports for long-haul flights into Italy. Milan's Linate airport handles European flights, and most European airlines also fly to Venice, Turin, Naples and Pisa (for Florence). Many airlines are now flying regularly to smaller cities such as Florence, Genoa, Bologna, Verona and Bergamo, while charter flights serve more obscure destinations in peak season such as Catania, Olbia and Rimini.

Part of the extension to Fiumicino airport, Rome

LONG-HAUL FLIGHTS

IF YOU ARE FLYING from the United States, TWA, Delta and United Airlines operate regular direct scheduled flights to Rome, with services from New York, Washington, Los Angeles, Boston and Chicago. Canadian Airlines flies from Montréal and Toronto, and Qantas flies from Sydney and Melbourne.

The Italian state airline, Alitalia, has a regular service between Rome and New York, San Francisco, Philadelphia, Boston, Chicago, Detroit, Washington, Montréal, Toronto and Sydney. It may, however, be more convenient and cheaper for

Alitalia flight tickets

long-haul passengers to take a budget flight to London, Frankfurt, Paris or Amsterdam and then continue with their journey to Italy (by aeroplane or train) from there.

NATIONAL FLIGHTS

ALITALIA AND ITS DOMESTIC arm, ATI, run regular services between many Italian cities. Long-haul passengers can easily transfer to domestic flights in Rome and Milan. Passengers from European destinations should find scheduled flights to most big cities, with the notable exceptions of Palermo and Catania in Sicily, where a change of

flight at one of the major airports is usually necessary. As internal flights are expensive, and busy at peak periods, it is worth trying the train as an alternative to domestic flights. Note that flights to airports in the north, particularly Milan and Turin, can be disrupted by fog in autumn and winter.

TICKETS AND FARES

APEX, PEX OR SUPERPEX fares generally offer the best deals on scheduled flights to Italy, but they must be purchased well in advance; at least 7 or 14 days in the UK and 21 days in the US. They are, however, subject to penalty clauses, so it is advisable to take out insurance against unforeseen cancellation.

If you are based in the UK it is well worth scouring the small ads of newspapers for cut-price charters and heavily-discounted scheduled flights.

AIRPORT
Rome (Fiumicino)
Rome (Ciampino)
Milan (Linate)
Milan (Malpensa)
Pisa (Galileo Galilei)
Venice (Marco Polo)
Venice (Treviso)

The entrance hall at Pisa airport

Most charters leave from Gatwick or Luton, and may land at a city's second (and often less convenient) airport. Fares tend to vary greatly during the year, but the most expensive periods are during the summer months and over the Christmas and Easter holidays. Where possible ask for available student discounts.

Shuttle bus to car hire lots at Fiumicino

PACKAGE HOLIDAYS

PACKAGE HOLIDAYS to Italy are usually cheaper than travelling independently, unless you are travelling on a tight budget and are prepared to make use of youth hostels and campsites. Rome, Florence and Venice are often offered as separate or linked package deals, and many operators have packages to the Tuscan and Umbrian countryside, Sicily, the Italian Lakes, the Italian Riviera, Naples and the Amalfi coast. In winter, ski packages are available to many Alpine resorts. Specialist packages, such as cooking, walking and art tours, are becoming increasingly common. In cities, different tour operators may use different hotels, so it is worth shopping around for the most pleasant (and centrally located) hotels. Many operators transport you free of charge from the airport to your hotel. Some will include a tour guide.

FLY-DRIVE DEALS

MANY TRAVEL AGENTS and car-hire firms will organize special fly-drive packages that enable you to book a flight and have a hire car waiting for you at your destination.

This is usually cheaper and involves fewer formalities than renting a car on arrival. Most major car hire firms such as Hertz, Avis and Budget (and many minor ones as well) have offices located at the major Italian airports.

The quayside at Venice's Marco Polo airport

INFORMATION	DISTANCE TO CITY CENTRE	TAXI FARE TO CITY CENTRE	PUBLIC TRANSPORT TO CITY CENTRE
(06-65 95 44 55	30 km (18 miles)	L75,000	FS 40 mins
(06-79 49 41	15 km (9 miles)	L40,000	M 50 mins
(02-738 02 33	7 km (4.5 miles)	L25–30,000	20 mins
(02-749 11 41	50 km (31 miles)	L100–120,000	1 hr
(050-50 07 07	2 km (1 mile)	L10–15,000 to Pisa	FS to Pisa: 5 mins FS to Florence: 1 hr
(041-260 92 60	10 km (6.5 miles)	L90,000 + Water Taxi	50 mins 20 mins
(0422-023 93	30 km (18 miles)	L80,000 to Venice	to Treviso: 20 mins to Venice: 30 mins

Arriving by Sea, Rail and Coach

Orient Express logo

ITALY IS SERVED BY AN EXTENSIVE network of roads, railways and international ferry lines. Road and rail links cross into the country from France, Switzerland, Austria and Slovenia, and there are through train services from as far afield as Moscow, London and Barcelona. Road connections into the country are generally of motorway standard, though delays can occur at some of the many Alpine passes and tunnels during bad weather or peak summer holiday periods.

Do-it-yourself help points with train information on screens

Ticket windows at Florence's Santa Maria Novella station

There are also direct services from Vienna, Spain and the south of France. Motor-rail connections exist from several northern European centres and the Channel ports.

Despite its convenience, international train travel is usually not much cheaper than air travel, particularly for longer journeys such as those from the United Kingdom. Special discount fares, however, are often available for senior travellers and for people under 26. Trains can be extremely busy during peak periods, particularly on Friday and Sunday evenings, and during the Christmas and Easter holiday periods. July and August can also be frantically busy, especially on routes from Germany and ports connecting with Greek ferries in the south. Reservations on most services are inexpensive and advisable.

ARRIVING BY CAR

MOST ROADS into Italy from the rest of Europe involve Alpine crossings by tunnel or mountain passes. The notable exceptions are the approach from Slovenia in the northeast (on the A4 motorway) and the route along the French Riviera that enters Italy as the A10 motorway at Ventimiglia.

The most popular route from Geneva and southeast France is via the Mont Blanc tunnel and A5 motorway, entering Italy close to Aosta and Turin. Another busy approach (from Switzerland) uses the St Bernard Pass and tunnel, also entering Italy close to Aosta.

Further east, the main route from Austria and southern Germany crosses the Brenner Pass and goes down to Verona on the A22 motorway via Trento and the Adige valley. Weather conditions rarely close the passes, but snow and fog can make progress slow on the winding roads through the mountains. Most motorways are toll-roads; you pay as you exit the motorway.

ARRIVING BY TRAIN

AFTER AIR TRAVEL, arriving by train is the least painful way to reach Italy. Countless through services (including many sleepers) link Italian towns and cities with places as far afield as Brussels, Moscow and Barcelona. Connections from Paris (and London) run to Milan, Venice or along Italy's west coast to Rome and Naples. Services also operate from German, Swiss and other northern European cities to Milan, Turin, Venice and Verona.

BINARIO 17

Platform sign

← uscita

Exit sign

Sleeping-car Voiture lits Schlafwagen Vettura letti

The sleeping car on an international Eurocity train

ARRIVING BY BOAT

MOST PEOPLE arriving in Italy by boat do so from Greece, which is linked by services from Corfu and Patras to Brindisi and other ports in southeast Italy. Services are particularly crowded in the summer months, as are the connecting train services from Brindisi to the rest of Italy.

Other international ferry connections include boats from Malta, Tunisia and other North African ports to Palermo, Naples and various southern Italian ports. Boats also run from towns in the south of France to Genoa, Livorno and ports on the Italian Riviera.

ARRIVING BY COACH

COACH TRAVEL to Italy is relatively cheap (though often not much cheaper than trains), but long journey times make it one of the least comfortable ways to travel. Some coach companies have now introduced plane-coach deals, whereby you can travel by coach on one leg of your trip and by air on the other. At the moment there are thrice-weekly services in summer from the UK to Turin, Milan, Bologna and Rome. The journey time from London to Milan is about 27 hours, and about 36 hours to Rome. A night on the road is thus unavoidable. **National Express Eurolines** run weekly coaches from London's Victoria Coach Station to all of Italy's major cities as far as Rome. Buses travel via Dover, Calais, Paris and Lyon and it

SITA coach arriving at the station in Florence

is useful to take some French francs with you for the probable stops en route.

Travelling Around by Ferry

ITALY'S LARGE NUMBER of off-shore islands mean that it has a large and well-developed network of ferries, as well as services to the rest of Europe and North Africa.

One of the Moby Lines car ferries that sail the Mediterranean

FERRIES

CAR FERRIES are a convenient link with the beautiful islands scattered off the Italian mainland. Boats for Sardinia leave from Civitavecchia (north of Rome), Livorno and Genoa, and depart for Sicily from Naples and Reggio di Calabria. Ferries run from the major Sicilian ports to the Egadi and the Aeolian archipelagoes, as well as to countless other small islands around Sicily (although ferries to the smaller islands do not always carry cars).

Boats also ply between Elba and Piombino, as well as the smaller islands of the Tuscan archipelago such as Capraia. Ferries run from ports close to Rome to Ponza and its surrounding islands, and from Naples to Capri and Ischia. On the east coast the Tremiti islands are linked to ports on the Gargano Peninsula.

Hydrofoils are increasingly complementing conventional ferries on many routes, particularly on the busy services to Capri and Ischia.

Queues for ferries to many destinations are common in summer, and you should book well ahead if you wish to travel to Sardinia in July or August, especially if taking a vehicle. Bookings can often be made through travel agents, as well as a ferry line's agents in your own country.

ROUTE	FERRY COMPANY	TELEPHONE INFORMATION
Piombino – Elba	Moby Lines	ℂ *0586-89 03 25* (Livorno)
Livorno – Elba	Navarma	ℂ *0565-91 81 01* (Piombino) ℂ *0586-380 68* (Livorno)
Genoa – Sardinia	Tirrenia	ℂ *070-66 60 65* (Cagliari) ℂ *0789-246 91* (Olbia) ℂ *010-25 80 41* (Genoa)
Livorno – Sardinia	Sardinia Ferries	ℂ *0789-252 00* (Olbia) ℂ *010-59 33 01* (Genoa)
	Navarma	ℂ *0789-279 27* (Olbia)
Genoa/Livorno – Palermo	Grandi Traghetti	ℂ *091-58 78 32* (Palermo)
Naples – Palermo	Tirrenia	ℂ *091-602 11 11* (Palermo)
Naples – Cagliari	Tirrenia	ℂ *070-66 60 65* (Cagliari)

Travelling Around by Train

FS Logo

Train travel is one of the best ways to explore Italy. Tickets are cheap, services frequent, and rolling stock some of the most modern in Europe. Services can be busy, but the days of rampant overcrowding are mostly over. Lines often run through lovely countryside, from mountain lakes to rolling plateaux, and they provide more convenient links between cities than roads or air travel. Only in the south, or deeply rural areas, are services slow and infrequent.

A Pendolino – Italy's fastest train

The atrium of Stazione Termini, at Piazza dei Cinquecento, Rome

THE NETWORK

The bulk of Italy's rail network is an integrated state-run system operated by the Ferrovie dello Stato (FS). A few privately run lines fill crucial gaps left by the FS, but through tickets are generally available where travel involves both networks. FS and private lines often (but not always) share the same main station *(stazione)*, and also charge similar fares.

TRAINS

The FS is in the process of changing the categories of trains, but in practice the same broad divisions will continue to apply. The fast Pendolino ("Leaning Train") and a handful of other special high-speed trains require pre-booking of seats. Intercity (IC) trains and Eurocity (EC) trains only stop at major stations and require the payment of a first- or second-class supplement *(un supplemento)* on top of the standard ticket (supplements can be bought on the train, but are more expensive). *Espresso* (Espr) and *Diretto* (Dir) trains make more stops and require no supplement (you may also find these

trains called *Regionali* and *Interregionali). Locali* stop at all stations.

Rolling stock has improved in recent years, especially on Intercity trains, which are now usually modern and air-conditioned. Branch line carriages can still be ancient. Facilities for the disabled exist on many Intercity trains.

FS train in Verona station

TICKETS AND FARES

Tickets (BIGLIETTI) are available as single *(andata)* or return *(andata e ritorno)* in first *(prima)* or second class *(seconda classe)*. They can be bought at some travel agents or at any station ticket office *(la biglietteria)*. Automatic ticket machines are being introduced, and increasingly

you can buy tickets for journeys of up to 250 km (155 miles) from newsstands or station tobacconists (such a ticket is known as *un biglietto a fascia chilometrica).* Be sure to validate all tickets on both outbound and return journeys, or you will be fined. A ticket's validity usually starts on the day of purchase, so be sure to specify the day of travel when buying tickets in advance. The fares are calculated on a kilometric basis and are among the cheapest in western Europe. Return fares offer a 15 per cent discount on trips of up to 250 km (155 miles).

PASSES

The FS provides three basic passes: the Biglietto Chilometrico, valid for two months, allowing 3,000 km (1,865 miles) of travel for up to five people for a maximum of 20 journeys; the Flexipass, permitting unlimited travel for four days within a nine-day period, eight days within a 21-day period, or 12 days within any month; and the Biglietto Turistico Libera Circolazione (BTLC), a travel-at-will pass for 8, 15, 21 or 30 days.

TIMETABLES

It is worth picking up a time-table *(un orario)* if you plan to use trains often. The official FS timetable is comprehensive but heavy and sells out very fast. A far better buy is the small *Pozzorario*, issued twice yearly. It is available from station kiosks and newsstands.

VALIDITY AND RESERVATIONS

Single or return tickets are valid for up to two months from the date of purchase. If a seat reservation is made with the ticket, however, the date you wish to travel will be stamped automatically on the ticket. Undated tickets for up to 250 km (155 miles) can also be purchased at newsstands, and must be validated on the day of travel. Reservations are a good idea on and around public holidays and can be made at most main stations for the high-speed, Intercity and Eurocity trains. Larger stations generally have separate windows for making reservations *(prenotazioni)*.

REDUCTIONS

Discounts of 20 per cent are available with a *Carta Famiglia* (Family Card), for families of up to four people; with a *Carta Verde*, for travellers aged between 12 and 26; and with a *Carta d'Argento*, for travellers over 60. Passes are not valid during Christmas and at certain periods in high summer. They can be bought from main line stations and are valid for a year. There is also the Rail Europe Family Card which allows up to 50 per cent for adults and 75 per cent for children under 12.

LEFT LUGGAGE

Main city stations usually have left luggage facilities. Most are manned (but the smaller stations have selfservice lockers), and you may need to present a passport or other form of identification when depositing or collecting bags. Fees are calculated per bag.

Left luggage logo

MACHINES FOR FS RAIL TICKETS

These self-service machines are simple and easy to use. Most have instructions in four languages on a printed panel.

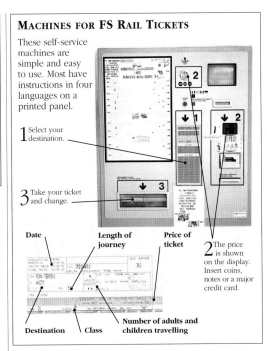

1 Select your destination.

3 Take your ticket and change.

2 The price is shown on the display. Insert coins, notes or a major credit card.

Date   Length of journey   Price of ticket

Destination   Class   Number of adults and children travelling

ITALY'S PRINCIPAL FS NETWORK

The Italian state rail network operates various different types of service. Check what is on offer before buying your ticket.

KEY

● Main stations

○ Other stations

▬ Principal rail route

- - Route over water

Travelling Around by Car

The classic Fiat 500

A MOTORING TOUR OF ITALY is the most practical way of exploring the country, though you should take into account high petrol prices, the difficulty of parking in many medieval towns and the Italians' occasionally erratic approach to driving. A car is invaluable in the countryside and for extensive touring, but less useful if you are only visiting a few major towns and cities, as the traffic congestion makes driving slow.

Automatic tollbooths on the motorway outside Florence

WHAT TO TAKE

DRIVERS FROM OUTSIDE Italy bringing their own foreign-registered cars into the country must be at least 18 years old and carry a Green Card (for insurance purposes), all the vehicle's registration documents, and a full, valid driving licence (*patente* in Italian). Any UK or other EU nationals without the standard EU "pink" licence will need an Italian translation of their licence, obtainable from most motoring organizations or from the Italian state tourist office in your home country. A red warning triangle must also be carried at all times, for use in the event of a breakdown.

PETROL

PETROL *(benzina)* in Italy is some of the most expensive in Europe (diesel, or *gasolio*, is a little cheaper). Although many petrol stations are now self-service, it is still common to be served by an attendant. Just say how much you want to spend or ask for *il pieno* (full tank). Most petrol stations follow normal shop hours so make sure you have a full tank before lunchtime or public

holidays. On motorways petrol stations tend to be open 24 hours a day. Credit cards are very rarely accepted.

ROADS

ITALY HAS A GOOD network of motorways, though many have a total of only four lanes, often leading to congestion.

Rules and Regulations

Italy uses standard European road signs. Drive on the right and give way to traffic from the right. Seat belts (la cintura) *are compulsory in the front and the back, and children should be properly restrained. The speed limit in urban areas is 50 km/h (30 mph); outside urban areas it is 110 km/h (70 mph) on dual carriage-ways and 90 km/h on all other secondary roads. On motor-ways* (autostrade) *the limit is 130 km/h (80 mph) for vehicles over 1100cc and 110 km/h (70 mph) for all vehicles under 1100cc. All documenta-tion must be carried with you.*

One-way street

Blue signs showing main roads and green signs showing motorways

Busy routes include the A1 from Bologna to Florence and between Bologna, Parma and Milan. Tolls are payable on all but a handful of motorways, again leading to congestion at tollbooths *(Alt Stazione)* at weekends and busy holiday periods. Payment is made at the end of the journey in cash or pre-paid magnetic cards called VIAcards, available from tobacconists and the ACI.

Secondary roads are known as Nazionali (N) or as Strade Statali (SS), and vary enormously in quality, the worst being in the south. Mountain roads are usually good, but distances can be deceptive on winding roads and in winter snow chains are obligatory on many higher routes. Some back roads (known as *strade bianche*, or "white roads") have only a gravel surface, but are still marked on motoring maps. These are slow, but usually passable to cars, if you drive carefully.

No stopping   **End of speed restriction**

Pedestrianized street – no traffic   **Give way to oncoming traffic**

No parking   **Danger (often with description)**

Car rental offices at Fiumicino airport, Rome

CAR HIRE

CAR HIRE *(autonoleggio)* is expensive in Italy, and should be organized beforehand through fly-drive deals *(see p627)* or pre-booked with firms who have branches in Italy. For on the spot hire Italian firms may be cheaper than big international names. Agencies are listed in Yellow Pages *(Pagine Gialle)* under Autonoleggio. Most airports have car hire offices on site.

To rent a car in Italy you must be over 21 and have held a valid driver's licence for at least a year. Visitors from outside the EU require an international licence, though in practice not all hire firms insist on this. Check the small print of the agreement for insurance cover.

DISCO ORARIO

ORA DI ARRIVO

Parking disc

CAR HIRE NUMBERS

Eurodollar (Rome)
📞 06-487 20 98.

Europcar (Rome)
📞 06-52 08 11.

Hertz (Rome)
📞 06-39 37 88 07.

Maggiore (Rome)
📞 06-22 93 51.

ACCIDENTS AND BREAKDOWNS

IF YOU HAVE AN ACCIDENT or a breakdown, switch on your hazard warning lights and place a warning triangle 50 m (164 ft) behind your car. Then (for breakdowns) call the ACI emergency number (116) or the emergency services (112 or 113). The ACI will tow any foreign-registered car free to

the nearest ACI-affiliated garage. They also do free repairs for members of affiliated associations, such as the AA and RAC in Britain.

If you have an accident keep calm, and do not admit liability or make any statements that might incriminate you later. Simply swap car and insurance details, names and addresses.

PARKING

PARKING IN MOST Italian cities and large towns is a problem. Many historic centres have restricted daytime access and baffling one-way systems. Other areas may be reserved for residents' parking (marked *riservato ai residenti*). Some towns have disc parking *(disco orario)*, with discs available from petrol stations or provided in hire cars, but spaces

go quickly. Cars can be towed away or clamped, especially in areas marked *zona rimozione* (particularly on street-cleaning days). Call the Municipal Police *(Vigili)* to retrieve your car.

SAFETY

CAR THEFT IS RIFE in Italy. Never leave anything in your car, and (if possible) always remove radio-cassette players. Leave your car in a guarded car park whenever you can. Be especially careful driving at night, when Italian driving is more cavalier than usual, and when many traffic lights switch to flashing amber. Hitching *(autostop)* is not a good idea (and is not common), certainly never for women on their own.

Official parking area patrolled by attendant

DISTANCE CHART

ROME											
286 178	ANCONA										**10** Distance in kilometres 10 Distance in miles
748 465	**617** 383	AOSTA									
383 238	**219** 136	**401** 249	BOLOGNA								
645 401	**494** 307	**449** 279	**280** 174	BOLZANO							
278 173	**262** 163	**470** 292	**106** 66	**228** 367	FLORENCE						
510 317	**506** 315	**245** 152	**291** 181	**422** 262	**225** 140	GENOA					
601 373	**614** 382	**1220** 758	**822** 511	**1097** 682	**871** 541	**1103** 685	LECCE				
575 357	**426** 265	**181** 113	**210** 130	**295** 183	**299** 186	**145** 90	**1029** 639	MILAN			
219 136	**409** 254	**959** 596	**594** 369	**856** 532	**489** 304	**714** 444	**393** 244	**786** 488	NAPLES		
673 418	**547** 340	**110** 68	**332** 206	**410** 255	**395** 245	**170** 106	**1150** 715	**138** 86	**884** 549	TURIN	
530 329	**364** 226	**442** 275	**154** 96	**214** 133	**255** 158	**397** 247	**967** 601	**273** 170	**741** 460	**402** 250	VENICE

Travelling within Cities

Pedestrian zone sign

THE BEST WAYS of getting around Italian cities differ from place to place. In Rome buses are most useful, in Milan the metro is more efficient, and in Venice you will need to take a boat to get about. Trams still run in some cities, such as Milan and Rome. Cars are a liability almost everywhere, unlike walking, which in many cases is the easiest way to negotiate the tight historic cores of Italian towns and cities. Florence has a large limited-traffic zone, and most towns now have a pedestrian area in the centre.

A Roman tram in the orange livery of ATAC

One of the distinctive orange city buses, central Verona

BUSES AND TRAMS

VIRTUALLY EVERY ITALIAN city and large town has a bus system. Most are cheap, comprehensive and as efficient as traffic and narrow streets will allow and vary only slightly from city to city. Bus stops are known as *fermate*, and increasingly (notably in Rome) list full details of the routes they serve. Buses *(autobus)* usually run from about 6am to midnight, and there are night buses *(servizio notturno)* in larger cities. Note that if you arrive in a town by train, stations are invariably linked to the centre by shuttle buses from the station forecourt (tickets are usually available from the station bar or tabacconist).

TICKETS

TICKETS *(biglietti)* must usually be bought before boarding the bus, and are available from kiosks belonging to the bus company (ATAC in Rome, ATAF in Florence), from bars, or from tobacconists *(tabacchi)* displaying the bus company's sticker. A few places, like Florence, also have on-street vending machines around the city's main transport hubs. It is worth buying more than one ticket at a time, especially as outlets often close in the afternoon or early evening. Discounted tickets *(un blocchetto)*, or day- or week-long visitors' tickets and passes *(una tessera* or *tesserino)* are also available. In some cities, notably Rome and Florence, tickets are valid for any number of journeys within a given time.

USING BUSES AND TRAMS

YOU BOARD BUSES via the front and rear doors, and exit via the central doors. Buses usually only have a driver and no conductor (though night buses may have a conductor from whom

Bus stop displaying the route

tickets can be bought). Tickets must therefore be validated by punching them in machines at the front or rear of the bus. There are large on-the-spot fines if you are caught without a properly validated ticket. Most larger cities have transport information offices at the main train station or larger piazzas which provide free maps, timetables and tickets.

The majority of city buses are painted bright orange and display the final destination *(capolinea)* on the front.

METROPOLITANA

Metro sign

UNDERGROUND systems, known as *metropolitana* (*la metro* for short), are found in Rome and Milan. Rome's network amounts to just two lines, A and B, which converge at Stazione Termini, the city's central railway station. Several stations are useful for key sights, although the system is designed primarily to ferry commuters. At peak times, however, the lines provide the best way of crossing the city quickly. Stations are fairly dingy – though rarely dangerous – and train carriages can be stiflingly hot in summer. In Milan the network is more extensive, with three principal lines – MM1 (the red line), MM2 (green) and MM3 (yellow) – that meet at the hub stations of Stazione Centrale, Duomo, Cadorna and Lima. These three lines

Termini Metro station, Rome

Waiting for a fare at an official rank in Florence

give easy access to the majority of the city's main sights.

Metro tickets in both cities are available from the same sources as bus and tram tickets, and from machines and ticket offices in underground stations. Tickets in Rome are valid for one journey only, though the special *BIG* ticket offers a day's travel on bus, tram and metro. In Milan, by contrast, ordinary metro tickets are valid for 75 minutes for any number of journeys and can also be used on the buses and trams.

It is unwise to buy tickets from people outside stations, as they are invariably already used or otherwise invalid.

Stay on the pavement at all costs

Marginally less dangerous to cross

usually indicated by yellow signs). Don't try to do too much, however, especially in the searing heat of summer, and always carry your valuables safely, preferably well out of sight. The best times to walk are in the cool of the morning, or in the early evening, when you can join the Italians in the ritualistic pre-dinner stroll known as the *passeggiata*.

TAXIS

ONLY ACCEPT RIDES in official taxis, which are usually either yellow (in Rome) or white (in Florence), and have

a "Taxi" sign on the roof. Contrary to rumour, most drivers are honest (if not terribly friendly), but there is a wide range of supplements that can be legitimately levied. These vary, but generally an extra charge is made for each piece of luggage placed in the boot, for rides between 10pm and 7am, on Sundays and public holidays, and for journeys to and from airports. It is worth fixing a price before you set off to or from airports, especially in Rome or Naples.

In the event of any dispute, note the cab's number and ask the nearest policeman to arbitrate. It is hard to hail a cab in the street, but they can be found at the station, main piazza or close to key tourist sights. If you call a cab, the meter will run from your call.

CYCLE HIRE

MANY TOWNS and cities, especially those popular with visitors, have stands and shops offering bikes and scooters for rent. You can usually rent hourly or by the day, and you may have to leave your passport in the shop as a deposit. Be very careful, however, if riding a bike in the busy traffic of the larger towns and cities.

WALKING

WALKING can be a wonderful way to explore Italy's historic towns and cities, most of whose historic centres are smaller than you might expect. Traffic can be a curse, however, especially in narrow streets (Rome is worst in this respect), but many cities are introducing pedestrianized areas or cutting down on car access around key tourist sights. Italian towns have plenty of shady squares and cafés to escape the heat of the summer sun, or to take time out to watch the world go by and enjoy a drink.

Churches and cathedrals also provide cool retreats from the rigours of sightseeing. Most sights are well signposted (churches, museums and other places of interest are

INTER-CITY TRANSPORT: COACHES

Long-haul buses (*pullman* or *corriere*) between towns operate in a similar way to local buses, though you can usually buy tickets on board, and services are often run by different companies in different-coloured buses (blue is the most common colour for *pullman*, orange for city buses). Coaches in some

Rome – Gubbio bus

areas may be run by several companies (notably around Florence and in Tuscany), and not all operate from the same termini. Services often depart from outside railway stations, or from a town's main piazza. If in doubt, ask at local tourist offices. A reduced service may operate at weekends, when offices are shut.

Rome	Tuscany	National
Cotral	Lazzi	Lazzi
(06-591 55 51.	(055-21 51 54.	(055-21 51 55.
Lazzi	Sita	Sita
(06-884 08 40.	(055-48 36 51.	(055-21 47 21.
Appian	Tra-In	
(06-488 41 51.	(0577-20 41 11.	

Travelling Around Venice

FOR VISITORS TO VENICE, the *vaporetti* or waterbuses *(see pp130–31)* provide an entertaining form of public transport, although most journeys within the city can usually be covered more quickly on foot. The main route through the city for the *vaporetti* is the Grand Canal. Waterbuses also supply a useful service connecting outlying points on the periphery of Venice, and linking the city to the islands in the lagoon. The most important service from a visitor's point of view is the No. 1. This operates from one end of the Grand Canal to the other and travels slowly enough for you to admire the parade of palaces at the waterside *(see pp84–9)*.

Vaporetto stop at the Giardini Pubblici, Venice

A *vaporetto* pulling into San Marco

The smaller, sleeker and quicker *motoscafo*

THE BOATS

THE ORIGINAL *vaporetti* were steam-powered (*vaporetto* means little steamer); today they are diesel-run motor boats. Although all the boats tend to be called *vaporetti*, the word only really applies to the large wide boats used on slow routes, such as No. 1. These boats provide the best views. *Motoscafi* are the slimmer, smaller and faster boats which look old but go at a fair pace. *Motonavi* are two-tier boats which run to the islands.

TYPES OF TICKET

THE PRICE of a ticket depends not on the length of your journey but on the particular line you are taking.

Tickets that are purchased on board, rather than at the kiosk found at each stop, are more expensive. If you buy a book of 10 or 20 tickets, the cost is no cheaper than single tickets, but it avoids queuing at a ticket office for each journey.

You can save money, however, by buying a 24-hour or 72-hour ticket, which entitles the holder to unlimited travel on most lines. If you are staying more than just a few days, you can also save money by buying a weekly or monthly season ticket (*abbonamento*) which is available from ticket offices. Holders of Rolling Venice cards (offering information packs and discounts to 14- to 30-year-olds) can buy a *Tre Giorni Giovane*, or three-day youth pass.

The new "Isles Ticket" enables you to travel on the No. 12 for a one-way run and stay for the day on the islands of Murano, Mazzorbo, Burano and Torcello (but you must buy a ticket for the return trip).

You may have to buy a ticket for each piece of large luggage, and you must remember to date-stamp your tickets.

HOURS OF SERVICE

THE MAIN ROUTES run every 10 to 20 minutes until the early evening. Services are reduced at night, particularly after 1am. From June to September the services are more frequent and certain routes are extended. Details of main lines are also given in the booklet *Un Ospite di Venezia*. From May to September the main routes and island boats are very crowded.

VAPORETTO INFORMATION

ACTV (Information Office)
3880 Corte dell'Albero
San Marco, Venice. **Map** 6 F2.
[041-528 78 86.

TRAGHETTI

TRAGHETTI are gondola ferries that cross the Grand Canal at seven different points, providing a useful service for pedestrians. Few tourists make use of this cheap (L600 per trip), constant service. Points where *traghetti* cross the Grand Canal are marked on the Street Finder maps *(see pp120–29)*. A gondola on yellow street signs points to *traghetti* stops.

A two-tier *motonave* on its way to Torcello

GONDOLAS

GONDOLAS are a luxury form of transport used only by visitors and Venetians at weddings. Before boarding, check the official tariffs and agree a price with the gondolier. Official costs are around L70,000 for 50 minutes, rising to L90,000 after 8pm. During the low season, you may also be able to negotiate a lower fee, and a journey shorter than the usual 50 minutes.

WATER TAXIS

FOR THOSE with little time and sufficient funds, the fastest and most practical means of getting from A to B is by water taxi. The craft are sleek, white or polished wood motorboats, all equipped with a cabin. They zip to and from the airport in only 20 minutes. There are 16 water taxi ranks, including one at the airport and the Lido. Beware of extra charges for luggage, waiting,

A water taxi

night service and for calling out a taxi. When the *vaporetti* go on strike, taxis are scarce.

WATER TAXI STANDS

Radio Taxi (all of Venice)
[041-522 23 03.

Ferrovia (Santa Lucia)
Map 1 C5. [041-71 62 86.

Piazzale Roma
Map 5 B1. [041-71 69 22.

San Marco
Map 7 B3. [041-522 97 50.

Crossing the Grand Canal by *traghetto*

THE MAIN ROUTES

① Confusingly called the *Accelerato*, this is the slow boat down the Grand Canal, stopping at every landing stage. The route starts at Piazzale Roma, travels the length of the Grand Canal, then from San Marco it heads east to the Lido.

⑧② The No. 82 is the faster route down the Grand Canal, making only eight stops. It goes westwards as far as Tronchetto (the car park island), then eastwards along the Giudecca canal to San Zaccaria and vice versa. In season the line is extended from San Marco to the Lido.

⑤② Keeping to the periphery of Venice, the No. 52 takes in the island of Murano and has been extended to the Lido. The circular route provides a scenic tour of Venice, but change boats at Fondamente Nuove to complete the circuit.

⑫ This line departs from the Fondamente Nuove and runs to the main islands in the northern lagoon: Murano, Mazzorbo, Burano and Torcello. The service only runs about once an hour.

USING THE VAPORETTI

1 Tickets are available at most landing stages, some bars, shops and tobacconists displaying the ACTV sign. The price of a ticket remains the same whether you are going one stop or travelling the whole line, but some routes are more expensive than others, and some prices go up in summer.

2 Signs on the landing stage tell you at which end you should board the boat.

3 Tickets should be punched at the automatic machines on the landing stages before each journey. Inspectors rarely board the boats and this makes it surprisingly easy for tourists (and Venetians) to hop on and off the boats without a validated ticket. However, there are steep fines for any passengers caught without tickets.

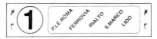

4 An indicator board at the front of each boat gives the line number and main stops. (Ignore the black numbers on the boat's side.)

5 Each landing stage has its name clearly marked on a yellow board. Most stops have two landing stages and it is quite easy, particularly if it is crowded and you can't see which way the boat is facing, to board a boat travelling in the wrong direction. It is helpful to watch which direction the boat is approaching from; if in doubt, check with the boatman.

General Index

E

Acknowledgments

DORLING KINDERSLEY would like to thank the following people whose contributions and assistance have made the preparation of this book possible.

CONTRIBUTORS
Paul Duncan is an expert on art and architectural history and has published a guide to Sicily as well as one on Italy's hilltowns.
Tim Jepson, formerly Rome correspondent for the *Sunday Telegraph*, has written guides to Tuscany, Umbria, Rome and Venice, a complete guide to Italy, *Italy by Train* and *Wild Italy*, a guide to Italy's nature reserves.
Andrew Gumbel, former Reuters correspondent in Rome, has written a number of guide books and is the correspondent for the *Independent* in Rome.
Christopher Catling has written guides to Florence and Tuscany, the Veneto and the Italian Lakes and is particularly interested in archaeology.
Sam Cole works for Reuters in Rome, where he has lived for some years, and contributes regularly to guidebooks on Rome and the Lazio region.

ADDITIONAL CONTRIBUTORS
Dominic Robertson, Mick Hamer, Richard Langham Smith.

ADDITIONAL PHOTOGRAPHY
Peter Chadwick, Andy Crawford, Philip Dowell, Mike Dunning, Philip Enticknap, Steve Gorton, Dave King, Neil Mersh, Roger Moss, Poppy, Kim Sayer, James Stevenson, Clive Streeter, David Ward, Matthew Ward.

ADDITIONAL ILLUSTRATIONS
Andrea Corbella, Richard Draper, Kevin Jones Associates, Chris Orr and Associates, Robbie Polley, Martin Woodward.

CARTOGRAPHIC RESEARCH
Jane Hugill, Samantha James, Jennifer Skelley.

DESIGN AND EDITORIAL ASSISTANCE
Ros Belford, Hilary Bird, Isabel Boucher, Caroline Brooke, Margaret Chang, Elspeth Collier, Cooling Brown Partnership, Gary Cross, Mandy Dredge, Michael Ellis, Danny Farnham, Angela-Marie Graham, Caroline Greene, Vanessa Hamilton, Tim Hollis, Tim Jepson, Steve Knowlden, Sarah Martin, Ferdie McDonald, Adam Moore, Jennifer Mussett, Alice Peebles, Jake Reimann, David Roberts, Evelyn Robertson, Carolyn Ryden, Simon Ryder, Giuseppina Russo, Alison Stace, Elaine Verweymeren, Ingrid Vienings.

DORLING KINDERSLEY would also like to thank the following for their assistance: Azienda Autonoma di Soggiorno Cura e Turismo, Napoli; Azienda Promozione Turistica del Trentino, Trento; Osservatorio Geofisico dell'Università di Modena; Bell'Italia; Enotria Winecellars.

PHOTOGRAPHY PERMISSION
DORLING KINDERSLEY would like to thank the following for their assistance and kind permission to photograph at their establishments:
Assessorato Beni Culturali Comune di Padova. Le Soprintendenze Archeologiche di Agrigento, di Enna, di Etruria Meridionale, per il Lazio, di Napoli, di Pompei, di Reggio Calabria e di Roma.
Le Soprintendenze per i Beni Ambientali e Architettonici di Bolzano, di Napoli, di Potenza, della Provincia di Firenze e Pistoia, di Ravenna, di Roma, di Siena e di Urbino. Le Soprintendenze per i Beni Ambientali, Architettonici, Artistici e Storici di Caserta, di Cosenza, di Palermo, di Pisa, di Salerno e di Venezia. Le Soprintendenze per i Beni Artistici e Storici della Provincia di Firenze e Pistoia, di Milano e di Roma. Also all the other churches, museums, hotels, restaurants, shops, galleries and sights too numerous to thank individually.

PICTURE CREDITS
t = top; tl = top left; tc = top centre; tr = top right; cla = centre left above; ca = centre above; cra = centre right above; cl = centre left; c = centre; cr = centre right; clb = centre left below; cb = centre below; crb = centre right below; bl = bottom left; b = bottom; bc = bottom centre; br = bottom right.

Every effort has been made to trace the copyright holders and we apologize in advance for any unintentional omissions. We would be pleased to insert the appropriate acknowledgments in any subsequent edition of this publication.

Works of art have been reproduced with the permission of the following copyright holders: © ADAGP, Paris and DACS, London 1996 *Bird in Space* by Constantin Brancusi 101cl; © DACS, 1996 *Mother and Son* by Carlo Carrà 190t.

DORLING KINDERSLEY would like to thank the following for their assistance: Eric Crighton: 79cra, FIAT: 212c, Gucci Ltd: 35cr, Prada, Milan: 35c, National Archaeological Museum, Naples: 479b, National Maritime Museum 36c, Royal Botanic Gardens, Kew: 79ca, Science Museum: 36cla, Telecom Italia: 620tc.

The publisher would like to thank the following individuals, companies and picture libraries for permission to reproduce their photographs:

ACCADEMIA ITALIANA: Sue Bond 479c; AFE, Rome: 34clb, 34cb, 35tl; Giuseppe Carfagna 188b, 194b,

210tl, 210b, 214tl, 216b, 217t, 227t; Claudio Cerquetti 64t, 65bl, 65t; E Lodi/Vision 66ca; Enrico Martino 54cl, 62tr; Roberto Merlo 228b, 231t, 231b; Piero Servo 259t, 261b; Gustavo Tomsich 219b; ARCHIVIO APT MONREGALESE 221t; ACTION PLUS: Mike Hewitt 66ca; Glyn Kirk 66b, 67ca, 67tr; ALITALIA: 626t, 626b; ALLSPORT Simon Bruty: 67tl; ANCIENT ART AND ARCHITECTURE: 39t, 465br; ARCHIV FÜR KUNST UND GESCHICHTE, London: 24bl, 30b, *Rossini* (1820), Camuccini, Museo Teatrale alla Scala, Milan 32br, 33bl, 37br, *Pope Sixtus IV Naming Platina Prefect of the Library*, Melozzo da Forlì (1477), Pinacoteca Vaticana, Rome 38, 40tl, *Statue of Augustus from Prima Porta* (1st century AD) 45tl, *The Gift of Constantine* (1246), Oratorio di San Silvestro, Rome 46cl, *Frederick I Barbarossa as a Crusader* (1188), Biblioteca Apostolica Vaticana, Rome 49bl, 52tl, *Giving the Keys to St Peter*, Perugino (1482), Sistine Chapel, Vatican, Rome 52cla, 52bl, *Machiavelli*, Santi di Tito, Palazzo Vecchio, Florence 53br, *Andrea Palladio*, Meyer 54cb, *Goethe in the Campagna*, Tischbein (1787), Stadelsches Kunstinstitut, Frankfurt 56cl, *Venetian Carnival in the Eighteenth Century*, Anon (19th century) 56clb, *Bonaparte Crossing the Alps*, David, Schloss Charlottenburg, Berlin 57cr, 57bl, 102t, 102b, 191b, 192b, 346–7, 450b, *Archimedes*, Museo Capitolino, Rome 465bl, 489t, 493c; Stefan Diller *St Francis Appearing to the Brothers at Arles* (1295–1300), San Francesco, Assisi 49tl; Erich Lessing *Margrave Gualtieri of Saluzzo Chooses the Poor Farmer's Daughter, Griseldis, for his Wife*, di Stefano, Galleria dell'Accademia Carrara, Bergamo 30crb, *The Vision of St Augustine* (1502), Carpaccio, Chiesa di San Giorgio degli Schiavoni, Venice 53cr, 214b, 260b, 475b; ARCHIVIO IGDA, Milan: 196t, 196c, 197b, 505bl, 505br; EMPORIO ARMANI: 20cl, 35tc; ARTEMIDE, GB Ltd: 35clb.

MARIO BETTELLA 519c, 526c; FRANK BLACKBURN: 259c; OSVALDO BÖHM, VENICE: 85t, 90c, 107t; BRIDGEMAN ART LIBRARY, London: Ambrosiana, Milan 189t; Bargello, Florence 271b, 275c; Bibliothèque Nationale, Paris: *Marco Polo with Elephants and Camels Arriving at Hormuz, Gulf of Persia, from India*, Livre des Merveilles Fr 2810 f.14v 37t; British Museum, London *Etruscan Vase Showing Boxers Fighting* 41tl, *Flask Decorated with Christian Symbols* 46tl, *Greek Attic Red-Figure Vase depicting Odysseus with the Sirens*, Stamnos 465cb; Galleria dell'Accademia Carrara, Bergamo 193t; Galleria degli Uffizi, Florence 22tl, 25tl, 25br, *Self Portrait*, Raphael Sanzio of Urbino 53bl, 279b, 281b: K & B News Photo, Florence 268tl; Santa Maria Novella, Florence 289b; Museo Civico, Prato 318b; Louvre, Paris *Statuette of Herakles Brandishing his Club*,

Classical Greek, Argive period 464t; Mausoleo di Galla Placidia, Ravenna 260tr; Museo di San Marco, Florence 289b; Musée d'Orsay, Paris - Giraudon *Les Romains de la Decadence*, Thomas Couture 385t; Museo delle Sinopie, Camposanto, Pisa 23clb; Palazzo dei Normanni, Palermo *Scene with Centaurs from the Room of King Ruggero* 507b; Pinacoteca di Brera, Milan 190c, 190b, 191t; Private Collection *Theodoric I* (455–526 AD) *Ostrogothic King of Italy* 46b; San Francesco, Arezzo 23tr; San Francesco, Assisi 345c; San Sebastiano, Venice 25crb; San Zaccaria, Venice 29c, 29tr, 95c; Santa Croce, Florence 276bl, 277cb; Santa Maria Gloriosa dei Frari, Venice 24tr; Santa Maria Novella, Florence 23cla; Scrovegni (Arena) Chapel, Padua 22tr; Scuola di San Giorgio degli Schiavoni, Venice 116b; Staatliche Museen, Berlin *Septimius Severus and Family* 45b; Vatican Museums and Galleries, Rome 411b; Walker Art Gallery, Liverpool *Aeschylus and Hygieia* 464b; BRITISH MUSEUM, London: 42cl.

CEPHAS PICTURE LIBRARY Mick Rock: 2–3, 19t, 20t, 176tr, 177b, 177tr, 234–5, 243tl, 243tr, 456–7, 610–1; JL CHARMET, Paris: 343br, 479t; CIGA HOTELS: 87cb; FOTO ELIO E STEFANO CIOL: 73cra, 158bl, 158br, 159bl, 159bc, 159br; COMUNE DI ASTI: 64cl; STEPHANI COLASANTI: 72bl; JOE CORNISH: 18t, 78tr, 132, 154t, 236–7, 304, 354, 445b, 521b; GIANCARLO COSTA: 9c, 30t, 31cr, 31tr, 31tl, 71c, 171c, 176tl, 457c, 537c, 611c.

IL DAGHERROTIPO: Archivio Arte 199t; Archivio Storico 31b, 198b, 253b; Salvatore Barba 490t; Alberto Berni 217bl; Riccardo Catani 485c; Marco Cerruti 172t, 205b, 207b, 208b; Antonio Cittadini 182b, 186b, 194t ; Gianni Dolfini 534b; Riccardo d'Errico 66tr, 239t, 260c; Maurizio Fraschetti 480; Diane Haines 167br, 625br; Maurizio Leoni 63c; Marco Melodia 490cb, 491b, 531t, 624bl, 624cl; Stefano Occhibelli 65c, 246; Giorgio Oddi 239cr, 244t, 497tr; Bruno Pantaloni 67bl; Donato Fierro Perez 517cb; Marco Ravasini 164t, 533c; Giovanni Rinaldi 62bl, 63tl, 173bl, 223b, 357t, 363t, 450c, 466, 483t, 490bl, 490br, 491c, 517cr, 535t, 535c; Lorenzo Scaramella 452c; Stefania Servili 166t; JAMES DARELL: 338; CM DIXON: 411cb; CHRIS DONAGHUE THE OXFORD PHOTO LIBRARY: 113t.

ELECTA: 150c, 151c, 151t; ET ARCHIVE: 32bc, 41c, 42tl, 45cr, 48cr–49cl, 53tl, 55tl, 59b, 465t, 515b; MARY EVANS PICTURE LIBRARY: 30clb, 31cl, 37ca, 58b, 58crb, 59cr, 60cb, 76tr, 237c, 310t, 316t, 381ca, 383bl, 399b, 432c, 495cr, 534t.

ARCHIVIO STORICO FIAT, TURIN: 60tr; FERRARI: 34b; APT FOLIGNATE E NOCERA UMBRA: 351t; WERNER FORMAN ARCHIVE: 41br, 47tr, 425br; CONSORZIO FRASASSI: 362b.

STUDIO GAVIRATI, Gubbio: 342c; APT GENOVA: Roberto Merlo 230bl; GIRAUDON, Paris: *Aphrodite Persuading Helen to Follow Paris to Troy,* Museo Nazionale di Villa Giulia, Rome 41clb, *Pharmacy,* Museo della Civiltà Romana 44cb, *Grandes Chroniques de France; Coronation of Charlemagne in St Peter's by Leon III,* Musée Goya, Castres 47tl, *Taking of Constantinople,* Basilica of St John the Evangelist, Ravenna 49cr, *Dante's Hell with Commentary of Guiniforte delli Bargigi (*Ms2017 fol 245), Bibliothèque Nationale, Paris 50cb, *Portrait of St Ignatius of Loyola,* Rubens, Musée Brukenthal, Sibiu 55ca, *Charles III's Fleet at Naples 6th October 1759,* Joli de Dipi, Museo del Prado, Madrid 56tr, *Inauguration of the Naples-Portici Railway,* Fergola (1839), Museo Nazionale di San Martino, Naples 58clb, *Piedmontese and French at the Battle of San Martino in 1859* Anon, Museo Centrale del Risorgimento, Rome 59tl, 102c, 103t, 191c, 260tl; ALINARI-GIRAUDON: *St Mark Appearing to the Venetians Looking for His Body,* Tintoretto (1568), Brera Art Gallery, Milan 25tr, *Shrine,* House of the Vettii, Pompeii 45cb, *St Gregory in his Study (*Inv 285), Pinacoteca Nazionale, Bologna 47bl, *Portrait of Victor Emmanuel II,* Dugoni (1866), Galleria d'Arte Moderna, Palazzo Pitti, Florence 58tl, 103b, 190t, *Louis II of Gonzaga and his Court,* Andrea Mantegna (1466–74), Museo di Palazzo Ducale, Mantova 200–201, 279tl-tr, *History of Pope Alexander III: Building of the City of Alexandria,* Aretino Spinello (1407), Palazzo Pubblico, Siena 51cr; ALINARI-SEAT-GIRAUDON: 219c; FLAMMARION-GIRAUDON: *Poem by Donizo in Honour of Queen Matilda,* Biblioteca Apostolica, Vatican 48ca; LAUROS-GIRAUDON: *Portrait of Francis Petrarch* 50b, *Liber notabilium Philippi Septimi, francorum regis a libris Galieni extractus (*Ms 334 569 fig17), Guy of Pavia (1345), Musée Condé, Chantilly 51b, *Gallery of Views of Ancient Rome,* Pannini (1758), Musée du Louvre, Paris 56cr–57cl, *Portrait of the Artist,* Bernini, Private Collection 54tl, *Four Angels and Symbols of the Evangelists,* 28tr–29tcr; ORSI-BATTAGLINI-GIRAUDON: *Madonna of the Shadow,* Museum of San Marco, Florence 28c, *Supplice de Savonarola* Anon 52cl; THE RONALD GRANT ARCHIVE: 61b; Paramount *The Godfather Part III* (1990) 519b; Riama *La Dolce Vita* (1960) 61tl; TCF *Boccaccio '70* (1962) 19cl, *The Name of the Rose* (1986) 30cla; PALAZZO VENIER DEI LEONI, PEGGY GUGGENHEIM COLLECTION, VENICE: 87cla.

PHOTO HALUPKA: 116t; ROBERT HARDING PICTURE LIBRARY: 1c, 66tl, 185b, 262, 380cl, 404, 409b, 615b, 624b; Richard Ashworth 21t; Dumrath 261c; HP Merton 160, 624tr; Roy Rainford 483cr; JOHN HESELTINE: 451t; MICHAEL HOLFORD: 43ca, 374b; HOTEL PORTA ROSSA: 540t; HOTEL VILLA PAGODA: 539t; THE HULTON DEUTSCH COLLECTION: 60br, 85cla,

86cla, 86br, 151br, 365c; Keystone 60ca, 61tc; Reuter/Luciano Mellace 35tr.
THE IMAGE BANK, London: 324b; Marcella Pedone 181b; Andrea Pistolesi 247b; Guido Rossi 10b, 43cb; IMPACT: 305b; INDEX, Florence: 274c, 317t, 317cr; ISTITUTO E MUSEO DI STORIA DELLA SCIENZA DI FIRENZE: Franca Principe 36b, 277c.

TIM JEPSON: 341t.

FRANK LANE PICTURE AGENCY: 208t, 209t, 209c, 209b; M Melodia/Panda 490ca.

MAGNUM, London: Abbas 61clb; THE MANSELL COLLECTION: 48cl, 383tl; MARCONI LTD 36t; MASTERSTUDIO, Pescara: 488c; MIRROR SYNDICATION INTERNATIONAL: 36clb; MOBY LINES: 629b; FOTO MODENA: 258t, 361c; TONY MOTT: 449b, 454t; MUSEO DIOCESANO DI ROSSANO 504t.

NHPA: Laurie Campbell 79crb; Gerard Lacz 79br; Silvestris Fotoservice 79cr; BY COURTESY OF THE NATIONAL PORTRAIT GALLERY, London: (detail) *Percy Bysshe Shelley,* Amelia Curran (1819) 56tl; GRAZIA NERI: 48tl; Marco Bruzzo 64br; Cameraphoto 104bl; Marcello Mencarini 84br; NIPPON TELEVISION NETWORK: 414c–415c, 414t, 414b–415bl, 415t, 415br, 416b; PETER NOBLE: 308t, 326–7, 331b, 616b.

L'OCCHIO DI CRISTALLO/STUDIO FOTOGRAFICO DI GIORGIO OLIVERO: 221b; APT ORVIETO: Massimo Roncella 348t; OXFORD SCIENTIFIC FILMS: Stan Osolinski 337c.

PADOVA - MUSEI CIVICI - CAPPELLA SCROVEGNI: 73cr, 150t, 150cla, 150clb, 151cra, 151crb, 151bl; PADOVA - MUSEI CIVICI AGLI EREMITANI: 152t, 152c; LUCIANO PEDICINI - ARCHIVIO DELL'ARTE: 352b, 394t, 459t, 470tl, 474t, 474ca, 474cb, 474b, 475t, 475ca, 475cr, 477t, 514b; APT PESARO - LE MARCHE: 358c; PICTURES COLOUR LIBRARY: 530b, 532l; ANDREA PISTOLESI: 16; POPPERFOTO: 60tl, 61ca, 61cb.

SARAH QUILL, Venice: 86t, 90b, 96tl.

RETROGRAPH ARCHIVE: 33c; REX FEATURES: 33t.

SCALA, Florence: 22b, 23b, 24br, 25ca, 25bl, 32tl, *Portrait of Claudio Monteverdi,* Domenico Feti, Accademia, Venice 32bl, *Portolan of Italy* (16th century), Museo Correr, Venice 39b, *Etruscan Bronze Liver,* Museo Civico, Piacenza 40t, *Earrings,* Museo Etrusco Guarnacci, Volterra 40br, 40cr–41cl, *Crater from Pescia Romana,* Museo Archeologico, Grosseto 41bc, *Terracotta Vase in the Shape of an Elephant,* Museo Nazionale, Naples 42cr, *Cicero denounces Catiline,* Palazzo Madama, Rome 43tl, 43bl, *Circus Scene Mosaic - Gladiator Fight,* Galleria Borghese, Rome 44t,

44br, *Theodolinda Melts the Gold for the New Church* (15th century), Famiglia Zavattari, Duomo, Monza 46clb, 46cr–47cl, 47b, *Tomb Relief depicting a School*, Matteo Gandoni, Museo Civico, Bologna 48b, *Detail from an Ambo of Frederick II* (13th century), Cattedrale, Bitonto 49cb, *Guidoriccio da Fogliano at the Siege of Note Massi*, Simone Martini, Palazzo Pubblico, Siena 50cl, 51tl, *Return of Gregory XI from Avignon* Giorgio Vasari, Sala Regia, Vatican 51cb, 52br, 52cr–53cl, 53crb, *Clement VII in Conversation with Charles V*, Giorgio Vasari, Palazzo Vecchio, Florence 54cla, *Portrait of Pierluigi da Palestrina*, Istituto dei Padri dell'Oratorio, Rome 54br, *Revolt at Masaniello*, Domenico Gargiulo, Museo di San Martino, Naples 55crb, 56br, 57tl, 57crb, 58cla, 58cr–59cl, 59crb, 91c, 96c, 114br, 140c, 214tr, 218b, 252t, 255t, 257t, 261t, 266c, 266b, 267t, 268c, 268b, 269t, 269b, 272, 274tr, 275tr, 275b, 278t, 278c, 278b, 279ca, 279cb, 280t, 280b, 281t, 282c, 283bl, 284t, 284b, 285t, 285b, 286t, 286c, 287t, 288bl, 290t, 290cl, 290cra, 290crb, 290b, 291cla, 291clb, 291cr, 291bl, 291br, 293bl, 294tr, 294tl, 294c, 295t, 295cl, 295b, 315c, 315b, 320t, 320cla, 320c, 320ca, 320cr-321cl, 320cb, 320b, 321cr, 321cb, 321cra, 321t, 321b, 322t, 322b, 328b, 330t, 331cl, 334cla, 335b, 344tl, 344c, 345b, 348b, 349c, 360t, 360b, 361t, 361bl, 367br, 374c, 390bl, 392t, 394c, 401c, 406tl, 406c, 406b, 407t, 408b, 409t, 410t, 410cb, 411c, 413t, 413c, 413b, 417t, 417b, 495c, 497tl, 513b, 514tr, 520t, 521t, 522b, 533b; SCIENCE PHOTO LIBRARY: 11t; Argonne National Laboratory 37cr; JOHN FERRO SIMS: 20b, 21b, 80, 170–171, 355b, 364–365, 444, 526b; AGENZIA SINTESI, ROME: 616tl; MARIO SOSTER DI ALAGNA: 541c; FRANK SPOONER PICTURES: Diffidenti 532b; Gamma 61cr; Daniel Simon 189b; SPORTING PICTURES: 66clb, 66crb, 67cb, 67cra; TONY STONE IMAGES: 79cla; Stephen Studd 27tr, 179cr; AGENZIA FOTOGRAFICA STRADELLA, Milan: Bersanetti 185c;

Lamberto Caenazzo 530t; Francesco Gavazzini 208c; F Giaccone 510c; Mozzati 360clb; Massimo Pacifico 491t; Ettore Re 483crb; Ghigo Roli 483b; Giulio Vegi 517t; Amedeo Vergani 202, 206b, 226t, 249t; SYGMA: 63tr.

TASTING ITALY: Martin Brigdale 625t; TATE GALLERY PUBLICATIONS: 60bl; APT DELL'ALTA VALLE DEL TEVERE: Museo del Duomo 50tl; TOURING CLUB OF ITALY: 196b, Cresci 518t; ARCHIVIO CITTÀ DI TORINO Settore Turismo: 213t, 213b; Davide Bogliacino 205t; FOTOTECA APT del TRENTINO: Foto di Banal 168t; Foto di Faganello 167t, 169c.

VENICE-SIMPLON ORIENT EXPRESS: 628tl; VILLA CRESPI: 576b.

CHARLIE WAITE: 17b; EDIZIONE WHITE STAR: Marcello Bertinetti 81b; Giulio Veggi 8–9, 70–71, 133b; FIONA WILD: 524–5; PETER WILSON: 5t, 88–89; WORLD PICTURES: 536–7.

Front Endpaper:
JOE CORNISH: Lcrb, Rc, Rtcr; IL DAGHERROTIPO: Marco Melodia Lbl; Stefano Occhibelli Rtl; Giovanni Rinaldi Rbl; JAMES DARELL: Rcl; ROBERT HARDING PICTURE LIBRARY: Lc, H.P. Merton Rtcl; JOHN FERRO SIMS: Ltr, Rbc; AGENZIA FOTOGRAFICA STRADELLA, Milan: Amadeo Vergani Ltl.

Back Endpaper:
ROBERT HARDING PICTURE LIBRARY: Rolf Richardson Lt.

COVER:
FERRARI: bl; GIRAUDON: Nicolò Orsi Battaglini crb; HULTON DEUTSCH COLLECTION: Reuter cra.

BACK COVER:
PETER WILSON: bl.

Phrase Book

IN EMERGENCY

Help!	Aiuto!	eye-**yoo**-toh
Stop!	Fermate!	fair-**mah**-teh
Call a doctor.	Chiama un medico.	kee-**ah**-mah oon **meh**-dee-koh
Call an ambulance.	Chiama un' ambulanza.	kee-**ah**-mah oon am-boo-**lan**-tsa
Call the police.	Chiama la polizia.	kee-**ah**-mah lah pol-ee-**tsee**-ah
Call the fire brigade.	Chiama i pompieri.	kee-**ah**-mah ee pom-pee-**air**-ee
Where is the telephone?	Dov'è il telefono?	dov-**eh** eel teh-**leh**-foh-noh?
The nearest hospital?	L'ospedale più vicino?	loss-peh-**dah**-leh pee-oo vee-**chee**-noh?

COMMUNICATION ESSENTIALS

Yes/No	Sì/No	see/noh
Please	Per favore	pair fah-**vor**-eh
Thank you	Grazie	**grah**-tsee-eh
Excuse me	Mi scusi	mee **skoo**-zee
Hello	Buon giorno	bwon **jor**-noh
Goodbye	Arrivederci	ah-ree-veh-**dair**-chee
Good evening	Buona sera	**bwon**-ah **sair**-ah
morning	la mattina	lah mah-**tee**-nah
afternoon	il pomeriggio	eel poh-mah-**ree**-joh
evening	la sera	lah **sair**-ah
yesterday	ieri	ee-**air**-ee
today	oggi	**oh**-jee
tomorrow	domani	doh-**mah**-nee
here	qui	kwee
there	la	lah
What?	Quale?	**kwah**-leh?
When?	Quando?	**kwan**-doh?
Why?	Perchè?	pair-**keh**?
Where?	Dove?	**doh**-veh?

USEFUL PHRASES

How are you?	Come sta?	**koh**-meh stah?
Very well, thank you.	Molto bene, grazie.	**moll**-toh **beh**-neh **grah**-tsee-eh
Pleased to meet you.	Piacere di conoscerla.	pee-ah-**chair**-eh dee coh-**noh**-shair-lah
See you later.	A più tardi.	ah pee-oo **tar**-dee
That's fine.	Va bene.	va **beh**-neh
Where is/are ...?	Dov'è/Dove sono ...?	dov-**eh**/doveh **soh**-noh?
How long does it take to get to ...?	Quanto tempo ci vuole per andare a ...?	**kwan**-toh **tem**-poh chee voo-**oh**-leh pair an-**dar**-eh ah ...?
How do I get to ...?	Come faccio per arrivare a ...?	koh-meh **fah**-choh pair arri-**var**-eh ah..?
Do you speak English?	Parla inglese?	**par**-lah een-**gleh**-zeh?
I don't understand.	Non capisco.	non ka-**pee**-skoh
Could you speak more slowly, please?	Può parlare più lentamente, per favore?	pwoh par-**lah**-reh pee-oo len-ta-**men**-teh pair fah-**vor**-eh?
I'm sorry.	Mi dispiace.	mee dee-spee-**ah**-cheh

USEFUL WORDS

big	grande	**gran**-deh
small	piccolo	**pee**-koh-loh
hot	caldo	**kal**-doh
cold	freddo	**fred**-doh
good	buono	**bwoh**-noh
bad	cattivo	kat-**tee**-voh
enough	basta	**bas**-tah
well	bene	**beh**-neh
open	aperto	ah-**pair**-toh
closed	chiuso	kee-**oo**-zoh
left	a sinistra	ah see-**nee**-strah
right	a destra	ah **dess**-trah
straight on	sempre dritto	**sem**-preh **dree**-toh
near	vicino	vee-**chee**-noh
far	lontano	lon-**tah**-noh
up	su	soo
down	giù	joo
early	presto	**press**-toh
late	tardi	**tar**-dee
entrance	entrata	en-**trah**-tah
exit	uscita	oo-**shee**-ta
toilet	il gabinetto	eel gab-bee-**net**-toh
free, unoccupied	libero	**lee**-bair-oh
free, no charge	gratuito	grah-**too**-ee-toh

MAKING A TELEPHONE CALL

I'd like to place a long-distance call.	Vorrei fare una interurbana.	vor-**ray far**-eh oona in-tair-oor-**bah**-nah
I'd like to make a reverse-charge call.	Vorrei fare una telefonata a carico del destinatario.	vor-**ray far**-eh oona teh-leh-fon-**ah**-tah ah **kar**-ee-koh dell dess-tee-nah-**tar**-ree-oh
I'll try again later.	Ritelefono più tardi.	ree-teh-**leh**-foh-noh pee-oo **tar**-dee
Can I leave a message?	Posso lasciare un messaggio?	**poss**-oh lash-**ah**-reh oon mess-**sah**-joh?
Hold on.	Un attimo, per favore	oon **ah**-tee-moh, pair fah-**vor**-eh
Could you speak up a little please?	Può parlare più forte, per favore?	pwoh par-**lah**-reh pee-oo for-teh, pair fah-**vor**-eh?
local call	telefonata locale	te-leh-fon-**ah**-tah loh-cah-leh

SHOPPING

How much does this cost?	Quant'è, per favore?	kwan-**teh**, pair fah-**vor**-eh?
I would like ...	Vorrei ...	vor-**ray**...
Do you have ...?	Avete ...?	ah-**veh**-teh... ?
I'm just looking.	Sto soltanto guardando.	stoh sol-**tan**-toh gwar-**dan**-doh
Do you take credit cards?	Accettate carte di credito?	ah-chet-**tah**-teh **kar**-teh dee **creh**-dee-toh?
What time do you open/close?	A che ora apre/ chiude?	ah keh **or**-ah **ah**-preh/kee-**oo**-deh?
this one	questo	**kweh**-stoh
that one	quello	**kwell**-oh
expensive	caro	**kar**-oh
cheap	a buon prezzo	ah bwon **pret**-soh
size, clothes	la taglia	lah **tah**-lee-ah
size, shoes	il numero	eel **noo**-mair-oh
white	bianco	bee-**ang**-koh
black	nero	**neh**-roh
red	rosso	**ross**-oh
yellow	giallo	**jal**-loh
green	verde	**vair**-deh
blue	blu	bloo

TYPES OF SHOP

antique dealer	l'antiquario	lan-tee-**kwah**-ree-oh
bakery	il forno /il panificio	eel **forn**-oh /eel pan-ee-**fee**-choh
bank	la banca	lah **bang**-kah
bookshop	la libreria	lah lee-breh-**ree**-ah
butcher	la macelleria	lah mah-chell-eh-**ree**-ah
cake shop	la pasticceria	lah pas-tee-chair-**ee**-ah
chemist	la farmacia	lah far-mah-**chee**-ah
delicatessen	la salumeria	lah sah-loo-meh-**ree**-ah
department store	il grande magazzino	eel **gran**-deh mag-gad-**zee**-noh
fishmonger	il pescivendolo	eel pesh-ee-**ven**-doh-loh
florist	il fioraio	eel fee-or-**eye**-oh
greengrocer	il fruttivendolo	eel froo-tee-**ven**-doh-loh
grocery	alimentari	ah-lee-men-**tah**-ree
hairdresser	il parrucchiere	eel par-oo-kee-**air**-eh
ice cream parlour	la gelateria	lah jel-lah-tair-**ee**-ah
market	il mercato	eel mair-**kah**-toh
newsstand	l'edicola	leh-**dee**-koh-lah
post office	l'ufficio postale	loo-**fee**-choh pos-**tah**-leh
shoe shop	il negozio di scarpe	eel neh-**goh**-tsioh dee **skar**-peh
supermarket	il supermercato	eel su-pair-mair-**kah**-toh
tobacconist	il tabaccaio	eel tah-bak-**eye**-oh
travel agency	l'agenzia di viaggi	lah-jen-**tsee**-ah dee vee-**ad**-jee

SIGHTSEEING

art gallery	la pinacoteca	lah peena-koh-**teh**-kah
bus stop	la fermata dell'autobus	lah fair-**mah**-tah dell **ow**-toh-booss
church	la chiesa la basilica	lah kee-**eh**-zah lah bah-**seel**-i-kah
closed for holidays	chiuso per le ferie	kee-oo-zoh pair leh **fair**-ee-eh
garden	il giardino	eel jar-**dee**-no
library	la biblioteca	lah beeb-lee-oh-**teh**-kah
museum	il museo	eel moo-**zeh**-oh
railway station	la stazione	lah stah-tsee-**oh**-neh
tourist information	l'ufficio di turismo	loo-**fee**-choh dee too-**ree**-smoh

STAYING IN A HOTEL

Do you have any vacant rooms?	**Avete camere libere?**	ah-**veh**-teh **kah**-mair-eh **lee**-bair-eh?
double room	**una camera doppia**	oona **kah**-mair-ah **doh**-pee-ah
with double bed	**con letto matrimoniale**	kon **let**-toh mah-tree-moh-nee-**ah**-leh
twin room	**una camera con due letti**	oona **kah**-mair-ah kon **doo**-eh **let**-tee
single room	**una camera singola**	oona **kah**-mair-ah **sing**-goh-lah
room with a bath, shower	**una camera con bagno, con doccia**	oona **kah**-mair-ah kon **ban**-yoh, kon **dot**-chah
porter	**il facchino**	eel fah-**kee**-noh
key	**la chiave**	lah kee-**ah**-veh
I have a reservation.	**Ho fatto una prenotazione.**	oh **fat**-toh oona preh-noh-tah-tsee-**oh**-neh

EATING OUT

Have you got a table for ...?	**Avete una tavola per ... ?**	ah-**veh**-teh oona **tah**-voh-lah pair ...?
I'd like to reserve a table.	**Vorrei riservare una tavola.**	vor-**ray** ree-sair-**vah**-reh oona **tah**-voh-lah
breakfast	**colazione**	koh-lah-tsee-**oh**-neh
lunch	**pranzo**	**pran**-tsoh
dinner	**cena**	**cheh**-nah
The bill, please.	**Il conto, per favore.**	eel **kon**-toh pair fah-**vor**-eh
I am a vegetarian.	**Sono vegetariano/a.**	**soh**-noh veh-jeh-tar-ee-**ah**-noh/nah
waitress	**cameriera**	kah-mair-ee-**air**-ah
waiter	**cameriere**	kah-mair-ee-**air**-eh
fixed price menu	**il menù a prezzo fisso**	eel meh-**noo** ah **pret**-soh **fee**-soh
dish of the day	**piatto del giorno**	pee-**ah**-toh dell **jor**-no
starter	**antipasto**	an-tee-**pass**-toh
first course	**il primo**	eel **pree**-moh
main course	**il secondo**	eel seh-**kon**-doh
vegetables	**il contorno**	eel kon-**tor**-noh
dessert	**il dolce**	eel **doll**-cheh
cover charge	**il coperto**	eel koh-**pair**-toh
wine list	**la lista dei vini**	lah **lee**-stah day **vee**-nee
rare	**al sangue**	al **sang**-gweh
medium	**al puntino**	al poon-**tee**-noh
well done	**ben cotto**	ben **kot**-toh
glass	**il bicchiere**	eel bee-kee-**air**-eh
bottle	**la bottiglia**	lah bot-**teel**-yah
knife	**il coltello**	eel kol-**tell**-oh
fork	**la forchetta**	lah for-**ket**-tah
spoon	**il cucchiaio**	eel koo-kee-**eye**-oh

MENU DECODER

l'acqua minerale gassata/naturale	lah-kwah mee-nair-**ah**-leh gah-**zah**-tah/nah-too-rah-leh	mineral water fizzy/still
agnello	ah-**niell**-oh	lamb
aceto	ah-**cheh**-toh	vinegar
aglio	al-ee-oh	garlic
al forno	al **for**-noh	baked
alla griglia	ah-lah **greel**-yah	grilled
l'aragosta	lah-rah-**goss**-tah	lobster
arrosto	ar-**ross**-toh	roast
la birra	lah **beer**-rah	beer
la bistecca	lah bee-**stek**-kah	steak
il brodo	eel **broh**-doh	broth
il burro	eel **boor**-oh	butter
il caffè	eel kah-**feh**	coffee
i calamari	ee kah-lah-**mah**-ree	squid
i carciofi	ee kar-**choff**-ee	artichokes
la carne	la **kar**-neh	meat
carne di maiale	**kar**-neh dee mah-**yah**-leh	pork
la cipolla	la chip-**oh**-lah	onion
i contorni	ee kon-**tor**-nee	vegetables
i fagioli	ee fah-**joh**-lee	beans
il fegato	eel **fay**-gah-toh	liver
il finocchio	eel fee-**nok**-ee-oh	fennel
il formaggio	eel for-**mad**-joh	cheese
le fragole	leh frah-goh-leh	strawberries
il fritto misto	eel free-toh **mees**-toh	mixed fried dish
la frutta	la **froot**-tah	fruit
frutti di mare	**froo**-tee dee **mah**-reh	seafood
i funghi	ee **foon**-ghee	mushrooms
i gamberi	ee **gam**-bair-ee	prawns
il gelato	eel jel-**lah**-toh	ice cream
l'insalata	leen-sah-lah-tah	salad

il latte	eel **laht**-teh	milk
lesso	**less**-oh	boiled
il manzo	eel **man**-tsoh	beef
la melanzana	lah meh-lan-**tsah**-nah	aubergine
la minestra	lah mee-**ness**-trah	soup
l'olio	loh-lee-oh	oil
il pane	eel **pah**-neh	bread
le patate	leh pah-**tah**-teh	potatoes
le patatine fritte	leh pah-pah-**teen**-eh **free**-teh	chips
il pepe	eel **peh**-peh	pepper
la pesca	lah **pess**-kah	peach
il pesce	eel **pesh**-eh	fish
il pollo	eel **poll**-oh	chicken
il pomodoro	eel poh-moh-**dor**-oh	tomato
il prosciutto cotto/crudo	eel pro-**shoo**-toh **kot**-toh/**kroo**-doh	ham cooked/cured
il riso	eel ree-zoh	rice
il sale	eel **sah**-leh	salt
la salsiccia	lah sal-**see**-chah	sausage
le seppie	leh **sep**-pee-eh	cuttlefish
secco	**sek**-koh	dry
la sogliola	lah **soll**-yoh-lah	sole
i spinaci	ee spee-**nah**-chee	spinach
succo d'arancia/ di limone	**soo**-koh dah-**ran**-chah/ dee lee-**moh**-neh	orange/lemon juice
il tè	eel **teh**	tea
la tisana	lah tee-**zah**-nah	herbal tea
il tonno	eel **ton**-noh	tuna
la torta	lah **tor**-tah	cake/tart
l'uovo	loo-**oh**-voh	egg
vino bianco	**vee**-noh bee-**ang**-koh	white wine
vino rosso	**vee**-noh **ross**-oh	red wine
il vitello	eel vee-**tell**-oh	veal
le vongole	leh **von**-goh-leh	clams
lo zucchero	loh **zoo**-kair-oh	sugar
gli zucchini	lyee dzu-**kee**-nee	courgettes
la zuppa	lah **tsoo**-pah	soup

NUMBERS

1	**uno**	**oo**-noh
2	**due**	**doo**-eh
3	**tre**	treh
4	**quattro**	**kwat**-roh
5	**cinque**	**ching**-kweh
6	**sei**	**say**-ee
7	**sette**	**set**-teh
8	**otto**	**ot**-toh
9	**nove**	**noh**-veh
10	**dieci**	dee-**eh**-chee
11	**undici**	**oon**-dee-chee
12	**dodici**	**doh**-dee-chee
13	**tredici**	**tray**-dee-chee
14	**quattordici**	kwat-**tor**-dee-chee
15	**quindici**	**kwin**-dee-chee
16	**sedici**	**say**-dee-chee
17	**diciassette**	dee-chah-**set**-teh
18	**diciotto**	dee-**chot**-toh
19	**diciannove**	dee-chah-**noh**-veh
20	**venti**	**ven**-tee
30	**trenta**	**tren**-tah
40	**quaranta**	kwah-**ran**-tah
50	**cinquanta**	ching-**kwan**-tah
60	**sessanta**	sess-**an**-tah
70	**settanta**	set-**tan**-tah
80	**ottanta**	ot-**tan**-tah
90	**novanta**	noh-**van**-tah
100	**cento**	**chen**-toh
1,000	**mille**	**mee**-leh
2,000	**duemila**	**doo**-eh **mee**-lah
5,000	**cinquemila**	**ching**-kweh **mee**-lah
1,000,000	**un milione**	oon meel-**yoh**-neh

TIME

one minute	**un minuto**	oon mee-**noo**-toh
one hour	**un'ora**	oon **or**-ah
half an hour	**mezz'ora**	medz-**or**-ah
a day	**un giorno**	oon **jor**-noh
a week	**una settimana**	oona set-tee-**mah**-nah
Monday	**lunedì**	loo-neh-**dee**
Tuesday	**martedì**	mar-teh-**dee**
Wednesday	**mercoledì**	mair-koh-leh-**dee**
Thursday	**giovedì**	joh-veh-**dee**
Friday	**venerdì**	ven-air-**dee**
Saturday	**sabato**	**sah**-bah-toh
Sunday	**domenica**	doh-**meh**-nee-kah

Central Rome

THE VATICAN AND TRASTEVERE
Pages 404–419
Street Finder maps 1, 5–6

AROUND PIAZZA NAVONA
Pages 386–395
Street Finder maps 2, 3

USEFUL BUS AND TRAM ROUTES

Villa Borghese

Roma Nord **FS**
Flaminio **M**

M Spagna

San Lorenzo
fuori le Mura

Mausoleo
di Augusto

M Barberini

Castel Sant'
Angelo

Termini
FS **M**

Vaticano

Ponte
Umberto I

Via del
Tritone

Piazza
Colonna

Pantheon

Gesù

Piazza
Venezia

M Colosseo

Porta
Maggiore

Villa Farnesina

San Giovanni

Teatro di
Marcello

Trastevere

Circo Massimo
M

Bocca della
Verità

FS Ostiense
M Piramide

KEY

— Bus route 23
— Bus route 30b
— Bus route 56
— Bus route 64
— Bus route 119